The Dryden Press Series in Management

Arthur G. Bedeian, Consulting Editor

Albanese and Van Fleet
Organizational Behavior: A Managerial
Viewpoint

Bedeian
Organizations: Theory and Analysis, Text and
Cases, Second Edition

Bedeian and Glueck
Management, Third Edition

Boone and Kurtz
Contemporary Business,
Third Edition

Bowman and Branchaw
Business Report Writing

Chen and McGarrah
Productivity Management:
Text and Cases

Compaine and Litro
Business: An Introduction

Gaither
Production and Operations Management: A
Problem-Solving and Decision-Making
Approach, Second Edition

Higgins
Organizational Policy and Strategic
Management: Text and
Cases, Second Edition

Hodgetts
Management: Theory, Process and
Practice, Third Edition

Hodgetts
Modern Human Relations at Work,
Second Edition

Holley and Jennings
Personnel Management: Functions
and Issues

Holley and Jennings
The Labor Relations Process,
Second Edition

Huseman, Lahiff, and Hatfield
Business Communication: Strategies
and Skills

Huseman, Lahiff, and Hatfield
Readings in Business Communication

Jauch, Coltrin, Bedeian, and Glueck
The Managerial Experience: Cases,
Exercises, and Readings,
Third Edition

Lee
Introduction to Management Science

Miner
Theories of Organizational Behavior

Miner
Theories of Organizational Structure
and Process

Paine and Anderson
Strategic Management

Paine and Naumes
Organizational Strategy and Policy:
Text and Cases, Third Edition

Penrose
Applications in Business Communication

Ray and Eison
Supervision

Robinson
The Internationalization of Business:
An Introduction

Robinson
International Business Management,
Second Edition

Smith
Management System: Analysis and
Applications

Stone
Understanding Personnel Management

Tombari
Business and Society: Strategies for the
Environment and Public Policy

Trueman
Quantitative Methods in Decision-Making
in Business

Zikmund
Business Research Methods

Dedicated to LYNDA, who appears between the lines

Acquisitions Editor: Anne Elizabeth Smith
Developmental Editor: Susan Meyers
Project Editor: Russell Hahn
Managing Editor: Jane Perkins
Design Director: Alan Wendt
Production Manager: Mary Jarvis
Copyeditor: Mary Englehart
Compositor: Progressive Typographers Inc.
Text Type: 9½/11 Serifa 55

Library of Congress Cataloging in Publication Data

Gaither, Norman.
    Production and operations management.

    Includes bibliographies and index.
    1. Production management.   I. Title.
TS155.G17   1983   658.5   83-11587
ISBN 0-03-062568-8

Printed in the United States of America
456-016-109876543

Address orders to:
383 Madison Avenue
New York, New York 10017

Address editorial correspondence to:
One Salt Creek Lane
Hinsdale, IL 60521

CBS College Publishing
The Dryden Press
Holt, Rinehart and Winston
Saunders College Publishing

Production and Operations Management

A Problem-Solving and Decision-Making Approach

Second Edition

Norman Gaither

College of Business Administration
Texas A & M University

THE DRYDEN PRESS
Chicago New York Philadelphia San Francisco Montreal Toronto
London Sydney Tokyo Mexico City Rio de Janeiro Madrid

Production and Operations Management

A Problem-Solving and Decision-Making Approach

Second Edition

Preface

The American Assembly of Collegiate Schools of Business (AACSB) requires that all accredited schools include Production and Operations Management (POM) in their common body of knowledge. Schools of business in growing numbers have included POM courses in their academic programs at both the undergraduate and graduate levels. This book is developed to meet the need for comprehensive text materials in these and other POM courses.

The second edition retains the distinctive features of the first edition:

1. *Operations Function Perspective.* The text places the student squarely in the production/operations function in a variety of organizations. The concepts, issues, and problems of operations managers are emphasized by requiring students to identify operational problems, analyze the available alternatives, and recommend solutions.

2. *Nontheoretical Approach.* The text presents the quantitative analysis of POM decisions side by side with managerial issues and concepts for a balanced view of POM problems. When quantitative approaches are appropriate, the text presents these approaches in a nontheoretical way. This objective is accomplished by emphasizing operational problems rather than the solution techniques and by using examples to demonstrate the procedures of the techniques.

3. *Emphasis of POM in Services.* POM is cast in a variety of settings. The term *operations* implies that producing goods and services in both private and public organizations should be included within the scope of POM. The text presents operational problems in such service sectors as transportation; communications; utilities; wholesaling; retailing; finance, insurance, and real estate; and a variety of governmental agencies.

4. *Pragmatic View of POM.* Most of the problems and examples in the text have been abstracted from actual problems that have been analyzed by the author or his associates. The view presented is one of realism about real world organizations from years of industrial experience and a continuing consulting relationship with manufacturing, service, and governmental organizations.

5. *Class-Tested Supporting Materials.* All of the problems, examples, and cases in the text have been assigned to POM classes for several semesters. These materials are debugged and ready for use with the assurance that the problems can be solved using the information presented in the text. The computer programs, statistical tables, and other supporting materials have similarly been class tested.

6. *Graduated-Learning Process.* Chapters that include quantitative topics are presented in a framework particularly suitable for learning by business students. Concepts are presented and discussed, concepts are reinforced through examples, many problems are presented at the ends of the chapters, and answers to the odd-numbered problems are provided as an appendix. This process builds understanding and confidence to the point that students should be able to test their ability to solve problems without the assistance provided through supplied solutions and answers.

Our goal in the second edition is to make our text even better. Toward this end, we have made the following changes and additions to the first edition:

1. *Japanese Management Approaches.* Japanese manufacturing strategy, personnel relations and practices, robotry, quality control, and other concepts are integrated throughout the second edition. The view is one of comparison and understanding, rather than one of directly adapting Japanese methods to our productive systems. Although much is to be learned from the Japanese, adapting their methods to our systems must be approached with a realistic understanding of the environments in which such methods must operate.

2. *Proactive Approach to Production Planning.* Part Three of the second edition, "Planning Production to Meet Demand: A Proactive Approach," consolidates most of the topics on inventories, materials management, and scheduling from the first edition into one section with a somewhat different thrust. This new organizational scheme, which better depicts how a proactive production planning system should actually work, is apparent in the chapters on proactive production planning, materials management and independent demand inventory systems, scheduling manufacturing and service operations, and resource requirements planning systems.

3. *Financial Analysis of POM.* The concepts and techniques of financial analysis are included as a supplement to Chapter 4, "Product Design and Process Planning." In an environment of scarce funds, high interest rates, and volatile financial conditions, financial analysis has surfaced as a topic of critical importance in POM.

4. *Problem Sets and Cases.* A strength of the first edition was its problem sets. The second edition has even more problems and cases with a greater range of rigor. Like the first edition, the second edition's problem sets are aimed at pragmatic

POM problems, can be worked directly from the information in the chapters, and exhibit a progression of rigor as one proceeds through a set. Many new problems and cases have been added in the second edition. These new problems, combined with some of those retained from the first edition, form a very comprehensive problem set for a POM text.

5. *Emphasis on Behavioral Concepts.* Readers of the second edition will immediately notice that the behavioral concepts are intertwined with other issues as early as Chapter 1. As the text unfolds, these concepts are integrated in such a way that they are not overemphasized but rather combine to form a more balanced view of operations management. Chapter 12, ''Human Resource Management and Productivity,'' for example, emphasizes that job designs should be based upon technical operating efficiency, the needs of workers, and motivational concepts.

6. *Supporting Materials.* The second edition retains the supporting materials of the first edition and adds something new. *The Instructor's Resource Manual* includes a comprehensive set of materials to assist instructors in teaching the course, ranging from suggested course schedules, chapter teaching notes, example exams, and objective exam questions to transparency masters of key figures not included in the text to help spice up lectures. *The Instructor's Solutions Manual* includes complete solutions for all of the problems in the text in large ORATOR type as transparency masters. The second edition is accompanied by something new — an *Interactive POM Computer Library.* This library includes fully documented computer programs that are intended for innocent computer users. Being totally prompted by the programs, students can use the programs to solve problems or cases assigned by instructors as they proceed through the text. The accompanying manual, tape, and diskettes are available for most mainframe and micro computers.

Generally, students should have completed courses in college algebra and introductory statistics as prerequisites to courses using this text. Although the mathematical and statistical concepts in the text are not complex, students with a basic background in these topics tend to perform better.

As this second edition is completed, numerous persons deserve special recognition for their contributions to the project. Among these persons are:

1. My faculty colleagues and students at Northern Arizona University who contributed to the first edition of the book.

2. My faculty colleagues and students at Texas A & M University who have participated in Bana 364, the Production and Operations core course. These individuals not only made many suggestions for the improvements that are incorporated into the second edition of this book, but they also shared their thoughts and philosophies of teaching the POM core course. Special mention is made of Don Aldrich, Ted Anthony, Bob Davis, Dave Olson, and Warren Rose.

3. The many friends and associates who have contributed both formal and informal reviews of the second edition manuscript. A special mention goes to those reviewers who were actively involved in the second edition project: Frank C. Barnes, University of North Carolina at Charlotte; Herbert Blake, Jr., California

berg, Bernard M. Baruch College (CUNY); Jeff E. Heyl, Arizona State University and Northern Arizona University; Russell E. Jacobson, University of Wisconsin – Whitewater; Barry E. King, Ohio State University; Paul S. Marlin, University of Missouri at St. Louis; T. H. Mattheiss, University of Alabama; Albert C. Phelps, University of Wisconsin – Eau Claire; Brooke Saladin, University of Georgia; Billy M. Thornton, Colorado State University; Richard Westphal, University of Wisconsin – Whitewater.

To these and all of the other persons who have contributed to this work, I am grateful.

Norman Gaither
Texas A & M University
October 1983

Contents

Part One

Production and Operations Management:

Introduction and Overview

Today is indeed an exciting time for the study of operations management. So many things have happened recently and are still happening that this field has become one of the most challenging in the world of business. Our national leaders are expressing concern that manufacturers from foreign countries are seriously threatening the future of our basic industries such as automobiles, steel, electronics, and computers. The top managements of our leading corporations are urging their operations managers to get back to the basics of factory management so that this country's manufacturing costs and product quality can compete with those of manufacturers from Asia, Europe, and other parts of the world. Many of our industries are in a period of rapid technological change as robotics and other computer-based mechanical and electronic innovations are applied to operations.

In such a heady environment, the study of operations management could not be more important to you or relevant to your career opportunities. If you should choose to enter the operations management field as a professional outlet for your college training, what you will learn in this course will prove to be an important introduction to the field. If you should choose to enter another field such as accounting, marketing, finance, or engineering, what we shall study in this text can be important to you because your chosen field will most certainly interact with operations management and its problems, opportunities, and challenges.

Part One of this text provides the following:

1. An overview of the operations management field — its historical development, the nature of operations managers' jobs, contemporary developments, production functions, and the nature of productive systems.

2. A review of some of the disciplines that underlie the field — decision-making techniques such as decision trees, payoff tables, break-even analysis, and cost benefit analysis and forecasting techniques and approaches.

3. A framework for studying operations management. The principal types of decisions that operations managers must make form the basis for organizing the remainder of the text — Foundations of Operations Strategy: Planning Products, Processes, and Facilities; Planning Production to Meet Demand: A Proactive Approach; and Planning and Controlling Operations.

Chapter Outline

Production and Operations Management Defined

Milestone Historical Developments in POM

The Post–Civil War Period (1865–1900)
Scientific Management (1875–1925)
Human Relations Movement (1925–1960)
Operations Research (1940–Present)
Computers (1955–Present)

Contemporary Developments and POM Practice

The Nature of Operations Managers' Jobs

Productive Systems

Systems Concepts
Productive Systems Concepts
A Productive System Model
Productive System Diversity

The Production Function

Summary

Review and Discussion Questions

Selected Bibliography

1

POM:

An Evolutionary Perspective

*Here and elsewhere we shall not obtain the best insight into
things until we actually see them growing from the beginning.*
Aristotle, 352 B.C.

This book is about production and operations management. **The definition of
production and operations management (POM) is the planning, organizing,
staffing, directing, and controlling of all of the activities of productive systems
—those portions of organizations that convert inputs into products and services.** In one sense, managers in POM, whom we shall simply call *operations
managers,* do the same basic things that other managers do—plan, organize, staff,
direct, and control. But the activities of productive systems are often so different
from the activities of finance, marketing, engineering, and other functions that the
ways in which operations managers manage can be distinctly different. In general,
productive systems take raw materials, personnel, machines, buildings, and other
resources and *produce* products and services for you and me, the consumers.

The management of productive systems today is different from what it was
yesterday, and changes are already in the works that will modify the ways in which
these operations managers go about their jobs next year. Because POM has evolved
over the years to its present form by continually changing and adapting to the
challenges of each new era, two factors are important to its understanding:

1. Operations managers today go about their jobs in ways that were developed by
   managers who preceded them decades, and even centuries, ago. Many of today's
   POM practices were originated by management pioneers who *broke the trail* as
   they encountered the new problems of their times.

5

2. Today's operations managers are facing new problems that are affecting the ways that they are managing. The old ways of the past are being modified and new methods are being developed as managers attempt to meet the pressures and challenges of today.

POM today is therefore an interesting blend of time-tested practices from the past that have been retained because they work, and a continuing search for different ways to manage productive systems in order to solve the new problems that occur day after day.

In this chapter we shall explore both the past and the present so that we may develop a useful background for this introductory study of POM.

Milestone Historical Developments in POM

For consideration of their impact on POM, we have selected five historical eras: the post–Civil War period, the scientific management movement, the human relations movement, the operations research movement, and the coming of computers. Although the study of these eras or movements does not explain all we know about POM, it does trace those developments that underlie the ways in which today's operations managers manage.

Post–Civil War Period (1865–1900)

A new industrial era for the United States was ushered in with the coming of the twentieth century. The earlier post–Civil War period had set the stage for the great expansion of productive capacity of the new century. The abolition of slave labor and the exodus of farm laborers to the cities provided a large work force for the rapidly developing urban industrial centers.

The end of the Civil War witnessed the beginning of modern forms of capital through the establishment of joint-stock companies. This development led to the eventual separation of the capitalist from the employer, with managers becoming salaried employees of the financiers who owned the capital. During this post–Civil War period J. P. Morgan, Jay Gould, Cornelius Vanderbilt, and others built industrial empires. These entrepreneurs and the vast accumulation of capital in this period created a great U.S. productive capacity that was to mushroom at the turn of the century.

The rapid expansion and settlement of the West created the need for numerous products and a means to deliver them to product-hungry settlers of the West. The post–Civil War period produced the large railroads, the first great U.S. industry. Rail lines were extended; new territories were developed; and with the coming of the twentieth century, an effective and economical transportation system, national in scope, was in operation.

By 1900 all these developments—increased capital and productive capacity, the expanded urban work force, new Western markets, and an effective national transportation system—set the stage for the great production explosion of the early twentieth century.

Table 1.1
Scientific Management: The Players and Their Parts

Contributor	Life Span	Contributions
1. Frederick Winslow Taylor	1856 – 1915	Scientific management principles, exception principle, time study, methods analysis, standards, planning, control
2. Frank B. Gilbreth	1868 – 1924	Motion study, methods, therbligs, construction contracting, consulting
3. Lillian M. Gilbreth	1878 – 1973	Fatigue studies, human factor in work, employee selection and training
4. Henry L. Gantt	1861 – 1919	Gantt charts, incentive pay systems, humanistic approach to labor, training
5. Carl G. Barth	1860 – 1939	Mathematical analysis, slide rule, feeds and speeds studies, consulting to automobile industry
6. Harrington Emerson	1885 – 1931	Principles of efficiency, million dollars a day savings in railroads, methods of control
7. Morris L. Cooke	1872 – 1960	Applied scientific management in educational and governmental organizations

Scientific Management (1875 – 1925)

The economic and social environments of the new century were the crucible in which scientific management was formulated. The one great missing link was management — the ability of managers to develop this great production machine to satisfy the massive markets of the day. A nucleus of men and women — business executives, consultants, educators, and researchers — developed the methods and philosophy called *scientific management*. Table 1.1 presents the main characters of the scientific management era.

Frederick Winslow Taylor is known as the father of scientific management. This title is well deserved when one considers his personal accomplishments in the face of great obstacles. Although Taylor did not originate most of the techniques that he used to analyze shop management problems of his day (time study, motion study, and methods study), he brought their use into focus and popularized the notions of efficiency and productivity as had never been done before.

Taylor was born in Pennsylvania, the son of a prosperous attorney. With a plan to follow in his father's professional footsteps, he attended preparatory school and applied such energy in his studies that he gradually impaired his eyesight. Although he passed the entrance exams to Harvard Law School with honors, his poor health prevented him from continuing in the legal profession. He turned instead to a four-year apprentice program for pattern makers and machinists. It was here in industry that Taylor found outlets for his interests — scientific investigation, experimentation, and improving and reforming things on the basis of fact. Taylor found industrial conditions that he could not tolerate — worker soldiering (loafing), poor management, and lack of harmony between workers and managers.

Although jobs were scarce in 1878, Taylor found work as a common laborer at the Midvale Steel Company in Philadelphia. In six years he rose from laborer to clerk, to machinist, to gang boss of machinists, to foreman, to master mechanic of maintenance, and finally to chief engineer of the works. While advancing through these positions, he attended Stevens Institute of Technology and received a degree in mechanical engineering. Taylor owed his rapid advancement at Midvale Steel in large part to his scientific investigations into improvements in efficient worker use that resulted in great labor cost savings.

Taylor's *shop system,* a systematic approach to improving labor efficiency, employed the following steps:

1. Skill, strength, and learning ability were determined for each worker so that individuals could be placed in jobs for which they were best suited.

2. Stopwatch studies were used to precisely set standard output per worker on each task. The expected output on each job was used for planning and scheduling work and for comparing different methods of performing tasks.

3. Instruction cards, routing sequences, and materials specifications were used to coordinate and organize the shop so that work methods and work flow were standardized and labor output standards could be met.

4. Supervision was improved through careful selection and training. Taylor frequently indicated that management was negligent in performing its functions. He believed that management had to accept planning, organizing, controlling, and methods determination responsibilities, rather than leave these important functions to the workers.

5. Incentive pay systems were installed to increase productivity and relieve foremen from their traditional function of driving the workers.

In 1893, Taylor left Midvale to form a private consulting practice in order to apply his system to a broader range of situations. Those analysts who followed Taylor were known as *efficiency experts, efficiency engineers,* and, finally, *industrial engineers.* In addition to the title of father of scientific management, Taylor is also known as the father of industrial engineering.

Taylor spent a total of twelve hours over a four-day period in the witness chair before a 1911 congressional investigating committee responding to labor, Congressmen, and newsmen on charges that scientific management treated labor unfairly. The great publicity from his testimony at these hearings and Louis Brandeis's call for the use of scientific management in the railroad industry to avoid railroad rate increases in 1910 gave scientific management the public attention it needed to gain widespread acceptance in a broad range of industrial settings in the United States and abroad.

The other scientific management pioneers found in Table 1.1 rallied to spread the gospel of efficiency. Each of these individuals contributed valuable techniques and approaches that eventually shaped scientific management into a powerful force to facilitate mass production. This force was so successfully applied during the U.S. buildup of output for World War I that after the war European countries imported scientific management methods to develop their factories.

Scientific management has dramatically affected today's management practices. Table 1.2 lists a few modern management concepts and practices that find their genesis in scientific management. Although this table emphasizes the techniques of the scientific management era, perhaps these are only symptomatic of the management philosophy or principles that permeate today's productive systems as Taylor so strongly advocated:

Table 1.2
Scientific Management Legacy: Some Practices and Concepts Found in Today's Organizational Functions

Organizational Function	Concepts and Practices from Scientific Management
1. Management	Exception principle; identifying management tasks that are distinctly different from worker tasks; placing responsibility for organizational performance on management; formal education of managers; staff experts; control systems as sensing mechanisms; decision making based on analysis; cost and budgeting systems
2. Industrial engineering	Time study; motion study; workplace layout and design; work sampling; standardization of tools and methods; slide rules and mnemonic devices; assembly line and mass production facilities
3. Personnel management	Incentive pay systems; scientific selection of employees to fit jobs; employee training; cooperation between workers and management
4. Operations scheduling and control	Labor and material standards; graphic scheduling devices; planning departments; standardization of product designs and methods

1. Systematic planning as a distinct management responsibility that must preclude production activity.
2. Control systems as sensing mechanisms to maintain established procedures and performance standards.
3. Scientific, or analytical, investigation of business problems rather than intuitive decisions.
4. Standards as benchmarks with which to compare management's and workers' performances.

Scientific management's struggle to find the *one best way* to operate factories leads logically to a questioning attitude on the part of managers in every phase of productive systems. The questioning attitude and analytical investigations are perhaps scientific management's greatest legacy to modern management.

The high water mark of scientific management occurred at the Ford Motor Company early in the twentieth century. Henry Ford (1863–1947) designed the "Model T" Ford automobile to be built on assembly lines that would soon become the basis for designing factories in the future. In Ford's assembly lines were embodied the chief elements of scientific management—standardized product designs, mass production, low manufacturing costs, mechanized assembly lines, specialization of labor, and interchangeable parts. Although Ford did not invent many of the production methods that he used, he did, perhaps more than any other industrial leader of his time, incorporate into his factories the best of that period's efficient production methods. In fact, he was responsible in large measure for popularizing assembly lines as *the* way to produce large volumes of low-cost products. Later, this popularity spread to other industries in this country and abroad. The technology of assembly lines expanded and grew throughout the buildup of production capacity in World War II.

Scientific management's thrust was at the lower level of the organization's hierarchy—the shop floor, the foremen, superintendents, and lower middle management. Taylor and his associates concentrated on the shop level because it was here that most management problems of the day were found. What was needed was production and efficiency. Scientific management methods met that challenge.

Human Relations Movement (1925 – 1960)

Factory workers of the Industrial Revolution were uneducated, unskilled, undisciplined, and starving peasants fresh off the farms. These workers had a basic dislike for factory work and wanted more security with little responsibility. Factory managers threatened their employees with punishment and developed rigid controls to force them to work hard. This legacy of a working environment structured around the threat of punishment, rigid controls, and coercion carried over into the 1800s and early 1900s. Basic to this management method was the assumption that workers were naturally lazy and that they had to be placed into jobs designed to ensure that they would work hard and efficiently. Workers were viewed as part of the machinery of the factory.

In the 1925 – 1960 period, however, there began to emerge the view among managers that workers were human beings and should be treated with dignity while on the job. The *human relations movement* began in Illinois with the work of Elton Mayo, F. J. Roethlisberger, T. N. Whitehead, and W. J. Dickson at the Hawthorne, Illinois, plant of the Western Electric Company in the 1927 – 1932 period. These *Hawthorne Studies* were initially begun by industrial engineers and were aimed at determining the optimal level of lighting to get the most production from workers. When these studies produced confusing results about the relationship between physical environment and worker productivity, the researchers realized that human factors must be affecting productivity. This was perhaps the first time that researchers and managers alike recognized that psychological and sociological factors affected not only human motivation and attitude but productivity as well.

These early human relations studies and experiments soon gave way to a broad range of research into the behavior of workers in their job environments. The work and writings of Chester Barnard, Abraham Maslow, Frederick Herzberg, Douglas McGregor, Peter Drucker, and others disseminated to industrial managers a basic understanding of workers and their attitudes toward their work. From the work of these *behavioralists,* as they would soon be known, came a gradual change in the way managers thought about and treated workers. We are still learning how to utilize the great potential present in industrial workers today. That they have underutilized capabilities is not questioned, but how to tap this reservoir of energy and skill remains the objective of many research experiments being carried out today.

Operations Research (1940 – Present)

With the advent of World War II, military, government, and industrial organizations in the United States and Europe grew to immense proportions. The European campaign of World War II used enormous quantities of resources that had to be deployed in efficient ways in order to accomplish a specific set of objectives in an extremely dynamic environment. Perhaps never before had organizations faced such complex management decisions. These particular organizational situations created the need for a problem-solving approach aimed at solving management's problems with a top-of-the-organization perspective.

Table 1.3
Characteristics of Operations Research (OR)

1. OR approaches problem solving and decision making from the total system's perspective.
2. OR does not necessarily use interdisciplinary teams, but it is interdisciplinary; it draws on techniques from sciences such as biology, physics, chemistry, mathematics, and economics and applies the appropriate techniques from each field to the system being studied.
3. OR does not experiment with the system itself but constructs a model of the system upon which to conduct experiments.
4. Model building and mathematical manipulation provide the methodology that has perhaps been the key contribution of OR.
5. The primary focus is on decision making.
6. Computers are used extensively.

Because of this complexity, *operations research* teams were formed in all branches of the military services. These teams utilized many of the academic disciplines of the time. The concepts of the *total systems approach, interdisciplinary teams,* and the *utilization of complex mathematical techniques* evolved as a result of the hectic and chaotic conditions existing in the huge military organizations involved in World War II. Operations research (OR) met the needs of the time.

After the war, operations research was introduced into the private sectors. In Britain, the government quickly assigned operational research teams to nationalized industries — iron and steel, coal, road and rail transport, textiles, agriculture, brickmaking, and shoe industries. In the United States, the adoption of operations research in business was somewhat slower. Competition among private firms tended to inhibit the exchange of information on applications, a problem that was unimportant in Britain because of nationalization.

After World War II, military operations researchers and their approaches to complex organizational problems found their way back to universities, industry, government agencies, and consulting firms. They introduced operations research into the curriculums of colleges and universities, developed consulting firms that specialized in operations research, and formed operations research societies. As time passed, operations research matured, and its characteristics (shown in Table 1.3) became those that we know today.

Operations research during the World War II period was best known for its total systems approach and its interdisciplinary teams providing problem-solving support for top management. During the postwar era, and perhaps today, operations research has been known chiefly for its quantitative techniques, such as linear programming, PERT/CPM, and forecasting techniques. The following question arises in most classes in POM: How widespread is the use of operations research techniques today? One study of 1,398 manufacturing firms with 250 or more employees indicated that about half these firms used one or more of these techniques in their daily operations.[1] This study also showed that quite small firms utilizing low levels of technology rarely used the techniques. As firms become larger and use higher levels of technology, adoption of the techniques is much more intense. These techniques are used, and we should know about their use in POM.

---

[1] Norman Gaither, "The Adoption of Operations Research Techniques by Manufacturing Organizations," *Decision Sciences* 6(October 1975): 808.

Operations research helps operations managers make decisions when problems are complex and when the cost of a wrong decision is high and long lasting. Problems such as the following are commonly analyzed by using operations research techniques:

1. A company has 12 manufacturing plants that ship products to 48 warehouses nationwide. How many units of each product should be shipped from each plant to each warehouse? In other words, what is the optimal shipping plan to maximize profits?

2. A firm contemplates building a $157 million production facility. The project involves company resources, 2 prime contractors, and 75 subcontractors over a 4-year period. How can the company plan the completion of each activity of the project and the use of workers, materials, and contractors so that the cost and duration of the project are minimized?

Operations research, like scientific management, seeks to replace intuitive decision making for large complex problems with an approach that identifies the optimal, or best, alternative through analysis. Operations managers, like managers of other functional areas in organizations, have adopted the approaches and techniques of operations research to improve their decision making.

But while scientific management, human relations, and operations research have affected the ways that managers in POM manage today, perhaps no other development is as important to these managers as the growing presence of computers in their jobs.

Computers (1955 – Present)

Since the first computer was installed at the General Electric Appliance Park in Louisville, Kentucky, in 1954, the number of annual business installations has grown enormously. The growth of the industry is perhaps epitomized by the International Business Machines Corporation (IBM). Though late to enter the field, in the early 1950s, IBM's 650, developed in 1954, proved to be the biggest seller through 1959, a five-year period when IBM sold and serviced over two thirds of the computer market.

Table 1.4 shows the evolution of commercial computers through three generations. Although some would argue that today's models should be considered a fourth generation, computers at present still exhibit the same basic features described in the third generation models. Actually, changes in computer designs have accelerated in recent years to the point that the generation terminology has ceased to be meaningful. The more recent product improvements are aimed at making computer services available to almost any customer at reasonable prices. Chief among these developments are low-cost and powerful mini- and microcomputers, standard computer programs, computer graphics, and data transmission equipment.

Colleges and universities throughout the United States have incorporated into their curriculums computer science courses that include computer languages, systems analysis, and applications of computers. Consequently, many employees of industry and government today have formal training in computers when they are hired. It is not surprising that these employees are more comfortable with computers, tending to use them more and thus expanding the applications of the computers in their organizations.

Table 1.4
Early Commercial Computers

Generation	Period	Representative Models (IBM)	Distinguishing Features and Improvements
First	1951–1959	IBM 701 IBM 650	Used vacuum tubes; large in size; required massive air conditioning; used binary programming language
Second	1960–1965	IBM 1401 IBM 1620 IBM 7090	Used transistors to replace vacuum tubes; smaller; less expensive; required little power and air conditioning; required less maintenance; improved language compilers
Third	1963–1982	IBM 360 IBM 370	Used miniaturized circuits; great programming assistance; operating aids; data communication, parallel processing, remote terminal processing; faster; less expensive; mini- and microprocessors

Table 1.5
The Evolving Uses of Computers in POM

Time Period	Key Applications	Examples of Applications
1951–1959	Clerical duties	Payrolls, billings, inventory transactions, cost reports
1960–1969	Analysis and optimization studies	Linear programming, scheduling, large-scale project planning
1970–present	Massive data storage, retrieval, and manipulation	Dynamic systems of forecasting, scheduling, inventory planning, material acquisition, and computer-aided design and computer-aided manufacture (CAD/CAM)

Computers are a growing force in POM. If properly used, an organization's computer can be an asset to any management as a large reservoir of information, enormous computational capability, and instantaneous and accurate information retrieval. Production and operations managers have learned to work with the computer system on a daily basis, not as slaves chained to the system who must supply information and accept any output in return but rather as computing-system users who use the tool to better manage the organization.

Table 1.5 traces the evolving uses of computers in POM. Early in the development of computers, they were used as cost reduction devices, replacing clerical jobs with machines. In the 1960s and increasingly in the 1970s and 1980s, computers were, are, and will be used to expand the capabilities of managers to store massive quantities of data and to manipulate and retrieve these data. The everyday management of inventories, scheduling, purchasing, and other activities within POM is increasingly dependent upon information that comes from computer-based information systems. The day now appears to be in sight when businesses and other organizations without computers will be the exceptions.

Scientific management, human relations, operations research, and computers have all affected *and are continuing to affect* the ways that managers in POM manage today. The combined effect of these developments has been so subtle that we do not easily recognize their aggregate impact; nevertheless, managers' jobs today are dramatically influenced by these advances. Clearer than these influences from the past, perhaps, is the challenge for managers in POM today to modify existing practices and adapt to the developments around them.

Contemporary Developments and POM Practice

Contemporary developments are presented here so that you can sense the changing nature of POM and so that you can become sensitive to the influence of these factors upon the POM topics that are presented in this text as you proceed through the course.

Unquestionably, several important developments that are critically affecting what POM is becoming are known today. Table 1.6 lists ten such contemporary developments.

Dominance of Service Systems

The emergence of a variety of private and public organizations to supply services to our growing population is perhaps the most dramatic fact of today's organizations. Managers are adapting many of the planning, analyzing, and controlling techniques traditionally used in goods-producing systems to these new systems that produce intangible outputs. But many traditional techniques do not apply, and new ones must be developed and tested.

Governmental Regulation

The intensity and variety of governmental regulation of productive systems is approaching staggering proportions. OSHA, EPA, affirmative action plans, and other federal standards and regulations are joined by a host of state and local agencies to form a long line of regulators and inspectors outside POM doors. The degree to which these complex and sometimes conflicting regulations constrain managers' flexibility in overseeing the activities of their organizations is at times mind-boggling. It appears that these frustrations may continue, given the tendency of bureaucracy to perpetuate itself. POM decisions are certainly not likely to get any simpler. In fact, increased regulation will likely occur; and more complex decisions are to be expected by tomorrow's managers.

Table 1.6
Some Contemporary Developments Affecting Production and Operations Management

1. Dominance of service systems	6. Universal use of computers
2. Governmental regulation	7. Consumers' demands upon POM
3. Scarcity of productive resources	8. Automation, robotry, and computerized controls
4. Spiraling inflation and financial instability	9. International scope of productive systems
5. Workers' attitudes toward work	10. Foreign imports in U.S. markets

Scarcity of Productive Resources

The scarcity of productive resources recently led one marketing executive to comment: "Manufacturing personnel used to call me and ask what they *should* produce. Now I call them and ask what they *can* produce." Certain raw materials, personnel skills, coal, natural gas, water, oil products, and other resources are periodically unavailable today and will probably become scarcer in the future. Rising costs and periodic gaps in supply motivate managers to develop better ways of using these resources and to spend increasing sums of money on plans to reduce the uncertainty of their supply.

Spiraling Inflation and Financial Instability

Just as inflation is increasing the cost of such personal needs as housing, food, gasoline, and clothing, so also are the costs of operating productive systems increasing. Labor, materials, machinery, buildings, supplies, utilities, insurance, taxes, interest, and transportation — the costs of all these items are escalating. How does this inflation affect POM?

If we were to assume that competing organizations' costs were all rising at about the same rate, prices for these organizations' outputs ordinarily would also be expected to increase at about the same rate. Each of the competing firms' costs and prices, therefore, would be in a state of dynamic equilibrium. There would be little worry in this idyllic, but unrealistic, arrangement. Competing firms, however, may be in West Germany, Japan, or Taiwan, where costs of many resources are lower than domestic costs. Low-cost imports put enormous pressure on domestic firms to reduce costs if they are to survive.

High inflation rates have combined with high and fluctuating interest rates, scarcity of debt financing, and general instability of the financial markets. Such conditions have made industrial expansion difficult because new debt and stock issues have been prohibitively expensive and the availability of funds has been uncertain.

Workers' Attitudes toward Work

Managers in POM can no longer take workers for granted. Workers' needs for interesting work, participation, and a sense of personal worth have to be accommodated. The alternative is to experience the costs of increasing turnover, absenteeism, and decreasing quality of outputs. As more and more young workers who have a variety of alternatives to working at any particular job come into the work force, this problem may increase in importance.

Universal Use of Computers

Computers are no longer the fad they seemed in the 1960s. Now they are among the facts of life; no one reasonably doubts that they are here to stay. True, computers have not made middle managers obsolete as they were predicted to do in the late 1950s, but computers are found in greater numbers than almost anyone expected only a few years ago. They are now available to any U.S. organization at economical cost, and their effective use can be a key factor in the success and survival of organizations.

Consumers' Demands upon POM

Increasingly, consumers demand more from productive systems. Special product or service designs, accelerated delivery dates, custom packaging, specific shipping requirements, and last-minute order changes are examples of these demands. Managers' performance in POM is decreasingly measured in terms of budget performance, cost per unit of output, or any other single measure. On the contrary, managers today are judged good managers if their productive systems are highly efficient (low cost) *and* responsive to customers' demands.

Automation, Robotry, and Computerized Controls

The technology of automation, robotry, and computerization is developing rapidly throughout the world. These developments facilitate the replacement of human effort with mechanical devices, thereby yielding cost savings. Moreover, these devices can sometimes perform operations faster, more safely, and more precisely than people can. In some cases operations that were not feasible when attempted by human beings can now be performed by *smart machines*. CAD/CAM (computer-aided design/computer-aided manufacturing) is growing in importance in the United States and other industrialized countries. Japan leads all other countries in the use of robots and other computer-assisted devices — a factor that is creating severe competitive pressures on U.S. industries.

International Scope of Productive Systems

That productive systems are now operating in an environment international in scope cannot be seriously doubted. Numerous examples demonstrate this fact. One firm imports textile fabric from the Far East, imports labor from Mexico, operates a garment factory in El Paso, Texas, and exports most of its products to Western Europe. This example represents a growing list of firms that are citizens of an international business community that is becoming increasingly important in trade. This development is expected to intensify in the future as countries become interdependent economically, sociologically, and even militarily.

Foreign Imports in U.S. Markets

The leaders of U.S. manufacturing firms are genuinely concerned about the successes of foreign manufacturers in U.S. markets today. These firms, most notably the Japanese companies, have built efficient manufacturing systems that can produce very high quality products at very low costs and in high volumes. Such tough competitors are forcing U.S. manufacturers to rethink the way that they have managed their factories and many are investing heavily in overhauling their production lines to improve both the quality and cost of their products.

These contemporary developments clearly demonstrate that productive systems cannot stand still. Because the work of operations managers is so closely linked to productive systems, POM jobs must also be adaptive and open to innovation.

Figure 1.1
A Comparison of Operations Managers with Executives

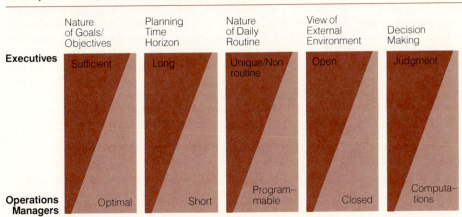

The Nature of Operations Managers' Jobs

What you have learned about management in other college courses has probably been about general management—the management of entire organizations. This view from the executive suite provides a good starting point for exploring POM. Here, we will compare and contrast the management practices of executives with those of operations managers. This comparison should bring us to a better understanding of what operations managers do, and the understanding of what operations managers do is the essence of understanding POM.

Figure 1.1 compares operations managers with executives along five dimensions —nature of goals and objectives, planning time horizon, nature of daily routine, view of external environment, and decision making.

Nature of Goals and Objectives

Executives do not necessarily strive for maximization of profits, minimization of costs, maximization of the number of souls saved, or the optimization or extreme of any single measure of organizational success. Rather, top executives tend to establish a set of goals and objectives that are satisfying (or *satisficing*) rather than optimizing, because they realize that long-term survival and stability are just as important as short-run optimization. Additionally, top executives are generally rewarded for the growth, stability, and survival of their organizations. Operations managers, on the other hand, tend to be more intent on a smaller set of objectives that are intended to be near optimal. Examples are: maximize profits, minimize costs, maximize sales, and maximize the number of satisfied customers. Operations managers tend to be rewarded on the basis of their ability to attain these optimizing goals.

Planning Time Horizon

While operations managers are concerned with what is likely to happen five or ten years from now (the long run), they must also be concerned with the immediate performance of their departments. When they alone must explain poor performance on a monthly or even weekly basis, it is no wonder that they tend to be concerned with short-term success. Top executives, on the other hand, are naturally concerned with short-run performance; but they tend to be more involved in and responsible for long-run planning for future success—stability, growth, and survival. Top executives' intense concern for the long run tends to result in the philosophy that operations managers are principally responsible for short-run execution and success, and top management is responsible for long-run organizational performance.

Nature of Daily Routine

The daily activities of executives tend to be nonroutine. In some situations every day's schedule can be unique. Much of this variety is by design, because most of the routine daily activities have been delegated to subordinates. This delegating leaves the executives free for such critical organizational duties as long-range planning, assisting subordinates in making unusual or very important decisions, and evaluating the organization's effectiveness.

Even though executives ordinarily experience a variety of daily activities, not all of their activities are of the mountain-top classification. Even executives have a certain amount of routine tasks that must be performed on a daily basis—opening the morning mail, signing required documents, initialing weekly reports. However, these routine duties tend to be a minor part of top managers' daily schedules.

Operations managers, on the other hand, will have some unusual activities, but on the whole their daily schedule tends to be much more predictable. Much of the stable nature of their jobs stems from the characteristically stable processes that they are responsible for. For example, managers of process engineering and maintenance departments are inseparably tied to a production process that is stable from day to day. The nonroutine parts of their jobs usually occur when the process is out of control or when new processes are being designed, but these interruptions are the exceptions rather than the rule.

Interestingly, when asked to describe their jobs, most operations managers emphasize interruptions, novel projects, and the daily unique situations and downplay the routine parts of their jobs. This is probably because the unusual tends to stand out in memory more than the ordinary. But on balance the daily schedules of operations managers are more predictable than those of top executives.

View of External Environment

Operations managers strive to minimize the number of interruptions to the production processes over which they exercise control. These managers therefore must take a somewhat *closed view of the external environment*. Although operations managers recognize that organizations must respond to changes in the external environment if they are to succeed and survive, they also know that planned gradual and periodic change, not continuous, highly fluctuating change, is necessary for effective and efficient internal operations.

Executives, on the other hand, tend to operate with an *open view of the external environment*. An open or adaptive view is one that continuously responds to stimuli from the external environment. Since executives must strive for long-run organizational growth and survival and aim at a satisficing performance level, this is not surprising. If organizations are to survive, they must adapt to changes in their external environments. In the long run, organizations that fail to respond to these changes usually die.

The fact that organizations need both closed and open views should be evident. Organizations must be relatively closed at lower levels to allow stable internal operations that promote short-run efficiency and effectiveness, and they must be relatively open at upper levels to allow long-run growth and survival.

Decision Making

The decision-making environment of executives is highly uncertain because of the long-run effects that decisions have on the organization, the interaction of an enormous number of variables, and the unique nature of each decision. One executive jokingly commented that if he had a crystal ball to establish what was going to happen with certainty five to ten years from now, what variables were important, and the values of each of those variables, he could probably make effective decisions most of the time. But, alas, most executives do not have an operative crystal ball. Therefore, how do they make decisions?

Most executives make decisions based upon *judgment* to a dominant degree. Judgment here means using all of the available data, formulating the necessary linkages about what is known and unknown about the decision and how these all relate, and finally deciding on a course of action. Past experience, knowledge, savvy, maturity, intelligence, common sense, and maybe even intuition are all important characteristics of executives who must engage in judgmental decision making.

The operations manager, by contrast, makes some decisions that (1) have a relatively short time horizon, (2) are about problems that have only a few variables, and (3) deal with recurring types of problems. Because of the short duration of the decisions, the planning horizon is more predictable and certain. The limited number of variables and the recurring nature of the problems allow operations managers to better understand the relationships among the variables and predict the probable outcomes from alternative courses of action. Many operations managers' decisions are based to a large degree upon computations of various complexities. Naturally, operations managers utilize judgment in decision making just as executives use computations. But computations are the dominant basis for operations decisions whereas judgment tends to be most important for executive decisions.

Although managers in POM may be like all other managers in that they plan, organize, staff, direct, control, and make decisions concerning these activities, they are distinctly different in many ways. They are typically directly involved in the production of organizations' goods and services. They are involved in a variety of functions such as engineering, maintenance, production, and warehousing. These differences are important in understanding what managers in POM do. Because operations managers manage all of the activities of productive systems, we can also better understand POM by understanding the nature of productive systems.

Productive Systems

As fields of scientific study such as physics, biology, and medicine develop and mature over time, their focus invariably moves from initial discoveries directly to intense investigations into highly specific areas. Very narrow topics are treated in great depth, using analyses supported by enormous data-gathering efforts. This natural tendency to move into deep analysis of apparently insignificant parts of the whole is useful in helping develop knowledge and understand specific details. There is evidence that most fields of scientific endeavor eventually move from in-depth analysis of the specialized parts to a phase of synthesis and integration.[2]

This development from microanalysis to macroanalysis can be observed in POM. The scientific management movement in the late 1800s and early 1900s sought to break productive systems down into indivisible parts and apply various tools of analysis to these microcomponents. The operations research (OR) approach from the 1940s to the present has focused on the productive system as a whole. The movement in POM toward integration and synthesis goes beyond the OR efforts, however, to include all facets of the operations manager's job.

Russell Ackoff, a pioneer in operations research and systems theory, documents this movement toward the *systems approach:*

World War II marked an end of an era of Western culture that began with the Renaissance, the Machine Age, and the beginning of a new era, the Systems Age.

In the Machine Age man sought to take the work apart, to analyze its contents and our experiences of them down to ultimate indivisible parts: atoms, chemical elements, cells, instincts, elementary perception, and so on. These elements were taken to be related to causal laws, laws which made the world behave like a machine. This mechanistic concept of the world left no place in science for the study of free will, goal seeking, and purposes. . . .

With World War II we began to shift into the Systems Age. A system is a whole that cannot be taken apart without loss of its essential characteristics, and hence it must be studied as a whole. Now, instead of explaining a whole in terms of its parts, parts began to be explained in terms of the whole.[3]

Let us examine some of the important systems concepts to gain an understanding of the operation of organizations in general and productive systems in particular.

Systems Concepts

Four systems concepts are essential to understanding productive systems: system, closed system, open system, and suboptimality. Table 1.7 defines each of these important systems concepts. Notice that the definition of a system contains two essential parts—the presence of interdependent components, or subsystems, and the system is designed to achieve objectives.

The *interdependence of the subsystems* means that when one subsystem is acted upon by some force, all other parts of the system are affected to some degree because of the relationships among all the components of the subsystems. If man-

---

[2] Thomas S. Kuhn, *The Structure of Scientific Revolutions* (Chicago: University of Chicago Press, 1962), 23.

[3] Russell L. Ackoff, ''A Note on Systems Science,'' *Interfaces* 2(August 1972): 40.

Table 1.7
Systems Concepts

Concept	Definition
1. System	An organized complex of interdependent components or subsystems designed to achieve objectives
2. Closed system	A system that does not interact with its external environment
3. Open system	A system that has a continuous action and reaction with its external environment
4. Suboptimality	The condition that exists when the extreme optimization of one component or subsystem results in less than optimal performance of the larger system and vice versa

agement intends to act upon any part of the organization, it must consider the impact that this action will have on all the other parts of the organization.

Too often managers make decisions concerning one small part of an organization while ignoring the impact that this course of action will have on other areas of the organization. The central message of the systems approach is that managers should examine the overall impact of decisions across all parts of the organization before they act.

A *closed system* view is one where the internal operations of the system are assumed to be isolated and insulated from their external environmental forces; consequently, the system is considered sufficiently independent so that its problems can be analyzed, tasks assigned, and formal relationships established without regard to the external environment. Mechanical systems such as clockworks are good examples of closed systems. Until modern times, organizations were viewed by their managers as closed systems. This closed-system view allowed managers to regiment and design the internal workings of organizations that operated like a clockworks: predictable, efficient, and easy to manage.

As the rate of change in our external environments accelerated in modern times, this pure closed-system view lost favor because of the high incidence of organization failures. These failures resulted principally from the external environment's ceasing to demand the goods and services offered. Managers of today's organizations have now accepted this important truth: In order for organizations to survive in the long run, they must continually respond to the stimuli from their external environment.

Customers, laws, competitors, suppliers, governmental regulations, social changes, technological developments, economic trends, and other factors are the necessary stimuli that cause organizations to respond, change, and adapt — and in the process survive. Organizations that are viewed as open systems have much in common with biological systems such as cells. These systems are in a dynamic relationship with their environment and receive various inputs, convert these inputs in some way, and export outputs. These open systems change the structures and processes of their internal components as changes in inputs and demand for outputs are sensed. The changing or adaptive nature of organizations is the key for long-run organizational survival, a concept basic to the systems approach.

We must recognize that the concept of open and closed systems is a matter of degree. All systems are both open and closed, depending upon our position of reference. Earlier, we emphasized this important point: Organizational success means both long-run survival and intermediate and short-run performance. Long-

Table 1.8
Inherent Sources of Organizational Suboptimality

Organizational Functional Subsystem	Typical Subsystem Goals
1. Production	Minimize costs
	Minimize interruptions to production
	Minimize the number of products
	Maintain stable levels of production
	Standardize product designs
2. Marketing	Maximize number of units sold
	Maximize market share
	Develop custom-designed products
	Develop new products
3. Accounting and finance	Maximize after-tax profits
	Minimize financial risks
	Maintain liquid cash position
	Maintain organizational survival and growth
4. General management	Maximize long-run profits
	Maintain organizational survival and growth
	Develop and increase profits over time

run survival is achieved in large part from the open system view — developing an organization that continually changes and adapts to its environment. Short-run performance results principally from predictability, rationality, and stability — the conditions present in the closed system. Productive systems, which are subsystems of the larger system — the organization — must operate to a degree as closed systems if intermediate and short-run performance goals are to be achieved.

As social systems all organizations have built-in forces that foster *suboptimality* of the larger system through the continual struggle for optimization of the subsystems. Table 1.8 shows three typical functions found in goods-producing organizations — production, marketing, and accounting/finance. These functions or subsystems have distinctly different subsystems goals. Can you see the potential for the suboptimality of the larger system? For example, the marketing subsystem strives to develop new products and to custom-design them to individual customers' needs. This is an important element in the marketing subsystem's ability to build a larger market for the system, and building larger markets is the principal basis for rewarding marketing subsystem personnel.

The production subsystem resists the custom designs and the great variety of products that the marketing subsystem continually proposes. Why? Because these actions can shorten production runs and increase the number and frequency of product changeovers on the production line, which increase per-unit costs; and low per-unit cost is the principal basis of rewarding production subsystem personnel. If these two subsystems were left to fight out their differences through influence or other means, one of the subsystems could be optimized at the other's expense. Thus, the larger system (firm) would be suboptimized. What is needed in this example is for the general management goals as shown in item 4 of Table 1.8 to dominate all of the subsystems' goals: Balance the goals of the subsystems so that the larger system's goals are achieved.

With these important systems concepts of the systems approach in mind, we can now examine the operation of productive systems.

Productive Systems Concepts

We can view all systems as subsystems of some larger system. For example, in the field of astronomy, we can view the earth either as a whole system or as a subsystem of our solar system. If our interest is in studying the earth alone (with very little interest in the other subsystems of our solar system), we will draw the system boundary around the earth. We will then refer to the earth as a system. If, on the other hand, our interest is in the earth and its relationships with the other subsystems of our solar system, we will draw the system boundary around the entire solar system. In this case we will refer to the earth as a subsystem.

Similarly, we could refer to a productive system as either a subsystem or a system depending upon where we draw the system boundary. For the purpose of examining the inner workings of productive systems, let us draw our system boundary around only the productive system, excluding the other organizational functions. We shall therefore refer to the productive system as a system.

Table 1.9 contains the definition of three important productive system concepts — a productive system, a conversion subsystem, and a control subsystem. Productive systems receive *inputs* in the form of materials, personnel, capital, utilities, and information. These inputs are changed in a *conversion subsystem* into the desired products and services, which are called *outputs*. A portion of the output is monitored in the *control subsystem* to determine if it meets the expected levels of quantity, cost, quality, or other criteria. If the output is acceptable across all of the appropriate criteria or standards, no changes are required in either the inputs or the conversion subsystem. If, however, it does not meet the appropriate standards, managerial corrective action is required in the inputs, the conversion subsystem, or both. The control subsystem ensures a uniform level of output performance by providing feedback information to management concerning the output so that corrective managerial action can be directed as required.

Figure 1.2 shows a comprehensive view of productive systems. Inputs are classified into three general classes — environmental, market, and primary resources.

Table 1.9
Productive Systems Concepts

Concept	Definition
1. Productive system	A system whose function is to convert a set of inputs into a set of desired outputs
2. Conversion subsystem	A subsystem of the larger productive system where inputs are converted into outputs
3. Control subsystem	A subsystem of the larger productive system where a portion of the outputs is monitored for feedback signals to provide corrective action if required

Figure 1.2
A Productive System Model

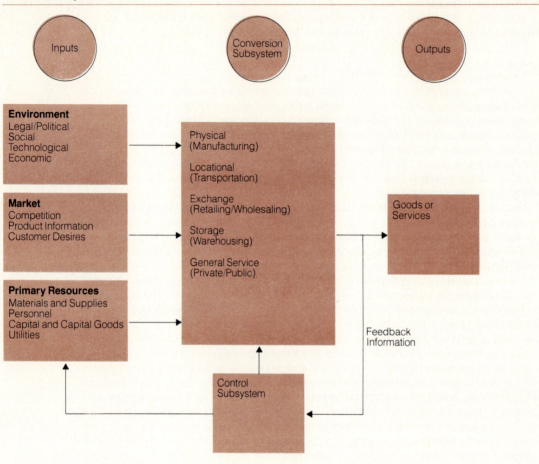

Environmental inputs generally are informational in character and tend to provide operations managers with knowledge about required or desired changes in the productive system. *Legal or political inputs* may place constraints within which the system must operate. All organizations must reckon with governmental regulation, which seems to be accelerating at a staggering pace.

Social and economic inputs can aid operations managers in sensing trends that will affect the productive system in the future. For example, a business firm learned that a local social organization had identified a group of local hard-core unemployed. Since the managers of the business perceived that their organization was a subsystem of a larger system, the community, they worked with the social organization to put several of these disadvantaged people to work as employees. These managers realized at least two major accomplishments: Valuable personnel resources were employed by the firm, and the community's welfare rolls were reduced.

Economic-trend information can also be important for the success of any productive system. For example, a company recently learned that its machine parts supplier planned a major price increase in thirty days. This information allowed the company's purchasing department to rush through an order, thus saving the company thousands of dollars.

Technological inputs may come from trade journals, government bulletins, trade association newsletters, vendors or suppliers, and other sources. This information provides managers with knowledge about important breakthroughs in technology that affect machinery, tools, or processes. Like environmental inputs, *market inputs* tend to be informational in character. Information concerning competition, product design, customer desires, and other market inputs guide POM in responding to the needs of the market.

Inputs that directly support the production and delivery of goods and services are referred to as *primary resources*. These are materials and supplies, personnel, capital and capital goods, and utilities (water, gas, oil, coal, electricity). Purchasing departments and personnel departments are established principally for the provision of materials, supplies, and personnel. Engineering departments are established principally for product design, and finance departments for the acquisition of capital goods and capital funds.

A growing area of concern in POM is the supply and conservation of energy inputs. Enormous efforts are being applied today to design and utilize alternative energy systems. These activities will undoubtedly continue in the future.

Outputs of productive systems can take two forms, tangible or intangible. An enormous array of *tangible goods* is produced each day — automobiles, hair dryers, toothpicks, calculators, rubber bands, clothes, tractors, vertical boring mills, typewriters, agricultural products, and so on endlessly. Likewise, the *intangible outputs — services —* that pour out from productive systems seem inexhaustible: education, trash hauling, haircuts, tax accounting, public and private health delivery systems, lodging, transportation, and so on. All of these goods and services are not the end but the beginning of productive systems. It is because of the outputs that productive systems are established. Lewis Carroll wrote in the 1800s in *Alice in Wonderland,* "If you don't know where you are going it doesn't matter how you get there." Likewise, if the outputs are inappropriate or unwanted, the productive system can hardly be effectively designed and operated.

Interestingly, we often overlook indirect outputs of productive systems. Taxes, waste and pollution, technological advances, wages and salaries, and community outreach activities are examples of indirect outputs. Although they do not receive the same attention as the goods and services outputs that generate the revenues which perpetuate the system, the indirect outputs are a cause of both concern and pride. An awareness that such factors are indeed outputs of our productive systems causes operations managers to more effectively manage the total scope of their jobs.

Productive System Diversity

All organizations have at least one productive system. As a college or university student you have had exposure to a wide variety of organizations. You can probably describe the inputs and outputs of these diverse organizations. Can you, however, describe the conversion subsystem of the various organizations with which you are familiar? This is a little more difficult.

Study the conversion subsystems in Figure 1.2 carefully. Notice the five classes of conversion subsystems that are specified: physical, locational, exchange, storage, and general service. The physical class covers the generation of all tangible goods. The locational, exchange, storage, and general service classes cover all of the services. The general service class is a broad one that covers a large number of private and governmental productive systems whose outputs do not fall in the locational, exchange, or storage classes.

Table 1.10 gives several examples of productive systems. Notice the variety in the classes of conversion subsystems presented. The inputs, outputs, and conversion subsystems are not difficult to identify in productive systems that generate physical or tangible goods. The components of service systems, both private and public, are more difficult to recognize. Why is it necessary or desirable to view these service systems as productive systems?

Because the number of persons employed in service systems accounts for almost two thirds of the total work force today. Also, about two thirds of the U.S. GNP originates in the service sectors of transportation (3.7 percent), communications (2.5 percent), utilities (2.4 percent), wholesaling (7.9 percent), retailing (10.0 percent), finance, insurance, and real estate (13.8 percent), miscellaneous services (12.0 percent), and governmental agencies (13.2 percent). This trend is not expected to diminish throughout the 1980s and 1990s.[4] This great mushrooming of service systems needs the management approaches and techniques that have benefited goods-producing systems for several decades: inventory control, material and personnel scheduling, forecasting, allocation techniques, cost controls, quality control, and others. Being able to fit service systems into the productive system framework of inputs, conversion subsystems, and outputs facilitates the straightforward application of the tried and proven POM approaches and techniques. This system framework also facilitates the development of new approaches and techniques to fit the new and sometimes strange service system situations.

How productive systems are manifested as parts of organizations differs considerably from firm to firm. Let us examine some diverse organizational schemes for these production functions.

The Production Function

The core of a productive system is its conversion subsystem wherein workers, materials, and machines are used to convert inputs into products and services. This process of conversion is at the heart of production and operations management and is present in some form in all organizations. *Where* this conversion process is carried out and *what we call* the department or function where it is located varies greatly among organizations. Be assured, however, that every organization, regardless of its purpose, has a production function whose departments and personnel play a central role in achieving the objectives of the organization.

---

[4] U.S. Department of Commerce, *U.S. Service Industries in World Markets* (Washington, DC: Government Printing Office, December 1976).

Table 1.10
Some Typical Productive Systems

Productive System	Primary Inputs	Conversion Subsystem	Outputs
1. Pet food factory	Grain, water, fish meal, personnel, tools, machines, paper bags, cans, buildings, utilities	Converts raw materials into finished goods (physical)	Pet food products
2. Hamburger stand	Meat, bread, vegetables, spices, supplies, personnel, utilities, machines, cartons, napkins, buildings, hungry customers	Transforms raw materials into fast-food products and packages (physical)	Satisfied customers and fast-food products
3. Automobile factory	Purchased parts, raw materials, supplies, paints, tools, equipment, personnel, buildings, utilities	Transforms raw materials into finished automobiles through fabrication and assembly operations (physical)	Automobiles
4. Trucking firm	Trucks, personnel, buildings, fuel, goods to be shipped, packaging supplies, truck parts, utilities	Packages and transports goods from sources to destinations (locational)	Delivered goods
5. Department store	Buildings, displays, shopping carts, machines, stock goods, personnel, supplies, utilities	Attracts customers, stores goods, sells products (exchange)	Marketed goods
6. Public accounting firm	Supplies, personnel, information, computers, buildings, office furniture, machines, utilities	Attracts customers, compiles data, supplies management information, computes taxes (private service)	Management information and tax services
7. Automobile body shop	Damaged autos, paints, supplies, machines, tools, buildings, personnel, utilities	Transforms damaged auto bodies into facsimiles of the originals (private service)	Repaired automobile bodies
8. College or university	Students, books, supplies, personnel, buildings, utilities	Transmits information and develops skills and knowledge (private/public service)	Educated persons
9. County sheriff's department	Supplies, personnel, equipment, automobiles, office furniture, buildings, utilities	Detects crimes, brings criminals to justice, keeps the peace (public service)	Acceptable crime rates and peaceful communities
10. National Marine Fisheries Service	Supplies, personnel, ships, computers, aircraft, utilities, office furniture, equipment	Detects offenders of federal fishery laws, brings them to justice, preserves fishery resources (public service)	Optimal stock of fish resources

Table 1.11
Production Functions and Jobs in Diverse Organizations

Type of Firm	Production Function Departments and Jobs		Name of Production Function's Department	Productive System Activities in Other Departments (Jobs/Department)
	Line Jobs	Staff Jobs		
Manufacturing	V.P. Manufacturing Plant Manager Production Manager Superintendent Foreman Team Leader Crew Chief	Manufacturing Engineer Industrial Engineer Quality Control Manager Quality Control Engineer Materials Manager Inventory Analyst Production Scheduler	Manufacturing	Purchasing Agent — Purchasing Buyer — Purchasing Personnel Specialist — Personnel Product Designer — Marketing or Engineering Budget Analyst — Accounting Shipping Specialist — Shipping
Retailing	V.P. Operations Store Manager Operations Manager Departmental Supervisor Sales Clerk Stocking Clerk	Customer Service Manager Security Manager Maintenance Manager Supplies Specialist Warehouse Manager	Operations	Purchasing Agent — Merchandising Buyer — Merchandising Merchandise Control Analyst — Merchandising Budget Analyst — Accounting Inspector — Merchandising
Trucking	Owner V.P. Operations Branch Manager Dock Supervisor Truck Operations Manager Driver Dock Worker	Rates Specialist Maintenance Director Truck Scheduler Repair Mechanic Dispatcher	Operations	Personnel Manager — Personnel Stores Manager — Administrative Services Budget Analyst — Accounting Systems Analyst — Accounting Purchasing Manager — Administrative Services

Table 1.11 compares the jobs and names of the production function departments of three different types of firms. This table shows the typical job titles given to the line and staff jobs within the production function, the name of the department where the production function is housed, and the jobs in other departments that are also a part of the larger productive system but not directly assigned to the production function. Notice that services such as retailing, trucking, and banking tend to use the word *operations* rather than *production* for the name of the production function department, and also that the types of jobs that are considered line jobs tend to depend upon the purpose of the organization. For example, line jobs in trucking are responsible for loading, hauling, and unloading freight, but line jobs in retailing are responsible for moving, stocking, and selling merchandise.

Although the departmental names and job titles of production functions differ among diverse organizations, such production functions are nevertheless present and constitute important parts of these organizations.

Summary

The post–Civil War period, the scientific management era, the human relations movement, operations research, and computers represent five important historical developments for POM. As POM has adapted to these events of the past, so also is POM attempting to meet such contemporary challenges as the emergence and dominance of service systems, governmental regulations, and foreign competition. Such is the nature of POM that it evolves to meet the challenges of each new era, and in the process keeps the tried and proven methods of the past and develops new ones for today's needs.

Operations managers' jobs are different from the jobs of general managers because of their close ties to productive systems. These systems convert inputs such as materials, labor, capital, and utilities into outputs that are their products and services. A great variety of productive systems exists in today's organizations. Understanding how this universe of organizations fits into the productive system framework (inputs, conversion subsystem, and outputs) facilitates an improved management of these systems.

All organizations, regardless of their purposes, have production functions—departments where the conversion process actually occurs. The location of these departments within organizations and the types of jobs in these departments vary greatly among organizations. Although such variance is nearly as great as the diversity of purposes among organizations, production functions and their personnel play central roles in achieving the objectives of their organizations.

Review and Discussion Questions

1. Define *POM*.
2. Describe Frederick Winslow Taylor's shop management approach.
3. Why was scientific management in the early 1900s aimed at the shop level?
4. Who were the foremost pioneers in scientific management, and what were their contributions?

5. Write a brief biography of Frederick Winslow Taylor.

6. What are the characteristics of operations research?

7. To what extent are operations research techniques used in today's organizations?

8. Arrange the ten contemporary developments listed in Table 1.6 in the order of their importance (in your opinion).

9. In what ways is operations management different from executive management?

10. Define a *system*. What implications to the management of organizations are present in this definition?

11. Define a *closed system*. Define an *open system*. How can organizations operate with both the open and closed systems views?

12. Define *suboptimality*. Give an example of suboptimality in organizations. What inherent forces are present in organizations that can lead to suboptimality?

13. Define a *productive system*. How does the concept of a productive system help in the understanding of POM?

14. What are the inputs to productive systems? How can they be classified?

15. Define *conversion subsystems*. How can they be classified?

16. Define *outputs of productive systems*. Why does all productive activity begin, rather than end, with outputs?

17. Define *control subsystems*. Do all organizations have them? Describe some of them. What do they control?

18. Describe the primary inputs, outputs, and conversion subsystems of the following organizations: **a.** Dry-cleaning business, **b.** television factory, **c.** medical clinic, **d.** local fire department, and **e.** public employment office.

19. Name two organizations that have no production functions. Defend your answer.

Selected Bibliography

Ackoff, Russell L. "A Note on Systems Science." *Interfaces* 2(August 1972): 40.

Boulding, Kenneth E. "General Systems Theory: The Skeleton of Science." *Management Science* 2(April 1956): 197–208.

Churchman, C. W. *Systems Approach*. New York: Dell, 1969.

Copely, F. B. *Frederick W. Taylor*, vol. 2. New York: Harper & Bros., 1923.

Gaither, Norman. "The Adoption of Operations Research Techniques by Manufacturing Organizations." *Decision Sciences* 6(October 1975): 797–813.

George, Claude S., Jr. *The History of Management Thought*. Englewood Cliffs, NJ: Prentice-Hall, 1968.

Kast, Fremont E., and James E. Rosenzweig. *Organization and Management: A Systems Approach*. New York: McGraw-Hill, 1974.

Kuhn, Thomas S. *The Structure of Scientific Revolutions*. Chicago: University of Chicago Press, 1962.

McClosky, Joseph F., and Florence N. Trefethen. *Operations Research for Management*. Baltimore: Johns Hopkins Press, 1954.

Miller, James G. "Living Systems: Basic Concepts." *Behavioral Science* 10(July 1965): 195.

Selznick, Phillip. "Foundations of the Theory of Organization." *American Sociological Review* 13(February 1948): 25–35.

Taylor, Frederick Winslow. *Shop Management.* New York: Harper & Bros., 1911.

——. *The Principles of Scientific Management.* New York: Harper & Bros., 1923.

Thompson, James D. *Organizations in Action.* New York: McGraw-Hill, 1967.

von Bertalanffy, Ludwig. "The Theory of Open Systems in Physics and Biology." *Science,* January 13, 1950, 23–29.

Wren, Daniel A. *The Evolution of Management Thought.* New York: Ronald Press, 1972.

Chapter Outline

Three Classes of POM Decisions

The Decision-Making Process
Define and Describe the Problems
Define the Objectives or Measures of Effectiveness
Generate Alternative Solution Approaches
Analyze the Alternatives
Weigh and Decide among the Alternatives
Formulate a Plan for Implementation
Formulate a Contingency Plan
Execute and Control the Plan
Follow Up and Provide Feedback

Characteristics of Decisions
Degree of Uncertainty
Degree of Complexity
Decision Time Frame
Returns Relative to Cost of Analysis
Degree of Recurrence
Intensity of Decision Impact
Duration of Decision Impact
Characteristics of POM Decisions

Levels of Analysis
Intuition
Quick-and-Dirty
Intensive Computations
Computer Model Building
Task Force
Levels of Analysis Appropriateness
Levels of Analysis in POM Decisions

Techniques for Structuring and Analyzing Decisions
Cost Analysis
Break-even Analysis
Decision Trees
Payoff Tables
Cost-Benefit Analysis

Summary

Review and Discussion Questions

Problems

Case: Shale-Co Inc.

Selected Bibliography

2

Decision Making in POM:

The Process and Methods

*What part does decision making play in managing? I shall
find it convenient to take mild liberties with the English
language by using decision making as though it were
synonymous with managing.*
Herbert A. Simon, 1960

We may not totally agree with those who would define managers solely as decision makers. But who would deny the important part that decision making plays in management? In the last chapter we defined production and operations management (POM) in terms of what operations managers do. They plan, organize, staff, direct, and control all of the activities of productive systems—those portions of organizations that convert inputs into products and services. This definition states in very general terms *what* POM is, but *how* operations managers manage may be just as important to understanding POM as what operations managers do. Perhaps no other approach helps us understand how operations managers manage than the examination of the decisions in POM, because, in large part, operations managers manage by making decisions about all of the activities and elements of productive systems.

Three Classes of POM Decisions

Classifying POM decisions into neat compartments is difficult. Although numerous authors have used a variety of schemes for studying POM, at best these schemes seem arbitrary and at worst they may portray unreal perspectives of POM. In my experience as a manager of production organizations, decisions tended to fall into three general categories:

Type 1 Decisions—Decisions about products, processes, and facilities. These decisions are strategic events that have long-term importance for the organization.

Type 2 Decisions—Decisions about planning production to meet demand. These decisions are necessary if the on-going production of goods and services is to continuously satisfy the demands of the market.

Type 3 Decisions—Decisions about planning and controlling operations. These decisions concern the day-to-day activities of workers, product quality issues, and machines.

Type 1 decisions are about operations strategies, the really big decisions of POM. These decisions are so important that we typically get together all of the interested parties, study the business opportunities carefully, and arrive at a decision that puts our organization in the best position of achieving its long-term goals. Examples of this type of planning decision are: deciding to launch a new product development project; selecting a production process for a new product; deciding how to allocate scarce raw materials, utilities, production capacity, and personnel among product lines or projects; and deciding what new facilities are needed and where to locate them. It seems that such decisions are in the works all the time. Those of us who are not tied directly to the supervision of workers in operations spend a good part of our time studying problems of this type. In the meantime, production is going on every day, and we must also be concerned with making decisions about the on-going activities of production.

Type 2 decisions must resolve all of the issues concerning planning production to meet the demands of the market. The principal responsibility of operations is to take the orders for products and services from customers, which the marketing function has generated, and deliver products and services in such a way that we have *satisfied customers* at reasonable costs. In carrying out this responsibility, numerous planning and controlling decisions are made. Examples of this type of decision are: deciding on an intermediate-range plan for production capacity so that the aggregate market demand is met; deciding inventory policies that govern the amount of product inventory to carry; deciding what products and what quantities of each to include in next month's production schedule; deciding whether to increase production capacity next month by having the foundry department work overtime; and deciding on a plan for purchasing raw materials to support next month's production schedule. Such decisions are fundamental to the success of the production function and the entire organization.

Type 3 decisions are concerned with a variety of day-to-day problems in operations. The facts of life for operations managers are that their workers do not always behave and perform as expected, product quality tends to vary, and production machinery tends to break down and usually does so when it is least expected. Operations managers engage in planning, analyzing, and controlling activities so that poor worker performance, inferior product quality, and excessive machine breakdowns do not interfere with the profitable operation of the productive system. Examples of this type of decision are: deciding what to do about a department's failure to meet the planned labor cost target; developing labor cost standards for a revised product design that is about to go into production; deciding how to arrange the equipment in the painting department; deciding what the new quality control acceptance criteria should be for a product that has had a change in design; and deciding how often to perform preventive maintenance on a key piece of production machinery. These and other day-to-day decisions about the workers, product quality, and production machinery may be the most pervasive aspect of an operations manager's job.

This book is organized with this general framework in mind: Type 1 decisions — planning products, processes, and facilities; Type 2 decisions — planning production to meet demand; and Type 3 decisions — planning and controlling operations. Table 2.1 outlines the remainder of the book in terms of this framework.

In the cases where topics seem to belong to more than one type of decision, our choice is to include them as early in the text as possible and then to reintroduce

Table 2.1
Framework of This Book in Terms of POM Decisions

Type of Decision	Chapter	Nature of Chapter Content
Type 1 Decisions: Planning Products, Processes, and Facilities (Part Two)	4. Product Design and Process Planning	Planning the design of products or services and production processes
	5. Allocating Scarce Resources in POM	Planning for the optimal distribution of scarce resources among product lines or projects
	6. Long-Range Capacity Planning and Facility Location	Answering the *how much* and *where* questions about long-range production capacity
	7. Project Management in POM	Planning and controlling large-scale projects
Type 2 Decisions: Planning Production to Meet Demand (Part Three)	8. Proactive Production Planning	Planning and controlling production with production control departments
	9. Materials Management and Independent Demand Inventory Systems	Planning and controlling finished goods inventories and managing all facets of the materials system
	10. Scheduling Manufacturing and Service Operations	Making short-range decisions about what to produce and when to produce
	11. Resource Requirements Planning Systems	Integrating scheduling, capacity utilization, and materials acquisition
Type 3 Decisions: Planning and Controlling Operations (Part Four)	12. Human Resource Management and Productivity	Planning for the effective and efficient use of human resources in operations
	13. Facility Layout	Planning the arrangement of facilities
	14. Quality Control	Planning and controlling the quality of products and services
	15. Maintenance Management and Reliability	Planning for maintaining the machines and facilities of production

them when appropriate in later sections. When a topic can appear in more than one part, we include it where its use is dominant. See if you don't agree, as we proceed through the text, that this arrangement not only gives a realistic view of POM but also progressively develops your understanding of POM.

All of us can profit from improving our decision-making batting average — you, I, and all kinds of managers. What follows is a discussion of the systematic decision-making process — a surefire way to improve our decision-making results.

The Decision-Making Process

Are good decision makers born, or can the techniques of good decision making be learned? A growing number of managers have learned to improve their decision-making abilities through reading, attending management development seminars, and employing consultants who assist individuals and groups in learning decision-making techniques. These managers give glowing testimony to the great value that systematic decision-making techniques have brought to their managerial capabilities.

When we think of decision making, we typically envision a manager at some *moment of truth* deciding or choosing a specific course of action. The mystique surrounding this highly charged moment can be so magnetic that it is sometimes hard to remember this is only the climax to decision making and not the total decision-making experience. While we cannot minimize the importance of this deciding phase of decision making, we must yet recognize that the process of arriving at this moment of choosing is of at least equal importance.

Table 2.2 lists nine steps in the systematic process of decision making. Let us examine each of these steps.

Define and Describe the Problem(s)

One anonymous philosopher stated that "a problem well defined is half solved." This truth is echoed by practicing managers who know that they must constantly remind subordinates and associates that actions tend to be aimed at the symptoms and not the causes of problems.

Problem definition and description involve much investigation in some cases to determine the causes rather than the obvious symptoms. Digging through records, gathering data, interviewing, asking questions, analyzing, and other laborious

---

Table 2.2
The Systematic Process of Decision Making

1. Define and describe the problem(s).	5. Weigh and decide among the alternatives.
2. Define the objective(s) or measure(s) of effectiveness.	6. Formulate a plan for implementation.
3. Generate alternative solution approaches.	7. Formulate a contingency plan.
4. Analyze the alternatives.	8. Execute and control the plan.
	9. Follow up and provide feedback.

activities are required if the true underlying problems are to be defined. This process is somewhat complicated at times by several problems operating simultaneously.

For example, a manufacturing process was under investigation because it was producing products of inferior quality. It was initially believed that the tooling for some newly installed machines was responsible (the cause). Engineers fell upon that tooling like bears on a newly found beehive—measuring, disassembling, reassembling, revising, redesigning, and so on. Guess what? After correcting the tooling deficiencies, the quality of the output did not improve. It was found later that the incoming raw material was marginally out of tolerance. A modest amount of investigation to thoroughly define the problems before a course of action was delineated could have avoided much wasted effort in this instance.

Managers do tend to operate on symptoms rather than causes. If you are to be a truly effective decision maker, in decision-making situations you must always, figuratively speaking, keep a flashing neon sign nearby that repeatedly asks: Problem or symptom?

Define the Objective(s) or Measure(s) of Effectiveness

How will you know when you have solved the problem? This question implies that a systematic decision process must have a control step that monitors the process for effectiveness. The last step of this process, following up and providing feedback, is this control step; and it requires some standard or benchmark to measure progress against.

Few decisions in the complex worlds of business and government are so simple that a singular objective or measure of effectiveness is adequate. All too often we must state multiple objectives and multiple measures of effectiveness for these real world decisions.

One decision of this type is the *trade-off decision*—a decision that involves two or more measures of effectiveness on parallel scales. For example, Figure 2.1 represents three manufacturing process alternatives—A, B, and C. The manager must select one. Each process involves a trade-off of cost per unit against quality.

Figure 2.1
A Manufacturing Trade-off Decision: Cost per Unit vs. Quality

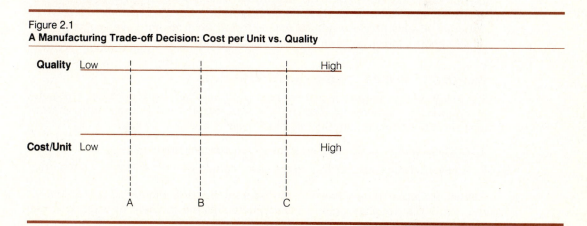

The manager must trade some higher quality for some lower cost per unit. In other words, the manager can get higher quality only by selecting a process that has a higher cost per unit. This situation forces the manager to select two measures of effectiveness: cost per unit and quality level.

Generate Alternative Solution Approaches

Once we have clearly defined the problem and stated objectives and measures of effectiveness of a decision, we are ready to move into perhaps the most creative phase of the decision-making process—generating alternatives, as many as possible and as rapidly as possible. This is the time to *brainstorm* the issue without regard to feasibility. We may generate alternative approaches that seem counterintuitive, unorthodox, and even weird by some people's standards. Some novel approaches can come from this process, and some ridiculous suggestions made here can result in modifications to feasible alternatives that are finally accepted for analysis and comparison at the next step.

Once we have developed a long list of alternatives, then we can shorten the list by eliminating alternatives that have no promise of feasibility, combining those that have commonality, and modifying others. Those alternatives that survive this step should reflect our best thinking about feasible alternatives for solving the problem.

Analyze the Alternatives

Analysis involves these distinct phases—data gathering, computing, and outputting (or results). Each of these phases is performed on each feasible alternative. Data can be gathered from historical records, observations, or other sources. The sources and form of the data typically vary among alternatives. The novel features of each alternative may also require that widely different *computations* be performed in order to arrive at comparable outputs or results across all alternatives. Cost analysis, linear programming, and a legion of other methods may be applied here to effectively manipulate the data into comparable results.

The results, or output, of the analysis should be comparable across all of the alternatives. They should be in the same units of measurement (pounds, dollars, and so on) if at all possible. Nothing is more exasperating to managers than to receive an elaborate display of the results of sophisticated analyses for several alternatives with the bottom lines being in units of oranges, apples, pears, and cabbages.

Weigh and Decide among the Alternatives

The results of the analysis step are but one input into the actual decision. This point is important to understand, as there are two potentially dangerous and common misconceptions concerning the role of analysis in decision making:

1. Analysis tells directly what alternative must be selected.

2. Analysis is such a minor step in decision making that we can skip it altogether.

Neither of these extremes could be further from the truth. Figure 2.2 shows some of the inputs that impinge upon decision makers at the *moment of truth,* when an

Figure 2.2
Deciding among Alternatives

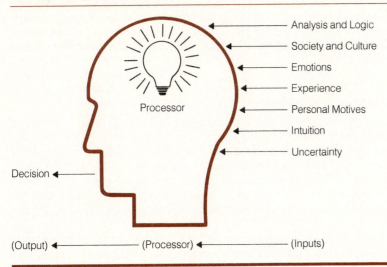

Analysis and Logic

Society and Culture

Emotions

Experience

Personal Motives

Intuition

Uncertainty

Processor

Decision

(Output) ◄─────── (Processor) ◄─────── (Inputs)

alternative must be selected. Analysis is of primary importance to most decisions, but it is by no means the only input. Tradition, society, culture, emotions, experience, personal motives, intuition, uncertainty, and other inputs all affect the decision. The weight given to analysis in decisions varies according to the characteristics of the decisions. These characteristics will be covered in more detail later in this chapter.

Formulate a Plan for Implementation

Few decisions are automatically carried out when no thought is given to implementation. This important truth is typically overlooked in most college and university courses. All too often we assume that a plan for action is centered on the objective —in other words, on *what* must be accomplished rather than on *how* the objective is to be achieved.

Some organizations have recognized the importance of implementing management decisions and have established *planning and programming functions* to aid management in formalizing *implementation*. These functions record for major decisions the tasks that must be performed, who is assigned the responsibility of carrying out each task, when each task is to be completed, and the resources required for each task. All parties to the decision are given periodic reports on the status of each phase of the program for implementation.

Not all decisions require this degree of formality to insure implementation. The benefits or results of the decisions may be so minor that they do not justify the expense of a formal plan; or the program may be assigned to only one person, thus greatly simplifying implementation. But regardless of the simplicity or complexity of implementation, all decisions require the delineation of a program for implementation. Tasks, task assignments, and a timetable for completion of tasks are necessary ingredients for any management decision. When you are sitting at a conference table at some future time and a decision is finally reached, remember this critical step in the decision process.

Formulate a Contingency Plan

Plans do not always go as expected. Our original estimates of such factors as market size, manufacturing costs, technology developments, and product or service performance are later found to be wide of the mark. *Contingency plans* are developed to allow managers to accomplish their objectives in a given decision, just in case the factors that are subject to uncertainty turn against us. We can not always control the outcomes of such variables, but we can avoid their effects by developing a plan for dealing with such variables before they scuttle our entire plan for carrying out the decision.

The idea behind contingency plans is simple: identify the principal factors that can go wrong in carrying out a decision and develop a plan of corrective action that will allow us to carry out the decision just in case these uncertain factors work against us. These plans remain in *standby status* until we determine that they must be activated. Such plans assume a constant monitoring of the progress of the implementing of decisions and provide managers with the best insurance against having to use the alibi: "The decision failed because of bad luck."

Execute and Control the Plan

Periodic reports should be given on the status of carrying out decisions. If the plan for implementing the decision is on schedule and each task is producing the desired results, no corrective action is required. If, however, timetables are slipping, the results of tasks are less than expected, or new information suggests program modifications, then corrective action is required either to change the decision itself or to modify the plan for implementation to insure that the objectives of the decision can be achieved.

Follow Up and Provide Feedback

Once the alternative is decided upon and the decision is implemented, one last step is required in the systematic decision-making process — a final review and assessment of the decision process. Was the correct decision made? Was the appropriate alternative selected? Was the implementation program an effective one? What could have been changed in the implementation program to improve the outcomes? Were there other alternatives that should have been suggested? Is there corrective action that can now be taken to improve the outcomes of the decision process? Were the correct problems identified? These questions and others should be answered so that the most effective decision can be achieved in a specific case and so that the organization's decision-making skills can be polished and improved.

The *systematic decision-making process* as we have outlined it above may seem rather long and unnecessarily complex for many managerial decisions. Experience shows, however, that all of the steps are present to varying degrees in all effective decisions. Practicing managers have used this process so extensively that the steps in the process have become internalized and used by force of habit. Simple and routine decisions may typically require an abbreviated and informal version of the process, whereas complex and unique decisions may require a strict and formal application of the process.

If effective management decision making can be learned, as so many managers and management theorists maintain, this systematic decision-making process is essential to acquiring this important expertise.

Much of what will follow in this book centers on the analysis-of-alternatives step in the larger decision-making process and in the great multitude of POM decisions. The logic scheme is: First, present the larger systematic decision-making process, as we have done here. Second, present the great variety of POM decision situations or POM problems that require analysis and solution. Finally, in each decision situation, present several approaches to the analysis of alternatives. Keep in mind as we proceed that in practice we would typically use the entire decision process, but from here forward, for the purpose of brevity, we will concentrate on POM decision applications and the various approaches to the analysis of specific alternatives or problems.

The characteristics of decisions differ greatly. Consequently, how we make decisions tends to differ, depending upon the characteristics of the decisions.

Characteristics of Decisions

Although the systematic decision-making process is applied to all decisions, the amount of analysis, amount of money spent on data gathering, degree of formality of implementation, and other specific details of the ways we would make decisions differ, depending upon the presence of the characteristics of the decisions found in Table 2.3. For example, the amount of analysis applied to a nonrecurring decision with limited intensity and duration of impact would differ tremendously from one that was recurring with high intensity and long duration of impact. To understand

Table 2.3
Some Characteristics of Decisions

1. Degree of uncertainty	4. Expected returns relative to cost of analysis
2. Degree of complexity	5. Degree of recurrence
3. Decision time frame	6. Intensity of decision impact
	7. Duration of decision impact

the characteristics of a decision is to a large degree to know the specifics of how to perform each step of the decision process.

Degree of Uncertainty

Uncertainty in decisions typically includes the lack of knowledge about what variables are important, the relationships between the variables, and the values of the variables. Uncertainty is typically dealt with by managers either subjectively or objectively. *Subjective* methods usually involve operating as if conditions of certainty were present by selecting the most important variables while ignoring the effect of all others, assuming the most likely relationships between the most important variables, and estimating as precisely as possible the values of the most important variables. When the analysis is completed while assuming conditions of certainty, the manager usually allows for uncertainty by dropping back and taking a somewhat more conservative stance than the analysis under assumptions of certainty may have indicated.

Objective methods of dealing with uncertainty usually involve (1) spending money, time, and human effort to gather data to reduce the level of uncertainty; (2) developing analyses based upon three or more levels of optimism — pessimistic, most likely, and optimistic; and (3) developing or estimating the probability of each outcome. The results of this latter analysis can be left in the form of outcome values (typically dollars), probabilities, or a combination of both into expected values.

Degree of Complexity

Decision complexity refers to the number of variables, the network of relationships between the variables, and the relationships between decisions. A complex decision is described as one that involves a great number of variables, many of them in complicated relationships to one another, and one that stands in a series of decisions that must be made in some specific sequence.

Decision Time Frame

The amount of time available to make a decision may be the overriding determinant of how a decision can be made. Some decisions must be made almost instantaneously. Failing to decide in cases like these is to decide not to decide (a fact that some decision makers do not grasp). These decisions with short time frames may not allow any consideration or analysis beyond a few minutes. Conversely, some decisions can take many weeks, months, or even years to complete.

Returns Relative to Cost of Analysis

The amount of money that should be spent on analysis is to a large degree a function of the returns expected from the decision. If few negative or positive consequences are expected from a decision, little analysis can be economically justified. Conversely, expected monumental consequences from decisions justify enormous outlays for data gathering and analysis.

Degree of Recurrence

Some major decisions are nonrecurring. These decisions may receive intense organization attention throughout the decision process, but when the process is completed, the attention and activity end. Some other decisions, on the other hand, have a high degree of recurrence or repeatability. These decisions initially receive a high degree of organization attention and activity. Once the decision is reached, a pattern is set for all similar future decisions. These recurring decisions are said to be *programmed*, and they subsequently receive only routine attention and activity. An example of this type of recurring production decision is how much to produce of a particular product. Intense analysis may initially be performed to establish economic production quantities. This decision becomes programmed as part of the scheduling system and tends to be routinely applied until changes occur that require scrutiny of the original decision. Nonrecurring lesser decisions typically do not receive a high degree of organization attention and activity.

Intensity of Decision Impact

When decisions have prospects of either a high return if a good decision is made or high negative consequences if a poor decision is made, they are described as having an intense impact. When decisions exhibit neither of these properties or exhibit them only to a limited degree, they are described as having a nonintense impact.

Duration of Decision Impact

The time span over which the outcome of decisions is expected to endure is an important consideration in the attention, activity, and formality that an organization devotes to them. For example, a decision concerning the location of the annual management meeting ordinarily receives much less emphasis than a decision concerning the selection of a production process design. A good or poor outcome concerning the former decision will be over momentarily and never be felt again. The latter decision may, however, have lasting effects that extend twenty or more years. The decisions with long-lasting consequences typically receive the highest level of decision effort.

Characteristics of POM Decisions

All of the characteristics listed in Table 2.3 tend to be present in varying degrees in all decisions. Figure 2.3 shows that *Type 1 decisions* tend to involve high degrees of uncertainty and complexity, long time spans for both duration of decision impact and analysis of the decisions, high expected returns relative to the cost of analysis, high intensity of decision impact, and nonrecurrence. Each *Type 3 decision,* conversely, tends to involve a low degree of uncertainty and complexity, a relatively short time span for both duration of the decision impact and analysis of the decision, low expected returns relative to the cost of analysis, low intensity of decision impact, and recurrence. The element of recurrence is one characteristic that attracts the attention of decision makers in POM.

Figure 2.3
The Degree of the Presence of Decision Characteristics in Type 1, Type 2, and Type 3 Decisions

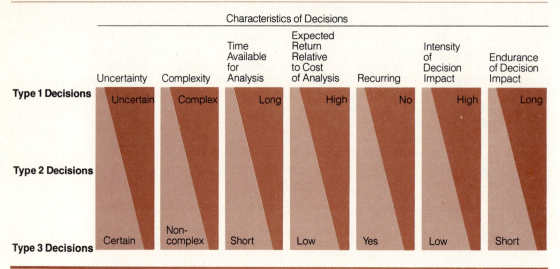

Several levels of analysis of decision alternatives are possible. When is each appropriate? How are these various possible levels of analysis related to the characteristics of decisions? What levels of analysis tend to be used in Type 1, Type 2, and Type 3 decisions? The answers to these questions conclude our treatment of the systematic decision-making process.

Levels of Analysis

The full range of analytical possibilities is grouped into five classes: intuition, quick-and-dirty, intensive computations, model building, and task force.

Intuition

To call intuition a level of analysis is perhaps a misnomer. Making decisions on the basis of *intuition* is to apply no analysis at all to decisions. This approach uses hunches, gut feelings, or instinctive leanings to arrive at spur-of-the-moment decisions. When would you ever want to use this approach? Most managers would advise that you use it only when you cannot use any other basis or when the decision outcome is unimportant.

Practically speaking, there are almost always other possible bases for decisions. This is not to say that intuition is never used by managers, because, as Figure 2.2 shows, it is present to varying degrees in all decisions. Additionally, when decisions must be made instantaneously, thus circumventing all other levels of analysis, intuition may be all that is left for the decision maker.

Crisis managers sometimes insist that all decisions must be made quickly. That is how they justify low levels of analysis, low degrees of participation in decision making by others, and poor decisions. They explain away these decisions with the excuse: "There wasn't enough time to. . . ."

Quick-and-Dirty

The *quick-and-dirty* level of analysis typically assumes away most complexity and uncertainty. Simple calculations are performed on only the most critical variables, while the simplest of relationships are assumed. This level of analysis can usually be performed in a few minutes or a couple of hours at the most. This may be the method that many of the day-to-day decisions are based upon in organizations.

Intensive Computations

When the relative importance of the decision is high, *intensive computations* are typically the lowest acceptable level of analysis. Many variables are quantified, manipulated, and compared in order to assess decision alternatives. These analyses typically involve one or more persons gathering and examining volumes of data and assembling, calculating, and comparing various alternatives. Desk-top calculators or interactive computer terminals for calculating are the dominant machines that are utilized.

Computer Model Building

The *model building* method of analysis involves the construction of a mathematical model that is a simplified abstraction from the real system under study.[1] This model is then programmed into a computer language so that it can be manipulated. By *manipulation* we mean sensitivity analysis—varying the variable values in the model so that we can observe the effects upon the outputs of the model. There are a great variety of canned computer programs that are useful models. (See the computer programs in Appendix C of this book: PERT/CPM, Linear Programming, and Queuing models.)

Computer models can also be custom-designed by analysts to specifically fit the decision situation under study. The computer allows analysts to examine large numbers of variables simultaneously, retrieve enormous blocks of data, and do these functions almost instantaneously. Still, model building takes more time and usually costs more than lower levels of analysis.

Task Force

A *task force* is a group of high-level personnel who are assigned to collectively analyze a decision and arrive at a consensus on a recommended course of action. All of the various levels of analysis that were mentioned before are likely to be used in

---

[1] Frank S. Budnick, Richard Mojena, and Thomas E. Vollman, *Principles of Operations Research* (Homewood, IL: Richard D. Irwin, 1977), 12–13.

Table 2.4
When the Various Levels of Analysis Are Likely to Be Used

Decision Characteristic	Levels of Analysis				
	Intuition	Quick-and-Dirty	Intensive Computations	Computer Model Building	Task Force
1. Degree of uncertainty			Moderate	High	Very high
2. Degree of complexity			Moderate	High	Very high
3. Decision time frame	Very short	Short	Moderate	Long	Very long
4. Return/cost of analysis	Very low	Low	Moderate	High	Very high
5. Degree of recurrence	Very low	Low	Moderate	High	Very high
6. Intensity of decision impact	Very low	Low	Moderate/high	High	Very high
7. Duration of decision impact	Very short	Short	Moderate/long	Long	Very long

Table 2.5
Frequency of Use of the Levels of Analysis for Type 1, Type 2, and Type 3 Decisions

Level of Analysis	Frequency of Use of the Levels of Analysis		
	Type 1 Decision	Type 2 Decision	Type 3 Decision
1. Intuition	Very low	Very low	Very low
2. Quick-and-dirty	Low	Moderate	Moderate
3. Intensive computations	High	High	High
4. Computer model building	Moderate/high	Moderate	Low
5. Task force	Moderate	Low	Very low

this effort. This team usually has the mandate of the highest executive officers and carries the highest priority over most other activities of the organization. Large amounts of data are processed, many alternatives are analyzed, many specialists are called into the effort as required, and the study typically spans several months or even years. Since task forces are the most intensive level of analysis of decisions, they are typically reserved for only the most critical organizational decisions.

Table 2.4 summarizes when the various levels of analysis are likely to be used in terms of the characteristics of decisions. Intuition may be used when any of these characteristics are present: The decision time frame is short, the return to cost of analysis is low, the decision is nonrecurring, the intensity of decision impact is low, the duration of decision impact is low, and no other level of analysis is feasible. At the other extreme, the task force may be appropriate when all the characteristics of decisions are present to a high degree.

Table 2.5 summarizes the frequency with which Type 1, Type 2, and Type 3 decisions tend to be analyzed by use of the various levels of analysis. Type 1 decisions predominantly involve intensive computations and computer model building and, to a reduced degree, task forces. Type 3 decisions principally involve intensive computations and, to a lesser degree, quick-and-dirty and model building. The recurring characteristics of Type 3 decisions support higher levels of analysis. Task force, model building, and intensive computations may therefore be used. Even though one of these decisions may involve only a few cents per unit of output, hundreds of thousands of these outputs may be produced in the future. Thus, the recurrence characteristic makes the cumulative impact and duration very high.

The levels of analysis and the specific techniques that we use to study decision alternatives can be critical to effective decisions. Let us now continue the emphasis upon analysis by considering some common techniques for structuring and analyzing POM decision alternatives.

Techniques for Structuring and Analyzing Decisions

The techniques that we shall explain and demonstrate in this section are general techniques that can be applied to a multitude of decisions. In later chapters we shall develop techniques that are highly specialized to analyze specific POM decisions. The techniques that are presented here can be used not only to analyze but also to structure decisions.

Have you had to make a decision where the amount of information, number of alternatives, and number of possible outcomes were so large that it seemed that you could not comprehend the whole problem at one time? Some POM decisions are of this magnitude. The ability to logically formulate these problems into understandable schemes can go a long way toward making a successful decision. Cost analysis, break-even analysis, decision trees, payoff tables, and cost-benefit analysis are important techniques for structuring and analyzing many POM decisions.

Cost Analysis

Cost analysis is perhaps the method used most often in organizations of all types for analyzing and comparing decision alternatives. Its frequency of use is probably tied to the fact that almost all decision alternatives can be compared according to their cost over some planning horizon or unit of measure. In this method of analysis the final display of the results typically is one summary sheet that shows the costs for each alternative arranged in vertical columns. The final cost per unit or total cost for the period for each alternative is displayed at the bottom of each column across the bottom line of the page. Table 2.6 shows a summary sheet of a simple cost analysis.

Table 2.6
Simple Cost Analysis Summary

	Product A	Product B	Product C
Labor cost/unit	$3.00	$3.50	$3.25
Material cost/unit	2.50	1.90	2.05
Variable O.H./unit	1.40	1.10	1.05
Total variable cost/unit	$6.90	$6.50	$6.35

If management has determined that total variable cost per unit is an important input to a decision concerning the three products of this table, then this method of analysis can be a useful tool.

If you use this method as the basis for a recommendation to management, you should be ready for these questions: How sure are you of your figures? How high or how low would you expect Product B total variable costs to be? These questions suggest that the cost analysis does not deal directly with uncertainty. This is one of its key weaknesses. The method can, however, be modified to deal with uncertainty in a straightforward way. Table 2.7 shows a summary sheet that explains how certain analysts are of their figures.

This modification of cost analysis allows the manager to determine the *degree of uncertainty* that is present in each of the costs in the analysis. For example, the material cost per unit for Product B is the same for Estimates *o*, *m*, and *p*. This zero range between *o* and *p* indicates high confidence in the $1.90 figure. On the other hand, the labor cost per unit for Product A has a difference of $.25 between *o* and *p*. This range between *o* and *p* is a measure of the analyst's uncertainty about the labor cost per unit for Product A.

The *o*, *p*, and *m* measures in this modified form of cost analysis reflect the analyst's optimistic estimates (how favorable are the costs likely to be if everything falls into place and everything goes well?), most likely estimates (what will the costs be if things go as we expect them to?), and pessimistic estimates (how unfavorable are the costs likely to be if we experience unexpected but not catastrophic outcomes?).

Cost analysis is the simplest and best understood method of comparing decision alternatives. The high frequency of its use attests to its effectiveness as a decision-making tool.

Break-even Analysis

By now you have probably had a minimum of three or four exposures to break-even analysis in accounting, economics, or other courses. We will not "reinvent the wheel" here by going through the whole topic again. We will, however, work our way through an example to refresh your memory on break-even concepts and demonstrate how break-even analysis can be used to analyze and compare decision alternatives in POM.

Table 2.8 contains variable definitions and formulas for straight-line break-even analysis. Example 2.1 compares three production processes that are decision alternatives.

Table 2.7
Cost Analysis Summary

	Product A			Product B			Product C		
	o	m	p	o	m	p	o	m	p
Labor cost/unit	$2.90	$3.00	$3.15	$3.45	$3.50	$3.55	$3.15	$3.25	$3.25
Material cost/unit	2.45	2.50	2.55	1.90	1.90	1.90	1.95	2.05	2.15
Variable O.H./unit	1.40	1.40	1.45	1.05	1.10	1.15	.95	1.05	1.15
Total variable cost/unit	$6.75	$6.90	$7.15	$6.40	$6.50	$6.60	$6.05	$6.35	$6.55

Note that o = optimistic, m = most likely, and p = pessimistic.

Table 2.8
Break-even Analysis Variable Definitions and Formulas

p = Selling price per unit	Q = Number of units produced and sold per period
v = Variable cost per unit	P = Pretax profits per period
FC = Total fixed cost per period	TR = Total revenue per period
TVC = Total variable cost per period	TC = Total cost per period

At break-even (P = 0)

1. $TR = pQ$
2. $TC = FC + TVC$
3. $TVC = vQ$
4. $P = TR - TC = pQ - (FC + vQ)$
5. $Q = (P + FC)/(p - v)$

6. $FC = pQ - vQ = Q(p - v)$
7. $Q = FC/(p - v)$
8. $TVC = TR - FC = pQ - FC$
9. $v = \dfrac{TR - FC}{Q} = \dfrac{pQ - FC}{Q} = p - \dfrac{FC}{Q}$
10. $TR = FC + TVC = FC + vQ$
11. $p = (FC + vQ)/Q = FC/Q + v$

Example 2.1

Break-even Analysis: Selecting a Production Process

Three production processes—A, B, and C—have the following cost structure:

Process	FC/Year	v
A	$100,000	$2.50
B	80,000	4.00
C	75,000	5.00

a. What is the most economical process for a volume of 10,000 units per year?

b. How many units per year must be sold with each process to have annual profits of $40,000 if the selling price is $6 per unit?

Solution

a. $TC = FC + v(Q)$

Process A $TC = \$100,000 + \$2.50(10,000) = \$125,000/year$
Process B $TC = \$80,000 + \$4(10,000) = \$120,000/year$
Process C $TC = \$75,000 + \$5(10,000) = \$125,000/year$

Process B has the lowest annual cost.

b.
$$Q = (P + FC)/(p - v)$$

Process A $Q = (\$40,000 + \$100,000)/(\$6 - \$2.50) = \dfrac{\$140,000}{\$3.50} = 40,000$ units

Process B $Q = (\$40,000 + \$80,000)/(\$6 - \$4) = \dfrac{\$120,000}{\$2} = 60,000$ units

Process C $Q = (\$40,000 + \$75,000)/(\$6 - \$5) = \dfrac{\$115,000}{\$1} = 115,000$ units

Break-even analysis is widely used to analyze and compare decision alternatives. It does have some key weaknesses, however, when compared to other methods. A primary weakness is the technique's inability to deal in a direct way with uncertainty. All of the costs, volumes, and other information of the technique must be assumed to be known with certainty. Another disadvantage of the tool is that the costs are assumed to hold over the entire range of possible volumes. This is seldom the case; nonlinear, discontinuous, or disjointed lines will account for this complexity, but their analysis may be too complex for practical solutions.

Break-even analysis can be displayed either algebraically as we have done in Example 2.1 or graphically as in the familiar break-even charts. In either form, both the components and the results are easily explained. This is an important advantage, because *managers would often rather live with a problem that they can't solve than implement a solution that they don't understand.*

Decision Trees

Cost analysis and break-even analysis have been presented as tools of analysis when simple single-phase decisions are to be made. *Single-phase decisions* are decisions that occur at one point in time with no thought of any other decisions that must precede or succeed them.

Multiphase decisions are a bit more complicated to organize than single-phase ones because they involve several decisions that are dependent upon one another and ones that must be made in a sequence. Decision trees were developed for multiphase decisions as aids to analysts who must see clearly what decisions must be made, in what sequence the decisions must occur, and the interdependence of the decisions. This ability to structure the way we think about multiphase decisions simplifies analyzing the decision alternatives.

Example 2.2 demonstrates the essentials of *decision tree analysis*. This form of analysis gives managers:

1. A way of structuring complex multiphase decisions by mapping decisions from the present to the future.

2. A direct way of dealing with uncertain outcomes.

3. An objective way of evaluating the relative value of each decision alternative.

Example 2.2

Decision Tree:
A New Product-Marketing Decision

Joe Sharpie has developed a promising new product. Joe faces three choices: He can sell the new product to a well-known company for $20,000, do a market test and then make a decision, or arrange financing and market the product.

    The market test will cost Joe $10,000, and he believes that there is about a fifty-fifty chance that a favorable market will be found. If the test is unfavorable, he figures he can still sell his idea for $12,000. If the test is favorable, he figures he can sell his idea for $40,000. But even if a favorable market is found, the chance of an ultimately successful product is about two out of five. A successful product will net a half-million dollars. Even with an unfavorable test, a successful product can be expected about once in every ten new product introductions. If Joe markets the product without a test, there is only a one in four chance of its being successful. A product failure costs $100,000. What should Joe do?

Solution

a. Draw a tree from left to right with squares (□) for decision points (acts) and circles (○) for outcome junctions (events). These decision points and outcome junctions are often referred to as *nodes* or *forks:*

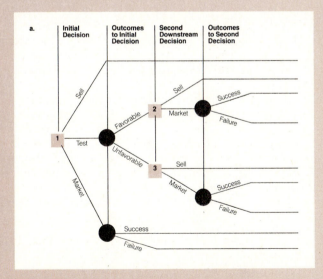

b. Write the values of each possible outcome (profits or losses) in the right margin and write the probability of multiple outcomes in parentheses on the branches that follow the circles:

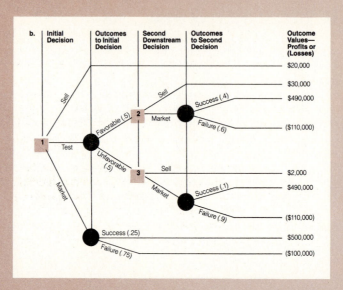

c. Working from right to left, compute the expected value (EV) at each circle for outcomes to second decisions. Do this by summing the products of the probabilities and outcome values. Write the EVs to the right of each circle. For example, the EV of the outcomes to market—decision ② —is computed:

EV = .4($490,000) + .6(−$110,000) = $196,000 − $66,000 = $130,000

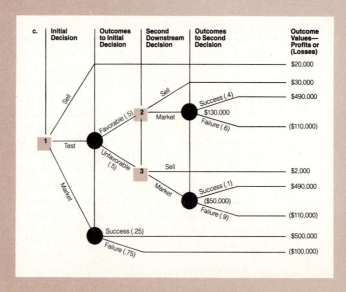

d. Continuing to work from right to left, decide which alternative of the second decisions (☐2 and ☐3) has the highest EV. Write the selected EV to the right of the decision boxes and truncate or prune (─/─) all other branches.

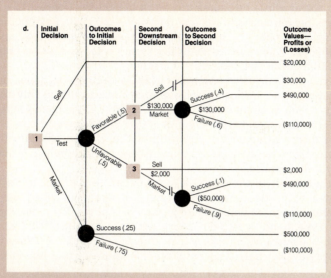

e. Continuing to work from right to left, repeat steps *c* and *d* for initial decision. The EV for outcomes to test is computed:

EV = .5($130,000) + .5($2,000) = $65,000 + $1,000 = $66,000

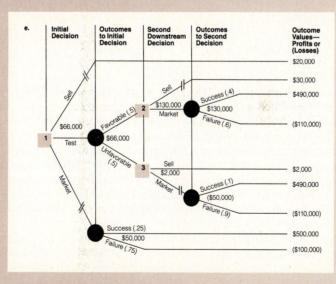

f. The EV for the initial decision is $66,000. The sequence of decisions is deduced by following the untruncated branches of the tree from left to right: Test. If favorable, market. If unfavorable, sell.

A note of caution should be given in regard to the interpretation of the expected values (EV) of decision tree analysis. One error that we might make is to interpret the EV for each decision literally and absolutely. The EVs are only relative measures of value and not *absolute* measures. Consider the profits (losses) in Example 2.2. These are possible outcomes to the test decision — $30,000, $490,000, ($110,000), or $2,000. Only one of these values will ultimately be returned to the decision maker. The EV of $66,000 will never be returned to the firm. The EV is only a relative measure of value of the test decision alternative.

Expected value as a decision criterion varies in effectiveness depending upon the decision situation. When a decision is a one-time shot (occurring only once, never to be repeated), which is usually the case with Type 1 decisions in POM, expected value is at best only a relative measure of value. In these situations, care must be taken by the decision maker not to interpret the EVs as absolute returns from decision alternatives, because, as we demonstrated in Example 2.2, these EVs will probably never materialize.

On the other hand, expected value as a decision criterion tends to be more meaningful when the decision is recurring. For example, when the number of standby machines is to be determined on the basis of weekly breakdown information or other Type 2 and Type 3 decisions in POM (day-to-day POM activities), the average value of each decision alternative tends to approach the EVs as the decision is applied over several trials. This point will be demonstrated in detail in the next section.

But even if expected values or probabilities are not included on decision trees, the value of decision trees as a useful way of organizing the way we think about complex multiphase decisions is important. This tool allows decision makers to see clearly what decisions must be made, in what sequence they must occur, and the interdependence of decisions. Expected value, if interpreted correctly, is a fringe benefit.

Payoff Tables

Whereas decision trees are typically used to analyze nonrecurring decisions, payoff tables are valuable tools of analysis when recurring decisions are encountered. Decision makers often find themselves facing decisions about the selection of alternatives for meeting a number of possible states of nature for a single time period. For example, retailers must decide how many units of a particular product to stock for the next month, given the many possible levels of demand for the product. Or production managers must select the number of standby machines to have in the next quarter, given that the number of machines likely to break down is uncertain. In such situations operations managers must evaluate the many alternatives available for meeting the uncertain states of nature.

How do operations managers choose among the alternatives? They usually use one of these rules or criteria: (1) Choose the alternative with the greatest expected profits. (2) Choose the alternative with the least total expected long and short costs.

(3) Choose the alternative with the least total expected costs. Because operations managers ordinarily prefer to maximize expected profits, *Rule 1* is usually preferred. *Rule 2* is also often used by operations managers, and if profits are involved it gives results equivalent to Rule 1. When profits are not involved, as in governmental agencies and not-for-profit organizations, or when revenues cannot be precisely attributed to specific products or units being stocked, *Rule 3* is frequently used.

The choice of criterion used for deciding among the alternatives can affect the alternative eventually selected for the decision. It is important, therefore, to give careful thought to the rule or criterion that is most appropriate for the decision situation under analysis. Example 2.3 demonstrates how payoff tables are used by operations managers when different decision criteria are the basis for selecting alternatives for meeting uncertain states of nature.

Example 2.3

Payoff Tables: A Retail Stocking Decision

The Gee Whiz Retailers are trying to decide how many #325 electronic calculators to stock during the next month. The sales history of this item is as follows:

Month	Units Demanded (SN)	Probability of Levels of Demand P(SN)
1	100	.1
1	200	.1
4	300	.4
3	400	.3
1	450	.1
Totals 10		1.0

Minimizing the Total Expected Long and Short Costs

Whenever the demand for this calculator exceeds the number stocked during the month, the lost profits, or short cost, is $5 per unit. Whenever a unit is not sold during the month and must be carried over into the next month as inventory, the carrying cost, or long cost, is $2 per unit. If the firm wishes to select the stocking alternative that minimizes the total expected long and short costs, which alternative should be selected?

Solution

First, complete a payoff table that minimizes the total expected long and short costs.

	States of Nature					Total Expected Long and Short Costs
S_j \ SN_i	100	200	300	400	450	$EC = \Sigma[P(SN_i) \times C_{ij}]$
100	$ 0	$500	$1,000	$1,500	$1,750	$1,075
200	200	0	500	1,000	1,250	645
300	400	200	0	500	750	285
400	600	400	200	0	250	205 ←
450	700	500	300	100	0	270
$P(SN_i)$	.1	.1	.4	.3	.1	

Strategies

Note: C_{ij} is the costs of S_j and SN_i.

The procedures of payoff tables can be illustrated by explaining the three shaded elements of the table in detail, using S_j to mean *stocking strategies* and SN_i to mean *states of nature* or uncertain levels of demand:

S of 200 and SN of 400: The $1,000 found in this position means that if a stocking strategy of 200 units is selected and a demand of 400 units is experienced, this would put the firm 200 units short during the period. Since short costs are $5 per unit, the period short costs are $5 per unit times 200 units, which equals $1,000.

S of 300 and SN of 300: The 0 found in this position means that since the strategy exactly meets the state of nature, there are neither short nor long costs.

S of 400 and SN of 100: The $600 found in this position means that if a stocking strategy of 400 units is selected and a demand of 100 units is experienced, this will yield an excess in inventory of 300 units at the end of the period. The period long cost is 300 units times $2 per unit, which equals $600.

All other elements of the payoff table are computed similarly. The expected cost column (EC) of the table is completed by summing along each strategy row (S_j) the products of the states of nature (SN_i) and their C_{ij}. For instance, the EC of $S_j = 400$ units is computed this way:

$$EC = .1(600) + .1(400) + .4(200) + .3(0) + .1(250) = 60 + 40 + 80 + 0 + 25 = 205$$

Maximizing the Total Expected Profits

Gee Whiz knows that the #325 calculator sells for $15 per unit and has a cost of goods sold of $10 per unit. Whenever this highly profitable item is not sold during the month and must be carried over into the next month, the carrying cost, or long cost, is $2 per unit. If the firm wishes to select the stocking alternative that maximizes the total expected profits (per-unit profit is loosely interpreted to mean the difference between the sales price and the cost of goods sold per unit), which alternative should be selected?

Solution

First, complete a payoff table that maximizes the total expected profits.

			States of Nature				Total Expected Profits
S_j \\ SN_i		100	200	300	400	450	$EP = \Sigma[P(SN_i) \times \pi_{ij}]$
Strategies	100	$500	$ 500	$ 500	$ 500	$ 500	$ 500
	200	300	1,000	1,000	1,000	1,000	930
	300	100	800	1,500	1,500	1,500	1,290
	400	(100)	600	1,300	2,000	2,000	1,370 ←
	450	(200)	500	1,200	1,900	2,250	1,305
	$P(SN_i)$	.1	.1	.4	.3	.1	

Note: π_{ij} is the profits of S_j and SN_i.

The shaded elements of the table are explained below:

S of 200 and SN of 400: The $1,000 found in this position means that if a strategy of 200 units is selected and a demand of 400 units is experienced, revenues would equal $15(200) or $3,000 and cost of goods sold would be $10(200) or $2,000 for a profit of $1,000 for the month.

S of 300 and SN of 300: The $1,500 found in this position means that the strategy exactly meets the state of nature; revenues would be $15(300) or $4,500 and cost of goods sold would be $10(300) or $3,000 for a profit of $1,500 for the month.

S of 400 and SN of 100: The ($100) means that if a strategy of 400 units is selected and a demand of 100 units is experienced, revenues would be $15(100) or $1,500, cost of goods sold would be $10(100) or $1,000, and long costs would be $2(300) or $600. Profits would then be ($100) for the month.

All other elements of the payoff table are computed similarly.

The expected profit column (EP) is completed by summing along each strategy row (S_j) the products of the states of nature (SN_i) and their π_{ij}. For instance, the EP of $S_j = 400$ units is computed this way:

$$EP = .1(-100) + .1(600) + .4(1,300) + .3(2,000) + .1(2,000)$$
$$= -10 + 60 + 520 + 600 + 200 = 1370$$

The stocking strategy that is recommended for Gee Whiz is 400 units of the #325 calculators. This alternative is preferred regardless of whether the total expected profits or the total expected long and short costs criterion is used. The equivalence of the two analyses is evident from a comparison of their payoff tables. For instance, it can be seen that the difference between the optimal strategy of 400 units and any other stocking strategy is the same in both analyses: for a strategy of 200 units, costs increase ($645 − $205 = $440) and profits decrease ($1,370 − 930 = $440) by the same amount. The criterion of minimizing the total expected costs (cost of goods sold, long costs, and short costs) would be inappropriate in this example because of the presence of revenues. Such an analysis would result in selecting a stocking strategy of 300 units that would yield a monthly expected profit of only $1,290, which can be seen to be $80 less than the stocking strategy of 400 units in the payoff table above.

Notice that the expected costs columns and expected profits columns of the payoff tables in Example 2.3 are interpreted as the average monthly costs and profits for each of the five stocking strategies. The best alternative is to stock 400 units because this alternative has the least expected costs and greatest expected profits. Notice that payoff tables also allow operations managers to compare the expected costs and expected profits for all the alternatives. Such comparisons allow managers to take other qualitative factors into account. For example, if there were compelling qualitative factors that favored the 300-unit strategy in Example 2.3, they could weigh these factors against the $80 that would be forgone by moving from the 400-unit strategy to the 300-unit strategy.

Example 2.3 uses cost functions that are simple linear functions: there are no fixed costs and the variable costs are constant for each unit produced. Could you use this technique to work problems with more complex cost functions? For example:

Short cost $= 1,000 + .1X^2 + .05XY + .08Y^2$

where

$X =$ the number of units short for one class of customers during the month

$Y =$ the number of units short for another class of customers during the month

Payoff tables allow the use of more complex long and short cost functions such as these.

One complication that students regularly encounter is the presence of *opportunity costs.* Such costs are incurred when, for example, not enough units are stocked at the beginning of the period and demand exceeds the number of units that have been stocked sometime during the period. The nature of these costs is in the form of profits forgone. In this type of problem we are often confused about how to incorporate these opportunity costs into our payoff tables. Two equally acceptable approaches to these problems are demonstrated in Example 2.3:

1. Minimize the total expected long and short costs where short costs represent the profit per unit. Long costs are incorporated as usual.

2. Maximize the total expected profits. Notice in Example 2.3 that for stocking strategy 200, whenever demand is 200, 300, 400, and 450, the profits are $1,000. In this treatment, whenever demand exceeds supply, the number of units sold is the number of units stocked, and the profits are implicitly penalized by remaining the same regardless of increased demand. Therefore, the implicit unit short cost is the entire per-unit profit. Long costs are incorporated as usual.

Payoff tables are an effective tool for analyzing single-period decisions under conditions of uncertainty. Their flexibility in evaluating a multitude of POM stocking decisions is perhaps their greatest strength. Cash, maintenance parts, workers, inventory items, production capacity, standby machines, and service capacity are all single-period stocking decisions that can be analyzed by payoff tables when demand levels or states of nature are uncertain. The greatest weakness of payoff tables is that the states of nature and alternatives must be discrete or accumulated into discrete classes.

Cost-Benefit Analysis

Some organizations must occasionally analyze decision alternatives where the ultimate effect of each alternative upon costs or profits is not clear. For example, consider the firm that is considering three alternative computers, each with different costs and different benefits. *Cost analysis* alone is an insufficient basis for deciding among the alternatives. Each computer brings to the organization unique benefits that may ultimately affect long-run profits or costs. But how much?

Cost-benefit analysis was developed to a fine art and popularized under the Kennedy and Johnson administrations by Defense Secretary Robert McNamara. This method has since become the standard tool for evaluating highly diverse government programs across most federal agencies.

The procedural steps for analyzing projects with cost-benefit analysis are:

1. Establish objectives that the projects are to meet.
2. Develop alternative projects for attaining the objectives.
3. Establish factors for evaluating alternative projects.
4. Develop a benefit model.
5. Develop a cost analysis of each project.
6. Develop a benefit analysis of each project.
7. Compare and choose among the alternative projects.

To illustrate how each of these steps is carried out, let us work through Example 2.4, a simple cost-benefit analysis of three different computing systems.

Example 2.4

Cost-Benefit Analysis: Selecting a Computer System

A company proposes to acquire a computer system. Three possible designs are being considered —A, B, and C. The firm wishes to use cost-benefit analysis to analyze the three alternatives. Julie Goodwork, a financial analyst for the firm, estimates these costs:

	A	B	C
Initial cost	$ 500,000	$ 300,000	$ 500,000
Operating costs for five years	800,000	1,000,000	600,000
Costs for software	150,000	——	50,000
Total costs	$1,450,000	$1,300,000	$1,150,000

Compu Inc., a local computer consulting firm, estimates the equivalent dollar benefits from each system:

$$B_i = 100,000X_1 + 50,000X_2 + 10,000X_3$$

where

	X_1	X_2	X_3
A	1.0	1.0	1.0
B	.6	.9	1.0
C	.9	.8	.7

Which project offers the best balance between costs and benefits? Follow the procedure for cost-benefit analysis (Steps 1–7 above) to analyze this decision.

Solution

1. Objective: To gain the greatest organizational benefit for the computing dollars.

2. Projects: A, B, and C.

3. Evaluation factors: X_1 = Software capability
   X_2 = Speed
   X_3 = Amount of facilities required

4. Benefit model: $B_i = 100,000X_1 + 50,000X_2 + 10,000X_3$

5. Cost analysis: A = $1,450,000
   B = $1,300,000
   C = $1,150,000

6. Benefit analysis: B_A = 100,000(1.0) + 50,000(1.0) + 10,000(1.0) = $160,000
   B_B = 100,000(.6) + 50,000(.9) + 10,000(1.0) = $115,000
   B_C = 100,000(.9) + 50,000(.8) + 10,000(.7) = $137,000

7. Compare and decide:

Project	Cost	Benefit	Benefit/Cost
A	$1,450,000	$160,000	.110
B	$1,300,000	$115,000	.088
C	$1,150,000	$137,000	.119

Select Project C because it has the highest benefit-to-cost ratio.

This example neatly develops the benefit model as $B = f(x_1, x_2, x_3)$. In actual practice the establishment of the benefit model is the most difficult part of the analysis. How do you, for example, develop a model that gives comparable benefits that are quantifiable along several factors for three public service projects: an urban renewal project, a new water system, and a new public swimming pool? The dilemmas posed in trying to compare the benefits for competing projects sometimes digress into a simple listing of the benefits for each project along with their costs. To select the winner, qualitative judgments are made when the alternative projects are compared.

Governmental agencies have set a number of guidelines to assist analysts in setting project benefits. Other organizations have adopted the general approach and terminology, if not the total package, to analyze decision alternatives with long-run abstract cost and benefit impacts that are difficult or impossible to quantify.

Summary

In this chapter we have explored the decision process as it applies to POM. Type 1 decisions — planning products, processes, and facilities, Type 2 decisions — planning production to meet demand, and Type 3 decisions — planning and controlling operations, were described as a helpful way of viewing decision making in POM.

Decision making is a major part of managers' jobs in POM. To understand POM therefore requires a thorough understanding of decisions in POM. The systematic decision-making process was recommended as a way to organize and formalize our decisions. This process includes these steps: Define and describe the problem(s), define the objective(s) or measure(s) of effectiveness, generate alternative solution approaches, analyze the alternatives, weigh and decide among the alternatives, formulate a plan for implementation, formulate a contingency plan, execute and control the plan, and follow up and provide feedback. All of these steps are important if effective decisions are to be achieved.

This book recognizes the importance of the entire systematic decision-making process, but, since space is limited, the remainder of the book will emphasize analysis of decision alternatives and POM decision situations. The degree of analysis and the formality of the decision process depend upon the characteristics of particular decisions. Some of these decision characteristics are: degree of uncertainty, degree of complexity, decision time frame, returns/cost of analysis, degree of recurrence, intensity of decision impact, and duration of decision impact.

Decisions may justify several levels of analysis: intuition, quick-and-dirty, intensive computations, model building, and task force. Type 1 decisions predominantly involve intensive computations and, to a reduced degree, model building and task forces. Type 2 and Type 3 decisions principally involve intensive computations and, to lesser degrees, quick-and-dirty and model building.

Several general techniques have been presented to structure and analyze decision alternatives in POM — cost analysis, break-even analysis, decision trees, payoff tables, and cost-benefit analysis. These techniques can help managers become more effective decision makers because they clarify the analysis of decision alternatives and thus simplify the way we think about complex decisions.

Review and Discussion Questions

1. Define a Type 1 decision. Give an example for: **a.** retailer, **b.** manufacturer, and **c.** government agency.

2. Define a Type 2 decision. Give an example for: **a.** computer center, **b.** university, and **c.** manufacturer.

3. Define a Type 3 decision. Give an example for: **a.** museum, **b.** ship, and **c.** hot dog stand.

4. What is systematic decision making? What steps are included?

5. Name seven characteristics of decisions.

6. What decision characteristics would make it appropriate to analyze decision alternatives using these levels of analysis: **a.** intuition, **b.** quick-and-dirty, **c.** intensive computations, **d.** model building, and **e.** task force?

7. Under what conditions would it be appropriate to use these decision-making tools: **a.** cost analysis, **b.** break-even analysis, **c.** decision trees, **d.** payoff tables, and **e.** cost-benefit analysis?

8. What are the major inputs into a manager's choice among alternatives?

9. What is a trade-off decision?

10. How do managers typically deal with uncertainty in decisions?

11. Under what conditions would a manager analyze a Type 2 decision as thoroughly as a Type 1 decision?

12. Discuss this statement: There is no room for intuition in systematic decision making.

13. Under what conditions does the EV of a decision alternative approach the absolute value of that course of action?

14. What is typically the most difficult part of a cost-benefit analysis?

Problems

Break-even Analysis

1. The EZ Haul Trucking Company hauls local freight in San Jose, California. Its terminal operations have the following costs: Fixed costs per year = $250,000, variable cost per ton-mile = $15.25, and freight rate per ton-mile = $17.35. **a.** Compute EZ's break-even point in ton-miles. **b.** Compute EZ's break-even point in sales dollars.

2. The Nononsense Publishing Company intends to publish a textbook in production and operations management. Fixed costs are $25,000 per year, variable costs per unit are $10, and selling price per unit is $12. **a.** How many units must be sold per year to break even? **b.** How much annual revenue is required to break even? **c.** If annual sales are 20,000 units, what are the annual profits? **d.** What variable cost per unit would result in $25,000 annual profits if annual sales are 20,000 units?

3. The Clutch Engineering Company is proposing to locate a branch office in one of two West Coast locations, A or B. These two sites have quite different estimated operating costs:

	A	B
Engineering labor cost	$15.00/hour	$17.00/hour
Materials and supplies (tied to engineering hours)	$2.40/hour	$1.80/hour
Variable overhead	$5.50/hour	$6.40/hour
Total annual fixed cost	$180,000	$190,000
Price to customers	$30.00/hour	$33.50/hour

a. Which location would result in the more profitable operation if approximately 30,000 hours per year of engineering time could be sold? **b.** Compute the break-even point in engineering hours per year for both locations. **c.** Compute the break-even point in annual sales dollars per year for both locations.

Decision Trees

4. Joy Rich has $100,000 to invest. She can invest in either stocks or certificates of deposit. Stocks will return 10 percent if business conditions continue as they are, 20 percent if they improve, and 3 percent if there is a mild recession. Certificates of deposit return 8 percent regardless of business conditions. There is a 15 percent probability of a business upturn, a 30 percent probability of a mild recession, and a 55 percent probability of no change in economic conditions. **a.** Use a decision tree to recommend to Joy how she should invest her $100,000. **b.** What will she earn on her investment if she follows your recommendation?

5. The purchasing department of the Flybynight Aircraft Company is developing plans for buying next year's requirements for stainless steel stock. Three alternatives are being considered — a blanket contract, a national contract, or individual orders. Five hundred thousand pounds of stock will be purchased next year. The firm estimates the costs and the associated probabilities for each of the three decision alternatives as follows:

	Probability	Cost per Pound
Blanket contract	.50	$.50
	.30	.60
	.20	.70
National contract	.75	.60
	.25	.50
Individual orders	1.00	.70

a. Use a decision tree to analyze the decision alternatives. **b.** How should the firm purchase the steel stock? **c.** What will be the cost of the steel if the firm follows your recommendation?

6. The Howsweetitis Manufacturing Company is considering expanding its production capacity to meet a growing demand for its product line of toilet bowl deodorizers. The alternatives are to build a new plant, expand the old plant, or do nothing. The marketing department estimates a 35 percent probability of a market upturn, a 40 percent probability of a stable market, and a 25 percent probability of a market downturn. Georgia Swain, the firm's capital appropriations analyst, estimates the following annual returns for these alternatives:

	Market Upturn	Stable Market	Market Downturn
Build new plant	$690,000	$(130,000)	$(150,000)
Expand old plant	490,000	(45,000)	(65,000)
Do nothing	50,000	0	(20,000)

a. Use a decision tree to analyze these decision alternatives. **b.** What should How-sweetitis do? **c.** What returns will accrue to the company if your recommendation is followed?

7. Shootthemoon Aerospace Inc. is about to submit a proposal for a research contract to develop a new product for a government agency. The firm can bid three levels of price. Shootthemoon estimates the probability of winning the research contract and the value to the firm as follows:

Level of Price	Probability of Winning Research Contract	Research Contract Value
High	.25	$200,000
Mid	.50	250,000
Low	.75	300,000

The profits tend to decline as the price increases on the research contract because Shootthemoon would tend to expand the goals that it wished to accomplish on the higher priced contracts and much of the additional expense would have to be absorbed by the company. The firm will lose $50,000 if it does not get the research contract. It is also trying to decide whether to bid on a production contract that will be released later this year. The firm has ample capacity to respond on both contracts. The firm estimates that the value to itself for the production contract is $750,000 if the contract is won, but an unsuccessful bid would result in a $100,000 loss. James Trenton, the estimator, estimates the probability of winning the production contract as follows:

	Probability of Winning Production Contract
Research contract won	.60
Research contract lost	.30

a. Use a decision tree to analyze the decision alternatives. **b.** What should Shootthemoon do? **c.** What will be the value of this decision if Shootthemoon follows your recommendation?

8. The Sunshine Manufacturing Company has developed a unique new product and must now decide between two facility plans. The first alternative is to build a large new facility immediately. The second alternative is to build a small plant initially and to expand it to a larger facility three years later if the market has proved favorable. The marketing department has provided the following probability estimates for a ten-year plan:

First Three-Year Demand	Next Seven-Year Demand	Probability
Unfavorable	Unfavorable	.2
Unfavorable	Favorable	.0
Favorable	Favorable	.7
Favorable	Unfavorable	.1

If the small plant is expanded, the probability of demand over the remaining seven years is $7/8$ for favorable and $1/8$ for unfavorable. The following payoffs for all of the outcomes has been provided by the accounting department:

Demand	Facility Plan	Payoffs
Fav-fav	1	$5,000,000
Fav-unfav	1	2,500,000
Unfav-unfav	1	1,000,000
Fav-fav	2-expanded	4,000,000
Fav-unfav	2-expanded	100,000
Fav-fav	2-not expanded	1,500,000
Fav-unfav	2-not expanded	500,000
Unfav-unfav	2-not expanded	300,000

With these estimates, analyze Sunshine's facility decision. **a.** Perform a complete decision tree analysis. **b.** What strategy do you recommend to Sunshine? **c.** What payoffs will result from your recommendation?

Payoff Tables

9. The Mashnbruise Produce Company sells lettuce in the wholesale market. It believes the next period demand can be approximated from similar past periods:

Thousands of Pounds Demanded	Number of Past Periods
20	10
25	20
40	50
60	20

The selling price is $100 per thousand pounds, the cost is $60 per thousand pounds, and any lettuce not sold in the period can be sold for animal feed for $10 per thousand pounds. How many pounds of lettuce should be stocked to maximize total expected profits per period?

10. A northern California nonprofit counseling service must staff caseworkers to meet an uncertain demand for its services. Each caseworker can process five cases during each month. Records show that the following number of cases were processed in past months:

Cases	Number of Past Months
40	10
60	20
70	40
90	20
100	10

The average cost per caseworker is $1,000 per month. When cases cannot be processed because of an insufficient number of caseworkers, temporary professional help can be obtained from a local contractor at a cost of $500 per case. How many caseworkers should be employed for the next month so that the total expected cost of caseworkers and contract counseling services per month are minimized? (Hint: Set up the tables so the strategies and states of nature are the number of case-workers — 8, 12, 14, 18, and 20.)

11. Wilma Strict, the principal of Learnalot High School, is trying to determine how many classrooms to plan for the upcoming school term. The analyst from the superintendent's office estimates the following:

Classrooms Needed	Probability
100	.1
120	.2
130	.3
150	.2
160	.2

The principal operates from a budget that provides an incentive for her to minimize facility costs. She is charged monthly costs for unused classrooms based on this formula:

$$LC = \$10{,}000 + \$200(X), \text{ where } X = \text{Number of unused classrooms.}$$

If Wilma is short on classrooms, she can rent temporary ones for $1,000 per month per classroom. How many classrooms should she provide for the next school term so that the monthly total expected long and short costs are minimized?

12. Big Store sells A60 Strongcharge automobile batteries. Batteries are ordered weekly for delivery on Monday morning. The sales price for an A60 is $65 and its cost for Big Store is $45. If too many batteries are ordered and stock must be carried over the weekend, corporate headquarters charges Big Store $15 per battery for increased insurance, finance, and warehouse occupation costs. If Big Store is out of stock, it forgoes the profits from missed sales. How many A60 batteries should Big Store order each week if the weekly sales pattern is as shown below?

Number of Batteries Demanded	Probability
20	.2
30	.3
40	.4
45	.1

a. Work this problem by first minimizing the weekly total expected long and short costs (carrying and opportunity costs). b. Next, work the problem by maximizing the total expected profits. c. Show the equivalence of your solutions in parts a and b.

13. The maintenance department of the Gripealot Manufacturing Company presently provides twenty standby machines for the fabrication department. Fabrication has over one hundred machines of the same design in service. When these machines break down, it costs $50 to install each standby machine. When breakdowns occur and no standby machines are available, lost production costs (LPC) result:

$$LPC = 400 + 50X + X^2, \text{ where } X = \text{Number of standby machines short per week}$$

Weekly LPC tend to justify a sizable bank of standby machines. On the other hand, the weekly cost of holding unused standby machines forces a balance in management's strategy. The cost per week of carrying standby machines (CC) when all are not used is:

$CC = Y^2 + 10Y - 40Z$, where Y = Number of standby machines provided per week

Z = Number of machines that have failed during the week

Maintenance records show the following pattern of breakdowns on these machines:

Breakdowns per Week	Number of Weeks
10	10
20	25
30	35
40	30

How many standby machines should be provided to minimize the total expected costs (installation, lost production, and carrying costs)?

14. The Handtomouth Finance Company keeps cash on hand to meet short-term loans. If the firm keeps too much cash on hand, it forgoes some interest income that it could have earned in alternative investments; that is, idle cash has an opportunity, or long, cost. If Handtomouth keeps too little cash on hand, it must go to other lending institutions for cash, and this results in extra operating costs (short costs). The estimates of demand for the next period are:

Demand or SN (Thousands)	Frequency	P(SN)
$100	$\frac{1}{10}$	.1
200	$\frac{2}{10}$	.2
250	$\frac{3}{10}$	.3
300	$\frac{1}{10}$	.1
400	$\frac{3}{10}$	.3

The firm's estimates of long and short costs are:

$SC = \$1,000 + .1X \qquad LC = \$500 + .05Y$

where:

SC = Total period short costs
LC = Total period long costs
  X = Total number of units (thousands of dollars) short during the period
  Y = Total number of units (thousands of dollars) long during the period

How much cash should Handtomouth keep on hand for the next period to minimize total expected long and short costs?

Cost-Benefit Analysis

15. The Coco County Sheriff's Department is operating under a severe funds shortage. The department has proposed to the county board of supervisors two costly projects aimed at improving its community services. Because of the shortage of funds, the board has informed Sheriff James Brown that one of the projects might possibly be approved if the sheriff can show through a cost-benefit analysis that it is superior to the other. Under no circumstances will both projects be approved. John Forthright, Sheriff Brown's financial analyst, estimates the following annual costs for the two projects:

Project	Annual Costs
Expand jail services	$175,000
Expand patrol services	190,000

"So far, so good," Sheriff Brown thinks. "But what about the benefit side of the analysis?" How can the sheriff evaluate and compare the benefits from the two different projects? At the board of supervisors' suggestion, he has appointed a citizens' committee to perform the benefit analysis and has received the following results:

	Project Values	
Important Factors	Jail	Patrol
X_1: Crime prevention	500	5,000
X_2: Legal liability	5,000	2,000
X_3: Publicity	1,000	1,500
X_4: Voter response	1,800	1,200

The committee concluded that these benefit factors were related as follows:

$$\text{Benefits} = 10X_1 + 10X_2 + 20X_3 + 30X_4$$

a. Prepare a cost-benefit analysis appropriate for Sheriff Brown to submit to the Coco County board of supervisors. b. Which project should he recommend?

Case
Shale-Co Inc.

Jim Sludge is owner of Shale-Co Inc., a medium-sized oil property development firm in Dynamite, Wyoming. Jim is trying to decide what to do with Shale-Co's shale oil properties in Dynamite. He has been offered $10 million for the properties by a large oil company. But Jim wonders if he might make even more if he developed the properties himself. One of the reasons for his reluctance to sell is that Shale-Co has already plowed $10 million into the properties and if he sells now, only a break-even situation would be realized.

Jim's staff has prepared two development proposals:

1. *Develop the Properties Now.* The cost of developing the properties would be $12 million. The likelihood of finding oil in the following quantities is: plentiful, .3; adequate, .4; and scarce, .3. With the expected world market conditions (OPEC, conservation, economy, regulation, etc.), Jim's staff estimates that the likelihood of the following levels of market demand for oil is: high, .6; medium, .3; and low, .1. The estimated differences between revenues and operating expenses if the properties are developed are:

Quantity of Oil Found	Market Demand		
	High	Medium	Low
Plentiful	$27.4	$23.1	$19.1
Adequate	22.3	15.6	11.1
Scarce	15.3	11.2	7.1

Note: Values are in millions of dollars.

Jim thinks that he can sell the properties after they are developed, but the sales price would depend upon the amount of oil found: plentiful, $22.6 million; adequate, $15.5 million; and scarce, $6.2 million.

2. *Build a Pilot Plant, Develop or Sell Later.* A pilot processing plant built to determine if the properties are commercially feasible would cost $3.1 million, and if the properties were developed later another $11 million would be required. If the pilot plant results were favorable, Jim thinks the properties could be sold for $17.5 million and that the likelihood of such an outcome would be about 50-50. If the pilot plant's results were unfavorable, Jim thinks that he would not be able to sell the properties. The likelihood of finding the three oil quantities would depend upon the outcome of the pilot plant studies:

Outcome of Pilot Plant Results	Quantity of Oil Found		
	Plentiful	Adequate	Scarce
Favorable	.6	.3	.1
Unfavorable	.2	.3	.5

If the properties were developed after the pilot plant's results are known, the differences between revenues and operating expenses exhibited in the first proposal would also apply to this proposal.

Assignment

1. Discuss the appropriateness of using decision trees to analyze decisions such as Shale-Co's problem. What are the strengths and weaknesses of the technique in such analyses?

2. Use a decision tree analysis as the basis for recommending a course of action to Jim Sludge. Complete the tree, its payoffs, probabilities, and expected values.

3. What alternatives do you recommend for Shale-Co? Specify the alternatives that Shale-Co should follow.

4. What payoffs should Shale-Co expect to receive if your recommendations in No. 3 are followed?

5. Do your recommendations in No. 3 take into consideration the attitude of Jim Sludge toward risk? How might your recommendations be affected if you included such a factor in your analysis?

Selected Bibliography

Budnick, Frank S., Richard Mojena, and Thomas E. Vollman *Principles of Operations Research*. Homewood, IL: Richard D. Irwin, 1977.

Drucker, Peter F. *The Effective Executive*. New York: Harper & Row, 1967.

Horowitz, I. *Decision Making and the Theory of the Firm*. Columbus, Ohio: Charles E. Merrill, 1969.

Jedamus, P., and R. Frame. *Business Decision Theory*. New York: McGraw-Hill, 1969.

Kast, Fremont E., and James E. Rosenzweig. *Organization and Management: A Systems Approach*. New York: McGraw-Hill, 1974.

McMillan, C., and R. F. Gonzalez. *Systems Analysis*. Homewood, IL: Richard D. Irwin, 1974.

Parker, Le Ross. "Test Your Decisions with Follow-up." *Administrative Management* 28(October 1967): 56–57.

Scanlon, Burt K. "Make Sure Your Decisions Get Carried Out." *Business Management* 32(September 1967): 63–64.

Schlaifer, Robert. "Decision Theory and Management Theory." In *Toward a Unified Theory of Management,* edited by Harold Koontz. New York: McGraw-Hill, 1964.

Simon, Herbert. *The New Science of Management*. Englewood Cliffs, NJ: Prentice-Hall, 1977.

"Ways to Sharpen Decision-Making." *Iron Age* 1(August 1968): 21.

Chapter Outline

Introduction
Some Reasons Productive Systems Forecast

Qualitative Forecasting Methods
Jury of Executive Opinion
Sales Force Composite
Survey of Users' Expectations

Quantitative Forecasting Methods
Forecast Accuracy
Long-Run Forecasts
Cycles, Trends, and Seasonality
Regression Analysis
Short-Run Forecasts
Impulse Response versus Noise Dampening
Moving Average Method
Exponential Smoothing Method

Forecasting Practices
Use of Forecasting Techniques

Optional Forecasting Topics
Forecast Ranging
Incorporating Seasonality into Time Series Forecasts

Summary

Review and Discussion Questions

Problems

Case: Swank Retailers

Selected Bibliography

3

Forecasting in POM:
The Starting Point for All Planning

Study the past if you would devine the future.
Confucius, 490 B.C.

Forecasting is an integral part of all managerial planning. **When managers plan, they determine in the present what courses of action their organizations will take in the future. The first step in planning is therefore <u>forecasting</u> or estimating the future demand for products and services and the resources necessary to produce these outputs.**

In most organizations the first and dominant forecasting activity involves the estimation of future demand levels for the ultimate goods and services to be produced. In business firms these demand estimates are called *sales forecasts*. From these forecasts comes the information necessary for operations managers to make planning decisions about the products, processes, and facilities that are the long-run strategic choices of their organizations. Such long-run decisions are explored in Part Two of this book. Similarly, sales forecasts are the basis for operations managers' decisions about planning production to meet demand, which are the intermediate and short-run decisions that allow productive systems to respond to the needs of the market. Such intermediate and short-run decisions are explored in Part Three of this book. Forecasting, whether long-run, short-run, or intermediate-run, is therefore absolutely fundamental to the day-to-day planning decisions of operations managers.

Ordinarily, operations start with the sales forecasts and from these are planned the amount of resources needed to produce the products and services included in the forecasts. There are situations that develop in POM, however, that reverse this sequence. When resources such as skilled workers, raw materials, capital funds, and utilities are scarce—a current and worsening fact of life for many operations managers—then the forecasting sequence may be turned around. In these cases operations managers first forecast how many resources of each type are available and the resulting production capacity. From these forecasts the sales forecasts are developed. The key question that forecasting seeks to answer in this reversed sequence is how much *can be produced,* rather than how much *can be sold.*

Operations managers plan, and in the process forecast, because they see this activity as an effective means of achieving organizational objectives—maximizing profits, minimizing costs, saving souls, getting reelected, and so on. But why is forecasting required to effectively achieve these objectives? Table 3.1 outlines some of the underlying reasons that organizations forecast.

Operations managers must learn to live with change. If changes never occurred, wouldn't managers' jobs be a snap? They could show up in the morning, turn the productive system on, and watch it continue uninterrupted to meet customers' demands for goods and services. But, alas, since demand is variable to greater or lesser degrees, forecasting must provide operations managers with the advance information they need in order to change the productive system.

Productive systems do not respond instantaneously to changes in demand for their goods and services. Suppose, for example, that a brewery is now producing 500,000 cases of beer per day. If the marketing department senses that the demand for the firm's beer will double to 1,000,000 cases of beer per day three months from now, the production department will need some lead time to hire and train new employees, increase inflow of materials and supplies, and expand production capacity. Forecasts should allow operations managers enough lead time to respond to changes in demand in order to avoid unsatisfied demand in the case of demand increases and excess inventories or capacity in the case of demand decreases.

Table 3.1
Some Reasons That Productive Systems Forecast

1. Because demand for products and services varies from month to month, production rates must be scaled up or down to meet these variable demands.

2. Productive systems need some reaction time to change production rates. Forecasts provide operations managers with estimates of future demands for products and services, thereby providing reaction times for changing production rates.

3. Related activities can be better coordinated when adequate lead times are provided. Forecasts allow operations managers to look ahead and plan related activities so that waste, inefficiency, and conflicts are better controlled.

4. When forecasts allow operations managers to look ahead and anticipate needed changes in the productive system, orderly change in the system can be planned. Such plans avoid the hectic last-minute changes that are often made in a crisis environment.

5. Forecasts of sales demands are the beginning and driving force of the financial budget control process, a process that is crucial to the effective management of all types of organizations.

Operations managers must coordinate related activities. Forecasting allows managers to move resources from one activity to another as one activity level decreases and another increases. Suppose, for example, that a sales manager oversees two geographical regions. By looking ahead and forecasting the number of salespersons required during the next time period in each of the two regions, the manager sees that one region needs five fewer salespersons and a few weeks later the other region needs five more salespersons—an almost perfect match. Notice how forecasting allows the manager to transfer resources from one activity to another, thus avoiding the expense associated with the needless layoff and hiring of employees. I wish that I could tell you that through effective forecasting all organizations avoid the inefficiency associated with the continual layoff and hiring of employees and other inefficient use of resources, but organizations are not yet perfect—a point that should encourage young, bright graduates of colleges and universities who are looking for managerial opportunities.

Knowing when changes in demand for outputs are likely to occur lets managers gradually and efficiently modify the productive system. Adequate *lead time* is the enemy of *crisis management*—the style of managers who manage so that every situation is a crisis or an emergency. Although necessary in such disasters as hurricanes and attempted suicides, crisis management typically results in wasted effort, foul-ups, increased costs, damaged customer relations, and reduced morale, rather than effective forecasting and planning. As an employee who was a victim of crisis management said, "There's never enough time to do it right, but there's always enough time to do it over." Planning and forecasting provides enough lead time to use systematic management planning rather than crisis management.

Along about October of every year in business organizations (earlier for governments) there begins the budgeting process for the following fiscal year. In this long process each major department typically assists in some degree in the preparation of the sales forecast for the firm's or division's goods and services. The sales forecast is done first and becomes the engine that drives the budget process. The operating departments then deduce the number of employees, the amounts of materials and supplies, the required capital goods, and so on to produce the forecast goods and services in each time period. These resources are costed—converted from units to dollars of expenses for each month—and when combined with the sales revenues (in for-profit organizations) they project the monthly profits for the next year. This plan, for which the sales forecast is the initial step, becomes the key planning and control instrument for the organization.

In governmental organizations the budgeting process has developed to the level of a fine art. It has been said that in some governmental units the weight of the paper generated for the budget planning and control activity far outweighs the value of their ultimate services. The performance of many departments and agencies is evaluated in large part on the basis of budget compliance rather than the acceptability of the services to constituents. Such budgets are not tied directly to forecasts of future constituent demand as in businesses. Rather, last year's expenditures are often increased to reflect increased inflation and costs of any new programs. The proponents of *zero-based budgeting* promise that this new tool will cause each budget to be built not on last year's foundation but on programs demanded by constituents. Similarly, *sunset laws* are designed to systematically kill off old programs, thus breaking any chain of continuity of unneeded programs. In spite of these and other budget innovations, federal governmental agencies seem quite immune to any such viruses of change. Budgets of the government in Washington, D.C., are only nebulously tied to forecast demand for services and forecast levels of tax income. State and local governments prepare budgets that are more directly tied to forecast income levels.

Forecasting is a continuous process. It does not occur once and remain struck in stone. Rather, as changes are sensed, operating forecasts are modified to allow managers to change productive systems. Accuracy is the chief attribute of good forecasts. The degree of accuracy determines in large part how efficiently productive systems will operate. If acceptable accuracy levels are to be realized, forecasts must be updated as new relevant information surfaces.

Not all forecasting situations are alike, and each requires a somewhat different approach. Let us now examine some forecasting methods commonly used by today's organizations.

Qualitative Forecasting Methods

Forecasting involves an interesting blend of considerations — the past, the present, and the most likely future. Figure 3.1 shows that forecasting ultimately includes a complex set of inputs before a decision is reached. The general economic climate of the firm, assessment of past and present events, analysis of future conditions, recommendations of others, and legal constraints constitute the bases for a rational approach to developing forecasts. This logic is continuously modified by decision makers' emotions, intuition, and personal motives and values as they exercise

Figure 3.1
The Forecasting Decision

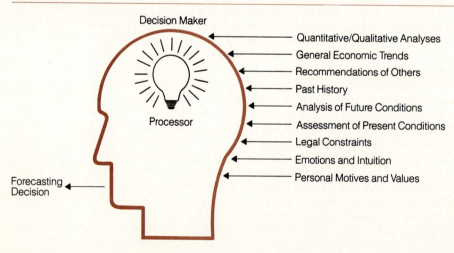

Table 3.2
Qualitative Forecasting Methods

1. **Jury of Executive Opinion Method.** Combines views of key executives to obtain a sounder sales forecast than might be made by a single estimator.
2. **Sales Force Composite Method.** Obtains the combined views of members of the sales force as to the future sales outlook. In some companies, each salesperson estimates the future sales in his or her territory. To ensure realistic estimates, successive management levels are likely to do careful reviews.
3. **Survey of Users' Expectations Method.** Involves asking product users about the quantities they expect to buy in the forecast period. By combining user responses, the interviewing firm can estimate total demand for the product (or service), and then determine the portion of that demand that it expects to fill.

Source: Adapted by permission from *Sales Forecasting Practices — An Appraisal,* National Industrial Conference Board, Bulletin 25, 1970.

judgment in reaching the forecasting decision. For most decisions quantitative analysis is but one input, although admittedly an important one, into this complex decision-making process.

Table 3.2 describes three *qualitative forecast methods* commonly used in estimating levels of long-run or short-run market demand in business organizations. Rarely do firms use only one of these methods. More often companies use one method in one forecasting situation and another method when different circumstances prevail. A drug manufacturer, for example, may use one of the quantitative methods for its regular products and jury of executive opinion for new products. Additionally, several methods may be applied to one forecasting problem to provide checks and balances in the forecasting process.

Jury of Executive Opinion

The *jury of executive opinion* is used most often in combination with other forecasting methods such as time series, sales force composite, and others. If there is strength in numbers, then this method promises to provide forecasts that are more accurate than is possible by individuals. But this method is not always better than the other methods. If the jury uses only opinion and intuition to estimate the future, then results must be carefully evaluated. This approach is no better than the bases for each of the juror's recommendations. Just as much analysis can be applied here as in the other approaches. The jury approach usually provides a compromise between extremely low and extremely high forecasts. The consensus reached may or may not be the best estimate of the future, but it is, at least, a middle ground. One technique that has recently developed to assist groups of executives in arriving at a consensus is the *delphi method.* In this method the executives anonymously answer a series of questions on successive rounds. The response of each participant is fed back to all participants on each round and the process is then repeated. As many as six rounds may be required before a consensus is reached on the forecast. This method can result in forecasts that most participants have ultimately agreed on in spite of initial disagreement. For an interesting account of using the delphi method in sales forecasting, see the Basu and Schroeder citation in the Selected Bibliography at the end of this chapter.

Sales Force Composite

The *sales force composite method* can be reliable *if* the salespersons' estimates are carefully scrutinized. Some of us tend to be either optimistic or pessimistic in our estimates of the future. Salespersons generally have optimistic personalities; they have to have them in order to be successful in their profession. This personality type may tend to develop highly optimistic (blue sky) forecasts. At the same time, if salespersons are rewarded on the basis of how much they exceed the forecast, they may tend to develop pessimistic (sandbagging) forecasts. Management must recognize these tendencies and adjust the forecasts accordingly if the method is to be reliable.

Survey of Users' Expectations

The *survey of users' expectations method* provides highly reliable information if the survey is feasible. There are some situations, however, where it is not feasible to attempt to contact the users of goods and services. Suppose, for example, that a new company is about to market a new product. The users in this case are unknown. Any information from prospective users will be unreliable if no experience ties users to the supplying firm. Additionally, consumer product firms that sell their products to a great multitude of users may find it difficult, if not impossible, to contact enough users to develop any intelligent information about future sales. Many industrial product firms that use this forecasting method do so because they have relatively few customers.

Most texts in POM do not mention the jury of executive opinion, the sales force composite, and the survey of users' expectations methods of sales forecasting. Although these methods may not be quantitatively sophisticated, the majority of forecasting applications in the real worlds of business and government use one or more of these methods. If you want to know more about these important forecasting approaches, read "Forecasting Sales" and "Sales Forecasting"—two of the articles listed in the Selected Bibliography at the end of this chapter.

Quantitative Forecasting Methods

All quantitative forecasting methods use past data to some extent to predict the future. Such an approach assumes, of course, that past data are relevant to the future, which is not the case in all forecasting situations. Take, for example, the company that developed the first diet beer product. Few past data and little experience were available or relevant to projecting future sales. Instances where the past data are of no particular help in estimating the future are rare and should not cause us to abandon analysis by throwing out the baby with the bath water.

The times when some form of quantitative analysis can be utilized outnumber the times when it is inappropriate. Some relevant data can almost always be found. The results of these methods are usually modified by other relevant information before a final forecasting decision is made. As Figure 3.1 shows, analysis that projects past data into the future may not be used alone to determine a forecast. Still, analyses are important inputs to forecasting decisions.

What follows will explain some long-range and short-range forecasting situations in POM and the details of some quantitative forecasting methods. The amount of space devoted to these methods is not necessarily directly proportional to the degree of use of the techniques by business and government relative to other methods, but only to the need to convey an understanding of the methods.

Forecast Accuracy

Forecast accuracy is how close forecasts are to actual, but after the fact, data. Because forecasts are made *before* actual data become known, their accuracy cannot be determined at the moment they are made. Only after the passage of time will we know how accurate our forecasts have been. If they are very close to the actual data, we say that they have *high accuracy* and that the *forecast error* was very low. If, on the other hand, they miss the mark and depart from the actual data, we say that they have *low accuracy* and very high forecast error. Forecast accuracy, unfortunately, cannot be determined until after the fact — after the future that we are forecasting becomes the past. Knowing whether a forecasting method has resulted in high-accuracy forecasts is fundamental to its continued use. We keep track of a forecasting method's accuracy by keeping a running tally of how far our forecasts have missed the actual data points over time. If the historical accuracy of a method's application has been low, we must consider whether to modify the method or select a new one. We usually monitor a forecasting method's accuracy with either *mean absolute deviation* (MAD) or *total absolute deviation* (TAD). We will use the latter measure, which we simply call *total absolute error*, in evaluating the accuracy of forecasting methods later in this chapter.

Long-Run Forecasts

Long-run forecasting means estimating future conditions over time spans that range from many months to many years. Estimates that span these long periods are necessary in POM to support most of the management decisions concerning planning products, processes, and facilities — the topics in Part Two of this text. Such decisions are so important to the long-term success of productive systems that intense organizational effort is applied to developing these forecasts.

Most of this effort involves estimating the future demand for products and services, or developing *sales forecasts.* From these sales forecasts comes most of the information that operations managers need to know about planning their productive systems. Specifically, long-run forecasts provide operations managers with information to make important decisions such as these:

1. Selecting a product design. The final design is dependent upon the expected sales volume. Enormous production engineering design work is necessary, for example, for mass-produced products to insure low-cost manufacture and ease of processing through automatic machines.

2. Selecting a production processing scheme for a new product. Because these

forecasts determine the long-run production capacity that is necessary, the process designs are dependent upon the forecasts.

3. Selecting a plan for the long-run supply of scarce materials. These forecasts allow operations managers to lock suppliers into long-run material supply contracts.

4. Selecting a long-run production capacity plan for all of an organization's product lines. How many manufacturing plants are needed and where should they be located?

5. Selecting a long-run plan for acquiring capital funds. Such a plan will be based upon a long-run production capacity plan, which is in turn based on long-run forecasts.

These and other estimates of long-run requirements of productive systems usually follow from long-run sales forecasts. To purchase and build new machines and buildings and develop new sources of materials and capital funds takes time. And long-run forecasts give managers the time to develop these requirements.

We shall now study some concepts and quantitative techniques of long-run forecasting.

Cycles, Trends, and Seasonality Developing forecasts that can span several years may involve historical data that exhibit cycles, trends, and seasonality. Figure 3.2 shows how past annual sales data tend to cycle about the long-run trend line. A *cycle* is a data pattern that covers several years before it repeats itself again. Long-run *trends* are described by a line through the cycles. Thus in Figure 3.2 annual sales are said to cycle about the trend line. *Seasonality* is a data pattern that occurs within each year. These seasonal fluctuations are usually not a major concern in long-run forecasting.

In Figure 3.2 ten periods of historical annual sales data are plotted on a graph. Long-run forecasts could be developed by graphically fitting a trend line to this past data and then extending the line forward into the future. The forecasts for Periods 11, 12, 13, and 14 could then be read off the vertical axis. This graphical approach to long-run forecasts is used in practice, but its principal drawback is our inability to accurately fit the trend line to the actual past data.

Regression analysis, although slightly more mathematically rigorous, provides a more accurate way to develop trend line forecasts. Later in this chapter we shall show how these trend line forecasts can be modified to reflect cycles and seasonality.

Regression Analysis *Regression analysis* is a type of quantitative forecasting that establishes a relationship between a dependent variable, for which future values will be forecast, and a group of other variables, called independent variables. We use our knowledge about the relationship between the dependent and independent variables and about the future values of the independent variables to estimate the future values of the dependent variables. Thus we forecast values of the dependent variables.

Time Series Forecasting We will first discuss a special case of simple linear regression analysis — *time series forecasting. Simple* means that only two variables are involved in the analysis — one dependent variable (the one we want to forecast

Figure 3.2
Long-Run Trend Forecasting

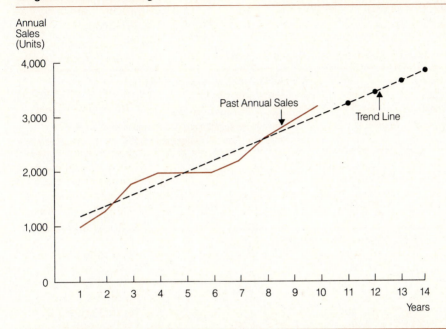

future values of) and one independent variable. In time series forecasts, the independent variable is time periods. Therefore, in time series forecasting we set the relationship between the dependent variable and past time periods and then use our knowledge about this relationship and values of the independent variable to forecast values of the dependent variable in future time periods.

Table 3.3 displays the variables, variable definitions, and formulas for simple linear regression analysis. The end product of simple linear regression analysis is the relationship between the dependent variable (Y) and the independent variable (X). The formula for this relationship is called the *regression equation:* $Y = a + bX$. The formulas listed in Table 3.3 show how to compute values of intercept (a) and slope (b). Once these constant values are known, a future value of X can be entered into the regression equation and a corresponding value of Y (the forecast) is set.

Conceptually, this procedure is the same as that of Figure 3.2 except that in regression analysis we derive the mathematical formula for the trend line ($Y = a + bX$) and mathematically compute the future values of the dependent variable, whereas in Figure 3.2 we graphically extend the trend line and read off values of the dependent variable from the vertical axis.

To better understand the detailed procedures of simple linear regression analysis, study Example 3.1, which develops a time series forecast. Use your calculator to check each calculation in the example. The example shows how operations managers can plan facility capacities by developing long-run forecasts for annual sales through time series forecasting.

Table 3.3
Simple Linear Regression Analysis Variable Definitions and Formulas

x = Independent variable values	$\bar{y}$ = Mean value of the dependent variable
y = Dependent variable values	a = Vertical axis intercept
n = Number of periods of data	b = Slope of the regression line
$\bar{x}$ = Mean value of the independent variable	Y = Forecast value in the regression equation $Y = a + bX$
	X = Projected value of independent variable value associated with Y

$$a = \frac{\Sigma x^2 \Sigma y - \Sigma x \Sigma xy}{n\Sigma x^2 - (\Sigma x)^2}$$

$$b = \frac{n\Sigma xy - \Sigma x \Sigma y}{n\Sigma x^2 - (\Sigma x)^2}$$

or

$$a = \bar{y} - b\,\bar{x}$$

$$b = \frac{\Sigma xy - n\,\bar{x}\,\bar{y}}{\Sigma x^2 - n(\bar{x})^2}$$

$$Y = a + bX$$

$$r = \frac{n\Sigma xy - \Sigma x \Sigma y}{\sqrt{[n\Sigma x^2 - (\Sigma x)^2][n\Sigma y^2 - (\Sigma y)^2]}}$$

Note: $\bar{x}$ and $\bar{y}$ must be carried out to *many* decimal places to achieve precision for *a* and *b*.

Example 3.1

Simple Linear Regression Analysis: Time Series Forecasting

Specific Motors produces electronic motors for power-actuated valves for the construction industry. Specific's production plant has operated at near capacity for over a year now. Jim White, the plant manager, thinks that the growth in sales will continue, and he wants to develop a long-run forecast to be used to plan facility requirements for the next three years. Sales records for the past ten years have been accumulated:

Annual Sales (Thousands of Units)

Year	Annual Sales	Year	Annual Sales
1	1,000	6	2,000
2	1,300	7	2,200
3	1,800	8	2,600
4	2,000	9	2,900
5	2,000	10	3,200

Study the formulas and variable definitions in Table 3.3 carefully, and construct the following table to establish the values to use in the formulas:

Year	Annual Sales (Thousands of Units) (y)	Time Periods (x)	x^2	xy	
1	1,000	1	1	1,000	
2	1,300	2	4	2,600	$\Sigma y = 21{,}000$
3	1,800	3	9	5,400	$\Sigma x = 55$
4	2,000	4	16	8,000	$\Sigma x^2 = 385$
5	2,000	5	25	10,000	$\Sigma xy = 133{,}300$
6	2,000	6	36	12,000	
7	2,200	7	49	15,400	$n = 10$
8	2,600	8	64	20,800	$\bar{x} = 55/10 = 5.5$
9	2,900	9	81	26,100	$\bar{y} = 21{,}000/10 = 2{,}100$
10	3,200	10	100	32,000	
Totals	21,000	55	385	133,300	

Solution

1. Let us now solve for the *a* and *b* values:

$$a = \frac{\Sigma x^2 \Sigma y - \Sigma x \Sigma xy}{n\Sigma x^2 - (\Sigma x)^2} = \frac{(385)(21{,}000) - (55)(133{,}300)}{10(385) - (55)^2}$$

$$= \frac{8{,}085{,}000 - 7{,}331{,}500}{3{,}850 - 3{,}025} = \frac{753{,}500}{825} = 913.333$$

$$b = \frac{n\Sigma xy - \Sigma x \Sigma y}{n\Sigma x^2 - (\Sigma x)^2} = \frac{(10)(133{,}300) - (55)(21{,}000)}{825}$$

$$= \frac{1{,}333{,}000 - 1{,}155{,}000}{825} = \frac{178{,}000}{825} = 215.758$$

or, alternatively, the other set of formulas for *a* and *b* may be used:

$$b = \frac{\Sigma xy - n\bar{x}\bar{y}}{\Sigma x^2 - n(\bar{x})^2} = \frac{133{,}300 - (10)(5.5)(2{,}100)}{385 - 10(5.5)^2}$$

$$= \frac{133{,}300 - 115{,}500}{385 - 302.5} = \frac{17{,}800}{82.5} = 215.758$$

$$a = \bar{y} - b\bar{x} = 2{,}100 - (215.758)(5.5) = 2{,}100 - 1{,}186.667 = 913.333$$

2. Now that we know the values of *a* and *b*, the regression equation ($Y = a + bX$) from Table 3.3 can be used to forecast future years' sales:

$$Y = a + bX = 913.333 + 215.758X$$

3. If we wish to forecast sales in thousands of units for the next three years, we would substitute 11, 12, and 13, the next three values for x, into the regression equation for X:

$$Y_{11} = 913.333 + 215.758\,(11) = 3,286.7$$

$$Y_{12} = 913.333 + 215.758\,(12) = 3,502.4$$

$$Y_{13} = 913.333 + 215.758\,(13) = 3,718.2$$

Simple Linear Regression Forecasting The independent variable in *simple linear regression analysis* does not have to be time periods as in time series forecasting. Rather, the independent variable can be any variable believed to be a good predictor of the dependent variable.

Example 3.2 demonstrates the procedures of simple linear regression analysis when the independent variable is not time periods. In this example a long-run forecast is developed to assist the manager in planning the number of engineers and facilities for the next year. This example also raises the question of the value of the predictive model developed through regression analysis. Coefficients of correlation and determination are measures of the precision of these forecasts.

Example 3.2

Simple Linear Regression Analysis

Jack Williams, the general manager of the Precision Engineering Corporation, thinks that his firm's engineering services supplied to highway construction firms are directly related to the amount of highway construction contracts let in his geographical area. He wonders if this is really so and if it is, can this information help him plan his operations better? Jack asked Bill Brandon, one of his engineers, to perform a simple linear regression analysis on historical data. Bill plans to do the following: **a.** Develop a regression equation for predicting the level of demand of Precision's services. **b.** Use the regression equation to predict the level of demand for the next four quarters. **c.** Determine how closely demand is related to the amount of construction contracts released.

Solution

a. Develop a regression equation:

1. Bill goes back through local, state, and federal records to gather the dollar amount of contracts released in the geographical area for two years by quarters.

2. He examines the demand for his firm's services over the same period.

3. The following data are prepared:

Year	Quarter	Sales of Precision Engineering Services (Thousands of Dollars)	Total Amount of Contracts Released (Thousands of Dollars)
1	Q_1	8	150
	Q_2	10	170
	Q_3	15	190
	Q_4	9	170
2	Q_1	12	180
	Q_2	13	190
	Q_3	12	200
	Q_4	16	220

4. Bill now develops the totals required to perform the regression analysis. The formulas and variable definitions are found in Table 3.3.

Time Period	Sales (y)	Contracts (x)	x^2	xy	y^2	
1	8	150	22,500	1,200	64	
2	10	170	28,900	1,700	100	$\Sigma y = 95$
3	15	190	36,100	2,850	225	$\Sigma x = 1,470$
4	9	170	28,900	1,530	81	$\Sigma x^2 = 273,300$
5	12	180	32,400	2,160	144	$\Sigma xy = 17,830$
6	13	190	36,100	2,470	169	$\Sigma y^2 = 1,183$
7	12	200	40,000	2,400	144	$n = 8$
8	16	220	48,400	3,520	256	
Totals	95	1,470	273,300	17,830	1,183	

5. Use these values in the formulas in Table 3.3 to compute a and b:

$$a = \frac{\Sigma x^2 \Sigma y - \Sigma x \Sigma xy}{n\Sigma x^2 - (\Sigma x)^2} = \frac{(273,300)(95) - (1,470)(17,830)}{8(273,300) - (1,470)^2} = \frac{25,963,500 - 26,210,100}{2,186,400 - 2,160,900}$$

$$= \frac{-246,600}{25,500} = -9.671$$

$$b = \frac{n\Sigma xy - \Sigma x \Sigma y}{n\Sigma x^2 - (\Sigma x)^2} = \frac{(8)(17,830) - (1,470)(95)}{25,500} = \frac{142,640 - 139,650}{25,500}$$

$$= \frac{2,990}{25,500} = .1173$$

6. The regression equation is therefore $Y = -9.671 + .1173X$.

b. Forecast the level of demand for the next four quarters:

1. Bill calls representatives of the contracting agencies and prepares estimates of the next four quarters' contract releases in thousands of dollars. These were 260, 290, 300, and 270.

2. Next, Bill forecasts the demand for Precision's engineering services (in thousands of dollars) for the next four quarters by using the regression equation $Y = -9.671 + .1173X$:

$$\begin{aligned}
Y_1 &= -9.671 + .1173(260) & Y_2 &= -9.671 + .1173(290)\\
&= -9.671 + 30.498 & &= -9.671 + 34.017\\
&= 20.827 & &= 24.346
\end{aligned}$$

$$\begin{aligned}
Y_3 &= -9.671 + .1173(300) & Y_4 &= -9.671 + .1173(270)\\
&= -9.671 + 35.190 & &= -9.671 + 31.671\\
&= 25.519 & &= 22.000
\end{aligned}$$

The total forecast (in thousands of dollars) for the next year is the total of the four quarter forecasts:

$$20.827 + 24.346 + 25.519 + 22.000 = \$92.7$$

c. Evaluate how closely demand is related to the amount of the construction contracts released:

$$r = \frac{n\Sigma xy - \Sigma x\Sigma y}{\sqrt{[n\Sigma x^2 - (\Sigma x)^2][n\Sigma y^2 - (\Sigma y)^2]}} = \frac{2{,}990}{\sqrt{[25{,}550][8(1{,}183) - (95)^2]}}$$

$$= \frac{2{,}990}{\sqrt{[25{,}500][9{,}464 - 9{,}025]}} = \frac{2{,}990}{\sqrt{(25{,}500)(439)}} = \frac{2{,}990}{\sqrt{11{,}194{,}500}}$$

$$= \frac{2{,}990}{3{,}345.8} = .894$$

$$r^2 = .799$$

The amount of contracts released explains approximately 80 percent ($r^2 = .799$) of the observed variation in quarterly demand for Precision's services.

Correlation Coefficient The *coefficient of correlation* (r) explains the relative importance of the association between y and x. The range of r is from -1 to $+1$. Minus 1 means a perfect negative relationship between the two variables; in other words, as y goes up, x goes down unit for unit and vice versa. Plus 1 means a perfect positive relationship between y and x; that is, as y goes up, x goes up unit for unit and vice versa. Zero means no relationship exists between y and x. If the formula for r in Table 3.3 will give only positive values to r, how can r take on negative values? This is made possible by assigning the sign of b in the regression analysis to r. In Example 3.2, $b = +.1173$; therefore $r = +.894$. This means that there is a strong positive relationship between demand for engineering services and amount of contracts released. A smaller value of r, say .25, would have indicated a weak relationship between demand for engineering services and amount of contracts released. The larger the absolute value of r, the better the regression equation forecasts accurate values of Y.

Although the coefficient of correlation is helpful in establishing confidence in our predictive model, terms such as *strong, moderate,* and *weak* are not very specific measures of relationship. The coefficient of determination offers some improvement in specificity.

Coefficient of Determination The *coefficient of determination* (r^2) is the square of the coefficient of correlation. The seemingly insignificant modification of r to r^2 allows us to shift from subjective measures of relationship between x and y to a more specific measure, *the percent of variation in y that is explained by x.* In other words, if $r^2 = 80$ percent, as in Example 3.2, we can say that the amount of contracts released (x) explains 80 percent of the variation in sales of engineering services (y). Twenty percent of the variation in sales of engineering services is not explained by the amount of contracts released and thus is attributed to other variables or chance variation.

Both the coefficients of correlation and determination are helpful measures of the strength of relationship between dependent and independent variables and thus of the value of regression equations as forecasting tools. The stronger the relationship, the more accurate the forecasts resulting from the regression equations are likely to be.

Advanced Regression Methods Simple linear regression analysis is severely limited in its ability to develop forecasts with high accuracy in the real worlds of government and business. Although there are instances where one independent variable explains enough of the dependent variable variation to provide management with forecasts having sufficient accuracy, more sophisticated models are usually required to increase forecasting accuracy. *Multiregression analysis* is used when two or more independent variables are incorporated into the analysis. An example of a multiregression equation is

$$Y = 15.5 + 2.9X_1 + 12.8X_2 - 1.2X_3 + 8.5X_4$$

where

Y = Annual sales in thousands of units

X_1 = National freight car loadings in millions

X_2 = Percent GNP growth $\times$ ten thousands

X_3 = Unemployment rate in region $\times$ ten thousands

X_4 = Population in county in thousands

Such an equation is used just as the simple regression equation ($Y = a + bX$): the values of the independent variables (X_1, X_2, X_3, and X_4) are substituted into the equation and the value of the dependent variable (Y) is directly calculated.

Another technique called *nonlinear multiregression analysis* is used when the relationship between the dependent variable and the independent variables is not linear. Other techniques such as *stepwise regression* and *partial and multiple correlation coefficients* are also part of the family of techniques called regression analysis. The concepts presented here generally apply to these more sophisticated techniques. Additionally, Y, X, and r all have their counterparts in the more complex models.

You have just received an introduction to regression analysis long-run forecasting methods. But you will need much more study beyond the scope of this course if you are to develop proficiency in applying this family of forecasting techniques.

There are times in POM when managers develop plans not for the long-run success of organizations, but to meet short-run goals such as high efficiency, cost and profit targets, and prompt customer deliveries. These plans require short-run forecasts.

Short-Run Forecasts

Short-run forecasts usually means estimates of future conditions over time spans that range from a few days to a few months. Short-run forecasts can span such brief periods that cycles, trends, and seasonality are unimportant influences. Here, therefore, we will develop short-run forecasts from data that are subject only to chance variation and ultrashort cyclical patterns.

Most short-run forecasts are sales forecasts. From these sales forecasts comes the information that operations managers need to know in order to make the decisions that we will explore in Parts Three and Four of this book: Planning Production to Meet Demand, and Planning and Controlling Operations. Specifically, short-run forecasts provide operations managers with information to make such decisions as these:

1. How much inventory of a particular product should be carried next month, given the short-run forecast?

2. How much of each product should be scheduled for production next week, given the amount that is in the sales forecast and the amount in inventory?

3. How much of each raw material should be ordered for delivery next week, given the amount of products in the production schedule and the amount in inventory?

4. How many workers should be scheduled to work on a straight-time and overtime basis next week, given the production schedule and the number of workers available?

5. How many maintenance workers should be scheduled to work next weekend, given the production schedule and our breakdown experience?

The continued efficient operation of productive systems requires accurate short-run forecasts. Two concepts are fundamental to these short-run forecasts—noise and impulse response.

Impulse Response versus Noise Dampening Short-run forecasting involves taking historical data from a few periods of the past and projecting the estimated values for these data one or more periods into the future. Forecasts that jump all over the map and reflect every little happenstance fluctuation in the past data are said to include *forecast noise*. These forecasts are highly erratic from period to period. If, on the other hand, analysis results in smooth forecasts with little period-to-period fluctuation, the forecasts are said to be *noise dampening*.

Forecasts that respond very fast to changes in the most recent historical data are described as having a *high impulse response*. On the other hand, when forecasts take several periods to reflect changes in historical data, these forecasts are said to have a *low impulse response*.

A forecasting system cannot be high both in noise-dampening ability and impulse response because we gain in impulse response only by giving up noise-dampening ability. In other words, a forecasting system that responds very fast to changes in the data, usually a desirable characteristic, necessarily picks up a great deal of noise associated with numerous chance variations in the data, which is usually undesirable. Conversely, a forecasting system that dampens noise does not respond fast to changes in the data. A trade-off between these two forecasting qualities is therefore always required.

We will refer to impulse response and noise as we study some short-run forecasting techniques.

Moving Average Method The *moving average method* averages the data from a few recent periods, and this average becomes the forecast for the next period. The key question is: How many periods of data do we include in the average? Example 3.3 addresses this question as it develops a system of short-run forecasts based upon the moving average method.

Example 3.3

Moving Average Short-Run Forecasting

The manager of the cash desk of a major corporation wishes to develop a short-run forecasting system to estimate the demand for cash from its many divisions and departments. Joseph Pennypinch, the manager of the cash desk, thinks that the overall demand for cash has been generally steady although it has fluctuated randomly from week to week. Orville Research, a forecasting expert from corporate headquarters, also known as OR, has recommended that Mr. Pennypinch use either a 3, 5, or 7 week average period moving average. The desk manager wonders which would be better. He decides to compare the precision of the 3, 5, and 7 week average period forecasts for the 10-week period that has just passed.

Solution

1. Compute the 3, 5, and 7 week Average Period (AP) moving average forecasts:

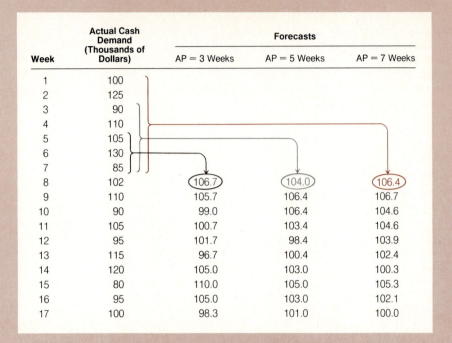

Week	Actual Cash Demand (Thousands of Dollars)	Forecasts		
		AP = 3 Weeks	AP = 5 Weeks	AP = 7 Weeks
1	100			
2	125			
3	90			
4	110			
5	105			
6	130			
7	85			
8	102	106.7	104.0	106.4
9	110	105.7	106.4	106.7
10	90	99.0	106.4	104.6
11	105	100.7	103.4	104.6
12	95	101.7	98.4	103.9
13	115	96.7	100.4	102.4
14	120	105.0	103.0	100.3
15	80	110.0	105.0	105.3
16	95	105.0	103.0	102.1
17	100	98.3	101.0	100.0

Sample computations — forecasts for the tenth week:

$$F_3 = \frac{85 + 102 + 110}{3} = 99.0 \qquad F_5 = \frac{105 + 130 + 85 + 102 + 110}{5} = 106.4$$

$$F_7 = \frac{90 + 110 + 105 + 130 + 85 + 102 + 110}{7} = 104.6$$

Note: In order to forecast for the tenth week, remember that the only historical weekly actual cash demand data you have to work with is Weeks 1–9. Therefore, you cannot include the actual data for the tenth week in computing the tenth-week forecasts.

2. Next, compute the total absolute forecast error for the three forecasts:

Week	Actual Cash Demand (Thousands of Dollars)	Forecasts					
		AP = 3 Weeks		AP = 5 Weeks		AP = 7 Weeks	
		Forecast	Error	Forecast	Error	Forecast	Error
8	102	106.7	4.7	104.0	2.0	106.4	4.4
9	110	105.7	4.3	106.4	3.6	106.7	3.3
10	90	99.0	9.0	106.4	16.4	104.6	14.6
11	105	100.7	4.3	103.4	1.6	104.6	.4
12	95	101.7	6.7	98.4	3.4	103.9	8.9
13	115	96.7	18.3	100.4	14.6	102.4	12.6
14	120	105.0	15.0	103.0	17.0	100.3	19.7
15	80	110.0	30.0	105.0	25.0	105.3	25.3
16	95	105.0	10.0	103.0	8.0	102.1	7.1
17	100	98.3	1.7	101.0	1.0	100.0	0
Total errors			104.0		92.6		96.3

3. Mr. Pennypinch should select an average period of 5 weeks because the total forecasting error tends to be less than with 3 or 7 weeks. The precision of the 7 week average period forecast is very close to the 5 week one; therefore, future checking is recommended.

4. OR now uses an AP of 5 weeks to forecast the cash demand for the next week, the eighteenth:

$$\text{Forecast} = \frac{115 + 120 + 80 + 95 + 100}{5} = 102, \text{ or } \$102,000$$

Figure 3.3 plots the three moving average forecasts against the actual data in Example 3.3. Note that the larger the averaging period, the smoother the forecast. In other words, the AP = 7 forecast has a low impulse response and a high noise-dampening ability, whereas the AP = 3 forecast has a high impulse response and a low noise-dampening ability. The AP = 5 forecast ranks somewhere between the other two forecasts in these two characteristics.

Figure 3.3
Moving Average Forecasts vs. Actual Cash Demand in Example 3.3

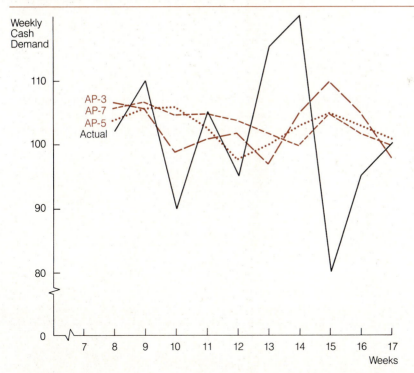

So which AP do we select? This is a qualitative decision.

	Noise-Dampening Ability	Impulse Response	Accuracy
AP = 3	Low	High	Low
AP = 5	Mid	Mid	High
AP = 7	High	Low	Mid

The ultimate selection of an AP would depend upon management's needs. What is more desirable, high impulse response or high noise-dampening ability? And how much accuracy can be given up to achieve either of these two characteristics? In the final analysis, the AP selected will depend upon a complete knowledge of the intended management use of the forecasts and the nature of the forecasting situation.

There are at least three drawbacks to the simple moving average method that we have presented: (1) all past periods in the AP are weighted equally, (2) no provision is made for seasonal patterns, and (3) several periods of historical data must be carried forward from period to period for calculating forecasts.

The first disadvantage can be overcome by assigning weights, the sum of which would equal one, to the past period data. For example:

	Actual Data	Weight
Week 7	85	.20
Week 8	102	.30
Week 9	110	.50

Forecast for the tenth week = .5(110) + .3(102) + .2(85)

= 55 + 30.6 + 17

= 102.6

This simple modification to the moving average method allows forecasters to specify the forecasting importance levels of past periods of data. Recent periods are typically more heavily weighted than older data.

Exponential Smoothing Method The variables, the variable definitions, and the formula for exponential smoothing forecasts are found in Table 3.4. *Exponential smoothing* takes the forecast for the current period and adds an error term to get the forecast for the next period. This error term is computed by multiplying the forecast error in the current period by a constant that is between zero and one. This constant alpha (α) is called the *smoothing constant*.

Table 3.4
**Formulas and Variable Definitions for
Exponential Smoothing Short-Run Forecasting**

F_t = next period's forecast A_{t-1} = current period's actual data

F_{t-1} = current period's forecast α = smoothing constant

New forecast = Current forecast + α (current actual − current forecast)

$F_t = F_{t-1} + \alpha (A_{t-1} - F_{t-1})$

Example 3.4 demonstrates how we might set a value of α in a real forecasting situation.

Example 3.4
Exponential Smoothing Short-Run Forecast

Joseph Pennypinch, from Example 3.3, liked the recommendations from OR, the corporate headquarters forecasting expert. As a goodwill gesture, OR was invited to the cash desk for consultation. OR was flattered, not to mention relieved to be out of sight of corporate headquarters for a short period. OR reviewed the moving average forecasts in Example 3.3 and suggested to Mr. Pennypinch that he try a similar experiment with ten periods of data using exponential smoothing. The only question was which alpha (α) is better: .1, .2, or .3?

Solution

1. First, study the formulas and variable definitions in Table 3.4. Compute the weekly forecasts for the eighth through the seventeenth weeks:

Week	Actual Cash Demand (Thousands of Dollars)	Forecasts $\alpha = .1$	$\alpha = .2$	$\alpha = .3$
7	85	85.0	85.0	85.0
8	102	85.0	85.0	85.0
9	110	86.7	88.4	90.1
10	90	89.0	92.7	96.1
11	105	89.1	92.2	94.3
12	95	90.7	94.8	97.5
13	115	91.1	94.8	96.8
14	120	93.5	98.8	102.3
15	80	96.2	103.0	107.6
16	95	94.6	98.4	99.3
17	100	94.6	97.7	98.0

All these seventh week forecasts were selected arbitrarily. Beginning forecasts are necessary to use exponential smoothing. Traditionally, we set these forecasts equal to the actual data value of the period.

Here are sample calculations for the tenth week forecasts:

$$F_{10} = F_9 + \alpha(A_9 - F_9)$$

$\alpha = .1$: $F_{10} = 86.7 + .1(110 - 86.7) = 89.0$

$\alpha = .2$: $F_{10} = 88.4 + .2(110 - 88.4) = 92.7$

$\alpha = .3$: $F_{10} = 90.1 + .3(110 - 90.1) = 96.1$

Note: When the tenth week forecasts are made, the only historical data available is through the ninth week. Only the ninth week actual data and the ninth week forecasts are used to compute the tenth week forecasts.

2. Next, compute the total absolute forecast error for the three forecasts:

Week	Actual Cash Demand (Thousands of Dollars)	Forecasts					
		$\alpha = .1$		$\alpha = .2$		$\alpha = .3$	
		Forecast	Error	Forecast	Error	Forecast	Error
8	102	85.0	17.0	85.0	17.0	85.0	17.0
9	110	86.7	23.3	88.4	21.6	90.1	19.9
10	90	89.0	1.0	92.7	2.7	96.1	6.1
11	105	89.1	15.9	92.2	12.8	94.3	10.7
12	95	90.7	4.3	94.8	.2	97.5	2.5
13	115	91.1	23.9	94.8	20.2	96.8	18.2
14	120	93.5	26.5	98.8	21.2	102.3	17.7
15	80	96.2	16.2	103.0	23.0	107.6	27.6
16	95	94.6	.4	98.4	3.4	99.3	4.3
17	100	94.6	5.4	97.7	2.3	98.0	2.0
Total errors			133.9		124.4		126.0

3. The smoothing constant $\alpha = .2$ gives slightly better accuracy when compared to $\alpha = .1$ and $\alpha = .3$.

4. Next, using $\alpha = .2$, compute the forecast (in thousands of dollars) for the eighteenth week:

$$F_{18} = F_{17} + .2(A_{17} - F_{17})$$

$$= 97.7 + .2(100 - 97.7) = 97.7 + .2(2.3) = 97.7 + .46 = 98.2$$

The selection of a value for alpha (α), the smoothing constant, is the only tricky part of the technique. Forecasters generally select values for α that work best for them in particular forecasting situations, as we have seen in Example 3.4. It is not always true that higher α levels result in more accurate forecasts. Each data set tends to have unique qualities, so that experimentation with different α levels is advised in order to maximize accuracy.

Figure 3.4 plots the exponential smoothing forecasts ($\alpha = .1, .2,$ and .3) against the actual weekly demand for cash from Example 3.4. When $\alpha = .1$, the forecast exhibits high noise-dampening ability but low impulse response. When $\alpha = .3$, the forecast exhibits higher impulse response but lower noise-dampening ability. This pattern is true over the entire $0 - 1.0$ range of α. The higher α is, the higher is its impulse response and the lower its noise-dampening ability and vice versa.

Figure 3.4
Exponential Smoothing Forecasts vs. Actual Cash Demand in Example 3.4

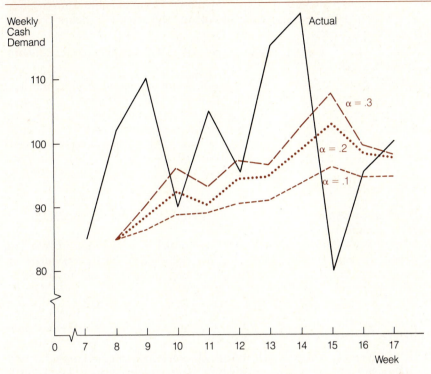

Let us summarize the results for selecting an α in Example 3.4:

	Noise-Dampening Ability	Impulse Response	Accuracy
$\alpha = .1$	High	Low	Mid
$\alpha = .2$	High/mid	Low/mid	High
$\alpha = .3$	Mid	Mid	High

As in the case of moving averages (AP), the selection of a level of α would be based on a knowledge of management's needs and the nature of the particular forecasting situation.

Exponential smoothing is really just one of a whole family of forecasting methods. We have presented only its simplest form here. At least four different sophistications can be offered:

1. *Double smoothing.* This allows the forecast to adapt to more complex cyclical patterns of the actual data.

2. *Variable smoothing constants.* This feature allows a tracking algorithm (usually MAD) to accumulate forecasting error and modify the value of α heuristically to minimize or control error.

3. *Nonhorizontal trends.* A trend term is added to the formulas to allow for nonhorizontal trend line data.

4. *Box–Jenkins.* Exponential smoothing is really just a special case of this approach. Its autocorrelation methods examine the actual historical data points and fit a mathematical function to these data. The mathematical function then becomes the forecasting model for future estimates. This method is available in many standard computer programming packages. The method is reported to be the most accurate of all the short-run forecasting methods, but about sixty data points are required, it requires some time to get forecast results, and it is moderately expensive to use.[1]

These and other developments in exponential smoothing forecasting make it a powerful force in short-run forecasting.

We have now worked our way through several of the most common forecasting methods. What is their value to you? This question can be partly answered by examining the extent to which these methods are used in today's organizations.

Forecasting Practices

Examine Table 3.5 carefully to compare the use of each forecasting technique across industrial products manufacturers, consumer products manufacturers, and service firms. Jury of executive opinion is used heavily across all firms, but to a lesser degree among consumer products companies. Survey of users' expectations is used only moderately across all firms, with industrial products manufacturers being the heaviest users. Time series projection is used moderately and uniformly across all firms. Other quantitative models are used only sparingly across all firms, with service companies being the heaviest users.

Across all firms the forecasting methods would rank according to heaviest use as follows, with the low-rank numbers indicating most use:

Forecasting Method	Rank
Jury of executive opinion	1
Sales force composite	2
Time series	3
Survey of users' expectations	4
Other quantitative models	5

[1] G. E. P. Box and G. M. Jenkins, *Time Series Analysis, Forecasting, and Control* (San Francisco: Holden-Day, 1970).

Table 3.5
Percentage of Firms Relying on Forecasting Methods

Forecasting Method	All Companies			Industrial Products Manufacturers			Consumer Products Manufacturers			Service Companies		
	Degree of Reliance			Degree of Reliance			Degree of Reliance			Degree of Reliance		
	Heavy	Moderate	Little	Heavy	Moderate	Little	Heavy	Moderate	Little	Heavy	Moderate	Little
Jury of executive opinion	48	32	20	47	34	19	53	24	23	42	38	20
Sales force composite	42	33	25	50	36	13	27	24	50	35	35	30
Survey of users' expectations	18	30	52	22	37	41	10	27	63	17	8	75
Time series projection	25	32	43	23	30	48	29	29	43	25	46	29
Predictive models	15	19	66	12	20	69	11	24	66	32	12	56

Source: Reprinted by permission from *Sales Forecasting Methods — An Appraisal,* National Industrial Conference Board, Bulletin 25, 1970. Based on information from 161 reporting companies — 93 industrial products manufacturers, 39 consumer products manufacturers, and 29 service firms (insurance, banking, transportation, utilities).

The forecasting techniques presented in this chapter have been demonstrated by working through several rather simple examples. Even these simple examples, however, require lengthy and time-consuming manual calculations. Real world governmental and business forecasters typically work with great quantities of data, and their complex techniques require more complex calculations. They do not, however, typically perform their forecasting calculations manually. Rather, they use computers to do the calculations. Numerous standard programs that are readily available at low cost cover the entire range of forecasting techniques. (See, for example, the statistical package for the social sciences — SPSS — discussed in a book of that title listed in the Selected Bibliography at the end of this chapter.)

Optional Forecasting Topics

Several refinements to the basic forecasting methods presented in this chapter exist to provide more usable forecasting information to management. Two additional topics are presented here — forecast ranging and seasonality in time series forecasting.

Forecast Ranging

Suppose that you have performed the forecasting analysis in Example 3.1 as part of your assignment from Jim White, Specific Motors, to recommend long-run forecasts for annual sales for three years into the future. You present your recommendations in thousands of units:

$$Y_{11} = 3,286.7 \qquad Y_{12} = 3,502.4 \qquad Y_{13} = 3,718.2$$

Mr. White considers the forecasts for a time that seems like an eternity and finally asks, "How sure are you of these figures?" Before you can respond, he asks, "How high and how low do you estimate the annual sales could be next year?"

When time series analysis generates forecasts for future periods, we must recognize that these are only estimates and that the actual annual sales to be subsequently realized may differ substantially from the forecasts. In fact, no one would be more surprised than the forecasters if they hit the forecasts on the nose. The presence of forecasting errors or chance variations is a fact of life for forecasters; it is a process permeated with uncertainty. How do forecasters deal with this uncertainty?

Figure 3.5 shows how we think about forecasting errors. Ten periods of data are used to develop a trend line. This analysis results in a forecast of 2,400 units for Time

Figure 3.5
Errors in Forecasting

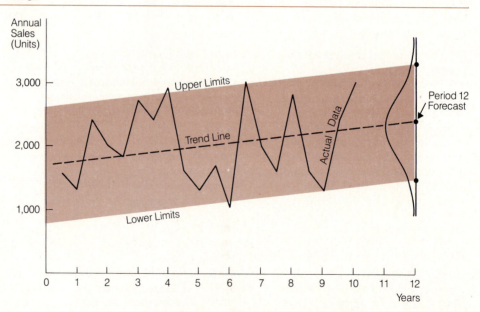

Period 12. The uncertainty surrounding this estimate is demonstrated by showing the forecast as a mean or central tendency of a frequency distribution of all of the possible values of annual sales during Time Period 12. By drawing upper and lower limits through the data parallel to the trend line such that actual annual sales only rarely exceed the limits, upper and lower limits can be estimated for the Time Period 12 forecast — 3,300 units and 1,500 units.

An analysis of this type allows us to deal with the uncertainty of our forecasts in a very direct way. Questions about our confidence in our forecasts can be answered by stating how high (upper limit) or how low (lower limit) the annual sales are likely to be. If these limits are far apart, the historical data are highly scattered around the trend line and we have less confidence in our forecasts. If, on the other hand, the limits are close together, the historical data have been closely grouped about the trend line and we have more confidence in our forecasts.

Although this graphical approach is sometimes used to set upper and lower limits or ranges of forecasts, a more precise method is available. Example 3.5 uses this formula to estimate ranges:

$$s_{yx} = \sqrt{\frac{\Sigma y^2 - a\Sigma y - b\Sigma xy}{n - 2}}$$

The expression s_{yx} is referred to by several names, including the *standard error of the forecast* and the *standard deviation of the forecast*. Whatever name is applied to it, s_{yx} is a measure of how historical data points have been dispersed about the trend line. If s_{yx} is large, the historical data points have been spread widely about the trend line and the upper and lower limits are far apart. If, on the other hand, s_{yx} is small, past data points have been tightly grouped about the trend line and the upper and lower limits are close together.

Example 3.5
Ranging Time Series Forecasts

The annual sales data of Specific Motors from Example 3.1 resulted in these values: $\Sigma y = 21,000$, $\Sigma xy = 133,300$, $a = 913.333$, $b = 215.758$, and $n = 10$. The distribution of forecast values for a future time period has a standard deviation (s_{yx}) which is a relative measure of how the distribution is dispersed (spread out). The distributions of all future time periods are assumed to be normal distributions if n (number of observations) is large (usually ≥ 30) or Student t distributions if n is small (usually < 30). Since we rarely have 30 or more observations in our data, and t and normal distributions tend to converge when n is large, it is assumed that we are dealing with t distributions.

Solution

1. From Example 3.1 we have computed all of these values: $\Sigma y = 21,000$; $\Sigma x = 55$; $\Sigma x^2 = 385$; $\Sigma xy = 133,300$; $n = 10$; $\bar{x} = 5.5$; and $\bar{y} = 2,100$. Let us now compute Σy^2:

Year	y (Thousands of Units)	y^2	Year	y (Thousands of Units)	y^2
1	1,000	1,000,000	6	2,000	4,000,000
2	1,300	1,690,000	7	2,200	4,840,000
3	1,800	3,240,000	8	2,600	6,760,000
4	2,000	4,000,000	9	2,900	8,410,000
5	2,000	4,000,000	10	3,200	10,240,000
			Totals	21,000	48,180,000

2. Now let us compute the value of s_{yx}:

$$s_{yx} = \sqrt{\frac{\Sigma y^2 - a\Sigma y - b\Sigma xy}{n-2}}$$

$$= \sqrt{\frac{48,180,000 - 913.333(21,000) - 215.758(133,300)}{10-2}}$$

$$= \sqrt{\frac{48,180,000 - 19,179,993 - 28,760,541.4}{8}} = \sqrt{\frac{239,465.6}{8}} = \sqrt{29,933.2}$$

$$= 173 \text{ thousand units}$$

3. Now that we have the value of s_{yx}, let us compute the upper and lower limits of the forecast for Time Period 11:

Upper limit $= Y_{11} + t\,s_{yx}$

Lower limit $= Y_{11} - t\,s_{yx}$

where t is the number of standard deviations out from the mean of the distribution to provide a given probability of exceeding these upper and lower limits through chance. Say, for example, that we wish to set the limits so that there is only a 10 percent probability of exceeding the limits by chance. Appendix B lists t values. Since the degrees of freedom (d.f.) $= n - 2$ and the level of significance is .10, the t value equals 1.860 and:

Upper limit $= 3,286.7 + 1.86(173) = 3,608.5$ thousand units

Lower limit $= 3,286.7 - 1.86(173) = 2,964.9$ thousand units

4. Now we can describe to Mr. White what we have: There is a 90 percent probability that our annual sales for next year will be between 3,608.5 and 2,964.9 thousand units. There is only a 10 percent probability that our sales will fall outside these limits. Our best estimate is 3,286.7 thousand units.

Forecast ranging allows analysts to face the reality of uncertainty that surrounds their forecasts by developing best estimate forecasts and the ranges that the actual data are likely to fall within.

Incorporating Seasonality into Time Series Forecasts

We can incorporate seasonality into short-run forecasts by using the same basic regression analysis formulas as in long-run forecasting. However, only a few periods of historical data are ordinarily used, and the trend line is usually extended only a short distance into the future. Additionally, the method establishes seasonal patterns in the historical data and uses these patterns to modify the trend forecasts. *Seasonal patterns* are by definition fluctuations that take place within one year and tend to be repeated annually. These seasons can be determined by weather, holidays, paydays, school events, and a multitude of other factors that can potentially affect demand for goods and services.

Example 3.6 demonstrates the procedures of seasonalized time series analysis. This example assumes that the last three years of data from Specific Motors in Example 3.1 are representative of what is expected in the near future.

Study Example 3.6 carefully, and use your calculator to check each calculation. The example follows these steps:

1. Select a representative historical data set.
2. Develop seasonal indexes for each time period in the forecasting horizon.
3. Use the seasonal indexes to deseasonalize the data; in other words, remove the seasonal patterns.
4. Perform a time series analysis on the deseasonalized data. This will result in a regression equation in the form $Y = a + bX$.
5. Use the regression equation to compute the short-run forecasts for the future. These are based on deseasonalized data; in other words, the seasonal patterns have been removed.
6. Use the seasonal indexes to modify the short-run forecasts, thereby reapplying the seasonal patterns to the forecasts.

Example 3.6
Seasonalized Time Series Analysis

Jim White, the plant manager of Specific Motors, is trying to plan cash, personnel, and materials and supplies requirements for each quarter of next year. The quarterly sales data for the past three years seem to fairly reflect the seasonal output pattern that should be expected in the future. If Mr. White could estimate quarterly sales for next year, the cash, personnel, and materials and supplies needs could be determined.

Solution

1. First, compute the seasonal indexes:

	Year	Q_1	Q_2	Q_3	Q_4	Annual Total
		\multicolumn{4}{c}{Quarterly Sales (Thousands of Units)}	
	8	520	730	820	530	2,600
	9	590	810	900	600	2,900
	10	650	900	1,000	650	3,200
Totals		1,760	2,440	2,720	1,780	8,700
Quarter average		586⅔	813⅔	906⅔	593⅓	725*
Seasonal indexes (S.I.)**		.809	1.122	1.251	.818	

* Overall quarter average = 8700/12 = 725.
** S.I. = Quarter average/overall quarter average.

2. Next, deseasonalize the data by dividing each quarterly value by its S.I.:

Deseasonalized Adjusted Quarterly Data

Years	Q_1	Q_2	Q_3	Q_4
8	642.8	650.6	655.5	647.9
9	729.3	721.9	719.4	733.5
10	803.5	802.1	799.4	794.6

3. Next, perform a time series analysis on the deseasonalized data (12 quarters) and forecast for the next 4 quarters:

Time Period	x	y	y^2	x^2	xy	
Year 8, Q_1	1	642.8	413,191.84	1	642.8	
Year 8, Q_2	2	650.6	423,280.36	4	1,301.2	
Year 8, Q_3	3	655.5	429,680.25	9	1,966.5	
Year 8, Q_4	4	647.9	419,774.41	16	2,591.6	
Year 9, Q_1	5	729.3	531,878.49	25	3,646.5	$\Sigma x = 78$
Year 9, Q_2	6	721.9	521,139.61	36	4,331.4	$\Sigma y = 8,700.5$
Year 9, Q_3	7	719.4	517,536.36	49	5,035.8	$\Sigma y^2 = 6,353,909.75$
Year 9, Q_4	8	733.5	538,022.25	64	5,868.0	$\Sigma x^2 = 650$
Year 10, Q_1	9	803.5	645,612.25	81	7,231.5	$\Sigma xy = 58,964.9$
Year 10, Q_2	10	802.1	643,364.41	100	8,021.0	$n = 12$
Year 10, Q_3	11	799.4	639,040.36	121	8,793.4	
Year 10, Q_4	12	794.6	631,389.16	144	9,535.2	
Totals	78	8,700.5	6,353,909.75	650	58,964.9	

4. Now use these values to substitute into the formulas found in Table 3.3:

$$a = \frac{\Sigma x^2 \Sigma y - \Sigma x \Sigma xy}{n \Sigma x^2 - (\Sigma x)^2} = \frac{650(8,700.5) - 78(58,964.9)}{12(650) - (78)^2} = 615.421$$

$$b = \frac{n\Sigma xy - \Sigma x \Sigma y}{n\Sigma x^2 - (\Sigma x)^2} = \frac{12(58,964.9) - 78(8,700.5)}{12(650) - (78)^2} = 16.865$$

$$Y = a + bX = 615.421 + 16.865X$$

5. Now, substitute the values 13, 14, 15, and 16, the next four values for x, into the regression equation:

$$Y_{13} = 615.421 + 16.865(13) = 834.666$$

$$Y_{14} = 615.421 + 16.865(14) = 851.531$$

$$Y_{15} = 615.421 + 16.865(15) = 868.396$$

$$Y_{16} = 615.421 + 16.865(16) = 885.261$$

These are the deseasonalized forecasts, in thousands of units, for the next four quarters.

6. Now use the seasonal indexes (S.I.) to seasonalize the forecasts:

Quarter	S.I.	Deseasonalized Forecasts	Seasonalized Forecasts [(S.I.) × Deseasonalized Forecasts] (Thousands of Units)
Q_1	.809	834.666	675.2
Q_2	1.122	851.531	955.4
Q_3	1.251	868.396	1,086.4
Q_4	.818	885.261	724.1

The method of developing seasonal indexes in Example 3.6 takes the ratio of each quarter's sales to the average sales for all 12 quarters of data. This method gives satisfactory results as long as the trend is relatively flat. In cases where the trend is steep, the method of this example may be subject to some error. In these cases seasonal indexes may be developed from the ratio of each quarter's sales to such measures as computed trend sales data or 12-month moving average sales.[2] The application of these ratios is procedurely similar to that of Example 3.6.

When we develop forecasts, as in Example 3.6, by using seasonalized time series analysis and we wish to range these forecasts, the procedure is straightforward. The deseasonalized forecasts would be ranged and then these forecasts, along with their upper and lower limits, would be seasonalized by multiplying them by their seasonal indexes.

The seasonalized time series analysis technique may seem somewhat laborious because of the complex formulas and numerous arithmetic calculations required.

---

[2] John R. Stockton and Charles T. Clark, *Business and Economic Statistics,* 5th ed. (Cincinnati: South-Western Publishing, 1975), Chap. 16.

Most applications of the technique in real world organizations utilize the computer to speed these analyses.

Summary

Forecasting is estimating future organizational activity levels through scientific investigation. Paramount above all other forecasts is the estimate of the demand for the goods and services of organizations. Business organizations call these estimates sales forecasts. Operations managers typically participate in preparing sales forecasts and are subsequently responsible for deducing forecasts for such items as personnel, cash, capital funds, materials and supplies, utilities, and inventories. Accurate forecasting in POM determines to a large degree the efficiency of the productive system in attaining its goals and objectives.

Long-run forecasting involves estimates that typically go from a few months to several years into the future. The most common long-run forecasting technique is regression analysis. This method develops a trend line through past data that is closest to the historical data points and projects this long-range trend line into the future time periods. The trend line projections yield long-range estimates of the forecast variable.

Short-run forecasting typically involves estimates of the future that are less than a few months in duration. Two commonly used techniques for short-run forecasting are moving averages and exponential smoothing. These techniques are applied to short-run forecasting situations that are vulnerable to day-to-day and week-to-week chance variation.

Five forecasting approaches mentioned in this chapter, ranked from most to least frequently used in business, are: jury of executive opinion, sales force composite, time series, survey of users' expectations, and other quantitative models.

Review and Discussion Questions

1. What is forecasting?
2. Name three underlying reasons that operations managers must forecast.
3. Name three qualitative forecasting methods used in business today.
4. What are the important inputs into forecasting decisions?
5. Describe briefly the steps in linear regression analysis.
6. What inputs are required in linear regression analysis? What are the outputs from this analysis?
7. What are the risks inherent in long-run forecasting?
8. What are the risks inherent in short-run forecasting?
9. Define *impulse response* and *noise dampening*. How are they related?
10. What are the key advantages of moving averages and exponential smoothing? What are the disadvantages?

11. Regression analysis is based on identifying independent variables and gathering historical data for these variables. Name some independent variables to forecast these dependent variables:
    a. Demand for hospital services
    b. Students entering colleges of business
    c. Local hamburger stand sales
    d. County sheriff's department services

Problems

Simple Regression

1. The We-Haul Trucking Company is authorized to haul local freight in the southern suburbs of Los Angeles. During the past five years the annual demand for We-Haul's services has grown steadily, requiring substantial outlays for trucking equipment. Laura Kennet, We-Haul's owner, has just managed to scrimp enough capital funds over the past five years to keep her head above water. These capital-raising projects have been spasmodic as the need for new equipment surfaced from time to time. Ms. Kennet realizes now that capital funds planning requires a long-range plan to provide steady and rational growth. Since she expects the past pattern of growth to continue, analyze the past five years of data using time series regression analysis to forecast the next two years' requirements for capital funds:

Year	Capital Funds (Thousands of Dollars)	Year	Capital Funds (Thousands of Dollars)
1	100	3	130
2	110	4	140
		5	160

2. The Halls of Ivy College, in a small town in upstate New York, is a private liberal arts college. Enrollments have grown steadily over the past six years since Marvin Conehead assumed the presidency. The number of students has grown sufficiently to warrant expanded library facilities. Dr. Conehead knows that the Board of Directors will not approve the library expansion unless it can be justified by forecast increased enrollments in the future. Enrollments for the past six years are:

Year	Student Enrollments (Thousands of Students)	Year	Student Enrollments (Thousands of Students)
1	2.5	4	3.2
2	2.8	5	3.3
3	2.9	6	3.4

Develop forecasts of enrollments for the next three years. Use time series regression analysis.

3. The Plymouth Foundation is a private research institute conducting research in solar energy in London, England. In the past, demand for research personnel has grown rapidly, and this trend is expected to continue indefinitely. Past data show this growth:

Year	Research Personnel	Year	Research Personnel
1	50	5	70
2	58	6	74
3	62	7	78
4	70		

Forecast next year's research personnel requirements for Plymouth. Use time series regression analysis.

4. Hank Besnette, the manager of Railroad Products Company (RPC), is in the process of projecting the firm's sales for the next three years. As a unit in the holding company's budget system, RPC is required to develop three-year sales forecasts, operating costs, and profits. Two years ago Mr. Besnette discovered that RPC's long-range sales were tied very closely to national freight car loadings, and he wonders if the railroad industry's projections of future freight car loadings can help him forecast his firm's sales. The following are seven years of historical data for RPC:

Year	RPC Annual Sales (Millions of Dollars)	National Freight Car Loadings (Millions)	Year	RPC Annual Sales (Millions of Dollars)	National Freight Car Loadings (Millions)
1	9.5	120	4	12.5	150
2	11.0	135	5	14.0	170
3	12.0	130	6	16.0	190
			7	18.0	220

a. Develop a simple linear regression analysis between RPC sales and national freight car loadings. Forecast RPC sales for the next three years if the railroad industry estimates freight car loadings of 250, 270, and 300 millions. **b.** What percentage of variation in RPC sales is explained by freight car loadings?

5. Juanita Cash, the operations planner for the First State Savings and Loan Company, is planning the next quarter's level of deposits. She suspects that First State's level of deposits is directly related to the interest rate paid on time deposits. The recent historical data for First State are as follows:

Year	Quarter	Deposits (Millions of Dollars)	Interest Rate (Percent)	Year	Quarter	Deposits (Millions of Dollars)	Interest Rate (Percent)
1	Q_2	10.0	4.50	2	Q_1	22.0	5.50
	Q_3	14.0	4.80		Q_2	16.3	5.00
	Q_4	18.5	5.25		Q_3	11.2	4.50

a. Use simple linear regression analysis between First State's deposits and the interest rate paid on deposits to forecast the next quarter's deposits level if the interest paid on deposits is expected to be 4.75 percent. **b.** What proportion of the variation in First State's deposit levels is explained by interest rates paid on deposits?

Moving Averages

6. The U.S. Coast Guard must enforce the fishing regulations set by the National Marine Fisheries Services within two hundred miles of the U.S. coastline. Because of spawning habits, weather, fishing seasons, and other reasons, the number of boats engaged in fishing in U.S. waters tends to be seasonal. Also, the number of employees required by the Coast Guard is seasonal. The historical quarterly patterns of employment by the Coast Guard are as follows:

Year	Quarter	Employees (Thousands)	Year	Quarter	Employees (Thousands)
1	Q_1	9.0	2	Q_1	9.3
	Q_2	12.2		Q_2	12.0
	Q_3	10.9		Q_3	11.0
	Q_4	9.5		Q_4	9.4

Use moving averages to forecast the number of employees required for the first quarter of the third year for AP = 4 and AP = 8.

7. Jane Fixitfast is the manager in charge of maintenance for Rest-International, a large hotel in Las Vegas, Nevada. She has observed that since the hotel is fairly new and is fully booked year round, maintenance calls occur randomly, with almost no trend or seasonality. She is developing a system to forecast one month ahead the number of maintenance calls she will receive. She plans to use moving averages but wonders what AP to use in order to minimize the total absolute forecasting error. Two years of historical data follow:

Month	Maintenance Calls	Month	Maintenance Calls	Month	Maintenance Calls	Month	Maintenance Calls
1	95	7	89	13	97	19	82
2	85	8	84	14	95	20	102
3	92	9	97	15	93	21	100
4	100	10	101	16	105	22	101
5	80	11	82	17	102	23	95
6	91	12	92	18	89	24	90

a. Develop moving average forecasts for the past ten months (Months 15–24) for AP = 2, 4, 6, and 8 months. **b.** Which AP results in the lowest absolute forecasting error? **c.** Use your recommended AP and forecast the number of maintenance calls for the next month (Month 25).

8. Jane Fixitfast of the Rest-International thinks that the moving average forecast from Problem 7 looks pretty good but wonders if recent past data are more important in forecasting than older data. She thinks that the most recent month should be weighted at .5 and that the preceding months' weights should be sequentially

reduced by a factor of .5 (i.e., .5, .25, .125, etc.). **a.** Develop the weights for the weighted moving average forecast. **b.** Use the weights developed in part a to forecast the number of maintenance calls for Month 25 from the data in Problem 7.

Exponential Smoothing

9. Bill O'Malley is a buyer in the purchasing department at Nilo Industries. His speciality is nonferrous metals. Bill is attempting to develop a system for forecasting monthly copper prices. He has accumulated sixteen months of historical price data:

Month	Copper Price/Pound	Month	Copper Price/Pound	Month	Copper Price/Pound	Month	Copper Price/Pound
1	$.85	5	$.83	9	$.95	13	$.83
2	.82	6	.85	10	.90	14	.81
3	.90	7	.89	11	.90	15	.87
4	.79	8	.81	12	.85	16	.85

a. Use exponential smoothing to forecast monthly copper prices. Compute what the forecasts would have been for all the months of historical data for $\alpha = .1$, $\alpha = .3$, and $\alpha = .5$ if the forecast for all α's in the first month was $.90. **b.** Which alpha (α) value results in the least total absolute forecast error over the 16-month period? **c.** Use the alpha (α) from part b to compute the forecast copper price for Month 17.

10. Bill O'Malley wishes to compare two forecasting systems to forecast copper prices from the data in Problem 9: moving averages (AP = 3) and exponential smoothing ($\alpha = .5$). **a.** Compute the two sets of monthly forecasts over the past ten months (7 through 16). The exponential smoothing forecast in Month 6 was $.832. **b.** Which forecast system has the least forecasting error? **c.** Plot on a graph the two forecast system results against the actual copper prices for the past ten months. What conclusions can you reach about the graph? **d.** Select the best system and forecast the copper prices for next month (Month 17).

Multiregression

11. Elaine Sharp, a production engineer for Machine Products Inc. (MPI), a large general job shop servicing automotive customers in the greater Detroit area, has just completed a linear multiregression analysis:

$$Y = 25.000 + .025X_1 + 100X_2 + 10.500X_3$$

where

Y = Number of production engineering hours per order

X_1 = Number of parts per order

X_2 = Inverse of the number of past orders for the part

X_3 = Number of gross pounds per part before machining

R^2 = .795

a. Estimate the number of production engineering hours required on the next order where X_1 = 1200, X_2 = ¼, X_3 = 2.5. **b.** What is the meaning of R^2 = .795?

Forecast Ranging

12. From Problem 2: **a.** Develop time series forecasts of enrollments for the next three years. **b.** Compute the value of the standard error of the forecast. **c.** What upper and lower limits can be estimated for the third-year forecast if a significance level of .05 is used?

13. From Problem 3: **a.** Use time series to forecast next year's research personnel requirements for Plymouth. **b.** What limits do you project for your forecast if the level of significance is .10? **c.** Explain in detail the meaning of your findings in part *b*.

14. From Problem 5, a simple linear regression forecast for the next quarter's deposits equals $13.368 million. **a.** Compute s_{yx}. **b.** Compute the upper and lower limits of your forecast from part *a* if the significance level is .10.

Seasonalized Forecasts

15. CHEMCO, a firm that provides in-transit warehouse space to major chemical manufacturers, has a facility at Evansbrook, Illinois. This warehouse stores strontium nitrate for three firms that ship from the CHEMCO warehouse to local distributors. To double its capacity if it needs it, CHEMCO can lease another nearby warehouse that has recently become available, but the decision must be made now. CHEMCO will lease the warehouse for one year if at any time during the year the maximum quarterly inventory is expected to exceed the present warehouse capacity, which is 28.5 million pounds. The recent past inventory levels are:

Year	Quarter	Inventory (Millions of Pounds)	Year	Quarter	Inventory (Millions of Pounds)	Year	Quarter	Inventory (Millions of Pounds)
1	Q_1	10	2	Q_1	12	3	Q_1	14
	Q_2	8		Q_2	10		Q_2	14
	Q_3	12		Q_3	16		Q_3	18
	Q_4	14		Q_4	20		Q_4	22

a. Use seasonalized time series analysis to forecast inventory levels for Q_1, Q_2, Q_3, and Q_4 for next year. **b.** Assume that when management refers to the maximum quarterly inventory levels, what it means is the upper limit of the quarterly forecasts with a probability of only .10 of exceeding the limit due to random variation. Find the upper limit or maximum quarterly inventory levels for next year. **c.** Should CHEMCO lease the warehouse?

16. From Problem 6: **a.** Use moving averages to forecast the number of employees required for the first quarter of the third year for AP = 4 and AP = 8. **b.** Are these forecasts seasonalized or deseasonalized? Why? **c.** Develop quarterly seasonal in-

dexes and apply them to the deseasonalized moving average forecasts ($AP = 4$ and $AP = 8$) from part *a*.

Integrative Problem

17. The APMC, Agricultural Products Machinery Corporation, manufactures automatic machinery for processing food products. One of its plants, located in San Leandro, California, manufactures automatic tomato pickers. Since the *beast*, as it is affectionately called by APMC, was first produced ten years ago, output has increased steadily until now the small plant is on a seven-day, three-shift production schedule. APMC now wishes to expand the facility at San Leandro to accommodate the maximum annual sales demand during the next five years (maximum, or only .05 probability of demand exceeding capacity). The historical records for production are:

Year	Production (Units)	Year	Production (Units)	Year	Production (Units)
1	100	4	200	7	220
2	130	5	200	8	260
3	180	6	200	9	290
				10	320

If the growth in sales of tomato pickers is expected to continue as in the past: **a.** Use time series regression to forecast production levels over the next five years. **b.** What is the maximum annual production (only .05 probability of exceeding the maximum) that you would expect during the five-year forecast period? **c.** Management at APMC suspects that the tomato picker demand is cyclical; demand goes through multiyear patterns. Plot the historical data on a graph, draw the trend line from part *a*, and estimate the effect that the cycles will have upon the planned facility expansion at San Leandro. **d.** Disregarding the cyclical fluctuations, estimate the upper and lower limits of the cumulative production of tomato pickers at San Leandro over the entire five-year period. (The standard deviation of the cumulative forecast $= \sqrt{k}\, s_{yx}$, where k = the number of time periods over which the forecast is accumulated.)

Case

Swank Retailers

Mary Demerick, chief operating officer of Swank Retailers in Phoenix, Arizona, is busy looking over the most recent sales information for the company. She has called a meeting of all salespersons in the region for one week from today, and she is attempting to estimate the sales levels that should be expected for their company over the next three months. She needs to have this information so that sales quotas can be set for the individual salespersons. Her staff has accumulated this historical sales data:

Year 1	Sales (Millions of Dollars)	Year 2	Sales (Millions of Dollars)	Year 3	Sales (Millions of Dollars)
Jan.	4.9	Jan.	5.1	Jan.	5.4
Feb.	6.1	Feb.	6.3	Feb.	7.5
Mar.	7.5	Mar.	7.9	Mar.	8.2
Apr.	7.4	Apr.	8.0	Apr.	8.7
May	5.2	May	5.5	May	6.1
Jun.	5.3	Jun.	5.9	Jun.	6.3
Jul.	5.6	Jul.	6.3	Jul.	6.9
Aug.	7.1	Aug.	7.7	Aug.	8.5
Sept.	8.0	Sept.	8.5	Sept.	9.0
Oct.	6.7	Oct.	7.1	Oct.	8.1
Nov.	8.2	Nov.	8.9	Nov.	10.2
Dec.	7.5	Dec.	8.7	Dec.	9.5

It is obvious to Ms. Demerick that Swank's sales have a definite seasonal pattern from month to month and that sales have been trending upward over the past three years. The nature of the retailing business causes the seasonal patterns and the population growth of the region is probably responsible for the overall growth in sales. Ms. Demerick expects these patterns and trends to continue.

Assignment

1. Plot the sales data on a graph and examine the pattern.

2. If exponential smoothing were applied to this sales data for the purpose of developing short-run forecasts, would you recommend a high or low α? Why?

3. Use an α of .8 and develop an exponential smoothing forecast for the next month's sales (Year 4, Jan.) if the Year 3, Jan. forecast is the same as actual sales.

4. Use seasonalized time series analysis to develop a forecast for the next three months' sales. How confident are you in your forecast? Develop a statistical statement expressing your confidence in the forecast.

5. Use total absolute deviation (TAD) over the last year as the basis for recommending either exponential smoothing ($\alpha = .8$) or seasonalized time series analysis as the forecasting system to be used by Swank Retailers.

6. Plot both the exponential smoothing and the seasonalized time series forecasts against the actual data for the most recent year on the graph. Is your graph consistent with your recommendation in No. 5?

Selected Bibliography

Basu, Shankar, and Roger G. Schroeder. "Incorporating Judgments in Sales Forecasts: Application of the Delphi Method at American Hoist & Derrick." *Interfaces* 7, no. 3(May 1977), 18–27.

Box, G. E. P., and G. M. Jenkins. *Time Series Analysis, Forecasting, and Control*. San Francisco: Holden-Day, 1970.

Brown, Robert G. *Smoothing, Forecasting and Prediction of Discrete Time Series*. Englewood Cliffs, NJ: Prentice-Hall, 1963.

Ezekial, Mordecai, and Karl Fox. *Methods of Correlation and Regression Analysis*. 3d ed. New York: Wiley, 1969.

"Forecasting Sales." *Studies in Business Policy*, no. 106. New York: National Industrial Conference Board, 1963.

Kerlinger, Fred N., and Elazar J. Pedhazur. *Multiple Regression in Behavioral Research*. New York: Holt, Rinehart & Winston, 1973.

Malinvaud, Edmond. *Statistical Methods of Econometrics*. New York: American Elsevier, 1970.

Nie, Norman, Dale H. Bent, and C. Hadlai Hull. *SPSS—Statistical Package for the Social Sciences*. New York: McGraw-Hill, 1970.

Parsons, Robert. *Statistical Analysis: Decision-Making Approach*. New York: Harper & Row, 1974.

"Sales Forecasting." *Experiences in Marketing Management*, no. 25. New York: National Industrial Conference Board, 1971.

Stockton, John R., and Charles T. Clark. *Business and Economic Statistics*. 5th ed. Cincinnati: South-Western Publishing, 1975.

Part Two

Foundations of Operations Strategy:
Planning Products, Processes, and Facilities

Chapter 4
Product Design and Process Planning
Goods and Services

Supplement to Chapter 4
Financial Analysis in POM

Chapter 5
Allocating Scarce Resources in POM
Constrained Decisions in Operations Strategy

Supplement to Chapter 5
Linear Programming Methods

Chapter 6
Long-Range Capacity Planning and Facility Location
Decisions with Long-Lasting Effects

Chapter 7
Project Management
Planning and Controlling Large Projects That Result from Operations Strategy

Part Two of this book is about the decisions involved in <u>operations strategy</u>, long-range plans that determine such things as what products will be produced, how they will be produced, how scarce resources will be allocated among the products, what production capacities will be provided, and where facilities will be located.

First, long-range corporate objectives are established that must be achieved through corporate teamwork. Next, top management develops strategies for achieving these long-range corporate objectives while considering the requirements to meet competition and the strengths and weaknesses of the functional areas of the organization. Then, the operations function identifies the long-range objectives that are necessary in operations if the business strategies are to be successful. Lastly, the operations function develops strategies for achieving its long-range objectives.

Setting operations strategy concerns long-range decisions about product designs, process designs, allocating scarce resources within operations, and capacity plans and facility location. These and other related strategic decisions in operations is what Part Two is about.

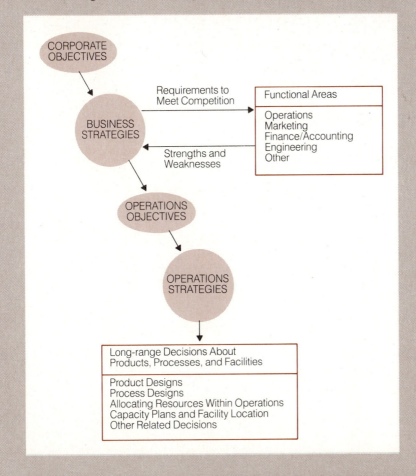

Chapter Outline

Introduction
Product Life Cycles and Patterns of Product/Service Design

Product/Service Design
Management of Product/Service Development
Development of Products
Development of Services
Terminating or Modifying Product/Service Development Projects
Product Engineering Design Concepts
Specifications
Standardization
Simplification
Quality Engineering

Process Planning
The Process Planning System
Relationship to Other POM Activities
Process Planning Information Flows
Metalworking Processes
Production Processes of Nonmetal Products
Automobile Tire Manufacturing Process Example
Radiological Clinic Process Example
Continuous Productive Systems
Characteristics
Intermittent Productive Systems
Characteristics
Automation—Special Purpose and General Purpose Machines
The Japanese *Yen* for Robots
American Robots
Techniques of Process Planning
Assembly Charts
Process Charts
Make-or-Buy Analysis
A Process Planning Horror Story

Product and Process Design in Business Strategy
Product and Process Design in the United States
Japanese Approach to Product and Process Design
Getting Manufacturing Strategy into U.S. Boardrooms

Summary

Review and Discussion Questions

Problems

Case: Brightco Manufacturing

Selected Bibliography

4

Product Design and Process Planning:

Goods and Services

Products should be designed, manufactured, and distributed
to meet the customer's desires and needs from his (her)
point of view.
L. P. Alford, 1940

All too often we think of organizations as static systems. Their products and services are designed and developed, their production processes planned and installed, and their markets established. We observe these organizations in their steady state, operating on an ongoing basis. But this static perspective of productive systems omits one of the most exciting and dynamic aspects of POM — determining *what* will be produced and *how* it will be produced. **Determining the design of products or services and the overall plan for processing or producing the products or services is at the heart of** <u>operations</u> strategy — **the long-range plans of an organization for producing its products and services. The foundation of an organization's operations strategy is expressed in its products, processes, and facilities.**

These designing, planning, and developing activities of POM occur rather dramatically in the birth stages of products/services and of productive systems. This innovative and creative work of POM, marketing, and engineering tends to be the principal organizational effort during the initial development of products and services. As most productive systems grow and mature, however, these activities typically assume a less dominant role, as Figure 4.1 indicates. Yet, the long-range survival of organizations requires that productive systems and their products and services adapt to meet the needs of today's and tomorrow's customers. POM is

117

Figure 4.1
Typical Pattern of Product/Service Design and Process Planning Activities

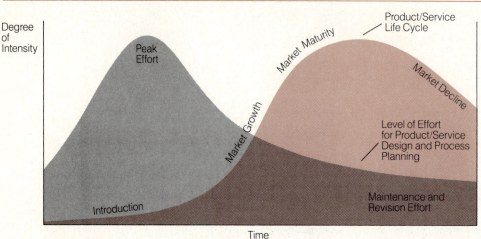

therefore continually involved in these designing, planning, and developing activities, even for mature products.

The system of developing a product or service from a bright idea in someone's mind to the point where the product or service is produced and delivered to the ultimate customer can be a long and complex one. Figure 4.2 describes this system.

Ideas for new products or services and revisions of existing products and services come from a variety of sources — sales, customers, engineering, marketing, production, competitors, and so on almost endlessly. The actual processes for producing products and services, however, most often come from persons closely associated with operations — production engineers, production managers, and others.

New product and service ideas are mere thoughts until they are evaluated by the market. Only after preliminary market surveys do managers usually begin to design prototype products and services. As the development of products and services proceeds, an almost constant vigil is maintained within potential markets to test acceptability to customers. This market sensing is usually performed by the marketing function of business organizations or by outside specialty consulting firms.

Product/service design and process planning are the main subjects of this chapter. Although the marketing and the process development aspects of this system are obviously important, these activities can usually be expected to be performed by marketers and engineers. Our primary interest in *product/service design* is the effect it has on the planning and design of the processes of productive systems.

Many interactions exist between the design and development of products and services on the one hand and the design and development of the productive system that produces these outputs on the other. As Figure 4.2 shows, these interactions

Figure 4.2
Designing and Developing New Products/Services and New Production Processes

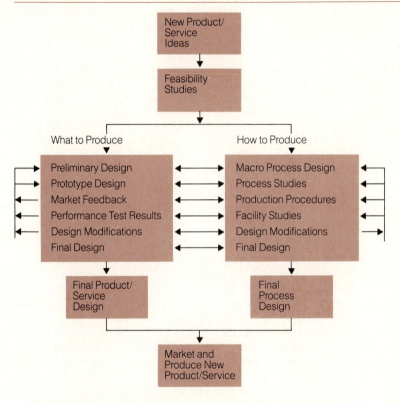

occur back and forth continuously as products/services and processes are being designed and developed in parallel.

The product/service design is inseparably related to the technological processes, the layout of facilities, the design of workers' jobs, quality control, and most of the other features of productive systems. The technological processes that are eventually selected must accommodate the product/service design. Conversely, the product/service design must take into account the economic feasibility of producing these outputs with known technology. Finally, the facility layout and design of workers' jobs depends upon the ultimate technological processes selected and their sequence. Once individual jobs are designed, facility layouts are complete, processes are selected, and products are designed, *the efficiency of the productive system is in large measure set.* All too often operations managers neglect to become involved early enough in product/service design, thus abdicating their ability to design and operate efficient productive systems.

I know of one plant manager who was aware of a new product his company was developing. He maintained only a casual relationship with those directly responsible for evolving the idea into a manufactured product. When he was formally handed the new product that marketing and the market were happy with, he was shocked to learn that the design could not be manufactured in his facility through the use of existing technologies. The design was locked in because of the previous market testing and customer contacts. Precision investment casting, a new technological process unfamiliar to his personnel, had to be developed at great expense and time delay to his operation. Such disasters can be avoided if operations managers recognize the interrelationships among product/service design, technological processes, facility layout, individual job design, and other operations activities. If efficient operations are to materialize, operations managers must get involved early and stay involved until the products and services have completely traversed the evolution from idea to produced product/service.

Let us now explore this procedure of product/service design in more detail from a POM perspective.

Product/Service Design

The product/service design and development process has been compared to that of giving birth to a new baby — conception, gestation, labor, birth, and postnatal care. Although the analogy is perhaps valid in terms of the basic phases of both systems, at least one major difference exists. The system of bringing forth a baby into the world is controlled by biological processes that, once begun, proceed almost automatically and in large part beyond conscious human control. The product/service design and development system, on the other hand, requires continual management effort to insure that the evolving product meets the needs of the market and can be produced efficiently.

Management of Product/Service Development

Figure 4.3 shows some of the important steps in this birth process of manufactured products. Tangible or physical products must consist of specific materials and must be produced to exact engineering specifications. When completed, they must perform in precise and predictable ways.

Once a product idea has materialized, initial technical and economic studies determine the feasibility of establishing a project for designing and developing the product. These studies seek to answer two questions: Can the product be technologically produced, and can the product be produced to further such organizational objectives as profits, costs, social utility, and so on?

If initial *feasibility studies* are favorable, engineers bring forth an initial *prototype design*. This prototype design should perform the basic functions that the final design will be required to perform: form, fit, and function. Prototypes do not necessarily possess the same weight, color, physical dimensions, materials, and other features of later designs, nor will they typically be made by the same processes. A prototype air-powered starter for diesel engines, for example, may be machined from steel by vertical boring machines and other general purpose high-precision

Figure 4.3
The Design and Development of Products

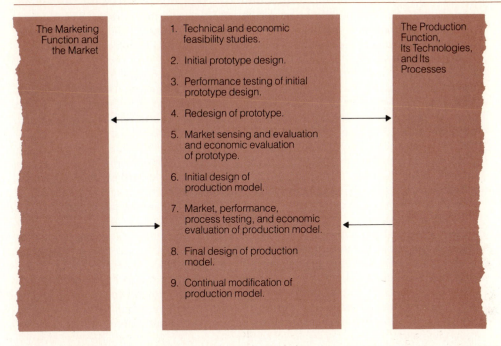

The Marketing Function and the Market		The Production Function, Its Technologies, and Its Processes
	1. Technical and economic feasibility studies.	
	2. Initial prototype design.	
	3. Performance testing of initial prototype design.	
	4. Redesign of prototype.	
	5. Market sensing and evaluation and economic evaluation of prototype.	
	6. Initial design of production model.	
	7. Market, performance, process testing, and economic evaluation of production model.	
	8. Final design of production model.	
	9. Continual modification of production model.	

machining processes with little concern for physical size, weight, corrosion characteristics, and cost. As long as the unit successfully starts engines, the prototype design is judged to perform the basic functions of the final design.

Prototypes typically undergo extensive testing to determine the performance characteristics of the design. As tests show deficiencies, the prototype design is modified until this design-test-redesign process produces a satisfactorily performing prototype.

When the prototype meets management expectations, the project is evaluated by its perceived target market. This *market evaluation* can be accomplished by demonstrations to potential customers, by market surveys, or by other means. The objective of these activities is to determine the acceptability and desirability of the product in the marketplace.

If the response of the perceived market to the prototype is favorable, *economic studies* are usually performed to estimate volume, costs, and profits for the product. If the estimated product profitability is acceptable to management, the project will enter the production design phase. This activity converts the prototype design, which is based solely on performance objectives, to a design that additionally exhibits low cost and producibility and has the weight, dimensions, color, appearance, corrosion resistance, and other characteristics desired in the final product.

The initial production design will evolve to a final production design through performance testing, production trials and testing, market testing, and economic studies. The final design will exhibit low cost, competitive reliability, acceptable performance, and the ability to be produced efficiently in the desired quantities. Actually, *final design* is a misnomer, since no design is ever final. Product designs are dynamic because they must be modified to adapt to frequently changing conditions and markets.

This system of designing and developing physical products walks a tight line between marketing and the market on the one hand and the technologies and processes of the production function on the other. Although the market is the engine that drives the system and necessarily must receive the principal emphasis, the capacity and capabilities of the production function, its technologies, and its processes must also be ever-present elements. How absurd it would be to propose a product that exhibits market acceptance if, because of its design, it could not be successfully produced. Conversely, it would be equally absurd to design and develop products that are readily producible but that cannot be successfully marketed. Physical products must therefore be designed for two masters — the market and the productive system.

Services are designed and developed systematically with a procedure similar to the one described above for physical products. Figure 4.4 describes this system. Although the design and development of services tend to be somewhat more informal than for physical products, nonetheless a system of design and development does exist. This system differs from physical products because few performance tests are performed, market surveys tend to be preferred over market tests, and personnel of the productive system are usually dominant in importance over its technologies.

Figure 4.4
The Design and Development of Services

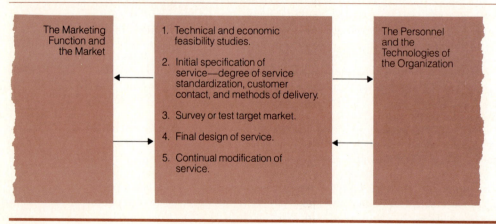

The Marketing Function and the Market

1. Technical and economic feasibility studies.

2. Initial specification of service—degree of service standardization, customer contact, and methods of delivery.

3. Survey or test target market.

4. Final design of service.

5. Continual modification of service.

The Personnel and the Technologies of the Organization

The *design of services* tends to be aimed more at questions of the degree of standardization of the service, the degree of customer contact, and methods of delivering the service rather than at engineering specifications and productive process technologies. Additionally, because services usually are intangible, market acceptability is usually determined from surveys rather than from testing and demonstration.

Service organizations produce and deliver their services predominantly through the medium of the people of the productive system. This is contrasted to the predominantly technological systems that produce physical products. Since people are flexible and trainable, they can adapt to almost any service requirement the market dictates. Therefore, people usually impose less rigid constraints on service design and development than processing technologies impose on physical products. The final design of the service eventually gives way to large-scale personnel training programs as the service enters the production and delivery phase of this system.

Because of a diversity of services, some organizations fall between the two extremes of pure physical products and pure services described in Figures 4.3 and 4.4. If the degree of customer contact is low, if the degree of standardization of service is high, and if high production technology is basic to the service, then the service tends to be designed and developed much like the physical products of Figure 4.3. Examples of these types of services are a new item for a fast-food restaurant, a standardized payroll system for a high-volume computer center, and a new course for a state university. However, if the degree of customer contact is high, if the degree of standardization of service is low, and if the service is not based on high production technologies, then the service tends to be developed as shown in Figure 4.4. Examples of these types of services are legal services in an attorney's office, interior decorating services, and the services of a public mental health clinic.

A final note on developing new products and services: We must be concerned with how to stop or modify projects for developing products and services. Otherwise, every design project will evolve into a produced product. When you consider that only about one out of ten new products is successful, new product development projects must be scrutinized carefully to determine at the earliest possible moment if the product is likely to be unsuccessful in its present form. Figure 4.5 shows that each step in the procedure for designing products/services requires a decision: Should the project be continued? If the answer is no, the project should be either killed or modified. It is best to kill projects early so that human effort and development money can be directed toward more promising projects. Unfortunately, this is easier said than done because managers, engineers, and marketers become emotionally caught up in their pet projects and are thus reluctant to dispose of them. This fact demonstrates the advisability of impartial management review boards for periodic reviews of the progress of new product/service projects.

Product Engineering Design Concepts

A command of designing and developing products and services requires an understanding of these key engineering concepts—specifications, standardization, simplification, and quality engineering. These concepts are fundamental to designing products and services. While this course is not intended for training engineers, it is important to understand that engineers affect the efficient operation of productive

Figure 4.5
Killing or Modifying Product/Service Development Projects

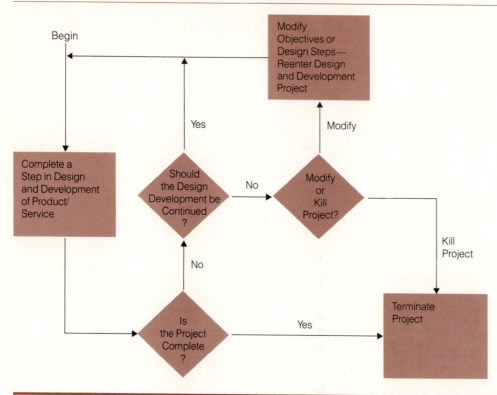

systems through their work on final product/service designs. Engineering concepts are thus important determinants of the features of productive systems and therefore of POM.

Specifications Eli Whitney, although perhaps best known for his invention of the cotton gin, also invented and developed a system of *interchangeable parts*. This system required each part of a rifle, which Whitney was manufacturing under contract to the U.S. government in 1798, to be manufactured to specific *tolerances*. The rifles could be assembled by fitting a set of components together with the assurance that all components would fit and the assembled rifle would function as the product designers intended.

Engineering tolerances are specified for each dimension of a physical product in a range from minimum to maximum dimensions. A motor shaft diameter, for example, could be specified as 4.000 ± .001 inches. This means that the minimum diameter is 3.999 inches and the maximum diameter is 4.001 inches. Tolerances are specified to facilitate assembly and manufacture as well as to provide for proper functioning of

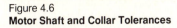

Figure 4.6
Motor Shaft and Collar Tolerances

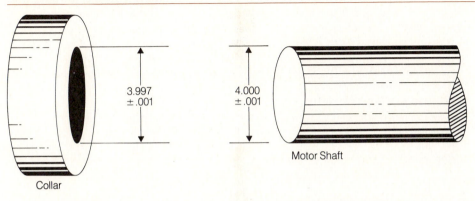

3.997
± .001

4.000
± .001

Motor Shaft

Collar

the final product. Figure 4.6 shows that a collar that must be pressed (forced) onto a motor shaft must have a *force fit*. This means that the maximum inside diameter of the collar (3.997 + .001 = 3.998) must be less than the minimum outside diameter of the motor shaft (4.000 − .001 = 3.999). This force fit allows the collar to stay attached to the shaft when assembled. However, the minimum inside diameter of the collar (3.997 − .001 = 3.996) and the maximum outside diameter of the shaft (4.000 + .001 = 4.001) must not be so far apart that the components cannot be assembled or will be damaged during assembly.

Other features of physical products can also be specified: viscosity, surface finish, pH rating, particle size distribution, hardness, steel composition, strength requirements, and so on. These specifications provide purchasing departments and production departments with precise information about the characteristics of each component of physical products to be acquired or produced. All of these specifications must be systematically related to provide for both ease of production and effective functioning of the finished products.

Although specifications are also a part of service design and development, their presence is perhaps less obvious. Productive systems that produce services use machines, supplies, and materials. These elements all require engineering tolerance specifications and specifications of other physical characteristics in order to make or purchase them. Additionally, services must be described in a detailed way to assure their conformity to the intended function, timeliness, cost, and quality. Therefore, services must have specifications prescribed, although these specifications in some cases may be less precise than the specifications of physical products.

Standardization Two extremes exist in product/service design. At one extreme each customer receives a tailor-made product or service, customized for his or her particular needs. In this extreme case each unit of output is unique. At the other extreme only one model of a product or service is generated by a productive system. As Henry Ford reportedly said, "You can have any color of a Model T that you want,

Table 4.1
Results of Economies of Standardization of Product/Service Design

1. Fewer items in finished goods inventory, thus less obsolescence and damage and fewer lost inventory goods.
2. Lower levels of finished goods inventory, thus reducing costs of carrying inventory and storage space.
3. Fewer items in raw materials inventory, thus less obsolescence and damage and fewer lost inventory goods.
4. Lower levels of raw materials inventory, thus reducing cost of carrying inventory and storage space.
5. Longer production runs, thus reducing setup costs per unit and lowering variable costs through employee learning.
6. Improved quality control because of less component diversity and greater inspection efficiency.
7. More automation opportunities in the productive system, thus reducing labor cost per unit of output.
8. Reduced raw material prices by allowing purchasing to acquire fewer types of materials in larger quantities.
9. Reduced amounts of equipment.
10. Less idle time for employees and equipment.
11. Lower training costs for employees.
12. Prompt deliveries through fewer out-of-stock conditions.

as long as it's black.'' The Model T era at Ford Motor Company is a classic example in the extreme of standardization in product design.

Marketing functions within firms usually push for diversity of product models because this allows marketing to appeal to a broader range of customers and thus enhance sales. Production functions, on the other hand, usually pull for a high degree of standardization of product models because this usually allows companies to operate with lower costs. These economies in product/service design standardization are outlined in Table 4.1.

Although the reduced labor, materials, and overhead costs that are made possible through product/service design standardization are certainly attractive, we must realistically recognize that many markets today are so competitive and segmented that a variety of product models are absolutely necessary. Yet, in spite of product differentiation, operations managers strive for some degree of product/service design standardization so that as many of the economies listed in Table 4.1 can be realized as intensely as possible.

Modular designs allow operations managers a variety of final product models with only a few basic components. A manufacturer of transmissions, for example, might use only three basic gear designs within its transmissions but arrange the gears to provide numerous transmissions with differing performance characteristics. This approach has promise of offering both productive system economies through standardizing subassembly designs and final product design variety, thus appealing to more customers. Although some additional costs can be incurred in final assembly operations, the concept of modular design is an attractive alternative to either tailor-made products/services or single-model product/service designs.

Services can also be standardized to yield most of the standardization economies listed in Table 4.1. One exception should be noted, however. Large finished-goods inventories are rare in most service organizations.

The largest single economy to be expected from service design standardization is usually reduced labor costs. Since wages tend to dominate the variable costs of most services, labor costs constitute an important consideration.

The natural intrusion of the customer into the productive system usually means lower levels of standardization for service organizations than for physical products.

The degree of customer contact and the importance of customer–service interaction at the point of service delivery will have an unavoidable influence on the degree of service design standardization possible. High customer contact, such as that in expensive restaurants, is typically related to customized menus, whereas low customer contact such as in a fast-food stand is typically related to highly standardized menus.

Simplification *Simplification* of product/service design is the elimination of complex features of a product/service so that the intended function is performed but with reduced operations cost while maintaining or even increasing customer satisfaction. Customer satisfaction may be increased through product/service design simplification by making a product/service easier to recognize, buy, install, maintain, or use.

Reduced operating costs can result from product/service design simplification when labor costs are reduced through easier assembly and through eliminated or simplified operations, and when material costs are reduced through substituted materials, materials are in simpler configurations, and fewer materials are wasted as scrap. Figure 4.7 shows how Design A, which is made of a machined aluminum

Figure 4.7
Product Design Simplification: Machined Aluminum Casting vs. Plastic Molding

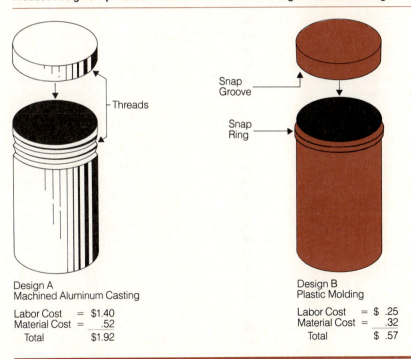

Threads

Snap
Groove

Snap
Ring

Design A
Machined Aluminum Casting

Labor Cost	=	$1.40
Material Cost	=	.52
Total		$1.92

Design B
Plastic Molding

Labor Cost	=	$ .25
Material Cost	=	.32
Total		$ .57

casting, was simplified to Design B, which is a two-piece plastic molding. Design A has a high material cost and requires many machining operations, thus resulting in both high labor costs and high material costs. Design B requires less labor and lower material costs and thus is the preferred design. Both designs perform the intended function of the part equally well.

Service designs can also be simplified. The objective of service design simplification is to reduce the costs of operating the productive system — the same as the objectives of simplifying the designs of physical products. Although physical product design simplification programs may seek to reduce operations costs while maintaining product function quality, these dual objectives are not always compatible. In fact, the simplification of services may result in reduced perceived quality of outputs.

Services are usually simplified by transferring some of the work from the productive system to customers, eliminating or reducing the range of services offered, or increasing the response time of services to customers. Examples of these are:

1. U.S. Postal Service — standardized envelope size, elimination of low-cost classes of mail, reduced number of deliveries, and the elimination of weekend deliveries.
2. Discount merchandise stores — self-service of customers by modifying facility layout and operations practices.
3. Restaurants — elimination of waitresses and waiters by installing self-service counters.
4. Telephone companies — reduction of the number of operators by initiating direct dialing procedures.
5. Universities — reduction of operating costs by increasing class sizes, offering fewer course choices, and using televised lectures for multiple locations.
6. Service stations — reduction of number of service attendants by eliminating oil changes, lubrication, and maintenance services and by installing self-service gasoline pumps.

These and other service design simplifications result in a reduction of operating costs along with a potential customer-perceived reduction in service quality. We are not implying that these simplifications are always unwelcomed by customers. Reduced service quality may be accompanied by price reductions or lack of price increases; these quality versus price trade-offs may receive enthusiastic customer acceptance in some cases.

Quality Engineering Four aspects of quality are important considerations in product design — maintainability, reliability, durability, and reproducibility.

Maintainability To remain in top running condition, physical products must be maintained. The ease with which these maintenance activities can be performed is perceived to be an element of product quality by users of these products. Take, for example, an American-made automobile and one made in Japan. In order to change the oil filter at home, as many of us do these days, on the American car you must lie on your back, slide under a car that is approximately 9 inches from the ground, twist and slide your arm past a hot exhaust pipe, and finally writhe and contort your body to turn the oil filter. When the filter is finally removed, the hot oil runs down your arm and onto the hot exhaust pipe as well as your clean driveway. How many times have you said, ''I wish that blanketyblank engineer who designed this thing had to work on it!''? The Japanese car's oil filter can be changed by standing above the engine and dropping the filter into a waiting pan below the car. We usually perceive that this convenience of maintenance is an essential element of product quality, which, in turn, is an important part of product design.

Reliability Reliability, or dependability, means the ability of a product to perform under prescribed conditions as desired without excessive frequency of failures. Reliability in engineering terms means the probability that a product or component of a product will not fail on any given trial. A reliability of .999, for example, indicates that a failure would ordinarily be expected once in 1,000 trials. A product composed of three independent components with reliabilities of .95, .90, and .99 would have a combined reliability of $.95 \times .90 \times .99 = .846$. This chain multiplication of component reliabilities further emphasizes the necessity of stringent design of components if the products are to have the desired level of reliability. Reliability is usually improved through precision design and manufacturing of parts. Precision is usually achieved by increasing production costs. Care is therefore exercised in determining customer willingness to pay more or increased reliability.

Durability Durability means the ability of products to function under prescribed conditions without failing from excessive wear. Automobile batteries and tires, for example, have very predictable lives. These lives have been purposely set by the engineering design of these products. Longer-wearing materials, corrosive resistant materials, and improved configurations are examples of how engineers can design products to wear longer. This decision of how much durability to design into products may also involve a cost-and-price versus durability trade-off. Durability may be increased only by increasing price, and customers may not always be willing to pay more for more durable products. Furthermore, companies can be reluctant to design more durable products because this will materially reduce the *aftermarket,* or secondary, sales of their products that result from product wear. Balances must be struck between durability and price on the one hand and durability and future aftermarket sales on the other.

Reproducibility Reproducibility means the ability of the productive system to consistently produce products of the desired quality. Reproducibility must be considered when engineers design products since all other aspects of quality are directly affected unless the productive system can effectively and efficiently produce the products at a consistent quality level. Selecting materials, setting tolerances, and specifying processing procedures are examples of elements of product design that can directly affect reproducibility. When products are in the final stages of the design procedure, *pilot runs* of the product through the proposed processes test the reproducibility of the design. Similarly, as materials, processes, and facilities change over time, a continuous monitoring of product quality gives engineers feedback concerning design modifications needed to improve reproducibility.

Service designs also must consider such aspects of quality as reliablility and reproducibility. Unless services are delivered to customers in a dependable and consistent fashion, customers will consider these services unreliable and therefore of low quality. Because personnel usually deliver services directly to customers, perceived service reliability can usually be improved through better personnel training, coordination, and control. But many obvious breakdowns in service delivery can be avoided by better service design. An example of improving service reliability through service redesign is offering computer users the opportunity to read in their own card decks and remove their printouts from line printers. Computer users usually welcome this service design modification because it helps to reduce the possibility of computer operators' errors or neglect, thus improving service reliability.

Product/service designs and all the concepts of these designs discussed thus far are a fundamental part of POM that affects all other elements of productive systems. A fuller understanding of this critical POM activity, however, is possible only after the technological processes of productive systems are considered.

Process Planning

PROCESS PLANNING means the complete determination of the specific technological process steps and their sequence for the productive system to produce the products/services of the desired quality, in the required quantity, and at the budgeted cost. Process planning can occur dramatically in one flurry of activity before facilities and equipment are constructed, purchased, installed, and operated to mass produce new products. Process planning can also occur routinely, on a daily basis, as special customer orders are processed through existing productive system facilities and processes. Regardless of the significance of particular process planning activities, the general procedures are the same.

It seems logical that product/service design and process planning would be determined simultaneously. This is, however, seldom achieved. In actual practice these initial determinations are made somewhat independently; subsequent modifications reflect their interdependence. Product/service designs are initially made with the processes of the productive system generally assumed to be fixed. Process planning is done while initially assuming that product/service designs are fixed. Modifications to these initial designs and process plans are then made while simultaneously considering both product/service design and process plans.

The *interdependence of product/service design and process planning* is dramatically emphasized by an account of the invention of the first automatic tomato picker. A large West Coast manufacturer of food processing equipment became aware of the difficulties of manually picking tomatoes. In the 1940s the company developed an automatic tomato picker mounted on a harvesterlike mobile unit. It cut the tomato vine off at the ground, then conveyed the vine up onto a picking table where seated workers picked the tomatoes from the vine. The tomatoes were then conveyed off the back of the unit and into a trailing truck while the denuded vine was thrown back into the field. The tomato picker worked beautifully, except for just one problem: It burst every tomato it touched. The automatic tomato picker was driven to the back of a lot and parked.

The company immediately began to study the genetics and characteristics of tomato varieties. This study soon evolved into a product development project that was to last nearly ten years. In the middle 1950s the results of the project were complete. A new strain of tomato with an extremely tough skin was successfully grown. The automatic tomato picker was again tried and proved totally successful, as this time there was no tomato damage. Since the vast majority of tomatoes are used for soups, juices, and paste rather than for table tomatoes, the new tough-skinned variety could be used for these products.

This example of how the characteristics of the product materially affect the processes of the productive system and vice versa is not unlike other experiences that occur daily in a diverse array of organizations, and this interdependence will be stressed and reinforced as we continue in this chapter.

Process planning is a central part of POM that involves specific steps. Although these procedures tend to differ somewhat from organization to organization, the general format is the same.

The Process Planning System

Process planning brings together knowledge about product designs, resources of the productive system, and markets and then develops a plan for producing the products/services. Figure 4.8 shows that process planning is the basis for the design

Figure 4.8
Process Planning: Its Relation to Other POM Activities

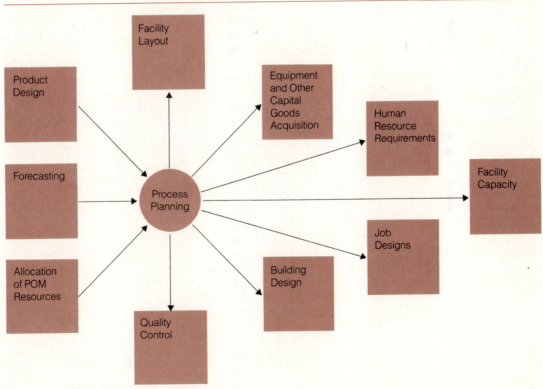

of buildings, layout of facilities, and selection of production equipment. Additionally, process planning ultimately affects quality control, human resource requirements, job designs, and facility capacity. In short, this important activity determines in large measure the details of *how* products/services will be produced.

What is process planning? What inputs are supplied? What are the outputs of process planning? Figure 4.9 answers these questions. The information inputs to process planning basically originate in the market and the productive system. The market directly or indirectly determines the basic product/service design, product/service volume, quality requirements, and conditions under which the product must be marketed. Furthermore, the product/service design affects the major technologies required to produce the products and services. Knowledge about the availability of land, personnel, and capital; economics of production; and technologies of productive systems allows operations managers to plan processes that are feasible as well as effective and efficient.

Process planning involves studies about product/service design, technological processes, production procedures, and facilities. These studies result in a complete determination of the technological process steps to be used and their sequence; the selection of equipment, design of buildings, and layout facilities; and number of personnel required, their skill levels, and supervision requirements.

Who does process planning? In complex manufacturing situations, this procedure may involve several departments, such as manufacturing engineering, plant engi-

Figure 4.9
The Process Planning System

INPUTS	PROCESS PLANNING	OUTPUTS
1. Product Information Product Design Product Volume Market Environment Quality Requirements Major Technologies Selection	**1. Product Design Studies** Production Specifications Alternate Materials Alternate Assembly Methods Alternate Designs	**1. Technological Processes** Specific Process Steps Sequence of Process Steps
2. Productive System Information Resource Availability Production Economics Technology Capabilities	**2. Process Studies** Major Technological Steps Minor Technological Steps	**2. Facilities** Building Design Layout of Facilities Selection of Equipment
	3. Production Procedures Studies Production Sequence Materials Specifications Personnel Requirements Make or Buy Decisions Equipment Selection	**3. Personnel Estimates** Skill Level Requirements Number of Personnel Supervision Requirements
	4. Facilities Studies Building Alternatives Layout of Facilities	

Figure 4.10
Process Planning Information Flows in Manufacturing

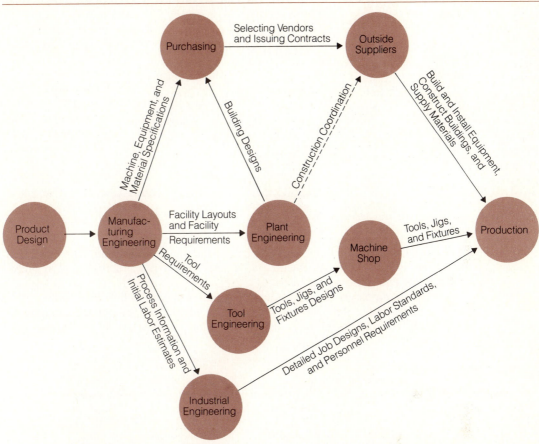

neering, tool engineering, purchasing, industrial engineering, design engineering, and of course production. Figure 4.10 shows how these functions work together to bring the product design into production through process planning. In less complex situations a single person may perform all of the activities of process planning.

Fundamental to process planning are the basic technological processes of organizations. A complete command of these processes in one's industry is an absolute must for effective process planning. Although it is impossible (and probably in a sense undesirable) to convey an in-depth knowledge of all of the possible technological processes of organizations here, some knowledge about the immensity of the scope of these processes is helpful. Table 4.2 lists the ways that the five basic processes of metalworking can be performed. Several years of intensive study would be required in order to begin to understand the intricacies of all these processes.

Table 4.2
Metalworking Processes

Casting and Molding	Machining	Metal Working	Assembly	Finishing
Sand casting	Turning	Forging	Soldering	Cleaning
Shell casting	Drilling	Extruding	Brazing	Blasting
Investment casting	Milling	Punching	Welding	Deburring
Die casting	Shaping	Trimming	Mechanical fastening	Painting
Permanent mold casting	Cutoff	Drawing	Cementing	Plating
Powered metal molding	Broaching	Rolling	Press fitting	Heat treating
Compression molding	Grinding	Forming	Shrink fitting	Buffing
Transfer	Honing	Coining		Polishing
Extrusion		Swaging		
Injection molding		Spinning		
Laminating				

Source: Donald F. Eary and Gerald E. Johnson, *Process Engineering for Manufacturing* (Englewood Cliffs, NJ: Prentice-Hall, 1962), 3. Adapted by permission of Prentice-Hall.

They are, however, the domain of process, product, manufacturing, tool, and industrial engineers. Organizations employ these engineers to use their specialized knowledge about these processes.

If you are employed in a metalworking industry, you will undoubtedly absorb some knowledge of the processes of casting and molding, machining, metalworking, assembly, and finishing. Table 4.3 lists some of these processes for five other

Table 4.3
Some Production Processes of Nonmetal Products

Chemicals, Petroleum, Paper, Plastics, Rubber	Woods	Mining, Quarrying, Stone, Clay, Glass	Food	Textiles
Grinding	Debarking	Excavating	Crushing	Spinning
Screening	Slabbing	Loading	Grinding	Yarn twisting
Cooking	Sawing	Crushing	Pressing	Polishing
Evaporating	Slitting	Grinding	Molding	Braiding
Concentrating	Planing	Screening	Sterilizing	Knitting
Neutralizing	Rasping	Washing	Pasteurizing	Weaving
Compounding	Sanding	Drying	Homogenizing	Drying
Cracking	Turning	Cooking	Cooking	Washing
Distilling	Jointing	Extracting	Freezing	Trimming
Calendering	Drilling	Smelting	Canning	Printing
Curing	Shaping		Evaporating	Shrinking
Extruding	Painting		Concentrating	Cooking
Molding	Kilning		Distilling	
	Curing			

industries. Although managers are not expected to be experts in the processes of their firms, neither are they expected to be totally ignorant of the subject. Fortunately most jobs afford opportunities to become informed about underlying technologies through daily on-the-job encounters. This practical knowledge comes through years of experience for most of us.

Process planning involves products and services alike. Figure 4.11 shows how some of the basic processes of the rubber industry listed in Table 4.3 are linked together to form a facility to produce automobile tires. Process planning is also performed in productive systems that produce services. Figure 4.12 shows how the basic processes of radiology are linked together to form a radiological clinic.

Before process planning studies are complete, a determination must be made on how the technological processes will be linked together. Will the process linkings

Figure 4.11
Basic Processes of Building Automobile Tires

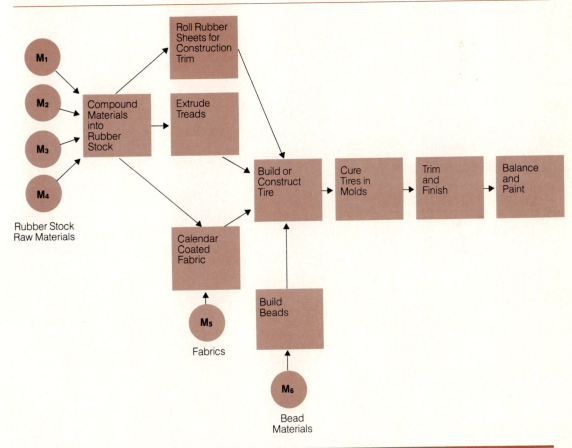

Figure 4.12
Basic Processes of a Radiological Clinic

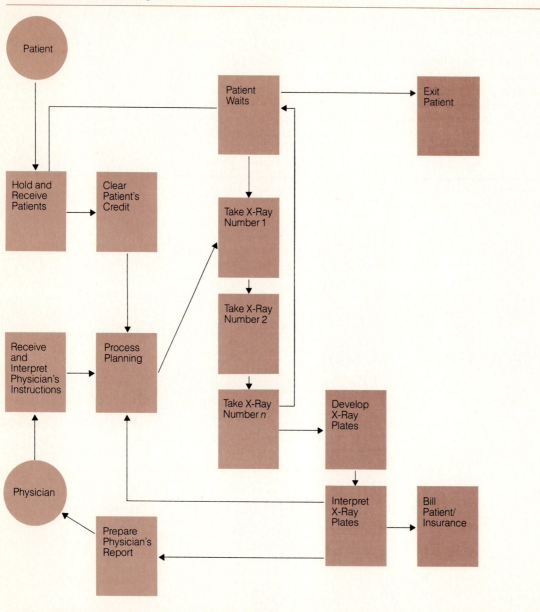

allow products to flow through facilities in rather straight, smooth lines? If so, the arrangement is described as a *continuous* productive system. Or will each product flow through facilities in a unique, zigzag, disjointed pattern? These arrangements are described as an *intermittent* productive system.

Continuous Productive Systems

The term *continuous productive systems* is sometimes used synonymously with *assembly lines*. This arrangement of processes, equipment, and personnel was, until after World War I, uniquely American. Since World War II, assembly line techniques have been applied in every industrialized country on the globe. Table 4.4 describes the characteristics of these productive systems. These continuous systems offer what many organizations relish most: high volume output at a lower per-unit cost.

Continuous productive systems encompass a broader class of productive systems than just assembly lines. They can also include such systems as petroleum refineries, chemical processing plants, and car washing facilities. These and other continuous productive systems usually require higher initial investment levels because of more expensive fixed-position materials handling equipment, and highly specialized processing equipment. Additionally, these systems are limited in their ability to adapt to changing product designs, when rapidly changing designs seem to be a sign of the times. Offsetting these drawbacks are the advantages of low labor skill, reduced worker training, and reduced supervision.

It is ironic that assembly lines have been developed to a fine art in some foreign countries (Japan, Taiwan, Sweden, and so on) that now pose a competitive threat to American industries which have used these same production techniques for over half a century. It is paradoxical that our own techniques are being used to threaten the soundness of our domestic industry at a time when some of us in America are

---

Table 4.4
Characteristics of Continuous Productive Systems

1. There are only a few standard products/services, each with a high volume of demand.
2. The systems utilize special-purpose machines, designed to perform highly specialized operations on single product designs. Changeovers to different product designs are difficult and expensive.
3. Equipment is arranged so that products flow through facilities in direct paths. Departments are often established on the basis of products. These layouts are called *product layouts*.
4. Equipment for moving products and materials through facilities is usually fixed-position types such as conveyors.
5. Little or no inventory builds up between steps of the productive system.
6. Worker skill level tends to be uniformly low, requiring little job training.
7. Supervision tends to be easy, with low supervisor-to-worker ratios and few job instructions.
8. Process planning is complex but occurs only occasionally when major changeovers to new products are made.
9. The productive system cannot easily be changed to different product/service designs.
10. The systems offer the lowest per-unit cost for most standard high-volume products/services.

Source: Evan D. Scheele, William L. Westerman, and Robert J. Wimmert, *Principles and Design of Production Control Systems* (Englewood Cliffs, NJ: Prentice-Hall), 1960, 29–30. Adapted by permission of Prentice-Hall.

attacking assembly lines as the symbol of much that is wrong with our industrial society: job boredom, low product quality, high absenteeism, high turnover, unreasonable regimentation, and inflexibility.

The individual worker responses to assembly lines will be treated in detail in Chapter 12, when we examine job design. For now it is sufficient to say that most mass-produced standardized products and services in this country and abroad use continuous productive systems because no alternative system offers comparable high volume of output and low per-unit costs.

Intermittent Productive Systems

The term *intermittent productive systems* is sometimes used to mean job shops. These systems must accommodate many product designs to suit individual customers' tastes. This product variety would be too expensive to produce on a continuous system because of the frequent massive changeovers of entire productive systems when product designs change. Table 4.5 lists the characteristics of intermittent productive systems.

Intermittent productive systems can include such productive systems as hospitals, automobile repair shops, machine shops, and manufacturing plants. These systems best adjust to many product designs at low volume of output and require lower initial investment since general purpose processing equipment and mobile materials handling equipment are generally less expensive. These systems do, however, require greater employee skill, greater employee training, more supervision, more technically trained supervision, and more complex planning and control.

If you were attempting to decide between a continuous and an intermittent productive system for a particular product/service, the key factors would be the degree of product variety that the system must accommodate and the volume of

---

Table 4.5
Characteristics of Intermittent Productive Systems

1. There are many highly variable nonstandard products/services, each with a low volume of demand.
2. The systems utilize general-purpose machines designed to perform a great variety of general operations on a variety of products.
3. Equipment is arranged by the type of process performed. Products necessarily follow a variety of paths through facilities depending upon which processes are required. Departments are based on processes such as painting, forming, and machining. These layouts are called *process layouts*.
4. Equipment for moving products and materials through facilities is usually mobile, like forklift trucks.

5. Inventory buildups frequently occur between steps of the productive system.
6. Worker skill levels tend to vary but are generally high. Long training periods are required.
7. Supervision tends to be difficult, with high supervisor-to-worker ratios and complex job instructions.
8. Process planning is complex and performed often.
9. The productive system adapts easily to different product/service designs.
10. The systems offer the lowest per-unit cost for most nonstandard low-volume products/services.

Source: Evan D. Scheele, William L. Westerman, and Robert J. Wimmert, *Principles and Design of Production Control Systems* (Englewood Cliffs, NJ: Prentice-Hall, 1960), 31–32. Adapted by permission of Prentice-Hall.

output of each product/service design. If volume were expected to be high, with only a few standard product/service designs, your choice would typically be for a continuous system. If, on the other hand, many nonstandard product/service designs were anticipated, each at relatively low volumes of output, your choice would typically be for an intermittent system. Between these two extremes you are in a trade-off position: you can gain the advantages of one type of system only by giving up the advantages of the other.

In either continuous or intermittent productive systems, individual operations can be performed in varying degrees by machines. This use of machines to do work conventionally performed by human beings is usually referred to as automation.

Automation

Automation usually means the replacement of human effort with machine effort. Historically, however, automation has meant a process of systematically replacing people with machines, a process that conjures up feelings of hatred in the hearts of workers and labor unions. Even though workers are still concerned about their job security today, more and more we see cooperative efforts between management and labor unions to study the use of automation as a way of meeting an even greater immediate threat to job security — foreign competition.

Automatic machines fall into four general classes: mechanized aids, numerically controlled (N/C) machines, robots, and systems of automatic machines. Table 4.6 describes each of these classes, gives specific examples of each type of machine, indicates whether each class is special or general purpose, and if a class is preprogrammed, indicates whether it is nonadaptive or adaptive. Special-purpose machines may be used only on a specific operation or product, whereas general-purpose machines are capable of being changed or adjusted so that they may be used in a variety of operations or on many products. Preprogrammed means that the exact operation that the machine will perform is determined in its software or programs, which are prepared in advance of the actual running of the machine. Adaptive machines are capable of sensing the environment and changing their settings in response to variables in the environment.

Numerically controlled (N/C) machines were the heroes among automatic machines in the 1950–1980 period as a broad range of applications were developed for this important technological achievement. These machines are preprogrammed through punched paper tape, magnetic tape, or other input media to perform a cycle of operations repeatedly. The machines have a control system that advances the input medium, reads the instructions, and translates the instructions into machine operations. Machine settings are achieved by the control system rather than by human beings. H. B. Maynard tells of one of the early experiments with N/C:

One of the first demonstrations of a numerically controlled machine tool took place at MIT in the early 1950's. It was a Cincinnati vertical milling machine that had been modified at the servomechanism laboratory of MIT to operate from a punched-tape input. At the time, it was machining a wing-root fitting for a B47. The fitting was machined from a solid block of magnesium. The finished block was so complex that it weighed only 10 percent of the original block. The operator simply pushed a button to start the cycle. The machine then performed the roughing-cut cycle by operating in three planes simultaneously. When the cycle was completed, a bell rang to attract the attention of the operator.

Table 4.6
Classification of Automatic Machines

Types of Machines	Special Purpose	General Purpose	Preprogrammed		Description	Examples
			Nonadaptive	Adaptive		
1. Mechanized aids	X				Machines that replace human effort with machine effort. Typically perform from one to a few simple operations.	Magazine feed attachments for screw machines, quick centering and grasping devices for lathes, strip feeders for stamping machines, vibrating hoppers that weigh and drop precise charges of chemicals into waiting containers
2. Numerically controlled (N/C) machines	X	X	X		Machines with control systems that read instructions and translate instructions into machine operations. The control systems replace the changing of machine settings by human beings.	Lathes, boring mills, tire building machines, curing machines, weaving machines
3. Robots	X	X	X	X	Computer controlled machines that when programmed perform series of complex operations in humanlike ways. May work alongside human beings.	Welding machines for air compressor chassis; painting machines, drilling machines, and assembly machines in automobile factories; quality control sensing machines, assembly machines in TV manufacturing
4. Systems of automatic machines	X		X	X	Systems of machines most of which are automatic. Robots are used extensively along the line of machines that move products from step to step in automatic operations.	Assembly lines for automobiles, assembly lines for TV sets, assembly lines for motocycles, hot strip mills in steel industry, processing lines in oil refineries and chemical plants

The operator then brushed some chips away and pressed the button for the finishing-cut cycle, which the machine quickly completed. The only operations the operator performed were to place the part in the machine, start it, brush away some chips, and remove the finished part. The operator, incidentally, was a law student from Harvard. This was the first machine tool he had ever operated.[1]

Numerically controlled machines can do work faster and more safely and accurately than manually controlled machines. Although the programming does take some special training and skill, the production then is almost fully automatic. Low labor cost, high quality, and ease of converting to different product designs are the principal advantages of numerically controlled machines. The disadvantages are their high cost, their specially trained programmers, and the expense required to maintain them. The ability of these machines to be easily changed to different product designs makes them general-purpose machines.

Increasingly, however, numerically controlled machines are seen as an important step in the evolution of automatic machines as they have advanced toward the ultimate in automation — *robots.* Robotry is a fast-developing field in which human-like machines totally perform operations usually performed by human beings. Although this sounds as if it is right out of *Buck Rogers, Star Wars,* or *The Empire Strikes Back,* industry in general and the Japanese in particular are producing and using growing numbers of these machines for highly repetitive work. The brain of these machines is a microcomputer that when programmed guides the machine through its predetermined operations. The high cost of robots is perhaps the greatest obstacle to their widespread adoption. Nevertheless, as labor costs soar and the price of the robots falls as their numbers increase, these devices are sure to become as common in this country as they are now in Japan, Sweden, and other countries.

The Japanese Yen for Robots It was estimated in 1981 that 70 percent of the robots then in use in the world were made in Japan. About 130 Japanese companies are now manufacturing industrial robots, whereas only a handful of U.S. companies are so involved. Robotry has progressed to the point that Japanese manufacturers of robots have now formed The Japan Industrial Robot Association to promote a worldwide market for their robots.[2]

Matsushita Electric, the world's largest maker of consumer electronic goods, is moving fast into the use and production of industrial robots.

There are roughly 3,000 robots in Matsushita plants at present. A decade from now, the company plans to have more than 50,000 in its factories and expects other companies to move in the same direction. Thus, Matsushita began selling robots to other companies last year and a new line of assembly robots went on sale in June. Already, Matsushita claims about 10 percent of the Japanese robot market.

"The company is defraying the costs of developing its own machine tools and robots by selling them to other people," said Michael Connors, an analyst for Jardine Fleming Ltd., in Tokyo.

---

[1] H. B. Maynard, *Industrial Engineering Handbook* (New York: McGraw-Hill, 1963), 1/101.

[2] Leslie Loddeke, "Eighties May Be Decade of Japanese Robot Boom," *The Houston Chronicle,* July 12, 1981.

Display of Robots: Reprinted by permission of Prab Robots.

Vacuum cleaner housings are unloaded from an injection molding machine, broached and drilled.

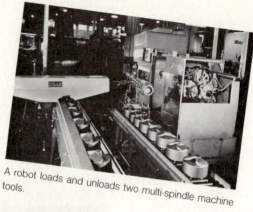

A robot loads and unloads two multi-spindle machine tools.

One U.S. robot manufacturer's line of industrial robots.

Robots tend single and multiple die presses for part transfer and unloading.

A robot transfers an automobile engine from assembly to final test.

Matsushita's sales of robotics and factory automation equipment will total about $80 million this year, according to Koichi Ogawa, a senior analyst for the Daiwa Securities Co. By 1987, the figure should grow to more than $400 million, Ogawa estimated. "This should be a real bright spot for Matsushita," he said.[3]

Not only do the Japanese make robots, they use them in great numbers as well. Automobile, television, motorcycle, and other mass production assembly lines all have major segments that are almost totally made up of robots. This extremely efficient system of producing large volumes of low-cost high-quality products for the world markets is the cornerstone of the Japanese business strategy. The success of the Japanese in world markets today cannot be questioned, and U.S. firms are working aggressively to close the gap in the use of robots as part of a larger effort aimed at meeting head on this threat from foreign competition.

American Robots Such firms as Cincinnati Milacron, Unimation Division of Condec Corporation, Prab Robots, Mobot Corporation, and Cross & Trecker are part of a group of robot manufacturers in the U.S. that numbered about 25–30 in 1981. Although U.S. firms produced only about 3,200 robots in 1981, according to the Robot Institute of America, great increases in output and use are expected in the near future. For example, "General Motors Corporation expects to boost the use of robots in its factories from about 300 in 1981 to some 14,000 by 1990. GM plans to have 2,500 robots in operation by 1983 and 5,000 by 1985."[4]

Considerable labor union resistance to robots is expected in the United States. Unions such as the International Union of Electrical Workers and The United Auto Workers are already developing plans to obtain these concessions from companies:

1. Advance notice of dismissal of workers whose jobs will be eliminated by robots.

2. Retraining of displaced workers.

3. Unionizing companies that supply robots.

Thus far, labor unrest over loss of job security because of robots seems to be giving way to mutual cooperation between management and the unions, as both of these groups are genuinely fearful of the foreign competition that already uses robots extensively. The mood seems to be: "If we can't beat them with business as usual, let's beat them at their own game."

One fact seems certain as we look forward to the late 1980s and beyond: Robots and other types of automatic machines will be an integral part of all process design in the United States and other industrialized countries. Any other approach to process design will place such designs in jeopardy as foreign and domestic competition accelerates in the use of robotry.

We have now examined process planning systems, basic processes of industry, types of productive systems, and productive machines. Let us now turn to some techniques that are commonly used to develop process plans for products/services.

---

[3] "Leading With Followership," *The Houston Chronicle*, Dec. 6, 1982, sec. 2, p. 1.

[4] "GM Plans Robot Boost," *The Houston Chronicle*, Feb. 1, 1981.

Techniques of Process Planning

Three techniques stand out in their frequency of use by process planners—assembly charts, process charts, and make-or-buy analyses.

Assembly Charts *Assembly charts* are typically used to provide an overall *macro-view* of how materials and subassemblies are united to form finished products. These charts list all major materials, components, subassembly operations, inspections, and assembly operations. Figure 4.13 is an assembly chart that shows the major steps in assembling an electronic hand-held calculator. Follow through these steps and try to visualize the actual operations for producing this familiar product.

Although assembly charts, sometimes called *gozinto charts* from the words *goes into,* can be used for products processed through either continuous or intermittent productive systems, they are more typically used for those products processed through assembly lines. This process planning tool is ideal for getting a bird's-eye view of the process for producing most assembled products. Additionally, they are also useful for planning productive systems for services when those services involve processing tangible goods such as in fast-food restaurants, dry-cleaning shops, and quick automobile tune-up shops.

Process Charts *Process charts* provide more detail for process planners than do assembly charts. Figure 4.14 shows the individual steps required to process 1,500 pounds of prepared materials through a mixing operation. This chart is a detailed analysis of only one of the operations required to produce aspirin tablets. This planning tool breaks the mixing operation down into fourteen elemental steps and segregates them into five classes—operation, transport, inspect, delay, and store. The frequency of occurrence of each class, distance traveled, and description and time for each step are recorded. When the heading of the chart is completed, the method of performing this mixing operation is thoroughly documented.

Process charts can be used to compare alternative methods of performing individual operations or groups of operations. Distance traveled and time to produce products can thus be reduced by examining alternative process charts for different production methods. This process planning tool can be used for products/services that are produced in either continuous or intermittent productive systems. Additionally, it is equally valuable for process planning when new products/services are being planned or when existing operations are being analyzed for improvement.

Process charts will surface again in Chapter 12 when we study the analysis of human performance in productive systems.

Make-or-Buy Analysis Some parts, components, subassemblies, and services can be purchased from suppliers at lower costs than if they were produced in-house. A question fundamental to process planning is: Should we produce it or should we buy it? *Make-or-buy analysis* provides process planners with economic comparisons of these alternatives. Example 4.1 shows how operations managers typically evaluate these make-or-buy decisions.

When outside suppliers specialize in particular processes, they often can produce products/services at lower costs than other organizations that must gear up technologically. A number of factors other than cost are also important in make-or-buy

Figure 4.13
Assembly Chart for OK-20 Hand-held Electronic Calculator

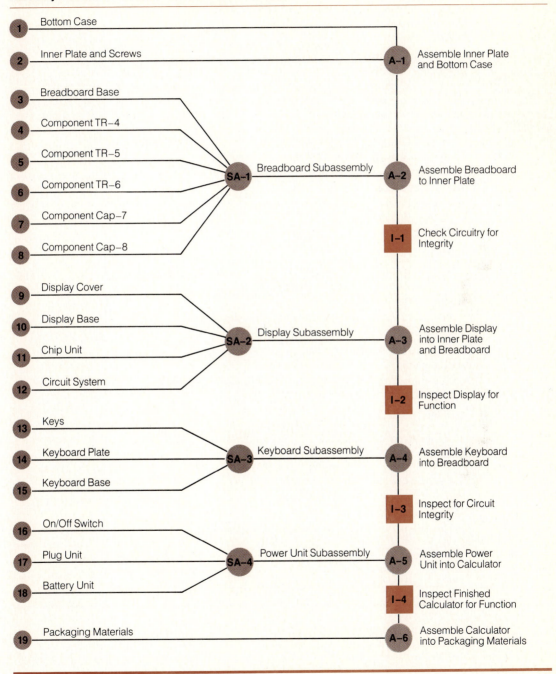

Figure 4.14
Process Chart for Mixing Aspirin

Operation	Mix aspirin materials
Product	Pronto aspirin (325)
Depts.	Mixing
Drawing No. —	Part No. 42200
Quantity	1500 pounds of mixed materials for Pronto 325 aspirin
Present X	Proposed

Sheet 1 of 1 Sheets
Charted By B. Brown
Date 3-16
Approved By M. Sharp
Date 3-17

Summary	
◯ Operation	5
⇨ Transport	5
▢ Inspect	1
D Delay	1
△ Store	2
Vertical Distance	—
Horizontal Distance	212
Time (Hours)	1.041

No.	Dist. Moved (Feet)	Worker Time (Hours)	Symbols	Description
1	15	.200	◯⇨▢DΔ	Unload packages of material from truck to dock and place on pallet.
2	42	.033	◯⇨▢DΔ	Truck packages of material to storage area.
3			◯⇨▢DΔ	Store materials until needed.
4	25	.025	◯⇨▢DΔ	Move packages to charge chute.
5		.330	◯⇨▢DΔ	Unpackage materials and pour into charge chute. Transport charge to mixer.
6	20	.030	◯⇨▢DΔ	Charge mixer and begin mixing cycle.
7		.100	◯⇨▢DΔ	Wait until mixer completes cycle.
8		.083	◯⇨▢DΔ	Dump mixer charge into receiving vehicle.
9		.017	◯⇨▢DΔ	Inspect materials for proper mixing.
10		.020	◯⇨▢DΔ	Transport vehicle to weighing and packaging station.
11	50	.033	◯⇨▢DΔ	Operate machine to weigh and package 1500 pounds of mixed materials.
12		.167	◯⇨▢DΔ	Transport materials to dock.
13	60	.033	◯⇨▢DΔ	Store materials until truck arrives.
14			◯⇨▢DΔ	

Example 4.1

A Make-or-Buy Decision

DRASCO, a medium-sized manufacturer of oilfield pumps, is located in Houston, Texas. The firm has developed a new model of its high-pressure secondary-recovery purge pump with improved performance. Bonnie Nelson, manager of process engineering, is trying to decide whether DRASCO should make or buy the electronically controlled input valve for the new pump. Her engineers have developed the following estimates:

	Make (Process A)	Make (Process B)	Buy
Annual volume	10,000 units	10,000 units	10,000 units
Fixed cost/year	$100,000	$300,000	——
Variable cost/unit	$75	$70	$80

a. Should DRASCO make the valve using Process A, make the valve using Process B, or buy the valve? **b.** At what annual volume should DRASCO switch from buying to making the valve on Process A? **c.** At what annual volume should DRASCO switch from Process A to Process B?

Solution

a. Develop the annual cost of each alternative:

Total annual costs = Fixed costs + volume (variable cost)

$$\text{Process A} = \$100,000 + 10,000\,(75) = \$\ 850,000$$
$$\text{Process B} = 300,000 + 10,000\,(70) = 1,000,000$$
$$\text{Buy} = 0 + 10,000\,(80) = 800,000$$

If the annual volume is estimated to be stable at 10,000 units, DRASCO should buy the valve.

b. At what annual volume should DRASCO switch from buying to making the valve on Process A (Q = volume)?

Total annual cost using Process A = Total annual cost of buying
$$100,000 + Q(75) = Q(80)$$
$$5Q = 100,000$$
$$Q = 20,000 \text{ units}$$

DRASCO should switch when annual volume is greater than 20,000 units.

c. At what volume should DRASCO switch from Process A to Process B (Q = volume, TC = total annual costs)?

$$TC_A = TC_B$$
$$100,000 + Q(75) = 300,000 + Q(70)$$
$$5Q = 200,000$$
$$Q = 40,000 \text{ units}$$

DRASCO should switch when annual volume is greater than 40,000 units.

decisions. Can suppliers give us the needed volume and quality? Volume and quality may be as important as cost in make-or-buy decisions. POM teams usually visit candidate suppliers to assure themselves that these outside shops can measure up to volume and quality requirements. If a supplier is selected, it can expect periodic visits from customers' engineers regarding delivery and quality performance.

A Process Planning Horror Story

Not all process planning efforts are successful. Perhaps this Soviet newspaper account from *Izvestia* of a process planning fiasco will motivate us to approach this important POM activity with more enthusiasm and commitment:

The fiasco began in 1969, when Russia bought a beer production line for canning kvass [a popular Russian beverage made from fermented bread and usually fruit flavored]. Its cost and capacity were not given, but an existing Soviet line that had been producing 120 million pints of kvass annually was torn out of the Ostankino beverage plant in Moscow and the imported beer line installed.

However, the engineers quickly "divined," as *Izvestia* said, that the line was "incomplete." Still needed were: equipment for removing empty cans from boxes, a rinsing unit, a unit to prepare the kvass, equipment to sort out rejects, a sterilizer, and equipment to pack filled cans.

Cost of the extra equipment was almost three times that of the original purchase price, *Izvestia* said.

An official of the Soviet Bank for Foreign Trade said he did believe that the specialists who requested the initial purchase of the beer-canning line were ignorant of the need to acquire additional equipment. They merely knew, he said, that it would be easier to get approval once initial equipment was delivered and standing idle.

And they got it. The extra equipment was imported and by 1971, the line was completed. Except a new problem was found: no cans. Also no tin for making cans, and no lacquer to line them, and no pull-tab tops to seal them.

Quickly shed was the luxury of pull-top cans. People could use a nail to punch holes in tops. The Research Institute for the Canning Industry developed a lacquer, the Food Ministry got some cans, and the line worked — briefly.

It produced 7,128 cans of kvass, of which 7,128 were rejected.

The cans could not take the pressure of pasteurizing the carbonated kvass. Not a single type of tin made in the Soviet Union is suitable for kvass cans.

Someone decided to save the line by canning kvass concentrate, a syrupy noncarbonated liquid.

"In the summer of 1973, the Ostankino fruit beverage plant celebrated its complete victory over foreign technology," *Izvestia* wrote. Canned kvass concentrate began to flow off the line. Instead of 4,000 cans an hour as planned, 4,872 were produced — but it took four months. The syrup clogged nozzles designed to pass beer. So in 1975, it was back to canning plain kvass.

Contracts for importing the right kind of tin — 600 tons of it were signed. Except then it was found the Soviet Union has no equipment for forming cans from the foreign tin.

There the line rests — "Still there is no canned kvass," said the *Izvestia* article.[5]

---

[5] Robert C. Toth, "Russians Just Can't Can That Brew," *Los Angeles Times*, Sept. 26, 1976. Copyright, 1976, *Los Angeles Times*. Reprinted by permission.

Product and Process Design in Business Strategy

Deciding what products and services to produce and how to produce them is an important part of a firm's overall business strategy—the long-range plans for the profitability, survival, and stability of the firm. Perhaps as never before, the soundness of the business strategies of U.S. firms is being questioned around the world. One of the reasons for questioning our business strategies is a seemingly endless surrender of market share by U.S. products to Japanese products in world markets.

When puzzling over why the Japanese are so successful at producing and selling such products as automobiles, television sets, and cameras, we have become accustomed to such pat answers as these:

1. Those little people over there just work harder than our workers.
2. We bombed out all of their industry in World War II; therefore, their machinery and production processes are technologically superior to ours.
3. Japanese labor works for less money than ours.
4. Japanese managers use more participative management styles, which results in more committed workers.
5. Japanese quality is better than ours because they have more conscientious workers.
6. The Japanese have been producing small cars longer than we have.
7. The Japanese government subsidizes its industries; thus, companies can produce at a loss and still remain afloat.

Although each of these answers may be valid to a greater or lesser degree, it is equally true that all of these answers when taken together do not fully explain why the Japanese have been so successful in the past decade. Some U.S. experts today believe that their success is directly tied to the way that they approach product and process design. To better understand the Japanese approach, let us first examine how U.S. firms typically decide what to produce and how to produce.

Product and Process Design in the United States

Deciding what to produce and how to produce in U.S. firms is dominated by two organization functions—marketing and finance. Marketing provides marketing information that becomes the principal basis for product designs. This marketing information includes such things as what features customers want in the products, what they are willing to pay for such features, the expected demand for these products, and when these products will be needed. Once the basic product design is determined, it is turned over to production to determine how to make it. Notice the *reactive* nature of production's role in this process. The finance functions in these firms provide the guidelines for the amount of capital funds that production may have in order to design, develop, and build the required processes and facilities to produce the product. All too often, our finance functions' focus is on short-range monetary returns. True, production can recommend modifications to the basic product design and propose exceptions to the capital funding policies, but make no mistake about it, marketing and finance swing the big sticks when these business strategies are planned in most U.S. corporate boardrooms.

Japanese Approach to Product and Process Design

Years ago, the leaders of Japan's industry determined that their country had certain strengths that could be used to compete in the larger world markets. Among these strengths, from their perspective, were an abundance of willing workers, low-cost labor, teamwork managerial styles, and an absence of destructive competition. To best use these strengths, they believed that they should concentrate on certain types of products:

1. Products that were in the mature stage of their product life cycle.
2. Products that were produced in very high volumes.
3. Products whose sales were price sensitive so that low manufacturing costs could provide a market advantage.
4. Products whose technological production processes were well known.
5. Products that could tolerate a high degree of product design standardization.

From the beginning modern Japanese industry studied, analyzed, and spent enormous sums of money to build a system of manufacturing that would allow it to compete in the growing world markets. It was thought that once this system of manufacturing was perfected, products could be found that would fit the system. They were right. General Motors, General Electric, and Kodak all know that Toyota, Sony, and Minolta are fierce competitors that have captured large shares of markets once dominated by the giants of U.S. industry.

Now, picture what it must be like to sit in on a boardroom discussion at Nissan, Nikon, or Honda. Which function do you think would dominate the decisions on what to produce and how to produce it — marketing, finance, or production? In the Japanese approach marketing and finance react to production. Production is *proactive* in their approach and determines the basic process design. It is the responsibility of marketing to go into the world markets and find products that can be easily manufactured by their productive systems. Marketing must be very selective and many promising products must be passed over because their markets have not yet developed to the necessary stage of maturity. Finance's responsibility is to acquire and provide the capital funds necessary to support the firm's long-range business strategy, which is dominated by their mass production manufacturing strategy.

This "bottoms-up" approach has allowed Japanese firms to plow great sums of money into automatic machinery and robots; into long-run material supply and shipping contracts; into the development of no-layoff personnel policies, benevolent management attitudes, long-range production engineering projects aimed at reducing costs; and into other activities. All of this effort is aimed at one central goal — build the most efficient manufacturing system possible so that continuous employment results. This common goal is shared by workers, management, unions, and government.

How can the Japanese spend all of this money on developing their manufacturing systems and U.S. firms don't seem to have sufficient funds to do so? The answer to this question lies partly in the type of products that the Japanese have chosen to produce. Products that are in their mature stage of market development are essentially set in their design, with no major design innovations likely and their markets fully developed. Because money need not be spent for product and market development, the Japanese firms have enormous funds to spend on manufacturing improvements. Matsushita Electric calls this strategy *followership*.

Japanese companies as a whole have employed the strategy [followership] in one form or another, in industry after industry. Often latecomers, they have used astute marketing techniques, product differentiation, and low-cost manufacturing as the keys to international success in such businesses as motorcycles, television sets, and cars.

Matsushita has long had a reputation for such followership, though some call it simply caution. It has let other companies blaze the trail with new products. Then, once a market starts to develop, Matsushita moves in and grabs a large share of the developing market. Typically, Matsushita's product line is a bit different and a bit less expensive than those of its competitors'. . . .

The classic example of this in recent years was Matsushita's move into the video cassette recorder market in the mid-1970s. It trailed Sony's Betamax (a beta-format VCR) into the market by nearly a year. But today Matsushita is the leading producer of video cassette recorders using the VHS format — and VHS machines represent 70 percent of the global VCR market.[6]

In the mid-1980s a new twist to Japanese business strategy has emerged. They have taken what they have learned from executing their mass production of mature products of the 1970s and 1980s and are applying it to a new arena. Specifically, their ability to develop automated assembly lines that produce products of exceptional quality has been applied to high technology products such as computers. The Japanese, who have been so successful at using their production technology as a competitive weapon against their U.S. counterparts, now appear to be going for the jugular of the Silicon Valley, the heart of the U.S. computer industry's research and development activity. It remains to be seen whether the Japanese manufacturers can be as successful in these new ventures as they have been in carrying out their business strategies of the past. Nevertheless, their attention to detail, their automated assembly lines, and the superior quality of their products continue to pose a challenge to U.S. industrial firms.

Getting Manufacturing Strategy into U.S. Boardrooms

Now the difficult question: How do we compete with the Japanese? There are no easy and simple solutions because if there were, U.S. firms would already have solved the problem. What is needed, perhaps more than anything else, is to put operations strategy on an equal footing with marketing and financial strategy in U.S. boardrooms. In past eras when the United States was the preeminent producer in the world, manufacturing strategy was the central power in corporations. But we have gotten away from our emphasis on production as the glamourous professions of marketing and finance grew and developed in the 1950–1980 period when markets and product innovation exploded.

---

[6] "Leading With Followership," *The Houston Chronicle*, Dec. 6, 1982, sec. 2, p. 1.

As Leighton F. Smith, of Arthur Andersen & Co., states: "Japanese manufacturers today are beating their U.S. counterparts over the head with a borrowed club — and we handed it to them a quarter-century ago when we freely exported our production technology. Now is perhaps the time to do some borrowing of our own."[7]

Summary

Product/service design and planning processes for producing these outputs are critical POM activities. The markets on the one hand and the technologies of productive systems on the other provide the constrained area within which products must be designed, developed, and produced. Product/service design and process planning are inseparably related. Each affects the other. Their ultimate determination must be made simultaneously.

Product design and development is a system that spans technical and economic studies through prototype design, production design, and finally the maintenance activity of continual design modification. Service design and development is very similar to that procedure used for tangible products, except that few performance tests are performed, market surveys tend to be preferred over market tests, and personnel of the productive system are dominant in importance over its technologies.

Specifications, standardization, simplification, and quality engineering are engineering concepts that must be incorporated into product/service designs. These important concepts apply equally well to either products or services.

Process planning means the complete determination of the specific technological process steps and their sequences — in other words, how products/services will be produced. Process planning occurs dramatically in the beginnings of new products/services and then routinely as productive systems revert to a steady state. This key POM activity ties together many of the other elements of POM. Product design, forecasting, and allocation of POM resources are basic to process planning. Process planning then determines in large measure building designs, facility layout, equipment selection, quality control programs, job design, and facility capacity.

Productive systems can be broken into two major classes — continuous and intermittent. Continuous productive systems are usually appropriate for products/services with very high volume and standardized designs. These systems have processes, equipment, and personnel arranged so that products flow in direct, smooth paths through facilities. Intermittent systems, on the other hand, are usually appropriate for products/services with low volume and nonstandardized designs. These systems have processes, equipment, and personnel arranged according to processes. Products therefore tend to flow through these facilities in indirect, irregular paths.

In process planning, the specific machines selected can take over varying degrees of work conventionally performed by human beings. Mechanized aids, preprogrammed nonadaptive machines, and preprogrammed adaptive machines span the automation spectrum from the simple to the complex.

---

[7] Leighton F. Smith, "Just-in case vs. Just-in-time Production Systems," presented at the APICS Educational Liaison Workshop, St. Charles, IL, June 29–July 1, 1981, 12.

Assembly charts and process charts are frequently used to aid process planners in their efforts to design processes that effectively and efficiently produce products/services of the desired quality, in the required quantity, and at the determined cost. Make-or-buy analysis compares processing products in-house to buying them from outside suppliers.

If U.S. firms are to compete successfully with Japanese firms in domestic and world markets, they must be willing to learn from their competitors. Japanese firms are doing well what many of these same U.S. firms used to do — use manufacturing efficiency as a weapon in world markets. U.S. firms must bring operations strategy back into the boardrooms when business strategy is developed and decisions on product design and process planning are made.

Review and Discussion Questions

1. How are product/service design and process planning activities related to product life cycles?

2. What are the eight basic steps in the system of bringing a product/service from a bright idea to a delivered product/service?

3. Why are product/service design and process planning fundamental to efficient productive systems?

4. Compare the steps in developing products and services. How are they alike? How are they different?

5. What are product specifications?

6. What is product/service standardization? Give an example of product standardization. Give an example of service standardization.

7. What is product/service simplification? Why is simplification desirable? Give an example of product simplification. Give an example of service simplification.

8. Define *process planning*.

9. Name four basic areas that are studied in process planning.

10. Name five characteristics of continuous productive systems.

11. Name five characteristics of intermittent productive systems.

12. If a manager were trying to decide between a continuous and an intermittent productive system for producing a product/service, what two key factors would be important to the decision?

13. What is automation? What are four classes of automatic machines?

14. Compare assembly charts and process charts. How are they alike? How are they different?

15. Compare and contrast the Japanese and American approaches to product and process design.

16. Why are Japanese firms so successful in world markets today? Name six important reasons for their success.

17. What can U.S. firms do to compete more effectively with their Japanese counterparts in world markets?

Problems

Assembly Charts

1. Prepare an assembly chart for a flashlight with two batteries.

2. Prepare an assembly chart for a long-sleeved sports shirt with a collar and one pocket.

3. Prepare an assembly chart for a bicycle with these basic components: frame, front wheel, back wheel, brakes, power, and guidance.

Process Charts

4. Prepare a process chart for replacing a flat automobile tire with a spare tire from the trunk.

5. Prepare a process chart for enrolling at your college or university.

6. Prepare a process chart for making a bed (use sheets and a pillowcase).

Make-or-Buy Analysis

7. A small manufacturer has developed a new product that requires heat treating. The firm is now trying to decide if it should gear up to do its own in-house heat treating or purchase these services from a local company. It has developed the following estimates:

	Heat Treat In-House	Purchase Heat Treat Services
Annual volume	5,000 units	5,000 units
Fixed cost/year	$25,000	——
Variable cost/unit	$10	$17.50

Should the company buy the heat treating services?

8. Oklahoma Instruments (OI) makes hand-held electronic calculators. A new model has been developed that requires a new design of display units. OI is trying to decide if it should make or buy the display units based on these estimates:

	Buy	Make (Process X)	Make (Process Y)
Annual volume	100,000 units	100,000 units	100,000 units
Fixed cost/year	——	$300,000	$500,000
Variable cost/unit	$10	$8	$7

a. What should OI do — buy; make, using Process X; or make, using process Y? b. At what volume should OI switch from buying to making, using Process X? c. At what volume should OI switch from Process X to Process Y?

9. The Beautiful Dreamer Mattress Company buys its spring foundation assemblies (SFA's) from the Springy Company. The present contract between the two companies requires the supply of SFA's on this basis:

Chapter 4   Product Design and Process Planning   155

Year	Volume (Units)	Price/Unit	Tooling Charges
1	100,000	$35.00	$10,000
2	200,000	37.50	20,000
3	250,000	39.50	30,000
4	350,000	42.00	35,000
5	400,000	45.00	50,000

Springy has informed Beautiful Dreamer that it has just filed for bankruptcy and it cannot honor its previous supply agreements past the first year. Beautiful Dreamer's process engineers have designed two in-house alternative production process plans with these costs:

	Robotry Process			Conventional Process		
Year	First Cost	Tooling Charges	Cost/Unit	First Cost	Tooling Charges	Cost/Unit
2	$5,000,000	$20,000	$22.50	$2,000,000	$30,000	$27.50
3		30,000	25.00		40,000	32.00
4		35,000	27.50		45,000	36.00
5		50,000	30.00		60,000	42.00

Assuming that the volume of SFA's will be the same as projected in the Springy contract, use graphs and cost analysis to determine: **a.** What should Beautiful Dreamer do now, install the robotry or the conventional process design? Why? **b.** During what years would the robotry process begin to show a cost advantage over Springy and the conventional process design? **c.** If Beautiful Dreamer follows your recommendation in part a, how much money will be saved over that which would have been paid to Springy over the four-year period?

Process Selection

10. Runemthru University currently has 950 students in its MBA program. The present program is a lockstep approach that its students refer to as the "assembly line." In this system students "flow" through the program, each taking the same courses as every other student and in the same sequence. Polyanna Aloof, the Dean, estimates that the annual fixed cost of the MBA program is $900,000 and the variable cost per student per year is $1,000. Ms. Aloof is considering a faculty proposal for modifying the MBA program to improve its academic standards. The suggested changes would allow students flexibility in selecting courses and the sequence in which the courses are taken. Under the new program, Ms. Aloof estimates that the annual fixed cost would be only $500,000, but the variable cost per student per year would be $1,600.

If the school receives budget allocations of $2,000 per MBA student: **a.** What is the present surplus or deficit of the MBA program? **b.** What enrollment is required in the present program in order to balance the budget? **c.** How many students would need to be in the proposed MBA program for Ms. Aloof to be indifferent between the two programs if only budget factors are considered? **d.** How many MBA students would be required in the proposed program in order for its total annual cost to be the same as in the present program?

Case

Brightco Manufacturing

Brightco manufactures signal products for highway, railway, and marine use. The company has just closed out one of its line of products and now has some production capacity available. One of two product alternatives will be developed—a *marine signal kit* to be sold through marine products distributors or a *triangular reflective highway signal* to be sold to a mass merchandiser.

Brightco thinks that there is a 20 percent likelihood that the marine product cannot be successfully developed and that the idea would have to be scrapped. If the product development is only marginally successful, a likelihood of 30 percent, the product idea can be sold to a firm for about $50,000. The product development project is expected to cost $200,000, and if it is successful, a production process development project will be undertaken. Two processing alternatives, Process A and Process B, are being considered. Process A is a fully automated assembly line and Process B is a job shop arrangement. The differences between revenues and operating expenses for the processes at three levels of market acceptance for the product are expected to be:

	Level of Market Acceptance		
	High (P = .3)	Medium (P = .4)	Low (P = .3)
Process A	$1,500,000	$600,000	$(500,000)
Process B	1,000,000	700,000	400,000

The highway product has these likelihoods of successful development: successful, 70 percent; marginal, 20 percent; and unsuccessful, 10 percent. If the product cannot be developed, the idea will obviously have to be scrapped. If the development project is only marginally successful, the product can be produced on existing production equipment and marketed through existing marketing channels, or the product idea can perhaps be sold to a company for about $100,000, a likelihood of only about 60 percent. If the product line is produced and marketed, the differences between revenues and operating expenses at two levels of market acceptance are expected to be:

	Levels of Market Acceptance	
	Medium (P = .4)	Low (P = .6)
Produce and market marginal product	$600,00	$200,000

If the product development project is successful, a mass merchandiser has agreed to a long-term purchase contract for all of Brightco's production of the highway product. Two processing alternatives are being considered for this production, with these expected differences between revenues and operating expenses at two yield levels:

	Levels of Production Yields			
	High Yields		Low Yields	
	Value	Likelihood (P)	Value	Likelihood (P)
Process X	$ 800,000	.5	$600,000	.5
Process Y	1,100,000	.3	400,000	.7

The product development project for the triangle signal is expected to cost $300,000 and the process development project would cost about $150,000.

Assignment

1. Describe the nature of Brightco's problem. What issues must they decide? What is the general structure of their decision?

2. Which analysis techniques are most appropriate for analyzing this decision? Defend your answer.

3. Analyze Brightco's problem and recommend a course of action. What are the strengths and weaknesses of your analysis approach?

4. What risks are present if Brightco follows your recommendation in No. 3? How would your recommendation be modified if you knew that Brightco's management was a risk taker or a risk avoider?

Selected Bibliography

Albus, James S., and John M. Evans. "Robot Systems." *Scientific American*, February 1976, 77–86.

Booz, Allen, and Hamilton, Management Research Department, "Management of New Products," 1960. As cited in *The Product Planning System,* by Lewis N. Goslin. Homewood, IL: Richard D. Irwin, 1967, 3.

Bright, James R. *Automation and Management.* Boston: Division of Research, Harvard Business School, 1958.

Cook, Nathan H. "Computer-Managed Parts Manufacture." *Scientific American*, February 1975, 26.

Cornish, Harry L., Jr., and William L. Horton. *Computerized Process Control: A Management Decision.* New York: Hobbs, Dorman, 1968.

Decker, Robert. "Computer Aided Design and Manufacturing at GM." *Datamation*, May 1979, 159–165.

Eary, Donald F., and Gerald E. Johnson. *Process Engineering for Manufacturing.* Englewood Cliffs, NJ: Prentice-Hall, 1962.

Hise, Richard, and A. McGinnis. "Product Elimination: Practices, Policies and Ethics." *Business Horizons,* June 1975, 25–32.

Levitt, Theodore. "Production Line Approach to Service." *Harvard Business Review* 50(September–October 1972): 41–52.

Levitt, T. "The Industrialization of Services." *Harvard Business Review* 54(1976): 41–52.

Maynard, H. B. *Industrial Engineering Handbook.* New York: McGraw-Hill, 1963, 1/101.

Niebel, B. W., and A. B. Draper. *Product Design and Process Engineering.* New York: McGraw-Hill, 1974.

Papen, G. W. "Minimizing Manufacturing Costs through Effective Design." *Proceedings: Sixth Annual Industrial Engineering Institute.* Berkeley–Los Angeles, 1954.

Sasser, W. Earl, R. Paul Olsen, and D. Daryle Wyckoff. *Management of Service Operations: Text, Cases, and Readings.* Boston: Allyn and Bacon, 1978.

Scheele, Evan D., William L. Westerman, and Robert J. Wimmert. *Principles and Design of Production Control Systems.* Englewood Cliffs, NJ: Prentice-Hall, 1960.

Uman, David B. *New Product Programs: Their Planning and Control.* New York: American Management Association, 1969.

Utterback, J., and W. J. Abernathy. "A Dynamic Model of Process and Product Innovation." *Omega* 3, no. 6(1976): 639–656.

Vonalven, William H. *Reliability Engineering.* Englewood Cliffs, NJ: Prentice-Hall, 1964.

Wallenstein, Gerd D. *Concept and Practice of Product Planning.* New York: American Management Association, 1968.

Financial Analysis in POM

Operations managers are usually among the first to sense the need for *capital goods*. These goods are anything bought by a business that have an expected life of more than one year and are not bought and sold in the ordinary course of operations. These goods include such items as production machinery, buildings, computers, trucks and cars, and office equipment.

Operations managers often initiate proposals for buying capital goods because:

1. New products or services require new production equipment and buildings.

2. Existing production equipment and buildings are old and worn out and must be replaced with new ones.

3. Present production equipment has become obsolete and must be replaced with new and technologically superior designs.

4. Sales growth has resulted in the need for more production capacity that requires additional production machinery and buildings.

Sensing the need for capital goods is one thing; justifying that need to top-level executives who must approve such spending is quite another. Because of the scarcity of funds in most businesses and because of the volatility of interest rates and scarcity of funds in capital markets in the last decade, proposals for capital goods have undergone increased scrutiny by top management. If operations managers expect to win funds for capital goods, they must develop to a fine art the tools of financial analysis for justifying the acquisition of capital goods.

Financial Analysis Concepts

Table 4S.1 presents and defines some of the terms and concepts used in financial analysis in POM.

Depreciation

Depreciation is perhaps the least understood concept in financial analysis. Central to the confusion is the *noncash* nature of depreciation expense. The noncash nature of annual depreciation charges means that no cash has actually been spent for depreciation; the cash for the asset was paid at the time of the original purchase of the asset. Depreciation does not *directly* affect profits; rather, depreciation affects profits only indirectly through income tax savings. Example 4S.1 shows this impact. Note that in the example a $40,000 tax bill would have been paid by the business if there were no depreciation charged. With a $20,000 depreciation charge, however, the business paid only $32,000 in taxes, a savings of $8,000.

The 1981 Tax Act, which is administered by the Internal Revenue Service (IRS), has greatly simplified the methods that may be used to depreciate assets that were put into service after 1980. The act classifies assets into three categories. The *3-year category* consists of automobiles and light trucks and items used for research and experimentation. The *15-year category* consists of buildings. The *5-year category*

Table 4S.1
Financial Analysis Concepts and Definitions

Capital Good — An asset with a life of more than one year that is not bought and sold in the ordinary course of business.

Cutoff Rate — The minimum rate of return on similar investments, set by management.

Depreciation — The annual noncash expense charged against profits to reduce taxes.

Economic Life — The period over which an asset is expected to remain economically productive.

First Cost — The total selling price of a capital good plus any delivery costs or costs of installation, tooling, and so on.

IRS Depreciation Category — The IRS classifies all capital goods put into service after 1980 into either 3, 5, or 15 years of depreciation for tax purposes.

Operating Expenses — The annual cost of operating the capital good, including labor, supplies, utilities, maintenance, and so on.

Opportunity Costs — The highest return that will be forgone if the funds are invested in a particular capital good.

Salvage Value — The market value of a capital good at the end of its economic life.

Taxes — Federal income taxes (this usually means corporate income taxes).

Example 4S.1

The Effects of Depreciation upon Cash Flows

	Without Depreciation	With Depreciation
Profits before depreciation and taxes	$100,000	$100,000
Less depreciation	0	20,000
Taxable income	100,000	80,000
Taxes ($t = .4$)	40,000	32,000
Profits after taxes	60,000	68,000
Tax savings due to depreciation ($t \times$ depreciation)	——	8,000

Note: t is the tax rate, or 40 percent in this example.

includes all other assets such as production equipment. Table 4S.2 shows the accelerated depreciation that firms may use for the three categories of assets.

The depreciation schedules in Table 4S.2 do not consider any salvage value and the whole percentage may be applied in the first year for 3-year and 5-year assets even if purchased as late as December 31. The 15-year schedule is for buildings purchased in January. The schedules for assets purchased in other months are contained in The 1981 Tax Act. Example 4S.2 shows how these schedules are used in computing the annual depreciation charges for an asset in the 5-year category.

Table 4S.2
Accelerated Depreciation Schedules in The 1981 Tax Act

Years	Percentage of Asset's First Cost That Can Be Charged in Each Year of Its Life		
	3-Year Assets	5-Year Assets	15-Year Assets
1	25%	15%	12%
2	38	22	10
3	37	21	9
4		21	8
5		21	7
6–9			6
10–15			5

Example 4S.2

Computing Annual Depreciation Charges from The 1981 Tax Act

The Blackbird Coal Company purchased a crusher, a piece of machinery for reducing the size of chunks of coal, for $5,000 on November 1. The crusher is in the 5-year category of assets according to the IRS. What are the annual depreciation charges allowed by the IRS for the crusher?

Year	Annual Depreciation	Accumulated Depreciation
1	$ 750	$ 750
2	1,100	1,850
3	1,050	2,900
4	1,050	3,950
5	1,050	5,000

Time Value of Money

The concept of the *time value of money* is based on two principles:

1. A sum of money in hand today will be worth more one year from now because of the earning power that money has in savings accounts and other forms of investments. The future value (f) of money is always more than the present value (p) by an amount that is equal to the *compounded interest* earned.

2. A sum of money in hand now is worth less than the sum one year from now because the sum of money one year from now implicitly includes compounded interest plus the value of the sum today. The future value must be stripped of its implicit interest earnings through discounting to compute the value of the sum today.

In compound interest calculations in business, an interest rate (i) may be selected for use in compounding or discounting that reflects any one of the following:

1. The *interest rate* that can be earned on such safe investments as savings accounts and government bonds. In this case *i* is an opportunity cost — the earnings passed up in other investments so that the money can be invested in the asset under consideration.

2. The *cutoff rate,* which is the lowest rate of return that management will accept on new investment opportunities for a business.

3. The current or *target rate of return* on the firm's assets.

4. The firm's *weighted cost of capital,* which is based on the inclusion of debt, stock issued by the firm, and retained earnings.

Regardless of the interpretation of the meaning of *i*, it is referred to as the *discount rate* in financial analysis.

Table 4S.3
Compound Interest Concepts and Definitions

Annuity — A series of payments of equal amounts for a specified number of time periods.

Compounding — The arithmetic process of computing the final value of a payment or a stream of annuity payments when the interest is added.

Discounting — The reverse of compounding: finding the present value of future cash flows.

Future Value — The value at some specific time in the future of a present payment or a stream of annuity payments compounded at the discount rate.

Discount Rate — The interest rate applied in compound interest calculations in capital budgeting. It always refers to an annual interest rate basis.

Present Value — The value today of a stream of annuity payments or a future payment discounted at the discount rate.

Table 4S.3 exhibits some of the concepts and their definitions that are fundamental to a study of the time value of money. These concepts will be used in Examples 4S.3 and 4S.4 to demonstrate the calculation of present values and future values. Before we begin the examples, however, turn to the end of this supplement and become familiar with the compound interest tables. These tables are used in the examples of this section.

The factors in the compound interest tables are all multiplied by a known value such as p, f, or a to give the unknown value such as p, f, or a. For example, $(f/p)_5^{10}$ is the factor multiplied by the present value (p), which is known, to give the future value (f), which is unknown. In this scheme the known value is always found to the right of the slash mark (/) and the unknown value is always to the left. In the factor above, the discount rate is 10 percent and the total span of time over which the interest is compounded is 5 years. Now, take out your calculator, put a paper clip to mark the Compound Interest Tables at the end of this supplement, and follow through the calculations in Examples 4S.3 and 4S.4.

Example 4S.3

Future-Value Calculations

1. What is the future value of $1,000 invested today at 10 percent compounded annually for 5 years? Given: $p = \$1,000$, $i = 10\%$, and $n = 5$. Find: $f = ?$

Solution

$$f = p(f/p)_n^i = 1,000(f/p)_5^{10} = 1,000(1.611) = \$1,611$$

	1,000					$1,611
End of Year	0	1	2	3	4	5

2. What is the future value 5 years from now of a stream of five $300 annuities paid in at the end of each year and compounded annually at 10 percent? Given: a = $300, i = 10%, and n = 5. Find: f =?

Solution

$$f = a(f/a)_n^i = a(f/a)_5^{10} = 300(6.105) = \$1,831.50$$

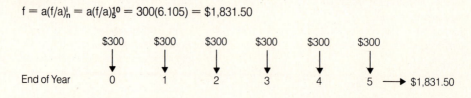

| | $300 | $300 | $300 | $300 | $300 | $300 |
| End of Year | 0 | 1 | 2 | 3 | 4 | 5 → $1,831.50 |

Example 4S.4

Present-Value Calculations

1. How much would you have to pay in today to get $1,000 back 5 years from now if your payment is compounded annually at 10 percent? Given: f = $1,000, i = 10%, and n = 5. Find: p = ?

Solution

$$p = f(p/f)_n^i = f(p/f)_5^{10} = 1,000(.6209) = \$620.90$$

| | $620.90 | | | | $1,000 |
| End of Year | 0 | 1 | 2 | 3 | 4 | 5 |

2. What is the present value today of a sum worth $1,611 five years from now discounted annually at 10 percent? Note that this is the exact reverse of No. 1 in Example 4S.3. It demonstrates that discounting is the exact reverse process of compounding. Given: f = $1,611, i = 10%, and n = 5. Find: p = ?

Solution

$$p = f(p/f)_n^i = f(p/f)_5^{10} = 1,611(.6209) = \$1,000$$

Therefore, the future value of $1,000 is $1,611 and the present value of $1,611 is $1,000.

3. What is the present value of a stream of five $300 annuities paid in at the end of each year for 5 years? The annuities are discounted annually at 10 percent. Given: a = $300, i = 10%, and n = 5. Find: p =?

Solution

$$p = a(p/a)_n^i = a(p/a)_5^{10} = 300(3.791) = \$1,137.30$$

$$\$1,137.30$$

In order to understand why the time value of money and depreciation are important concepts in financial analysis in POM, let us now study some of the ways that operations managers actually choose among capital goods.

Methods of Financial Analysis

Among the methods of financial analysis used in business today, the following types will be studied and evaluated here: payback period, net present value (NPV), and profitability index (PI). These methods may be used either to analyze and justify the purchase of individual capital goods or to analyze and compare several capital goods.

Payback Period

This method answers the question: How long does it take to get back our original investment less the salvage value through savings in operating expenses or other profit improvements for each capital good? The assumptions that underly this method are: (1) Investments that return the original investment faster are more profitable. (2) Investments with fast paybacks are less risky. (3) Investments with fast paybacks allow the firm to reinvest its capital in new revenue-generating projects and thus relieve capital funds shortages.

The payback period can be computed while using returns either before taxes or after taxes. An after-tax basis is more realistic and is preferred in most analyses. Example 4S.5 works through a comparison of investment alternatives using the payback period method. As Table 4S.4 summarizes, the payback period is quick and easy to compute, easily explained and understood, and considered a standard tool in financial analysis in business.

Ease of understanding is an important feature of the payback period method. A few years ago I hopped a plane to New York to meet with the board of directors of a major chemical manufacturer. I presented a proposal to build a new $20 million production facility in Florida. In summarizing, I explained that the investment promised a 12 percent internal rate of return (IRR, the discount rate that equates discounted cash inflows to cash outflows). I shall never forget the response of the chairman of the board, who was also a major stockholder in the corporation (he

Example 4S.5

Comparing Three Investments — A, B, and C — Using the Payback Period

	End of Year Cash Flows		
Year	Investment A	Investment B	Investment C
0	($10,000)*	($20,000)*	($30,000)*
1	5,000	5,000	10,000
2	5,000	5,000	10,000
3	5,000	5,000	10,000
4	——	5,000	10,000
5	——	5,000	10,000
6	——	——	——
7	——	——	——
8	——	——	——
	15,000	25,000	50,000

* Note: ( ) means an outflow, usually first cost minus salvage value if it occurs at the end of Year 0 or at the beginning of Year 1.

Solution

Payback period: 2 years   4 years   3 years

made or lost over $1 million when the corporation's stock price increased or decreased $1): He loudly asked, "What the hell does that mean?" While the financial vice-president was desperately trying to explain the meaning of IRR, I was shuffling through my stack of transparencies for a payback period explanation. I finally found it and flashed it up on the screen. The tension was immediately eased, the chairman of the board and the remainder of the board eventually approved the project, and I learned a valuable lesson in presenting the results of analytical studies. First, present the results in simple and understandable terms. Second, present the results in more detail and with more sophisticated techniques if required. This approach is also called the KISS Principle (Keep It Simple, Stupid!), a principle that is commonly applied in business.

The payback period method is criticized by financial theorists because it doesn't consider any returns after the payback period and it doesn't consider the time value of money. Although one cannot deny the severity of these shortcomings, the method must have something going for it considering its almost universal use in business.

Perhaps the greatest potential shortcoming of the payback period is that it tends to pass over investments that are big long-range winners in favor of investments with modest short-range returns. Can businesses continually go for short-range

Table 4S.4
Pros and Cons of Payback Period Method

Advantages	Disadvantages
1. Quick and easy to compute; requires no compound interest or other complex calculations.	1. Does not consider returns after the payback period.
2. Easily explained and understood.	2. Does not compound or discount future earnings or costs; does not consider time value of money.
3. Universally used; considered a standard tool.	3. Builds a short-range investment bias.
4. Most effective for firms with cash shortages.	4. Inappropriate for capital assets with net cash outflows. For
5. Adapts to comparisons of investments of unequal first costs.	example, a new machine performing a new operation may have cash outflows throughout its entire life, and a payback period cannot be calculated.

payoffs or must they sometimes forgo short-range performance for long-range opportunities? The answer given by most businesses is that a balance must be struck in selecting investment alternatives between short-range and long-range performers. When used as the sole criterion for capital budgeting, the payback period may not allow this balance.

Net Present Value (NPV)

This method of financial analysis discounts the value of the stream of after-tax cash flows back to the present. The capital good with the *least NPV* is preferred if we want the one with the least cost, and the one with the *greatest NPV* is preferred if we want the one with the greatest profits. The word *net* suggests that all cash flows are taken into account, both inflows and outflows.

NPV overcomes most of the disadvantages of the payback period method, as Table 4S.5 shows. It considers the time value of money and it considers all of the cash flows over the entire life of the asset. But it is more difficult to use, explain, and understand than the payback period. Moreover, when capital goods with unequal

Table 4S.5
Pros and Cons of Net Present Value Method

Advantages	Disadvantages
1. Considers time value of money; discounts future returns and costs back to the present.	1. Requires complex compound interest calculations.
2. Commonly used in business.	2. More difficult to explain and understand.
3. Considers all cash flows over the entire economic life of a capital good.	3. The selection of a discount rate is critical. Widely disparate rates can result in different investment decisions.
	4. Can be inappropriate for comparing investments with unequal first costs.

first costs are being compared, the method can give confusing results. In these cases the profitability index (PI) may be used. This method will be discussed in the next section. Because The 1981 Tax Act lumps all similar capital goods into the same 3-, 5-, or 15-year categories, the lives of capital goods that would be compared by NPV will ordinarily be considered equal. In many cases, therefore, this act has eliminated a traditional objection to the use of NPV when capital goods have unequal lives.

Study Example 4S.6 and try to relate this example to the advantages and disadvantages of NPV from Table 4S.5.

Example 4S.6

Net Present Value (NPV) Method

Use NPV to select either Investment A or Investment B, if the discount rate is 10 percent:

Year	End-of-Year After-Tax Cash Flows	
	Investment A	Investment B
0	($15,000)*	($15,000)*
1	7,000	10,000
2	6,000	5,000
3	6,000	5,000
4	6,000	5,000

* Note: (   ) means a cash outflow.

Solution

	Investment A				
Year	End-of-Year After-Tax Cash Flows		Present-Value Factors $(p/f)_n^{10}$		Present Value
0	($15,000)	$\times$	1.0000	=	($15,000)
1	7,000	$\times$	.9091	=	6,364
2	6,000	$\times$	.8264	=	4,958
3	6,000	$\times$	.7513	=	4,508
4	6,000	$\times$	.6830	=	4,098
			NPV_A =		$4,928

Investment B

Year	End-of-Year After-Tax Cash Flows		Present-Value Factors $(p/f)_n^{10}$		Present Value
0	($15,000)	×	1.0000	=	($15,000)
1	10,000	×	.9091	=	9,091
2	5,000	×	.8264	=	4,132
3	5,000	×	.7513	=	3,757
4	5,000	×	.6830	=	3,415
				$NPV_B =$	$5,395

Investment B is preferred. This results in spite of equal total cash inflows and equal first costs, because earlier cash inflows are discounted less severely than later ones.

Profitability Index (PI)

When capital goods that are being compared have unequal first costs and net cash inflows, NPV is an inappropriate financial analysis method. NPV could, for example, show that these two investments are equally attractive:

	Capital Good A	Capital Good B
First cost	$1,000,000	$200,000
NPV	100,000	100,000

We would obviously prefer Investment B because its return compared to its first cost is much greater than that of Investment A. The PI modifies the NPV to overcome this deficiency when there are unequal first costs and net cash inflows:

$$PI = \frac{\text{First cost} + \text{NPV}}{\text{First cost}}$$

$$PI_A = \frac{\text{First cost} + \text{NPV}_A}{\text{First cost}} = \frac{1,000,000 + 100,000}{1,000,000} = 1.10$$

$$PI_B = \frac{\text{First cost} + \text{NPV}_B}{\text{First cost}} = \frac{200,000 + 100,000}{200,000} = 1.50$$

Because Investment B has a greater PI, it is preferred.

When capital goods have unequal first costs and net cash outflows, NPV ordinarily is effective in comparing their cash flows and PI would not necessarily be preferred to NPV.

Table 4S.6
A Comparison of Financial Analysis Methods: Which Methods Are Appropriate?

Financial Analysis Method	Equal Lives and Equal First Costs	Unequal First Costs	Cash Inflow ≥ Cash Outflow	Cash Outflow ≥ Cash Inflow
1. Payback period	X	X	X	
2. NPV	X	X*	X*	X
3. PI	X	X	X	

* Note: NPV is appropriate for comparing investments with unequal first costs only when the objective is to minimize the cash outflows over the economic lives. NPV is inappropriate when investments with unequal first costs have net cash inflows.

Evaluation of Methods

All of the financial analysis methods presented in this section are used in business today, each with varying frequency. Because no single method applies universally in all situations, analysts must thoroughly understand the conditions under which each method is appropriate. Table 4S.6 summarizes the conditions appropriate for the use of each method when alternative investments are to be compared.

Now that we are equipped with an understanding of financial analysis concepts and methods, let us focus on some concrete examples of classic financial decisions in POM.

Classic Financial Analysis Decisions in POM

Three financial analysis decisions stand out in frequency of occurrence in POM: Equipment replacement, choice of equipment, and make or buy. These types of investment decisions are demonstrated in Examples 4S.7, 4S.8, and 4S.9. When studying these examples, you may find it helpful to refer to Table 4S.6 to determine which financial analysis methods are appropriate in each example.

Example 4S.7

An Equipment Replacement Decision

Margaret Cooper is director of the product research department at Aerojet-Specific Corporation. She manages the department's personnel in their duties in determining the level of pressure at which the firm's products fail. One piece of equipment is critical in these tests — a 250-ton high-speed hydraulic press. The press is now 15 years old, has been fully depreciated, and has a salvage value of $2,000. A new press is being considered that will reduce maintenance costs, reduce downtime, and increase the speed of the pressing operation. The new press falls into the 5-year IRS depreciation category and is expected to have an economic life of 5 years. It has a first cost of $200,000, an annual operating cost savings of $60,000, and a salvage value of $30,000.

The firm would use a discount rate of 10 percent and a tax rate of 40 percent. **a.** Use net present value to determine if Ms. Cooper should recommend buying the new press. **b.** Use the payback method to determine if Ms. Cooper should recommend buying the new press if management uses 4 years as the maximum after-tax payback period for similar investments.

Solution

a. Net present value of new press:

1. First, compute the tax savings from depreciation:

Year	IRS Depreciation Allowable	Annual Depreciation	Accumulated Depreciation	Tax Savings ($t \times$ Annual Depreciation)
1	15%	$30,000	$ 30,000	$12,000
2	22	44,000	74,000	17,600
3	21	42,000	116,000	16,800
4	21	42,000	158,000	16,800
5	21	42,000	200,000	16,800

2. Now, compute the NPV:

	Before-Tax Amount	After-Tax Amount	Year of Occurrence	Present-Value Factor	Present Value
Cash Outflow:					
First cost	($200,000)	($200,000)	0	1.000	($200,000)
Cash Inflows:					
Cost savings	60,000	36,000	1–5	$(p/a)_5^{10} = 3.791$	136,476
Depreciation tax					
savings	30,000	12,000	1	$(p/f)_1^{10} =$ .9091	10,909
	44,000	17,600	2	$(p/f)_2^{10} =$ .8264	14,545
	42,000	16,800	3	$(p/f)_3^{10} =$ .7513	12,622
	42,000	16,800	4	$(p/f)_4^{10} =$ .6830	11,474
	42,000	16,800	5	$(p/f)_5^{10} =$ .6209	10,431
Salvage value (new)	30,000	30,000	5	$(p/f)_5^{10} =$ .6209	18,627
Salvage value (old)	2,000	2,000	0	1.000	2,000
				NPV =	$ 17,084

Yes, the firm should buy the new press because a NPV of $17,084 means that the investment will return the 10 percent discount rate and still have a present value of cash inflows in excess of first cost.

b. Payback period:

Year	Depreciation Tax Savings	After-Tax Operating Cost Savings	First Cost less Salvage Value	Annual After-Tax Cash Flows	Accumulated After-Tax Cash Inflows
0	—	—	($168,000)	($168,000)	—
1	$12,000	$36,000	—	48,000	$ 48,000
2	17,600	36,000	—	53,600	101,600
3	16,800	36,000	—	52,800	154,400
4	16,800	36,000	—	52,800	207,200
5	16,800	36,000	—	52,800	260,000

The payback period is 3.3 years [3 + (168,000 − 154,400)/52,800], which is within management's maximum payback period for similar investments. The firm should therefore purchase the new press.

Example 4S.8

A Choice of Equipment Decision

Cal-Coop, a large agricultural corporation operating in the Imperial Valley of California, is now outfitting one of its divisions with tomato-harvesting equipment. Two designs are being considered: S, which is semiautomatic, and A, which is almost fully automatic. The two designs, both with equal capacities, exhibit the following costs:

	Design S	Design A
First cost	$400,000	$700,000
IRS life category	5-year	5-year
Estimated economic life	5 years	5 years
Labor cost per year	$85,000	$10,000
Annual maintenance and supplies	10,000	5,000
Salvage value	40,000	150,000

If Cal-Coop uses a standard 3½-year payback period for similar investments and its tax rate is 40 percent, use the payback period to choose between the two equipment designs. The payback period can be used only if we assume that one of the two designs will be selected. Then we must determine if the additional investment required for Design A can be justified on the basis of annual labor cost savings and annual maintenance and supplies cost savings.

Solution

1. Compute depreciation for both designs:

Design	Year	IRS Depreciation Allowable	Annual Depreciation	Accumulated Depreciation	Tax Savings ($t \times$ Annual Depreciation)
	1	15%	$60,000	$ 60,000	$24,000
	2	22	88,000	148,000	35,200
S	3	21	84,000	232,000	33,600
	4	21	84,000	316,000	33,600
	5	21	84,000	400,000	33,600
	1	15%	$105,000	$105,000	$42,000
	2	22	154,000	259,000	61,600
A	3	21	147,000	406,000	58,800
	4	21	147,000	553,000	58,800
	5	21	147,000	700,000	58,800

2. Next, compute the tax savings from depreciation of the additional first cost for Design A over Design B:

Year	Tax Savings, Design A	Tax Savings, Design S	Difference in Tax Savings of A over B
1	$42,000	$24,000	$18,000
2	61,600	35,200	26,400
3	58,800	33,600	25,200
4	58,800	33,600	25,200
5	58,800	33,600	25,200

3. Next, compute the payback period for the additional investment for Design A. The annual after-tax cost savings of the automatic design over the semiautomatic design and the additional first cost are:

$$\text{Annual cost savings} = (1 - t) \text{ (Annual operating cost savings)}$$
$$= (1 - .4)(\text{Labor savings} + \text{Maintenance and supplies savings})$$
$$= (.6)(\$75,000 + \$5,000) = .6(\$80,000) = \$48,000$$

$$\text{Additional first cost} = (\text{First cost less salvage value for A}) - (\text{First cost less salvage value for B})$$
$$= (700,000 - 150,000) - (400,000 - 40,000)$$
$$= (550,000) - (360,000) = \$190,000$$

Year	Depreciation Tax Savings	After-Tax Operating Cost Savings	Additional First Cost	Annual After-Tax Cash Flows	Accumulated After-Tax Cash Inflows
0	—	—	($190,000)	($190,000)	—
1	$18,000	$48,000	—	66,000	$ 66,000
2	26,400	48,000	—	74,400	140,400
3	25,200	48,000	—	73,200	213,600
4	25,200	48,000	—	73,200	286,800
5	25,200	48,000	—	73,200	360,000

The payback period is 2.7 years [2 + (190,000 − 140,400)/73,200]. The additional outlay for the automatic design is therefore within management's payback period guideline of 3½ years and Design A should be purchased.

Example 4S.9

A Make-or-Buy Decision

NIKO manufactures hand-held electronic calculators. When the firm was small and growing, it purchased most of the components that go into calculators from outside suppliers. Now that NIKO has grown to the point that funds for capital investment are available from profits, various investment opportunities are being investigated. One such opportunity involves establishing a production department for manufacturing electronic chips, a major component used in calculators and currently purchased from Florida Instruments. The present purchase price of chips is $4.25 per calculator. NIKO estimates that the department fully equipped will cost $1.5 million; the equipment falls into the 5-year IRS depreciation category; a 5-year economic life is expected; the variable cost, including labor, materials, and overhead, will total $3 per calculator; the salvage value of the equipment will be $300,000; and 500,000 calculators per year can be sold. If a tax rate of 40 percent and a discount rate of 10 percent are used: **a.** Use NPV to determine if NIKO should make or buy the chips. **b.** Use the payback period after taxes to determine if NIKO should make or buy the chips if management uses a 3-year maximum payback period for similar investments.

Solution

a. Compute the NPV:

1. First, compute the tax savings from depreciation:

Year	IRS Depreciation Allowable	Annual Depreciation	Accumulated Depreciation	Tax Savings ($t \times$ Annual Depreciation)
1	15%	$225,000	$ 225,000	$ 90,000
2	22	330,000	555,000	132,000
3	21	315,000	870,000	126,000
4	21	315,000	1,185,000	126,000
5	21	315,000	1,500,000	126,000

2. Compute the NPV:

	Before-Tax Amount	After-Tax Amount	Year of Occurrence	Present-Value Factor	Present Value
Cash outflow:					
First cost	($1,500,000)	($1,500,000)	0	1.000	($1,500,000)
Cash inflows:					
Cost savings					
($1.25/unit)	625,000	375,000	1–5	$(p/a)_5^{10} = 3.791$	1,421,625
Depreciation tax					
savings	225,000	90,000	1	$(p/f)_1^{10} = .9091$	81,819
	330,000	132,000	2	$(p/f)_2^{10} = .8264$	109,085
	315,000	126,000	3	$(p/f)_3^{10} = .7513$	94,664
	315,000	126,000	4	$(p/f)_4^{10} = .6830$	86,058
	315,000	126,000	5	$(p/f)_5^{10} = .6209$	78,233
Salvage value	300,000	300,000	5	$(p/f)_5^{10} = .6209$	186,270
				NPV =	$557,754

A NPV of $557,754 indicates that making the chips returns the 10 percent discount rate and $557,754 over the first cost. NIKO therefore should make the chips.

b. Payback period:

Year	Depreciation Tax Savings	After-Tax Operating Cost Savings	Additional First Cost	Annual After-Tax Cash Flow	Accumulated After-Tax Cash Inflows
			($1,200,000)	($1,200,000)	——
1	$ 90,000	$375,000	——	465,000	$ 465,000
2	132,000	375,000	——	507,000	972,000
3	126,000	375,000	——	501,000	1,473,000
4	126,000	375,000	——	501,000	1,974,000
5	126,000	375,000	——	501,000	2,475,000

The payback period is 2.5 years [2 +(1,200,000 − 972,000)/501,000]. The project is therefore within management's maximum payback period of 3 years for similar investments.

The NPV and payback period both confirm that the chips should be made rather than bought.

Note that in these examples when changes in operating expenses are converted from pretax to after-tax amounts a $(1 - t)$ factor is used. Let's use an example to demonstrate when $t = .4$:

	Situation A	Situation B
Pretax profits	$100,000	$100,000
Operating expenses	——	10,000
Taxable profits	$100,000	$ 90,000
Taxes	40,000	36,000
After-tax profits	$ 60,000	$ 54,000
After-tax impact of operating expenses		(6,000)

These two situations (A and B) are identical except that Situation A does not have the $10,000 in operating expenses. How do their after-tax profits differ? They differ by $6,000, which equals $(1 - t) \times$ pretax operating expenses, or $(.6) \times \$10,000$. Anytime you encounter operating expenses or operating expense savings in financial analysis, these are converted to after-tax amounts by multiplying them by $(1 - t)$. Depreciation, on the other hand, has been demonstrated to use t as the factor for converting pretax depreciation to after-tax savings.

The classic investment decisions demonstrated in these examples are realistic decisions that are made periodically in POM. These decisions are important for many reasons but particularly because they are long-lasting. How a company spends its investment dollars determines in large part its future course in terms of productive capacity, diversification, expansion, and other elements of operations strategy. Wrong investment decisions in POM must be lived with for a long time by managers. Good investment decisions generate improved profits well into the future. The longevity of these decisions and a continuing condition of scarce and expensive capital funds cause companies today to scrutinize these decisions closely. The analysis methods presented in this chapter can serve you well in analyzing and justifying capital funds outlays in POM.

Compound Interest Tables

			(5%)			
	TO FIND F, GIVEN P: $(1 + i)^n$	TO FIND P, GIVEN F: $\dfrac{1}{(1 + i)^n}$	TO FIND A, GIVEN F: $\dfrac{i}{(1 + i)^n - 1}$	TO FIND A, GIVEN P: $\dfrac{i(1 + i)^n}{(1 + i)^n - 1}$	TO FIND F, GIVEN A: $\dfrac{(1 + i)^n - 1}{i}$	TO FIND P, GIVEN A: $\dfrac{(1 + i)^n - 1}{i(1 + i)^n}$
n	$(f/p)_n^5$	$(p/f)_n^5$	$(a/f)_n^5$	$(a/p)_n^5$	$(f/a)_n^5$	$(p/a)_n^5$
1	1.050	0.9524	1.00000	1.05000	1.000	0.952
2	1.102	0.9070	0.48780	0.53780	2.050	1.859
3	1.158	0.8638	0.31721	0.36721	3.152	2.723
4	1.216	0.8227	0.23201	0.28201	4.310	3.546
5	1.276	0.7835	0.18097	0.23097	5.526	4.329
6	1.340	0.7462	0.14702	0.19702	6.802	5.076
7	1.407	0.7107	0.12282	0.17282	8.142	5.786
8	1.477	0.6768	0.10472	0.15472	9.549	6.463
9	1.551	0.6446	0.09069	0.14069	11.027	7.108
10	1.629	0.6139	0.07950	0.12950	12.578	7.722
11	1.710	0.5847	0.07039	0.12039	14.207	8.306
12	1.796	0.5568	0.06283	0.11283	15.917	8.863
13	1.886	0.5303	0.05646	0.10646	17.713	9.394
14	1.980	0.5051	0.05102	0.10102	19.599	9.899
15	2.079	0.4810	0.04634	0.09634	21.579	10.380
16	2.183	0.4581	0.04227	0.09227	23.657	10.838
17	2.292	0.4363	0.03870	0.08870	25.840	11.274
18	2.407	0.4155	0.03555	0.08555	28.132	11.690
19	2.527	0.3957	0.03275	0.08275	30.539	12.085
20	2.653	0.3769	0.03024	0.08024	33.066	12.462

			(10%)			
	TO FIND F, GIVEN P: $(1 + i)^n$	TO FIND P, GIVEN F: $\dfrac{1}{(1 + i)^n}$	TO FIND A, GIVEN F: $\dfrac{i}{(1 + i)^n - 1}$	TO FIND A, GIVEN P: $\dfrac{i(1 + i)^n}{(1 + i)^n - 1}$	TO FIND F, GIVEN A: $\dfrac{(1 + i)^n - 1}{i}$	TO FIND P, GIVEN A: $\dfrac{(1 + i)^n - 1}{i(1 + i)^n}$
n	$(f/p)_n^{10}$	$(p/f)_n^{10}$	$(a/f)_n^{10}$	$(a/p)_n^{10}$	$(f/a)_n^{10}$	$(p/a)_n^{10}$
1	1.100	0.9091	1.00000	1.10000	1.000	0.909
2	1.210	0.8264	0.47619	0.57619	2.100	1.736
3	1.331	0.7513	0.30211	0.40211	3.310	2.487
4	1.464	0.6830	0.21547	0.31547	4.641	3.170
5	1.611	0.6209	0.16380	0.26380	6.105	3.791
6	1.772	0.5645	0.12961	0.22961	7.716	4.355
7	1.949	0.5132	0.10541	0.20541	9.487	4.868
8	2.144	0.4665	0.08744	0.18744	11.436	5.335
9	2.358	0.4241	0.07364	0.17364	13.579	5.759
10	2.594	0.3855	0.06275	0.16275	15.937	6.145
11	2.853	0.3505	0.05396	0.15396	18.531	6.495
12	3.138	0.3186	0.04676	0.14676	21.384	6.814
13	3.452	0.2897	0.04078	0.14078	24.523	7.103
14	3.797	0.2633	0.03575	0.13575	27.975	7.367
15	4.177	0.2394	0.03147	0.13147	31.772	7.606
16	4.595	0.2176	0.02782	0.12782	35.950	7.824
17	5.054	0.1978	0.02466	0.12466	40.545	8.022
18	5.560	0.1799	0.02193	0.12193	45.599	8.201
19	6.116	0.1635	0.01955	0.11955	51.159	8.365
20	6.727	0.1486	0.01746	0.11746	57.275	8.514

Compound Interest Tables (continued)

	TO FIND F, GIVEN P: $(1 + i)^n$	TO FIND P, GIVEN F: $\dfrac{1}{(1 + i)^n}$	TO FIND A, GIVEN F: $\dfrac{i}{(1 + i)^n - 1}$	TO FIND A, GIVEN P: $\dfrac{i(1 + i)^n}{(1 + i)^n - 1}$	TO FIND F, GIVEN A: $\dfrac{(1 + i)^n - 1}{i}$	TO FIND P, GIVEN A: $\dfrac{(1 + i)^n - 1}{i(1 + i)^n}$
				(15%)		
n	$(f/p)_n^{15}$	$(p/f)_n^{15}$	$(a/f)_n^{15}$	$(a/p)_n^{15}$	$(f/a)_n^{15}$	$(p/a)_n^{15}$
1	1.150	0.8696	1.00000	1.15000	1.000	0.870
2	1.322	0.7561	0.46512	0.61512	2.150	1.626
3	1.521	0.6575	0.28798	0.43798	3.472	2.283
4	1.749	0.5718	0.20027	0.35027	4.993	2.855
5	2.011	0.4972	0.14832	0.29832	6.742	3.352
6	2.313	0.4323	0.11424	0.26424	8.754	3.784
7	2.660	0.3759	0.09036	0.24036	11.067	4.160
8	3.059	0.3269	0.07285	0.22285	13.727	4.487
9	3.518	0.2843	0.05957	0.20957	16.786	4.772
10	4.046	0.2472	0.04925	0.19925	20.304	5.019
11	4.652	0.2149	0.04107	0.19107	24.349	5.234
12	5.350	0.1869	0.03448	0.18448	29.002	5.421
13	6.153	0.1625	0.02911	0.17911	34.352	5.583
14	7.076	0.1413	0.02469	0.17469	40.505	5.724
15	8.137	0.1229	0.02102	0.17102	47.580	5.847
16	9.358	0.1069	0.01795	0.16795	55.717	5.954
17	10.761	0.0929	0.01537	0.16537	65.075	6.047
18	12.375	0.0808	0.01319	0.16319	75.836	6.128
19	14.232	0.0703	0.01134	0.16134	88.212	6.198
20	16.367	0.0611	0.00976	0.15976	102.444	6.259

	TO FIND F, GIVEN P: $(1 + i)^n$	TO FIND P, GIVEN F: $\dfrac{1}{(1 + i)^n}$	TO FIND A, GIVEN F: $\dfrac{i}{(1 + i)^n - 1}$	TO FIND A, GIVEN P: $\dfrac{i(1 + i)^n}{(1 + i)^n - 1}$	TO FIND F, GIVEN A: $\dfrac{(1 + i)^n - 1}{i}$	TO FIND P, GIVEN A: $\dfrac{(1 + i)^n - 1}{i(1 + i)^n}$
				(20%)		
n	$(f/p)_n^{20}$	$(p/f)_n^{20}$	$(a/f)_n^{20}$	$(a/p)_n^{20}$	$(f/a)_n^{20}$	$(p/a)_n^{20}$
1	1.200	0.8333	1.00000	1.20000	1.000	0.833
2	1.440	0.6944	0.45455	0.65455	2.200	1.528
3	1.728	0.5787	0.27473	0.47473	3.640	2.106
4	2.074	0.4823	0.18629	0.38629	5.368	2.589
5	2.488	0.4019	0.13438	0.33438	7.442	2.991
6	2.986	0.3349	0.10071	0.30071	9.930	3.326
7	3.583	0.2791	0.07742	0.27742	12.916	3.605
8	4.300	0.2326	0.06061	0.26061	16.499	3.837
9	5.160	0.1938	0.04808	0.24808	20.799	4.031
10	6.192	0.1615	0.03852	0.23852	25.959	4.192
11	7.430	0.1346	0.03110	0.23110	32.150	4.327
12	8.916	0.1122	0.02526	0.22526	39.581	4.439
13	10.699	0.0935	0.02062	0.22062	48.497	4.533
14	12.839	0.0779	0.01689	0.21689	59.196	4.611
15	15.407	0.0649	0.01388	0.21388	72.035	4.675
16	18.488	0.0541	0.01144	0.21144	87.442	4.730
17	22.186	0.0451	0.00944	0.20944	105.931	4.775
18	26.623	0.0376	0.00781	0.20781	128.117	4.812
19	31.948	0.0313	0.00646	0.20646	154.740	4.843
20	38.338	0.0261	0.00536	0.20536	186.688	4.870

Review and Discussion Questions

1. Define *capital goods*. Give five examples of capital goods in POM.

2. Define the following terms: *depreciation, salvage value, first cost, taxes, operating expenses.*

3. Define the following terms: *compound interest rate, cutoff rate.*

4. Why is depreciation a noncash expense?

5. Does depreciation directly affect profits? Why or why not?

6. Define the following terms: *annuity, discount rate, future value, compounding, discounting, present value.*

7. Name the advantages and disadvantages of these financial analysis methods: **a.** payback period, **b.** net present value (NPV).

8. What disadvantages of the payback method does NPV overcome?

9. What disadvantages of NPV does PI overcome?

10. Under what conditions should the NPV not be used?

11. Under what conditions should the PI not be used?

Problems

Depreciation

1. Design Corporation is an engineering service company servicing the greater Phoenix area construction contractors with structural testing. A new core failure machine has been purchased for $75,000. The new machine falls in the 5-year IRS depreciation category. The machine is expected to have a salvage value of $10,000 at the end of 5 years. If the firm is in the 30 percent tax bracket, what are the annual tax savings from depreciation of the machine?

2. The purchasing department of Expando Corporation, a company that produces highway bridge expandable joints, has just purchased a new minicomputer for instantaneously accessing inventory records. The computer costs $25,000, it is expected to have a salvage value of $5,000 at the end of its 5-year economic life, and it falls into the 5-year IRS depreciation category. What are the annual depreciation charges over its economic life?

3. The maintenance shop at the Bilt-Rite garment factory needs a new welding machine. A new one costs $1,750 and falls into the 5-year IRS depreciation category. If the machine is expected to have a salvage value of $50 at the end of 5 years and the firm's tax rate is 45 percent, what are the annual tax savings from depreciation of the welding machine?

4. The Speed-Flyte Corporation conducts air tunnel tests for aircraft and other airborne products. A new test facility is proposed that will cost $400,000 and will have a salvage value of $70,000 at the end of 3 years. What are the annual depreciation charges if the facility falls into the 3-year IRS depreciation category?

5. The Jones Arms Company is proposing to build a new building for manufacturing clay pigeons. The building is planned for completion in January, will have a first cost of $500,000, and will have a salvage value of $50,000 at the end of its economic life. What are the annual depreciation charges if the firm's tax rate is 45 percent?

Compound Interest

6. What is the future value of these sums? **a.** Present value = $5,000, in 5 years at 10 percent compounded annually. **b.** Five annuities of $500 paid in at the end of each year at 5 percent compounded annually at the end of 5 years. **c.** Six annuities of $1,000 paid in at the end of each year at 20 percent compounded annually at the end of 6 years.

7. What is the present value of these sums? **a.** Future value = $1,000 in 5 years at 10 percent compounded annually. **b.** Five annuities of $1,000 paid in at the end of each year at 5 percent compounded annually. **c.** Six annuities of $1,000 paid in at the beginning of each year at 20 percent compounded annually.

8. What single payment 10 years from now is equivalent to a $10,000 payment 2 years from now, if the discount rate is 15 percent compounded annually?

9. What five annuities beginning today are equivalent to two payments of $10,000, one made at the end of 2 years and the other one at the end of 4 years, if the discount rate is 10 percent compounded annually?

Financial Analysis Decisions

10. The OK Trucking Company has a fleet of over-the-road trucks operating in southeastern Oklahoma. The fleet was purchased new 10 years ago and is obsolete and badly deteriorated. OK estimates that a new fleet would cost $800,000 and would save $200,000 per year in operating and maintenance expenses. If taxes are ignored, the old fleet has zero salvage value, the fleet falls into the IRS 5-year depreciation category, and the new fleet is expected to have a salvage value of $150,000 at the end of 5 years, what is the payback period of the new fleet?

11. Bill Binton operates a small manufacturing company in Detroit. His firm manufactures side-view mirrors for one of the major auto manufacturers. He presently buys the bolts that are used to assemble the mirrors, but he wonders if he should make them since this business is expected to remain strong. He uses ten million bolts per year at a price of $.01 each. He can buy, install, and debug a machine for $25,000. The machine will have an economic life of 5 years and a salvage value of $5000, and will fall into the IRS 5-year depreciation category. Bill estimates that labor, material, and overhead would cost about $.009 per bolt. He will buy the machine only if it pays itself out in savings after taxes in 3½ years or less at a tax rate of 30 percent. Use payback period after taxes to recommend whether the bolts should be purchased or manufactured.

12. The Geotherm Research Corporation located in Jakes Pass, Idaho performs geothermal energy conversion research on federal and state contracts. The firm is experiencing a substantial growth and wishes to replace its old experimental machines with new ones. The new machinery will cost $500,000 and will improve operating efficiency by $100,000 per year. If Geotherm has a tax rate of 45 percent, the machinery falls into the 3-year IRS depreciation category, a 10 percent cutoff rate is used, an economic life of 5 years is expected, and the old machinery and new machinery is expected to have a salvage value of zero, use NPV to recommend if the new machinery should be purchased.

13. The Riskway Grocery Corporation is considering building a new retail grocery store in Denton, Texas. The present store is inefficient to operate, is fully depreciated, has limited parking, and is not attractive in appearance. A new store at a nearby location will cost $1,750,000 to build, will have an expected salvage value in 15 years of

$200,000, falls into the 15-year IRS depreciation category, and will have improved profits due to increased revenues and decreased operating expenses of $250,000 per year. If Riskway has a tax rate of 40 percent, the salvage value of the old store is $100,000, and the discount rate is 10 percent compounded annually, use NPV to recommend if the new store should be built.

14. The Cloud Kist Almond Wholesaling Company of Morgan Hill, California warehouses enormous quantities of almonds and sells them to retailers. The company is building a new warehouse facility and some disagreement has arisen concerning what type of forklift trucks to buy for the facility. Two designs appear to be the least costly to operate: electric and propane. The trucks have these characteristics:

	Electric	Propane
First cost	$14,500	$7,800
Economic life	8 years	8 years
IRS depreciation category	5 years	5 years
Salvage value	$1,000	$2,000
Annual fuel cost	300	2,500
Annual maintenance cost	1,500	200

If the discount rate is 15 percent, the tax rate is 40 percent, and NPV is used, recommend which forklift design Cloud Kist should purchase.

15. Debits Inc., a CPA firm, is about to buy a computer. Management is torn between two designs, each with unique costs and savings:

	Computer Y	Computer Z
First cost	$50,000	$75,000
Economic life	5 years	5 years
IRS depreciation category	5 years	5 years
Salvage value	$ 5,000	$10,000
Annual operating cost	12,000	14,000
Annual savings through increased efficiency	15,000	20,000

Use after-tax payback period to recommend which computer should be purchased if the company's tax rate is 35 percent and if the maximum payback period allowed is 5 years.

16. The Quikut Lawn Mower Company of Grassy Knoll, Indiana manufactures lawn mowers that are sold to several large merchandisers. The firm buys the drive assembly unit from another large manufacturer in Chicago for $7.49 each. Recently management at Quikut has wondered if it would be a good investment to bring this drive assembly unit in-house and make it themselves. A new building for the manufacture of these units would have these characteristics: a first cost of $300,000 with an economic life of 15 years beginning in January, zero salvage value, and a 15-year IRS depreciation category. The building can be used for other products beyond the economic life of the machinery and equipment. Machinery and equipment would have a first cost of $450,000, an economic life of 5 years, a salvage value of $40,000, and a 5-year IRS depreciation category. Quikut figures that labor, material, and overhead will cost about $5.90 per unit and that 200,000 units per year will be needed for at least 5 years. If a 15 percent discount rate compounded annually, a tax rate of 40 percent, and NPV are used, should Quikut make or buy the unit?

17. The electronic maintenance and calibration department at Whatsamattayou Hospital in Glen Falls, New York is trying to decide which design of electronic diagnostic
unit to purchase. Two designs, A and B, appear to have about the same performance
features, but their unique designs result in different costs:

	Design A	Design B
First cost	$50,000	$25,000
Economic life	5 years	5 years
IRS depreciation category	5 years	5 years
Salvage value	0	0
Annual operating cost savings	$30,000	$14,000

If the tax rate is 45 percent and the discount rate is 20 percent, use PI to determine
which design should be purchased.

Selected Bibliography

Anthony, Robert N., and Glen A. Welsch. *Fundamentals of Management Accounting.*
Homewood, IL: Richard D. Irwin, 1974.

Grant, E. L., and W. G. Ireson. *Principles of Engineering Economy.* New York: Ronald
Press, 1960.

Thuesen, H. G., and W. J. Fabrycky. *Engineering Economy.* Englewood Cliffs, NJ: Prentice-Hall, 1964.

Van Horne, James C. *Financial Management and Policy.* Englewood Cliffs, NJ: Prentice-
Hall, 1974.

Weston, J. Fred, and Eugene F. Brigham. *Essentials of Managerial Finance.* New York:
Holt, Rinehart, & Winston, 1977.

Chapter Outline

Introduction

Scarce POM Resources
Constrained POM Decisions
Linear Programming (LP) in POM

Recognizing LP Problems

LP Applications in POM
Characteristics of LP Problems in POM
LP-1, a Maximization LP Problem
LP-2, a Minimization LP Problem

Formulating LP Problems

Steps in Setting Up LP Problems
Formulating LP-1
Formulating LP-2
Guidelines for Formulating LP Problems

Solving LP Problems

Graphical LP Solutions
Simplex Method LP Solutions
Transportation Method LP Solutions
Assignment Method LP Solutions

Real LP Problems in POM

Characteristics of Real LP Problems
Case 5.1: Oklahoma Crude Oil Company

Summary

Review and Discussion Questions

Problems

Case: Sunshine Tomato Soup Shippers

Selected Bibliography

5

Allocating Scarce Resources in POM:

Constrained Decisions in Operations Strategy

A management system is a process of people interacting to apply resources to achieve goals.
M. Scott Myers, 1971

Scarcity is a fact of life. There just are not enough resources to go around to satisfy all of our wants. Paul Samuelson, the noted author and economist, defines economic scarcity as:

The basic fact of life is that there exists only a finite amount of human and nonhuman resources, which the best technical knowledge is capable of using to produce only a limited maximum amount of each and every good. And thus far, nowhere on the globe is the supply of goods so plentiful or the tastes of the populace so limited that every person can have more than enough of everything he might fancy.[1]

Operations managers are acutely aware of the scarcity of the resources used to generate products and services of productive systems: personnel, machines and equipment, cash and capital funds, materials and supplies, utilities, floor space, and other resources. There never seems to be enough of these means of production to do all that managers wish to accomplish.

Managers work toward organizational goals, as M. Scott Myers states in the opening quote of this chapter.[2] The means of achieving these organizational goals is

---

[1] Paul A. Samuelson, *Economics: An Introductory Analysis* (New York: McGraw-Hill, 1967), 21.

[2] M. Scott Myers, ''The Human Factor in Management Systems,'' *Journal of Systems Management* (November 1971), 13.

resources. The limited availability of POM resources today results, in some cases, in the "tail wagging the dog," the scarcity of resources affecting the ultimate degree of objective achievement. In other words, the ultimate success of organizations (objective achievement) is determined in large measure by the availability of resources.

The availability of resources in POM was not always so critical to managers as it is today. Shortly after World War II production was assumed to be automatic. Marketers developed new markets, new products were designed, and the productive system was expected to generate the products and services that the customers demanded with a minimum amount of deviation from delivery schedules, quality standards, and cost standards. These expectations were generally realized because of the abundance of resources then available to productive systems. This resource availability resulted in part from the highly developed wartime work force, materials and supply stockpiles, and excess postwar productive capacity.

Conditions have changed today. Suppliers of materials do not necessarily beat a path to the door of productive systems. The dominant question in some cases has become: Can we get the quantity of materials when we need them? It used to be: Which supplier has the best price? Similarly, the delivery times on machine tools such as lathes, boring mills, and other metalworking equipment are well over one year. There is growing competition for top human resource talent, from managers to hourly workers. Some geographical areas appear to be saturated with people looking for jobs, but in most areas employers will tell you that there is a shortage of qualified personnel at all levels. The shortage of energy (natural gas, electricity, gasoline, and other fuels) is an ever-present and growing concern to all types of productive systems. Shortages of water in some states sometimes curtail productive system output.

These and other resource scarcities can cause hectic shifts in operations strategies to meet objectives; additionally, resource prices are skyrocketing. The limited quantity of resources available and their high prices act as a double-barreled incentive to use them to the greatest advantage in achieving organizational objectives. Today, perhaps more than ever before, operations managers understand that operations strategies must be set and objectives must be achieved within constraints imposed upon their organizations.

Today's business profits are limited by the set of prevailing constraints. As Figure 5.1 shows, a business can achieve profits only to the degree that the firm's constraints allow — the amount of products and services demanded by the market and the availability of productive systems' resources such as personnel, materials and supplies, cash, and utilities.

There are five classic types of constrained decision problems commonly found in POM: product mix, ingredient mix, transportation, time period, and assignment. Table 5.1 describes each of these problem types by posing three questions about each: What is the single management objective? What information do we need to know to achieve our objective? And what factors restrain us from achieving our objective?

The first question concerns our objective: What are we trying to accomplish? We may want to maximize profits, maximize contribution (profits plus fixed costs), minimize costs, maximize the number of souls saved, maximize the weight gain in hogs, or any other conceivable organizational objective. Although most POM decisions in business will seek to maximize profits (or contribution) or minimize costs,

Figure 5.1
The Profits/Constraints Dynamic Balance

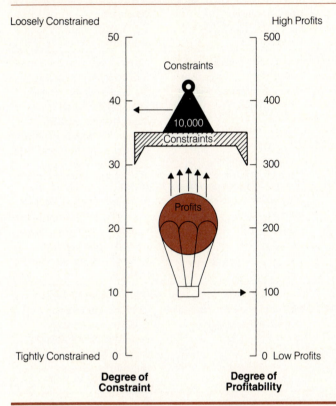

Loosely Constrained

High Profits

Tightly Constrained

Low Profits

**Degree of
Constraint**

**Degree of
Profitability**

the special nature of particular organizations makes other objectives important. For example, a governmental organization may wish to maximize the total daily calorie intake of school age children, maximize the total annual tonnage yield of king crab from Alaskan waters, or minimize the total days of schedule delinquency over the life of a large construction project.

The second question posed in Table 5.1 concerns what we need to know to make an optimal decision, one that best achieves our objective within the framework of our constraints. This information (values of our decision variables) allows us to choose courses of action for our constrained decision problems.

The final question in Table 5.1 concerns the constraints of our decisions. Understanding what factors restrain us from maximizing profits, for example, is basic to effective decisions. These constraints define the ball park within which our ultimate decisions must fall. The ball park typically is large, and a large number of potential decisions are possible. The trick is to select the decision that best achieves our

Table 5.1
Five Common Constrained Decisions in POM — Typical Features

Decision Type	Objective (What Is the Single Management Objective?)	Decision Variables (What Information Do We Need to Know to Achieve Our Objective?)	Constraints (What Factors Restrain Us from Achieving Our Objective?)
1. Product mix	To select the mix of products or services that results in maximum profits for the planning period.	How much to produce and market of each product or service for the planning period.	*Market* — the maximum amount of each product or service demanded and the minimum amount policy will allow. *Capacity* — the maximum amount of resources available (personnel, materials, machines, utilities, cash, floor space).
2. Ingredient mix	To select the mix of ingredients going into final products that results in minimum operating costs for the planning period.	How much of each raw material or ingredient to use in the planning period.	*Market* — the amount of final products demanded. *Technology* — the relationship between ingredients and final products. *Capacity* — the maximum amount of ingredient processing available.
3. Transportation	To select the distribution plan from sources to destinations that results in minimum shipping costs for the planning period.	How much product to ship from each source to each destination for the planning period.	*Destination requirements* — the minimum or exact amount of products required at each destination. *Source capacity* — the exact or maximum amount of products available at each source.
4. Time period	To select the amount of products or services to be produced on both straight time and overtime labor during each month of the year to minimize costs of labor and carrying inventory.	How much to produce on straight time labor and overtime labor during each month of the year.	*Market* — the amount of products demanded in each month. *Capacity* — the maximum amount of products that can be produced with straight time and overtime labor in each month. *Inventory space* — the maximum storage capacity in each month.
5. Assignment	To assign personnel to jobs so that the total labor cost for all jobs is minimized during the planning period.	Which job each person is assigned to.	Each job must be assigned to a person, and each person must be assigned to a job.

objectives within the limits set by the constraints. Although most POM business constraints involve either market demand limitations or productive capacity limitations caused by resource scarcity, constraints are by no means limited to these two areas. Governmental regulations, quality requirements, technological relationship requirements, and a host of other types of constraints are possible. Governmental and nonprofit organizational decisions usually involve constraints similar to those of business except that market demand typically is described as constituent demand.

When very simple organizational problems arise where objective achievement is constrained by limited resources and other restrictions, managers can respond in a variety of ways. One way is to ignore the constraints and worry about them later. This tactic usually is effective when resources can be substituted for one another without too much impact on costs. In more complex problems, however, management cannot ignore the constraints because the outcome to the problem is not straightforward and obvious; therefore, new forms of analysis have evolved to take into account these constraints in decision making.

Read the five types of constrained POM decisions of operations managers in Table 5.1. Read the objective first, then the decision variables, and finally the constraints for each type of decision. Visualize how managers analyze these problems when they involve numerous constraints; large quantities of data; many products, services, warehouses, designs, time periods, and other decision elements; numerous decision alternatives; and other complications.

The complexity of these and other constrained POM decisions prompted the development of a whole family of new analysis techniques to assist managers in choosing among decision alternatives. This family of techniques generally falls under the title of *mathematical programming* and includes such tools as linear programming, nonlinear programming, stochastic programming, and integer programming. Among these mathematical programming techniques, linear programming (LP) stands out in its frequency of use across a variety of organizations.

LP is a powerful tool in POM — powerful because of the variety of uses to which it is put by managers. Table 5.2 shows the diversity of operational problems in POM to which LP is being successfully applied. Other operations research techniques such

---

Table 5.2
POM Applications of Linear Programming (LP)

POM Applications	Percent of LP Applications
1. Production planning and control	15
2. Product mix	11
3. Location and logistics	11
4. Capacity allocation	11
5. Assignment of personnel to jobs	10
6. Capital investment analysis	8
7. Inventory analysis	7
8. Materials allocation	7
9. Ingredient blending	7
10. Facility, equipment, and methods design	5
11. Other	8
Total	100

Source: Norman Gaither, "The Adoption of Operations Research Techniques by Manufacturing Organizations," *Decision Sciences* 6 (October 1975): 809. Reprinted by permission of the American Institute of Decision Sciences.

as PERT/CPM, computer simulation, and queuing theory that will be covered in other chapters of this book cannot claim the great breadth of application that LP enjoys.

Much of this chapter is about LP: recognizing LP problems, formulating LP problems, solving LP problems, and interpreting LP solutions (what do you have after you are finished?). Devoting an entire chapter to one analytical technique may seem a travesty unless you have actually been in POM decision situations. The ability to think in terms of optimizing an objective within a set of constraints in real POM decision situations will definitely set you apart as a competent analyst. This *thinking* is at the heart of linear programming. And besides, there are occasions when LP can be applied to POM decisions to achieve substantial increases in profits. LP can therefore be a valuable technique for analyzing POM decisions and for assisting you in developing good decision-making thinking processes.

The first step is recognizing problems that are appropriate for LP solutions.

Recognizing LP Problems

This section is perhaps the most important part of this chapter. Even if you completely master LP solutions and interpretation of the final results that will soon follow, if you cannot recognize LP problems when they occur, what have you accomplished? Being able to recognize problems for which LP solutions are appropriate is fundamental—the very least that you should master and retain from this chapter.

What are the characteristics of problems suitable for LP solutions? Table 5.3 outlines briefly the five basic problem characteristics. When *all* of these requirements are met, LP can be a suitable tool of analysis. Read these problem features carefully and note that if any one of these characteristics is missing from a POM problem situation, LP should not be used.

Examples 5.1 and 5.2 are examples of LP problems in POM. Follow through these examples carefully and see if you can recognize the objective, the range of alternatives available to POM, and the nature of the constraints (the first three characteristics of LP problems). Don't worry about the mathematical requirements just yet.

Table 5.3
Characteristics of LP Problems in POM

1. A well-defined single objective must be stated.
2. There must be alternative courses of action.
3. The total achievement of the objective must be constrained by scarce resources or other restraints.
4. The objective and each of the constraints must be expressed as mathematical functions. The variables in these functions must be interrelated so that they are mathematically compatible.
5. The objective and constraint functions must be linear (first-degree mathematical expressions, all variable exponents equal to one with no cross products of variables; e.g., xy or zy).*

* Maximizing profits is typically stated as the objective in business LP problems. Profit functions are not usually linear functions, but contribution functions are. Therefore, although we tend to use the term *maximize profits*, we ordinarily mean *maximize contribution*, which is *profits plus fixed costs*.

Example 5.1

LP-1: Problem Recognition

The Precision Engineering Service Company uses both engineers and technicians to work on design projects for its customers. Engineers cost more per hour, but they require less supervision and less secretarial assistance than technicians. Engineers cost $10 per hour and technicians $5 per hour. Each hour of engineering time requires ¼ hour of supervision and ¾ hour of secretarial assistance. Each hour of technician time requires ½ hour of supervision and 1 hour of secretarial assistance. The company bid and won a large design project several months ago and now must determine how many engineering and technician hours to use on the project. It bid a total labor cost of $10,000, and management will not tolerate labor cost overruns because of a severe cash shortage. Underruns, however, are acceptable. A maximum of 600 hours of supervision and 1,500 hours of secretarial assistance is available for this project because of demands for supervision and secretarial assistance from other projects. If Precision charges its customer hourly rates when labor is used so that each hour of technician time yields $4 in profit and each hour of engineering time yields $3 in profit, how many hours of engineering and technician time should be allocated to the project?

1. Is there a single managerial objective?
   Yes. To maximize profits on the engineering design project.

2. Are there alternative courses of managerial action?
   Yes. Management can use either all engineering hours or all technician hours at the extremes or several intermediate mixes of engineering and technician hours between the extremes.

3. Is the total achievement of the objective constrained by scarce resources or other restraints? If so, what is the nature of the constraints?
   Yes. Profits are constrained downward by the total maximum amount of supervision and secretarial hours available and the maximum amount of cash available for labor costs.

Disregarding the mathematical requirements of an LP problem, this example is the type appropriate for LP solutions.

Example 5.2

LP-2: Problem Recognition

The Pour-More Foundry buys scrap metal from two sources, A and B. The scrap is melted down, and lead and copper are extracted and used in the foundry processes. Each railroad car of scrap from Source A yields 1 ton of copper and 1 ton of lead and costs $1,000 per car. Each railroad car of scrap from Source B costs $1,500 per car and yields 2 tons of lead and 1 ton of copper. If the foundry needs at least 4 tons of lead and 2.5 tons of copper per month, how many railroad cars of scrap should be purchased from Sources A and B per month?

1. Is there a single managerial objective?
   Yes. Although the objective is not explicitly stated, management wishes to minimize the monthly costs for the scrap metal from which lead and copper are extracted.

2. Are there alternative courses of managerial action?

Yes. Management can buy all of its scrap from either Source A or Source B at the extreme, or a wide range of mixes of railroad carloads from both A and B.

3. Is the total achievement of the objective constrained by scarce resources or other restraints? If so, what is the nature of the constraints?

Yes. Monthly costs are constrained upward by the minimum amount of lead and copper that must be purchased monthly.

Disregarding the mathematical requirements of an LP problem, this example is the type appropriate for LP solutions.

Once we have the feel of what an LP problem is and is not, the next step is formulating (setting up) the problem in the LP format. After we have gained experience in formulating LP problems, we will have actually reinforced our ability to recognize real world LP problems, because an intimate knowledge of the structure of LP helps us identify LP characteristics in real operational problems.

Formulating LP Problems

Although both recognition and formulation of LP problems tend to become intuitive after we gain experience, in the beginning a method to follow helps us to formulate them more effectively. Table 5.4 lists the steps to follow in formulating LP problems. These steps structure problems in a way that helps us better understand the problems we are dealing with. Additionally, the problems are then in a form necessary for LP solutions.

Example 5.3 follows the LP formulating steps and sets up Problem LP-1, which was discussed earlier. Read LP-1 carefully again and reassure yourself that it is in fact an LP problem. Follow through the example carefully to make sure that you understand the procedures for setting up LP problems. Figure 5.2 shows how the steps in formulating LP problems are placed in Problem LP-1.

Table 5.4
Steps in Setting Up LP Problems

1. Define the objective.
2. Define the decision variables.
3. Write the mathematical function for the objective (objective function).
4. Write a one- or two-word description of each constraint.
5. Write the right-hand side (RHS) of each constraint, including the units of measure.
6. Write =, ≤, or ≥ for each constraint.
7. Write in all of the decision variables on the left-hand side of each constraint.
8. Write the coefficient for each decision variable in each constraint.

Example 5.3

Formulating LP-1

We set up Problem LP-1:

1. **Define the objective.** Precision Engineering seeks to maximize profits. The problem is therefore a maximization problem.

2. **Define the decision variables.** What information does Precision Engineering need to know to maximize profits? The company needs to know how many engineer and technician hours to use on the design project. Therefore, let

   X_1 = number of engineering hours to be used on the project
   X_2 = number of technician hours to be used on the project

   X_1 and X_2 are the decision variables. When we know their values, the problem will be solved.

3. **Write the mathematical objective function.** Let Z equal the profits. Then Z is a function of X_1 and X_2. In other words, profits (Z) depend upon how many engineer hours (X_1) and technician hours (X_2) are used on the project. $Z = C_1X_1 + C_2X_2$, where C_1 and C_2 are the respective profits per hour of engineer and technician time. $C_1 =$ \$3 per hour of engineering time, $C_2 =$ \$4 per hour of technician time, and $Z = 3X_1 + 4X_2$, where Z = total dollars of profit for the project, $3X_1$ = total dollars of profit for engineers, and $4X_2$ = total dollars of profit for technicians. Since we wish to maximize profits, the final objective function becomes Max $Z = 3X_1 + 4X_2$. This function suggests that we should select values of the decision variables (X_1 = number of engineering hours and X_2 = number of technician hours) that result in maximum profits (Z). If it were not for the supervision, secretarial, and cash constraints soon to follow, X_1 and X_2 would approach infinity and result in infinite profits.

4. **Write a one- or two-word description of each constraint.** There are three constraining factors that restrain Precision Engineering from reaching infinite profits — supervision time available, secretarial time available, and cash for labor costs. Therefore, *supervision, secretarial,* and *cash* are terms that describe the three constraints.

5. **Write the RHS of each constraint.** The RHS of each constraint is the maximum amount ($\leq$), exact amount ($=$), or minimum amount ($\geq$) of each constraint. In this problem the maximum amount of supervision is 600 hours, the maximum amount of cash is \$10,000, and the maximum amount of secretarial time available is 1,500 hours.

6. **Write all $\leq, =, \geq$ for each constraint.** Since all of the constraints in this problem are maximum amounts, all constraints are the $\leq$ type. In other words, the amount of supervision that X_1 and X_2 use must be less than or equal to 600 hours, the amount of cash that X_1 and X_2 use must be less than or equal to \$10,000, and the amount of secretarial hours that X_1 and X_2 use must be less than or equal to 1,500.

7. **Write in *all* of the decision variables on the left-hand side of each constraint.** In this problem there are only two decision variables — X_1 and X_2. If there were more X's, they would all have been written in with enough space between them to allow us to write in their coefficients in the next step. It may be that not all decision variables appear in each constraint; this is taken care of in the next step by assigning zero coefficients to decision variables that do not belong in a constraint.

8. **Write the coefficients for each decision variable in each constraint.** Consider the first constraint, supervision. What is the coefficient of X_1 in this constraint? It is the amount of supervision per unit of X_1. In other words, it is the amount of supervision hours used per hour of engineer time, or one fourth. Similarly, the coefficient of X_2 in this first constraint is the amount of supervision hours used per hour of technician time, or one half. The coefficients of X_1 and X_2 in the cash constraint are \$10 and \$5, and the coefficients of X_1 and X_2 in the secretarial constraint are ¾ hour and 1 hour.

Study Figure 5.2 carefully to see where each of the above steps is placed.

Figure 5.3 shows how the LP formulating steps are applied to Problem LP-2, found earlier in Example 5.2. Read LP-2 again carefully and follow through Figure 5.3 step by step, as we did above in Example 5.3. Notice that LP-2 is a minimization problem and that the constraints are of the $\geq$ type.

Some observations are in order about LP problems in general. Let us use the LP-1 and LP-2 formulations to focus our comments:

Figure 5.2
Setting up Problem LP-1

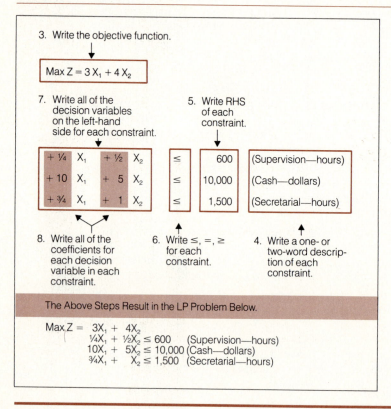

3. Write the objective function.

$$\text{Max } Z = 3X_1 + 4X_2$$

7. Write all of the decision variables on the left-hand side for each constraint.

5. Write RHS of each constraint.

$+ \frac{1}{4}\ X_1$	$+ \frac{1}{2}\ X_2$	$\leq$	600	(Supervision—hours)
$+ 10\ X_1$	$+ 5\ X_2$	$\leq$	10,000	(Cash—dollars)
$+ \frac{3}{4}\ X_1$	$+ 1\ X_2$	$\leq$	1,500	(Secretarial—hours)

8. Write all of the coefficients for each decision variable in each constraint.

6. Write $\leq$, $=$, $\geq$ for each constraint.

4. Write a one- or two-word description of each constraint.

The Above Steps Result in the LP Problem Below.

$$\text{Max } Z = 3X_1 + 4X_2$$
$$\tfrac{1}{4}X_1 + \tfrac{1}{2}X_2 \leq 600 \quad \text{(Supervision—hours)}$$
$$10X_1 + 5X_2 \leq 10,000 \quad \text{(Cash—dollars)}$$
$$\tfrac{3}{4}X_1 + X_2 \leq 1,500 \quad \text{(Secretarial—hours)}$$

LP-1

Max Z = $3X_1 + 4X_2$

$\quad\quad \frac{1}{4}X_1 + \frac{1}{2}X_2 \le 600$ (supervision-hours)

$\quad\quad 10X_1 + 5X_2 \le 10,000$ (cash-dollars)

$\quad\quad \frac{3}{4}X_1 + X_2 \le 1,500$ (secretarial-hours)

LP-2

Min Z = $1,000X_1 + 1,5000X_2$

$\quad\quad X_1 + \quad 2X_2 \ge 4$ (lead-tons)

$\quad\quad X_1 + \quad\quad X_2 \ge 2\frac{1}{2}$ (copper-tons)

1. The units of each term in a constraint must be the same as the RHS. For example, $\frac{1}{4}X_1$ in LP-1 must have the same units as 600:

Figure 5.3
Setting up Problem LP-2

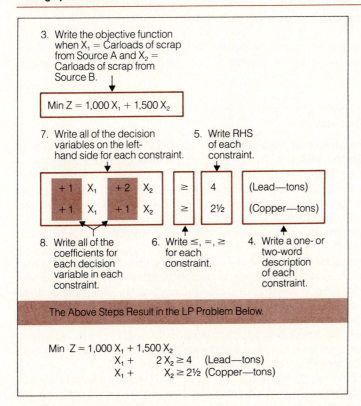

3. Write the objective function when X_1 = Carloads of scrap from Source A and X_2 = Carloads of scrap from Source B.

Min Z = $1,000\,X_1 + 1,500\,X_2$

7. Write all of the decision variables on the left-hand side for each constraint.

5. Write RHS of each constraint.

| +1 | X_1 | +2 | X_2 | $\ge$ | 4 | (Lead—tons) |
| +1 | X_1 | +1 | X_2 | $\ge$ | 2½ | (Copper—tons) |

8. Write all of the coefficients for each decision variable in each constraint.

6. Write $\le, =, \ge$ for each constraint.

4. Write a one- or two-word description of each constraint.

The Above Steps Result in the LP Problem Below.

Min Z = $1,000\,X_1 + 1,500\,X_2$

$\quad\quad X_1 + \quad 2\,X_2 \ge 4 \quad$ (Lead—tons)

$\quad\quad X_1 + \quad\quad X_2 \ge 2\frac{1}{2}$ (Copper—tons)

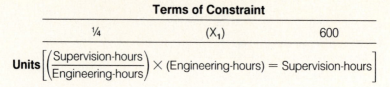

Therefore, Supervision-hours = Supervision-hours.

2. The units of each term in the objective function must be the same as Z. For example, $1{,}500X_2$ in LP-2 must be the same as Z:

	Terms of Objective Function	
Z	1,500	(X_2)

Units [$ = ($/carload) × (carloads)]

Therefore, $ = $.

3. The units between constraints do not *have* to be the same. For example, in LP-1, 600 supervision hours and $10,000 are different units. The units *may* be the same between constraints, as LP-2 demonstrates, but they do not *have* to be.

Now that you have a grasp of how to recognize LP problems and how to set up or formulate LP problems, you are ready to examine how LP problems are analyzed and solved.

Solving LP Problems

Constrained operational decisions have been recognized and structured for analysis for several decades. In the 1930s W. W. Leontief developed his input-output economic analyses that were structured similarly to today's LP format. In the 1930s and 1940s F. L. Hitchcock and T. C. Koopsmans developed a method for structuring *and* solving transportation-type LP problems. In 1947 George Dantzig developed the simplex method of linear programming. Dantzig's simplex method was probably the beginning of the development of the present-day field of *mathematical programming.*

Before modern LP solution methods were developed, managers routinely made constrained decisions by selecting courses of action (setting values for decision variables) and then checking to see if their decisions were within their constraints (did not violate their constraints). Operations managers today conceptually follow the same procedure, particularly in noncomplex constrained operational decisions. The constraints may not be developed into mathematical functions in these simple decision situations, but managers are aware of their constraints and they make sure their decisions are possible within their organizations' restrictions.

When POM constrained decisions are a little more complex and managers wish to take account of their constraints more thoroughly, two simple minor solution approaches can be used: *trial and error* and *total enumeration*. In trial and error, analysts develop the mathematical objective and constraint functions, select good decision outcomes, compare these solutions with the constraints, determine whether these solutions are within the constraints, and repeat the process until an acceptable solution is developed. This solution approach is limited to situations where fast answers are needed and where imprecision can be tolerated. *Total enumeration* involves working out all the possible solutions within the problem's constraints and then selecting the best solution. Total enumeration is practical only in problems of small proportions, those with few decision variables and constraints.

Another early minor LP solution method was developed to solve facility location problems in POM. A physical model was built over a map of the geographical areas under examination. A string was threaded through a hole in the map over each proposed location, and a weight proportional to the location's total cost was tied to the end of the string. All of the strings were then connected on the top surface of the map by a sliding knot apparatus. When all of the weights were dropped simultaneously, the knot was pulled to a location point that minimized the total costs. While this "drop the string" method is archaic by today's standards, the time and effort plowed into these early methods emphasize the importance that managers place on the need for LP solution techniques.

The *graphical solution* approach conceptually demonstrates the process of LP solutions to those who have no experience with LP—perhaps better than any other method. Graphical solutions are therefore intended as a teaching tool to assist you in understanding the process of LP solutions. The simplex, transportation, and assignment methods are the practical LP solution tools that will subsequently follow.

Graphical LP Solutions

Table 5.5 outlines the steps in the graphical method of solving LP problems. These steps are demonstrated in Example 5.4, a maximization problem, and Example 5.5, a minimization problem. Study these two examples and make sure you understand the basics of these solutions: plotting the constraint equations, outlining the solution area, circling the solution points, and, finally, selecting the optimal solution.

Table 5.5
Steps in the Graphical Solution Method

---

1. Formulate the objective and constraint functions.
2. Draw a graph with one variable on the horizontal axis and one on the vertical axis.
3. Plot each of the constraints as if they were equalities.
4. Outline the solution area.
5. Circle the potential solution points. These are the intersections of the constraints on the perimeter of the solution area.

6. Substitute each of the potential solution point values of the two decision variables into the objective function and solve for Z.
7. Select the solution that optimizes Z.

Example 5.4

Graphical Solution of LP-1

Problem LP-1 is used to demonstrate the steps in the graphical solution of a maximization problem. Read LP-1 again.

1. **Formulate the objective and constraint functions.** When LP-1 was set up in Example 5.3 earlier in this chapter, the decision variables were: X_1 = number of engineering hours to be used on the project, and X_2 = number of technician hours to be used on the project. The objective and constraint functions were:

$$\text{Max } Z = 3X_1 + 4X_2$$
$$\tfrac{1}{4}X_1 + \tfrac{1}{2}X_2 \leq 600 \text{ (supervision-hours)}$$
$$10X_1 + 5X_2 \leq 10,000 \text{ (cash-dollars)}$$
$$\tfrac{3}{4}X_1 + X_2 \leq 1,500 \text{ (secretarial-hours)}$$

2. **Draw a graph. 3. Plot the constraint functions. 4. Outline the solution area. 5. Circle the potential solution points on the perimeter of the solution area. (See Figure 5.4.)**

Note that the constraints are plotted by treating each constraint as an equality, letting $X_2 = 0$, solving for X_1, and vice versa. This gives two points for each constraint. When these two points are connected with a straight line, the constraint is completely defined.

Note that all possible values of X_1 and X_2 must fall inside *all* constraints (toward zero) because the constraints are $\leq$. While any point within the shaded area satisfies the constraints, only Points A, B, and C are candidates for the optimal solution because they are intersections of constraints and lie on the outer perimeter of the solution area.

Note also that Points A and C are formed by the intersection of a constraint and one of the axes. This is possible because the axes are implied constraints. In other words, X_1 cannot be negative; therefore, the vertical axis, $X_1 = 0$, is treated as a constraint. Similarly, the horizontal axis, $X_2 = 0$, is also treated as a constraint.

Points A, B, and C are three potential solutions to Problem LP-1:

A: $X_1 = 0$ and $X_2 = 1,200$ B: $X_1 = 533\tfrac{1}{3}$ and $X_2 = 933\tfrac{1}{3}$ C: $X_1 = 1,000$ and $X_2 = 0$

How do we determine Point B accurately? If the coordinates cannot be read precisely, the two constraint equations can be solved simultaneously for X_1 and X_2:

The two equations	Multiply the first constraint by -10 and add the two equations together:	Substitute the value for X_1 back into either constraint and solve for X_2:
$\tfrac{1}{4}X_1 + \tfrac{1}{2}X_2 = 600$	$-2.5X_1 - 5X_2 = -6,000$	$10(533\tfrac{1}{3}) + 5X_2 = 10,000$
$10X_1 + 5X_2 = 10,000$	$\underline{10X_1 + 5X_2 = \ 10,000}$	$5,333\tfrac{1}{3} + 5X_2 = 10,000$
	$7.5X_1 \qquad = \quad 4,000$	$5X_2 = 4,666\tfrac{2}{3}$
	$X_1 = 4,000/7.5$	$X_2 = \dfrac{4,666\tfrac{2}{3}}{5}$
	$= 533\tfrac{1}{3}$	$= 933\tfrac{1}{3}$

Figure 5.4
Graphical Solution of LP-1

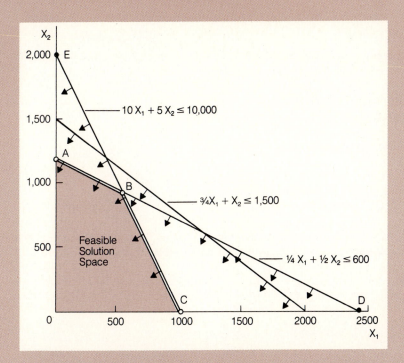

The intersection of the two constraints is therefore $X_1 = 533\frac{1}{3}$ and $X_2 = 933\frac{1}{3}$. Points A, B, and C are potential solutions to Problem LP-1. Which one is optimal, or best?

6. **Substitute the solution point values of the two decision variables into the objective function and solve for Z:**

Point A:
$X_1 = 0$ and $X_2 = 1,200$
$Z = 3X_1 + 4X_2$
$= 3(0) + 4(1,200)$
$= 4,800$

Point B:
$X_1 = 533\frac{1}{3}$ and $X_2 = 933\frac{1}{3}$
$Z = 3X_1 + 4X_2$
$= 3(533\frac{1}{3}) + 4(933\frac{1}{3})$
$= 1,600 + 3,733\frac{1}{3}$
$= 5,333\frac{1}{3}$

Point C:
$X_1 = 1,000$ and $X_2 = 0$
$Z = 3X_1 + 4X_2$
$= 3(1,000) + 4(0)$
$= 3,000$

7. **Select the solution that optimizes Z:**
   To maximize Z, the optimal solution is Point B, where $X_1 = 533\frac{1}{3}$ engineering-hours, $X_2 = 933\frac{1}{3}$ technician-hours, and $Z = \$5,333\frac{1}{3}$ profits.

Example 5.5

Graphical Solution of LP-2

Problem LP-2 is used to demonstrate the steps in the graphical solution of a minimization LP problem. Read LP-2 again.

1. **Formulate the objective and constraint functions.** Recall that LP-2 was set up in Figure 5.3 earlier in this chapter with these decision variables:

X_1 = carloads of scrap from Source A per month
X_2 = carloads of scrap from Source B per month

The objective and constraint functions were:

$$\text{Min } Z = 1{,}000X_1 + 1{,}500X_2$$
$$X_1 + 2X_2 \geq 4 \text{ (lead-tons)}$$
$$X_1 + X_2 \geq 2\tfrac{1}{2} \text{ (copper-tons)}$$

2. **Draw a graph. 3. Plot the constraint functions. 4. Outline the solution area. 5. Circle the potential solution points on the perimeter of the solution area. (See Figure 5.5.)**

Note that since both constraints are $\geq$, all possible values of X_1 and X_2 must lie outside both constraints, away from the origin. Point D is not possible because it violates the first constraint. Similarly, Point E violates the second constraint.

Points A, B, and C are three potential solutions to Problem LP-2:

A: $X_1 = 0$ and $X_2 = 2.5$ B: $X_1 = 1$ and $X_2 = 1.5$ C: $X_1 = 4$ and $X_2 = 0$

6. **Substitute the solution point values of the two decision values into the objective function and solve for Z:**

Point A:
$X_1 = 0$ and $X_2 = 2.5$
$Z = 1{,}000X_1 + 1{,}500X_2$
$= 1{,}000(0) + 1{,}500(2.5)$
$= 3{,}750$

Point B:
$X_1 = 1$ and $X_2 = 1.5$
$Z = 1{,}000X_1 + 1{,}500X_2$
$= 1{,}000(1) + 1{,}500(1.5)$
$= 1{,}000 + 2{,}250$
$= 3{,}250$

Point C:
$X_1 = 4$ and $X_2 = 0$
$Z = 1{,}000X_1 + 1{,}500X_2$
$= 1{,}000(4) + 1{,}500(0)$
$= 4{,}000$

7. **Select the solution that optimizes Z:**
    To minimize Z, the optimal solution is Point B, where $X_1 = 1$ carload of scrap from Source A per month, $X_2 = 1.5$ carloads of scrap from Source B per month, and $Z = \$3{,}250$ total scrap cost per month.

Figure 5.5
Graphical Solution of LP-2

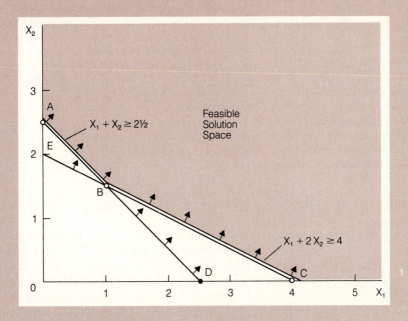

The graphical solution identifies solutions at the intersections of the constraints and methodically substitutes the values of the decision variables of these solutions into the objective function, until the optimal solution (maximum or minimum Z) is found. These steps are also approximately followed in the other solution methods that will soon follow.

The graphical method is severely limited in its use in real LP problems primarily because only two, or three at most, decision variables are allowed. The number of axes possible (three) limits the number of decision variables in this method. It is needless to emphasize that real world LP problems seldom contain only two or three decision variables. On the contrary, real LP problems in POM often contain numerous variables, thus eliminating the graphical method from consideration in many problems.

Simplex Method LP Solutions

The *simplex method* is an analytical tool that is adaptable to numerous constrained decisions. It provides managers with precise solutions to complex problems that have many variables and constraints. Since its development in the 1940s, the simplex method has accumulated a large following among industrial and academic

Exhibit 5.1
Scientific American **Praises the Simplex Method of Linear Programming**

The simplex algorithm has enormous economic importance in government and industry. The algorithm determines the most profitable or least expensive course of action under a number of constraints. It is applied extensively in petroleum refining, papermaking, food distribution, agriculture, steelmaking and metalworking (see "The Allocation of Resources by Linear Programming," by Robert G. Bland; *Scientific American,* June, 1981).

Suppose a paper company makes 50 grades of paper, each grade requiring different quantities of wood pulp, chemical sizing, bleach and clay coating. If the company devoted production exclusively to its most profitable grade of paper (white bond, say), the supply of bleach might be exhausted long before the other resources were used up. Indeed, if at least some bleach is needed for all grades of paper, the allocation of all the bleach to the production of white bond would halt the manufacture of the other grades in spite of ample inventories of the remaining resources. The task of maximizing the paper company's return on its investment in the various resources is one of determining just how to allocate the resources most effectively to the entire range of products.

Source: *Scientific American,* September 1982, 106.

analysts. Exhibit 5.1 illustrates the esteem in which the method is held in the scientific community.

Although the simplex method is long and difficult to use on large LP problems, most real LP problems in POM are worked on computers anyway. Numerous standard computer programs are available to generate solutions to large LP problems quickly and accurately. Among these are IBM's MPSX, LINDO, and the LP program in Appendix C of this book. A general familiarity with data processing will allow you to use these programs to input data and almost instantaneously receive solutions. Even though computer solutions are *the* method of solving real LP problems in POM, some experience with manual simplex solutions is desirable in order to better understand how to input data and interpret LP solutions when the computer is used. The details of simplex solutions are included in the supplement to this chapter.

Transportation Method LP Solutions

One of the earliest LP solution methods was the *transportation method*. This method can solve only a special form of LP problem, but when this type of LP problem occurs, the transportation method solves these problems efficiently. The simplex method can solve any LP problem that the transportation method can solve, but not vice versa. If computer solutions are used, the simplex method is usually preferred, because many computer programs are based upon the simplex method inputs. If, however, you find yourself in some remote location, such as the North Slope in Alaska, without access to a computer, and if a small transportation LP problem occurs, you would ordinarily prefer the transportation method over the simplex method. The transportation solution method is also demonstrated in the supplement to this chapter.

A transportation LP problem is of a special form where the objective is usually to minimize the cost for shipping products from several sources to several destinations. The constraints are usually of the = type for source capacity and destination demand. Example 5.6 is an LP problem of this form. Note that the coefficients of the decision variables in the constraints are either zero or one. Additionally, the pattern of the appearance of the decision variables in the constraints in the example is characteristic of transportation problems.

Example 5.6

A Transportation LP Problem

The Green Up Fertilizer Company ships fertilizer from two plants to three customers. The shipping cost per ton of fertilizer from each plant to each customer is:

	Customer		
Plant	A	B	C
1	$15	$30	$20
2	$20	$25	$15

Plant 1 has a monthly capacity of 1,000 tons and Plant 2 has a monthly capacity of 2,000 tons. The monthly customer demand is: A = 500 tons, B = 1,500 tons, and C = 1,000 tons. Formulate an LP problem to determine how much fertilizer should be shipped from each plant to each customer per month to minimize monthly shipping costs.

1. **Define the objective.** Minimize monthly shipping costs.

2. **Define the decision variables:**

   X_1 = tons of fertilizer to be shipped from 1 to A per month
   X_2 = tons of fertilizer to be shipped from 1 to B per month
   X_3 = tons of fertilizer to be shipped from 1 to C per month
   X_4 = tons of fertilizer to be shipped from 2 to A per month
   X_5 = tons of fertilizer to be shipped from 2 to B per month
   X_6 = tons of fertilizer to be shipped from 2 to C per month

3. **Write a mathematical function for the objective:**

   $$\text{Min } Z = 15X_1 + 30X_2 + 20X_3 + 20X_4 + 25X_5 + 15X_6$$

4. **Write the constraints:**

   $$X_1 + X_2 + X_3 = 1{,}000 \text{ (Plant 1 capacity in tons)}$$
   $$X_4 + X_5 + X_6 = 2{,}000 \text{ (Plant 2 capacity in tons)}$$
   $$X_1 + X_4 = 500 \text{ (Customer A demand in tons)}$$
   $$X_2 + X_5 = 1{,}500 \text{ (Customer B demand in tons)}$$
   $$X_3 + X_6 = 1{,}000 \text{ (Customer C demand in tons)}$$

The resultant LP problem is:

$$\text{Min } Z = 15X_1 + 30X_2 + 20X_3 + 20X_4 + 25X_5 + 15X_6$$
$$X_1 + X_2 + X_3 = 1{,}000$$
$$X_4 + X_5 + X_6 = 2{,}000$$
$$X_1 + X_4 = 500$$
$$X_2 + X_5 = 1{,}500$$
$$X_3 + X_6 = 1{,}000$$

Assignment Method LP Solutions

Another LP problem of a special form occasionally occurs in POM: the *assignment problem*. These problems usually seek to assign jobs or personnel to machines or departments. For example, suppose that three persons must be assigned to three projects, each project must be assigned to only one person, and each person must be assigned to only one project. The costs are shown below. A straightforward solution method for assignment problems is included in the supplement to this chapter.

Project	Persons		
	A	B	C
1	$20	$30	$10
2	40	30	40
3	30	20	30

Real LP Problems in POM

Real LP problems in POM typically have numerous variables, numerous constraints, and other complex characteristics. A realistic LP problem in POM is presented and formulated in Case 5.1 so that you can deepen your comprehension of LP in POM.

Case 5.1

Oklahoma Crude Oil Company

An oil refinery in Oklahoma buys domestic crude oil from five sources: Oklahoma, Texas, Kansas, New Mexico, and Colorado. Six end products are produced: regular gasoline, premium gasoline, low-lead gasoline, diesel fuel, heating oil, and lubricating oil base. The accompanying table shows the crude oil distribution to each end product, the crude oil costs, and the market requirements for each end product.

Product	Crude Oil Source					Monthly Market Requirements (Thousands of Gallons)
	Oklahoma	Texas	Kansas	New Mexico	Colorado	
Regular gasoline	40%	30%	30%	20%	30%	5,000
Premium gasoline	20	30	40	30	20	3,000
Low-lead gasoline	20	10	——	30	10	3,000
Diesel fuel	10	10	10	——	20	2,000
Heating oil	——	10	10	20	10	1,000
Lubricating oil base	10	10	10	——	10	2,000
Totals	100%	100%	100%	100%	100%	16,000
Delivered cost/gallon	$.20	$.14	$.15	$.18	$.12	

The sources of crude oil are captive within the company, and any quantity of each of the crudes can be purchased to satisfy the needs of this refinery up to these maximums:

Crude Source	Maximum Monthly Supply (Thousands of Gallons)	Crude Source	Maximum Monthly Supply (Thousands of Gallons)
Oklahoma crude	8,000	New Mexico crude	3,000
Texas crude	4,000	Colorado crude	6,000
Kansas crude	5,000		

How much crude oil should be purchased from each source to at least satisfy the market and to minimize crude oil costs?

1. Define the decision variables:

X_1 = thousands of gallons of Oklahoma crude to be purchased per month
X_2 = thousands of gallons of Texas crude to be purchased per month
X_3 = thousands of gallons of Kansas crude to be purchased per month
X_4 = thousands of gallons of New Mexico crude to be purchased per month
X_5 = thousands of gallons of Colorado crude to be purchased per month

2. Set up the LP problem:

$$\text{Min } Z = 200X_1 + 140X_2 + 150X_3 + 180X_4 + 120X_5$$

$.4X_1 + .3X_2 + .3X_3 + .2X_4 + .3X_5 \geq 5,000$ (regular gasoline market requirement in thousands of gallons)

$.2X_1 + .3X_2 + .4X_3 + .3X_4 + .2X_5 \geq 3,000$ (premium gasoline market requirement in thousands of gallons)

$.2X_1 + .1X_2 \qquad + .3X_4 + .1X_5 \geq 3,000$ (low-lead gasoline market requirement in thousands of gallons)

$.1X_1 + .1X_2 + .1X_3 \qquad + .2X_5 \geq 2,000$ (diesel fuel market requirement in thousands of gallons)

$.1X_2 + .1X_3 + .2X_4 + .1X_5 \geq 1,000$ (heating oil market requirement in thousands of gallons)

$.1X_1 + .1X_2 + .1X_3 \qquad + .1X_5 \geq 2,000$ (lubricating oil base market requirement in thousands of gallons)

$X_1 \qquad \leq 8,000$ (Oklahoma crude supply in thousands of gallons)

$X_2 \qquad \leq 4,000$ (Texas crude supply in thousands of gallons)

$X_3 \qquad \leq 5,000$ (Kansas crude supply in thousands of gallons)

$X_4 \qquad \leq 3,000$ (New Mexico crude supply in thousands of gallons)

$X_5 \leq 6,000$ (Colorado crude supply in thousands of gallons)

The problem in Case 5.1 has five decision variables and eleven constraints. Many hours of laborious desk work would be required to manually solve such problems with the simplex method. Only about half an hour would be required to input the data for computer solutions. The speed and accuracy of computers just about rules out manual solutions today for realistic LP problems in POM such as these.

Summary

The resources of productive systems—personnel, machines and equipment, cash and capital funds, materials and supplies, utilities, and others—are scarce. Both scarcity and rising resource prices cause shifts in POM strategies so that these resources can be used to the greatest advantage in achieving organizational objectives.

Today, perhaps more than ever before, operations managers understand that most decisions must be made and objectives achieved within constraints imposed on organizations. Customer demand for products and services, limited productive resources, governmental regulations, quality requirements, and technological limitations are examples of typical decision constraints in POM. Within these and other constraints, managers seek to achieve such objectives as profit maximization and cost minimization.

The complexity of these constrained POM decisions prompted the development of a family of new analysis techniques. Among them, linear programming (LP) stands out in its frequency of use across various organizations. This chapter discusses several aspects of LP—recognizing LP problems, formulating LP problems, solving LP problems, and interpreting LP solutions.

LP problems have a singular well-defined objective, alternative courses of action, constraints, and linear objective and constraint mathematical functions. All of these characteristics must be present in decisions before LP is an appropriate tool of analysis. LP problems are solved with the graphical, simplex, transportation, and assignment methods. Among these solution methods, the simplex method stands out in frequency of use, breadth of application, and adaptability to computer programs. Computer solutions are *the* solution approach to real LP problems in POM.

This text and most others provide simple LP problems for solution solely to clarify the solution procedures. More complex real LP problems are typically solved on computers. Careful attention to problem recognition, formulation, and solution interpretation is perhaps more important than solution details.

Review and Discussion Questions

1. What are productive system resources?
2. What effects do scarce resources have upon POM today?
3. Name five classical POM constrained decisions. Briefly describe each.
4. Define these terms: *objective function, constraint function, decision variable, objective function value, maximization LP problem, minimization LP problem.*

5. Name five characteristics of LP problems.

6. Name eight steps in formulating, or setting up, LP problems.

7. Name four solution methods to LP problems.

8. Describe the elements of a transportation LP problem.

9. Which LP solution method is used most often in POM? Why?

10. Why is the graphical method almost never used for real LP problems in POM?

Problems

LP-A. Agri-Gro, a large modern farming corporation in West Texas, plants milo and soybeans on a large tract of nonirrigated land. Soybeans require a special soil that is scarce, and only 100 acres are available for this crop. Milo can be planted on any of Agri-Gro's land but requires more fertilizer to condition the land. Agri-Gro is particularly worried about an adequate supply of fertilizer this year because the firm's supplier has been on strike for four months and only 200,000 pounds are available for this season's planting. Milo takes 2,000 pounds of fertilizer per acre and soybeans take 1,000 pounds of fertilizer per acre. How many acres should Agri-Gro plant in soybeans and milo, considering the shortages of fertilizer and land suitable for soybeans, if the profit per acre is $700 for soybeans and $500 for milo?

LP-B. Calchem is a supplier of specialty chemical products to petroleum and chemical industries in the San Francisco Bay area of northern California. Martha Sellmore, sales manager for Calchem, is trying to determine how the typical salesperson should divide time between petroleum and chemical industry customers. The following information seems pertinent to the sales manager:

	Petroleum Industry Customers	Chemical Industry Customers
1. Average profit per sales call	$500	$200
2. Salesperson's time required per sales call	8 hours	⅔ hours
3. Average entertainment cost per sales call	$40	$30

If less than 8 hours per day per salesperson is required for sales calls, other administrative duties can be performed to fill out the day. A maximum of $60 per salesperson per day for entertainment cost is allowed under company policy. How many daily sales calls to petroleum and chemical industry customers should each salesperson make, on the average, to maximize daily profits?

LP-C. Therm-co, a small private energy research firm in Tucson, Arizona, is planning the number of research personnel to assign to a new solar research project for the first and second quarters of this year. Because the firm has other research contracts, the number of personnel available for the new project during these two periods is severely limited. Maximums of 15 and 10 personnel are available during the first and second quarters, respectively. Additionally, a total personnel allowance of 20 personnel for the project means that a maximum of 20 personnel can be assigned to the project for the two periods (for example, if 15 personnel were assigned to the project during the first quarter, a maximum of 5 could be assigned during the second quarter). If the profit per person working on the project is estimated at $20,000 during the first quarter and $30,000 during the second quarter, how many personnel should be assigned to the project during each of the two periods?

LP-D. Moon City, a progressive municipal government in the western United States, is trying to decide among three community development projects — urban renewal, social health services expansion, and fire department services expansion. It is estimated that for each dollar spent next year in these three projects the equivalent dollar amount in social returns is:

Project	Social Returns
Urban renewal	$.40
Health services	.30
Fire department	.35

Moon City can allocate no more than a total of $10 million to these projects. The nature of these projects sets these limitations on next year's spending:

Project	Minimum Cost Allocation	Maximum Cost Allocation
Urban renewal	No limit	$7 million
Health services	$3 million	No limit
Fire department	No limit	$8 million

Considering the project spending constraints, how much should Moon City spend on each of the three projects to maximize the social returns?

LP-E. Fat Quick, a huge cattle feedlot operation near Chicago, Illinois, blends feeds mechanically to generate low-cost feeds for its cattle. Oats and corn are the principal ingredients of the cattle feed. The current costs for oats and corn are $.05 and $.03 per pound, respectively. Fat Quick requires a minimum of 4,000 calories, 10,000 units of minerals, and 5,000 units of vitamins per day for each head of cattle. Each pound of oats and corn supplies these quantities:

Feed	Calories per Pound	Mineral Units per Pound	Vitamin Units per Pound
Oats	100	200	200
Corn	100	400	100

How many pounds of oats and corn should be fed to each cow per day to minimize feed costs?

LP-F. A manufacturer of electrical consumer products, with its headquarters in Burlington, Iowa, produces electric irons at Manufacturing Plants 1, 2, and 3. The irons are shipped to Warehouses A, B, C, and D. The shipping cost per iron, the monthly warehouse requirements, and the monthly plant production levels are:

| | Destination | | | | Monthly Plant Production |
	A	B	C	D	Level (Units)
Plant 1	$.20	$.25	$.15	$.20	10,000
Plant 2	.15	.30	.20	.15	20,000
Plant 3	.15	.20	.20	.25	10,000
Monthly Warehouse Requirement (Units)	12,000	8,000	15,000	5,000	

How many electric irons should be shipped per month from each plant to each warehouse to minimize monthly shipping costs?

LP-G. The Error Prone Publishing Company is a medium-sized printing house in Gone Astray, Texas. It prints hardback and paperback books for publishing companies on a project basis. The printing industry backlog is now great and Error Prone can pick and choose from the available customers to develop the best mix of hardback and paperback books for their particular production environment. Because of their unique product-line design (one color, fixed book length, fixed book size, standard paper, etc.), Error Prone expects to earn $10 for each hardback and $6 for each paperback in contribution (fixed costs + pretax profits). The book cover department processes hardback books more slowly than paperback books. The cover department can complete eight paperback covers per minute but only four hardback covers per minute. The cover department cannot make both types of covers simultaneously, but it can easily switch from one type to the other. The printing line, on the other hand, can actually print hardbacks slightly faster than paperbacks because of the flimsy nature of the paperback paper stock. The printing department can produce six hardbacks per minute or it can produce four paperbacks per minute. The printing line can also easily be changed from one type of book to the other. Hardback books require a special framing operation that has a capacity of three and a half books per minute. For control purposes Error Prone's management requires that any books that begin production in any 8-hour shift must be processed through the last operation in the plant before the end of that shift, so that no in-process inventory can accumulate between shifts. How many paperbacks and hardbacks should be produced per shift to maximize contribution?

LP-H. Jesse Hopkins owns and operates the Moon Slick Specialty Oil Products Company in Cedar County, Nebraska. Jesse is now developing a business plan for the next quarter for his three principal products: Moon Slick #1, #2, and #3. The costs per barrel of these products are $3, $4, and $2, respectively, and Jesse would prefer to sell all #3 if he had complete freedom of choice. His salesman indicates, however, that the way his two regions have been buying the Moon Slick products, it is doubtful that #3 alone would satisfy his two major industries: mining/quarrying and construction. Mining/quarrying should use at least 500 barrels of either #1 or #2. This industry can use either product in a pinch, but generally prefers #1. In fact, these customers could use #1 exclusively, but if only #2 were available, at least 100 barrels would be needed. Construction should use at least 400 barrels of either #1 or #3. This industry can use either product, but also prefers #1. These customers could also use #1 exclusively, but if only #3 were available, at least 133⅓ barrels would be needed. The Moon Slick processing plant has a maximum quarterly capacity of only 5,000 processing hours available in this quarter, and the three products require 2, 5, and 4 hours per barrel, respectively. Additionally, Jesse has a policy of producing amounts of products sufficient to maintain steady employment for his employees. He figures that exactly 1,000 hours of employee work per quarter just about keeps all of his experienced and loyal employees working. A barrel of each product requires 1 hour of an employee's time.

How much of each product should be produced and sold during this quarter to minimize Moon Slick's costs?

Recognizing LP Problems

1. The Unfettered Lumber Mill in northern Alabama sells all of its products — oak, sycamore, and juniper hardwood slabs — to a local furniture manufacturer. The customer will take any amount of each of the three hardwoods as long as the total equals 500,000 board feet a year. The customer will pay $150 for sycamore, $170 for oak, and $300 for juniper per 1,000 board feet. The mix between the three wood types is determined by the mix of woods found in the forest by the mill's contract woodcutters. The mill and log costs are $100 for 1,000 board feet of sycamore and oak, but $200 for the same amount of juniper. If the mill wishes to maximize annual profits, how much oak, sycamore, and juniper should it process each year? (**a**) Review the requirements for a LP problem listed in Table 5.3 and determine if this problem meets each of these requirements. (**b**) Is LP appropriate to use in this problem?

2. An expert diet planner for the U.S. Department of Health, Education, and Welfare (HEW) wishes to plan the ideal breakfast for first-grade schoolchildren. The diet would minimize the cost for a national breakfast program by providing a choice among three meals — A, B, and C. The dietetic quality of the three meals is:

Meal	Calories	Mineral Index	Costs/Meal
A	750	5.00	$1.25
B	1,200	7.00	$1.50
C	3,000	8.00	$3.00

What mix of A, B, and C meals provides the best balance of calories and minerals for minimum costs? (**a**) Review the requirements for a LP problem listed in Table 5.3 and determine if each requirement is met. (**b**) Is LP appropriate to use in this problem?

Formulating LP Problems

3. Formulate the objective function and constraint functions for Problem LP-A of this section. Define the decision variables.

4. Formulate the objective function and constraint functions for Problem LP-B of this section. Define the decision variables.

5. Formulate the objective function and constraint functions for Problem LP-C of this section. Define the decision variables.

6. Formulate the objective function and constraint functions for Problem LP-D of this section. Define the decision variables.

7. Formulate the objective function and constraint functions for Problem LP-E of this section. Define the decision variables.

8. Formulate the objective function and constraint functions for Problem LP-F of this section. Define the decision variables.

9. Formulate the objective function and constraint functions for Problem LP-G of this section. Define the decision variables.

10. Formulate the objective function and constraint functions for Problem LP-H of this section. Define the decision variables.

Solving LP Problems Graphically

11. Solve Problem LP-A graphically. What is the optimal solution? Explain what the solution means in terms of the original problem.

12. Solve Problem LP-B graphically. What is the optimal solution? Explain what the solution means in terms of the original problem.

13. Solve Problem LP-C graphically. What is the optimal solution? Explain what the solution means in terms of the original problem.

14. Solve Problem LP-E graphically. What is the optimal solution? Explain what the solution means in terms of the original problem.

15. Solve Problem LP-G graphically. What is the optimal solution? Explain what the solution means in terms of the original problem.

Case:

Sunshine Tomato Soup Shippers

The Sunshine Tomato Soup Shippers produces tomato soup at five West Coast locations. The soup is shipped to four regional warehouses. The accompanying table shows the transportation cost per case from each cannery to each regional warehouse, the maximum and minimum monthly warehouse requirements, and the maximum monthly capacities of each of the canneries. The company wishes to ship all of its cannery capacity to the regional warehouses so that both the maximum and minimum monthly warehouse requirements are satisfied and the monthly total transportation cost is minimized.

	Destinations				Maximum Monthly Cannery Capacities (Cases)
Sources	Seattle, Washington	Los Angeles, California	Denver, Colorado	Dallas, Texas	
San Jose, California	$1.50	$ .70	$2.00	$2.50	50,000
Stockton, California	1.60	.80	1.80	2.50	80,000
Phoenix, Arizona	2.80	.60	1.20	1.50	60,000
Eugene, Oregon	.50	1.20	2.20	3.50	40,000
Bakersfield, California	1.80	.40	1.80	2.20	100,000
Maximum monthly warehouse requirements (cases)	90,000	100,000	80,000	100,000	
Minimum monthly warehouse requirements (cases)	60,000	80,000	50,000	70,000	

Assignment

1. Formulate the information in this case into a LP format. Define the decision variables, write the objective function, and write the constraint functions.

2. Using the LP computer program in Appendix C of this book, or another computer package such as MPSX or LINDO, solve the problem that you have formulated in No. 1.

3. Fully interpret the meaning of the solution that you obtained in No. 2. In other words, what should the management at Sunshine Tomato Soup Shippers do? Fully explain the meaning of the slack variable values.

4. Discuss the changes that would occur in the solution if there were slightly more or less minimum warehouse requirement amounts and slightly more or less maximum warehouse requirement amounts.

5. Is the solution that you identified in No. 2 the only optimal solution to this problem? If another optimal solution does exist, what variable or variables (shipping path from a source to a destination) would be used under the alternate solution?

6. Discuss the changes that would be expected in the optimal solution if any unused shipping path were used.

7. Explain the caution that must be observed in answering Nos. 4, 5, and 6.

Selected Bibliography

Balsey, H. L. *Quantitative Research Methods for Business and Economics.* New York: Random House, 1970.

Dallenback, H. G., and E. J. Bell. *Users' Guide to Linear Programming.* Englewood Cliffs, NJ: Prentice-Hall, 1970.

Gaither, Norman. "The Adoption of Operations Research Techniques by Manufacturing Organizations." *Decision Sciences* 6(October 1975):797–813.

Goss, S. I. *Illustrated Guide to Linear Programming.* New York: McGraw-Hill, 1970.

Kwak, N. K. *Mathematical Programming with Business Applications.* New York: McGraw-Hill, 1973.

Lee, Sang M., and Lawrence J. Moore. *Introduction to Decision Science.* New York: Petrocelli-Charter, 1975.

Levin, Richard I., and Charles A. Kirkpatrick. *Quantitative Approaches to Management.* New York: McGraw-Hill, 1978.

Naylor, Thomas H., Eugene T. Byrne, and John R. Vernon. *Introduction to Linear Programming: Methods and Cases.* Belmont, CA: Wadsworth, 1971.

Shamblin, James E., and G. T. Stevens, Jr. *Operations Research.* New York: McGraw-Hill, 1974.

Stockton, R. S. *Introduction to Linear Programming.* Homewood, IL: Richard D. Irwin, 1971.

Strum, J. E. *Introduction to Linear Programming.* San Francisco: Holden-Day, 1972.

Thierauf, Robert J., and Robert C. Klekamp. *Decision Making through Operations Research.* New York: Wiley, 1975.

Throsby, C. D. *Elementary Linear Programming.* New York: Random House, 1970.

Wagner, Harvey M. *Principles of Management Science, with Applications to Executive Decisions.* Englewood Cliffs, NJ: Prentice-Hall, 1970.

Linear Programming Solution Methods

Although the graphical solution method that was presented in Chapter 5 is a useful learning device for those with limited knowledge of LP, other methods are used daily in the worlds of business and government to solve real LP problems. Preeminent among these methods are *simplex*, *transportation*, and *assignment*.

Simplex Method

Students can have difficulty in grasping the mechanics of the simplex method even in solving super-simple LP problems. It is not mathematically complex, because only simple addition, subtraction, multiplication, and division computations are performed; but it is long, repetitive, and sometimes frustrating. It takes diligence and patience to correctly work even the simplest LP problems with the simplex method.

Simplex does not mean *simple*. But on the bright side, the simplex method is used term after term by thousands of students just like you, and you can do it too. The main thing is to keep your eye on the big picture: understand the overall procedures of the simplex method because it is easy to get bogged down in the nitty-gritty details and lose sight of the overall process. Pay attention to the small details; this is necessary. But also constantly keep in mind the overall simplex method process.

The best way to learn the simplex method is to use it to work LP problems. "Experience is the best teacher" certainly applies here.

Simplex Maximization Solutions

Table 5S.1 presents the steps in the simplex method. Read them carefully and don't worry too much about being confused. Remember, get the big picture. Working through an example will demonstrate the meaning of each of these steps. Example 5S.1 uses the simplex method to solve Problem LP-1 while methodically following the steps of the simplex method. Work through every step in this example meticulously; this is absolutely necessary to an understanding of the method. Notice that the step numbers in this example correspond to the step numbers in Table 5S.1. You will not need a calculator, because calculators compute in decimals that require rounding or truncating. These sources of error are unacceptable in the simplex method, and therefore all calculations are carried out in fractions.

Table 5S.1
Steps in the Simplex Solution Method

---

1. Formulate the objective and constraint functions.
2. Add slack variables to convert each constraint to an equality (=).
3. Add artificial variables to constraints that were originally ≥ or = to produce a starting solution.
4. Set up the first tableau, starting solution.

5. Check solution for optimality. If optimal, stop. If not, continue.
6. Select a variable to enter to improve the solution.
7. Select a variable to leave the solution.
8. Perform row operations to complete the solution.
9. Return to Step 5 and continue until optimality is achieved.

Example 5S.1

Simplex Solution of LP-1

The Precision Engineering Service Company uses both engineers and technicians to work on design projects for its customers. Engineers cost more per hour, but they require less supervision and less secretarial assistance than technicians. Engineers cost $10 per hour and technicians $5 per hour. Each hour of engineering time requires ¼ hour of supervision time and ¾ hour of secretarial assistance. Each hour of technician time requires ½ hour of supervision time and 1 hour of secretarial assistance. The company bid and won a large design project several months ago and now must determine how many engineering and technician hours to use on the project. It bid a total labor cost of $10,000, and management will not tolerate labor cost overruns because of a severe cash shortage. Underruns, however, are OK. A maximum of 600 hours of supervision and 1,500 hours of secretarial assistance is available for this project because of demands for supervision and secretarial assistance from other projects. If Precision charges its customer hourly rates when labor is used so that each hour of technician time yields $4 in profit and each hour of engineering time yields $3 in profit, how many hours of engineering and technician time should be allocated to the project?

1. **Formulate the objective and constraint functions:**

   LP-1 was formulated earlier as:

   $$\text{Max } Z = 3X_1 + 4X_2$$
   $$\tfrac{1}{4}X_1 + \tfrac{1}{2}X_2 \le 600 \text{ (supervision-hours)}$$
   $$10X_1 + 5X_2 \le 10,000 \text{ (cash-dollars)}$$
   $$\tfrac{3}{4}X_1 + X_2 \le 1,500 \text{ (secretarial-hours)}$$

   where

   $X_1 =$ the number of engineering-hours to be used on the project
   $X_2 =$ the number of technician-hours to be used on the project

2. **Add slack variables to convert each constraint to an equality (=):**

   a. $\tfrac{1}{4}X_1 + \tfrac{1}{2}X_2 \le 600$ (supervision-hours)

   Note that the left-hand side of the expression is always less than or equal to the right-hand side (RHS). If the expression is to be an equality (=), something must be added to the left-hand side to increase its value up to the level of the RHS. We will add a slack variable S_1 to take up the slack between the value of the left-hand side and the RHS. S_1 will take on a value of zero if the left-hand side exactly equals 600 and a value of 600 if X_1 and X_2 equal zero. When X_1 and X_2 take on values greater than zero, the value of S_1 will decrease accordingly so that the left-hand side of the expression always exactly equals 600.

   $$\tfrac{1}{4}X_1 + \tfrac{1}{2}X_2 + S_1 = 600$$

   Note that the subscript 1 in S_1 denotes that S_1 is the slack variable for the first constraint. When we proceed with and complete the simplex solution, and S_1 takes on some specific value at the end, we will automatically know that S_1 belongs to the first constraint — unused supervision-hours. Similarly, S_2 will belong to the second constraint — unused cash-dollars.

   b. The second constraint is converted to an equality by adding a slack variable S_2 to the left-hand side:

   $$10X_1 + 5X_2 + S_2 = 10,000$$

   c. The third constraint is converted to an equality by adding a slack variable S_3 to the left-hand side:

   $$\tfrac{3}{4}X_1 + X_2 + S_3 = 1,500$$

We now have the LP problem:

$$
\begin{aligned}
\text{Max } Z = {} & 3X_1 + 4X_2 \\
& \tfrac{1}{4}X_1 + \tfrac{1}{2}X_2 + S_1 && = 600 \\
& 10X_1 + 5X_2 \phantom{{}+{}} + S_2 && = 10{,}000 \\
& \tfrac{3}{4}X_1 + X_2 + && + S_3 = 1{,}500
\end{aligned}
$$

3. **Add artificial variables to constraints that were originally $\geq$ or $=$ to produce a starting solution:** since the constraints in this problem were $\leq$, no artificial variables are required.

4. **Set up first tableau starting solution:**
   A *tableau* simply means a *table*. Each solution will be a tableau or a table.

   a. First let all variables appear in the objective function and constraint functions:

$$
\begin{aligned}
\text{Max } Z = {} & 3X_1 + 4X_2 + OS_1 + OS_2 + OS_3 \\
& \tfrac{1}{4}X_1 + \tfrac{1}{2}X_2 + S_1 + OS_2 + OS_3 = 600 \\
& 10X_1 + 5X_2 + OS_1 + S_2 + OS_3 = 10{,}000 \\
& \tfrac{3}{4}X_1 + X_2 + OS_1 + OS_2 + S_3 = 1{,}500
\end{aligned}
$$

   This is achieved by assigning zero coefficients to all variables not appearing in these functions.

   b. Now put the problem in the tableau format. The format is achieved by entering the set of coefficients for all the variables into the framework below:

First Tableau

C			3	4	0	0	0	
	SOL	b	X_1	X_2	S_1	S_2	S_3	ϕ
0	S_1	600	$\tfrac{1}{4}$	$\tfrac{1}{2}$	1	0	0	
0	S_2	10,000	10	5	0	1	0	
0	S_3	1,500	$\tfrac{3}{4}$	1	0	0	1	
	Z	0	0	0	0	0	0	
	(C − Z)		3	4	0	0	0	

   c. Constraints. The RHS value of each constraint is placed in Column b and the coefficients of the variables in the constraint are placed under the variables' columns.

   d. Objective function. The coefficients of the variables in the objective function are placed in Row C above the appropriate variable column.

   e. SOL column. Note that the matrix under S_1, S_2, and S_3 is an *identity matrix,* a NW to SE diagonal of ones, with all other elements being zero. The variables over the identity matrix are always in the SOL column:

SOL	S_1	S_2	S_3
S_1	1	0	0
S_2	0	1	0
S_3	0	0	1

This condition will always hold: **A variable found in the SOL column will have a one at the intersection of its row and column and all other elements in its column will be zero.** This condition holds for all tableaus. When we are trying to determine what variables go into the SOL column later in this section, this rule can be helpful. Just look at all of the columns in the tableau and find the column that has a *one* in the first row with all other elements zero, and the variable of that column goes into the SOL column in the first row. All other SOL elements are determined in the same way.

f. C column. The zeros under the C column and opposite S_1, S_2, and S_3 are taken from Row C elements above S_1, S_2, and S_3. This will always hold — **the values in the C column are the coefficients in the objective function that correspond to the variables found in the SOL column of the tableau.**

g. Row Z. The elements in Row Z are all computed. Since the elements in the C column were zero, all the elements in Row Z were zero; however, the elements in the C column will not always be zero. Each element in Row Z is computed as follows:

$$Z_b = (0)(600) + (0)(10{,}000) + (0)(1{,}500) = 0$$
$$Z_{x_1} = (0)(\tfrac{1}{4}) + (0)(10) + (0)(\tfrac{3}{4}) = 0$$
$$Z_{x_2} = (0)(\tfrac{1}{2}) + (0)(5) + (0)(1) = 0$$
$$Z_{S_1} = (0)(1) + (0)(0) + (0)(0) = 0$$
$$Z_{S_2} = (0)(0) + (0)(1) + (0)(0) = 0$$
$$Z_{S_3} = (0)(0) + (0)(0) + (0)(1) = 0$$

This step will become clearer in subsequent tableaus.

h. Row (C − Z). These values are computed by subtracting each element in Row Z from its counterpart in Row C:

$$(C - Z)_{x_1} = 3 - 0 = 3$$
$$(C - Z)_{x_2} = 4 - 0 = 4$$
$$(C - Z)_{S_1} = 0 - 0 = 0$$
$$(C - Z)_{S_2} = 0 - 0 = 0$$
$$(C - Z)_{S_3} = 0 - 0 = 0$$

i. The starting solution. This completes the explanation of the starting solution tableau. This starting solution is:

$$X_1 = \quad 0 \text{ engineering-hours}$$
$$X_2 = \quad 0 \text{ technician-hours}$$
$$S_1 = \quad 600 \text{ unused supervision-hours}$$
$$S_2 = 10{,}000 \text{ unused cash-dollars}$$
$$S_3 = \quad 1{,}500 \text{ unused secretarial-hours}$$
$$Z = \quad 0 \text{ profit-dollars}$$

Simplex tableau solutions always give the variables in the solution under the SOL column. Their associated values are found opposite them in Column b; therefore $S_1 = 600$, $S_2 = 10{,}000$, and $S_3 = 1{,}500$. **All other variables not in the SOL column are equal to zero.** The value of Z is found in Column b and Row Z.

5. **Check solution for optimality. If optimal, stop. If not, continue:**
Solutions are optimal when all of the values in Row (C − Z) are either zero or negative. When any of the values in this row are nonzero positive numbers, the solution can be improved by continuing and the solution is not optimal. In our first tableau of LP-1, both X_1 and X_2 have Row (C − Z) elements that are nonzero and positive. It is therefore not optimal, and we must continue to the next tableau.

6. **Select a variable to enter to improve the solution:**
Select the variable to enter that has the largest positive element in Row (C − Z). X_2 will enter since its Row (C − Z) element is the largest positive value in Row (C − Z).

7. **Select a variable to leave the solution:**

First Tableau (continued)

C			3	4	0	0	0		
	SOL	b	X_1	X_2	S_1	S_2	S_3	ϕ	
0	S_1	600	¼	(½)	1	0	0	$600/½ = 1{,}200$	← Leaving Variable
0	S_2	10,000	10	5	0	1	0	$10{,}000/5 = 2{,}000$	(Smallest Positive)
0	S_3	1,500	¾	1	0	0	1	$1{,}500/1 = 1{,}500$	
	Z	0	0	0	0	0	0		
	(C − Z)		3	4	0	0	0		

↑
Entering Variable
(Largest Positive)

The variable to leave this starting solution is determined by entering the column of the entering variable, X_2, dividing the number in each row into its b value, and recording this value in the ϕ column to the right. The leaving variable has the smallest positive ϕ value. If zero values or ties occur, do not worry. In the case of a tie, arbitrarily select one of the tying variables to leave, and in the case of a zero, let that variable leave. **(Remember that a positive number divided by zero is a very large number at the limit.)**

8. **Perform row operations to complete the solution:**
This is perhaps the most confusing point in the simplex method. Table 5S.2 lists the steps in performing row operations. These steps will be followed to construct the second tableau.

   a. Identify the pivot element. It is found at the intersection of the entering variable column (X_2) and the leaving variable row (S_1): the pivot element is (½).

   b. Divide the pivot row, element by element, by the pivot element. Enter this new row in the next tableau: The first constraint row (600 ¼ ½ 1 0 0) is divided by ½ and the result is entered in the second tableau in the first row position. The variable in the SOL column in this row is the new entering variable X_2, and its coefficient (4) in Row C is entered in Column C.

Table 5S.2
Steps in Performing Row Operations

1. Identify the *pivot element* in the present tableau, which is found at the intersection of the column of the entering variable and the row of the leaving variable. Circle this element. Row operations convert the pivot column in this present tableau, element by element, to a new column in the new tableau. This new column always has these features: the element that is the pivot element in the present tableau will be a *one* in the new tableau, and all other elements in that column in the new tableau will be *zero*.

2. We convert the pivot element in the present tableau to a *one* in the new tableau by dividing the entire pivot row in the present tableau by the pivot element (element by element). This new row with a one in the pivot element is entered into the new tableau in the same row position as the pivot row of the present tableau.

3. Next, we convert all other elements in the pivot column of the present tableau to *zero* in the new tableau. This is done by performing a separate operation on each remaining row of the present tableau. This operation involves the development of a special transitional row that is added to a row in the present tableau. Each row in the present tableau for which we wish to convert its pivot column element to zero requires its own unique transitional row. This transitional row is developed by first determining the value of the element that we want to transform to zero. We then take the negative of the value of this element and multiply it by the row obtained in Step 2 above, element by element. When this transitional row is added to the row of the present tableau, a new row results that has a zero in the pivot column. This new row is entered in the new tableau in the same row position as it occupied in the present tableau before it was transformed.

Second Tableau

C			3	4	0	0	0	
	SOL	b	X_1	X_2	S_1	S_2	S_3	ϕ
4	X_2	1,200	½	1	2	0	0	
0	S_2							
0	S_3							
	Z							
	C − Z							

c. Reduce the other elements in the pivot column (X_2) to zero. Transform the second row in the first tableau (10,000 10 5 0 1 0) by multiplying the new row in the second tableau (1,200 ½ 1 2 0 0) by a negative 5 and adding this transitional row to the second row of the first tableau:

Multiply the row first entered in the second tableau by −5:

$$-5(1,200) \quad -5(½) \quad -5(1) \quad -5(2) \quad -5(0) \quad -5(0)$$

This gives values of

$$-6,000 \quad -\tfrac{5}{2} \quad -5 \quad -10 \quad 0 \quad 0$$

which are added to the row being transformed

$$10,000 \quad 10 \quad 5 \quad 0 \quad 1 \quad 0$$

to get values of

$$4,000 \quad \tfrac{15}{2} \quad 0 \quad -10 \quad 1 \quad 0$$

The third row in the first tableau (1,500 ¾ 1 0 0 1) is now transformed by multiplying the row first entered in the new tableau (1,200 ½ 1 2 0 0) by a negative 1 and adding this transitional row to the third row of the first tableau:

Multiply the row first entered in the second tableau by −1:

$$-1(1,200) \quad -1(½) \quad -1(1) \quad -1(2) \quad -1(0) \quad -1(0)$$

This gives values of

$$-1,200 \qquad -½ \qquad -1 \qquad -2 \qquad 0 \qquad 0$$

which are added to the row being transformed

$$1,500 \qquad ¾ \qquad 1 \qquad 0 \qquad 0 \qquad 1$$

to get values of

$$300 \qquad ¼ \qquad 0 \qquad -2 \qquad 0 \qquad 1$$

d. These rows are entered into the second tableau in the second and third row positions. The variables in the SOL column for these rows do not change:

Second Tableau (continued)

C			3	4	0	0	0	
	SOL	b	X_1	X_2	S_1	S_2	S_3	ϕ
4	X_2	1,200	½	1	2	0	0	
0	S_2	4,000	15½	0	−10	1	0	
0	S_3	300	¼	0	−2	0	1	
	Z	4,800	2	4	8	0	0	
	(C − Z)	1	0	−8	0	0	

e. Row Z is computed as follows:

$$Z_b = (4)(1,200) + (0)(4,000) + (0)(300) = 4,800$$
$$Z_{X_1} = (4)(½) + (0)(15½) + (0)(¼) = 2$$
$$Z_{X_2} = (4)(1) + (0)(0) + (0)(0) = 4$$
$$Z_{S_1} = (4)(2) + (0)(-10) + (0)(-2) = 8$$
$$Z_{S_2} = (4)(0) + (0)(1) + (0)(0) = 0$$
$$Z_{S_3} = (4)(0) + 0(1) + (0)(0) = 0$$

Row (C − Z) is again computed by subtracting each element in Row Z from its counterpart in Row C.

f. The solution to the second tableau is:

$X_1 =$ 0 engineering-hours
$X_2 =$ 1,200 technician-hours
$S_1 =$ 0 unused supervision-hours
$S_2 =$ 4,000 unused cash-dollars
$S_3 =$ 300 unused secretarial-hours
$Z =$ 4,800 profit-dollars

The values of X_2, S_2, S_3, and Z are found within the body of the second tableau, X_1 and S_1 are not in the SOL column; therefore, they both equal zero. **Does this solution look familiar? It should, because it is identical to Point A in Example 5.4 of the graphical method.**

9. **Return to Step 5 and continue until optimalilty is achieved:**

5, 6, and 7. Check solution for optimality. If optimal stop. If not, continue. Select a variable to enter the solution. Select a variable to leave the solution:

Second Tableau (continued)

C			3	4	0	0	0	
	SOL	b	X_1	X_2	S_1	S_2	S_3	ϕ
4	X_2	1,200	½	1	2	0	0	1,200/½ = 2,400
0	S_2	4,000	(15/2)	0	−10	1	0	4,000/15/2 = 533⅓ ← Leaving Variable
0	S_3	300	¼	0	−2	0	1	300/¼ = 1,200 (Smallest Positive)
	Z	4,800	2	4	8	0	0	
	(C − Z)		1	0	−8	0	0	

↑
Entering Variable
(Largest Positive)

The second tableau is not optimal since all Row $(C - Z)$ elements are not zero or negative. X_1 enters and because the ϕ value for the second row is the smallest positive, S_2 leaves.

8. **Perform row operations to complete the solution:**

a. The pivot element is 15/2 because that element is at the intersection of the entering variable column and the leaving variable row.

b. Divide the pivot row (second constraint row) of the second tableau through by the pivot element (15/2). Enter this new row into the third tableau in the same second row position:

Third Tableau

C			3	4	0	0	0	
	SOL	b	X_1	X_2	S_1	S_2	S_3	ϕ
4	X_2							
3	X_1	533⅓	1	0	−20/15	2/15	0	
0	S_3							
	Z							
	(C − Z)							

c. Multiply this new row by a negative ½ to transform the first constraint row in the second tableau:

−½(533⅓) −½(1) −½(0) −½(−20/15) −½(2/15) −½(0)

This gives value of

−266⅔ −½ 0 10/15 −1/15 0

which are added to

1200 ½ 1 2 0 0

to give

933⅓ 0 1 40/15 −1/15 0

Multiply the first row entered in the third tableau by −¼:

−¼(533⅓) −¼(1) −¼(0) −¼(−20/15) −¼(2/15) −¼(0)

This gives values of

−133⅓ −¼ 0 ⅓ −1/30 0

which are added to

300 ¼ 0 −2 0 1

to give

166⅔ 0 0 −5/3 −1/30 1

d. These rows are now entered into the first and third row positions of the third tableau:

Third Tableau (continued)

C			3	4	0	0	0	
	SOL	**b**	**X_1**	**X_2**	**S_1**	**S_2**	**S_3**	ϕ
4	**X_2**	**933⅓**	0	1	40/15	−1/15	0	
3	**X_1**	**533⅓**	1	0	−20/15	2/15	0	
0	**S_3**	**166⅔**	0	0	−5/3	−1/30	1	
	Z	**5,333⅓**	3	4	100/15	2/15	0	
		(C − Z)	0	0	−100/15	−2/15	0	

e. Compute Rows Z and (C − Z) to complete the third tableau. Row Z is computed as follows:

$$Z_b = (4)(933\tfrac{1}{3}) + (3)(533\tfrac{1}{3}) + (0)(166\tfrac{2}{3}) = 5{,}333\tfrac{1}{3}$$
$$Z_{x_1} = (4)(0) + (3)(1) + (0)(0) = 3$$
$$Z_{x_2} = (4)(1) + (3)(0) + (0)(0) = 4$$
$$Z_{S_1} = (4)(\tfrac{40}{15}) + (3)(-\tfrac{20}{15}) + (0)(-\tfrac{5}{3}) = \tfrac{100}{15}$$
$$Z_{S_2} = (4)(-\tfrac{1}{15}) + (3)(\tfrac{2}{15}) + (0)(-\tfrac{1}{30}) = \tfrac{2}{15}$$
$$Z_{S_3} = (4)(0) + (3)(0) + (0)(0) = 0$$

Row $(C - Z)$ is again computed by subtracting each element in Row Z from its counterpart in Row C.

 f. The solution to the third tableau is:

$X_1 =$ 533⅓ engineering-hours
$X_2 =$ 933⅓ technician-hours
$S_1 =$ 0 unused supervision-hours
$S_2 =$ 0 unused cash-dollars
$S_3 =$ 166⅔ unused secretarial-hours
 $Z =$ 5,333⅓ profit-dollars

Does this solution look familiar? It should, because it is identical to Point B in Example 5.4 of the graphical method.

9. **Return to Step 5 and continue until optimality is achieved. Check solution for optimality. If optimal, stop. If not, continue.**

The third tableau is optimal because all the elements in Row $(C - Z)$ are either negative or zero. The solution is complete. Note that the simplex method does not guarantee whole number (integer) answers. This is not normally a serious obstacle. If only integer answers can be tolerated, numerous integer programming computer programs can overcome this difficulty.

The graphical solution of maximization Problem LP-1, Example 5.4, identified three solution points — A, B, and C. Each of these solutions was first identified as intersections of the constraints, and then each was substituted into the objective function to determine a value of Z. Finally, the optimal solution (maximum profit) was selected. The simplex method solution to LP-1 follows this same general process with one exception. The first tableau begins with Z = 0, and each subsequent tableau methodically exhibits higher values of Z. You can be assured that each tableau will exhibit progressively higher profits. This progression to better and better solutions is the only conceptual departure of the simplex method from the general process of the graphical method.

Simplex Minimization Solutions

The graphical solution of minimization Problem LP-2, Example 5.5, identified three solution points — A, B, and C. The optimal solution to the problem was then determined by investigating Points A, B, and C. The simplex solution to this problem begins the first tableau with a very large value of Z. Subsequent tableaus exhibit progressively lower values for Z until optimality is achieved. This progression from high to low values of Z is characteristic of the simplex solution of minimization LP problems.

There are only two basic differences between maximization and minimization LP problem solutions with the simplex method:

1. Minimization LP problems are more likely to have $\geq$ and $=$ constraints, although the procedures for treating them apply to both minimization and maximization LP problems.

2. Minimization LP problems have different objective functions; Z is minimized.

In either minimization or maximization problems $\geq$ and $=$ constraints are accommodated by adding artificial variables to these constraints. For example, in the case of $\geq$ constraints:

$$
\begin{aligned}
&1.\ X_1 + 2X_2 && \geq 500 \\
&2.\ X_1 + 2X_2 && = 500 + S_1 \\
&3.\ X_1 + 2X_2 && - S_1 = 500 \\
&4.\ X_1 + 2X_2 + A_1 && - S_1 = 500
\end{aligned}
$$

Note that in Step 2 above, a slack variable (S_1) is added to the right-hand side, which must always be less than or equal to the left-hand side. The addition of S_1 to the smaller side of the expression allows us to convert the $\geq$ to $=$. In Step 3 the S_1 is moved to the left-hand side by subtracting S_1 from both sides. In Step 4 an artificial variable (A_1) is added to the left-hand side. Why do we do this? The only reason is to get a starting simplex solution. Remember when we said earlier that a requirement for each tableau was that the variable with a column which has a one in the first row and all other elements in its column are zero is the variable that must go in the SOL column in the first row? What happens if no variable exists that has a column meeting this requirement? This is exactly the situation we have with $\geq$ or $=$ constraints. A $\geq$ constraint has a -1 coefficient for S_1 and this does not meet the requirement. Similarly, an $=$ constraint does not have a slack variable (as we shall soon see below); therefore, we shall not be able to meet the requirement here either. When such conditions exist, we must add an artificial variable to $\geq$ or $=$ rows to meet the requirement and obtain a starting solution (complete the first tableau). The artificial variables appear in the SOL column of the first tableau and are then methodically driven from the solution in subsequent tableaus. The artificial variables have absolutely no meaning and we will not be concerned with them again.

When $=$ constraints occur, an artificial variable must also be added. For example:

$$
\begin{aligned}
3X_1 + 2X_2 && = 1{,}000 \\
3X_1 + 2X_2 + A_2 && = 1{,}000
\end{aligned}
$$

Again, the purpose of A_2 is to achieve a starting simplex solution; A_2 will have no subsequent meaning.

The second basic difference is accommodated by converting objective functions from the *min* to the *max* form. For example:

$$
\text{Min } Z = 5X_1 + 3X_2 \quad \text{becomes} \quad \text{Max } Z = -5X_1 - 3X_2
$$

This is achieved by multiplying each term of the Min Z objective function by a -1. Minimization LP problems, after this conversion, are then solved as maximization problems. The exact same tableau procedures apply. After this conversion, slack variables and artificial variables are added to the objective function as required. Slack variables are assigned zero coefficients in the objective function as before. But what about the artificial variables? What coefficients should be assigned to the artificial variables? Would you believe a $-M$, where the M is a very large number? Now what the M actually represents is subject to speculation, but legend has it that Harvey Wagner first used the *Big M Method* in LP studies at the Mercury Motors Division of the Ford Motor Company more than 20 years ago. Regardless of its origin, each artificial variable is always assigned a $-M$ coefficient in the objective function in either max or min LP problems when the objective function conversion described above is used.[1] This $-M$ in Row C of the simplex tableau avoids an artificial variable entering back into the solution since $(C - Z)$ will always be zero or negative because the C value is $-M$ . . . , a negative very large number, say minus infinity. Since whatever is subtracted from minus infinity is either negative or zero, the artificial variable will never reenter the solution.

Example 5S.2 solves Problem LP-2, a minimization problem, using the simplex method.

Example 5S.2

Solving a Minimization Problem (LP-2) Using the Simplex Method

The Pour-More Foundry buys scrap metal from two sources, A and B. The scrap is melted down, and lead and copper are extracted and used in the foundry processes. Each railroad car of scrap from Source A yields 1 ton of copper and 1 ton of lead and costs $1,000 per car. Each railroad car of scrap from Source B costs $1,500 per car and yields 2 tons of lead and 1 ton of copper. If the foundry needs at least 4 tons of lead and 2.5 tons of copper per month, how many carloads of scrap should be purchased from Sources A and B per month? We have previously formulated LP-2 as follows:

$$\text{Min } Z = 1,000X_1 + 1,500X_2$$
$$X_1 + 2X_2 \geq 4 \text{ (lead-tons)}$$
$$X_1 + X_2 \geq 2\tfrac{1}{2} \text{ (copper-tons)}$$

where X_1 = carloads of scrap purchased monthly from Source A and X_2 = carloads of scrap purchased monthly from Source B.

---

[1] If this conversion of the objective function is not used, the objective function is left in its original form and the rule for the entering variable for minimization problems becomes: the entering variable is the one with the most negative number in Row $(C - Z)$. The artificial variables must then be assigned $+M$ coefficients in the objective function. All other procedures remain the same as in maximization problems. We prefer the conversion described above because the procedures are all exactly the same for both maximization and minimization problems, and we shall follow this convention throughout.

1. **Add slack variables to constraints to convert from $\geq$ to $=$:**

$$\text{Min } Z = 1{,}000X_1 + 1{,}500X_2$$
$$X_1 + 2X_2 - S_1 \qquad = 4$$
$$X_1 + X_2 \qquad - S_2 = 2\tfrac{1}{2}$$

2. **Multiply objective function by -1 to convert to a maximization problem:**

$$\text{Max } Z = -1{,}000X_1 - 1{,}500X_2$$
$$X_1 + 2X_2 - S_1 \qquad = 4$$
$$X_1 + X_2 \qquad - S_2 = 2\tfrac{1}{2}$$

3. **Add artificial variables to constraints to obtain a starting solution, and include all variables in all functions:**

$$\text{Max } Z = -1{,}000X_1 - 1{,}500X_2 - MA_1 - MA_2 + OS_1 + OS_2$$
$$X_1 + 2X_2 + A_1 + OA_2 - S_1 + OS_2 = 4$$
$$X_1 + X_2 + OA_1 + A_2 + OS_1 - S_2 = 2\tfrac{1}{2}$$

4. **Place in first tableau and solve:**

First Tableau

C			$-1{,}000$	$-1{,}500$	$-M$	$-M$	0	0	
	SOL	b	X_1	X_2	A_1	A_2	S_1	S_2	ϕ
$-M$	A_1	4	1	(2)	1	0	-1	0	$4/2 = 2$ ← Leaving
$-M$	A_2	$2\tfrac{1}{2}$	1	1	0	1	0	-1	$2\tfrac{1}{2}/1 = 2\tfrac{1}{2}$ Variable
	Z	$-6\tfrac{1}{2}M$	$-2M$	$-3M$	$-M$	$-M$	M	M	
	(C − Z)		$2M$ $-1{,}000$	$3M$ $-1{,}500$	0	0	$-M$	$-M$	

↑
Entering
Variable

-2	$-\tfrac{1}{2}$	-1	$-\tfrac{1}{2}$	0	$\tfrac{1}{2}$	0
$2\tfrac{1}{2}$	1	1	0	1	0	-1
$\tfrac{1}{2}$	$\tfrac{1}{2}$	0	$-\tfrac{1}{2}$	1	$\tfrac{1}{2}$	-1

Second Tableau

C			$-1{,}000$	$-1{,}500$	$-M$	$-M$	0	0	
	SOL	b	X_1	X_2	A_1	A_2	S_1	S_2	ϕ
$-1{,}500$	X_2	2	$\tfrac{1}{2}$	1	$\tfrac{1}{2}$	0	$-\tfrac{1}{2}$	0	4
$-M$	A_2	$\tfrac{1}{2}$	$\tfrac{1}{2}$	0	$-\tfrac{1}{2}$	1	$\tfrac{1}{2}$	-1	1 ← Leaving
	Z	$-\tfrac{1}{2}M$ $-3{,}000$	$-\tfrac{1}{2}M$ -750	$-1{,}500$	$\tfrac{1}{2}M$ -750	$-M$	$-\tfrac{1}{2}M$ $+750$	M	Variable
	(C − Z)		$\tfrac{1}{2}M$ -250	0	$-\tfrac{3}{2}M$ $+750$	0	$\tfrac{1}{2}M$ -750	$-M$	

↑
Entering
Variable

$-\frac{1}{2}$	$-\frac{1}{2}$	0	$\frac{1}{2}$	-1	$-\frac{1}{2}$	1
2	$\frac{1}{2}$	1	$\frac{1}{2}$	0	$-\frac{1}{2}$	0
$1\frac{1}{2}$	0	1	1	-1	-1	1

Third Tableau

C				$-1,000$	$-1,500$	$-M$	$-M$	0	0	
	SOL	b		X_1	X_2	A_1	A_2	S_1	S_2	ϕ
$-1,500$	X_2	$1\frac{1}{2}$		0	1	1	-1	-1	1	
$-1,000$	X_1	1		1	0	-1	2	1	-2	
	Z	$-3,250$		$-1,000$	$-1,500$	-500	-500	500	500	
		$(C - Z)$		0	0	$-M$ $+500$	$-M$ $+500$	-500	-500	

The third tableau is optimal because all elements in Row $(C - Z)$ are zero or negative.

5. Interpret the solution:

The solution is deduced from the SOL and b columns of the last tableau. All variables that do not appear in the SOL column are equal to zero:

$$X_1 = 1 \qquad X_2 = 1\frac{1}{2} \qquad S_1 = 0 \qquad S_2 = 0 \qquad Z = 3,250$$

The Pour-More Foundry should purchase 1 carload of scrap per month from Source A and $1\frac{1}{2}$ carloads of scrap per month from Source B. The total monthly scrap cost will be $3,250, and no excess lead or copper above the minimum requirements will result.

Pay particular attention to the conversion of $\geq$ constraints to the first tableau form by adding artificial variables and subtracting slack variables. Note also that the subscripts of the artificial and slack variables correspond to the order of the constraints. A_1 and S_1 belong to the first constraint, and A_2 and S_2 belong to the second constraint.

The key complication in minimization problems is the more frequent inclusion of artificial variables. Negative M's, negative very large numbers, appear in the C row and column and consequently in Row Z and Row $(C - Z)$. If these M's are treated as any other very large number and are added, subtracted, and multiplied while the appropriate signs are observed, the minimization problems are as straightforward to solve as the maximization problems.

Interpreting Simplex Solutions

Example 5S.1 used the simplex method to solve Problem LP-1. Let us now examine LP-1 and the last tableau from this example to determine what information is available to POM decision makers.

LP-1 was formulated as:

$$\text{Max } Z = 3X_1 + 4X_2$$
$$\tfrac{1}{4}X_1 + \tfrac{1}{2}X_2 + S_1 \qquad\qquad = \quad 600 \text{ (supervision-hours)}$$
$$10X_1 + 5X_2 \qquad + S_2 \qquad = 10{,}000 \text{ (cash-dollars)}$$
$$\tfrac{3}{4}X_1 + \ X_2 \qquad\qquad + S_3 = \ 1{,}500 \text{ (secretarial-hours)}$$

where

X_1 = engineering-hours to be used on the project
X_2 = technician-hours to be used on the project
S_1 = unused supervision-hours
S_2 = unused cash-dollars
S_3 = unused secretarial-hours
Z = profits on the project

The last tableau in the simplex solution to LP-1 in Example 5S.1 was:

Third Tableau

C			3	4	0	0	0	
	SOL	b	X_1	X_2	S_1	S_2	S_3	ϕ
4	X_2	$933\tfrac{1}{3}$	0	1	$^{40}/_{15}$	$-\tfrac{1}{15}$	0	
3	X_1	$533\tfrac{1}{3}$	1	0	$-^{20}/_{15}$	$\tfrac{2}{15}$	0	
0	S_3	$166\tfrac{2}{3}$	0	0	$-\tfrac{5}{3}$	$-\tfrac{1}{30}$	1	
	Z	$5{,}333\tfrac{1}{3}$	3	4	$^{100}/_{15}$	$\tfrac{2}{15}$	0	
	(C − Z)		0	0	$-^{100}/_{15}$	$-\tfrac{2}{15}$	0	

$Z = 5{,}333\tfrac{1}{3}$ $S_1 = \ 0$
$X_1 = \ 533\tfrac{1}{3}$ $S_2 = \ 0$
$X_2 = \ 933\tfrac{1}{3}$ $S_3 = 166\tfrac{2}{3}$

The solution to LP-1 is deduced as follows: X_1, X_2, S_3, and Z are in the SOL column and their values are shown in Column b. Because S_1 and S_2 are not found in the SOL column, their values are zero. This solution indicates that management should use $533\tfrac{1}{3}$ engineering-hours and $933\tfrac{1}{3}$ technician-hours, yielding a profit of $5,333.33 for the project. All available supervision and cash would be used and $166\tfrac{2}{3}$ secretarial-hours would be unused. Let's check this:

$$\tfrac{1}{4}X_1 + \ \tfrac{1}{2}X_2 + S_1 = 600 \text{ (supervision-hours)}$$
$$\tfrac{1}{4}(533\tfrac{1}{3}) + \tfrac{1}{2}(933\tfrac{1}{3}) + \ 0 = 600$$
$$133\tfrac{1}{3} + \quad 466\tfrac{2}{3} \qquad = 600$$
$$600 \qquad = 600$$

The engineering- and technician-hours have used up all of the available supervision-hours; therefore, $S_1 = 0$.

$$10X_1 + \quad 5X_2 + S_2 = 10{,}000 \text{ (cash-dollars)}$$
$$10(533\tfrac{1}{3}) + 5(933\tfrac{1}{3}) + \quad 0 = 10{,}000$$
$$5{,}333\tfrac{1}{3} + 4{,}666\tfrac{2}{3} \qquad = 10{,}000$$
$$\qquad\qquad 10{,}000 \qquad = 10{,}000$$

The engineering- and technician-hours have also used up all of the available cash. Therefore, $S_2 = 0$.

$$\tfrac{3}{4}X_1 + \qquad X_2 + \qquad S_3 = 1{,}500$$
$$\tfrac{3}{4}(533\tfrac{1}{3}) + 1(933\tfrac{1}{3}) + (166\tfrac{2}{3}) = 1{,}500$$
$$400 + \qquad 933\tfrac{1}{3} + \quad 166\tfrac{2}{3} = 1{,}500$$
$$\qquad 1{,}333\tfrac{1}{3} + \quad 166\tfrac{2}{3} = 1{,}500$$

The engineering- and technician-hours have used up only $1{,}333\tfrac{1}{3}$ hours of the secretarial assistance available, which leaves $166\tfrac{2}{3}$ hours remaining unused.

This explains the solution to LP-1. There is, however, some additional information present in the last tableau of LP-1 that allows operations managers to shift resources around. This information is called *shadow prices* and is found in Row $(C - Z)$:

	X_1	X_2	S_1	S_2	S_3
$(C - Z)$	0	0	$-100\!/15$	$-\tfrac{2}{15}$	0

The zeros in the X_1 and X_2 columns mean that these variables are in the solution column, SOL. When nonzero numbers appear under the decision variables in Row $(C - Z)$, these values are the impact on Z of forcing one unit of a decision variable into the solution. In a maximization problem, a nonzero element would indicate how much Z would be reduced. In the case of a minimization problem, a nonzero element would show how much Z would be increased.

The elements under the slack variables S_1 and S_2 refer to the marginal value of one unit of each of the constraints. S_1 refers to the first constraint (the subscript is 1), supervision-hours. Since S_1 is not in the SOL column, $S_1 = 0$, which means that all of the supervision-hours are used. Management typically asks these questions:

1. How much would Z (profits) increase if we could find one more hour of supervision time (601 versus 600)?
2. How much would Z (profits) decrease if we had one less hour of supervision time (599 versus 600)?

The answer to both of these questions is found in Row $(C - Z)$ and the S_1 column: $100\!/15$ or $6.67. In other words, the new profits (Z) would be $5340.00 and $5326.67, respectively.

The element in Row $(C - Z)$ and the S_2 column indicates the impact upon Z if the right-hand side of the second constraint changes by one unit:

1. How much would Z (profits) increase if we could find one more dollar of cash (10,001 versus 10,000)?

2. How much would Z (profits) decrease if we had one less dollar of cash (9,999 versus 10,000)?

Again, the answer to both of these questions is $\frac{2}{15}$ or $.13. In other words, the new profits (Z) would be $5,333.46 and $5,333.21, respectively.

How much would we be willing to pay for some extra secretarial assistance? The element in Row $(C - Z)$ and the S_3 column indicates the answer to this question — nothing. This answer is also obvious from the solution to LP-1: if we have $166\frac{2}{3}$ hours of unused secretarial assistance, we would not pay anything for more of these hours.

An understanding of the shadow prices in Row $(C - Z)$ is valuable to management. This information allows managers to evaluate whether resources (supervision, secretarial, and cash in this example) should be shifted from other products or projects. If the cost of getting one unit of a resource is less than its shadow price, the resource should be acquired.

Interpreting simplex solutions of LP minimization problems is essentially the same as interpreting those of maximization problems. To demonstrate this similarity, let us examine Row $(C - Z)$ from the optimal tableau of Problem LP-2, a minimization problem:

	X_1	X_2	A_1	A_2	S_1	S_2
$(C - Z)$	0	0	$-M$ $+500$	$-M$ $+500$	-500	-500

The zeros under X_1 and X_2 mean that both X_1 and X_2 are in the solution. The values under A_1 and A_2 have no meaning. The 500 under S_1 means that if the lead requirement is raised or lowered one unit (1 ton per month), Z will change by $500. If the right-hand side of the first constraint were increased from 4 to 5, Z would increase from $3,250 to $3,750. If the right-hand side were decreased from 4 to 3, Z would decrease from $3,250 to $2,750. The meaning of the 500 under S_2 is similarly the marginal impact of 1 ton of copper upon Z.

The minimization and maximization LP problems are interpreted exactly the same way. It is usually helpful to have the original problem set up and in front of you when the last tableau is interpreted. The meanings of the variables in the solution and the shadow prices are then easier to understand.

Now, to further develop your ability to interpret simplex solutions, let us move on to a more realistic LP problem. Remember the Oklahoma Crude ingredient mix problem, Case 5.1, from Chapter 5? Example 5S.3 presents this problem and its simplex solution and fully interprets the meaning of the solution. Carefully reread the earlier problem before you begin this example.

Example 5S.3

Interpreting Simplex Solutions:
The Oklahoma Crude Oil Company
Ingredient Mix Problem

The variable definitions of the Oklahoma Crude Oil Company problem are:

X_1 = Thousands of gallons of Oklahoma crude to be purchased per month
X_2 = Thousands of gallons of Texas crude to be purchased per month
X_3 = Thousands of gallons of Kansas crude to be purchased per month
X_4 = Thousands of gallons of New Mexico crude to be purchased per month
X_5 = Thousands of gallons of Colorado crude to be purchased per month
S_1 = Excess regular gasoline over minimum market requirement in thousands of gallons
S_2 = Excess premium gasoline over minimum market requirement in thousands of gallons
S_3 = Excess low-lead gasoline over minimum market requirement in thousands of gallons
S_4 = Excess diesel fuel over minimum market requirement in thousands of gallons
S_5 = Excess heating oil over minimum market requirement in thousands of gallons
S_6 = Excess lubricating oil base over minimum market requirement in thousands of gallons
S_7 = Unused Oklahoma crude supply in thousands of gallons
S_8 = Unused Texas crude supply in thousands of gallons
S_9 = Unused Kansas crude supply in thousands of gallons
S_{10} = Unused New Mexico crude supply in thousands of gallons
S_{11} = Unused Colorado crude supply in thousands of gallons
$A_1, A_2, A_3, A_4, A_5,$ and A_6 = No meaning

$$\text{Min } Z = 200X_1 + 140X_2 + 150X_3 + 180X_4 + 120X_5$$

$$.4X_1 + .3X_2 + .3X_3 + .2X_4 + .3X_5 \geq 5{,}000 \text{ (regular gasoline market requirement)*}$$

$$.2X_1 + .3X_2 + .4X_3 + .3X_4 + .2X_5 \geq 3{,}000 \text{ (premium gasoline market requirement)}$$

$$.2X_1 + .1X_2 \qquad\quad + .3X_4 + .1X_5 \geq 3{,}000 \text{ (low-lead gasoline market requirement)}$$

$$.1X_1 + .1X_2 + .1X_3 \qquad\quad + .2X_5 \geq 2{,}000 \text{ (diesel fuel market requirement)}$$

$$.1X_2 + .1X_3 + .2X_4 + .1X_5 \geq 1{,}000 \text{ (heating oil market requirement)}$$

$$.1X_1 + .1X_2 + .1X_3 \qquad\quad + .1X_5 \geq 2{,}000 \text{ (lubricating oil base market requirement)}$$

$$X_1 \qquad\qquad\qquad\qquad\qquad\qquad \leq 8{,}000 \text{ (Oklahoma crude supply)}$$

$$X_2 \qquad\qquad\qquad\qquad\qquad \leq 4{,}000 \text{ (Texas crude supply)}$$

$$X_3 \qquad\qquad\qquad\qquad \leq 5{,}000 \text{ (Kansas crude supply)}$$

$$X_4 \qquad\qquad\qquad \leq 3{,}000 \text{ (New Mexico crude supply)}$$

$$X_5 \leq 6{,}000 \text{ (Colorado crude supply)}$$

---

* All requirements and supplies are in thousands of gallons.

A computer solution (last tableau) is presented in Table 5S.3.

Table 5S.3
Optimal Tableau from Ingredient Mix Problem: Oklahoma Crude Oil Company

C			-200	-140	-150	-180	-120	0	0	0	0
	SOL	b	X_1	X_2	X_3	X_4	X_5	S_1	S_2	S_3	S_4
-120	X_5	6,000	0	0	0	0	1	0	0	0	0
-180	X_4	1,333.33	0	0	0	1	0	0	0	-3.33	0
0	S_5	466.67	0	0	0	0	0	0	0	$-.67$	0
-150	X_3	2,000	0	0	1	0	0	0	0	0	0
0	S_2	2,200	0	0	0	0	0	0	1	-1	0
-140	X_2	4,000	0	1	0	0	0	0	0	0	0
-200	X_1	8,000	1	0	0	0	0	0	0	0	0
0	S_9	3,000	0	0	0	0	0	0	0	0	0
0	S_4	600	0	0	0	0	0	0	0	0	1
0	S_{10}	1,666.67	0	0	0	0	0	0	0	3.33	0
0	S_1	2,066.67	0	0	0	0	0	1	0	$-.67$	0
	Z	$-3,420,000$	-200	-140	-150	-180	-120	0	0	600	0
		(C − Z)	0	0	0	0	0	0	0	-600	0

a. What should management do? In other words, what is the complete meaning of the values of the decision variables, slack variables, artificial variables, and Z in the optimal solution to management decision makers? **b.** What is the meaning of each element in Row (C − Z)?

Solution

a. What should management do? What is the complete meaning of the values of the variables?

$X_1 =$ 8,000 (buy 8 million gallons of crude oil per month from Oklahoma)
$X_2 =$ 4,000 (buy 4 million gallons of crude oil per month from Texas)
$X_3 =$ 2,000 (buy 2 million gallons of crude oil per month from Kansas)
$X_4 =$ 1,333⅓ (buy 1⅓ million gallons of crude oil per month from New Mexico)
$X_5 =$ 6,000 (buy 6 million gallons of crude oil per month from Colorado)
$S_1 =$ 2,066⅔ (2,066,667 gallons of excess regular gasoline will be supplied monthly)
$S_2 =$ 2,200 (2,200,000 gallons of excess premium gasoline will be supplied monthly)

0	0	−M	−M	−M	−M	−M	−M	0	0	0	0	0
S_5	S_6	A_1	A_2	A_3	A_4	A_5	A_6	S_7	S_8	S_9	S_{10}	S_{11}
0	0	0	0	0	0	0	0	0	0	0	0	1
0	0	0	0	3.33	0	0	0	−.67	−.33	0	0	−.33
1	−1	0	0	.67	0	−1	1	−.23	−.07	0	0	−.07
0	−10	0	0	0	0	0	10	−1	−1	0	0	−1
0	−4	0	−1	1	0	0	4	−.4	−.2	0	0	−.3
0	0	0	0	0	0	0	0	0	1	0	0	0
0	0	0	0	0	0	0	0	1	0	0	0	0
0	10	0	0	0	0	0	−10	1	1	1	0	1
0	−1	0	0	0	−1	0	1	0	0	0	0	.1
0	0	0	0	−3.33	0	0	0	.67	.33	0	1	.33
0	−3	−1	0	.67	0	0	3	−.03	−.07	0	0	0
0	1,500	0	0	−600	0	0	−1,500	70	70	0	0	90
0	−1,500	−M	−M	−M +600	−M	−M	−M +1,500	−70	−70	0	0	−90

$S_3 =$ 0   (no excess low-lead gasoline will be supplied monthly)

$S_4 =$ 600   (600,000 gallons of excess diesel fuel will be supplied monthly)

$S_5 =$ 466⅔ (466,667 gallons of excess heating oil will be supplied monthly)

$S_6 =$ 0   (no excess lubricating oil base will be supplied monthly)

$S_7 =$ 0   (all Oklahoma crude oil available will be purchased monthly)

$S_8 =$ 0   (all Texas crude oil available will be purchased monthly)

$S_9 =$ 3,000 (3,000,000 gallons of Kansas crude oil will be available and not purchased monthly)

$S_{10} =$ 1,666⅔ (1,666,667 gallons of New Mexico crude oil will be available and not purchased monthly)

$S_{11} =$ 0   (all Colorado crude oil available will be purchased monthly)

$A_1, A_2, A_3, A_4, A_5,$ and A_6 = No meaning

$Z = 3,420,000$ ($3,420,000 crude oil cost per month will result)

b. Interpret Row $(C − Z)$:

    1. The values in the $A_1, A_2, A_3, A_4, A_5,$ and A_6 columns have no meaning.

2. The zeros in the X_1, X_2, X_3, X_4, and X_5 columns mean that all of these variables are in the solution.

3. The zeros in the S_1, S_2, S_4, S_5, S_9, and S_{10} columns mean that a 1,000-gallon change in the RHS of these constraints will not affect the monthly crude oil cost (Z), because each of these slack variables is in the solution. For example, $S_1 = 2,066\frac{2}{3}$ means that 2,066,667 gallons more than the 5,000,000 RHS of the regular gasoline minimum market requirement is supplied. Therefore, raising or lowering the RHS a small amount will not affect Z.

Column	Row (C − Z)	Interpretation
S_3	−600	If the low-lead gasoline monthly market requirement were increased by 1,000 gallons, Z would increase $600.
S_6	−1,500	If the lubricating oil base monthly market requirement were increased by 1,000 gallons, Z would increase $1,500.
S_7	−70	If the amount of Oklahoma crude available each month were increased by 1,000 gallons, Z would decrease by $70.
S_8	−70	If the amount of Texas crude available each month were increased by 1,000 gallons, Z would decrease by $70.
S_{11}	−90	If the amount of Colorado crude available each month were increased by 1,000 gallons, Z would decrease by $90.

Post Optimality Analysis

Post optimality analysis, or *sensitivity analysis* as it is often called, manipulates the elements of the last tableau of the simplex procedure to determine the sensitivity of the solution to changes in the original problem. Here are some of the questions that this analysis seeks to answer:

1. How will Z change if the RHS of any constraint changes? This analysis was treated earlier in this section. The values in Row (C − Z) under the slack variables provide this information.

2. If a decision variable is not in the optimal solution (equals zero), how will Z change if one unit of the decision variable is forced into the solution ($X_i = 1$)? This analysis was also treated earlier in this supplement. The values in Row (C − Z) under the decision variables provide this information.

3. Over what range can the RHS change and the shadow prices in Row (C − Z) remain valid?

4. How will Z change if one of the coefficients of a decision variable in the objective function changes by one unit?

5. How will Z change if one of the coefficients of a decision variable in a constraint changes by one unit?

These and other questions usually assume that all other parts of the original problem remain unchanged and only the singular change under consideration occurs. Parametric programming does seek to examine two or more of these changes simultaneously, but most other analyses assume singular changes.

These and other post optimality questions are deduced from the optimal tableau.

Although this is a popular topic with operations researchers, one rather obvious method for answering these and other post optimality questions exists: make the desired changes in the original problem, input the new problem to the computer, and interpret the new results. This approach may be less sophisticated and slightly more expensive, but it is effective in answering management's post optimality questions.

Unusual Features of Some LP Problems

Two linear programming situations deserve special attention—degeneracy and alternate optimal solutions. *Degeneracy* is a condition in which there is a tie between two or more leaving variables in any max or min simplex tableau (not a condition of social degeneration). For example, consider this problem:

$$\text{Max } Z = 5X_1 + 10X_2$$
$$X_1 + 3X_2 \le 6$$
$$2X_1 + 2X_2 \le 4$$

First Tableau

C			5	10	0	0	
	SOL	b	X_1	X_2	S_1	S_2	ϕ
0	S_1	6	1	3	1	0	$6/3 = 2$
0	S_2	4	2	2	0	1	$4/2 = 2$
	Z	0	0	0	0	0	
	(C − Z)	5	10	0	0		

$$\uparrow$$
Entering
Variable

In the first tableau a tie for the leaving variable exists. Therefore, a condition of degeneracy is present. Why is this a problem? It usually poses absolutely no problem at all in arriving at an optimal solution. One of the variables is arbitrarily selected to leave, and the simplex method is continued. In rare instances, however, *looping* can occur. In other words, in the example above, if S_2 is selected to leave the first tableau, S_1 and X_2 are in the SOL column of the second tableau. S_1 could leave and S_2 could reenter the third tableau, and S_2 and X_2 would be in the SOL column. S_2 could leave and S_1 reenter the fourth tableau, and S_1 and X_2 would be in the fourth tableau. This switching could conceivably continue endlessly, thus prohibiting an optimal solution.

Looping situations almost never happen in nontrivial real LP problems in POM. When they do, a simple solution is to add or subtract an infinitesimally small amount to either the RHS or coefficient in the ϕ ratio to break the tie. For example, the original problem could be modified as follows:

$$\text{Max } Z = 5X_1 + 10X_2$$
$$X_1 + 3X_2 \leq 6.0001$$
$$2X_1 + 2X_2 \leq 4$$

This slight modification breaks the tie of leaving variables and removes the degeneracy condition. Purists would argue that we have needlessly introduced imprecision into the problem. But experience teaches us that this amount of imprecision is usually present anyway in most computer solutions because of rounding and truncation of solutions.

In summary, degeneracy conditions are usually ignored, and one of the tying leaving variables is selected arbitrarily to leave the tableau. Looping almost never occurs in real LP problems in POM.

Alternate optimal solutions exist when an element under a variable in Row $(C - Z)$ is zero and that variable is not in the solution. For example, consider this problem:

$$\text{Max } Z = X_1 + 7X_2$$
$$X_1 + 7X_2 \leq 14$$
$$7X_1 + X_2 \leq 14$$

Second Tableau

C			1	7	0	0		
	SOL	**b**	X_1	X_2	S_1	S_2	ϕ	
7	X_2	2	$1/7$	1	$1/7$	0	$2/1/7 = 14$	Leaving
0	S_2	12	$(48/7)$	0	$-1/7$	1	$12/48/7 = 1\frac{3}{4}$	← Variable
	Z	14	1	7	1	0		
	(C − Z)		0	0	−1	0		

↑
Entering
Variable

Note that the zero under X_1 in Row $(C - Z)$ of this optimal tableau indicates that X_1 can enter the solution ($X_2 = 2$, $X_1 = 0$, $Z = 14$) with no change in Z. Let X_1 enter to check this out. X_1 enters and S_2 leaves:

$-1/7(1\frac{3}{4})$	$-1/7(1)$	$-1/7(0)$	$-1/7(-1/48)$	$-1/7(7/48)$
$-1/4$	$-1/7$	0	$1/336$	$-7/336$
2	$1/7$	1	$1/7$	0
$1\frac{3}{4}$	0	1	$49/336$	$-7/336$

A new alternate optimal solution emerges in the third tableau where $X_1 = 1\frac{3}{4}$, $X_2 = 1\frac{3}{4}$, and $Z = 14$. Z has not changed. Note that the zero in Row $(C - Z)$ under S_2 in the third tableau indicates also that an alternate optimal solution exists, the one in the second tableau.

Third Tableau

C			1	7	0	0	
	SOL	b	X_1	X_2	S_1	S_2	ϕ
7	X_2	$1\frac{3}{4}$	0	1	$\frac{49}{336}$	$-\frac{7}{336}$	
1	X_1	$1\frac{3}{4}$	1	0	$-\frac{1}{48}$	$\frac{7}{48}$	
	Z	14	1	7	1	0	
	(C − Z)		0	0	−1	0	

So what does all of this mean? Only that we should always examine Row (C − Z) to inspect for alternate optimal solutions. Why? Because these alternatives offer management the ultimate in flexibility—alternatives with the same profits or costs.

Now, let us turn to a solution method designed to solve a special type of LP problem—the transportation problem.

Transportation Method

Earlier in this chapter we discussed selecting a set of shipments from sources to destinations that minimized period transportation costs. These and problems with similar characteristics can be analyzed by either the simplex method or the transportation method. We present the essential elements of the transportation method here.

Characteristics of Transportation Problems

Transportation problems have these characteristics:

1. A finite and homogeneous set of discrete units must be shipped from several sources to several destinations in a particular time period.

2. Each source has a precise number of units that must be shipped in the time period.

3. Each destination has a precise number of units that must be received in the time period.

4. Each discrete unit to be shipped has a specific transportation cost from each source to each destination.

5. The objective is to minimize the total transportation costs for the time period.

6. The decision variables represent the number of units to be shipped from each source to each destination during the time period.

Such problems were first formulated in the 1940s and the solution procedures that will be presented in this section were developed in the 1950s. Although the characteristics listed above accurately depict the problems as they were originally formulated and solved, later formulations and solutions allow a much broader range of problems. As we shall see later in this section, problems with ≥ and ≤ constraints, maximization objectives, demands greater than supply, and other characteristics are now routinely described as *transportation problems*. Solution procedures that are called the *transportation method* also are used to routinely solve such expanded problems.

The term *transportation problem* is in some cases a misnomer because the problem may not involve any transportation or movement of materials at all. It is true that the early formulations of these problems were aimed at problems in which materials were actually being shipped from several sources to several destinations. When we use the term today, we are referring to any LP problem that fits the unique structure referred to and described in Example 5.6 of Chapter 5. See Problem 21 at the end of this supplement for an example of such a nontransportation type of problem.

Solution Procedures of the Transportation Method

The procedures of the transportation method are exhibited in Table 5S.4. To demonstrate these procedures, Example 5S.4 analyzes a problem of a manufacturing company that must select a new location for a factory to produce computer peripheral units. The key factor in this facility location decision is the costs of transportation between the various sources and destinations, a problem particularly well suited for solving by the transportation method.

Table 5S.4
Procedures of the Transportation Method

1. Formulate the problem in a transportation table.
2. Use the northwest corner rule or VAM to obtain a feasible starting solution.
3. Test the optimality of the solution by using the stepping-stone or MODI methods. If the solution is optimal, stop. If not, continue to the next step.
4. Develop a new transportation table that is an improved solution. Go back to Step 3.

Notice in Steps 2 and 3 of Table 5S.4 that two alternative ways can be used to either test a solution for optimality or obtain a starting solution. Example 5S.4 uses only the northwest corner rule and the stepping-stone method so that you can get the overall picture of how the transportation method works. Later the same problem will be worked with the MODI and VAM methods so that you can appreciate the relationships among the methods.

Example 5S.4 uses the well-known *stepping-stone method* to determine optimality and to develop improved solutions. A newer and more frequently used method is the *MODI method* (modified distribution method). This procedure is similar to the stepping-stone method, but it is more efficient in computing the improvement costs (circuit costs in the stepping-stone method) for the empty cells.

Example 5S.4

The Northwest Corner Rule and the Stepping-Stone Method

The Plain View Manufacturing Company presently has two factories at Amarillo and Waco, Texas and three warehouses at Dallas, San Antonio, and Houston, Texas. In recent months Plain View has been unable to produce and ship enough of its product (a computer peripheral unit) to satisfy the market demand at the warehouses. A new factory is proposed to increase factory capacity, but two alternative locations (Huntsville and Austin, Texas) seem equally attractive in all respects except transportation costs. Bill Mayer, Plain View's president, wants to locate the factory at either Huntsville or Austin, whichever location results in the lowest monthly transportation costs for Plain View. The monthly shipping costs for Plain View will be $4,200 if the new factory is located at Austin. Mayer wants to determine what Plain View's monthly shipping costs will be if the factory is located at Huntsville.

The monthly capacities of the old and new factories, the monthly warehouse requirements, and the transportation costs per unit from each factory to each warehouse are:

Factory	Monthly Capacity (Units)
Amarillo	400
Waco	1,000
Huntsville or Austin	600
Total	2,000

Warehouse	Monthly Warehouse Requirements (Units)
San Antonio	300
Dallas	900
Houston	800
Total	2,000

Transportation Costs

	Warehouses		
Factory	San Antonio	Dallas	Houston
Amarillo	$3.00	$2.00	$4.00
Waco	2.00	2.00	3.00
Huntsville	2.00	2.00	1.00

a. Use the transportation method to determine the total monthly transportation costs if the new factory is located at Huntsville. **b.** Which location is preferred for the new factory, Huntsville or Austin? **c.** If the Huntsville location is preferred, how many units per month should be shipped from each factory to each warehouse after the new factory is built? Follow the steps in Table 5S.4 for the transportation method. These steps are illustrated in Figure 5S.1.

Solution

1 and 2. Formulate the problem in a transportation table and use the northwest corner rule to obtain a starting solution. Note that the monthly factory capacities are placed on the right-hand side of the table opposite the appropriate factory row. Similarly, warehouse requirements are placed along the bottom of the table under the appropriate warehouse column. The per-unit shipping cost is shown in a box within each factory-warehouse cell. Note also that the total capacity for all factories equals the total warehouse requirements.

This starting solution shows how many units are shipped from each factory to each warehouse. When a cell is empty, zero units are to be shipped. The initial solution is obtained by beginning in the northwest cell (Amarillo-San Antonio) and allocating as many units as possible to this cell and proceeding likewise from left to right and downward. Only 300 units are possible

Figure 5S.1
Transportation Tables of Example 5S.4

Step 3—First, evaluate the Amarillo–Houston empty cell:
Circuit cost = + 4 − 3 + 2 − 2 = +$1.00. Place this cost in a circle.

To From	San Antonio	Dallas	Houston	Factory Totals
Amarillo	**300** `3`	**100** `2` (−)	(+1) `4` (+)	400
Waco	`2`	**800** `2` (+)	**200** `3` (−)	1,000
Huntsville	`2`	`2`	**600** `1`	600
Warehouse Totals	300	900	800	2,000 2,000

Next, evaluate the Waco–San Antonio empty cell:
Circuit cost = + 2 − 3 + 2 − 2 = −$1.00. Place this cost in a circle.

To From	San Antonio	Dallas	Houston	Factory Totals
Amarillo	**300** `3` (−)	**100** `2` (+)	`4`	400
Waco	(−1) `2` (+)	**800** `2` (−)	**200** `3`	1,000
Huntsville	`2`	`2`	**600** `1`	600
Warehouse Totals	300	900	800	2,000 2,000

Next, evaluate the Huntsville–San Antonio empty cell:
Circuit cost = + 2 − 3 + 2 − 2 + 3 − 1 = + $1.00. Place this cost in a circle.

To From	San Antonio	Dallas	Houston	Factory Totals
Amarillo	**300** `3` (−)	**100** `2` (+)	`4`	400
Waco	`2`	**800** `2` (−)	**200** `3` (+)	1,000
Huntsville	(+1) `2` (+)	`2`	**600** `1` (−)	600
Warehouse Totals	300	900	800	2,000 2,000

Next, evaluate the Huntsville–Dallas empty cell:
Circuit cost = + 2 − 2 + 3 − 1 = + $2.00. Place this cost in a circle.

To From	San Antonio	Dallas	Houston	Factory Totals
Amarillo	**300** `3`	**100** `2`	`4`	400
Waco	`2`	**800** `2` (−)	**200** `3` (+)	1,000
Huntsville	`2`	(+2) `2` (+)	**600** `1` (−)	600
Warehouse Totals	300	900	800	2,000 2,000

Steps 1 and 2—Starting Solution Using the Northwest Corner Rule

From \ To	San Antonio	Dallas	Houston	Factory Totals
Amarillo	**300** ╳ 3	**100** 2	4	400
Waco	2	**800** ╳ 2	**200** ╳ 3	1,000
Huntsville	2	2	**600** ╳ 1	600
Warehouse Totals	300	900	800	2,000 / 2,000

Transportation Table #1

From \ To	San Antonio	Dallas	Houston	Factory Totals
Amarillo	**300** 3	**100** 2	(+1) 4	400
Waco	(-1) 2	**800** 2	**200** 3	1,000
Huntsville	(+1) 2	(+2) 2	**600** 1	600
Warehouse Totals	300	900	800	2,000 / 2,000

The monthly costs of Transportation Table #1 are:

Factory	Warehouse	Units to Be Shipped per Month	Monthly Transportation Cost ($)
Amarillo	San Antonio	300	$ 900
Amarillo	Dallas	100	200
Waco	Dallas	800	1,600
Waco	Houston	200	600
Huntsville	Houston	600	600
	Totals	2,000	$3,900

Transportation Table #2

From \ To	San Antonio	Dallas	Houston	Factory Totals
Amarillo	(+1) 3	**400** 2	(+1) 4	400
Waco	**300** 2	**500** 2	**200** 3	1,000
Huntsville	(+2) 2	(+2) 2	**600** 1	600
Warehouse Totals	300	900	800	2,000 / 2,000

The monthly costs of Transportation Table #2 are:

Factory	Warehouse	Units to Be Shipped per Month	Monthly Transportation Cost ($)
Amarillo	Dallas	400	$ 800
Waco	San Antonio	300	600
Waco	Dallas	500	1,000
Waco	Houston	200	600
Huntsville	Houston	600	600
	Totals	2,000	$3,600

1. Select an empty cell from the transportation table.
2. Draw a closed circuit between that empty cell and other stones (occupied cells) by using only straight vertical or horizontal lines. The circuit may skip over stones or other empty cells, but the corners of the circuit may occur only at stones (occupied cells) and the empty cell that is being evaluated.
3. Beginning at the empty cell being evaluated, move clockwise and alternatively assign positive (+) and negative (−) signs to the costs of the cells at the corners of the circuit from Step 2.
4. Total the per-unit costs of the cells at the corners of the

circuit. The circuit total corresponds to the Row (C − Z) values of the simplex method, and these values mean the amount of change in total shipping costs that can be realized by moving one unit to the empty cell under examination. Positive values mean costs will rise; negative values mean costs will fall.
5. Return to Step 1 and continue until all empty cells have been evaluated. The new cell to enter the solution is the cell whose circuit has the most negative circuit total cost.
6. If all circuit totals are positive or zero, the solution is optimal. If negative circuit totals exist, develop an improved solution.

in the Amarillo-San Antonio cell because this amount satisfies the San Antonio warehouse requirement. Moving to the right, we can allocate only 100 units to the Amarillo-Dallas cell because this completes the Amarillo factory capacity of 400 units. Next, we move downward and allocate 800 units to the Waco-Dallas cell, right and allocate 200 units to the Waco-Houston cell, and so on until all 2,000 units have been allocated.

3. **Test the optimality of the solution by using the stepping-stone method.** This step requires systematically evaluating each of the empty cells in Transportation Table #1 to determine if monthly transportation costs can be reduced by moving any units into the empty cells.

    The stepping-stone evaluation method involves the steps in Table 5S.5.

    As shown in Figure 5S.1, Transportation Table #1 is not optimal because we have a negative circuit cost for the Waco-San Antonio cell and we can reduce monthly transportation costs by moving some units into this empty cell.

4. **Develop a new transportation table that is an improved solution.** An improved solution is obtained by moving as many units as possible into the empty cell of the last transportation table with the most negative circuit cost. But how many units can be moved into the Waco–San Antonio cell, which had a negative circuit cost in the last step? Let us again examine the stepping-stone circuit for this cell.

    The maximum number of units that can be moved into the Waco–San Antonio empty cell is 300 — the smallest number of units in a negative cell on the Waco–San Antonio stepping-stone circuit. To complete the improved solution, subtract the smallest number of units in negative cells, 300, from all negative cells and add this same number of units to the positive cells of the circuit. All other cells not on this circuit remain unchanged. This new solution is shown in Transportation Table #2 of Figure 5S.1.

    This solution is an improved one — $3,900 in Transportation Table #1 versus $3,600 in Transportation Table #2 — but is it optimal? Optimality can be determined once again by following the stepping-stone procedures. The stepping-stone circuit costs of the empty cells are shown in circles in Transportation Table #2 of Figure 5S.1. Because all stepping-stone circuit costs are positive or zero, the solution in Transportation Table #2 is optimal.

    Now let us answer the questions of Plain View's location problem:

a. If the factory is located at Huntsville, Plain View's total monthly transportation costs will be $3,600.

b. The Huntsville location is preferred because Plain View's monthly transportation costs are less than if Austin were selected ($3,600 versus $4,200).

c. Plain View should make these monthly shipments:

Factory	Warehouse	Number of Units
Amarillo	Dallas	400
Waco	San Antonio	300
Waco	Dallas	500
Waco	Houston	200
Huntsville	Houston	600
	Total	2,000

Example 5S.5 uses the MODI method to test Transportation Table #1 in Figure 5S.1 for optimality. Before you begin this example, however, perhaps it would be helpful if you would do two things. First, review the procedures of the transportation method from Table 5S.4 to get the overall view of the procedure again. Notice that the only way that the MODI method affects the procedures of the transportation method is in testing each transportation table for optimality. Everything else in the procedure stays the same — formulating the transportation tables, using either the northwest corner rule or VAM to obtain a starting solution, and developing new transportation tables that are improved solutions. Next, review Step 3 in Figure 5S.1. This step uses the stepping-stone method to check for optimality.

In Example 5S.5 we first compute the R_i and K_j for the table. R_1 is always set equal to zero; this allows us to compute all other values of R_i and K_j *for filled cells.* After we know these values, we can directly calculate the circuit costs for the empty cells of the transportation table, but without the necessity of drawing the stepping-stone circuits for *all* of these cells as in the stepping-stone method. Next, if there are any negative circuit costs, we would draw the stepping-stone circuit for the empty cell that has the most negative circuit cost, just as we did in Figure 5S.1, and develop a new transportation table with an improved solution as before. Although the R_i and K_j must be recomputed for each transportation table, the MODI method is more efficient than the stepping-stone method and tends to be used more frequently in practice.

The northwest corner rule provides a starting solution to transportation problems, but one that is arbitrary. In most problems this results in too many transportation tables. This source of inefficiency may not seem too important to you now after having worked through Example 5S.4 in just two transportation tables, but in problems of more realistic proportions, say 25 sources and 40 destinations, *many* tables would be required if we used the northwest corner rule to obtain a starting solution. *Vogel's Approximation Method (VAM)* was developed to obtain a more efficient starting solution. In fact, in many problems the starting solution is optimal.

Example 5S.5

MODI Method of Testing Transportation Tables for Optimality

Transportation Table #1

R_i \ K_j	To \ From	$K_1 = 3$ San Antonio	$K_2 = 2$ Dallas	$K_3 = 3$ Houston	Factory Totals
$R_1 = 0$	Amarillo	300 · 3	100 · 2	(+1) · 4	400
$R_2 = 0$	Waco	(−1) · 2	800 · 2	200 · 3	1,000
$R_3 = -2$	Huntsville	(+1) · 2	(+2) · 2	600 · 1	600
	Warehouse Totals	300	900	800	2,000 / 2,000

Calculating R_i and K_j for Filled Cells

$R_i + K_j = C_{ij}$, where C_{ij} represents the transportation cost of the ij cell

$R_1 = 0$

$R_1 + K_1 = C_{11}$

$0 + K_1 = 3, \quad K_1 = 3$

$R_1 + K_2 = C_{12}$

$0 + K_2 = 2, \quad K_2 = 2$

$R_2 + K_2 = C_{22}$

$R_2 + 2 = 2, \quad R_2 = 0$

$R_2 + K_3 = C_{23}$

$0 + K_3 = 3, \quad K_3 = 3$

$R_3 + K_3 = C_{33}$

$R_3 + 3 = 1, \quad R_3 = -2$

Calculating Circuit Costs for Unfilled Cells

$C_{ij} - R_i - K_j$

Amarillo – Houston
$$= C_{13} - R_1 - K_3$$
$$= 4 - 0 - 3 = +1$$

Waco – San Antonio
$$= C_{21} - R_2 - K_1$$
$$= 2 - 0 - 3 = -1$$

Huntsville – San Antonio
$$= C_{31} - R_3 - K_1$$
$$= 2 - (-2) - 3 = +1$$

Huntsville – Dallas
$$= C_{32} - R_3 - K_2$$
$$= 2 - (-2) - 2 = +2$$

Although the VAM method is more complicated than the northwest corner rule, in realistic problems that must be solved by hand, VAM is a much more practical way to obtain starting solutions.

Example 5S.6 develops a starting solution to the transportation problem of our previous example. In working through the procedures of the VAM method, refer to Table 5S.6, which explains the steps of the method that are applied in Example 5S.6. In Step 1 of the method in the example, the D_1 row and column are first completed. These values represent the difference between the lowest unit cost and next lowest

Example 5S.6

Starting Solutions with Vogel's Approximation Method (VAM)

From \ To	San Antonio	Dallas	Houston	Factory Totals	D_1	D_2	D_3	D_4
Amarillo	3	(3) 400 — 2	4	400	1	1	(1)	
Waco	(4) 300 — 2	(4) 500 — 2	(2) 200 — 3	1,000	0	0	0	(0)
Huntsville	2	2	(1) 600 — 1	600	1			
Warehouse Totals	300	900	800	2,000 / 2,000				
D_1	0	0	(2)					
D_2	1	0	(1)					
D_3	1	0						
D_4								

D_i Column Calculations

D_1 $2-2=0$, $2-2=0$, $3-1=$ ②
D_2 $3-2=1$, $2-2=0$, $4-3=$ ①
D_3 $3-2=1$, $2-2=0$
D_4

D_i Row Calculations

D_1 $3-2=1$, $2-2=0$, $2-1=1$
D_2 $3-2=1$, $2-2=0$
D_3 $3-2=$ ①, $2-2=0$
D_4 $2-2=$ ⓪

Units Allocated at Iteration (i)

(1) 600/Huntsville – Houston
(2) 200/Waco – Houston
(3) 400/Amarillo – Dallas
(4) 500/Waco – Dallas
    300/Waco – San Antonio

Table 5S.6
Steps of the VAM Method

1. For each row and column of the transportation table, compute the difference between the lowest unit cost and the next lowest unit cost and record this difference. Place the row differences in a column to the right of the table under a heading of D_I and the column differences in a row across the bottom of the table with a heading of D_i, where i represents the number of times you have done this step.
2. Select either the row or column with the largest difference. If ties occur, arbitrarily select between tying elements.
3. Allocate as many units as possible to the cell with the lowest cost in the row or column selected in Step 2.
4. If the units in a row or column have been exhausted in Step 3, that row or column may be eliminated from further consideration in subsequent calculations by drawing a line through it.
5. When differences cannot be calculated in Step 1 because only one row or one column remains, this is not an unusual occurrence as we near the end of the process. Calculate the differences that are possible and continue.
6. Return to Step 1 and continue until the units in all of the rows and columns have been allocated.

unit cost for each row and column. In Step 2 the Houston column has the largest difference on the first iteration and it is selected. In Step 3 the Huntsville-Houston cell has the lowest unit cost within the Houston column, and we therefore allocate 600 units to that cell, the most possible. Because all of the Huntsville row has been allocated, you may draw a line all the way through this row and it is eliminated from further consideration. This completes the first iteration.

Next, we begin the second iteration in the D_2 row and column. There are several ties for the largest difference in the D_2 row and column—the Amarillo and Waco rows and the San Antonio and Houston columns. The Houston column is selected arbitrarily, and 200 units are allocated to the Waco-Houston cell within the Houston column because this cell has the lowest remaining unit cost. This allocation exhausts the Houston column and a line may be drawn through the column. This completes the second iteration. The third and fourth iterations are similarly completed.

The starting solution obtained in this example is the same optimal solution obtained in Figure 5S.1 of Example 5S.4. This is not always the case and although the VAM method does yield an efficient starting solution when compared to the northwest corner method, it still must be considered only a starting solution and all of the steps of the transportation method listed in Table 5S.4 must be followed. In other words, in Example 5S.6, after the last iteration we would need to use either the stepping-stone or the MODI method to test the solution for optimality and proceed with the entire transportation method.

The reason that the VAM method yields better starting solutions than the northwest corner rule is that the northwest corner rule does not consider any cost information when the starting solution is determined—units are arbitrarily allocated on a northwest diagonal regardless of the costs. In the VAM method an opportunity cost principle is applied. At each iteration the difference between the lowest unit cost and the next lowest unit cost is the opportunity cost of not allocating units to a row or column. By selecting the largest difference, the largest opportunity cost is avoided. By taking into account the costs of alternative allocations, the VAM method yields very good starting solutions that are sometimes optimal, particularly in simple problems.

Figure 5S.2
An Unbalanced Transportation Problem

From \ To	1	2	3	Dummy Destination	Source Totals
A	3.5	2.0 / 1,000	4.0	0	1,000
B	4.0	2.5 / 2,000	1.5 / 3,000	0	5,000
C	2.0 / 1,000	3.0 / 1,000	3.0	0 / 2,000	4,000
Destination Totals	1,000	4,000	3,000	2,000	10,000 / 10,000

Unbalanced Problems

Example 5S.4 involved a problem where the total number of units to be shipped from sources exactly equaled the number of units required at destinations. This is called a *balanced transportation problem*. It is not unusual to have an *unbalanced transportation problem*, where the number of units that can be shipped from sources exceeds the number required at destinations or vice versa. Figure 5S.2 is the optimal transportation table of such an unbalanced transportation problem.

A dummy destination column is entered into the table to account for the difference between destination requirements and source shipments. Note that the shipping cost from any source to the dummy destination is zero. The only function of the fictitious destination is to balance the problem. The interpretation of the 2,000 units in the Source C – dummy destination cell is that 2,000 units of the capacity at Source C will not be shipped. The dummy destination column therefore serves the same purpose as slack variables in the simplex method. All other solution procedures (the northwest corner rule, VAM, the stepping-stone or MODI methods) discussed earlier are followed to solve unbalanced transportation problems. The interpretation of the final solution is exactly the same in either balanced or unbalanced problems, with the exception of the dummy row or column interpretation.

Degeneracy

Degeneracy is another complication that can be encountered in transportation problems. The number of occupied cells in a transportation table must be equal to the number of sources plus the number of destinations minus one. Thus, in Example 5S.4 all transportation tables always had 5 occupied cells (3 sources + 3 destinations − 1 = 5). Degeneracy is present when less than this minimum number of occupied cells occurs. Degeneracy, if present, interferes with the drawing of stepping-stone circuits when the stepping-stone method is used, or it makes it impossible to compute the R_i and K_j if the MODI method is used to check for optimality of transportation tables, and special procedures are necessary to successfully complete these procedures.

If degeneracy occurs in the initial transportation table solution after employing either the VAM method or the northwest corner rule, a zero is assigned to one of the empty cells. The empty cell selected is usually one that creates an unbroken chain of occupied cells from NW to SE across the transportation table. The zero cell is treated as an occupied cell with zero units occupying the cell when stepping-stone circuits are drawn or R_i or K_j are calculated. This manipulation allows us to complete our check for optimality without changing the nature of the transportation problem.

When degeneracy occurs in transportation tables beyond the initial solution, a slightly different procedure is used. Figure 5S.3 shows Transportation Tables 1 and 2 of a transportation problem where degeneracy exists. Notice that the initial solution to this transportation problem has 6 occupied cells, exactly the required minimum (3 sources + 4 destinations − 1 = 6). The stepping-stone circuit of the San Diego – Seattle cell (superimposed on Transportation Table 1) has the most negative circuit cost of any empty cell in this table, and an improved solution must

Figure 5S.3
A Degenerate Transportation Table

Transportation Table 1

From \ To	Seattle	Denver	New Orleans	New York	Factory Totals
Miami	5,000 · 1.2 (−)	5,000 · .7 (+)	.5	.6	10,000
Chicago	.7	5,000 · .5 (−)	10,000 · .5	5,000 · .6 (+)	20,000
San Diego	.5 (+)	.7	.8	15,000 · 1.2 (−)	15,000
Warehouse Totals	5,000	10,000	10,000	20,000	45,000 / 45,000

Transportation Table 2

From \ To	Seattle	Denver	New Orleans	New York	Factory Totals
Miami	0 · 1.2	10,000 · .7	.5	.6	10,000
Chicago	.7	.5	10,000 · .5	10,000 · .6	20,000
San Diego	5,000 · .5	.7	.8	10,000 · 1.2	15,000
Warehouse Totals	5,000	10,000	10,000	20,000	45,000 / 45,000

be developed from this circuit. Remember that we first identify the smallest number of units in the negative cells (5,000 units) and then subtract this number from all negative cells and add it to all positive cells on the circuit.

Ordinarily, this procedure makes one occupied cell go to zero units, but in this circuit both the Miami–Seattle and Chicago–Denver cells go to zero. That is what causes the solution in Transportation Table 2 to be degenerate, a condition comparable to a tie for leaving variables in the simplex method. We handle this degenerate situation in the transportation method by assigning a zero number of units to either one of the cells reduced to zero units. In Figure 5S.3 the zero is assigned to either the Miami–Seattle cell or the Chicago–Denver cell. The zero is then treated as an occupied cell, but with zero units, when applying either the stepping-stone or the MODI method of checking subsequent transportation tables for optimality. All other procedures of the transportation method are followed as before.

When more than two occupied cells are eliminated, more than one zero must be assigned to these cells to overcome the condition of degeneracy. Add enough zero cells so that the number of occupied cells equals the number of sources plus the number of destinations minus one. These problems are otherwise solved as before, with standard transportation method procedures.

Assignment Method

The *assignment method* is another method for solving LP problems. Like the transportation method, the assignment method is easier to work than the simplex method, but it can be used only on LP problems with special characteristics. These characteristics are even more restrictive than those of the transportation method:

1. *n* objects must be assigned to *n* destinations.
2. Each object must be assigned to some destination.
3. Each destination must be assigned an object.
4. The objective is to minimize the total cost of the assignment.

These problems can be solved by the transportation method where the units to be "shipped" is 1 for all rows and columns and the number of rows equals the number of columns. In this formulation the "sources" are the objects to be assigned. Although this formulation is straightforward, its solution with the transportation method can become difficult owing to extreme cases of degeneracy. Because of this complication, the assignment method offers computational advantages for solving assignment problems.

Example 5S.7 demonstrates the procedures of the assignment method. In this example, the Mercury Electric Motor Company needs to assign five motor overhaul jobs to five motor rewinding centers. The assignment method is a good method for solving such problems because it guarantees assignments that result in minimum processing cost, maximum profit, or minimum processing time for all of the jobs and the method is simple and efficient to use.

Example 5S.7 demonstrates the minimization algorithm that is appropriate for minimizing costs or processing times. If we wished to maximize profits, we would multiply all the profits in the first table by minus one (-1) and then follow the same procedures as in the minimization case. Regardless of whether the problem is of the maximization or minimization type, the optimal job assignment — or job assignments, since multiple optimal solutions are possible — results from the use of the assignment method.

Example 5S.7

Using the Assignment Method to Assign *n* Jobs to *n* Work Centers

Mercury Electric Motor Company overhauls very large electric motors used in industrial plants in its region. Bill Tobey has just received five electric motor overhaul jobs and is trying to decide to which rewinding work centers the jobs should be assigned. Because some of the work centers specialize in certain types of jobs, the cost for processing each job varies from work center to work center. Bill has estimated the processing costs for the five jobs at five rewinding work centers, and uses the assignment method to make a minimum cost assignment of the jobs to work centers, following this procedure:

1. Place the cost information for assigning the jobs to work centers in an assignment table format. This is shown in Step 1 of Figure 5S.4.

2. Subtract the smallest cost in each row from all other costs in that row. The resulting table is shown in Step 2 in Figure 5S.4.

3. Subtract the smallest cost in each column from all other costs in that column. See Step 3 in Figure 5S.4.

4. Draw the least number of vertical or horizontal straight lines to cover the zero cells. See Step 4 in Figure 5S.4. Note that several different schemes may be possible, but the same number of minimum lines should result. If *n* lines (five in this example) were the minimum number of lines to cover the zero cells, the optimal solution would have been reached. If that were the case, the optimal job assignments would be found at the zero cells. Because less than *n* or only four lines were required, we must perform a modification to the table in Step 4 in Figure 5S.4.

5. Select the smallest cost not covered by lines in the table in Step 4 of Figure 5S.4 (the smallest cost is 50). Subtract this cost from all uncovered costs and add this cost to cells at the intersections of lines in Step 4. Then transfer these new costs and the costs that are unchanged in Step 4 to a new table in Step 5. Redraw the lines to cover the zero cells. Because five lines are required in Step 5, the solution is optimal. If fewer than five lines had been required, Step 5 would have to be repeated.

The zero cells in Step 5 of Figure 5S.4 indicate these assignments:

Possible Assignments			The Optimal Assignment		
Job	Work Centers		Job	Work Center	Processing Cost (from 1st Table)
A	1 or 5		A	5	$250
B	2, 4, or 5		B	4	300
C	2, 3, 4, or 5		C	3	100
D	2		D	2	100
E	1		E	1	150
				Total cost	$900

Figure 5S.4
Tables of the Assignment Method in Example 5S.7

1

Work Centers

Jobs	1	2	3	4	5
A	$150	$300	$225	$350	$250
B	300	200	400	300	250
C	150	100	100	200	150
D	300	100	200	250	200
E	150	350	230	375	260

2

Work Centers

Jobs	1	2	3	4	5
A	0	150	75	200	100
B	100	0	200	100	50
C	50	0	0	100	50
D	200	0	100	150	100
E	0	200	80	225	110

3

Work Centers

Jobs	1	2	3	4	5
A	0	150	75	100	50
B	100	0	200	0	0
C	50	0	0	0	0
D	200	0	100	50	50
E	0	200	80	125	60

4

Work Centers

Jobs	1	2	3	4	5
A	0	150	75	100	50
B	100	0	200	0	0
C	50	0	0	0	0
D	200	0	100	50	50
E	0	200	80	125	60

5

Work Centers

Jobs	1	2	3	4	5
A	0	100	25	50	0
B	150	0	200	0	0
C	100	0	0	0	0
D	250	0	100	50	50
E	0	150	30	75	10

Review and Discussion Questions

1. Where in the optimal simplex tableau is the LP solution found?
2. Where are the shadow prices in the optimal simplex tableau?
3. What are shadow prices? What information do they provide managers?
4. Why must row operations be performed in the simplex method?
5. What purpose do artificial variables serve?
6. What are slack variables? What purpose do they serve?
7. What determines the subscripts for artificial and slack variables?
8. What are the characteristics of transportation problems?
9. What are the procedures of the transportation method?
10. What are the procedures of the northwest corner rule? Why do we use the northwest corner rule?
11. What methods may we use to test a transportation table for optimality?
12. What advantage does the MODI method have over the stepping-stone method? Explain.
13. What advantage does the VAM method have over the northwest corner rule? Explain.
14. What is an unbalanced transportation problem? What modifications are necessary in our ordinary transportation method when working unbalanced problems?
15. Why is degeneracy a problem in the transportation method? What specific difficulties are encountered in the northwest corner rule, stepping-stone method, and the MODI method?
16. What are the characteristics of assignment problems?
17. Describe the procedures of the assignment method.

Problems

Simplex Method

Performing Row Operations

1. Perform row operations on this second tableau and complete the third tableau. Is the third tableau optimal? If not, which variables will enter and leave the third tableau?

Second Tableau

C			100	200	0	0	
	SOL	b	X_1	X_2	S_1	S_2	ϕ
200	X_2	500	¼	1	1	0	
0	S_2	750	3/2	0	−½	1	
	Z	100,000	50	200	200	0	
	(C − Z)		50	0	−200	0	

2. Perform row operations on this second tableau. Complete the third tableau. Is the third tableau optimal? If not, which variables will enter and leave the third tableau?

Second Tableau

C			60	70	80	0	0	0	
	SOL	b	X_1	X_2	X_3	S_1	S_2	S_3	ϕ
0	S_1	50	⅛	½	0	1	0	0	
0	S_2	200	1	½	0	0	1	0	
80	X_3	60	¼	¼	1	0	0	½	
	Z	4,800	20	20	80	0	0	40	
	(C – Z)		40	50	0	0	0	–40	

3. Perform row operations on this third tableau. Complete the fourth tableau. Is the fourth tableau optimal? If not, which variables will enter and leave the fourth tableau?

Third Tableau

C			–20	–30	–M	–M	–M	0	0	0	
	SOL	b	X_1	X_2	A_1	A_2	A_3	S_1	S_2	S_3	ϕ
–20	X_1	100	1	1	0	1	0	0	¼	0	
0	S_1	200	0	1	3	½	0	1	½	½	
–M	A_3	200	0	1	1	0	1	0	1	½	
	Z	–200M –2,000	–20	–M –20	–M	–20	–M	0	–M –5	–½M	
	(C – Z)		0	M –10	0	–M –20	0	0	M +5	½M	

Simplex Solutions

(LP-A, B, C, D, E, F, G, and H problems are found at the end of Chapter 5.)

4. Solve LP-A using the simplex method. What is the optimal solution?

5. Solve LP-B using the simplex method. What is the optimal solution?

6. Solve LP-C using the simplex method. What is the optimal solution?

7. Solve LP-D using the simplex method. What is the optimal solution?

8. Solve LP-E using the simplex method. What is the optimal solution? (Hint: Convert the objective function to cents.)

9. Solve LP-G using the simplex method. What is the optimal solution?

10. Solve LP-H using the simplex method. What is the optimal solution?

Interpreting Simplex Solutions

11. Below are the variable definitions and last (optimal) tableau for Problem LP-A: **a.** What should management do? In other words, what is the complete meaning to management decision makers of the values of X_1, X_2, S_1, S_2, and Z in the optimal solution? **b.** What is the meaning of each of the elements in Row (C − Z)?

X_1 = Acres planted in soybeans this season
X_2 = Acres planted in milo this season
S_1 = Unused soybean acreage in acres
S_2 = Unused fertilizer in pounds
Z = This season's profits on soybeans and milo in dollars

Optimal Tableau

C			700	500	0	0	
	SOL	b	X_1	X_2	S_1	S_2	ϕ
700	X_1	**100**	1	0	1	0	
500	X_2	**50**	0	1	−½	¹⁄₂₀₀₀	
	Z	**95,000**	700	500	450	¼	
	(C − Z)	0	0	−450	−¼	

12. Below are the variable definitions and last (optimal) tableau for Problem LP-B: **a.** What should management do? In other words, what is the complete meaning of the values of X_1, X_2, S_1, S_2, and Z in the optimal solution to management decision makers? **b.** What is the meaning of each of the elements in Row (C − Z)?

X_1 = Daily sales calls per salesperson to petroleum industry customers
X_2 = Daily sales calls per salesperson to chemical industry customers
S_1 = Daily unused hours per salesperson on sales calls
S_2 = Daily unused entertainment costs per salesperson
Z = Average daily profits per salesperson in dollars

Optimal Tableau

C			500	200	0	0	
	SOL	b	X_1	X_2	S_1	S_2	ϕ
500	X_1	$^6/_{10}$	1	0	$^{18}/_{80}$	−$^1/_{50}$	
200	X_2	$1^2/_{10}$	0	1	−$^3/_{10}$	$^3/_{50}$	
	Z	540	500	200	52½	2	
	(C − Z)	0	0	−52½	−2	

13. Below are the variable definitions and last (optimal) tableau for Problem LP-C: **a.** What should management do? In other words, what is the complete meaning to management decision makers of the values of X_1, X_2, S_1, S_2, and Z in the optimal solution? **b.** What is the meaning of each of the elements in Row (C − Z)?

X_1 = Personnel assigned to the new project during the first quarter
X_2 = Personnel assigned to the new project during the second quarter
S_1 = Unused total personnel allowance
S_2 = Unassigned first quarter personnel
S_3 = Unassigned second quarter personnel
Z = Total profits on the new project in dollars

Optimal Tableau

C			20,000	30,000	0	0	0	
	SOL	b	X_1	X_2	S_1	S_2	S_3	ϕ
20,000	X_1	10	1	0	1	0	−1	
0	S_2	5	0	0	−1	1	1	
30,000	X_2	10	0	1	0	0	1	
	Z	500,000	20,000	30,000	20,000	0	10,000	
	(C − Z)		0	0	−20,000	0	−10,000	

14. Below are the variable definitions and last (optimal) tableau for Problem LP-D: **a.** What should management do? In other words, what is the complete meaning to management decision makers of the values of X_1, X_2, X_3, S_1, A_2, S_2, S_3, S_4, and Z in the optimal solution? **b.** What is the meaning of each element in Row (C − Z)?

X_1 = Next year's spending on urban renewal in millions of dollars
X_2 = Next year's spending on health services in millions of dollars
X_3 = Next year's spending on fire department in millions of dollars
S_1 = Unused urban renewal spending below the upper limit in millions of dollars
A_2 = No meaning
S_2 = Excess health services spending above the lower limit in millions of dollars
S_3 = Unused fire department spending below the upper limit in millions of dollars
S_4 = Unused total spending in millions of dollars
Z = Total social returns for the three projects for next year in millions of dollars

Optimal Tableau

C			.4	.3	.35	0	−M	0	0	0	
	SOL	b	X_1	X_2	X_3	S_1	A_2	S_3	S_4	S_2	ϕ
.4	X_1	7	1	0	0	1	0	0	0	0	
.3	X_2	3	0	1	0	0	1	0	0	−1	
0	S_3	8	0	0	0	1	1	1	−1	−1	
.35	X_3	0	0	0	1	−1	−1	0	1	1	
	Z	3.7	.4	.3	.35	.05	−.05	0	.35	.05	
	(C − Z)		0	0	0	−.05	−M +.05	0	−.35	−.05	

15. Below are the variable definitions and last (optimal) tableau for Problem LP-E: **a.** What should management do? In other words, what is the complete meaning to management decision makers of the values of X_1, X_2, A_1, A_2, A_3, S_1, S_2, S_3, and Z in the optimal solution? **b.** What is the meaning of each element in Row (C − Z)?

X_1 = Pounds of oats fed to each head of cattle daily
X_2 = Pounds of corn fed to each head of cattle daily
A_1 = No meaning
A_2 = No meaning
A_3 = No meaning
S_1 = Excess calories per head of cattle daily in calories
S_2 = Excess minerals per head of cattle daily in units
S_3 = Excess vitamins per head of cattle daily in units
Z = Daily feeding cost per head of cattle in cents

Optimal Tableau

C			−5	−3	−M	−M	−M	0	0	0	
	SOL	b	X_1	X_2	A_1	A_2	A_3	S_1	S_2	S_3	ϕ
0	S_2	4,000	0	0	6	−1	−2	−6	1	2	
−3	X_2	30	0	1	1/50	0	−1/100	−1/50	0	1/100	
−5	X_1	10	1	0	−1/100	0	1/100	1/100	0	−1/100	
	Z	−140	−5	−3	−1/100	0	−1/50	1/100	0	1/50	
	(C − Z)		0	0	−M +1/100	−M	−M +1/50	−1/100	0	−1/50	

16. Below are the variable definitions for Problem LP-F. The last (optimal) tableau is found in Table 5S.7. **a.** What should management do? In other words, what is the complete meaning to management decision makers of the values of the decision variables, artificial variables, and Z in the optimal solution? **b.** What is the meaning of each element in Row (C − Z)?

A_1, A_2, A_3, A_4, A_5, A_6, and A_7 = No meaning

The decision variables are the numbers of electric irons shipped from these sources to these destinations:

Decision Variable	Source	Destination	Decision Variable	Source	Destination
X_1	1	A	X_7	2	C
X_2	1	B	X_8	2	D
X_3	1	C	X_9	3	A
X_4	1	D	X_{10}	3	B
X_5	2	A	X_{11}	3	C
X_6	2	B	X_{12}	3	D

Table 5S.7
Optimal Tableau of LP-F

C			-.2	-.25	-.15	-.2	-.15	-.3	-.2	-.15	-.15	-.2	-.2	-.25	-M	-M	-M	-M	-M	-M	-M
	SOL	b	X_1	X_2	X_3	X_4	X_5	X_6	X_7	X_8	X_9	X_{10}	X_{11}	X_{12}	A_1	A_2	A_3	A_4	A_5	A_6	A_7
-.15	X_5	10,000	1	1	0	0	1	1	0	0	0	0	-1	-1	1	1	0	0	0	-1	-1
-.15	X_8	5,000	0	0	0	1	0	0	0	1	0	0	0	1	0	0	0	0	0	0	1
-.15	X_9	2,000	0	-1	0	0	0	-1	0	0	1	0	1	1	0	0	1	0	-1	0	0
-M	A_4	0	0	0	0	0	0	0	0	0	0	0	0	0	-1	-1	-1	1	1	1	1
-.20	X_{10}	8,000	0	1	0	0	0	1	0	0	0	1	0	0	0	0	0	0	1	0	0
-.20	X_7	5,000	-1	-1	0	-1	0	0	1	0	0	0	1	0	-1	0	0	0	0	1	0
-.15	X_3	10,000	1	1	1	1	0	0	0	0	0	0	0	0	1	0	0	0	0	0	0
	Z	-6,650	-.1	-.15	-.15	-.1	-.15	-.2	-.2	-.15	-.15	-.2	-.2	-.15	M	M	M	-M	-M	-M	-M
	(C - Z)		-.1	-.1	0	-.1	0	-.1	0	0	0	0	0	-.1	-2M	-2M	-2M	0	0	0	0

17. Below are the variable definitions and last (optimal) tableau for Problem LP-G: **a.** What should management do? In other words, what is the complete meaning to management decision makers of the values of X_1, X_2, S_1, S_2, S_3, and Z in the optimal solution? **b.** What is the meaning of each of the elements in Row $(C - Z)$?

Optimal Tableau

C			10	6	0	0	0
	SOL	b	X_1	X_2	S_1	S_2	S_3
6	X_2	960	0	1	−4	6	0
0	S_3	$68\frac{4}{7}$	0	0	$-12\frac{4}{7}$	$\frac{6}{7}$	1
10	X_1	1,440	1	0	6	−3	0
	Z	20,160	10	6	36	6	0
	(C − Z)		0	0	−36	−6	0

$X_1 =$ Number of hardback books to be produced per shift
$X_2 =$ Number of paperback books to be produced per shift
$S_1 =$ Unused minutes of cover capacity per shift
$S_2 =$ Unused minutes of printing line capacity per shift
$S_3 =$ Unused minutes of framing capacity per shift
$Z =$ Contribution dollars per shift

18. Below are the variable definitions and last (optimal) tableau for Problem LP-H: **a.** What should management do? In other words, what is the complete meaning to management decision makers of the values of X_1, X_2, X_3, S_1, S_2, S_3, A_1, A_2, A_4, and Z in the optimal solution? **b.** What is the meaning of each of the elements in Row $(C - Z)$?

$X_1 =$ Barrels of Moon Slick #1 to be produced next quarter
$X_2 =$ Barrels of Moon Slick #2 to be produced next quarter
$X_3 =$ Barrels of Moon Slick #3 to be produced next quarter
$S_1 =$ Excess barrels of production sold to mining/quarrying
$S_2 =$ Excess barrels of production sold to construction
$S_3 =$ Unused quarterly processing capacity at the plant
A_1, A_2, and $A_4 =$ No meaning
$Z =$ Quarterly costs

Optimal Tableau

C			−3	−4	−2	−M	−M	0	−M	0	0
	SOL	b	X_1	X_2	X_3	A_1	A_2	S_3	A_4	S_1	S_2
0	S_2	600	0	1	$-3\frac{4}{5}$	0	−1	0	1	0	1
−3	X_1	1,000	1	1	$-1\frac{9}{5}$	0	0	0	1	0	0
0	S_3	3,000	0	3	$\frac{58}{5}$	0	0	1	−2	0	0
0	S_1	500	0	−4	$-1\frac{9}{5}$	−1	0	0	1	1	0
	Z	−3,000	−3	−3	$\frac{57}{5}$	0	0	0	−3	0	0
	(C − Z)		0	−1	$-\frac{67}{5}$	−M	−M	0	−M +3	0	0

Transportation Method

Northwest Corner Rule and Stepping-Stone Method

19. From the transportation table below: **a.** Use the northwest corner rule and the stepping-stone method to determine how many units should be shipped from each source to each destination to minimize period transportation costs. **b.** What period transportation costs will result from your recommendation in part *a*?

From \ To	1	2	3	Source Totals
A	$.50	$ .90	$.50	100
B	.80	1.00	.40	500
C	.90	.70	.80	900
Destination Totals	300	800	400	1,500 / 1,500

20. The Apex Company produces electric transformers for electrical distributors at two factories located in New York City and San Diego. Apex has four regional warehouses located in Seattle, Denver, Chicago, and Atlanta. The monthly warehouse requirements, monthly factory capacities, and per-unit transportation costs are:

Factory	Monthly Factory Capacity (Units)
New York City	12,000
San Diego	14,000

Warehouse	Monthly Warehouse Requirement (Units)
Seattle	9,000
Denver	10,000
Chicago	5,000
Atlanta	2,000

Source	Destination	Transportation Cost per Unit
New York City	Seattle	$3.00
	Denver	2.00
	Chicago	1.00
	Atlanta	1.00
San Diego	Seattle	1.00
	Denver	1.50
	Chicago	2.00
	Atlanta	2.00

a. Use the northwest corner rule and the stepping-stone method to determine how many units should be shipped from each source to each destination to minimize period transportation costs. **b.** What monthly transportation costs will result from your recommendation in part *a*?

21. Three fabrication departments—A, B, and C—produce three slightly different products that are processed further in four assembly departments—1, 2, 3, and 4. Each fabrication and assembly department has a unique monthly capacity, and it is desirable that each department operate at capacity. Although any of the three products coming from the three fabrication departments can be processed in any of the four assembly departments, the assembly cost per unit differs among the products. Additionally, the materials handling costs per unit differ among all the fabrication and assembly departments. The monthly fabrication department capacities, monthly assembly department capacities, and per-unit materials handling and assembly processing costs are:

Fabrication Department	Monthly Capacity (Units)
A	9,000
B	17,000
C	14,000

Assembly Department	Monthly Capacity (Units)
1	3,000
2	10,000
3	15,000
4	12,000

Fabrication Department	Assembly Department	Materials Handling Cost per Unit	Assembly Cost per Unit	Total Materials Handling and Assembly Cost per Unit
A	1	$.25	$.95	$1.20
	2	.15	.55	.70
	3	.10	.40	.50
	4	.15	.45	.60
B	1	.10	.60	.70
	2	.15	.35	.50
	3	.20	.30	.50
	4	.25	.35	.60
C	1	.10	.40	.50
	2	.15	.55	.70
	3	.30	.50	.80
	4	.40	.80	1.20

a. Use the northwest corner rule and the stepping-stone method to plan a monthly production schedule for the three fabrication and four assembly departments. In other words, how many units should be processed in each fabrication department and moved to and processed in each assembly department so that the monthly assembly and materials handling costs are minimized? b. What monthly assembly and materials handling costs will result from your recommendation in part a?

22. Three recycling plants—A, B, and C—receive and process scrap paper and ship paper stock to three regional warehouses—1, 2, and 3. The monthly recycling plant capacities, monthly regional warehouse requirements, and the shipping cost per 100 pounds are:

Recycling Plant	Monthly Capacity (100 Pounds)	Regional Warehouse	Monthly Requirement (100 Pounds)
A	500	1	300
B	1,200	2	900
C	800	3	800

Recycling Plant	Regional Warehouse	Shipping Cost per 100 Pounds
A	1	$3
	2	2
	3	4
B	1	4
	2	3
	3	1
C	1	2
	2	2
	3	3

a. Use the northwest corner rule and the stepping-stone method to determine how many pounds of paper stock should be shipped from each recycling plant to each regional warehouse per month to minimize monthly shipping costs. **b.** What monthly shipping costs will result from your answer in part *a*?

VAM and MODI Methods

23. Use the VAM method to obtain a starting solution and complete the transportation method by using the MODI method to test the solutions for optimality in Problem 21.

Assignment Method

24. Four jobs must be assigned to four work centers. Only one job can be assigned to each work center, and all jobs must be processed. The cost of processing each job through each work center is shown below:

		Work Centers			
		1	2	3	4
Jobs	A	$50	$45	$50	$65
	B	25	40	35	20
	C	65	60	55	65
	D	55	65	75	85

a. Use the assignment method to determine which jobs should be assigned to which work centers to minimize total processing costs. **b.** What is the cost of your assignments in part *a*?

25. a. Use the assignment method to assign these employees to these projects. **b.** What is the total cost of your assignment in part *a*?

	Projects			
	1	2	3	4
Al	$300	$325	$500	$350
Ben	400	525	575	600
Cal	350	400	600	500
Dan	400	350	450	450

(Employees label on left side)

26. Five customers must be assigned to five stockbrokers in a brokerage house. The estimated profits for the brokerage house for all possible assignments are shown below:

	Brokers				
	1	2	3	4	5
A	$500	$525	$550	$600	$700
B	625	575	700	550	800
C	825	650	450	750	775
D	590	650	525	690	750
E	450	750	660	390	550

(Customers label on left side)

a. Use the assignment method to assign the five customers to the five different brokers to maximize profits for the brokerage house. **b.** What are the profits from your assignment in part *a*?

Selected Bibliography

Anderson, David R., Dennis J. Sweeney, and Thomas A. Williams. *Essentials of Management Science: Applications to Decision Making.* St. Paul: West Publishing, 1978.

Budnick, Frank S., Richard Mojena, and Thomas E. Vollmann. *Principles of Operations Research for Management.* Homewood, Ill. Richard D. Irwin, 1977.

Levin, Richard I., and Charles A. Kirkpatrick. *Quantitative Approaches to Management.* 4th ed. New York: McGraw-Hill, 1978.

Chapter Outline

Introduction

Long-Range Capacity Planning

Definition of Production Capacity
Measurements of Capacity
Predicting Capacity Demand
Alternative Sources of Capacity
Economies of Scale
The Japanese story
Analyzing Capacity-Planning Decisions

Facility Location

Factors Affecting Location Decisions
Regional, Community, and Site Decisions
Types of Facilities and Their Dominant Locational Factors
Locating Customer/Constituent Service Facilities
Analyzing Retailing and Other Customer Service Facilities
Techniques for Analyzing Industrial Facility Locations
Common Types of Locational Problems
Annual Operating Cost Comparisons
Break-even Analysis
Linear Programming
Integrating Quantitative and Qualitative Factors into Location Decisions
Rating Scale
Relative Aggregate Scale

Summary

Review and Discussion Questions

Problems

Case: Sporting Charge Company

Selected Bibliography

6

Long-Range Capacity Planning and Facility Location:

Decisions with Long-Lasting Effects

We allocate basic facilities and capacities for production and distribution that commonly account for the largest fraction of the assets of an organization. [And] the location [decision] . . . represents the basic strategy for accessing markets and may have significant impact on such factors as revenues, costs, and service levels to customers and clients!
Elwood S. Buffa, 1976

Most facility planning decisions in operations management usually involve these issues:

1. How much capacity is needed and when is additional capacity needed?
2. Where should new facilities be located?

These issues are critically important in operations management for many reasons. First, the investment in facilities to produce goods and services today is enormous, and once you've sunk several million dollars in a production facility, you live with that decision, right or wrong, for a very long time. Such decisions are therefore not made lightly. Second, **the long-range operating strategies of an organization are expressed in their capacity plans. What is to be produced, where it is to be sold, what technologies will be employed, and other related questions reflect the long-range strategies of organizations, and these issues must be resolved at the highest levels of organizations.** The resolution of these issues is fundamentally related to long-range capacity plans, which also must be resolved at the top of organizations. Third, the operating efficiency of operations is dependent upon the capacity of the facilities. Maintenance costs, ease of scheduling, and economy of scale are among the factors affected by the capacity of facilities. Fourth, the capacity of facilities becomes a constraint on many other POM decisions. How much that can be economically produced in a specific time period is a limiting factor in many POM issues.

In this chapter we shall develop a framework for planning long-range facility capacities, explore some of the important issues in capacity planning today, and study some of the methods used to analyze facility location decisions in POM.

Long-Range Capacity Planning

Capacity-planning decisions usually involve these activities:

1. Estimating the capacities of the present facilities.
2. Predicting the long-range future capacity needs for all products and services.
3. Identifying and analyzing alternative sources of capacity to meet future capacity needs.
4. Selecting among the alternative sources of capacity.

Definition of Production Capacity

Capacity is the maximum production rate of an organization. Several factors underlying this definition make its use and understanding somewhat complex. First, day-to-day variations such as employee absences, equipment breakdowns, vacations, and material delivery delays combine to make the output rate of facilities uncertain. Second, the production rates of different products and services are not the same. Thus, 50,000 A's or 20,000 B's may be produced per month or some mix of A's and B's may be produced. The product mix must therefore be taken into account when capacity is estimated. Third, what level of capacity are we talking about? The maximum possible, the capacity based on a five-day-week work schedule, the practical capacity based on the use of existing facilities without the need to activate mothballed facilities, or some other level?

The Bureau of Economic Analysis defines *maximum practical capacity* as "that output attained within the normal operating schedule of shifts per day and days per week while bringing in high cost inefficient facilities."[1] This definition is also used by the Federal Reserve Board and *The Wall Street Journal*. This commonly used definition, like our definition at the beginning of this section, does not rule out the use of inefficient standby equipment in estimating capacity.

Measurements of Capacity

Now that we understand the definition of capacity, it is time to address the ways that capacity can be measured. For firms that produce only a single product or a few homogeneous products, the units used to measure *output rate capacity* are straightforward: automobiles per month, tons of coal per day, and barrels of beer per quarter are examples of such measures. When a mix consisting of such products as lawn mowers, grass seed, and lawn furniture is produced from a facility, however, the diversity of the products presents a problem in measuring capacity. In such cases an *aggregate unit of capacity* must be established. This aggregate measure of capacity must allow the output rates of the various products to be converted to a common unit of output measure. For example, such measures as tons per hour and sales

---

[1] "Survey of Current Business," *U.S. Department of Commerce Journal*, 1982.

dollars per month are often used as aggregate measures of capacity among diverse products.

In capacity planning for services, output measures are particularly difficult. In these cases *input rate capacity* measures may be used. For example, airlines use available-seat-miles per month, hospitals use available beds per month, tax services use available accountant-days per month, and engineering service firms use labor-hours per month.

"U.S. factory use plunged to 79.9 percent of capacity in December, the lowest rate since 1975": What does this mean? *Percentage of capacity utilization* measures relate output measures to inputs available. For example, a service bureau that had 10,000 labor-hours available during March only used 8,200 labor-hours to meet the demands of its customers. We divide the actual labor-hours used by the maximum labor-hours available during a normal schedule to arrive at the percentage of capacity utilization, or 82 percent in this example. Other commonly used percentage of capacity utilization calculations are: actual automobiles produced per quarter divided by the quarterly automobile production capacity, and occupied airline seats per month divided by the monthly airline seat capacity.

Predicting Capacity Demand

Predicting the sales levels of products and services five, ten, or twenty years into the future is very difficult. So much time is involved that fundamental changes in the economy, changes in consumer preferences, technological developments, demographic shifts, changes in governmental regulations, political and military events, and other developments can occur. Such shifts can dramatically affect the future demands for our products and services and the way that we produce them. As difficult as these forecasts are, we must nevertheless make them. Such long-range forecasts are necessary if we are to provide production capacity for our products and services because it takes as long as five years to design, build, and activate a production facility today. If new technology is to be developed and incorporated into our production machines in a new building, it can take as long as an additional five years. These long lead times required to provide production capacity necessitate long-range forecasts of the demands for our products and services.

Some products or services for which we must develop long-range capacity plans are new, and others will have become obsolete and no longer need to be produced. The mix of products and services that will require production capacity five or ten years from now may therefore be quite different from the present mix. The product life cycles (introduction — growth — maturity — decline) that we discussed in Chapter 4 must be projected forward into the future for all products and services. This consideration must be built into the marketing plans and estimates upon which the long-range forecasts and the capacity plans are to be based.

Technological developments must be anticipated because they can dramatically affect the way that we produce our products and services in the future. Robotics, electronic computerized process controls, and other contemporary achievements are examples of such developments in our recent past. Because these and other technological advances are sure to affect the capacity of our facilities in the future, such developments must be an integral part of our long-range capacity predictions.

As we indicated earlier, long-range forecasting is difficult, but such estimates are best developed in a realistic atmosphere in which technological developments, product life cycles, economic conditions, and other important factors are directly addressed. In this way these factors become an important part of our forecasts. They should not be swept under the rug, which is what we do if, like the ostrich, we stick our heads in the sand and ignore these factors or simplistically assume that they can have little effect on our forecasts.

Alternative Sources of Capacity

Once the long-range capacity needs are estimated through forecasting, many avenues exist to provide for the capacity. Firms may find themselves in either a capacity shortage situation, where present capacity is insufficient to meet the forecast demand for their products and services, or present capacity is in excess of the expected future needs. Long-range capacity planning may therefore require either reduction or expansion of present capacity levels. Table 6.1 lists some of the ways that managers can accommodate the changing long-range capacity needs of organizations.

Table 6.1
Ways of Changing Long-Range Capacity

Type of Capacity Change	Ways of Accommodating Long-Range Capacity Changes
Expansion	1. Subcontract with other companies to become suppliers of the expanding firm's components or entire products.
	2. Acquire other companies, facilities, or resources.
	3. Develop sites, build buildings, buy equipment.
	4. Expand, update, or modify existing facilities.
	5. Reactivate facilities on standby status.
Reduction	1. Sell off existing facilities, sell inventories, and lay off or transfer employees.
	2. Mothball facilities and place on standby status, sell inventories, and lay off or transfer employees.
	3. Develop and phase in new products as other products decline.

In cases where capacity reductions seem necessary, you may wonder why not leave well enough alone? Operations managers should be just as concerned when their capacities are excessive as when they are insufficient. Excessive capacities result in unnecessarily high operating costs for several reasons. First, much of the facility investment is not being profitably used and could be sold, rented, or otherwise used to produce alternative sources of income. In times when interest rates are in the 15 to 25 percent range, where they have been known to soar, businesses must make sure that every dollar of investment is being used to produce profits, either through producing products and services or through alternative investments. Second, operating expenses are excessive because of insurance costs, air-conditioning and heating costs, taxes, maintenance costs, security costs, and other costs that are directly related to the size and value of the facility. Third, as we shall discuss in the next section, facilities with production capacities greater than needed are often so unwieldy to operate that they are too inefficient to permit changeover to other product models. For these and other related reasons, labor, material, and overhead costs can be excessive when the production capacity of facilities is excessive. Operations managers therefore must adjust long-range capacities downward as required by declines in long-range demand for their products and services.

One avenue usually preferred by operations managers to maintain high levels of facility utilization in spite of declining long-range demand for their products and services is the phasing-in of new products to replace older and declining ones. Figure 6.1 shows how a firm might design and develop new products as old ones decline over time. This time-phasing may be a key motivating force behind the development of new products and services in that the excess production capacity resulting from declining product demand that is not replaced by demand for new products becomes a millstone of high operating costs supported by a declining revenue base. Such a strategy, as demonstrated in Figure 6.1, does maintain a relatively stable long-range facility capacity utilization.

Since the Great Depression of the 1930s in the United States, operations managers have tended to be more concerned with expanding capacity because of the extended growth patterns of our business sectors in this period. Although this tendency is now coming under increasing scrutiny because of the escalating cost of funds and increasing shortages of resources of all types, capacity expansions remain

Figure 6.1
Effects of Time-phasing Products upon Facility Capacity Utilization

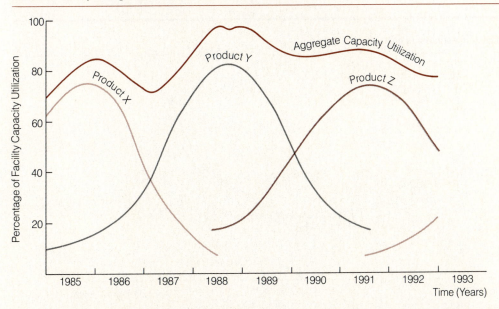

a major concern to operations managers today. As can be seen in Table 6.1, the alternatives for providing additional capacity include outside contracting, acquisition, building new facilities from scratch, updating existing facilities, and reactivating old ones. Deciding among the alternatives available in a particular situation has resulted in management using a number of different approaches to these decisions, ranging from the tried and proven methods of decision trees and present-value analysis to computer model building. Later in this chapter we shall discuss these decisions as well as the concepts and methods of analyzing such problems.

If operations managers decide upon building new facilities as the best alternative source of additional capacity, how to time-phase in the capacity remains an important issue.

Economies of Scale

For a given production facility, there is an annual volume of outputs that results in the least average unit cost. This level of output is called the facility's *best operating level.* Figure 6.2 illustrates this concept. Notice that as the annual volume of outputs increases outward from zero in a particular production facility, average unit costs fall. These declining costs result from fixed costs being spread over more and more units, longer production runs that result in a smaller proportion of labor being allocated to setups and machine changeovers, proportionally less material scrap, and other economies. Such savings, which are called *economies of scale,* continue to accrue as the volume of outputs increases to the best level of output for that particular facility.

Past this point, however, additional volume of outputs results in ever-increasing average unit costs. These increasing costs result from increased congestion of

Figure 6.2
Economies and Diseconomies of Scale

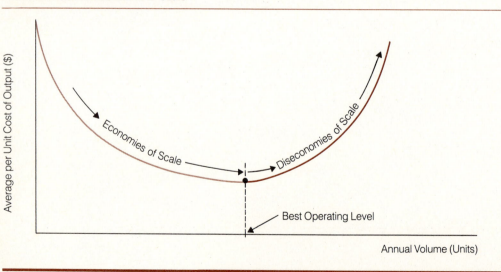

materials and workers, which contributes to increasing inefficiency, difficulty in scheduling, damaged goods, reduced morale, increased use of overtime, and other diseconomies. The impact of such factors, which are called *diseconomies of scale,* increases at an accelerating rate past the best operating level for the facility.

Because each facility has its own unique best operating level and, all other things being equal, facilities with higher best operating levels require greater investments, operations managers must decide between two general approaches to expanding long-range capacity:

1. Invest heavily in one large facility that requires a large initial investment, but one that will have a higher best operating level and that ultimately will fulfill the capacity needs of the firm. In other words, build the ultimate facility now and grow into it.

2. Plan to invest in an initial facility design now and expand or modify that facility as needed to raise the best operating levels to meet the long-range demand for products and services. In other words, expand long-range capacity incrementally as needed to match future capacity demands.

Figure 6.3 compares these strategies. Notice that facility designs A, B, and C

Figure 6.3
Increases in Incremental Facility Capacity

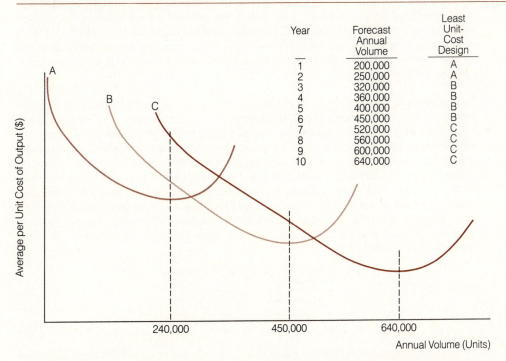

Year	Forecast Annual Volume	Least Unit-Cost Design
1	200,000	A
2	250,000	A
3	320,000	B
4	360,000	B
5	400,000	B
6	450,000	B
7	520,000	C
8	560,000	C
9	600,000	C
10	640,000	C

exhibit best operating levels at 240,000, 450,000, and 640,000 annual volume, respectively. Let us suppose, for example, that our long-range capacity needs were estimated to be 640,000 annual volume ten years from now. How do we best provide for this long-range capacity, incrementally or all at once?

As shown in Figure 6.3, the strategy of initially selecting Design A and subsequently modifying that design to Design B and then to Design C would seem to make sense because the average unit cost tends to be the lowest. Additionally, this incremental approach may be less risky because if our forecast capacity needs do not materialize, then the expansion program could be stopped in time to avoid unnecessary investment in unneeded expansion. On the other hand, one large construction project is likely to involve less investment and costs than several smaller projects because there would be no redundant construction work or interruptions of production. Because of inflation, construction costs may be less if we build all the needed capacity now. Furthermore, we avoid the risk of having to turn down future business if our long-range forecast turns out to be too low and our capacity is inadequate. But the chief concern about building the big facility now is that our funds will be tied up in excess capacity on which no return will be realized for several years. This results either in great additional interest expense or in income foregone owing to not having the funds committed to other types of investments that would generate revenue.

Choosing between expanding capacity all at once or incrementally is not a clear-cut choice for most firms. In cases of mature products with stable and predictable demand patterns, firms are more receptive to building the ultimate facility now. With new products, however, firms lean more toward an incremental expansion strategy because of the riskiness of forecasts and the unpredictable nature of their long-range demands. The eventual choice will differ from firm to firm because of the nature of their products, the availability of investment funds, their attitude toward risk, and other factors.

The Japanese Story Japanese manufacturers have preferred relatively smaller facilities with less capacity. They, unlike their U.S. counterparts, have leaned away from vertical integration, where all operations required to produce a product are under one roof, and more toward *subcontractor networks*. In these arrangements the parent manufacturers develop long-range contractual relationships with several suppliers to provide a large proportion of the production of parts, components, and subassemblies. This system allows the parent manufacturers to operate with lower levels of capacity within their own facilities because much of their capacity needs have been "farmed out" to their supplier subcontractors. This pattern of subcontractor networks is evident in the size of Japanese manufacturing firms, as shown in the accompanying table.[2]

Number of Employees	Number of Firms	Percent of Firms
1,000 or more	750	20%
30–999	60,000	30%
Less than 30	180,000	50%

[2] Leighton F. Smith, "Just-in-time Production Systems," presented at the APICS Educational Liaison Workshop, St. Charles, IL, June 29–July 1, 1981, 9.

The principal advantage of subcontractor networks is that parent manufacturers can conveniently vary their capacity when business cycles or other factors would otherwise necessitate the hiring and layoff of employees. Since increases or decreases in capacity are ordinarily absorbed by subcontractors, the parent manufacturers can provide their lifetime-employed work forces with stable employment, the main objective of these Japanese firms.

A recent survey of the U.S. automotive industry conducted by Arthur Andersen & Co. and the University of Michigan reports that industry leaders plan to reduce vertical integration in the 1980s, implying a greater reliance on subcontracting in the future.[3]

Analyzing Capacity-Planning Decisions

What methods of analysis are commonly used to assist managers in making decisions about long-range capacity expansions? *Break-even analysis,* discussed in Chapter 2, can be used to compare the cost functions of two or more facility alternatives. If we know the approximate volume of outputs for any given year, we can determine from this type of analysis which facility alternative exhibits the least cost. We can also determine the annual volume of outputs for which we would be indifferent between two facility alternatives. Example 2.1 and Problem 2 in Chapter 2 demonstrate the use of break-even analysis in capacity-planning decisions.

Decision trees are also routinely used in capacity-planning decisions. This method provides an excellent way of organizing the way we think about such problems in that we can see the alternatives available for supplying capacity and their relative costs. This information and the straightforward calculations of the method make decision trees one of the most popular solution procedures for this type of problem. Problems 6 and 8 in Chapter 2 exemplify the use of decision trees in analyzing capacity-planning decisions.

Present-value analysis is also particularly useful in long-range capacity planning. Its usefulness stems from the long-term nature of the planning, which can span as many as twenty or more years. Over such long periods of time, discounting future sums back to present values puts all future actions and their costs or profits on an equal footing for the purpose of comparison. This type of analysis avoids such a question as: Which is better, $50,000 five years from now or $75,000 eight years from now? Because all future sums are discounted to the present, all sums are compared according to their present values, and differences in the timing of cash flows therefore do not become an obstacle to their comparisons. Examples 4S.8 and 4S.9 and Problems 12, 13, 14, 16, and 17 from the Supplement to Chapter 4 demonstrate the use cf this approach to long-range capacity-planning problems.

In addition, *computer simulation* and *waiting line analysis* can be used to analyze capacity-planning decisions. These techniques are presented in Chapter 13. *Linear programming* is also used in these decisions; this approach is used later in this chapter to analyze alternative facility locations.

Regardless of the specific techniques employed to analyze long-range capacity-planning decisions, you may be assured that these decisions are among the most analyzed decisions that involve operations managers. The reasons for this involve-

---

[3] Ibid., 6.

ment reside in the importance that these decisions hold for these managers, as we discussed early in the chapter.

When existing facility capacities are inadequate to meet the long-range capacity needs and new facilities are to be built, rented, or purchased, an important issue that must be resolved is where to locate the new facilities.

Facility Location

Location decisions are particularly important—whether we are considering the location of warehouses, manufacturing plants, hospitals, fire stations, or retail outlets—because once the buildings are built, managers must live with their location decisions for a long time. The enormous first cost of most facilities and their subsequent low market value for resale purposes dictate that most organizations must continue to operate facilities for extended periods of time even though their locations are less than optimal.

Facility location decisions are not made lightly. On the contrary, they usually involve long and costly studies of alternative locations before the eventual site is selected. Those who have been through several of these location studies generally conclude that there is no clear-cut best location but rather that there are several good locations. If one site is clearly superior to all others in all respects, the location decision is an easy one. Typically, however, several site candidates, each with its strengths and weaknesses, emerge as good choices; and the location decision becomes a trade-off decision. You can gain one type of benefit only by giving up another. These trade-off decisions among sites can be agonizing and are usually resolved only after long and careful weighing of the pros and cons of each location.

Location decisions can be better understood by examining the factors that commonly affect the final selection of facility locations.

Factors Affecting Location Decisions

Selecting a facility location usually involves a sequence of decisions. This sequence can include a regional decision, a community decision, and a site decision. Figure 6.4 shows this location decision sequence.

First, management must decide the general geographical region where the facility is to be located. This *regional decision* may involve choosing among a few national regions, as in Figure 6.4, or among several regions within a much smaller geographical area. The scope of an organization's operations generally determines the size of the regions under consideration (county, state, or nation).

Regional location decisions are affected by the factors shown in Figure 6.4. Among them are market or customer concentrations; productive system input factors such as labor, materials, transportation, and utilities; construction and land costs; and climate. The relative importance of these factors varies greatly among the differing types of facilities to be located.

Once the geographical region decision has been made, we must decide among several communities within the region. Figure 6.4 also lists some of the factors affecting the community decision. Most of the factors taken into consideration in the regional decision are also present in the community decision. An exception is

Figure 6.4
The Facility Location Decision

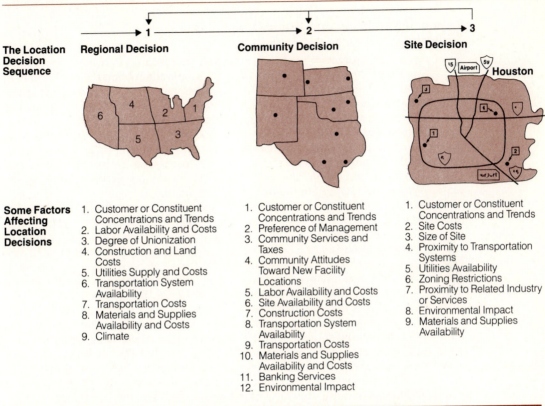

The Location Decision Sequence

Regional Decision	Community Decision	Site Decision
1	2	3

Some Factors Affecting Location Decisions

Regional Decision:
1. Customer or Constituent Concentrations and Trends
2. Labor Availability and Costs
3. Degree of Unionization
4. Construction and Land Costs
5. Utilities Supply and Costs
6. Transportation System Availability
7. Transportation Costs
8. Materials and Supplies Availability and Costs
9. Climate

Community Decision:
1. Customer or Constituent Concentrations and Trends
2. Preference of Management
3. Community Services and Taxes
4. Community Attitudes Toward New Facility Locations
5. Labor Availability and Costs
6. Site Availability and Costs
7. Construction Costs
8. Transportation System Availability
9. Transportation Costs
10. Materials and Supplies Availability and Costs
11. Banking Services
12. Environmental Impact

Site Decision:
1. Customer or Constituent Concentrations and Trends
2. Site Costs
3. Size of Site
4. Proximity to Transportation Systems
5. Utilities Availability
6. Zoning Restrictions
7. Proximity to Related Industry or Services
8. Environmental Impact
9. Materials and Supplies Availability

climate, because climate tends to be uniform within regions. For example, Philadelphia and Pittsburgh are generally believed to have comparable climates.

The *community decision* has some additional factors affecting the location choice. Community services and taxes, attitudes and incentives toward new facility locations, availability and costs of sites, environmental impact, banking services, and management preferences are important inputs in deciding among communities.

Finally, once a community has been selected, a site within that community must be chosen. Some additional factors emerge in *site selection:* size and cost of each site, proximity to transportation systems and related industries or services, availability of utilities and materials and supplies, and zoning restrictions.

The process of selecting a specific location is complex. The decision sequence can be looping — backtracking to rethink community selection after sites have been examined, for example. Also, the analysis can compare Site X in Community A with Site Y in Community B. But regardless of the decision sequence and its complexity, these and other factors affect the eventual choice of region, community, and site.

The type of organization and the nature of its products or services strongly affect the relative importance of each of these factors in location decisions.

Types of Facilities and Their Dominant Locational Factors

Have you ever wondered why several steel mills are located right next door to one another in Pennsylvania, why several large mass-merchandising mail order houses are located in Chicago, why most tire manufacturers are in Akron, why many automobile manufacturers are in Detroit, and why small convenience grocery stores are widely dispersed throughout communities? Are there compelling reasons why one type of facility with a particular product or service tends to be located close to its raw materials or centers of management, technical, and worker skills, while another facility with a different product or service is located close to its markets? These questions suggest that each type of facility under consideration has a few dominant factors that ultimately determine its location decision.

Table 6.2 rates the relative importance of some of the factors affecting location decisions for different types of facilities. Note, for example, that facilities for mining, quarrying, and heavy manufacturing tend to have Factors 3 to 6 and 8 to 10 rated as very important, while Factor 1 is rated as less important. These facilities usually are expensive to build, cover large geographical areas, and use great quantities of heavy and bulky raw materials. Additionally, their production processes discard large amounts of wastes, total finished outputs weigh much less than total raw material inputs, enormous quantities of utilities are absorbed, and products are shipped to only a few customers. These facilities consequently tend to be located near their raw material sources rather than near their markets so as to minimize the total transportation costs of inputs and outputs. Additionally, they tend to select sites where land and construction costs are relatively inexpensive and where waste disposal is not expected to harm the environment. The availability of an abundant supply of utilities and the proximity of railroad service are also necessary.

Light manufacturing facilities that make such items as electronic components, small mechanical parts, and assembled products do not typically locate near their raw material suppliers, because transportation costs of inputs are not typically dominant over transportation costs of outputs. In fact, these facilities do not necessarily locate near either raw material sources or markets. Rather, they strike a balance between transportation costs of inputs and outputs, and other locational factors therefore tend to dominate the location decision. The availability and cost of labor and the degree of unionization can be dominant because labor tends to be a large part of total product cost for this type of facility. Light manufacturing facilities do not typically locate near their markets because they usually ship their products to only a few regional warehouses of wholesalers, who then distribute through their retailing network to the ultimate users of the products. Thus, the shipment of outputs typically is in large quantities to a few locations and constitutes a relatively small part of total product costs.

The location of warehouses is perhaps the most straightforward location decision among the various types of facilities. The dominant factors are those affecting incoming and outgoing transportation costs. Although it is desirable and indeed frequently necessary to be near enough to markets to both communicate effectively

Table 6.2
Relative Importance of Location Factors in Types of Facilities

Factors Affecting Location Decisions	Mining, Quarrying, Heavy Manufacturing	Light Manufacturing	Warehousing	Retailing	Customer Services for Profit	Local Government Services	Health and Emergency Services
			Types of Facilities				
1. Proximity to concentrations of customers or constituents	C	C	B	A	A	A	A
2. Labor availability and costs	B	A	B	B	A	B	B
3. Degree of unionization	A	A	B	B	B	C	B
4. Construction and land costs	A	B	B	B	B	B	B
5. Proximity to transportation facilities	A	B	A	B	C	C	C
6. Incoming transportation costs	A	B	A	B	C	C	C
7. Outgoing transportation costs	B	B	A	C	C	C	C
8. Utilities availability and costs	A	B	C	C	C	C	C
9. Proximity to raw materials and supplies	A	B	C	C	C	C	C
10. Zoning restrictions and environmental impact	A	B	C	C	B	C	C

Note: A = very important, B = important, C = less important.

with recipients of outgoing products and react quickly to customer orders, transportation cost is the paramount locational factor for warehouses. These facilities are therefore often subjects of quantitative economic evaluations such as linear programming.

Retailing facilities are located near concentrations of target customers. All other locational factors are subordinate to this single factor. The studies of these facility locations typically involve the identification of target customer residential concentrations, traffic data on nearby streets, growth trends of communities and suburbs, discretionary spending levels of nearby neighborhoods, and other demographic information.

Facilities that provide customer services for profit, such as dry cleaners, laundromats, banks, welding shops, and hotels, are not unlike retailing facilities in their location decisions. These facilities are also located near concentrations of their target customers. These location studies therefore are also usually dominated by the identification of the target customers, their characteristics, and their present and future concentration locations. Because some service facilities can discard large quantities of waste paper, chemicals, and spent supplies, zoning restrictions and environmental impact can play more important roles than in retailing location decisions.

Local government service facilities also are usually located near concentrations of their constituents. Local government services are often grouped together so that constituents can economize in their time, effort, and transportation costs by making multiple calls with one trip. Additionally, these services are grouped in order to allow interagency interactions. For example, county jails tend to be located near county court buildings so as to minimize the transportation of prisoners between the jails and the courts.

Health and emergency services are traditionally located near concentrations of constituents because the key consideration in selecting locations is that such locations result in the lowest overall response times between the constituents and the services. The minimizing of property loss and loss of life is the overriding consideration in these locations. Fire stations are typically located near concentrations of residential constituents to minimize the time it takes for fire engines to arrive at fire scenes. Ambulance services are similarly located near these community neighborhood population centers to minimize the transportation time of patients to hospitals and health clinics. Hospitals are usually located near the centers of community population density concentrations.

The type of facility, the nature of its products and services, and the nature of its daily activities affect the importance that each locational factor plays in location decisions. Each location decision is unique because the nature of each facility and its daily operation is unique. The understanding of the factors that affect these decisions and of their relative importance in locating several classes of facilities provides a useful framework for analysis. A variety of analysis techniques that integrate the consideration of both qualitative and quantitative data have evolved.

Locating Customer/Constituent Service Facilities

Table 6.2 showed that the dominant factor in location decisions for some facilities is proximity to concentrations of customers. Facilities such as retailing, customer services for profit, local government services, and health and emergency services are types of facilities that attempt to locate near their customers/constituents.

Retailing and customer-service-for-profit organizations typically perform empirically based studies of alternative facility locations. Table 6.3 shows the basic steps in these studies. First, an organization's management must understand why customers buy its products and services. Next, market research must be performed to determine target customer characteristics. When large concentrations of target customers are identified, alternative locations near these concentrations can be considered. Enormous data-gathering activities can occur at this point in the study. Traffic patterns, local spending and income data, competition, and projected growth trends are estimated for each location. Revenues and operating costs are projected for each location. The projected profits based on empirical data become the basis for comparing the location alternatives under consideration.

Local government services typically do not systematically decide among locational alternatives for their facilities. To the contrary, geographical centers or

Table 6.3
Steps in Analyzing Retailing and Customer-Service-for-Profit Facility Location Decisions

1. **Consumer Behavior Research:** Why do customers buy our products and services?
2. **Market Research:** Who are our customers and what are their characteristics?
3. **Data Gathering for Each Location Alternative:** Where are concentrations of target customers? What are their traffic and spending patterns, growth trends, and degree of present and projected competition?
4. **Revenue Projections for Each Location Alternative:** What are the relevant national economy projections, discretionary spending projections, competition activity, and time-phased location revenue?
5. **Profit Projections for Each Location Alternative:** What are projected revenues less time-phased operating costs?

conglomerations of these services tend to evolve over time. This is not necessarily bad, because once citizens learn that governmental services are concentrated in one location with centralized parking and other conveniences, they can maximize their utility in using the services. Satellite centers may develop as geographical constituent population centers shift outward as cities grow. The continuing threat of suburb incorporation may motivate central cities' services to move outward in order to service these outlying districts better.

Health and emergency services can analyze alternative locations much as industrial facilities do. The principal difference between these studies is their objectives. Health and emergency services usually attempt to minimize the overall time or distance traveled in responding to constituents' requests, whereas industrial facilities are usually located to minimize costs or maximize profits.

Techniques for Analyzing Industrial Facility Locations

Industrial facility locations vary from simple situations to the super complex. Table 6.4 classifies locational problems into four basic classes from the simplest to the

Table 6.4
Some Common Types of Locational Problems

Class of Locational Problem	Analysis Objective
1. Locating *a single plant facility* that will be serviced by one or more sources and that will in turn supply one or more destinations.	Minimize total annual costs (incoming and outgoing transportation costs and operating costs) or maximize annual profits while considering all these costs.
2. Locating *one or more source facilities* that will combine with existing source facilities to supply several existing destinations.	Minimize total annual costs (outgoing transportation costs and operating costs) or maximize profits while considering all these costs.
3. Locating *one or more destination facilities* that will combine with existing destination facilities to be serviced by one or more existing sources.	Minimize total annual costs (incoming transportation costs and operating costs) or maximize profits while considering all these costs.
4. Locating *one or more plant facilities* that will combine with existing plant facilities to be serviced by one or more existing sources and that will in turn supply one or more existing destinations.	Minimize total annual costs (incoming and outgoing transportation costs and operating costs) or maximize annual profits while considering all these costs.

Table 6.5
Cost Comparisons for Three Alternative Manufacturing Locations — A Steel Mill

	St. Louis, Missouri			Cleveland, Ohio			Milwaukee, Wisconsin		
Cost Element	Year 1	Year 5	Year 10	Year 1	Year 5	Year 10	Year 1	Year 5	Year 10
Transportation in	$18.5	$22.9	$28.4	$17.4	$21.5	$26.8	$16.4	$19.9	$24.6
Transportation out	6.1	7.6	10.2	6.0	7.6	10.0	6.1	7.6	10.1
Labor	14.7	19.4	26.2	18.6	22.7	30.5	21.5	25.4	33.9
Raw materials	30.3	39.4	57.1	29.5	39.1	56.3	28.9	38.6	55.2
Supplies	4.2	4.5	5.9	4.4	4.9	5.9	4.6	4.9	6.2
Utilities	6.0	9.2	18.5	8.4	12.6	29.2	10.1	16.3	32.1
Variable overhead	5.9	6.8	7.5	6.1	7.2	8.2	6.0	7.6	8.6
Fixed overhead	9.6	10.5	14.2	10.2	11.6	14.9	10.4	12.3	15.3
Total Operating Cost	95.3	120.3	168.0	100.6	127.2	181.8	104.0	132.6	186.0
Projected Volume	1.201	1.489	2.001	1.201	1.489	2.001	1.201	1.489	2.001
Per-Unit Production Costs ($/ton)	$79.4	$80.8	$84.0	$83.8	$85.4	$90.4	$86.6	$89.1	$93.0

Note: Costs are in millions of dollars and volume is in millions of tons.

most complex. In the first class, organizations are assumed to wish to locate a single facility that will receive materials from several sources and in turn ship finished goods to several destinations. This type of problem is typically analyzed by *conventional cost analysis methods.*

Table 6.5 is a cost analysis for three alternative locations for a steel mill. The analysis develops all the estimated costs for operating the mill at each location for the present and future periods. Total operating costs are divided by the projected volume to yield per-unit production costs for each location alternative. Of the three alternatives St. Louis, Missouri, exhibits the minimum per-unit production costs for the first, fifth, and tenth years of operation. The St. Louis location would therefore be preferred.

Similarly, Figure 6.5 graphically compares the fixed and variable costs of three alternative locations for plastic film manufacturing. San Diego is preferred if the annual volume is below 18,000 tons. Seattle is preferred if the annual volume is above 18,000 tons and below 35,000 tons. San Jose is preferred if the annual volume is above 35,000 tons.

When one or more facilities are to be located along with similar existing facilities, analyses become more complex. Some form of linear programming is usually employed to simultaneously investigate all the possible combinations of material shipments either from present and proposed sources to the required destinations or from sources to present and proposed destinations. These types of problems are described in Table 6.4 in Classes 2 and 3.

Example 6.1 demonstrates that linear programming can be used to select a new warehouse location to team with two other existing ones to supply four customer centers (an example of Class 2 from Table 6.4). The objective in this example is to minimize the total annual transportation and handling costs in operating the three warehouses. The procedure is to assume that one of the location alternatives teams with the existing warehouses to supply the four customer centers. This problem is formulated and solved as an LP problem. Next, another location alternative is assumed to team with the existing warehouses. This problem is also formulated and solved as an LP problem. After all the location alternatives have been considered in like manner, the results of the LP solutions are compared. The least-cost location alternative is preferred.

Figure 6.5
Fixed and Variable Cost Relationships for Three Plastic Film Manufacturing Locations

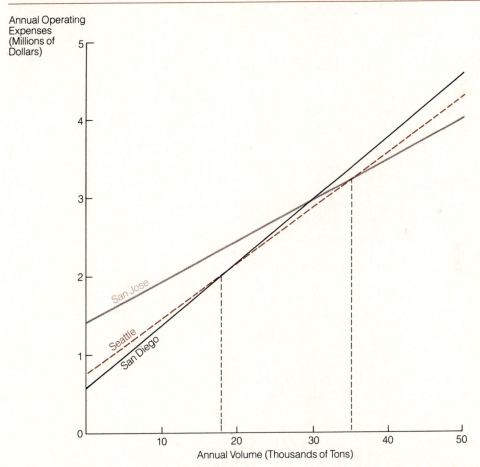

Annual Operating Expenses (Millions of Dollars)

Annual Volume (Thousands of Tons)

San Jose

Seattle

San Diego

Example 6.1

Using LP to Select an Industrial Facility Location

Eco-Steel, a steel bar stock wholesaler specializing in imported assorted steel stock, must soon add another warehouse to its New York City area system in order to supply an increased demand from its customers. Eco now has two warehouses supplying four clusters of machine shop customers in the region. Two location alternatives, L_3 and L_4, are proposed, each with monthly capacities of 12,000 pounds. The actual monthly capacities for existing Warehouses 1 and 2, the minimum demand for each of the customer clusters, A, B, C, and D, and the transportation and handling costs per pound for supplying are shown below:

Warehouse	Customer Clusters				Monthly Warehouse Capacity (Pounds)
	A	B	C	D	
Warehouse 1	$.10	$.10	$.15	$.20	12,000
Warehouse 2	.10	.10	.10	.20	12,000
Proposed Location L_3	.15	.15	.10	.10	12,000
Proposed Location L_4	.20	.10	.15	.15	12,000
Monthly Customer Demand (Pounds)	10,000	8,000	12,000	6,000	

a. If only one new warehouse will be built, which location (L_3 or L_4) will result in the lowest monthly transportation and handling costs? **b.** What total monthly transportation and handling costs will result from all warehouses to all customers if your recommendation from part a is followed? **c.** How much steel should be shipped from the new warehouse to each customer cluster per month?

Solution

a. First, assume that proposed Warehouse L_3 will be combined with existing Warehouses 1 and 2, and formulate the linear programming problem:

1. Define decision variables:

X_1 = Number of pounds of steel to be shipped from Warehouse 1 to Customer Cluster A per month

X_2 = Number of pounds of steel to be shipped from Warehouse 1 to Customer Cluster B per month

X_3 = Number of pounds of steel to be shipped from Warehouse 1 to Customer Cluster C per month

⋮

X_{12} = Number of pounds of steel to be shipped from Warehouse L_3 to Customer Cluster D per month.

2. Formulate the objective function:

$$\text{Min } Z = .10X_1 + .10X_2 + .15X_3 + .20X_4 + .10X_5 + .10X_6 \\ + .10X_7 + .20X_8 + .15X_9 + .15X_{10} + .10X_{11} + .10X_{12}$$

3. Formulate the constraints:

$$X_1 + X_2 + X_3 + X_4 = 12,000 \text{ — Warehouse 1 capacity}$$
$$X_5 + X_6 + X_7 + X_8 = 12,000 \text{ — Warehouse 2 capacity}$$
$$X_9 + X_{10} + X_{11} + X_{12} = 12,000 \text{ — Warehouse } L_3 \text{ capacity}$$
$$X_1 + X_5 + X_9 = 10,000 \text{ — Customer Cluster A requirements}$$
$$X_2 + X_6 + X_{10} = 8,000 \text{ — Customer Cluster B requirements}$$
$$X_3 + X_7 + X_{11} = 12,000 \text{ — Customer Cluster C requirements}$$
$$X_4 + X_8 + X_{12} = 6,000 \text{ — Customer Cluster D requirements}$$

4. This LP problem is solved by computer, with these results:

$X_1 = 10,000$	$X_4 = 0$	$X_7 = 6,000$	$X_{10} = 0$	$Z = \$3,600$
$X_2 = 2,000$	$X_5 = 0$	$X_8 = 0$	$X_{11} = 6,000$	
$X_3 = 0$	$X_6 = 6,000$	$X_9 = 0$	$X_{12} = 6,000$	

Next, assume that proposed Warehouse L_4 will be combined with existing Warehouses 1 and 2, and formulate the LP problem:

5. The objective function is:

$$\text{Min } Z = .10X_1 + .10X_2 + .15X_3 + .20X_4 + .10X_5 + .10X_6$$
$$+ .10X_7 + .20X_8 + .20X_9 + .10X_{10} + .15X_{11} + .15X_{12}$$

6. The constraints will not change from No. 3 above.

7. The solution to this new LP problem is:

$X_1 = 10,000$	$X_4 = 0$	$X_7 = 12,000$	$X_{10} = 6,000$	$Z = \$3,900$
$X_2 = 2,000$	$X_5 = 0$	$X_8 = 0$	$X_{11} = 0$	
$X_3 = 0$	$X_6 = 0$	$X_9 = 0$	$X_{12} = 6,000$	

Because the total monthly costs for L_3 are less than for L_4, Warehouse Location L_3 is preferred.

b. The total monthly transportation and handling costs for the three warehouses will be $3,600.

c. Eco should ship these quantities of steel per month from Warehouse L_3 to:
A = 0   B = 0   C = 6,000 pounds   D = 6,000 pounds

Example 6.2 uses the same procedure as Example 6.1 to demonstrate the location of a single new medical center that will combine with two other existing medical centers to service four municipal population centers. The selected location alternative minimizes total annual miles traveled from the four population centers to the three medical centers. This is an example of Class 3 from Table 6.4.

Example 6.2

Using LP to Select a Medical Facility Location Alternative

Metroville, a fast-growing city in the Midwest, is trying to decide between two alternative locations (L_C and L_D) for one new emergency medical facility. Two such facilities (A and B) are now in existence, and it would be desirable to select a location for the new one that would minimize the distance traveled per year by citizens from the four major population centers in the city (1, 2, 3, and 4) to the three emergency medical facilities. The medical facilities' capacities (in patients per year), the minimum population expected to demand medical services in each population center per year, and the distance from each population center to each medical facility (in miles) are given below:

Population Center	Medical Facilities				Minimum Population from Each Population Center Expected to Demand Emergency Care per Year
	A	B	L_C	L_D	
1	1 mile	1 mile	2 miles	2 miles	10,000
2	1	1½	2½	2½	20,000
3	1	1	1	½	20,000
4	3	2½	2	2	10,000
Medical Facility Capacities (Patients per Year)	20,000	20,000	20,000	20,000	

a. Since only one new medical facility will be built, which location (L_C or L_D) will result in the fewest total annual miles traveled one way between the population centers and the three emergency medical facilities? **b.** How many total miles will be traveled by Metroville's population one way to the emergency health facilities per year? **c.** How many people from each of the population centers will be serviced per year by the new facility?

Solution

a. First, assume that Facility L_C will be combined with existing Facilities A and B. Formulate this into an LP problem:

1. Define the decisions variables:

X_1 = Number of patient trips to be traveled per year between Population Center 1 and Medical Facility A

X_2 = Number of patient trips to be traveled per year between Population Center 1 and Medical Facility B

⋮

X_{12} = Number of patient trips to be traveled per year between Population Center 4 and Medical Center L_C

2. Formulate the objective function:

$$\text{Min } Z = X_1 + X_2 + 2X_3 + X_4 + 1\tfrac{1}{2}X_5 + 2\tfrac{1}{2}X_6$$
$$+ X_7 + X_8 + X_9 + 3X_{10} + 2\tfrac{1}{2}X_{11} + 2X_{12}$$

3. Formulate the constraints:

$$X_1 + X_2 + X_3 \geq 10,000 \text{ — demand from 1}$$
$$X_4 + X_5 + X_6 \geq 20,000 \text{ — demand from 2}$$
$$X_7 + X_8 + X_9 \geq 20,000 \text{ — demand from 3}$$
$$X_{10} + X_{11} + X_{12} \geq 10,000 \text{ — demand from 4}$$
$$X_1 + X_4 + X_7 + X_{10} \leq 20,000 \text{ — capacity of A}$$
$$X_2 + X_5 + X_8 + X_{11} \leq 20,000 \text{ — capacity of B}$$
$$X_3 + X_6 + X_9 + X_{12} \leq 20,000 \text{ — capacity of } L_C$$

4. This LP problem, solved by computer, produces this result:

$X_1 = 0$	$X_4 = 20,000$	$X_7 = 0$	$X_{10} = 0$	$Z = 70,000$ miles/year
$X_2 = 10,000$	$X_5 = 0$	$X_8 = 10,000$	$X_{11} = 0$	
$X_3 = 0$	$X_6 = 0$	$X_9 = 10,000$	$X_{12} = 10,000$	

Next, assume that facility L_D will be combined with existing medical facilities A and B. Formulate this LP problem:

5. The objective function is:

$$\text{Min } Z = X_1 + X_2 + 2X_3 + X_4 + 1\tfrac{1}{2}X_5 + 2\tfrac{1}{2}X_6$$
$$+ X_7 + X_8 + \tfrac{1}{2}X_9 + 3X_{10} + 2\tfrac{1}{2}X_{11} + 2X_{12}$$

6. The constraints will not change from No. 3 above.

7. The solution to this new LP problem is:

$X_1 = 0$	$X_4 = 20,000$	$X_7 = 0$	$X_{10} = 0$	$Z = 65,000$ miles/year
$X_2 = 10,000$	$X_5 = 0$	$X_8 = 10,000$	$X_{11} = 0$	
$X_3 = 0$	$X_6 = 0$	$X_9 = 10,000$	$X_{12} = 10,000$	

Because the miles traveled per year with L_D is less than for L_C, Location L_D is preferred.

b. The total annual miles traveled one way to emergency health facilities per year will be 65,000 miles.

c. Metroville's citizens will visit the new medical facility L_D next year from the population centers:
$$1 = 0 \quad 2 = 0 \quad 3 = 10,000 \quad 4 = 10,000$$

Class 4 from Table 6.4 is often referred to as the *transshipment problem* and is of an order of magnitude more complex than the other types of locational decisions considered thus far. There are several solution approaches to these and other complex locational problems. Harvey Wagner, A. M. Geoffrion, and G. W. Graves have developed advanced solution techniques for these problems.[4]

The LP location problems in the examples of this section really should be processed on computers. However, the supplement to Chapter 5 demonstrates how to work location problems and other transportation type problems manually while using the *transportation method* of linear programming.

Integrating Quantitative and Qualitative Factors into Location Decisions

The techniques for analyzing and comparing alternative locations have thus far dwelled on locating concentrations of customers, as in the case of most service organizations, or on minimizing travel time, distance, or costs, as in the case of industrial organizations, warehouses, and certain health and emergency services. These quantitative analyses provide invaluable quantitative inputs into location decisions, but many of these decisions may also involve factors that cannot be easily quantified.

Managers who make location decisions know that in some cases these qualitative factors can be dominant when compared to quantitative ones. Some of these qualitative factors are housing, cost of living, availability of labor, climate, community activities, education and health services, recreation, churches, union activities, local transportation systems, proximity of similar industrial facilities, and community attitudes. These factors all work together with quantitative factors such as annual operations costs to determine the acceptability of a particular location in such broad areas as family life, work life, recreation, religion, and so on.

Managers often wrestle with the task of trading off qualitative factors against quantitative ones. Methods for systematically displaying the relative advantages and disadvantages of each location alternative, both quantitative and qualitative, have evolved. Two general approaches are presented here. One approach is to develop quantitative and qualitative locational factor ratings independent of each other. This approach requires managers to subjectively weigh and relate the qualitative and quantitative factors for each location alternative in making their decisions.

Table 6.6 develops ratings for the locational factors for a steel mill. St. Louis, Missouri, obviously has a cost/ton advantage whereas Cleveland, Ohio, has a local transportation system advantage and Milwaukee, Wisconsin, has a labor availability advantage. Managers must process these comparisons through their unique mental calculus and arrive at a relative rating for each of the location alternatives.

Another approach is demonstrated in Table 6.7. Here, quantitative factors are placed on the same scale as qualitative factors, and an aggregate weighted score is developed for each location alternative. Because production cost per ton is a continuous measure (ranges from zero to infinity in minute increments), the relative

---

[4] Harvey Wagner, *Principles of Operations Research* (Englewood Cliffs, NJ: Prentice-Hall, 1975), 176–182; and A. M. Geoffrion and G. W. Graves, "Multicommodity Distribution System Design by Benders Decomposition," *Management Science* 20(January 1974): 822–844.

Table 6.6
**Rating Scale Approach to Comparing Alternative Locations
for Qualitative Factors for a Steel Mill**

Locational Factors	Locations		
	St. Louis, Missouri	Cleveland, Ohio	Milwaukee, Wisconsin
Economic Factors			
Annual Operating Costs	$95,300,000	$100,600,000	$104,000,000
Per-Unit Production Costs	$79.40/ton	$83.80/ton	$86.60/ton
Qualitative Factors			
Housing availability	3	3	4
Cost of living	3	3	2
Labor availability	3	3	5
Community activities	3	2	4
Education and health services	3	3	4
Recreation	4	2	5
Union activities	3	1	3
Local transportation systems	3	5	3
Proximity to similar industry	3	4	4
Community attitudes	5	5	5

Note: A five-point rating scale is used: 5 = excellent, 4 = good, 3 = average, 2 = below average,
1 = poor.

scores for this factor are computed by dividing the lowest cost ($79.40) by each of the location alternatives' costs per ton, thus reducing these continuous measures to relative measures (range from zero to one in minute increments). The qualitative factor scores are estimated on a zero-to-one scale. The relative weights (summing to one) are multiplied by these scores to yield weighted scores, and these are summed for each location alternative. This approach shows that Milwaukee, Wisconsin, barely squeezes out St. Louis, Missouri, as the preferred location (.870 versus .860). Approaches such as these can be helpful in comparing location alternatives, particularly when qualitative factors are important in the location decisions.

The concepts, locational factors, and analysis techniques for approaching facility location decisions presented in this chapter do not exhaust the subject. On the contrary, facility location can become a lifelong professional speciality through in-depth research into this intriguing subject. What is presented here serves only as an introduction to a large topic.

Summary

Long-range facility-planning decisions are made at the highest levels of organizations because of the enormous amount of capital funds required and the far-reaching impact that the decisions have upon future operations. Once that future capacity

Table 6.7
Relative Aggregate Scores Approach to Comparing Alternative Locations for a Steel Mill

Relevant Locational Factor	Weights of Factors	St. Louis, Missouri			Cleveland, Ohio			Milwaukee, Wisconsin		
		Economic Data	Scores	Weighted Scores	Economic Data	Scores	Weighted Scores	Economic Data	Scores	Weighted Scores
Production cost/ton	.60	$79.40	1.000*	.600	$83.80	.948*	.569	$86.60	.917*	.550
Cost of living	.05		.600**	.030		.650	.033		.500	.025
Labor availability	.20		.650	.130		.600	.120		.950	.190
Union activities	.10		.700	.070		.700	.070		.650	.065
Proximity to similar industry	.03		.600	.018		.650	.020		.850	.026
Local transportation	.02		.600	.012		.700	.014		.700	.014
Total Location Scores				.860			.826			.870

* These scores are determined by dividing the lowest cost/ton by the actual cost per ton:

$$\frac{79.40}{79.40} = 1.000 \qquad \frac{79.40}{83.80} = .9475 \qquad \frac{79.40}{86.60} = .9169$$

** Qualitative factor scores are estimated based on a maximum score of 1.000.

needs have been estimated, additional capacity can be obtained from subcontractors, acquisitions, building new facilities, expanding present facilities, and reactivating facilities that are on standby status. The alternative selected for additional capacity is usually selected after extensive analysis. Such techniques as break-even analysis, decision trees, present-value analysis, computer simulation, waiting line analysis, and linear programming are used to analyze and compare the alternatives. When new facilities are required, one fundamental issue in these decisions is where to locate the new facilities.

Location decisions are sequential — regional, community, and site. The factors affecting the selection of each element of a location are basic to understanding location decisions. These factors also become the basis for analyzing and comparing location alternatives. Each particular type of facility, whether heavy manufacturing, light manufacturing, warehousing, retailing, customer services for profit, local government services, or health and emergency services, has unique dominant locational factors. For example, warehouses are principally located to minimize transportation costs, whereas retailers are located to be close to concentrations of target customers.

Locations of single facilities usually are analyzed by comparing the per-unit operating costs for alternative locations. Similarly, the cost functions for alternative locations can be compared graphically. When a single facility is to be located to team with other like facilities and to be either supplied from suppliers or to supply customer centers, linear programming is typically used to identify the lowest-cost location alternative. Qualitative and quantitative factors can be combined in either rating scale or aggregate score comparisons.

Review and Discussion Questions

1. Name four activities that are usually involved in any long-range capacity-planning decisions.

2. Define *production capacity*. How does the Bureau of Economic Analysis define *maximum practical capacity*?

3. How is the measurement of capacity of services likely to differ from manufacturing capacity?

4. Define these terms: **a.** *output rate capacity*, **b.** *aggregate unit of capacity*, **c.** *input rate capacity*, and **d.** *percentage of capacity utilization*.

5. Name three ways that firms can reduce long-range capacity. Name five ways that firms can expand long-range capacity.

6. Define these terms: **a.** *best operating level*, **b.** *economies of scale*, **c.** *diseconomies of scale*, and **d.** *subcontractor networks*.

7. Name five techniques that are used to analyze long-range capacity decisions.

8. Name three sequential steps in location decisions.

9. What factors affect regional location decisions?

10. What factors affect community location decisions?

11. What factors affect site location decisions?

12. List the dominant factors affecting the location of these facilities: **a.** mining, quarry-

ing, and heavy manufacturing facilities, **b.** light manufacturing facilities, **c.** warehouses, **d.** retail and customer-service-for-profit facilities, and **e.** local government services and health and emergency services facilities.

13. Name five steps in analyzing retailing and customer-service-for-profit facility locations.

14. Describe four classes of location problems.

15. With what class of location problems can conventional cost comparisons and break-even analysis be appropriately used?

16. Name five qualitative factors commonly considered in facility location decisions.

17. Describe how managers may simultaneously consider both quantitative and qualitative factors in facility location analysis.

Problems

Long-Range Facility-Planning Decisions

1. The Nononsense Publishing Company intends to publish a textbook in production and operations management. Fixed costs are $25,000 per year, variable costs per unit are $10, and selling price per unit is $12. **a.** How many units must be sold per year to break even? **b.** How much annual revenue is required to break even? **c.** If annual sales are 20,000 units, what are the annual profits? **d.** What variable cost per unit would result in $25,000 annual profits if annual sales are 20,000 units?

2. The Howsweetitis Manufacturing Company is considering expanding its production capacity to meet a growing demand for its product line of toilet bowl deodorizers. The alternatives are to build a new plant, expand the old plant, or do nothing. The marketing department estimates a 35 percent probability of a market upturn, a 40 percent probability of a stable market, and a 25 percent probability of a market downturn. Georgia Swain, the firm's capital appropriations analyst, estimates the following annual returns for these alternatives:

	Market Upturn	Stable Market	Market Downturn
Build new plant	$690,000	$(130,000)	$(150,000)
Expand old plant	490,000	(45,000)	(65,000)
Do nothing	50,000	0	(20,000)

a. Use a decision tree analysis to analyze these decision alternatives. **b.** What should Howsweetitis do? **c.** What returns will accrue to the company if your recommendation is followed?

3. The Sunshine Manufacturing Company has developed a unique new product and must now decide between two facility plans. The first alternative is to build a large new facility immediately. The second alternative is to build a small plant initially and to expand it to a larger facility three years later if the market has proven favorable. Marketing has provided the following probability estimates for a ten-year plan:

First Three-Year Demand	Next Seven-Year Demand	Probability
Unfavorable	Unfavorable	.2
Unfavorable	Favorable	.0
Favorable	Favorable	.7
Favorable	Unfavorable	.1

If the small plant is expanded, the probability of demands over the remaining seven years is $\frac{7}{8}$ for favorable and $\frac{1}{8}$ for unfavorable. These payoffs for each outcome have been provided by the accounting department:

Demand	Facility Plan	Payoffs (Thousands of Dollars)
Fav-fav	1	$5,000
Fav-unfav	1	2,500
Unfav-unfav	1	1,000
Fav-fav	2 — expanded	4,000
Fav-unfav	2 — expanded	100
Fav-fav	2 — not expanded	1,500
Fav-unfav	2 — not expanded	500
Unfav-unfav	2 — not expanded	300

With these estimates, analyze Sunshine's facility decision and: **a.** perform a complete decision tree analysis, **b.** recommend a strategy to Sunshine, and **c.** determine what payoffs will result from your recommendation.

4. The OK Trucking Company has a fleet of over-the-road trucks operating in southeastern Oklahoma. The fleet was purchased new ten years ago and is becoming obsolete and badly deteriorated. OK estimates that a new fleet would cost $800,000 and would save $200,000 per year in operating and maintenance expenses. If taxes are ignored, the old fleet has zero salvage value, and the new fleet has a salvage value of $150,000, what is the pay-back period on the new fleet?

5. The Riskway Grocery Corporation is considering building a new retail grocery store in Denton, Texas. The present store is inefficient to operate, is fully depreciated, has limited parking, and is not attractive in appearance. A new store at a location nearby will cost $1,750,000 to build and equip, will have a salvage value of $200,000, and will have improved profits due to increased revenues and decreased operating expenses of $250,000 per year. If Riskway has a tax rate of .4, the economic life of the new facility is 15 years, the new store will be placed into service in January, the salvage value of the old store is $100,000, and the discount rate is 10 percent compounded annually, use net present value to recommend if the new facility should be acquired.

6. The Geotherm Research Corporation located in Jake Pass, Idaho performs geothermal energy conversion research on federal and several state contracts. The firm is experiencing substantial growth and wishes to replace its old experimental facility with a new one. The new facility will cost $50,000 and will improve operating efficiency by $100,000 per year. If Geotherm has a tax rate of .45, the new facility is expected to have an economic life of 3 years, there is a 10 percent cutoff rate, and the old facility has a salvage value of zero, use net present value to recommend if the new facility should be acquired.

7. A local law firm, Amburep Associates, wishes to locate its offices nearer the county hospital where their investigative activities tend to be concentrated. A real estate broker has a professional building to Amburep's liking near the hospital and has agreed to either sell the building outright or provide a 50-year lease agreement. Here is the information affecting the analysis:

	Lease	Buy
Salvage value	——	0
First cost	——	$100,000
Economic life	50 years	50 years
Annual depreciation	——	$2,000
Annual lease payment	$20,000	——
Tax rate	.4	.4

If the after-tax pay-back period is less than six years, Amburep will buy the building; if it is greater than six years, they will lease the building. What should Amburep do?

Facility Location Decisions

8. BANCO, a large banking corporation in Texas, is comparing two locational choices for a branch bank in Dallas: Fifth Street and University Avenue. BANCO estimates the annual volume of money transactions in millions of dollars at the two locations for three years as:

Fifth Street			University Avenue		
Year 1	Year 2	Year 3	Year 1	Year 2	Year 3
30.1	36.1	37.9	29.4	32.3	35.6

The annual operating expenses at the two locations are estimated as a percentage of the volume of money transactions:

Expense	Fifth Street	University Avenue
Labor	1.01	1.00
Supplies	.59	.59
Utilities	1.26	1.01
Variable overhead	3.10	2.80

The fixed costs per year in millions of dollars are estimated for the two locations:

Fifth Street			University Avenue		
Year 1	Year 2	Year 3	Year 1	Year 2	Year 3
.659	.501	.410	.620	.500	.450

If BANCO earns an average of 8 percent of annual money transactions as revenues, compare the two locations' three-year pretax profits.

9. Three proposed locations for a manufacturing plant have these estimated total annual costs:

Location	Annual Fixed Costs	Variable Costs per Unit
Dallas	$2,500,000	$10
Houston	3,500,000	8
San Antonio	2,000,000	12

Determine in what range of annual outputs each of these locations would be preferred: **a.** San Antonio, **b.** Dallas, **c.** Houston.

10. Two locations are being examined for the construction of a new manufacturing plant. Two production processes, A and B, are also being studied. The annual operating costs for each process at the two locations are:

Location	Process A		Process B	
	Fixed Costs	Variable Costs per Unit	Fixed Costs	Variable Costs per Unit
New York	$1,500,000	$5.90	$3,400,000	$3.80
Philadelphia	1,250,000	6.40	3,000,000	4.10

In what range of outputs would each location and production process be preferred?

11. The Big Shot Travel Trailer Manufacturing Company plans to establish another warehousing facility to strengthen its West Coast distribution system. Big Shot presently has three warehouses (San Diego, San Francisco, and Seattle). Two location alternatives are being considered for the new warehouse: Los Angeles and San Jose. The estimated shipping costs per trailer from the two manufacturing plants to each of the existing and proposed warehouses, the warehouses' annual trailer requirements, and the manufacturing plants' annual trailer capacities are shown below:

Manufacturing Plant	Warehouse Locations					Annual Plant Capacity (Trailers)
	San Diego (Existing)	San Francisco (Existing)	Seattle (Existing)	Los Angeles (Proposed)	San Jose (Proposed)	
Stockton	$170	$100	$190	$150	$120	50,000
Portland	200	160	130	180	170	50,000
Annual Warehouse Requirements (Trailers)	25,000	25,000	25,000	25,000	25,000	

If Big Shot wants to locate only one additional warehouse and wants to minimize the annual shipping costs from the two plants to the four warehouses: **a.** Write the objective function and constraints for two LP problems that evaluate each of the proposed warehouse locations. Be sure to define your variables. **b.** Use the computer program in Appendix C to solve the two LP problems. **c.** What annual shipping costs result from selecting Los Angeles? San Jose? **d.** Which of the two locations is preferable? **e.** How many trailers will be shipped from each plant to each warehouse?

12. The Arizona County Sheriff's Department is proposing to locate an additional substation to service its constituents. The department presently has three substations (1, 2, and 3) that service three constituent centers (A, B, and C). Two alternative new substations are being considered: L_4 and L_5. The estimated response time in minutes from each of the existing and proposed substations to the three constituent centers,

the minimum number of trips expected to each constituent center, and the maximum number of trips possible from each substation are shown below:

Substation	Constituent Centers			Annual Substation Capacity (Trips)
	A	B	C	
1	20 min.	5 min.	10 min.	10,000
2	20	10	5	10,000
3	5	20	20	20,000
L_4	8	12	12	10,000
L_5	12	10	8	10,000
Annual Minimum Constituent Center Requirements (Trips)	15,000	15,000	15,000	

If the Arizona County Sheriff's Department wants to locate only one additional substation and wants to minimize the total annual response time from the four substations to the three constituent centers: **a.** Write the objective function and constraints for two LP problems that evaluate each of the proposed substation locations. Be sure to define your variables. **b.** Use the computer program in Appendix C to solve the two LP problems. **c.** What annual total response time results from selecting L_4? L_5? **d.** Which of the two locations is preferred? **e.** How many trips will be made from each substation to each constituent center per year?

13. A large electronics R & D laboratory is investigating three alternative locations for a new facility. The rating scale and economic information for the locations are:

	Locations		
	Miami, Florida	Cleveland, Ohio	San Francisco, California
Economic factor			
Annual operating costs (% of revenue)	76.5	69.5	81.0
Qualitative factors			
Housing availability	5	2	3
Professional personnel availability and costs	5	3	5
Degree of unionization of hourly workers	5	2	3
Construction and labor costs	5	3	1
Urban transportation system	2	3	5
Proximity to customers	1	3	5
Zoning restrictions	3	5	1
Recreation	5	2	5
Cost of living	5	4	2

Note: A five-point rating scale is used: 5 = excellent, 4 = good, 3 = average, 2 = below average, 1 = poor.

Which location would you recommend? Why?

14. The Arkansas Cement Company plans to locate a new cement production facility at either Little Rock, Fort Smith, or Jonesboro. Six locational factors are important—

cost per ton, labor availability, union activities, local transportation, proximity to similar industry, and proximity to raw materials. The weighting of these factors and the scores for each location are shown below:

Locational Factor	Factor Weight	Locations		
		Fort Smith Score	Little Rock Score	Jonesboro Score
Cost per ton	.55	$55.40	$62.30	$59.10
Labor availability	.15	.70	.90	.50
Union activities	.15	.80	.40	.90
Local transportation	.08	.70	.70	.60
Proximity to similar industry	.05	.80	.80	.40
Proximity to raw materials	.02	.70	.80	.50

Use a relative aggregate score approach to compare the three alternative locations. Which location is preferred?

Case

Sporting Charge Company

The Sporting Charge Company produces powder for shotgun shells in its only plant in St. Louis, Missouri. The plant was originally built in 1889 and with the great explosion of consumer demand for its product, growing environmental pressures from being located in a large city, and out-of-control production costs, Sporting Charge is considering three new location alternatives for its central offices and manufacturing plant: Clear River, Florida; Deerco, Nevada; and another location in the suburban St. Louis area. The production processes at Sporting Charge require about 300 production workers and 200 engineering and management personnel, large amounts of water and other utilities, large expanses of land, large volumes of materials to be shipped in and out of the plant, and fire- and explosion-tolerant areas.

   The three locations under consideration have been analyzed by Sporting Charge's technical staff, and these operating costs have been developed for each location:

	Clear River, Florida	Deerco, Nevada	St. Louis, Missouri
Annual fixed costs	$5,000,000	$1,500,000	$3,500,000
Variable cost/pound	$.0200	$.0475	$.0290

These costs reflect all relocation costs, production costs, overhead costs, transportation costs, etc. Sporting Charge estimates these annual volumes for their powder over the next ten years:

Year	Powder Sales (Millions of Pounds)
1	70
5	140
10	200

The marketing staff for Sporting Charge does not think that sales volume or sales price will be affected by the location of the plant.

Assignment

1. What major factors should be considered in choosing one of the three location alternatives?

2. How would you weight the factors that you developed in No. 1 for Sporting Charge's plant? Which ones are more important and which ones should not be weighted heavily? Discuss and defend your answer.

3. Analyze the factors listed in No. 1 and recommend a course of action for Sporting Charge.

Selected Bibliography

Atkins, R. J., and R. H. Schriver. "New Approach to Facilities Location." *Harvard Business Review* 46(May–June 1968): 70–79.

Bechman, M. *Location Theory.* New York: Random House, 1968.

Belt, Bill. "Integrating Capacity Planning and Control." *Production and Inventory Management* 17(first quarter 1976): 9–25.

Buffa, E. S. *Operations Management: Problems and Models.* 3d ed., Chaps. 10 and 11. New York: Wiley, 1972.

Coyle, John J., and Edward J. Bardi. *The Management of Logistics.* 2d ed., 294–298. St. Paul: West Publishing, 1980.

Francis, R. L., and J. A. White. *Facility Layout and Location: An Analytical Approach.* Englewood Cliffs, NJ: Prentice-Hall, 1974.

Geoffrion, A. M. "Better Distribution Planning with Computer Models." *Harvard Business Review* (July–August 1976): 92–99.

Geoffrion, A. M., and G. W. Graves. "Multicommodity Distribution System Design by Benders Decomposition." *Management Science* 20(January 1974): 822–844.

Graziano, Vincent J. "Production Capacity Planning—Long Term." *Production and Inventory Planning* 15(second quarter 1974): 66–80.

Huettner, D. *Plant Size, Technological Change, and Investment Requirements.* New York: Praeger, 1974.

Khumawala, B. M., and D. C. Whybark. "A Comparison of Some Recent Warehouse Location Techniques." *Logistics Review* 7(1971).

Plossl, George W., and Oliver W. Wight. "Capacity Planning and Control." *Production and Inventory Management* 14(third quarter 1973): 31–67.

Reed, R. *Plant Location, Layout, and Maintenance.* Homewood, IL: Richard D. Irwin, 1967.

Schmenner, Roger W. "Before You Build a Big Factory." *Harvard Business Review* (July–August 1976): 100–104.

Skinner, Wickham. "The Focused Factory." *Harvard Business Review* (May–June 1974): 113–121.

Sullivan, William G., and W. Wayne Claycombe. "The Use of Decision Trees in Planning Plant Expansion." *SAM: Advanced Management Journal* 40, no. 1(winter 1975).

Weston, F. C., Jr. "Quantitative Analysis of Plant Location." *Industrial Engineering* 4(April 1972): 22–28.

Chapter Outline

Introduction

Managing Stable Productive Systems
The Large-Scale Project Challenge to Managers
The Evolution of Project Management

Project Management

The Project Team
Project Management Tasks
Scheduling and Controlling Projects with Project Teams

Project Scheduling and Control Techniques

Project Scheduling and Control Concepts
Case 7.1: Rocket Aerial Target System (RATS)
Scheduling and Control Charts
Project Schedules — Horizontal Bar Charts
Milestone Charts
Expenditures Charts
Personnel Charts
Materials Charts
Critical Path Method (CPM)
Characteristics of Complex Projects
A Manager's View of CPM
The CPM Management Information System
Steps in CPM Processing
CPM Networks
CPM Activity Status Reports
CPM Computations
Program Evaluation and Review Technique (PERT)
Project Cost Control Systems
PERT/Cost
Time/Cost Status Reports
Time/Cost Status Charts
PERT and CPM in Practice
Target Slack versus Project Slack
Activity Cost-Time Trade-offs
PERT/CPM Computer Programs

Summary

Review and Discussion Questions

Problems

Case: Maxwell Construction Company

Selected Bibliography

7

Project Management:
Planning and Controlling Large Projects That Result from Operations Strategy

*Modern operations research is a re-emergence of man's
age-old quest for order, predictability, measurement, and
control. In the development of management thought, the
search for science in managing is an old one and reflects the
search for certainty of performance in operations.*
Daniel Wren, 1972

Operations managers develop effective management schemes for planning and controlling the ongoing activities of their organizations. The predictability of most productive systems allows the establishment of specialty departments such as personnel, production, engineering, accounting, and purchasing to support the continuity of these stable productive processes. The entire organization of most productive systems is in fact built around the repetitive nature of the day-to-day generation and delivery of products and services.

Visualize the effects on these managers when they are confronted with a monumental challenge, the one-time large-scale project—for example, designing and developing a new product, introducing a new product or service to its market, locating and constructing a new manufacturing plant, or selecting and installing a new computer system for the organization. Such projects occur naturally as operations managers carry out their operations strategy—the long-range plan for producing an organization's products and services. These and other one-time large-scale projects are particularly challenging to operations managers because the delivery of the products and services of their organizations must continue, and most organizations are not designed to accommodate interruptions of such magnitude.

Organizations to plan, schedule, and control large-scale projects today are usually developed outside the normal productive system, thus minimizing interruptions to the generation and delivery of the systems' products and services. Although the management of large-scale projects is a challenge in POM, new approaches and techniques have evolved over the past three decades that have improved operations managers' ability to plan and control all phases of these massive undertakings.

Project management techniques have generally evolved from the military, to other governmental agencies, to aerospace companies, and to other private industry. The temptation to overcontrol, a legacy from military, governmental, and aerospace organizations, is balanced with a concern in POM for the cost of managing projects. As we proceed in this chapter, several project scheduling and control techniques will be presented and explained. Keep in mind that not all these techniques should be used in all situations. Each technique costs something, and no more time and money should be spent on techniques for scheduling and controlling projects than can be saved through more effective project management.

Project Management

New organization forms have been developed to assure both continuity of the productive system in its day-to-day activities and the successful completion of projects. Foremost among these new organization forms is the *project organization*. Figure 7.1 shows that project teams and their project managers are drawn from organizations' departments. Engineering, scheduling, quality control, personnel, purchasing, production, accounting, marketing, and other specialists are recruited from various departments of organizations and temporarily assigned, full or part-time, to project teams for the duration of the projects.

Figure 7.1
Project Organization

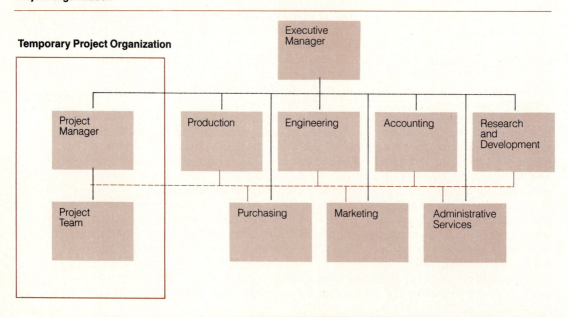

A project manager is usually appointed to head the team, coordinate its activities, coordinate other departments' activities on the project, and report directly to the top of the organization. This executive management exposure gives the project high visibility within the organization, assures the attention of the functional departments to the project, and encourages cooperation between the project team and other organizational units.

The project organization is usually established well in advance of beginning the project so that the project plan can be developed. Figure 7.2 shows the interrelationships among the planning, scheduling, and controlling functions of the project. Notice that the project plan is established before project activities begin and is modified as conditions change throughout the project. The plan is the blueprint and overall guide for achieving the successful completion of the project. Cash flow,

Figure 7.2
Planning, Scheduling, and Controlling Projects

Sequential Functions	Plan ⟶	Schedule ⟶	Control
Tasks	Develop Internal and External Resource Requirements and Time Phase Them to the Activities of the Project	Develop Detailed Guides for Each Resource Indicating Quantity, Quality, Timing, and Relationship to Other Resources Revise and Circulate Periodically and as Conditions Change	Sense Noncompliance of Resources with Schedules, Cost and Quality Standards, and Budgets Take Corrective Actions, Shift Resources, and Develop Alternatives to Achieve Time, Cost, and Quality Performance

Means of Task Accomplishment	Cash Flow Charts
	Personnel Requirement Charts
	Subcontractor Work Plans
	Material Delivery Plans
	Activity Descriptions
	Time and Cost Estimates
	Departmental Budgets
	Milestone Charts
	CPM/PERT
	   Engineering Designs
		Milestone Charts:
		   Departments
		   Subcontractors
		   Material Deliveries
		Cash Flow Schedule
		CPM/PERT:
		   Begin Activity Dates
		   Complete Activity Dates
		   Updated Activity Slack
			Departmental Budget Reports
			Activity Cost Reports
			Quality Compliance Reports
			Time Performance Reports:
			   Delinquent Activities
			   Activity Slack
			   Critical Path
			   Project Summary

Timing of Task	Before Project Is Begun Modified as Required during Project	Slightly before Project Is Begun Continued throughout Project	During Project

personnel, material delivery, and subcontractor work plans provide for the supply and timing of the project's resources. Departmental budgets, milestone charts, engineering specifications, and PERT/CPM provide for time, cost, and quality standards for each activity of the project and the coordination of its activities.

The scheduling and controlling functions of the project occur as the project proceeds. These ongoing functions use a diversity of scheduling and control devices to assure timely performance of the project's activities within cost and quality standards. The periodic generation of updated charts, reports, and schedules keeps all parties to the project informed about their particular work, when and how each activity must be done, corrective actions required, and particular problems to watch for.

The key ingredient in scheduling and controlling the project is the project team. Figure 7.3 shows that the project team is the hub around which the project accomplishment rotates. The project team supplies updated changes to project plan and project schedules through the management information system. The project team sends periodic time, cost, and quality performance reports to the project's internal and external resources. The project team receives back from its resources informa-

Figure 7.3
Scheduling and Controlling Projects with Project Teams

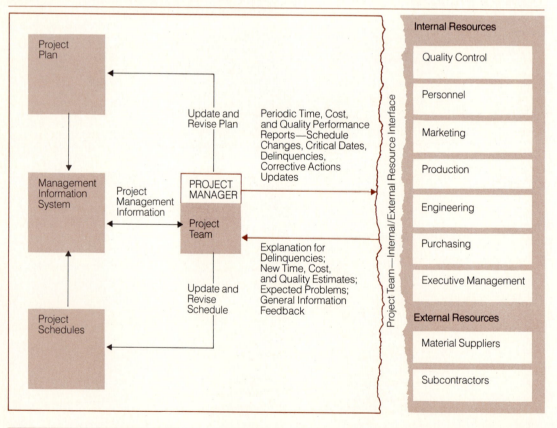

tion about progress on the project. This process continues throughout the project.

The concepts of the project team and its scheduling and control activities can be carried to the extreme in cases of massive projects. On projects like BART, Bay Area Rapid Transit in the San Francisco Bay area, the project organization, the project team, and its scheduling and control functions were formally imposed in massive proportions. The Minute Man Missile Program within the Boeing Corporation, the construction of the world's largest domed structure by the Mardian Construction Company, and the development of the fee and quota systems connected with the establishment of a 200-mile fishing conservation zone within the U.S. Department of Commerce are other examples of large formal project organizations. The size of these massive projects justifies the formality of project organizations, because the stakes are high. On the other hand, smaller, less massive projects may utilize the concepts of the project team and its scheduling and controlling functions, but impose them more informally and flexibly on the existing organization. The degree of formality and dominance of the project team over project activities must be determined by management's confidence in the existing organization's ability to successfully accomplish the project. If management believes that the project can be accomplished within the existing organization, then a very informal application of the project team and its scheduling and controlling activities can be developed. If, however, the project cannot be expeditiously completed within the existing organization, then much more formality should be exercised in establishing the scheduling and controlling procedures of the project team.

One rather interesting development concerns the permanent institutionalization of the project organization form in organizations that predominantly depend upon products best managed as projects. Aerospace firms, construction firms, computer firms, and other types of firms have used the project organization form for so long that it has become a permanent part of their organization structures. Project managers, project team members, and the project management information system continue to adapt and change to new project assignments. This development is being watched by management theorists with intense interest to determine the benefits and burdens resulting from these new organizational forms.

New techniques have evolved to facilitate the timely completion of project activities within time, cost, and quality standards of the project plan. Some of the most often used scheduling and control techniques will be presented here.

Project Scheduling and Control Techniques

Table 7.1 presents definitions of the terms we shall use in demonstrating the techniques of project scheduling and control. *These terms are the language of project management.* Additionally, we shall use them to explain the use of scheduling and control charts, CPM, PERT, and project cost control systems.

The use of each of these techniques is demonstrated from the information found in Case 7.1—Rocket Aerial Target System (RATS), a real world project. Read the case carefully and try to sense the climate that must have permeated this project, a sense of excitement and urgency. Can you imagine being relieved from your regular job and assigned to the project of designing, building, and flying rockets and seeing them shot down by guided missiles?

Table 7.1
Project Scheduling and Control Terms

1. **Activity** — An effort that is required to complete a part of the project.
2. **Activity duration** — In CPM, the best estimate of the time to complete an activity. In PERT, the expected time or average time to complete an activity.
3. **Critical activity** — An activity that has no room for schedule slippage; if it slips, the entire project completion will slip. An activity with zero slack.
4. **Critical path** — The chain of critical activities for the project. The longest path through the network.
5. **Dummy activity** — An activity that consumes no time but shows precedence between events.
6. **Earliest finish (EF)** — The earliest that an activity can finish, from the beginning of the project.
7. **Earliest start (ES)** — The earliest that an activity can start, from the beginning of the project.
8. **Event** — A beginning, completion point, or milestone accomplishment within the project. An activity begins and ends with an event.
9. **Latest finish (LF)** — The latest that an activity can finish, from the beginning of the project, without causing a delay in the completion of the project.
10. **Latest start (LS)** — The latest that an activity can start, from the beginning of the project, without causing a delay in the completion of the project.
11. **Most likely time (t_m)** — The time for completing an activity that is the consensus best estimate; used in PERT.
12. **Optimistic time (t_o)** — The time for completing an activity if all goes well; used in PERT.
13. **Pessimistic time (t_p)** — The time for completing an activity if bad luck is encountered; used in PERT.
14. **Predecessor activity** — An activity that must occur before another activity.
15. **Slack** — The amount of time that an activity or group of activities can slip without causing a delay in the completion of the project.
16. **Successor activity** — An activity that must occur after another activity.

Case 7.1

Rocket Aerial Target System (RATS)

In April, Norbert Gailer, vice-president of Operations for the Controlled Power Division of the Acme Corporation, received a telephone call from Ivor Kaney, vice-president of Marketing:

Ivor: Norb, how would you like the opportunity to double your business? I've run across a tremendous marketing opportunity that your operation just might be able to fill.

Norb: Let's hear about it.

Ivor: The army has just released an RFP[1] on an aerial target to be used on gunnery ranges for its heat-seeking missiles, the Red Eye and Chaparral. They call this system RATS; it is an expendable, low-cost, rocket propelled, aerial target. With your proven capability in solid propellant motors and the aggressive attitudes shown by your people since you took over down there, I thought you might be interested in going after this piece of new business.

---

[1] An RFP is a request for a proposal. RFPs are frequently issued by funding agencies such as government bureaus, think tanks, and so on to likely producers of the needed matter (product or ideas).

Norb: How much business are we talking about, Ivor?

Ivor: About ten million dollars a year.

Norb: You're right, it would just about double our business. Our sales this year are going to hit about nine and a half million. How much time do we have to respond on the RFP, and is it a development or a production contract?

Ivor: It's a production contract for the first year's requirement, thirty-five thousand birds.[2] The successful bidder will have proved its technical capability by flying four units at Fort Bliss during the first two weeks of September. The bid package is due on or before September 15.

Norb: Wow! That doesn't give us much time to react, considering that we're already busting our backsides on this XRN-20 contract.[3]

Ivor: Yes, I know, but you've got some darn good people down there, and you just might pull it off. I think it's well worth the try.

Norb: OK, Ivor, how about hopping a plane and bringing your experts on this project down here the first thing in the morning and talk it over with our people in more detail? We should be able to make a *go* or *no go* decision tomorrow.

Ivor: I'll see you at nine o'clock tomorrow morning.

Norb Gailer immediately called a staff meeting of his key people to get their ideas on proceeding with the project. It was generally agreed that this was a piece of business the operation should pursue. The question was, how could the operation go after this new business and still successfully produce and deliver its other products? It was conceded that the new business was so important that if the key personnel were satisfied with what they heard from marketing tomorrow morning, an all-out effort should be expended to win the contract.

The meeting the next morning resolved most of the operation's questions. Ivor Kaney informed Gailer that Corporate was so impressed with the prospects of RATS that the operation had Corporate's approval to spend up to a half million dollars in securing the contract, a very high-trust, high-priority allotment. All the department heads agreed that some sacrifice would have to be made by them to succeed in this new effort. Each of them would be asked to give up one or two key employees to serve on the project team. Gailer decided to commit the operation to an all-out effort on the project.

The next day the project team was announced:

1. Project manager — Cris Jacobs, a young recent MBA with an undergraduate degree in management. She was selected because she was perhaps the best administrator in the operation and she had great rapport with the other units of the company.

2. Flight Engineer — Jim Sherry, head of quality assurance/propulsion.

3. System Design Specialist — Robert Brannon, expert design engineer, brilliant development specialist.

4. Production Engineer — Jim Dawson, production manager of propulsion generator department.

---

[2] *Birds* are generally aircraft, here aircraft *targets*.

[3] It is common for RFPs to provide minimal turnaround time. Many have been known to arrive *after* the deadline for proposals.

5. Safety and Security Officer — Irene Thompson, director of loss prevention.

6. Cost Engineer — Wallace Potter, industrial engineer.

These individuals would be assigned to the project full-time for its duration. If the contract was won, all of them would carry their knowledge about RATS back to their home departments, thus aiding in the conversion from development to production.

The team developed the following list of project activities, time estimates, and precedence relationships as part of the project plan:

Activity	Precedence Relationships (Immediate Predecessor Activities)	Estimated Time to Complete Activity (Weeks)
Product Development		
a. Preliminary propulsion design	——	4
b. Preliminary flight system design	——	5
c. Static tests A	a	2
d. Propulsion design modifications	c	2
e. Static tests B	d	2
f. Flight tests A	b	3
g. Flight system design modifications	e, f	3
h. Flight tests B	g	3
i. Demonstration to customer	h	2
Bid Package		
j. Material and component costs	e, f	6
k. Labor and overhead costs	e, f	6
l. Process bid package through company	j, k	2
m. Delivery of bid package to customer	l	1

Scheduling and Control Charts

Scheduling and control charts are the most frequently used tools across a variety of organizations that manage projects. They serve as project planning, scheduling, and controlling devices. Each chart that we shall examine first plans and schedules some particular part of the project; in other words, what must be done and when it must be done. Second, each chart is updated as the project proceeds to indicate the amount of accomplishment toward the plan. In this way project managers can compare actual project work accomplishment with planned project progress. This procedure allows rational changes in management's use of resources to complete the project within time, cost, and quality targets. For example, if one activity is running well ahead of schedule while another is behind schedule, management may shift personnel, materials, and other resources from one activity to another in order to shorten the duration of particular activities.

Perhaps the most often used chart is the horizontal bar chart. These charts are in reality applications of Gantt charts (see Henry Gantt from the scientific management era—Chapter 1), which are also applied in Chapter 10 of this text. One particularly useful horizontal bar chart is depicted in Figure 7.4. This chart is prepared in advance of the project to plan and schedule the activities of the project. Open horizontal bars are drawn for each activity of the project along a time dimension. The letters at the beginning of each bar (left) indicate the activities that must be completed before that bar can begin.

After the open bar chart is initially prepared, managers can be assured that all the activities of the project are planned for, the order in which the activities must be performed is taken into account, the time estimates for completing each activity are included, and, finally, the overall estimated time for completing the project is developed. The open horizontal bar chart becomes the overall plan for the project.

As the project proceeds and activities are completed, actual activity progress is recorded by shading in the horizontal bars. How much of an activity bar to shade in is determined from estimates of the percent of completion of work involved in each activity. If an activity is estimated to be one third completed, for example, then one third of the horizontal bar is shaded in.

Periodically, these charts are updated and distributed to all project participants. A vertical line is drawn on the chart corresponding to the date of the status report. Activity progress can be compared to the status date. In Figure 7.4, for example, Activity g, Flight System Design Modifications, can be observed to be on schedule because the horizontal bar is shaded up to the status date vertical line. Activity j, Materials and Components Costs, is approximately one week behind schedule, because its horizontal bar is shaded to a point about one week behind the status date. Similarly, Activity k, Labor and Overhead Costs, is approximately one week ahead of schedule.

These status reports allow managers to observe the progress of the project's activities, identify problem areas, and develop corrective action to bring the project back on target. These reports can be used alone or in conjunction with other techniques. When projects are not very complex, costly, or long lasting, horizontal bar charts may be used alone to plan and control the timely completion of the project. On the other hand, on more complex and costly projects, the charts may be used as a summary of project status even though other more detailed techniques are also used.

The key advantages of horizontal bar charts are their ease of understanding, ease of modification, and low cost. Their chief disadvantages are that on complex projects the number of activities may require either unwieldy charts or aggregation of activities, and the charts may not adequately indicate the degree of interrelationships among the project's activities.

Other charts are used to plan and control the acquisition and use of resources such as cash, personnel, and materials. Figure 7.5 shows one example of a chart used to plan and control expenditures accumulated through June and a projection of expenditures over the remainder of the project.

Managers typically seek answers to these questions from the charts:

1. Are we on our spending targets now?
2. Do we expect to be on our spending targets at the end of the project?
3. If we do not expect to be on our spending targets at the end of the project, should management corrective action begin in order to bring spending in on target?

Figure 7.4
Horizontal Bar Chart—RATS Project Schedule Plan/Status Report Summary

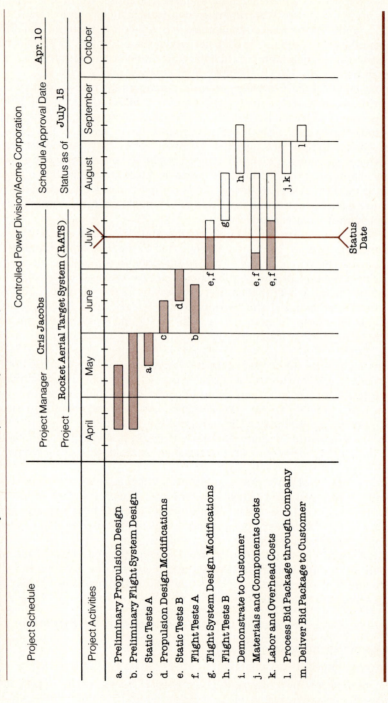

Figure 7.5
Expenditures Chart—RATS Project Expenditures Plan/Status Report: June 30

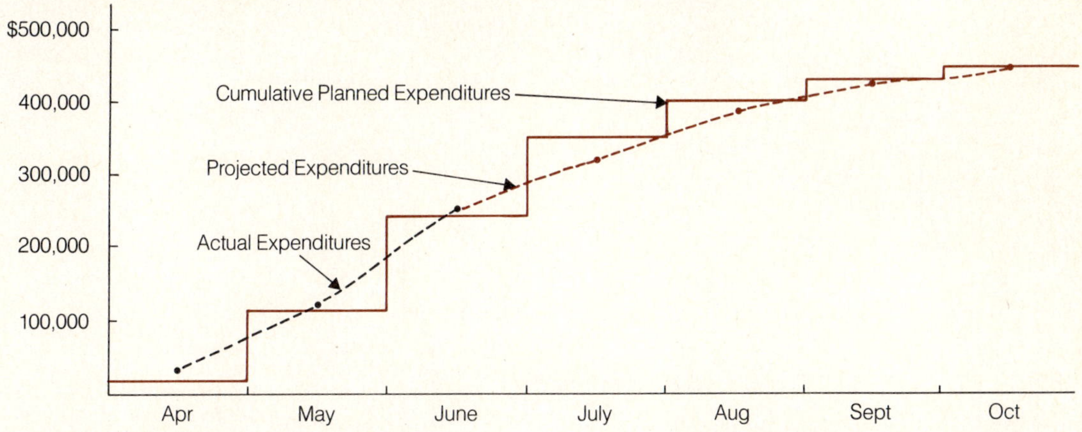

The answer to the last question is complex. There are situations when management purposely allows project expenditures to overshoot spending targets in order to build new technical features into the project, improve project time performance, and other imperatives.

While the chart in Figure 7.5 was used to plan and control expenditures for the entire RATS project, these charts can be and often are used to plan and control smaller parts of a project. For example, departmental expenditures, individual activity expenditures, and a multitude of other more detailed expenditure divisions could be used to back up the project summary in Figure 7.5. These finer breakdowns of expenditures allow managers to determine with more specificity where in the organization project expenditure problems are occurring. Managers can then find answers to such questions as: "Why are we $11,350 overspent on the project to date?"

Having the proper number of employees to work on a project is a knotty problem. Employees must be transferred from other departments to the project; people must be hired from outside the organization or recalled from a waiting list of previously laid-off employees or some other source, and then methodically removed from the project as their activities wind down. Since projects tend to be labor intensive—in other words, much of the cost of the projects tends to be labor cost—project progress is dependent to a large degree upon acquiring the number of trained employees when needed.

Figure 7.6 shows one chart used to plan and control two skill levels of employees on the RATS project. The project requires personnel peaks of 40 and 25 for Skills Levels One and Two, respectively. These charts are used by personnel departments and project teams to plan the acquisition of personnel and to develop corrective action as personnel needs change or as excess absenteeism, turnover, or other personnel related developments occur.

The delivery of materials, components, and subcontracted parts presents special

Figure 7.6
Personnel Chart — RATS Project Plan/Status Report: July 15

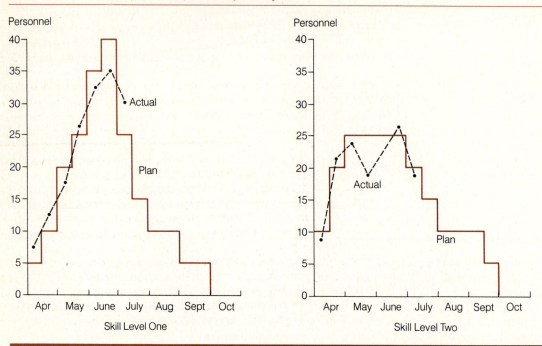

planning and control problems to project managers. First, the short duration and the unique nonrecurring nature of most projects rule out making components and parts in-house; therefore most materials, components, and parts are purchased from suppliers outside the organization. Second, projects typically need the materials "yesterday," as the saying goes, because of severe time pressures. Third, materials of projects can be sufficiently different from the organization's other purchased materials so that regular suppliers may be passed over in favor of new, untried suppliers specializing in these new materials. These reasons and others often account for a most chaotic materials acquisition process for projects.

In spite of the uncertainty associated with finding new suppliers and severe time pressures, organizations have learned to successfully manage the acquisition of projects' materials, components, and subcontracted parts. Figure 7.7 shows one chart approach to planning and controlling the acquisition of materials for the RATS project. This figure shows the key materials to be acquired for the project, when orders are to be placed (x), when expediting checks are to be made (✓), when the supplier plans to process the order (an open horizontal bar), actual supplier processing progress (shaded portion of horizontal bar), and planned deliveries (◬).

Materials charts allow project managers to plan and control the delivery of purchased and subcontracted materials and components by directing purchasing specialists' attention to suppliers and subcontractors of materials that are running

309

Figure 7.7
Materials Chart—RATS Project Key Materials Acquisition Plan/Status Report

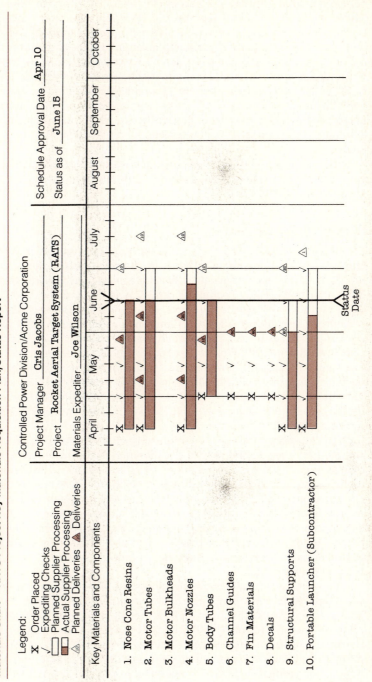

behind schedule. Figure 7.7 shows, for example, that Material Items Number 9 (Structural Supports) and Number 10 (Portable Launcher) are behind schedule. Corrective action may involve plant visits to assist suppliers and subcontractors to overcome their production problems, examination of engineering specifications to facilitate processing, or, as a last resort, reassigning the work to another supplier.

The charts presented here suggest that a wide range of these tools can be applied to an enormous number of project/planning and control situations. In fact, this flexibility probably is the key reason charts are used most frequently in project management, over all other techniques. Flexibility, low cost, and ease of understanding—all contribute to the almost universal use of charts in project management.

Some complex situations call for minute control of each elemental part of projects. CPM and PERT have evolved to fill this need for close microcontrol of the duration of projects.

Critical Path Method

Developed in 1957 by J. E. Kelly of Remington Rand and M. R. Walker of Du Pont to help schedule maintenance projects in chemical plants, the Critical Path Method (CPM) is today an important project-planning and control technique. Program Evaluation and Review Technique (PERT) was developed at about the same time as CPM by the Navy Special Projects Office in cooperation with the management consulting firm, Booz, Allen & Hamilton to plan and control the Polaris atomic powered submarine and its intercontinental ballistic missile systems. PERT and CPM are alike in most respects, except for a few extra refinements incorporated into PERT and not found in CPM. Because of the great similarity of the two methods and because many users of CPM also refer to their method as PERT (the two terms tend to be used interchangeably), CPM will be presented first and everything covered in regard to CPM will also apply to PERT. The refinements in PERT will be covered in the next section.

CPM is designed for unique complex projects with many activities where on-time completion is imperative. Where the planning and control charts of the last section offered overall macrocontrol, CPM is designed to provide intense microcontrol. The technique is expensive to develop and use and should be reserved for large, complex one-time-shot projects. In its original form, time performance was considered paramount; in other words, the legacy from government's use of CPM was the implicit assumption of unlimited funds. The federal government was racing to complete the Polaris program to avoid a possible Russian-imposed nuclear blackmail on the United States. Under this critical time pressure, it is no small wonder that unlimited funding was assumed.

CPM today is typically combined with other project cost control systems such as the charts of the previous section. The combination of macrocontrol from control charts and microcontrol from CPM offers management both the big picture and minute detailed control. This full range of control is necessary on projects such as these: (1) construction of a large dam on the Colorado River; (2) design and testing of the Space Shuttle System; and (3) design, development, and market testing of a new major product line. Such projects have the characteristics displayed in Table 7.2.

Table 7.2
Characteristics of Complex Projects

1. Hundreds and even thousands of activities.
2. Many participating individuals, departments, and organizations
3. High cost
4. High risk of time delays
5. Long time duration
6. Necessity of meeting strict time schedules

Figure 7.8 shows a manager's view of CPM: What information must I supply CPM, and what project management information do I receive in return?

Some projects just do not require the amount of detail provided by CPM because the projects do not fall into the category of complex projects described in Table 7.2. In these cases CPM typically would be passed over for scheduling and controlling techniques offering more macrocontrol. On complex projects, however, the outputs of CPM are absolutely necessary if the project is to be completed on time — duration of the project, identification of critical activities (activities that cannot slip without increasing the project's duration, or those activities with zero slack), and amount of slack for each activity (the amount of time that each activity can slip without affecting the project's duration).

CPM is not a scheduling and controlling system that is done once, set on the shelf, and never used again. Conversely, the system is dynamic. CPM continues to provide management with periodic reports as the project progresses. As Figure 7.9 shows, project managers update their original time estimates for completing each activity as time passes, and the computerized CPM system supplies management with current project management information: new estimates of project duration, a new list of critical activities, new activity estimates, and exception reports (e.g., new delinquent activities and compressed activities).

Now that we understand how CPM was developed, when to use it, when not to use it, what inputs must be provided, and what outputs it provides, let us examine how CPM transforms the inputs into the outputs. We shall now return to our RATS project from Case 7.1 to demonstrate the inner workings of CPM. Although we shall

Figure 7.8
A Manager's View of CPM

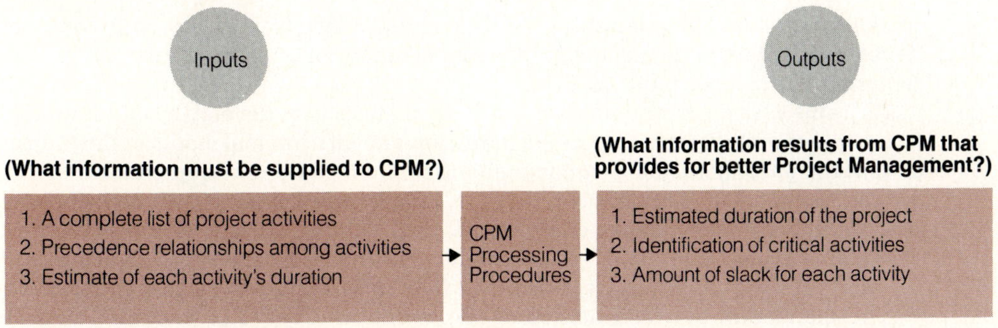

Inputs

Outputs

(What information must be supplied to CPM?)

1. A complete list of project activities
2. Precedence relationships among activities
3. Estimate of each activity's duration

CPM Processing Procedures

(What information results from CPM that provides for better Project Management?)

1. Estimated duration of the project
2. Identification of critical activities
3. Amount of slack for each activity

Figure 7.9
The CPM Management Information System

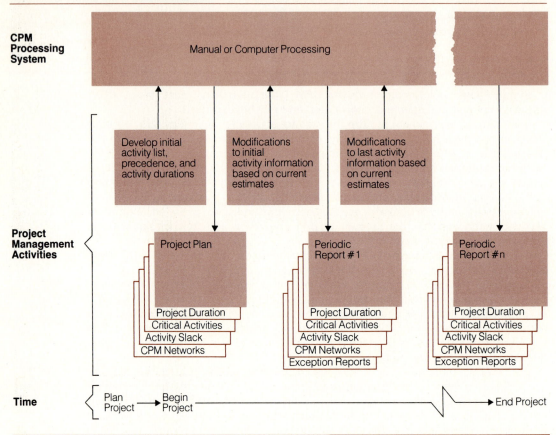

work through the CPM analysis of the RATS project step by step manually to better develop an understanding of the method, most organizations actually use computers to perform CPM's calculations.

As Table 7.3 shows, the first step in CPM analysis is to develop a CPM network. The purpose of this step is to provide management with a visual model of the project so that the interrelationships among activities can be better conceptualized. Before we can develop a CPM network for RATS, we must have a complete list of the project activities, their precedence relationships, and activity time duration estimates. These are developed in Table 7.4. The activity information comes directly from Case 7.1, and the event information is deduced from information about the activities.

The distinction between activities and events is clear. *Activities* are specific efforts required to complete a part of the project and are represented by straight (not

Table 7.3
Steps in CPM Processing

1. Develop a CPM network.
2. Compute ES, EF, LS, and LF for each activity.
3. Compute slack for each activity.

curved) lines. *Events* are the actual beginning or completion of activities and are represented by circles. For example, the project begins with Event Number 1 and is followed by Activity *a* (perform preliminary propulsion design) and Activity *b* (perform preliminary flight system design). Figure 7.10 is the CPM network for the RATS project, developed from the information in Table 7.4.

If each student in your class were to draw a CPM network from the activity information in Table 7.4, you can be sure that there would be great variation in the appearance of the networks. This is because there is a wide range of possible acceptable network representations of projects. No one network is *correct,* because there is a certain amount of art in drawing networks and consequently individual tastes and perspectives necessarily enter. All acceptable networks do, however,

Table 7.4
RATS Activities and Events

RATS Activity	Immediate Predecessor Activities	Activity Duration (Weeks)
a. Perform preliminary propulsion design.	—	4
b. Perform preliminary flight system design.	—	5
c. Perform Static Tests A.	a	2
d. Perform propulsion design modifications.	c	2
e. Perform Static Tests B.	d	2
f. Perform Flight Tests A.	b	3
g. Perform flight system design modifications.	e,f	3
h. Perform Flight Tests B.	g	3
i. Demonstrate RATS to customer.	h	2
j. Estimate material and component costs.	e,f	6
k. Estimate labor and overhead costs.	e,f	6
l. Process bid package through company.	j,k	2
m. Deliver bid package to customer.	l	1

RATS Event

1. Project is begun.
2. Preliminary propulsion design is completed.
3. Preliminary flight system design is completed.
4. Static Tests A are completed.
5. Propulsion design modifications are completed.
6. Static Tests B, Flight Tests A are completed.
7. Flight system design modifications are completed.
8. Flight Tests B are completed.
9. Material and component cost estimates are completed.
10. Labor and overhead cost estimates are completed.
11. Processing bid package through company is completed.
12. Bid package is delivered to customer; RATS demonstration to customer is completed; and project is finished.

Figure 7.10
CPM Network of RATS Project

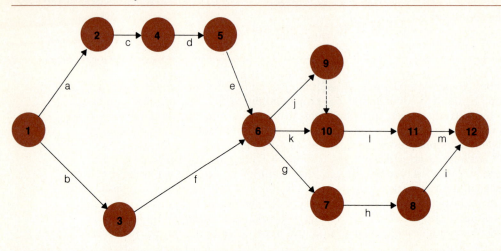

Figure 7.11
CPM Network Conventions

**Network
Representation**   **Interpretation**

1.    Activity *a* must be completed before Activity *b* can begin.

2. 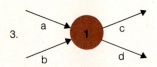   Activities *a* and *b* can occur concurrently but Activity *c* cannot begin until both *a* and *b* are completed.

3. 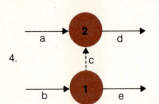   Activities *a* and *b*, *c* and *d* can occur concurrently, but both Activities *a* and *b* must be completed before either Activity *c* or *d* can begin.

4. 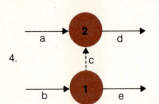   Activities *a* and *b*, *d* and *e* can occur concurrently, but both Activities *a* and *b* must be completed before Activity *d* can begin and Activity *b* must be completed before Activity *e* can begin. Activity *c* is a dummy activity (dashed). Dummy activities have zero time duration and show only precedence relationships.

abide by certain rules and conventions. Figure 7.11 demonstrates these conventions. Notice that Convention Number 4 in the figure uses a dummy activity. Dummy activities only indicate precedence relationships (order in which activities must be performed) between activities — nothing else. Follow through the complete RATS Project CPM network in Figure 7.10 and make sure you grasp the procedures of networking. Refer to the activities and events of RATS from Table 7.4 as required. Notice also that in Figure 7.10 all activities that begin or end a project begin or end in a single event. For example, Activities *a* and *b* both begin with Event 1 and Activities *m* and *i* end in Event 12. Beginning projects with a single event that always signifies the beginning of the project and ending projects with a single event that always signifies the ending of the project is traditional. This tradition avoids dangling arrows at the start and finish of projects.

Now we are ready to complete Step 2 from Table 7.3 in CPM, computing ES, EF, LS, and LF for each activity. The definitions of these terms can be found in Table 7.1. ES and EF are both computed for each activity by working forward through the network, or from left to right in Figure 7.10. LS and LF, on the other hand, are both computed for each activity by working backward through the network, or from right to left in Figure 7.10. Table 7.5 is a computer printout of a CPM activity status report for the RATS project that shows the project duration, customer requirement, activity duration, and activity slack.

In order to completely understand how the ES, EF, LS, and LF computations were

Table 7.5
CPM Activity Status Report

PROJECT: RATS
DATE: APRIL 10
PROJECT CRITICAL PATH IS 19 WEEKS
CUSTOMER REQUIREMENT IS 20 WEEKS

ACTIVITY	ACTIVITY DURATION (D)	EARLIEST START (ES)	EARLIEST FINISH (EF)	LATEST START (LS)	LATEST FINISH (LF)	SLACK (S)
a	4	0	4	0	4	0
b	5	0	5	2	7	2
c	2	4	6	4	6	0
d	2	6	8	6	8	0
e	2	8	10	8	10	0
f	3	5	8	7	10	2
g	3	10	13	11	14	1
h	3	13	16	14	17	1
i	2	16	18	17	19	1
j	6	10	16	10	16	0
k	6	10	16	10	16	0
l	2	16	18	16	18	0
m	1	18	19	18	19	0

Note: Time is in weeks.

Table 7.6
Computing ES and EF with the Left to Right Pass through the CPM Network (Figure 7.10)

Activity	ES Computation	ES	EF Computation	EF
a	$ES_a = 0^*$	0	$EF_a = ES_a + D_a = 0 + 4 = 4$	4
b	$ES_b = 0^*$	0	$EF_b = ES_b + D_b = 0 + 5 = 5$	5
c	$ES_c = EF_a = 4$	4	$EF_c = ES_c + D_c = 4 + 2 = 6$	6
d	$ES_d = EF_c = 6$	6	$EF_d = ES_d + D_d = 6 + 2 = 8$	8
e	$ES_e = EF_d = 8$	8	$EF_e = ES_e + D_e = 8 + 2 = 10$	10
f	$ES_f = EF_b = 5$	5	$EF_f = ES_f + D_f = 5 + 3 = 8$	8
g	$ES_g = EF_e = 10^{**}$	10	$EF_g = ES_g + D_g = 10 + 3 = 13$	13
h	$ES_h = EF_g = 13$	13	$EF_h = ES_h + D_h = 13 + 3 = 16$	16
i	$ES_i = EF_h = 16$	16	$EF_i = ES_i + D_i = 16 + 2 = 18$	18
j	$ES_j = EF_e = 10^{**}$	10	$EF_j = ES_j + D_j = 10 + 6 = 16$	16
k	$ES_k = EF_e = 10^{**}$	10	$EF_k = ES_k + D_k = 10 + 6 = 16$	16
l	$ES_l = EF_j$ or $EF_k = 16^{**}$	16	$EF_l = ES_l + D_l = 16 + 2 = 18$	18
m	$ES_m = EF_l = 18$	18	$EF_m = ES_m + D_m = 18 + 1 = 19$	19

* Note: The ES is zero when an activity begins the project.

** Note: Whenever two or more activities precede a common event, as with Events 6 and 10 in Figure 7.10, the ES's for all successor activities equal the greatest EF among the predecessor activities. Therefore, ES = greatest EF among all of an activity's immediate predecessors.

made that underlie Table 7.5, first work your way through the steps of Table 7.6 while carefully following along the CPM network in Figure 7.10. This will give a detailed understanding of the forward pass (left to right) calculations that yield the ES and EF values. Next, do the same thing with Table 7.7. This will cover the backward pass (right to left) calculations that yield the LF and LS values.

The values in the *Slack* column in Table 7.5 are computed by taking the difference either between LF and EF or between LS and ES. These slack values represent the number of weeks that an activity can slip before the duration of the project is affected (assuming that all other activities do not change). For example, the duration of the project is 19 weeks (the greatest LF or EF). If Activity b slips 2 weeks, Path b–f is now tied with Path a–c–d–e up to Event 6:

Path	Path Duration
a–c–d–e	$4 + 2 + 2 + 2 = 10$ weeks
b–f	$7 + 3 = 10$ weeks

This does not increase the duration of the project because it now takes 10 weeks to move from Event 1 to Event 6, the same as before. If, however, Activity b slips from 5

Table 7.7
Computing LF and LS with the Right to Left Pass through the CPM Network (Figure 7.10)

Activity	LF Computation	LF	LS Computation	LS
m	$LF_m = EF_m = 19^*$	19	$LS_m = LF_m - D_m = 19 - 1 = 18$	18
l	$LF_l = LS_m = 18$	18	$LS_l = LF_l - D_l = 18 - 2 = 16$	16
k	$LF_k = LS_l = 16$	16	$LS_k = LF_k - D_k = 16 - 6 = 10$	10
j	$LF_j = LS_l = 16$	16	$LS_j = LF_j - D_j = 16 - 6 = 10$	10
i	$LF_i = EF_m = 19^*$	19	$LS_i = LF_i - D_i = 19 - 2 = 17$	17
h	$LF_h = LS_i = 17$	17	$LS_h = LF_h - D_h = 17 - 3 = 14$	14
g	$LF_g = LS_h = 14$	14	$LS_g = LF_g - D_g = 14 - 3 = 11$	11
f	$LF_f = LS_j$ or $LS_k = 10^{**}$	10	$LS_f = LF_f - D_f = 10 - 3 = 7$	7
e	$LF_e = LS_j$ or $LS_k = 10^{**}$	10	$LS_e = LF_e - D_e = 10 - 2 = 8$	8
d	$LF_d = LS_e = 8$	8	$LS_d = LF_d - D_d = 8 - 2 = 6$	6
c	$LF_c = LS_d = 6$	6	$LS_c = LF_c - D_c = 6 - 2 = 4$	4
b	$LF_b = LS_f = 7$	7	$LS_b = LF_b - D_b = 7 - 5 = 2$	2
a	$LF_a = LS_c = 4$	4	$LS_a = LF_a - D_a = 4 - 4 = 0$	0

 * Note: The LF's of all activities ending in the last event of a project, such as Activities *m* and *i* ending in Event 12 in Figure 7.10, are equal to the greatest EF among these activities.

** Note: Whenever two or more activities succeed a common event, as with Event 6 in Figure 7.10, the LF's of the predecessor activities are equal to the least LS among the successor activities. Therefore, LF = least LS among all of an activity's immediate successors.

to 8 weeks, a slippage of 3 weeks, the duration of the entire project is increased from 19 to 20 weeks.

Path	Path Duration
b–f–j–l–m	$8 + 3 + 6 + 2 + 1 = 20$ weeks
b–f–k–l–m	$8 + 3 + 6 + 2 + 1 = 20$ weeks
b–f–g–h–i	$8 + 3 + 3 + 3 + 2 = 19$ weeks

All activities with zero slack are said to be *critical activities* and lie on *critical paths*. These activities cannot slip or the whole project will slip. The critical activities therefore receive the highest degree of project management attention:

Critical Activities	Critical Paths
a, c, d, e, j, k, l, and m	a–c–d–e–j–l–m
	a–c–d–e–k–l–m

Project management can also consider transferring resources (personnel, materials, machines, and so on) from noncritical activities to critical activities to reduce the total duration of the project. For example, let us suppose that some resources could be shifted from Activity b to Activity a, thus increasing the duration of b from 5 to 6½ weeks and decreasing the duration of a from 4 to 3½ weeks. Because activity b has a slack of 2 weeks, this will not affect the duration of the project; S_b will be reduced accordingly. Reducing the duration of Activity a by ½ week will, however, reduce the duration of the project from 19 to 18½ weeks, or a reduction of ½ week.

Suppose that resources could be shifted from Activity f to Activity i, thus changing the duration of these activities:

Activity	Duration before Transfer of Resources	Duration after Transfer of Resources
f	3	4
i	2	1

What effect will this change have upon the duration of the project? It will be unaffected, because Paths $k-l-m$ and $j-l-m$, parallel critical paths, are unaffected.

We now have demonstrated how CPM analysis develops management's CPM outputs—project duration, critical activities, and activity slack. These computations are developed in the beginning of the project as shown in Figure 7.9 and modified as new estimates are available as the project proceeds. Tables 7.4, 7.5, and Figure 7.10 result from the initial estimates and CPM computations.

As the project progresses, new activity estimates are supplied to the CPM processing system as shown in Figure 7.9. These updates result in new periodic reports supplied to project managers. Tables 7.8 and 7.9 are examples of these updated reports. Note in Table 7.8 that the durations of Activities k and j have changed. Activity k has compressed from 6 to 5 weeks, and j has slipped from 6 to 7 weeks. This change results in three significant effects: The duration of the project (largest EF and LF) is increased from 19 to 20 weeks; S_k is increased from zero to 2 weeks; and S_g, S_h, and S_i are increased from 1 to 2 weeks.

Table 7.9, a CPM exception report, highlights changes to previous management reports. From the delinquent activities report managers can immediately see that Activity j has slipped one week, resulting in the increase in S_k of one week, increase in ES_l of one week, increase in ES_m of one week, and increase in project duration of one week. The compressed activities report shows that although the duration of Activity k has been reduced one week, no other activities or the duration of the project are affected. These periodic reports provide project management with current information about the minute details of the project, thus allowing close microcontrol.

The critical path method assumes that the activities of the network are independent. This is critical to the use of the procedures of the method, but may or may not reflect the actual conditions of the project. Two activities may be directly related (for example, Activity d, propulsion design modifications, and Activity g, flight system design modifications); if so, the duration of one is dependent upon the duration of another.

Another assumption in the critical path method is that there are precise breaking points where one activity ends and another begins. This may not be true because one activity may begin before another preceding activity is completed as long as the

Table 7.8
CPM Activity Status Report

PROJECT: RATS
DATE: JULY 15
PROJECT CRITICAL PATH IS 20 WEEKS
CUSTOMER REQUIREMENT IS 20 WEEKS

INCOMPLETE ACTIVITY	ACTIVITY DURATION (D)	EARLIEST START (ES)	EARLIEST FINISH (EF)	LATEST START (LS)	LATEST FINISH (LF)	SLACK (S)
g	3	10	13	12	15	2
h	3	13	16	15	18	2
i	2	16	18	18	20	2
j	7	10	17	10	17	0
k	5	10	15	12	17	2
l	2	17	19	17	19	0
m	1	19	20	19	20	0

preparatory work required has been performed. The scope of work for real project activities may not totally fit this neat breaking point assumption.

The degree of dependence and overlap between real project activities will determine in part the usefulness of CPM as a project management tool. Most project managers understand these assumptions and continue to use CPM in spite of slight violations of the assumptions, feeling that the inflicted errors are minimal.

Perhaps the greatest problem with CPM is the temptation to apply the technique to noncomplex projects, an overkill legacy from the government and the aerospace

Table 7.9
CPM Exception Report—RATS Project July 15

DELINQUENT ACTIVITIES REPORT

DELINQUENT ACTIVITY	AMOUNT OF SLIPPAGE	OTHER AFFECTED ACTIVITIES	IMPACT ON OTHER ACTIVITIES	NET CHANGE IN PROJECT COMPLETION
j	1	k	S + 1	+1
		l	ES + 1	
		m	ES + 1	

COMPRESSED ACTIVITIES REPORT

COMPRESSED ACTIVITY	AMOUNT OF COMPRESSION	OTHER AFFECTED ACTIVITIES	IMPACT ON OTHER ACTIVITIES	NET CHANGE IN PROJECT COMPLETION
k	1	—	—	—

industry. This problem would be diminished if managers would carefully weigh the benefits to be gained from using CPM against the time and money costs in maintaining the CPM processing system. It appears that sanity is prevailing in this respect as real world managers are moving away from government-imposed overkill toward more selective use of this valuable microcontrol project scheduling and control technique.

Program Evaluation and Review Technique (PERT)

PERT is almost identical to CPM in regard to its functions, network diagrams, internal calculations, and resulting project management reports. The minor exceptions surround the activity time estimates.[4]

In CPM an activity's duration is based on a single time estimate. In PERT three time estimates are made for each activity — pessimistic time (t_p), if bad luck were encountered; most likely time (t_m), the consensus best estimate; and optimistic time (t_o), if all goes well. From these three time estimates a mean (t_e) and variance (V_t) are computed for each activity:

$$t_e = \frac{t_o + 4t_m + t_p}{6} \qquad V_t = \left(\frac{t_p - t_o}{6}\right)^2$$

PERT implicitly assumes that each activity has a distribution of possible times. The distribution is defined by its t_e and V_t, which are computed from t_o, t_m, and t_p.

Why does PERT use multiple activity time estimates? Because this allows the development of an average duration and a variance for each path in the network, thus totally defining the paths' duration distributions. Figure 7.12 shows how the duration distribution of Path $b-f-g-h-i$ from RATS is determined: The mean duration of the path is equal to the sum of the activity mean durations, and the variance of the path is equal to the sum of the activity variances.

When the duration distribution of a path is assumed to be normal and its mean and variance have been computed, we can make probabilistic statements about the path. For example: (1) There is only a 10 percent probability that the critical path will be greater than 35 weeks. (2) There is a 35 percent probability that the project can be completed in less than 50 weeks. The ability to make probabilistic statements about project path durations is the only material difference between CPM and PERT. PERT uses t_e, the mean time based on three activity duration time estimates for activity durations whereas CPM uses a single time estimate for activity durations, but all other calculations of the two methods are identical.

How much value is there in the probabilistic features of PERT? There are many practitioners who would argue that fewer and fewer organizations may be using the probabilistic capabilities unique to PERT because:

1. It is difficult enough to make one good time estimate for each activity as in CPM; three accurate time estimates, each with a different meaning, may be more than we can hope for.

---

[4] Note to instructors: For simplicity of presentation, the activity-on-arrow (AOA) convention is used for both CPM and PERT.

Figure 7.12
Activity and Path Duration Distributions

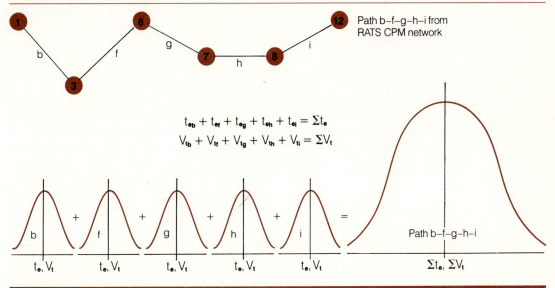

$$t_{eb} + t_{ef} + t_{eg} + t_{eh} + t_{ei} = \Sigma t_e$$
$$V_{tb} + V_{tf} + V_{tg} + V_{th} + V_{ti} = \Sigma V_t$$

2. Developing information inputs, processing the information, and interpreting the results in CPM are complex enough. Can we realistically expect our managers to use the probabilistic information in PERT?

3. Inaccuracies have surfaced in PERT probabilistic statements because of inaccurate time estimates and violations of the probability distribution assumptions underlying activity time estimates.

4. PERT is inherently more costly than CPM both in terms of dollars and in terms of management effort.

These and other reasons may have validity. In spite of PERT's possible shortcomings, however, it remains an important force in government and industry project scheduling and control.

Project Cost Control Systems

CPM and PERT are designed to offer project managers planning, scheduling, and control aimed at only one project performance dimension — time performance. Most organizations today, whether goods producing or service producing, private industry or governmental, must also plan and control for another project performance dimension—cost or project expenditures.

Figure 7.5, the cash flow chart from the RATS project expenditures plan/status report of June 30, is one approach to planning and controlling project expenditures. This chart has one distinct disadvantage, however: time performance control and cost performance control are not integrated. If both these project performance dimensions are important to project managers, wouldn't it be advisable to have a time and cost control system that showed time and cost performance simultaneously?

PERT/Cost was devised by the Department of Defense (DOD) and the National Aeronautics and Space Administration (NASA) in 1962 to tie together time and cost performance on government contracts. The term PERT/Cost is now commonly used not to identify the DOD and NASA system or any other specific cost system, but as a description of the general class of project time/cost planning and control systems. The term PERT/Cost is applied to a variety of systems in use today in business and

Table 7.10
RATS Time/Cost Status Report

ACTIVITY				TIME STATUS (WEEKS)		COST STATUS (THOUSANDS OF DOLLARS)		
AC- TIVITY CODE	ACCOUNT NUMBER	SCHED- ULED ACTIVITY DURATION	NEW ESTI- MATED DURATION	ESTIMATED VS. LATEST ALLOWABLE COM- PLETION DATE	ACTIVITY SLACK	SCHED- ULED ACTIVITY COST	ACTUAL COST TO DATE	ESTIMATED COST (OVER) OR UNDER TO COMPLETE ACTIVITY
a	R-100	4	4	*		36.5	40.0	(3.5)
b	R-101	5	5	*		60.0	66.0	(6.0)
c	R-102	2	2	*		35.0	30.5	4.5
d	R-103	2	2	*		28.5	28.5	--
e	R-104	2	2	*		42.0	40.0	2.0
f	R-105	3	3	*		67.5	65.0	2.5
g	R-106	3	3	7/15-7/15	2	52.0	31.0	5.0
h	R-107	3	3	8/7-8/7	2	39.5	--	--
i	R-108	2	2	9/1-9/1	2	63.5	--	--
j	R-109	6	7	8/22-8/22	0	14.0	4.5	(4.0)
k	R-110	6	5	8/7-8/22	2	9.5	5.0	2.0
l	R-111	2	2	9/7-9/7	0	1.0	--	--
m	R-112	1	1	9/15-9/15	0	1.0	--	--
							Total	2.5

Note: * means activity is complete.

government. We will examine some of these by developing time/cost planning and control reports and charts for the RATS project (Case 7.1).

One common PERT/Cost report is depicted in Table 7.10: the RATS Time/Cost Status Report. These computerized reports periodically show actual time and cost status compared to scheduled status for each activity of the project. For example, Activity c can be evaluated as: (1) the activity is completed. (2) The actual duration of the activity was the same as the scheduled duration. (3) An amount $4,500 less than scheduled cost was actually expended on the activity. Similarly, Activity j can be evaluated as: (1) The activity is incomplete. (2) The activity duration has slipped from 6 weeks as scheduled to an estimated 7 weeks. (3) The estimated completion date and the latest allowable completion date are the same—August 22. (4) There is zero slack for the activity. If the activity duration slips beyond the estimated 7 weeks, the entire project will also slip by an equal amount. (5) Although the actual activity cost is well below the scheduled activity cost, the activity is estimated to be overspent by $4,000 at the completion of the activity. These evaluations of the project's activities give project managers information to better manage the project's activities. These and similar reports can be designed to offer much more refined exhibition of costs. The cost status of Table 7.10 could, for example, be broken into Labor, Materials, and Overhead, or any other meaningful division of costs for each activity.

Computerized time/cost status reports such as depicted in Table 7.10 offer project managers the ultimate in project time and cost microcontrol. The microcontrol does not come free, however. Money and time must be used to: (1) design and implement the scheduling and control system; (2) provide computer services; (3) provide updated time and cost activity estimates on a daily, weekly, or biweekly basis; (4) distribute the reports and instruct project personnel on the use of the reports; and (5) maintain, revise, and redesign the system as required. These and other costs associated with the elaborate microcontrol systems suggest that managers must carefully weigh the advantages to be gained from the systems against their costs.

Charts and other visual devices are used to simultaneously assess the cost and time status of projects. Figure 7.13 is an example of a chart that summarizes a project's actual time and cost status compared to the project schedule. It shows that the RATS project on July 15 is about one week behind schedule and approximately $30,000 overspent. Expenditures are projected to be about the same as scheduled at the end of the project.

Charts offer a quick evaluation of projects' cost and time status, but not in the same detail or precision as offered by detailed computerized reports such as the one depicted in Table 7.10. The charts can, however, be broken down into much smaller coverage of the project. For example, charts for small groups of activities or even individual activities can be developed. These minute, detailed charts, however, do become burdensome to prepare and distribute to the project personnel.

Regardless of the format for time/cost status reports for projects, cost performance and time performance are both critically important elements of project management. The days when time performance dominated project management thinking are over for most organizations. Today cost performance is of at least equal importance in project management.

Figure 7.13
RATS Project Time/Cost Plan vs. Actual Performance Chart

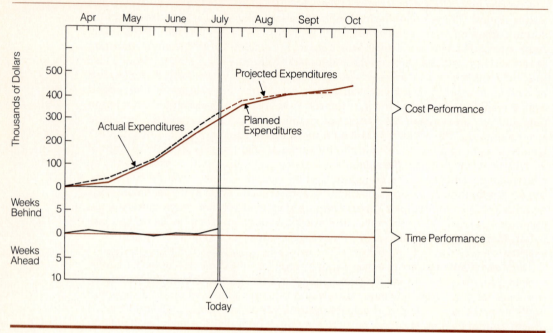

PERT/CPM in Practice

PERT/CPM is perhaps the most frequently used operations research technique across a wide variety of organizations. Table 7.11 indicates that it tends to be used across a narrow range of applications. Project planning and control dominates all

Table 7.11
Uses of PERT/CPM

Pert/CPM Use	Frequency of PERT/CPM Use (Percent)
1. Project planning and control	46
2. Production planning and control	22
3. Maintenance planning and control	18
4. All other	14

Source: Norman Gaither, "The Adoption of Operations Research Techniques by Manufacturing Organizations," *Decision Science* 6 (October 1975):809. Reprined by permission of the American Institute for Decision Sciences.

other applications, while production planning and control and maintenance planning and control round out 86 percent of the uses of PERT/CPM. All these applications have the characteristics of complex projects displayed in Table 7.2—many activities, high costs, high risk of time delays, long time duration, time performance imperatives, and so on. The frequency of use of PERT/CPM supports the view that these recent scheduling and control techniques offer project managers maybe not the certainty of project performance, as Wren states in the opening quote of the chapter, but the likelihood of satisfactory project completion.

Target Slack versus Project Slack Table 7.5, the initial CPM analysis of the RATS project, computes the slack for each activity—the amount of time that an activity can slip without causing a delay in the project completion. The slack expressed in this table is based on the duration of the critical path, which is 19 weeks. Notice that the customer requirement is 20 weeks, so that even if any critical activity slipped one week the customer requirement would still be met.

Each of the activities in Table 7.5, then, in reality has one additional week of slack if the standard is the customer requirement. Some organizations add this additional week of slack on to the project slack of each activity; thus activity slack is based upon a target project duration rather than critical path duration.

Table 7.8 shows that the critical path for the RATS project has slipped one week, and now the target duration and project duration are the same—20 weeks. There is now no question about the meaning of activity slack because each activity slack is expressed in terms of target project duration, which is equal to critical path duration.

Management typically favors the use of project slack rather than target slack because that typically gives an automatic built-in time cushion. However, both target project duration (contracts, customer requirements, and so on) and critical path duration are commonly used in organizations today. Interpreters of PERT/CPM status reports must understand the basis of activity slack if appropriate project management decisions are to be made.

PERT Statistics The three activity time estimates, the feature unique to PERT, allow us to compute:

$$\text{a mean } t_e = \frac{t_o + 4t_m + t_p}{6}, \qquad \text{and a variance, } V_t = \left(\frac{t_p - t_o}{6}\right)^2$$

for each activity. Table 7.12 develops these activity parameters for the RATS project. The last two columns contain the activity expected times (t_e—mean time or duration) and activity variances (V_t), respectively. These values are used to develop path probabilistic statements.

Example 7.1 analyzes one of the paths in the RATS project network, $a-c-d-e-j-l-m$. We want to know the probability of this path exceeding 20 weeks. Note that by summing the t_e and V_t for the activities along the path, we can define the distribution of the path's possible duration times. Once the mean and standard deviations are known about a particular path, the probability of exceeding or, conversely, completing a path within a certain time limit is straightforward.

Table 7.12
PERT Expected Time (t_e) and Variance (V_t) for RATS Project Activities

Activity	Optimistic Time (t_o)	Most Likely Time (t_m)	Pessimistic Time (t_p)	Expected Time or Duration $t_e = \dfrac{t_o + 4t_m + t_p}{6}$	Variance $v_t = \left(\dfrac{t_p - t_o}{6}\right)^2$
a. Preliminary propulsion design	3	4	5	4.00	.11
b. Preliminary flight system design	5	6	8	6.17	.25
c. Static Tests A	2	2	3	2.17	.03
d. Propulsion design modifications	1	2	3	2.00	.11
e. Static Tests B	1	2	3	2.00	.11
f. Flight Tests A	2	3	5	3.17	.25
g. Flight system design modifications	2	3	4	3.00	.11
h. Flight Tests B	3	3	6	3.50	.25
i. Demonstrate to customer	2	2	2	2.00	0
j. Material and component costs	5	6	8	6.17	.25
k. Labor and overhead costs	3	6	9	6.00	1.00
l. Process bid package through company	2	2	2	2.00	0
m. Deliver bid package to customer	1	1	1	1.00	0

Note: Time is in weeks.

Example 7.1

PERT Path Duration Distributions

Evaluate the probability of Path a–c–d–e–j–l–m of the RATS project taking longer than 20 weeks.

Solution

1. Compute the mean path duration. Sum the activity expected times (from Table 7.12) along the path:

Activity	t_e	Activity	t_e
a	4.00	j	6.17
c	2.17	l	2.00
d	2.00	m	1.00
e	2.00		$\Sigma t_e = 19.34$

2. Compute the path variance. Sum the activity variances (from Table 7.12) along the path:

Activity	V_t	Activity	V_t
a	.11	j	.25
c	.03	l	0
d	.11	m	0
e	.11		$\Sigma V_t = $ .61

3. Compute the standard deviation of path duration: $\sigma_t = \sqrt{\Sigma V_t} = \sqrt{.61} = .78$

4. Construct the path duration distribution:

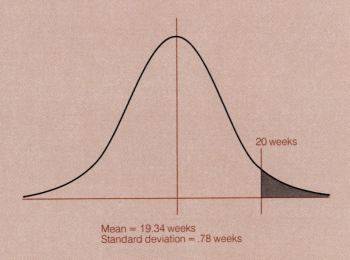

20 weeks

Mean = 19.34 weeks
Standard deviation = .78 weeks

5. Compute the probability of the path running longer than 20 weeks:

a. Find how many standard deviations (Z) 20 weeks is from the mean (19.34 weeks):

$$Z = \frac{x - \mu}{\sigma_t} = \frac{20 - 19.34}{.78} = .85$$

b. Turn to Appendix A, "Normal Probability Distribution," and read down the Z column of the table to .8 and across that row to the .05 column. The value in the body of the table (.80234) is the probability that the path duration will be less than or equal to 20 weeks. Therefore:

p (path duration > 20 weeks) = 1 − .80234 = .198

Activity Cost-Time Trade-offs Project managers occasionally may have the option of *crashing* activities, spending extra money to compress an activity's duration by using overtime, subcontracting, expediting materials, and so on. If projects are in danger of running over the allowable project duration, managers often consider crashing as a viable alternative.

Given that managers have several activities in the project that can be crashed, how does one decide which activities not to crash; which activities to crash, if any; and in what order? The general rules are:

1. Do not crash noncritical activities. (This normally will not reduce the project's duration.)
2. Crash only critical activities — activities on the critical path, those activities with zero slack.
3. Crash activities with the lowest crashing cost per unit of time first until the desired project duration is achieved.
4. When parallel critical paths exist, each of the parallel paths must be compressed. Compressing only one of the paths will not reduce the project duration.

PERT/CPM Computer Programs Most PERT/CPM applications today utilize computers to receive updated project activity time estimates, make the necessary internal calculations, and generate project management reports. Although our PERT/CPM calculations in this chapter have been performed manually, PERT/CPM applications are typically almost never calculated without computers.

Appendix C in this book has one such computer program that receives activity time estimates and gives back slack for each activity, duration and variance for critical paths, and other useful project management information. There are reportedly more than 60 such computer programs in use.[5] For those wishing to explore this topic further, an extensive list of reference sources of PERT/CPM computer programs is included in the selected bibliography at the end of this chapter.

Summary

New organization forms have evolved during recent years to simultaneously accommodate both complex projects and the generation and delivery of goods and services in productive systems. Foremost among these new forms is the project organization. Project teams are formed from personnel drawn from departments of organizations to manage and coordinate the activities of projects outside conventional organization structures.

The scheduling and control of complex projects are sufficiently difficult to have fostered a variety of planning and control techniques. Additionally, a set of commonly used terms has developed into a language unique to project planning — activities, events, critical path, slack, predecessor activity, networks, CPM, PERT, and the like.

---

[5] J. J. Moder and C. K. Phillips, *Project Management with CPM and PERT*, 2d ed. (New York: Reinhold, 1970).

Scheduling and control charts are the most frequently used among these techniques. Simplicity, flexibility, and low cost are the key strengths of these devices. These macrocontrol techniques offer project managers perhaps the quickest overall view of project performance at the lowest cost.

When more minutely detailed control is desired, CPM, PERT, and PERT/Cost can be used. PERT/CPM offers project managers an activity-by-activity planning and control system that is usually computerized. Periodic status reports give managers updated project duration, critical activities, activity slack, network diagrams, and exception reports from which to determine what must be done to assure successful project completion.

Review and Discussion Questions

1. Define *project management*.

2. Why is the management of one-time large-scale projects a challenge for most managers in productive systems? How do these managers meet this challenge?

3. What tasks must the project team do before the project begins?

4. What tasks must the project team do as the project progresses?

5. Why are the planning, scheduling, and controlling of materials, supplies, and subcontractors on projects more difficult than with these resources in production of the organization's usual goods and services?

6. Define these terms: **a.** *activity,* **b.** *event,* **c.** *critical activity,* **d.** *critical path,* **e.** *activity duration,* and **f.** *slack.*

7. Define these terms: **a.** *predecessor activity,* **b.** *dummy activity,* **c.** *earliest start,* **d.** *earliest finish,* **e.** *latest finish,* and **f.** *latest start.*

8. Define these terms: **a.** *most likely time* (t_m), **b.** *optimistic time* (t_o), and **c.** *pessimistic time* (t_p).

9. How does the activity duration differ between CPM and PERT?

10. Horizontal bar charts and other charting techniques offer operations managers macrocontrol of projects whereas CPM and PERT offer microcontrol. Explain.

11. Name four characteristics of complex projects.

12. What are the inputs (information supplied) and outputs (information returned) of CPM?

13. Name three steps in CPM processing.

Problems

Scheduling and Control Charts

1. The Buildrite Construction Company is developing plans to build a new medical building in downtown Denver, Colorado. Buildrite has established these project activities, their precedence relationships, and their estimated time durations:

Activity	Precedence Relationsips (Immediate Predecessor Activities)	Estimated Activity Duration (Weeks)
a. Demolition of present structures	——	4
b. Excavation and filling of site	a	5
c. Forming and pouring of footings and foundation	b	5
d. Construction of structural steel skeleton	c	6
e. Construction of concrete structure	d	8
f. Construction of exterior skin	e	12
g. Installation of plumbing system	e	5
h. Installation of electrical system	e	3
i. Installation of heating/cooling system	e	4
j. Construction of interior partitions	g, h, i	3
k. Installation of lighting fixtures, and finish work	j	5

Prepare a horizontal bar chart to plan the schedule for this construction project if work is to begin January 1.

2. The Brownkraft Paper Mill in Ohno, Maine, has been experiencing increasingly excessive downtime and maintenance costs because of long-term machinery deterioration. Something has to be done. Brownkraft has decided to shift its production to a nearby mill on a subcontracted basis and shut the Ohno Mill down in order to perform a massive repair and refurbishing program. These activities, their precedence relationships, and their estimated time durations have been established:

Activity	Precedence Relationships (Immediate Predecessor Activities)	Estimated Activity Duration (Days)
a. Development of machinery status reports	——	30
b. Engineering machinery renovations	a	60
c. Shutting down mill	b	7
d. Performance of mechanical renovations	c	90
e. Performance of electrical renovations	c	80
f. Performance of plumbing renovations	c	70
g. Test running refurbished facility	d, e, f	10
h. Debugging entire facility	g	7
i. Starting up mill	h	7

a. If the work is to begin June 1, prepare a horizontal bar chart to plan the schedule for this maintenance project. b. How long will the Ohno Mill be shut down?

3. From Figure 7.14, describe fully the status of Stratophonic's new product development project as of March 1.

4. From Figure 7.15, describe fully the spending status of Stratophonic's new product development project as of March 1.

5. From Figure 7.16, describe fully the status of project personnel on Stratophonic's new product development project as of March 1.

6. From Figure 7.17, describe fully the status of key materials deliveries of Stratophonic's new product development project as of March 1.

Figure 7.14
Project Schedule — New Product Development Project: Stratophonic Sound Inc.

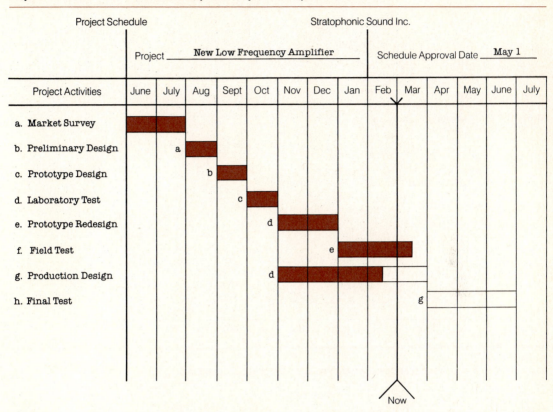

Figure 7.15
Expenditures Chart — New Product Development Project: Stratophonic Sound Inc.

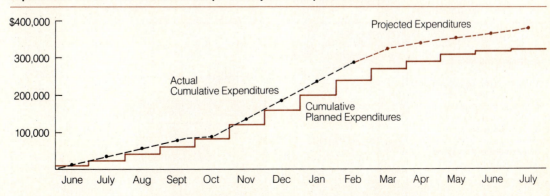

Figure 7.16
Personnel Chart — New Product Development Project: Stratophonic Sound Inc.

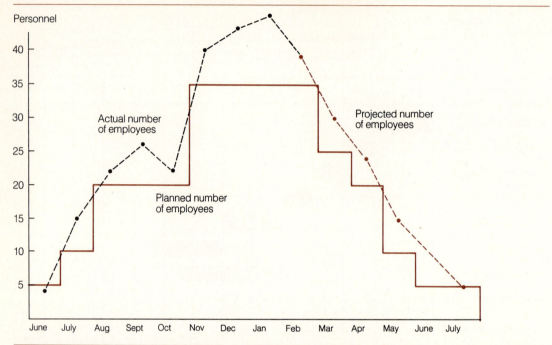

Figure 7.17
Materials Chart — New Product Development Project: Stratophonic Sound Inc.

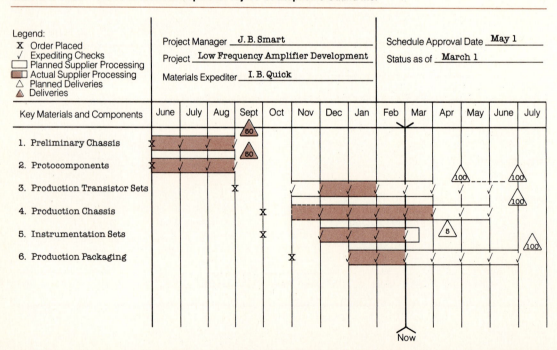

CPM

7. A project has the following activities and precedence relationships:

Activity	Immediate Predecessor Activities	Activity	Immediate Predecessor Activities
a	——	d	b
b	——	e	b
c	a	f	e
		g	d

Construct a CPM network for the project.

8. A project has the following activities and precedence relationships:

Activity	Immediate Predecessor Activities	Activity	Immediate Predecessor Activities
a	——	e	a
b	——	f	e, c
c	b	g	c, d, e
d	b	h	f, g

Construct a CPM network for the project.

9. A project has the following activities and precedence relationships:

Activity	Immediate Predecessor Activities	Activity	Immediate Predecessor Activities
a	——	g	d, e
b	——	h	a
c	——	i	h
d	b	j	i
e	c	k	b
f	c	l	h, k, f, g
		m	g, f

Construct a CPM network for the project.

10. A project has these activities, precedence relationships, and activity durations in weeks:

Activity	Immediate Predecessor Activities	Activity Duration (Weeks)	Activity	Immediate Predecessor Activities	Activity Duration (Weeks)
a	——	3	e	b	5
b	——	4	f	a	7
c	——	3	g	e, f	3
d	c	12			

a. Construct a CPM network for the project. **b.** Compute ES, EF, LS, LF and slack for each activity. **c.** What is the critical path? What is the project's estimated duration?

11. A project has these activities, precedence relationships, and activity durations in days:

Activity	Immediate Predecessor Activities	Activity Duration (Days)	Activity	Immediate Predecessor Activities	Activity Duration (Days)
a	——	10	f	b	17
b	——	15	g	b	12
c	a	10	h	d, f	9
d	a	20	i	h, g	7
e	c	15			

a. Construct a CPM network for the project. **b.** Compute ES, EF, LS, LF and slack for each activity. **c.** What is the critical path, and what is its duration?

12. A project has these activities, precedence relationships, and activity durations in weeks:

Activity	Immediate Predecessor Activities	Activity Duration (Weeks)	Activity	Immediate Predecessor Activities	Activity Duration (Weeks)
a	——	3	g	d	10
b	——	9	h	e, f	7
c	——	7	i	g, h	14
d	a	12	j	c	15
e	a, b	10	k	f, j	9
f	c	11			

a. Construct a CPM network for the project. **b.** Compute ES, EF, LS, LF, and slack for each activity. **c.** What is the critical path and its duration?

13. Larissa Gibbons is the manager of new product development at the Quality Underwear Company. She has just received this month's report on one of Quality's new products:

Time/Cost Status Report
  Reporting Date July 30
Project XR-15-Nylon Brief

Activity		Time Status (Weeks)				Cost Status (Thousands of Dollars)		
Activity Code	Account Number	Duration (D)	New D	Old/New Completion Date	Slack	Target Cost	Cost to Date	Estimated Cost (over) or under Target to Completion
a	X-100	10	10	★	—	10.5	8.5	2.0
b	X-110	12	12	★	—	12.0	13.5	(1.5)
c	X-120	5	6	8/15–8/22	0	10.0	9.0	(3.5)
d	X-130	16	18	12/15–1/7	0	22.0	5.5	(5.0)
e	X-140	12	10	10/1–9/15	4	6.5	0.0	1.0
f	X-150	5	5	11/1–11/1	3	5.0	0.0	1.0

★ Means activity is complete

Describe fully the status of time and cost performance of the project's activities.

PERT

14. An activity in a project has these time estimates: optimistic time (t_o) = 15 weeks, most likely time (t_m) = 20 weeks, and pessimistic time (t_p) = 22 weeks. **a.** Compute the activity's expected time or duration (t_e). **b.** Compute the activity's variance (V_t). **c.** Compute the activity's standard deviation (σ_t).

15. Project Path a–c–e–f has these activity time estimates in days:

Activity	Optimistic Time (t_o)	Most Likely Time (t_m)	Pessimistic Time (t_p)
a	20	25	30
c	25	30	32
e	15	17	20
f	18	18	18

a. Compute expected time or duration (t_e) for each activity. **b.** Compute the variance (V_t) for each activity. **c.** Compute the expected duration and variance for the path.

16. A project has the following activities, precedence relationships, and time estimates in weeks:

Activity	Immediate Predecessor Activities	Optimistic Time (t_o)	Most Likely Time (t_m)	Pessimistic Time (t_p)
a	——	15	20	25
b	——	8	10	12
c	a	25	30	40
d	b	15	15	15
e	b	22	25	27
f	e	15	20	22
g	d	20	20	22

a. Construct a PERT network. **b.** Compute the duration, ES, EF, LS, LF, and slack for each activity. **c.** What is the critical path? **d.** What is the probability that the project will take longer than 57 weeks to complete?

17. Three paths of a PERT network have these mean durations and variances in weeks:

Path	Mean Duration (Σt_e)	Variance (ΣV_t)
1	45	2.75
2	44	5.50
3	46	1.20

Which path offers the greatest risk of overrunning a contract deadline of 48 weeks?

Case

Maxwell Construction Company

The Maxwell Construction Company is a large company that specializes in industrial and governmental construction projects. The company bids on only the largest projects at premium prices and tends to get its fair share because it has gained a reputation for doing work of outstanding quality within the time constraints of its contracts. Maxwell is now in the process of bidding on the construction of an addition to the Western State University football stadium, a project that will go for about $20 million. The only problem is that the project falls at a time when Maxwell has won several other large contracts and does not want to overextend itself and spread its resources too thin. If the project could be completed within 300 days of the beginning of the project, the company would feel confident in pursuing the contract. The cost estimator for Maxwell has developed these estimates of activity durations and their precedence relationships:

Activity	Precedence Relationships (Immediate Predecessor Activities)	Activity Duration (Days)
a. Demolish and salvage existing structures	——	10
b. Excavate and grade site	a	15
c. Pour concrete footings and foundation	b	17
d. Install in-ground plumbing	b	20
e. Install underground electrical service	b	8
f. Preassemble mid-level steel skeleton	b	14
g. Construct and pour concrete substructure	c,d,e	16
h. Pour lower-level concrete floors	g	12
i. Erect mid-level steel skeleton	f, h	9
j. Erect mid-level concrete columns and cross beams	i	21
k. Install aboveground phase 2 plumbing	j	18
l. Install aboveground phase 2 electrical service	j	14
m. Pour mid-level concrete floors	k,l	23
n. Preassemble top-level steel skeleton	i	14
o. Erect top-level steel skeleton	m,n	23
p. Erect top-level concrete columns and cross beams	o	36
q. Pour top-level floors	p	37
r. Construct press box complex	q	45
s. Erect field lights	p	14
t. Construct restrooms	m,n	48
u. Install seats	q	21
v. Paint and finish walls, floors, and ceilings	u	14
w. Clean up structure and grounds	v	7

Assignment

1. Draw a CPM network diagram of the project.

2. Develop a horizontal bar chart that summarizes the plan for the project. Each activity should be "mapped out" on this chart. Discuss how this chart would be used as the project proceeds and how it would be used in the planning phases of the project.

3. Develop a CPM analysis of the project. What is the estimated duration of the project? What activities are on the critical path? How much can Activity u slip without affecting the project completion date?

4. Discuss how the CPM analysis results compare with your chart in No. 2. What are the advantages and disadvantages of CPM as a planning and controlling technique when compared with the project chart or horizontal bar chart?

5. Use the CPM computer program in Appendix C to analyze this case. What is the estimated duration of the project. What activities are on the critical path? How much can Activity u slip without affecting the project completion date?

6. Should the Maxwell Construction Company bid on the project? Does the project require more time than Maxwell has available?

Selected Bibliography

Original Descriptions

Kelley, James E., Jr., and Morgan R. Walker. "Critical Path Planning and Scheduling." *Proceedings of the Eastern Joint Computer Conference*, 160–173. Boston: 1959.

PERT, Program Evaluation Research Task, Phase I Summary Report, 646–669. Washington, DC: Special Projects Office, Bureau of Ordnance, 7, Department of the Navy, July 1958.

General Explanation and Applications

Baboulene, B. *Critical Path Made Easy*. London: Duckworth Press, 1970.

Burman, P. J. *Precedence Networks for Project Planning and Control*. London: McGraw-Hill, 1972.

Gaither, Norman. "The Adoption of Operations Research Techniques by Manufacturing Organizations." *Decision Science* 6(October 1975): 794–814.

Levin, R. I., and C. A. Kirkpatrick. *Planning and Control with PERT/CPM*. New York: McGraw-Hill, 1966.

MacCrimmon, K. R., and C. A. Ryavec. "An Analytical Study of the PERT Assumptions." *Operations Research* 12(January–February 1964): 16–37.

McLaren, K. G., and E. L. Buesnel. *Network Analysis in Project Management*. London: Cassell, 1969.

Wiest, Jerome D., and Ferdinand K. Levy. *A Management Guide to PERT/CPM*. Englewood Cliffs, NJ: Prentice-Hall, 1977.

Computer Applications

Archibald, R. D. "PERT and the Role of the Computer." *Computers and Automation* 12(July 1963): 26–30.

Jennett, Eric. "Availability of CPM Programs." *Project Management Quarterly* 1(July 1970): 10–13.

Khtaian, G. A. "Computer Project Management—Proposal, Design, and Programming Phases." *Journal of Systems Management* 27(August 1976): 12–21.

Miller, Robert W. "How to Plan and Control within PERT." *Harvard Business Review* 40(March–April 1962): 93–104.

Paulson, Boyd C. "Man–Computer Concepts for Project Management." *The Construction Institute,* Technical Report No. 148. Stanford, Calif.: Stanford University, August 1971.

Smith, Larry A., and Joan Mills. "Project Management Network Programs." *Project Management Quarterly* (June 1982): 18–29.

Solomon, N. B. "Automated Methods in PERT Processing." *Computers and Automation* 14(January 1965): 18–22.

Part Three

Planning Production to Meet Demand:
A Proactive Approach

Part Two of this text explored the ways that operations managers approach and analyze crucial operations strategy decisions. Designing products and production processes; allocating scarce resources to product lines, projects, and departments; planning long-range production capacities; locating facilities; and planning large-scale projects are so important that great attention and notoriety are focused on them. Important as these strategic planning decisions are in POM, we must not allow them to overshadow other ongoing decisions in POM that can be of at least equal importance.

POM is more than the mountaintop experiences of infrequent strategic decisions. After the dust has settled from these crucial decisions, operations managers must then continue to face one of the most compelling facts about their jobs: products and services must be produced and delivered on a daily basis so that customers' needs are satisfied at competitive costs.

When I visit with operations managers, they consistently say that the greatest source of pressure and tension in their jobs is the need to produce products and services to meet delivery promises and at the same time keep the lid on costs. The causes of this pressure are customers, bosses, marketing personnel, accounting personnel, and personal pride. These formidable pressures are ever-present reminders to operations managers that products and services must be gotten out the back door on time and within cost budgets. Toward this end, operations managers engage in production planning activities such as these:

1. Develop intermediate-range plans for providing aggregate production capacity sufficient to meet the estimated customer demands.

2. Establish production planning and control departments to guide the organization's activities toward its delivery promises, inventory targets, and production objectives.

3. Provide sufficient inventory of finished products to meet the dual objectives of efficient operations and satisfaction of customers needs.

4. Schedule the production of products and services necessary to meet the short-range needs of customers or to replenish depleted finished goods inventories and to efficiently load the production facilities.

5. Plan for the purchase, storage, and shipment of materials so that sufficient quantities of the right materials of the appropriate quality are available in time to support the short-range production schedules.

Although any one decision concerning these activities and the ongoing operation of the productive system may not in itself be critical to the long-range success of the organization, the cumulative effect of all of these ongoing decisions is immense. These decisions are therefore emphasized here in Part Three.

Chapter Outline

8

Proactive Production Planning:

An Overview of Aggregate Plans, Production Control
Departments, and Scheduling Systems

*The manufacturing business environment, in most cases, is
inherently unstable and turbulent. Change is the rule.
Change, in fact, is "the name of the game." The solution lies
not in methods to stabilize and freeze, but rather in an
enhancement of the ability to accept change and respond to
it promptly and correctly—and do it routinely, as a matter
of course.*[1]
Joseph Orlicky, 1975

This chapter is concerned with developing intermediate- and short-range production plans that result in getting products and services out of productive systems on time to satisfy customer demand. Two equally important goals impinge on operations managers in this activity—meeting customer due dates or promised delivery dates *and* arranging the bringing together of workers, materials, and machines to achieve high levels of efficiency within the productive system. **Both satisfied customers and internal operating efficiency are absolutely necessary to the survival and success of productive systems; production planning is aimed at both these essential goals.**

The driving force in production planning is the due dates for products and services. Timetables for delivering these outputs are usually determined by the delivery dates requested on customer purchase orders. When productive capacity, inventory deficiencies, or other obstacles prevent meeting of the customer requested dates, customers are contacted and alternative delivery dates are usually negotiated. Experienced operations managers know that customers prefer to have suppliers give promised delivery dates that they can count on. Nothing is more frustrating than to be promised that an order will be delivered on the first of the month and it doesn't arrive, and time passes and still it doesn't arrive. Finally, after this unhappy experience is repeated several times, the customer gives up on the

---

[1] Joseph Orlicky, *Material Requirements Planning* (New York: McGraw-Hill, 1975), 277.

supplier. Operations managers therefore usually prefer to give conservative promised delivery dates and then devise production schedules that will keep those promises. But the desire to win customers from competitors motivates these managers to make delivery promises that are favorable to the customer as well.

The quantity of products and services that *can* be promised during any one time period is a function of both productive capacity and economics. Such factors as machine capacity, size of the work force, and the availability of materials limit the number of products and services that can be produced in each time period. The capacity of a facility can be increased by buying more machines, hiring and training more workers, using overtime, developing additional material sources, expediting material deliveries, and so on; but these efforts take time and are often prohibitively expensive. Capacity is therefore dynamic: it can be changed over time, but at a cost.

Internal operating efficiency is promoted in production planning by promising delivery dates on customer orders that load the productive system in each time period without *overloading* or *underloading*. **A fully loaded facility is one that uses the planned complement of workers on straight time to operate all the system's most efficient machinery with material deliveries designed to smoothly support the continuity of these high output rates.** Under this preferred arrangement the rhythmic operation of the productive system results in low labor and material costs per unit; because output is usually high, the fixed cost per unit is also low.

When a system is overloaded, output rates are so high that the productive system strains at the seams because capacity has been increased beyond ordinary levels. These undesired consequences can result: (1) increased turnover and absenteeism of workers, (2) increased worker hiring and training costs, (3) increased use of worker overtime, (4) increased scrap rates and reduced quality of outputs, (5) increased material expediting and transportation costs, (6) use of less efficient standby machines, (7) use of more costly subcontracting services, (8) increased confusion and awkwardness in materials handling and work planning, (9) increased maintenance costs because machines cannot be shut down for preventive maintenance servicing, and (10) lowered worker and management morale if these conditions continue for long periods. These and other outcomes of overloading are avoided in production planning by promising deliveries of products and services that, when taken together, fully load but do not overload the productive system.

When productive systems are underloaded, the output rates are so low that the resources of production are underutilized. These outcomes often result: (1) temporary layoffs of workers, (2) increased fixed cost per unit because output rates are so low, and (3) decreased labor efficiency because of underutilized workers. Since capacity can be gradually scaled up or down as time passes, overloading and underloading of productive systems are not conditions that must necessarily occur when output rates must increase or decrease. The concept of a fully loaded facility in production planning therefore refers to fitting the short-term customer demand for products and services to the capacity of the productive system during each time period.

Toward the dual goals of satisfying customer demand on a timely basis and achieving high levels of internal operating efficiency through fully loading the production facilities, operations managers develop proactive production planning systems. These systems are forward-looking systems that plan which

products to produce, how to produce the products, how many to produce, and when to produce them. Because these systems are forward looking and continuously sense changes in their environments, they also adapt to change, which is a necessary characteristic for organizations that expect to survive.

Figure 8.1 illustrates how all of the long-range, intermediate-range, and short-range plans of these systems are connected. First, long-range capacity plans are developed. These plans, which were discussed in Chapter 6, reflect the *operations strategies* and set in motion the work required to build, buy, or develop buildings, to acquire machinery, and to develop major subcontractors, which are the principal means of production. These plans become the constraints on how many products and services *can* be produced in the intermediate- and short-range plans.

Next, an aggregate capacity plan is developed from the demand forecasts and the production capacity constraints imposed by the long-range capacity plans. This intermediate-range plan, which usually spans a time period of from six to twelve months, specifies the employment plans, machinery and utilities plans, subcontractor and material supply plans, and facility modification plans. The aggregate capacity plan, though not specifying the exact products that will be produced, does impose capacity constraints on the short-range production schedules that follow. We shall study the concepts and approaches of aggregate capacity planning later in this chapter.

Short-range production schedules specify the finished goods and components to be produced in each time period of the planning horizon, which usually spans a time period of from a week to a few months. These schedules specify the quantity of components or finished goods to be completed in each work center of the entire productive system during each day or week of the schedule. Before these schedules can be developed, estimated short-range demands must be developed from forecasts and in-hand orders for products and services. In the case of products, because these outputs can be inventoried or stored, we must know the status of our inventory for each product before we can determine how many of each needs to be produced. The concepts and issues involved in finished goods inventories are presented in Chapter 9.

Master production schedules are the short-range plans for completing finished goods, or *end items* as they are usually called, at the very front end of the productive system. Many detailed scheduling decisions back upstream in the production processes are caused by a master production schedule. Both master production schedules and detailed work center production scheduling decisions are treated in Chapter 10.

Resource requirements planning is a planning system that includes master production scheduling, capacity requirements planning (testing the master production schedule for capacity feasibility and developing a plan for loading the system), and material requirements planning (testing the master production schedule for material availability and developing a plan for acquiring the materials to support the master production schedule). And yet resource requirements planning is more than a sum of its parts, because it is a *planning system* that integrates all of its parts in such a way that it supplies operations managers with all of the information they need to plan and control production. In a sense, then, resource requirements planning is an *operations information system,* a system that will be discussed in Chapter 11.

Figure 8.1
A Proactive Production Planning System

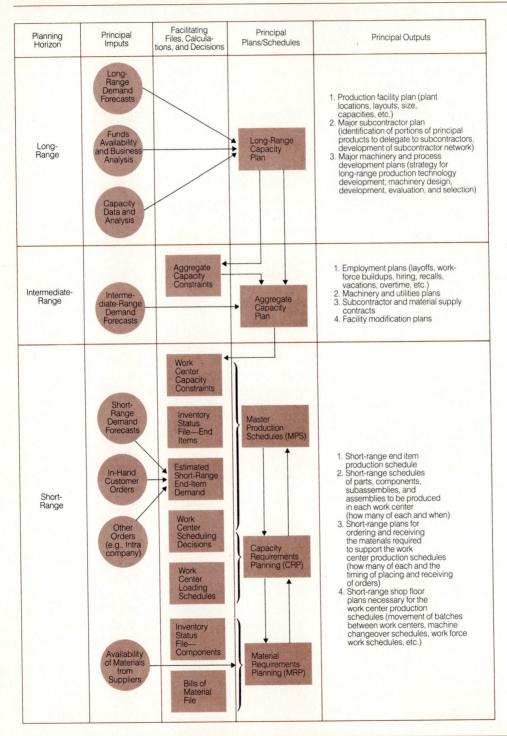

Planning Horizon	Principal Imputs	Facilitating Files, Calculations, and Decisions	Principal Plans/Schedules	Principal Outputs
Long-Range	Long-Range Demand Forecasts; Funds Availability and Business Analysis; Capacity Data and Analysis		Long-Range Capacity Plan	1. Production facility plan (plant locations, layouts, size, capacities, etc.) 2. Major subcontractor plan (identification of portions of principal products to delegate to subcontractors, development of subcontractor network) 3. Major machinery and process development plans (strategy for long-range production technology development; machinery design, development, evaluation, and selection)
Intermediate-Range	Intermediate-Range Demand Forecasts	Aggregate Capacity Constraints	Aggregate Capacity Plan	1. Employment plans (layoffs, work-force buildups, hiring, recalls, vacations, overtime, etc.) 2. Machinery and utilities plans 3. Subcontractor and material supply contracts 4. Facility modification plans
Short-Range	Short-Range Demand Forecasts; In-Hand Customer Orders; Other Orders (e.g., Intracompany); Availability of Materials from Suppliers	Work Center Capacity Constraints; Inventory Status File—End Items; Estimated Short-Range End-Item Demand; Work Center Scheduling Decisions; Work Center Loading Schedules; Inventory Status File—Components; Bills of Material File	Master Production Schedules (MPS); Capacity Requirements Planning (CRP); Material Requirements Planning (MRP)	1. Short-range end item production schedule 2. Short-range schedules of parts, components, subassemblies, and assemblies to be produced in each work center (how many of each and when) 3. Short-range plans for ordering and receiving the materials required to support the work center production schedules (how many of each and the timing of placing and receiving of orders) 4. Short-range shop floor plans necessary for the work center production schedules (movement of batches between work centers, machine changeover schedules, work force work schedules, etc.)

Aggregate Planning

If we possessed perfect information about demand for the products of a productive system for next year and if the demand were perfectly uniform from time period to time period, aggregate planning would be simple. We would hire just enough workers, buy just enough machines, and buy just enough materials to flow in to produce the exact amount of outputs in every time period to satisfy customer demand. Unfortunately, future demand is not known with certainty and is almost never uniform.

The forecasting techniques in Chapter 3 of this text are employed to estimate the quantity of products or services likely to be demanded in each time period of the planning horizon. *Aggregate planning* is the process of devising a plan for providing a productive capacity scheme to support these intermediate-range sales forecasts. Then, as forecast customer demand becomes known in the form of customers' orders, aggregate plans may have to be revised upward or downward to avoid either overloaded or underloaded facilities.

Aggregate planning is necessary in POM because: (1) it facilitates fully loaded facilities and minimizes overloading and underloading, thus enhancing internal operating efficiency; (2) adequate productive capacity is provided to meet promised customer delivery dates in most situations; (3) orderly and systematic transition of productive capacity to meet the peaks and valleys of expected customer demand is facilitated; and (4) in times of scarce productive resources, getting the most output for the amount of resources available is enhanced. Aggregate planning is the key to managing change in POM because the changing patterns of customer demand and the plans for providing productive resources that adapt to those changes are fundamental to aggregate planning.

In developing an intermediate-range aggregate capacity plan, management has several variables that may ordinarily be manipulated to vary the production capacity from month to month. Among these variables are: (1) the size of the work force; (2) the use of overtime, although managers do not like to include this as part of an intermediate-range plan, ordinarily preferring to reserve overtime for emergencies in short-range scheduling situations; (3) the use of undertime—the practice of providing workers with less than the normal hours of work per week, similarly a practice usually reserved for short-range planning on an emergency basis; and (4) the use of inventories, backorders, subcontractors, and leaving demand unfilled to buffer the difference between a rather uniform production capacity and variations in demand from month to month.

Aggregate planning is performed at the highest levels within production organizations. Vice-presidents of manufacturing, vice-presidents of operations, plant managers, directors of operations, and other executives regularly participate in aggregate planning. The fact that these executives are deeply involved in aggregate planning underscores its importance and the impact that it has on their organizations.

Aggregate planning as a process generally follows the steps shown in Table 8.1. After a study of these steps, we shall demonstrate them through the Brush and Roll Paint Company Case as we proceed through this section. After you have read the introductory scenario to the Brush and Roll Paint Company Case, we will begin to explore how to go about developing an aggregate capacity plan.

Table 8.1
Steps in Aggregate Planning

1. Begin with a sales forecast for each product or service that indicates the quantities to be sold in each time period (usually weeks, months, or quarters) over the planning horizon (usually 3 months, 6 months, or a year).
2. Total all of the individual product or service forecasts into one aggregate demand for the entire productive system. If the products are not straightforwardly additive because of heterogeneous units, a homogeneous unit of measure must be selected that both allows the forecasts to be added and links aggregate outputs to productive capacity.
3. Transform the aggregate demand for each time period into workers, materials, machines, and other elements of productive capacity required to satisfy aggregate demand.
4. Develop alternative resource schemes for supplying the necessary productive capacity to support the cumulative aggregate demand.
5. Select the capacity plan from among the alternatives considered that satisfies aggregate demand at lowest total operating cost.

Note: Step 5 assumes that the productive system is compelled by management policy to produce the sales forecast. There are occasions when capacity cannot be sufficiently increased or when it would be more profitable to produce less than the sales forecast. It is assumed, for the purposes of this chapter, that these issues have already been resolved and that the sales forecast is the production objective.

Case 8.1

Aggregate Planning at the Brush and Roll Paint Company

The Brush and Roll Paint Company is about to finalize its aggregate capacity plan for next year. The company produces three paint products—latex interior, latex enamel, and latex stain. The production plant is located in Cleveland, Ohio, where there is an abundance of workers who must be trained for a one-month period to perform the duties of material preparation, mixing, and canning—the principal operations of the production line.

The latex carrier, pigments, cans, boxes, and other materials required to produce Brush and Roll's products are also readily available from tried and proven suppliers in abundant quantities. The processing equipment in the production departments is operated on only one shift because Brush and Roll's management bought out a competitor last year, and so an excess of machine capacity is available. Similarly, ample warehouse space for holding finished goods inventory is available.

The capacity situation at Brush and Roll is this: Since the only limiting factor in capacity planning is the size of the work force, how many workers should be employed during each time period to provide the productive capacity to support the sales forecasts of the three paint products?

Three plans are currently being considered by Brush and Roll's president: (1) levelized capacity, (2) matching capacity with aggregate demand, and (3) compromise capacity (something between the other two "pure" plans). These three alternatives must be evaluated in terms of which plan results in the lowest total annual cost while considering three elements of cost: (1) cost of hiring workers from time period to time period over the entire year, (2) cost of laying off workers over the same period, (3) cost of carrying the finished goods inventory for the entire year.

The pertinent data for this analysis are presented below:

Working days per quarter: Q_1 and $Q_4 = 62$, Q_2 and $Q_3 = 63$
Labor standard per gallon of paint: 2.311 worker hours per gallon
Working hours per shift: 8 hours per shift per worker
Maximum machine and material capacity on one shift: 100,000 gallons per quarter

The key analyses that must be performed by Brush and Roll in developing an aggregate capacity plan are:

1. Develop an aggregate demand from individual product forecasts.

2. Develop an analysis of the three capacity plan alternatives in terms of their impact upon worker employment levels and finished goods inventories.

3. Compare the three alternatives in the number of workers hired, the number of workers laid off, and the average finished goods inventory levels for the entire year.

4. Select the capacity plan alternative with the lowest annual cost.

Aggregate Demand

The aggregation of all of an organization's products or services into one aggregate demand that is expressed in homogeneous units may or may not be straightforward. Consider these aggregate demand situations: (1) systems that produce only one product—ammonium nitrate fertilizer, sand, coal, and crude oil; (2) systems that produce multiple outputs that are readily converted into common production capacity units—barrels, tons, press strokes, labor hours, dollars, and machine hours; (3) systems that produce diverse products with different productive capacity units—electrical appliances, office supplies, and medical operations. This latter class of systems usually reduces its diverse outputs to common denominator production planning units by developing conversion statistics such as labor hours, machine hours, dollars, standard processing units, and so on. For example, lawn mowers and Rototillers could be reduced to a common denominator of labor hours by developing a historical relationship between the labor content of the two products: lawn mower = 21 labor hours and Rototiller = 17 labor hours. The aggregate plan for the two products would be the total labor hours for each time period required to produce the forecast quantity of the two products. This example assumes that labor hours is a good unit to measure productive capacity. Machine hours, pounds per product, or other common denominator units of measure might be better, but we could determine this only by being intimately familiar with a particular productive system. The precision of aggregate plans that use artificially contrived common denominator units of capacity is highly dependent upon the accuracy of the conversion factors.

Figure 8.2 shows how the Brush and Roll Paint Company develops an aggregate demand with a one-year planning horizon. The three individual product quarterly forecasts are added together to form the aggregate demand for all products, expressed in gallons per quarter. It is important to note that the nature of the capacity of the processing steps in the production of paint must also be expressed in gallons of paint per quarter. For example, the material preparation, mixing, and canning operations, in the Brush and Roll Paint Company, are known to have capacities expressed in gallons per quarter. The aggregate plan, which is also expressed in these same units, can therefore be readily compared to the capacities of the

Figure 8.2
Aggregating Individual Product Forecasts into Aggregate Demand: The Brush and Roll Paint Company

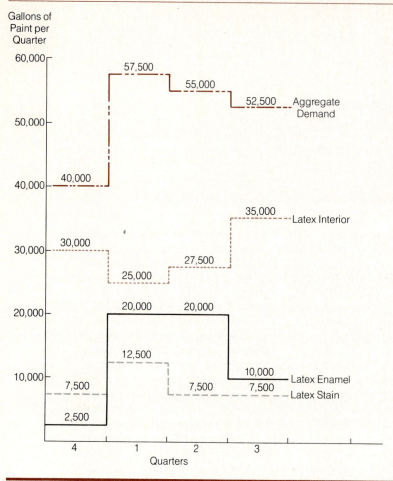

processing steps. These capacities can then be scaled up or down to approximately meet the aggregate demand.

Dimensions of Productive Capacity

As we have suggested, productive capacity is dynamic — it can be changed from time period to time period, but at a cost. An essential part of aggregate planning is a comprehensive understanding of each productive system's capacities. Of particular importance are the availability of productive resources, the relationships between these resources and capacities, and the time and cost requirements to scale these capacities up or down.

The sources of labor are present employees, new hires, workers who have been previously released and are on recall lists, and overtime. The local labor market may or may not be a limiting factor in building up the work force. In some localities there are severe shortages of workers in some higher skilled labor classes. When these shortages exist, expensive training programs must often be maintained to insure an adequate supply of skilled workers.

Union contracts can limit management's flexibility in hiring new employees and laying off experienced workers. For example, the United Auto Workers (UAW) has won Supplemental Unemployment Benefits (SUB), which guarantee experienced workers 90 percent of past earnings during layoff periods of less than one year. These and other similar union contract provisions tend to inhibit management from varying productive capacities drastically during the peaks and valleys of customer demand. Personnel departments and industrial relations departments, the experts in these matters, play an important role in scaling the work force up or down in aggregate planning. The instability of the U.S. auto industry in the 1980s highlights the importance of this role and the economic impact of such planning on both the company and the workers.

Material supply can usually be varied up or down without great difficulty. However, when new sources of supply must be developed by the purchasing department to support increased capacity, these consequences can occur: (1) increased scrap rates while new suppliers are debugging their production processes, (2) spasmodic supply rates as suppliers struggle to increase their outputs, (3) increased material costs as new suppliers incur start-up costs. These and other outcomes are normally expected during time periods when capacities must be escalated.

Of all the factors that limit productive capacity, machines are perhaps the most inflexible. Once a machine is operating 24 hours per day, 7 days per week, at its capacity, that is all the output you are going to get out of it. To get more output, you must either buy or rent another machine or you must subcontract out the machine operation to a subcontractor. Any one of these alternatives usually requires a long lead time.

In most productive systems, labor standards per unit of output are the fundamental bases for estimating the number of workers required to produce the aggregate demand. Similarly, the material standards or bills of material for each product determine the required quantities of material flows to support the production of the aggregate demand. Known machinery capacities, which are usually expressed in units per hour, become the basis for estimating the required number of machines of each type. These and other relationships between productive resources and capacities are unavoidable parts of aggregate planning.

How quickly can you scale the production capacity of an operation up or down, *and* what are the relative costs of accelerated changes and gradual changes to capacities? These questions suggest that if capacity is changed rapidly, more costs might be incurred than if capacities are allowed to shift gradually. In general, this is true. Productive capacity can be increased almost instantaneously in most situations by using worker overtime. But overtime is usually prohibitively expensive if continued for long periods because of worker fatigue, reduced morale of workers, premium labor rates, and a tendency of managers to become increasingly dependent upon this costly safety factor. On the other hand, an alternative to overtime may be the addition of another shift, say, for example, an evening shift. This alternative may take as long as a month or six weeks to execute if workers must be hired or trained, but it is usually less expensive than overtime if the additional capacity is planned for extended periods.

These time and cost characteristics of productive capacity form the basis for developing alternative strategies for providing future aggregate production capacity.

Some Traditional Aggregate Plans

Productive systems have developed traditional plans for responding to aggregate demand. Levelized capacity, matching capacity with aggregate demand, and compromise capacity are three plans that are commonly observed in POM practice.

Levelized Capacity When managers develop aggregate production plans that have uniform capacities per day from time period to time period, these plans are called *levelized capacity plans*. Figure 8.3 shows how the seasonal quarterly aggregate demand of the Brush and Roll Paint Company is met by a levelized capacity plan. Begin at the first quarter and follow through the computation of finished goods inventory levels.

In the first quarter, aggregate demand is less than production. Thus, finished goods inventory levels grow to a peak of 10,840 gallons at the end of the quarter. In the second and third quarters, production increases only slightly because the number of working days per quarter increases from 62 to 63, and inventories fall because production is less than aggregate demand. In the fourth quarter, production falls only slightly because the number of working days per quarter falls from 63 to 62, and inventory levels decline further until they are entirely depleted because demand still exceeds outputs. This is the underlying strategy of levelized capacity: operate productive systems at uniform production levels and let finished goods inventories rise and fall as they will to buffer the differences between aggregate demand and production levels from time period to time period.

The chief advantage of levelized capacity as an aggregate plan is that this approach usually promotes the development of internal operating efficiency above all other alternatives. This is because: (1) the costs of hiring and laying off workers and using overtime are practically eliminated; (2) the cost of locating and developing new sources of material supplies is minimized; (3) only the most efficient productive machinery is used; (4) labor and material costs per unit of output are low, as the rhythmic operation of the productive system has eliminated the continual start-up and shutdown of operations; (5) supervision is simplified since workers are typically on a 40-hour work week and are experienced in their jobs; (6) voluntary turnover and absenteeism may be lower. The Japanese use the concept of levelized capacity to the hilt through their ''lifetime employment'' personnel policies. It is believed that this idea results, at least in the Japanese system, in stable employment levels for personnel, reduced turnover and absenteeism, improved quality levels, and increased commitment of employees to company goals. Some U.S. companies are now adopting these employee guarantees, and this approach seems to favor levelized capacity as an aggregate planning strategy.

In short, operations managers like this approach because operating costs tend to be low, quality of outputs tends to be high and consistent, and production rates are usually dependable. Financial managers, however, typically do not prefer this

Figure 8.3
Levelized Capacity: The Brush and Roll Paint Company

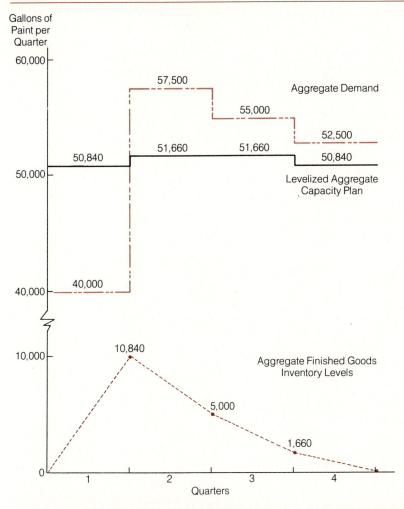

strategy. Can you guess why? You've probably already guessed that this approach typically results in higher finished goods inventory levels, thus tying up cash and increasing the cost of carrying these inventories.

A pragmatic question arises here: Whose budgets bear the cost of carrying these increased finished goods inventories? An important part of carrying cost is the cost of financing the inventory if the cash is borrowed or the *opportunity cost* (what could have been earned if the cash value were invested in alternative investments) if the inventory is internally financed. These costs are often jokingly referred to as *funny money* by some operations managers because POM budgets almost never reflect carrying costs. On the other hand, the direct reduction of labor and material costs through levelizing production appears dramatically in POM budgets. Carrying costs are real, however, and the resolution of this finance versus POM conflict usually depends, finally, upon the trade-off between additional carrying costs and the savings in labor and material costs that result from levelized capacity as an aggregate plan.

Matching Capacity with Aggregate Demand Another traditional aggregate plan is to approximately *match production capacity in each time period with the aggregate demand.* Figure 8.4 shows how the work force of the Brush and Roll Paint

Figure 8.4
Matching Capacity with Aggregate Demand: The Brush and Roll Paint Company

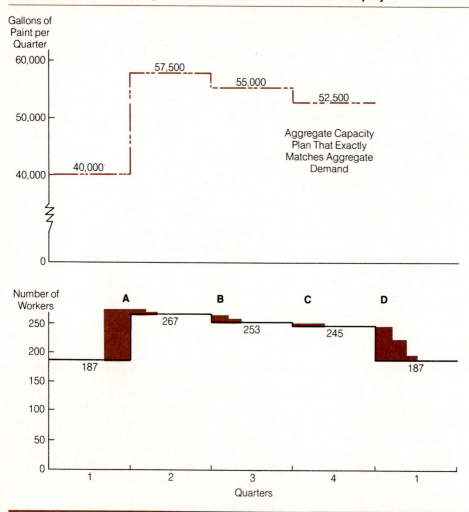

Company fluctuates to support this aggregate plan. Material flows and machinery capacity would similarly be allowed to change from quarter to quarter to just match the aggregate demand.

The labor standard at Brush and Roll is 2.311 worker hours per gallon of paint. The number of workers required in each quarter is therefore determined:

$$\text{Workers} = \frac{\text{Gallons of paint per quarter} \times \text{Labor standard per gallon}}{\text{Working days per quarter per worker} \times \text{Hours per day}}$$

(1st quarter) = (40,000 × 2.311) ÷ (62 × 8) = 187 workers

(2nd quarter) = (57,500 × 2.311) ÷ (63 × 8) = 264 workers

(3rd quarter) = (55,000 × 2.311) ÷ (63 × 8) = 253 workers

(4th quarter) = (52,500 × 2.311) ÷ (62 × 8) = 245 workers

Ideally, under this aggregate plan we would have exactly this number of workers in each quarter, and commensurate amounts of materials and machines would also be made available to support them. But this ideal work force is seldom achieved. For example, note that in Transition Period A in Figure 8.4 Brush and Roll must increase the work force by 77 workers (from 187 to 264) by the beginning of the second quarter. Approximately 85 workers must therefore be hired one month in advance of the second quarter, because they must be trained. Keep in mind that approximately 10 percent of the new hires are historically screened out as unacceptable during the first month of the second quarter. During Transition Periods B, C, and D, the work force must be scaled down 11, 8, and 58 workers, respectively. These reductions in work force seldom occur precisely at the point in time that production output rates are to be reduced according to the aggregate capacity plan. Among the causes of these delays are the reluctance of managers to release workers until the scale-down in outputs has actually been achieved and the desire to let *attrition*—the natural reduction in the size of the work force through retirements, voluntary worker terminations, transfers, and other worker initiated causes—reduce the work force.

The chief advantage of this plan is the lower levels of finished goods inventory that result. Carrying costs are therefore below those of the levelized capacity plan. However, labor and material costs tend to be higher because of the turmoil involved in frequently scaling the work force, material supplies, and production machine capacities up and down.

Compromise Capacity An aggregate plan intermediate to levelized capacity and matching capacity with aggregate demand is the *compromise* approach. This plan varies production capacity up or down slightly as aggregate demand varies, but frequent dramatic changes in production capacity are avoided. Figure 8.5 shows how the Brush and Roll Paint Company's work force varies under this aggregate plan.

Production capacity in this plan is varied only slightly from a levelized capacity plan. Begin again in Figure 8.5 at the first quarter. Output is at 48,333 gallons, which is greater than aggregate demand. Finished goods inventory therefore grows to a

Figure 8.5
Compromise Capacity: The Brush and Roll Paint Company

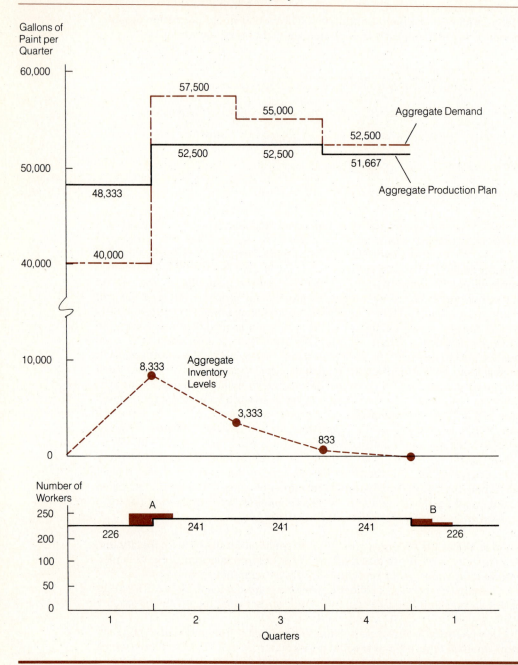

peak of 8,333 gallons at the end of the quarter. In the second and third quarters, inventory levels fall to 3,333 and 833 gallons, respectively, because production is now at 52,500 gallons while aggregate demand is 57,500 and 55,000 gallons. The finished goods inventory is totally depleted during the fourth quarter as aggregate demand still exceeds production.

Note that the production per day during the second, third, and fourth quarters is the same because 241 workers were employed during each of the quarters, but output declined from 52,500 to 51,667 between the third and fourth quarters. This is caused by a decline in working days per quarter (from 63 to 62) between the third and fourth quarters.

Further, notice that this compromise plan results in lower inventory levels when compared to the levelized capacity strategy of Figure 8.3. The work force also is more stable than in the matching capacity with aggregate demand strategy of Figure 8.4. Not only does the work force vary less at the extremes (226 and 241 versus 187 and 264), but the work force is scaled up and down fewer times per year (two versus four). The internal operating efficiency and inventory carrying costs also would be expected to be intermediate to the levelized capacity and matching capacity with aggregate demand plans; thus, a compromise has been struck.

These three traditional aggregate plans are discrete stops along the continuum of possible plans, but they demonstrate the necessary trade-off between internal operating efficiency and inventory carrying costs. Let us now evaluate these three alternative plans for the Brush and Roll Paint Company in order to select the aggregate plan with the lowest total incremental cost.

Selecting an Aggregate Planning Alternative

Table 8.2 develops and compares the number of workers hired per year, the number of workers laid off per year, and the average annual inventory level for each of the three plans.

The aggregate plan of outputs previously developed for each plan is included in Column 5. The number of workers required in each quarter was previously developed, in Figures 8.4 and 8.5, and is calculated again in Column 6. The number of workers hired and laid off in each quarter is thus deduced for each plan. Refer to Figures 8.3, 8.4, and 8.5 as needed to clarify your understanding of this table.

The average annual inventory, which is the basis for computing the annual carrying costs for each of the plans, is straightforwardly developed in Columns 9 through 13. These average inventory levels should be interpreted as the *extra* inventories required when using the matching capacity with aggregate demand strategy as a base; the relative inventory level of this strategy is zero.

Table 8.3 summarizes the incremental costs of the three aggregate plans. The annual cost of hiring and laying off workers and inventory carrying cost are computed and totaled for each plan. The levelized capacity plan is the lowest cost plan in this case. Although levelized capacity does seem to be favored among operations managers, it is not always the lowest cost alternative. This can be demonstrated by increasing inventory carrying costs and decreasing hiring and layoff costs.

Hiring costs typically include personnel department costs incurred in the hiring process, training of new workers, and the cost of scrapped products while workers are learning their jobs. *Layoff costs* usually include personnel department costs,

Table 8.2
Quarterly Production Plans for the Three Traditional Aggregate Plans—Brush and Roll Paint Company

(1) Aggregate Plan	(2) Quarter	(3) Aggregate Demand (Gallons)	(4) Working Days per Quarter	(5) Planned Outputs (Gallons)	(6) Workers Required $\frac{(5) \times 2.311}{8 \times (4)}$	(7) Workers Hired	(8) Workers Laid Off	(9) Inventory Additions or (Subtractions) [(5) − (3)]	(10) Beginning Inventory (Gallons)	(11) Ending Inventory (Gallons)	(12) Average Inventory per Quarter (Gallons) $\frac{(10)+(11)}{2}$	(13) Average Inventory per Year (Gallons) $\frac{\Sigma(12)}{4}$
Levelized capacity	1	40,000	62	50,840	237			10,840	0	10,840	5,420	4,375
	2	57,500	63	51,660	237			(5,840)	10,840	5,000	7,920	
	3	55,000	63	51,660	237			(3,340)	5,000	1,660	3,330	
	4	52,500	62	50,840	237			(1,660)	1,660	0	830	
Matching capacity with aggregate demand	1	40,000	62	40,000	187	85	58		0	0	0	0
	2	57,500	63	57,500	264		8		0	0	0	
	3	55,000	63	55,000	253		11		0	0	0	
	4	52,500	62	52,500	245		8		0	0	0	
Compromise capacity	1	40,000	62	48,333	226	17	15	8,333	0	8,333	4,167	3,125
	2	57,500	63	52,500	241		2	(5,000)	8,333	3,333	5,833	
	3	55,000	63	52,500	241			(2,500)	3,333	833	2,083	
	4	52,500	62	51,667	241			(833)	833	0	417	

Table 8.3
A Cost Comparison of Three Alternative Aggregate Plans—Brush and Roll Paint Company

(1) Aggregate Plan	(2) Total Annual Number of Workers Hired	(3) Total Annual Number of Workers Laid Off	(4) Average Annual Inventory (Gallons)	(5) Annual Hiring Cost [(2) × $250]	(6) Annual Layoff Cost [(3) × $300]	(7) Annual Inventory Carrying Cost [(4) × $5.00]	(8) Total Annual Incremental Operating Costs [(5) + (6) + (7)]
Levelized capacity	0	0	4,375	$ 0	$ 0	$21,875	$21,875
Matching capacity with aggregate demand	85	85	0	21,250	25,500	0	46,750
Compromise capacity	17	17	3,125	4,250	5,100	15,625	24,975

Note: The labor cost is the same for each of the plans; therefore, this cost is not included in this analysis.

termination pay, unemployment benefits, and so on. Although the Brush and Roll Paint Company considered only three alternative capacity plans that were differentiated only in hiring and layoff costs and annual inventory carrying costs, several other possibilities exist in practice.

For example, extra days per week, extra shifts per day, shifts longer than 8 hours, subcontracting, and a host of other alternatives exist that could supply the required productive capacity in any time period. Such alternatives may be differentiated according to overtime premium labor rates, evening and night shift premium labor rates, additional supervision and other overhead costs, subcontracting fees, and so on. Although Brush and Roll considered only three capacity alternatives and three elements of costs, many more capacity alternatives and more cost elements are usually considered in practice.

Aggregate Planning in Job Shops and Service Systems

Some service systems perform aggregate planning in almost exactly the same way as we did in the Brush and Roll Paint Company Case. In fact, in some of these systems that supply standardized services to customers, aggregate planning may be even simpler than in systems that produce products. Examples of these straightforward aggregate planning situations in service systems are fast-food shops, trucking firms, and banks and savings and loans. Aggregate planning in these systems presents no additional problems beyond those faced by most manufacturing systems.

Some systems that produce products face great difficulty in capacity planning. Job shops that produce products that are custom designed for individual customers find it particularly difficult to develop intermediate-range capacity plans. The knotty problem in aggregate planning for these organizations is that every product is different, and therefore each output requires different amounts of worker, material, and machine resources. Let us say, for example, that the XYZ Job Shop estimates 10 million dollars in sales for next year. How do you transform these dollars into workers, pounds of steel stock, and machine hours required in each time period? This is particularly difficult because all too often we cannot specify the designs of the products before the customer orders are received.

Some service systems that supply customized services to customers experience the same difficulty as job shops in specifying the nature and extent of services to be performed for each customer. Examples of these systems are hospitals, computer service centers, and automobile body repair shops. Another complicating factor with many of these customized service systems is that, unlike job shops, the customer may be an integral part of the productive system, and scaling productive capacity up or down may directly alter the perceived quality of the delivered services. Examples of these services are small private colleges and universities, exclusive dinner clubs, private country clubs, and private health clinics.

Also particularly worrisome to managers who must plan capacity levels for service systems and job shops is the absence of finished goods inventories as a buffer between system capacity and customer demand. This fact effectively takes away the aggregate plan of levelized outputs in many of these systems. This is particularly true in direct worker-to-customer services where no products are processed, stored, or transferred. Examples of these systems are income tax services, legal services, and emergency ambulance and fire fighting services. However, some of these systems have developed some techniques that encourage the use of levelized capacity aggregate plans. For example, the use of appointment schedules has tended to levelize the peaks and valleys of demand in medical clinics, thus facilitating levelized capacity plans. Similarly, after-hours windows at banks and savings and loans have facilitated levelized capacity plans. In spite of these innovations, however, many of these systems must develop capacity plans that nearly match the expected aggregate demand.

In service systems that deliver standardized services we would perform aggregate capacity planning as in the Brush and Roll Paint Company case, with the exception that finished goods inventories are infeasible. In custom-designed services and job shops, we would suggest a two-step approach to aggregate planning. First, develop aggregate demand forecasts in some homogeneous units of measure such as labor hours, machine capacity, and sales dollars. Second, try to discover common denominator units of capacity that are helpful in transforming aggregate demand into productive resource requirements. Some experimentation may be necessary to develop these conversion factors.

Next, particularly if the first suggestion is infeasible, develop alternative innovations for expanding the flexibility of productive resource capacities. Examples of these innovations are standby workers who are on call for peak demand periods, machines and buildings that can be activated during peak demand periods, subcontractors who respond quickly, and retired supervisors who wish to work only part-time and can be recalled for short periods. These standby resources provide operations managers a near levelized capacity aggregate plan with the extra capacity needed to respond to surges in demand.

Mathematical Aggregate Planning Models

Several aggregate planning methods have developed in recent years as the use of computers and the operations research discipline have grown. These methods seek to design capacity plans for productive systems that achieve organizations' objectives within the availability of their productive resources and aggregate demand constraints. A general description of four such methods is offered here to demonstrate their characteristics and general approaches: linear programming, linear decision rules (LDR), management coefficients, and computer search.

Linear Programming   *Linear programming* was presented in Chapter 5 as a technique for applying scarce resources optimally to competing demands. Perhaps nowhere else in POM do we see exemplified the power of linear programming to achieve the optimal use of resources than in aggregate planning. E. H. Bowman was one of the first analysts to apply linear programming to aggregate planning in 1956.[2] Since the 1950s numerous aggregate planning models using mathematical programming models have been processed using the computer.

These models typically seek to minimize total operating costs over the planning

---

[2] E. H. Bowman, "Production Planning by the Transportation Method of Linear Programming," *Journal of Operations Research Society* 4 (February 1956): 100–103.

horizon and include such costs as straight-time labor costs, overtime costs, subcontracting costs, worker hiring costs, worker layoff costs, and inventory carrying costs. The constraints of the models usually include such factors as the maximum capacity available in each time period from straight-time workers, overtime workers, subcontractors, and new workers and the minimum cumulative aggregate demand over the planning horizon. The *decision variables* (what managers need to know to construct a capacity plan) are the number of straight-time workers' hours, number of overtime workers' hours, subcontracted units, number of new workers to hire, and number of workers to lay off in each time period.

These models are accepted and understood more and more by managers today. Their frequency of use may also be increasing. Although linear programming does have some shortcomings, as we discussed in Chapter 5, it provides operations managers with a technique that selects a capacity plan that minimizes operating costs from among the host of alternative strategies. And it does this in complex intermediate-range planning decision situations. The need to include more realistic resource constraints, more product lines, a broader range of objectives, and more elements of operating costs continues to challenge today's operations analysts in applying linear programming to aggregate capacity planning decisions.

Linear Decision Rules (LDR) Holt, Modigliani, Muth, and Simon of the Carnegie Institute of Technology developed the *linear decision rule* in the 1950s.[3] LDR develops a single quadratic mathematical cost function for a particular productive system that includes these costs — regular payroll, hiring, layoff, overtime, inventory carrying, back order or shortage, and setup. This composite mathematical cost function covers each time period in the planning horizon and includes two principal decision variables — number of units of output to be produced and size of work force in each time period.

The quadratic composite mathematical cost function is differentiated by calculus methods to yield two linear mathematical functions, one is used to compute the number of units to produce during the next time period and another used to compute the work force size during the next time period. These two linear equations are typically used at the beginning of each period to plan the forthcoming production capacity and work force size; thus, the number of workers to be hired or laid off, number of overtime hours required, expected fluctuations in inventories, and machine changeovers can all be deduced.

LDR does allow nonlinear mathematical functions that may be a small improvement over linear programming. However, because the mathematical functions cannot be of a higher order than quadratic, cost functions must be laboriously and uniquely developed for each productive system, and since the values of the decision variables are unconstrained, the application of the technique is severely weakened.[4] However, the method has become a benchmark for measuring the performance of

---

[3] Charles C. Holt, Franco Modigliani, John F. Muth, and Herbert A. Simon, *Planning Production, Inventories, and Work Force* (Englewood Cliffs, NJ: Prentice-Hall, 1960).

[4] Leroy B. Schwarz and Robert E. Johnson, "An Appraisal of the Empirical Performance of the Linear Decision Rule for Aggregate Planning," *Management Science* 24 (April 1978): 844–849.

other methods, and it continues to be a useful teaching tool to demonstrate the thought processes in aggregate planning decisions.

Management Coefficients *Management coefficients* are a capacity planning technique that results in *heuristics* — useful guides to action. The basic assumption that underlies this approach is that managers develop capacity plans in practice by using complex criteria and gut feeling. This technique uses the historical data surrounding a manager's past capacity planning decisions and develops a predictive regression equation to be used to formulate future capacity plans.

This approach to capacity planning does not try to explain why managers make certain capacity planning decisions, given that certain market and operations conditions are present. It only attempts to describe the decision processes of individual managers. Although there is some evidence that the technique performs rather well under some circumstances, numerous obstacles to its widespread use exist.[5] Chief among these weaknesses is the dependence of the technique upon the individual expertise of analysts to effectively build a regression model that reflects a manager's decision-making behavior.

Computer Search *Computer search techniques* sequentially examine thousands of combinations of productive resources (overtime, layoffs, hiring, subcontracting, and so on) in each time period to meet the cumulative aggregate demand over a planning horizon. This method uses preprogrammed rules that control the way resources can be combined to select a low-cost capacity plan for each time period: What combination of productive resources should be used in each time period?

These computer programs select a combination of sources of capacity in each time period that meets aggregate demand, computes the operating cost, follows search rules to select another combination of sources of capacity, costs out this new combination, and continues this process sequentially until no significant improvement in operating costs is observed. The last combination of sources of capacity in each time period is the *capacity plan*.

These computer search methods are perhaps the most flexible of the mathematical aggregate planning models. There are almost no limitations on the type of cost functions that can be used, and they can be allowed to change from period to period or as conditions change. The models can include great numbers of costs, time periods, constraints and other features that allow the method to more accurately reflect the characteristics of the real productive systems. Although this technique is not, strictly speaking, an optimal model — that is, it does not guarantee the best solution — as computer technology continues to develop and improve in its ability to process greater numbers of search cycles, these methods should grow in application.

Mathematical models in aggregate planning do not dominate POM practice — not yet anyway. But you should know about these techniques because their approaches are fundamental and future models may become more important in capacity planning as you assume positions of responsibility in real world productive systems. Table 8.4 compares the advantages and disadvantages of the aggregate planning models discussed here.

―――――――――――
[5] E. H. Bowman, "Consistency and Optimality in Managerial Decision Making," *Management Science* 4 (January 1963): 100–103.

We have thus far discussed the major concepts, issues, and techniques of aggregate planning—the development of intermediate-range capacity plans for productive systems. These plans largely determine the volume of customer orders that *can be* economically produced during any specific time period. The upper limit of productive capacity directly impinges on the day-to-day scheduling of products and services, the detailed plan by which products or services will be produced in each department, day by day or week by week in the near future. Aggregate planning and detailed scheduling are therefore inseparably related. Let us now examine how we organize and approach these detailed scheduling activities in various productive systems.

Table 8.4
A Comparison of Mathematical Aggregate Planning Models

Technique	Advantages	Disadvantages
1. Linear programming	1. Easily understood. 2. Closely duplicates managers' decision processes—constrained optimization problems. 3. Selects an optimal capacity plan—lowest cost. 4. Can be easily applied periodically as new data become known, thus is dynamic.	1. Mathematical functions must be linear—may not be realistic. 2. Ignores economic lot sizes for production runs—may plan for very small lot sizes in some time periods. 3. Cost functions cannot easily change as capacity levels change, or from time period to time period.
2. Linear decision rules (LDR)	1. Develops an optimal capacity plan—lowest cost. 2. Allows quadratic cost functions—may be more realistic.	1. Quadratic functions ignore economies of scale—cost of hiring workers may actually decline when more workers are hired. 2. Mathematically complex. 3. Cost functions must be uniquely developed for each productive system. 4. The values of the variables are unconstrained—an unrealistic feature.
3. Management coefficients	1. Attempts to duplicate managers' decision-making processes—this feature has innate appeal. 2. Reduces variability in managerial decisions by eliminating human behavior variability.	1. Nonoptimal. 2. Manager being modeled may not be a good decision maker. 3. Depends upon expertise of analyst to creatively duplicate real manager behavior. 4. Each manager requires a new model.
4. Computer search	1. Allows any type of cost function. 2. Allows cost functions to change periodically and as capacity levels change. 3. Adapts to changing operational conditions.	1. Nonoptimal. 2. Computer capacities may limit both complexity and number of search cycles possible. 3. Expensive and requires expertise to use.

Production Planning and Control

Once the aggregate plan has set the intermediate-range capacity, some means must be devised to plan and control the exact mix of products and services to be produced in the days and weeks ahead. Production planning and control departments are established to develop and control these short-range schedules for the dual purposes of efficient internal operations and the timely satisfaction of customers' demands for products and services.

Production Planning and Control Departments

Productive systems use production planning and control departments to prepare detailed schedules for all production operations—the quantity of products, assemblies, subassemblies, or parts that must be completed at each processing step in future time periods. These departments engage in four traditional stages of production planning and control:

1. Routing—determining the processing steps and detailed tasks required to produce each completed product. The processing plan for producing a product becomes its routing.

2. Scheduling—determining what, how many, and when outputs are to be completed at each processing step in the productive system. A schedule is a short-term plan for an operation, work center, department, or plant that identifies what products in what quantities must be produced in each time period.

3. Dispatching—specific orders issued to production departments concerning movement of materials, due dates, and other directives to insure that schedules are met.

4. Expediting—a system of determining whether schedules are being met and taking corrective action, if necessary, to insure timely performance to schedules. Many of these monitoring activities are now done automatically through computerized progress reports.

The organizational location of production planning and control departments is highly variable. For example, one large automobile manufacturer has a corporate-wide central planning department located in Detroit that reports to the executive vice-president of operations. Individual plants also have production planning and control departments that officially report to local manufacturing executives, but also have administrative responsibility to corporate planning and control. This rather elaborate planning and control organizational scheme is necessary to plan and control one of the most complex productive systems—automobile manufacturing and assembly. At the other extreme, a nationally known pet food plant that employs 200 workers has a one-person production planning and control department that reports to the local manufacturing manager.

Another factor responsible for recent modification of where in organizations these departments are located is the trend to place all materials management functions under the responsibility of one materials manager. Several organization arrangements for these departments are observed in practice; three such schemes are shown in Figure 8.6.

Figure 8.6
Production Planning and Control: Three Organizational Schemes

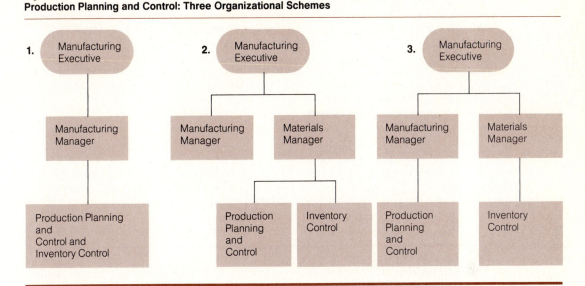

Production planning and control and inventory control functions traditionally have been either within the same department or in closely related organizational units. These two important functions are so inseparably related that when manufacturing executives speak of production control, inventory control, or production and inventory control (PIC), they often are referring to either or both functions. For the purposes of focusing on scheduling we will concentrate here only on the production planning and control function while recognizing its close organizational ties to inventory control.

Production planning and control functions exist to achieve these objectives:

1. Meet customer requests for delivery times when feasible.

2. When customer requests cannot be met because of insufficient finished goods inventory or insufficient production capacities, promise delivery dates that meet customer needs and that can be produced.

3. Minimize per-unit operating costs of production departments by preparing detailed schedules that optimally load processing operations in each time period.

4. Meet the preset goals for inventory levels.

To achieve these objectives, production planning and control obviously cannot work alone. On the contrary, marketing, production, purchasing, accounting/finance, personnel, engineering, and inventory control staffs must work cooperatively. Production's essential relationships with other organizational functions are emphasized by examining in Table 8.5 some of the key duties that production planning and control departments often perform. How are these duties tied together to achieve the objectives of improved customer service, high internal operating efficiency, and

Table 8.5
Some Duties of Production Planning and Control Departments

1. Receive customer orders from marketing.
2. Determine whether orders can be shipped from stock or must be produced.
3. Notify marketing of promised delivery dates.
4. If products must be produced, prepare routing sheets describing processing plans for the product.
5. Prepare material stock requisitions for inventory control to support the production of the product.
6. Fit the product's production into the production departments' detailed schedules. These are prepared well in advance of the production period and modified up to the freezing of the schedules.
7. Initiate the movement of materials into production to support production schedules.
8. Issue move tickets to transfer completed production orders from operation to operation in production departments.
9. Receive progress reports on production orders, evaluate the status of orders, and initiate corrective actions as required.
10. Initiate customer-requested changes.
11. Revise schedules when production operations' outputs do not conform to schedules or when customer changes are requested.
12. Serve as the information interface between production and marketing on the status of customer orders.
13. Keep accurate records on the status of schedules and customer orders.
14. Prepare cost estimates on new or revised products.

meeting inventory level targets? The answer to this question requires an understanding of the diversity among productive systems, because its answer is, in large part, dependent upon whether the system under study produces goods or services.

Controlling the Production of Goods and Services

Prior to World War II, manufacturing firms immediately came to mind when we mentioned *industry*. The preoccupation with producing goods was a natural outgrowth of the building of manufacturing plants to satisfy the enormous markets created by the development of the Western frontier in the late 1800s and the massive production buildup required to support the war effort of the 1940s. Between 1945 and the present, however, an interesting phenomenon has occurred. The generation of services is beginning to get equal billing with goods production when we think of industry.

The rise in importance of services is emphasized by these facts: (1) Services now generate from one half to two thirds of the United States' total gross national product (GNP). (2) Services now employ from two thirds to three fourths of all employees. (Note: The ranges in Items 1 and 2 result from a variety of measures of GNP and employment.) (3) Productivity (output per hour of human effort) in generating services has not increased as it has in manufacturing.[6] Service operations are now a potent force in our economy. Such systems employ the majority of U.S. workers and generate much of the GNP, but improved management of these operations is required to increase their productivity. Although many of the management techniques developed in manufacturing systems directly apply to service systems, the uniqueness of these systems often requires different management approaches if

---

[6] W. Earl Sasser, R. Paul Olsen, and D. Daryl Wyckoff, *Management of Service Operations* (Boston: Allyn and Bacon, 1978), 3–7.

the systems are to be operated effectively. Understanding how goods-producing systems and service-producing systems are alike and different is a starting point for designing production control systems.

Control Issues in Goods and Services A comparison of goods-producing systems and service-producing systems is difficult because of the great heterogeneity that exists within each of these classes. But unless some generalizations are drawn, hardly any description can be given and little understanding can occur. The nature of the inputs, conversion subsystems, and outputs will therefore be compared for four general classes of goods-producing and service-producing systems.

Table 8.6 compares the inputs to productive systems for these four classes:

Table 8.6
A Comparison of Productive Systems' Inputs: Goods and Services

Goods-Producing Systems		Service-Producing Systems	
Processing Industries (mining; quarrying; steel, copper, and chemical processing; and heavy manufacturing)	Light Manufacturing (electronic assembly, small mechanical devices, garments, and assembled products)	Materials/Technology Emphases (hospitals, fast-food restaurants, copy shops, and ambulance services)	Customer Service Emphasis (savings and loans, banks, tax services, and unemployment offices)
A full range of inputs; materials, personnel, capital goods, and utilities are used. Bulky and heavy materials must be received, handled, and stored. Employees are selected and employed primarily for their physical strengths or skills and technical knowledge. Capital goods play a critical role because of extremely high technology and mechanization of conversion systems. Capital goods can be freely substituted for personnel. Utilities are consumed in great quantities and usually require multienergy sources.	A full range of inputs; materials, personnel, capital goods, and utilities are used. Among these, however, personnel and materials receive greatest attention. Employees are used in great numbers and require careful selection and training to provide physical skills first and technical skills second. Relatively light materials are received, tested, handled, and stored in large quantities. Capital goods are substituted for personnel. Utilities are consumed in moderate quantities.	Although a full range of inputs is used, personnel and capital goods begin to emerge as dominant inputs to these systems. Employees are selected and trained both for physical and technical skills, but technical skills begin to surface as dominant. Specialty materials are received, tested, handled, and stored in relatively small quantities and require unsophisticated handling devices. Capital goods are selected more for their technological advantages rather than for their economic advantages in substituting for personnel. Utilities are a minor input. Hard-and-fast descriptions are difficult because of heterogeneity of systems within this class.	Personnel is the dominant input to these systems. Employees are carefully selected and trained for their interpersonal relations attributes. It is almost impossible to distinguish between operations personnel and marketing personnel because customers often are an integral part of the processes of operations. Therefore, personnel becomes the key input because customer relations depend primarily upon the impressions that employees create in the minds of customers. Materials and supplies, capital goods, and utilities play minor roles in these systems. Capital goods and technology cannot be freely substituted for personnel unless we first consider the impact upon customers.

processing industries and light manufacturing (goods-producing) and materials/ technology emphases and customer service emphasis (service-producing). Read this table and notice the key similarities and differences between the inputs to these four classes of productive systems. Goods-producing systems typically use a full range of inputs: materials, personnel, capital goods, and utilities; but service-producing systems' inputs tend to be dominated by personnel.

The conversion systems for the four classes of productive systems are described in Table 8.7. Note that goods-producing systems are dominated by the concern for routing and handling of materials and technologies of processing these materials. On the other hand, service-producing systems tend to be dominated by concerns for supervising personnel and meeting and waiting on customers. In goods-producing systems, processing times are determined in large part by machines and equipment, but in service-producing systems, customer-processing times are chiefly determined by personnel efficiency and the nature of individual customer service needs.

The outputs of productive systems are compared in Table 8.8. The key differences between the outputs of goods-producing systems and service-producing systems are in their use of inventories to buffer variability of demand and in the factors that affect quality of outputs. In goods-producing systems, finished goods

Table 8.7
A Comparison of Productive Systems' Conversion Subsystems: Goods and Services

Goods-Producing Systems		Service-Producing Systems	
Processing Industries (mining, quarrying; steel, copper, and chemical processing; and heavy manufacturing)	Light Manufacturing (electronic assembly, small mechanical devices, garments, and assembled products)	Materials/Technology Emphases (hospitals, fast-food restaurants, copy shops, and ambulance services)	Customer Service Emphasis (savings and loans, banks, tax services, and unemployment offices)
These conversion subsystems convert large volumes of difficult-to-handle raw materials into intermediate products. The dominant emphases are on the handling and routing of materials through these facilities and the processing technologies. Processing times and capacities are rigidly determined by high technology processing equipment. Standardized products require few machine changeovers.	These conversion subsystems convert large quantities of relatively light and easy-to-handle materials into products to be used by consumers. The dominant emphases are on routing and handling of materials and components and on supervising personnel and processing technologies. Processing times and capacities depend both upon personnel and upon processing equipment. Many product designs may require frequent changeover of machines.	Conversion of materials into finished products may or may not occur. Emphases are on supervising personnel, processing customers through facilities, and the unique materials or technologies of these systems. Dual processing facilities may exist for meeting and servicing customers on the one hand and moving materials and/or customers through the technical processes on the other. Great variety exists in the nature of these systems.	Conversion of materials into finished products does not occur. In fact, in a strict sense a conversion subsystem probably does not exist at all. The only conversion that possibly does occur is transforming unserved customers into served ones. The primary emphases are supervising personnel and meeting and waiting on customers. Processing times are determined primarily by the efficiency of personnel and the nature of individual customer service requirements.

Table 8.8
A Comparison of Productive Systems' Outputs: Goods and Services

Goods-Producing Systems		Service-Producing Systems	
Processing Industries (mining; quarrying; steel, copper, and chemicals processing; and heavy manufacturing)	Light Manufacturing (electronic assembly, small mechanical devices, garments, and assembled products)	Materials/Technology Emphases (hospitals, fast-food restaurants, copy shops, and ambulance services)	Customer Service Emphasis (savings and loans, banks, tax services, and unemployment offices)
The outputs of these systems are tangible products entering the intermediate markets where other firms use or sell them. They usually require little or no packaging. Extremes exist in importance of installation services required. Quality of outputs is dependent predominantly upon machinery settings and processing technologies. Inventories buffer differences between demand for products and short-run system capacities.	The outputs of these systems are tangible products entering either intermediate or consumer markets. They usually require packaging for either protection during shipment or customer appeal or both. Product installation in customer facilities is usually not required. Quality of outputs is dependent both upon employee technical skills and machine settings. Inventories buffer differences between demand for products and short-run system capacities.	The outputs of these systems are services, but the generation and delivery of the services may involve the technological processing of materials. Packaging may be used to enhance customer appeal, but those packaging materials can be discarded before the customer leaves the premises. Quality of outputs is dependent both upon interpersonal skills of employees who service customers and the technical skills of employees who process customers and materials. Inventories exist either not at all or only to a minute degree. Services are usually delivered immediately upon demand.	The outputs of these systems are services that are delivered directly to customers by employees. The outputs are generated by the technical expertise of the employees. The quality of outputs is predominantly determined by both interpersonal and technical skills of employees. Services are delivered immediately upon demand. Inventories of these services are not possible. The units of output are more difficult to identify.

inventories effectively allow these machine dominated systems to operate rather uniformly in levels of output. This is absolutely necessary because these systems are rather rigid in their ability to vary output levels because of the fixed nature of machine capacities. Service-producing systems, on the other hand, may be more flexible in their output levels because personnel levels can usually be varied to meet variability of demand. This is required since finished goods inventories are usually impossible. Quality of outputs is critically affected by machine settings and processing technologies in goods-producing systems but quality of outputs in service systems may be largely determined by personnel skills.

Understanding the differences and similarities between goods-producing and service-producing systems is helpful in designing production control methods for this patchwork of assorted systems. But operations managers must build into their production control methods the ability to deal with the uncertainties inherent in their particular system. Let us look briefly at how POM deals with uncertainty in both goods-producing and service-producing systems.

Coping with Uncertainty in Producing Goods and Services The nitty-gritty of controlling productive systems is devising standby or contingency plans that are enacted as required to keep operations on target in achieving objectives. Whether or not contingency plans are necessary depends upon the outcome of several factors that are subject to variability: demand variability, material delivery and quality variability, machine breakdowns and malfunctions, personnel behavior variability, and variability of utility supply.

Table 8.9 compares how each of the four classes of productive systems that were

Table 8.9
**Coping with Uncertainty in Controlling Productive
Systems: Goods and Services**

Major Source of Uncertainty in POM	Goods-Producing Systems		Service-Producing Systems	
	Processing Industries (mining; quarrying; steel, copper, and chemical processing; and heavy manufacturing)	Light Manufacturing (electronic assembly, small mechanical devices, garments, and assembled products)	Materials/Technology Emphases (hospitals, fast-food restaurants, copy shops, and ambulance services)	Customer Service Emphasis (savings and loans, banks, tax services, and unemployment offices)
Demand variability	Finished-goods inventories and standby facilities.	Finished-goods inventories, standby facilities, additional shifts, overtime, and subcontracting.	Standby facilities, standby personnel, additional shifts, overtime, customer waiting lines, off-hours services, appointment schedules, and autotellers.	Additional shifts, standby personnel, overtime, customer waiting lines, off-hours service, appointment schedules, and autotellers.
Material delivery variability	Raw material inventories, safety stocks, alternative suppliers.	Raw material inventories, safety stocks, and alternative suppliers.	Raw material inventories, emergency supply procedures, and safety stocks.	Usually a minor concern.
Material quality variability	Compensating processing steps or adjustments, the rejection of defective materials, and alternative suppliers.	Reworking defective parts, rejecting defective parts, safety stocks, and alternative suppliers.	Emergency supply procedures, rejecting defective materials, and safety stocks.	Usually a minor concern.
Machine breakdowns or malfunctions	Maintenance crews, standby machines, renting machine replacements, and subcontracting.	Maintenance crews, standby machines, renting machine replacements, and subcontracting.	Maintenance crews, standby machines, and renting machine replacements.	Standby machines, maintenance crews, and renting machine replacements.
Personnel behavior variability	Automatic machines, supervision, and employee development and training.	Automatic machines, supervision, and employee development and training.	Automatic machines, supervision, personnel selection, and employee development and training.	Supervision, personnel selection, and employee development and training.
Utility supplies variability	Alternative suppliers, standby systems, alternate fuels, and safety stocks.	Alternative suppliers, standby systems, alternate fuels, and safety stocks.	Alternative suppliers, standby systems, alternate fuels, and safety stocks.	Usually a minor concern, but the same means as other systems.

previously described copes with these major sources of uncertainty. After reading this table carefully, see if you agree that the *key* differences between service-producing systems and goods-producing systems are:

1. Demand variability — Goods producing systems use inventories, whereas service-producing systems must develop service levels to approximately match the variability of demand.
2. Material delivery and quality variability — Usually not a major concern of service-producing systems (retailers, restaurants, and other service systems with materials/technology emphases are notable exceptions).
3. Personnel behavior variability — Goods-producing systems control human behavior by using machine pacing and supervision, whereas service-producing systems use supervision, careful personnel selection, and employee training and development.
4. Utility supplies variability — Usually not a major concern of service-producing systems.

Productivity may not have improved in service systems as fast as in manufacturing because of the enormous impact that variability in human behavior has upon service systems, the unpredictability of human behavior, and the difficulty in effectively identifying units of output in services. These factors lead to both uncertainty of outcomes and difficulty in performance evaluation.

Although the control of goods-producing and service-producing systems differs, there are also commonalities. For example, both types of systems employ personnel, use materials, schedule operations, and control quality. The importance of each of these elements naturally differs among systems, as we have demonstrated above, but nevertheless they are present in most systems. This diversity among systems sets the stage for an interesting study of the ways that we schedule these systems.

Scheduling Systems

Enormous variety exists in how productive systems are scheduled in practice. The specific techniques employed, procedures used, and degree of sophistication achieved in scheduling are almost as varied as the productive systems themselves. For it is the unique features of individual productive systems that determine in large measure the best way to control their outputs. A detailed schedule for any productive system must be devised with two overriding objectives clearly in mind:

1. To produce sufficient quantities of each product at each processing step in the productive system during each future time period to meet customer or finished goods inventory needs.
2. To plan the production quantities, processing plans of production orders, priorities among production orders, and sequence of processing production orders that result in high internal operating efficiency of the productive system.

Attempts to achieve these objectives in a diversity of productive systems have led to three general control approaches to scheduling manufacturing systems —

Table 8.10
Control Systems in POM

Type of Control System	Description of Productive Systems Appropriate for Control System
1. Flow control	Very large quantities of identical products are processed through continuous productive systems. Changeovers are infrequent and chief scheduling concerns are coordinating raw material inputs with outputs. Examples are oil refining, chemical manufacture, and standardized services.
2. Batch control	Large quantities of identical products are produced on production lines. Lines must be periodically changed over from product to product to build finished goods inventories and meet customer demand. Examples are electrical appliance manufacture, apparel manufacture, and a university MBA class.
3. Order control	Production runs vary from single, unique products to only a few identical products per batch. Fixed location and process layouts are usually used. CPM, PERT, and other project-scheduling techniques and job-shop-scheduling techniques are frequently employed. Examples are bridge construction, general machine job shops, and hospital operating rooms.

flow control, batch control, and order control. Table 8.10 describes the control classes that form the underlying basis for different systems of scheduling.

Flow control scheduling systems attempt to plan when the desired quantities of products should be emitted from the productive system. Because these continuous productive systems have few changeovers, the primary scheduling concerns are production rates, output schedules or master production schedules (MPS), and material input schedules or material requirements planing (MRP) to support the output schedules.

Batch control scheduling systems are essentially the same as flow control systems except that they have an additional concern—determining the length of production runs before the production line is changed over to another product. *In this sense batch control systems are the general case and may be applied to both flow control and batch control situations.*

Order control scheduling systems are used to schedule job shops and other intermittent productive systems. The chief focus in these control systems is the *production order,* scheduling the desired quantity of products on a make-to-order basis through process layouts. These systems of scheduling are more complex to plan and execute than are continuous systems.

Project scheduling and control was discussed in Chapter 7, and CPM and PERT were illustrated as techniques for scheduling these one-of-a-kind projects. The scheduling of service systems is very important in POM, and we will discuss approaches to these production control methods in Chapter 10. But first, let us develop an overview of scheduling systems for scheduling continuous and intermittent production.

Scheduling Continuous Productive Systems

Read each of the characteristics of continuous productive systems and their scheduling implications in Table 8.11, which should be somewhat familiar to you because we discussed them in detail in the process planning section in Chapter 4. In continuous productive systems, products are standardized designs, products are usually produced for finished goods inventory, processing steps are coupled together, and production rates for individual products are usually greater than demand rates. These and the other characteristics in Table 8.11 shape the way that the productive systems are scheduled.

Scheduling systems in continuous productive systems for batch control are preoccupied with three principal concerns:

1. The output schedule from each production line or department that meets customer and finished goods inventory needs. This is the master production schedule (MPS).

2. The material schedule required to support the output schedule. This activity is materials requirements planning (MRP).

3. The length of production runs for each product, a schedule of changeovers, and the sequence of these production runs for the production line. This activity insures high internal operating efficiency and is built into the MPS.

Table 8.11
Continuous Productive Systems Characteristics and Scheduling Implications

Characteristics of Continuous Productive Systems	Scheduling Implications
1. Products are standard designs. The parts and raw materials, required processing steps, and sequence of operations are known.	Little preproduction planning concerning routing of products, job instructions, and processing plans is necessary.
2. Products are usually produced for inventory rather than to customer order.	Schedules can be based on near-economic production runs for products without pressure for emergency deliveries.
3. Processing steps are coupled together in sequences based on product layouts.	Production process is scheduled much like a pipeline, concentrating on raw material input schedules (MRP) and output schedules (MPS).
4. Workers and machines are specialized in only a few skills and operations.	Workers and machines cannot be readily shifted from operation to operation or from product to product.
5. Production rates are greater than demand rates for products.	The predominant scheduling concern is timing of production line changeovers and length of production runs.
6. Because operations are coupled together, material supply delays, mechanical breakdowns, and other factors that cause one operation to become idle also cause subsequent operations to shut down.	Production schedules must have liberal safety factors built in to allow for periodic idle time.
7. The pipeline nature of the production line results in materials, once they have entered the line, flowing continuously by near-automatic mechanical means from operation to operation until emitted at the end.	Production control does not ordinarily need to keep complex records of in-process material movements, authorize in-process material movements, or otherwise plan for the timing of in-process material movements along the line. The key planning and materials movement authorization activities concern the supply of materials to the line and discharge of finished units from the line.

Figure 8.7 shows how these concerns are met in scheduling continuous productive systems. When production of a particular product is necessary to meet customer orders or replenish inventory, a production order is issued to production scheduling. The existing schedule for each future time period, usually days or weeks, for the appropriate production line is reviewed. The relative priority assigned to the production order by marketing or inventory control, the production order quantity, the material availability, the economic production quantity, and the available time slots in future periods are simultaneously reviewed.

A compromise among all these factors is often required. For example, the time slots available to meet the priority assigned to the production order by marketing

Figure 8.7
Scheduling Continuous Productive Systems

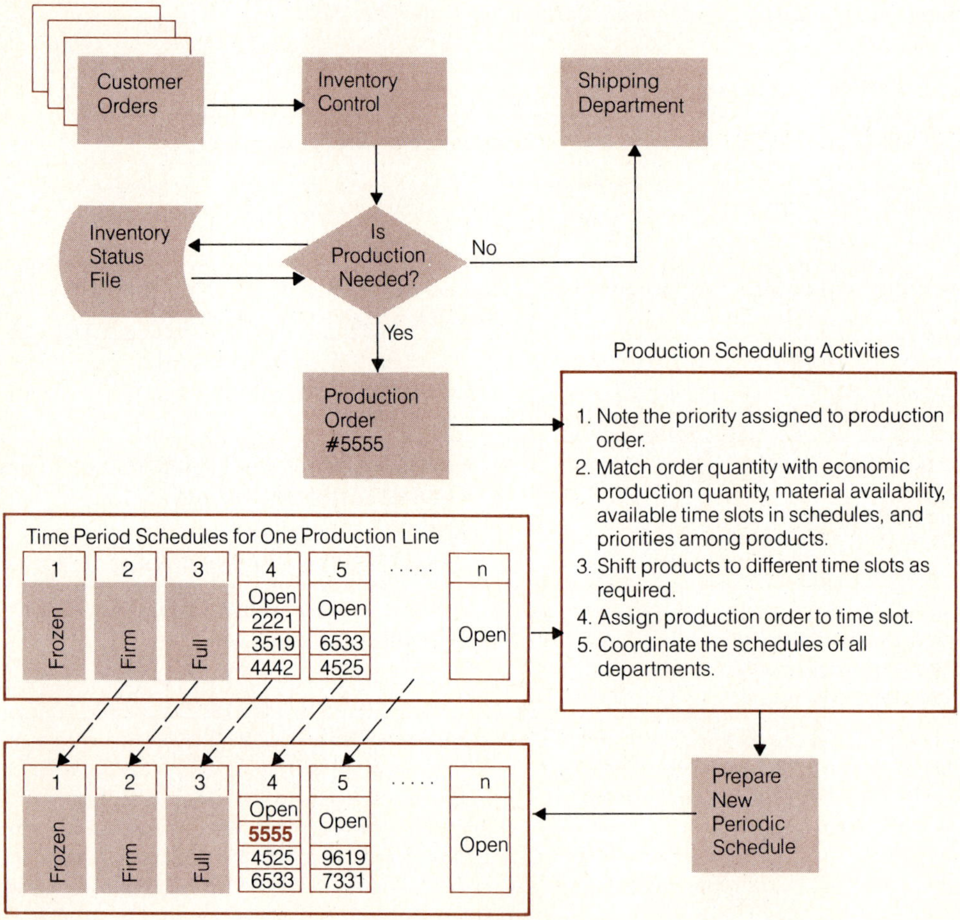

may not allow a long enough production run to be economical. Therefore, the production order may have to be split into two parts, giving up the economic advantages of longer production runs to meet the marketing priority assigned to the order. Compromises of this nature are common in most real world schedules.

Products are routinely shifted to later time slots as required to make room for higher priority orders. The more current the time period schedule for a production line, however, the less likely that it will be modified. As Figure 8.7 shows, the most immediate time period schedule (first time period) is frozen. This is necessary because all materials required to produce this first time period schedule are lined up on stream in the material flow system to support its production. Changes in these frozen schedules can be initiated only in the highest organizational levels.

The firm and full schedules of the second and third time periods are also set with material plans, but some flexibility does exist for production order substitutions if production orders with super-high priorities surface. Because open time slots are present in time period schedules beyond the third period, new production orders would ordinarily be scheduled in these open time slots.

Once an appropriate time slot is reserved for a production order, such as the #5555 order in Figure 8.7, it shows up on the next issued periodic schedule. The first period schedule of the previous periodic schedule is placed into production, and all other modified time period schedules are rolled up one time period.

Once detailed schedules are completed for each production line or each production department, all the production line schedules must be coordinated. Coordination is necessary because few production lines or departments operate independently of one another. The use of common materials, common machines, and assemblies produced in one department and used in another are all examples of why departmental schedules must be dovetailed.

Now let us study scheduling in intermittent systems.

Scheduling Intermittent Productive Systems

Job shops and other intermittent productive systems are far more complex to schedule than continuous systems. Table 8.12 describes some characteristics of intermittent productive systems and their scheduling implications. Where scheduling of continuous productive systems is principally concerned with developing output schedules for entire production lines, job shops must develop detailed schedules for controlling customer orders at each processing operation, work center, department, and plant. Not only are more detailed schedules required in intermittent productive systems, but the task of coordinating these schedules is far more difficult.

Because these productive systems usually produce to customer orders, production runs tend to be quite short with numerous machine changeovers. The number of paths through the facility for products and, in fact, for each product is large. Additionally, machines and workers are highly flexible and may be easily shifted between production orders. Flexibility, variability, and change therefore characterize these productive systems; schedules must be specific and detailed in each operation of the plant to bring order and rationality to such a potentially confusing situation.

Besides the complex schedules of intermittent systems, much more preproduc-

Table 8.12
Intermittent Productive Systems Characteristics and Scheduling Implications

Characteristics of Intermittent Productive Systems	Scheduling Implications
1. Similar operations are grouped with common supervision.	Numerous individual work center schedules must be developed and coordinated within production departments.
2. Products are diverse and custom-designed.	Much preproduction planning is necessary to establish routing, job instructions, and processing plans.
3. Processing steps are uncoupled and orders can follow a multitude of paths through productive systems.	A complex production control system must be developed to plan, execute, and follow up the movement of orders through the productive system.
4. In-process inventories build up between processing steps. Workers possess a variety of skills. Machines can adapt to a variety of products and operations.	Great flexibility is present in shifting workers and machines from order to order.
5. Work loads are typically unbalanced between processing steps.	An extra burden is put on schedules to fully load facility and minimize idle time and underloading.
6. When mechanical breakdowns, material delivery delays, and other interruptions occur, subsequent operations typically are not immediately affected.	Fewer allowances for idle time from these factors need to be included in schedules.
7. Numerous orders can build up at each processing step.	A system of priorities must be established that determines which order should be scheduled first at each work center.
8. Products are typically of the produce-to-order type.	Long lead times are necessary for manufacture and material deliveries. Raw material input schedules (MRP) and output schedules (MPS) are used.

tion planning, in-process control, and follow-up on each production order are required. Since products are made to order, product design and redesign must often be done before production can begin. The specific processing steps required to produce each product must be included in a processing plan and a routing through the facility must be set. After these process planning and routing activities are completed, production is soon begun and processing of the order must be carefully guided by production planning and control departments.

Material handlers are notified by production planning and control to move a production order to the next operation in its process plan by a *move ticket*. The order is accompanied with engineering drawings, specifications, or other job instructions necessary to process the order through that operation. The detailed schedule tells the production supervisor which order should be processed first at that operation and when the order should be finished. When the order is completed, the operator sends notification of completion of the order to production planning and control, a move ticket is issued for the next operation, and the detailed schedules are updated.

Figure 8.8 shows the key scheduling activities of production planning and control departments in intermittent productive systems. Production Order #9999 is placed

Figure 8.8
Scheduling Intermittent Productive Systems

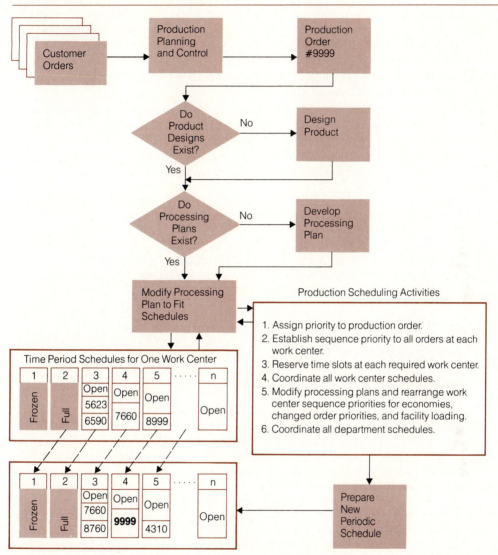

in time slots of each work center's time period schedules. The key differences between scheduling intermittent and continuous productive systems are:

1. Continuous system schedules are more macro because they principally deal with scheduling outputs from entire production lines. Intermittent scheduling systems must prepare detailed schedules for each operation, work center, department, and plant during each time period.

2. Coordination of work center schedules is far more difficult in intermittent systems because they are often interdependent.

3. In intermittent systems, priorities must be assigned to each production order based on marketing factors; but additionally, priorities must be set for processing orders that are waiting at each operation.

4. Much flexibility exists in shifting orders to different processing paths and modifying schedules in scheduling intermittent systems.

In spite of the complexity of scheduling job shops, much progress has been achieved in POM in the development of techniques that reduce throughput times and increase internal operating efficiencies in these systems. Some of the more commonly used approaches will be demonstrated in Chapter 10.

Although many service systems can and do approach scheduling in much the same way as manufacturing systems by using the continuous or intermittent scheduling systems described above, enough diversity exists in these systems to justify special treatment.

Scheduling Service Systems

Detailed schedules in productive systems whose outputs are services tend to be differentiated between custom and standard services.

Custom Services These systems are not unlike job shops in their characteristics. Consequently, their scheduling systems theoretically should be much like those found in intermittent manufacturing. However, in practice we find extremes in scheduling these systems. Small services, such as doctors' offices, small retailers, and local trucking companies, use almost no formal scheduling systems. Instead, such devices as appointment schedules, take-a-number systems, or first-come first served rules are often used to assign priorities among customers. Part-time workers and standby equipment are also frequently employed during unexpectedly high demand periods.

At the other extreme, service systems such as hospitals have developed sophisticated scheduling systems that may surpass those found in job shop manufacturing. Because these systems are also produce-to-order systems and therefore finished goods inventories cannot be maintained, capacities must be variable to meet wide variations in customer demand levels. Because customer demand is highly variable from week to week and because services must often be provided on short notice, these scheduling systems tend to work on a rather short planning horizon. It is not uncommon to observe schedules in these systems for only one week into the future.

The primary scheduling concerns in these custom service systems are:

1. Determining the expected customer demand for a short time into the future.

2. Preproduction planning to determine a process plan for each customer.

3. Reserving time slots in future time periods for key processing steps such as hospital room, lab tests, X ray, and surgery. The chief schedules in this system are the department loading schedules by time period. These schedules show which customers will be processed in each department by time period.

4. Scheduling personnel into the system to support the departmental schedules, often called work schedules. Scheduling nurses to departments in each week is an example of these work schedules.

Can you see the similarity in scheduling in hospitals and job shops? Several differences naturally exist — for example, setting priorities among patients at each work center in a hospital, though obviously based on different criteria than in a machine shop, would still follow the same general procedure.

Standard Services Much work has been devoted to developing scheduling systems in *standard services*. These productive systems are much like continuous manufacturing systems. Services are standard for most customers, and the processes employed are similar to production lines in that once they are begun they are carried through to completion without significant delays. They differ materially from continuous manufacturing productive systems in only one respect: They produce to order rather than for finished goods inventory.

Examples of these systems are trucking companies, fast-food restaurants, the U.S. Postal Service, and airlines. The principal scheduling tasks in these systems are:

1. Estimating the expected demand for short- to medium-term planning horizons.

2. Planning delivery routes and other output schedules over those horizons.

3. Planning work schedules that are based on these short-range forecasts of outputs.

4. Modifying near-term work schedules to reflect new demand information. This often requires standby equipment, standby personnel, and highly flexible personnel and equipment.

The degree of sophistication achieved in scheduling some of these productive systems has surpassed all other productive systems. The airlines, for example, have on-line computer-based scheduling systems that are among the most effective today.

Although service system scheduling has its own unique properties consistent with the idiosyncrasies of each particular system, the techniques employed, approaches used, and principal issues and concerns are not unlike scheduling manufacturing productive systems.

We have now discussed aggregate planning and detailed scheduling systems in a variety of POM settings. In Chapter 10 we shall build upon these concepts to demonstrate many techniques to assist schedulers in adopting schedules that are either optimal or near optimal.

Summary

Production planning is concerned with getting products and services out of production systems on time to meet customers' needs and doing so in ways that maintain high levels of internal operating efficiency. Forecasts of customer orders for goods and services are the starting point for these activities, but the orders that can be promised are functions of productive capacity.

Aggregate planning is the management activity that sets the planned capacity level for each time period in the planning horizon. Effective aggregate planning fully loads production facilities, provides adequate capacity to meet promised delivery dates, plans orderly transition of productive capacity to meet the peaks and valleys of demand, and maximizes the utilization of scarce productive resources.

Production planning and control departments engage in routing, scheduling, dispatching, and expediting of production orders through production facilities. The scheduling of continuous productive systems is principally concerned with developing output schedules for entire production lines; material schedules to support the output schedules; and length of production runs, changeover schedules, and sequence of production runs. Scheduling intermittent productive systems is more complex than scheduling continuous systems. The complexity stems principally from the number of schedules required (operation, work center, department, and plant levels) and the degree of coordination necessary among the multitude of schedules.

Service system scheduling is differentiated between custom and standard services. Custom services are scheduled much like job shops, and standard services are scheduled a great deal like continuous manufacturing systems, except that finished goods inventories are absent. Hospitals and airlines are the best examples of sophisticated scheduling of custom and standard services, respectively.

Review and Discussion Questions

1. Define *aggregate planning*.

2. What two fundamental goals must be achieved in aggregate planning, production planning and control, and detailed scheduling?

3. Describe how the following productive resources can be increased to support increased productive capacity: **a.** work force, **b.** materials, and **c.** machines.

4. List the advantages and disadvantages of these traditional capacity planning strategies: **a.** levelized capacity, **b.** matching capacity with aggregate demand, and **c.** compromise capacity.

5. Give three reasons why aggregate planning in job shops or service systems is typically difficult.

6. Describe these mathematical models for aggregate planning: **a.** linear programming, **b.** linear decision rule (LDR), **c.** management coefficients, and **d.** computer search.

7. Define *production planning and control*. What major activities does it engage in?

8. What is a schedule? What information does a production schedule provide?

9. Name five duties of production planning and control departments.

10. Describe productive systems commonly controlled with these control systems: **a.** flow control, **b.** batch control, and **c.** order control.

11. Name three key differences between scheduling continuous and intermittent productive systems.

12. How is scheduling differentiated among service systems? Give three examples of each type of service system.

13. Summarize the differences among inputs, conversion systems, and outputs of goods-producing and service-producing systems.

Problems

1. The Acme Engineering Company provides bridge design services to road construction companies. These projects are classified into three types of bridges — pedestrian, Class 1 vehicle traffic, and Class 2 vehicle traffic. Acme is planning its work force for next year and estimates that for every sales dollar .156 engineering design hour will be required. The forecast of next year's sales of bridge design is:

Type of Bridge	Sales (Thousands of Dollars)			
	1st Quarter	2nd Quarter	3rd Quarter	4th Quarter
Pedestrian	1,200	1,500	1,200	1,000
Class 1 vehicle	2,700	2,500	3,000	2,500
Class 2 vehicle	5,500	6,000	5,000	5,000

If there are 2,000 hours per year for each engineer, compute the number of engineers needed for each bridge type in each quarter and the total number of engineers needed in each quarter. Next, draw a composite graph that shows the number of enginers needed in each quarter for each bridge type and the aggregate demand (in engineers) for each quarter.

2. The Triple A Products Company produces three product lines: A_1, A_2, and A_3. Triple A is now doing its capacity planning for next year and wishes to develop an aggregate demand for its products. Billie Joe Kennedy, forecasting analyst, has developed a regression equation for each of the products' quarterly sales for next year:

Product	Quarterly Sales in Units
A_1	$Y = 550 + 333 X$
A_2	$Y = 1,000 - 250 X$
A_3	$Y = 250 + 267 X$

Y is quarterly sales in units and X is the quarter (1, 2, 3, 4). The number of machine hours required in the calendering operation, which is the bottleneck operation in the entire facility (this operation has the least capacity among all the operations in the entire facility), for each of the products is:

Product	Machine Hours per Product
A_1	.50
A_2	1.00
A_3	.30

a. Compute the quarterly sales in units for each of the three products. **b.** Compute the number of machine hours in the calendering operation required to produce each of the products per quarter and all of the total aggregate demand (machine hours) per quarter. **c.** Graph the information developed in part *b*.

3. The Zapcom Computer Company manufactures small business computers that are marketed nationally through a distributor network. Zapcom is now making its marketing and manufacturing plans for the next year, which are intermediate-range plans in their planning system. They have developed these sales forecasts and labor and machine standards for their products:

	Quarterly Sales (Units)				Labor Standard (Labor Hours/Unit)	Machine Standard (Machine Hours/Unit)
Product	1st Quarter	2nd Quarter	3rd Quarter	4th Quarter		
1. Z305 Business Computer	13,000	19,500	15,400	23,500	7.95	5.77
2. Z205 Business Computer	6,500	8,700	7,200	10,000	6.56	4.10
3. Z105 Business Calculator	12,500	23,500	16,500	25,000	3.22	2.55
4. Z1510 Floppy Diskette	8,700	12,200	10,500	15,750	4.90	3.15
5. Z1210 Floppy Diskette	4,500	6,000	4,900	7,000	3.11	2.10
6. Z620 CRT	11,500	14,700	12,800	16,500	2.60	1.50
7. Z520 CRT	10,500	14,000	11,500	17,500	2.20	1.21
8. ZROM Business Package	25,500	33,500	27,500	38,500	.56	.79

a. Compute the labor hours required for each quarter. **b.** Compute the machine hours required for each quarter. **c.** Graph the information developed in parts *a* and *b*.

4. The Rigid Strut Steel Company is trying to decide between two aggregate capacity plans, No. 1 and No. 2. The number of workers per quarter and average annual finished goods inventory in thousands of pounds for the two plans are shown below. If hiring costs are $1,200 per worker hired, layoff costs are $600 per worker laid off, and inventory carrying cost is $.015 per pound per year, compute the annual hiring, layoff, carrying, and total incremental costs for each plan. Which plan would you prefer?

Aggregate Plan	Quarter	Workers Required	Average Annual Inventory (Thousands of Pounds)	Aggregate Plan	Quarter	Workers Required	Average Annual Inventory (Thousands of Pounds)
No. 1	1	150	1,500	No. 2	1	155	2,950
	2	160			2	155	
	3	160			3	155	
	4	150			4	155	

5. In Problem 3, the Zapcom Computer Company, if the machine hours were sufficient and employees worked 13 weeks in each quarter and 40 hours in each week, determine how many employees would be required in each quarter, using these aggregate plans: **a.** levelized capacity, **b.** matching capacity with aggregate demand.

6. The CM Underwear Company makes boys' stretch-fit briefs — one size fits all. CM is presently considering two capacity plans for next year — levelized capacity and matching capacity with aggregate demand. The quarterly aggregate demand and the working days per quarter are shown for the two plans. The labor standard per brief is .250 hour, hiring cost is $200 per worker hired, layoff cost is $200 per worker laid off, and carrying cost for finished goods is $.60 per brief per year.

Aggregate Plan	Quarter	Aggregate Demand (Thousands of Briefs)	Working Days per Quarter	Aggregate Plan	Quarter	Aggregate Demand (Thousands of Briefs)	Working Days per Quarter
Levelized capacity	1	150	62	Matching capacity with aggregate demand	1	150	62
	2	200	63		2	200	63
	3	400	63		3	400	63
	4	200	62		4	200	62

If the beginning inventory levels are 35,600 briefs for the levelized capacity plan and zero for the matching plan, which plan exhibits the lowest total incremental operating costs?

7. The Brush and Roll Paint Company, of Case 8.1 in the chapter, has just discovered more current and accurate information. The new data are:

Information Item	New Data
Aggregate demand	No change
Labor standard	2.650 worker hours per gallon
Working days per quarter	$Q_1 = 60$, $Q_2 = 65$, $Q_3 = 60$, $Q_4 = 65$
Beginning inventory	Zero in matching plan, 5,000 gallons in levelized plan
Working hours per shift	No change
Maximum capacity	No change
Carrying cost	$4 per gallon per year
Hiring cost	$200 per worker hired
Layoff cost	$250 per worker laid off
Unsatisfactory hires	No change — an extra 10 percent must be hired during each hiring transition period
Training period	No change (one month)

Evaluate only the levelized capacity and matching capacity with aggregate demand alternatives of the Brush and Roll Paint Company case, using this new data.

8. In Problem 1, The Acme Engineering Company, two aggregate plans are now being evaluated: levelized capacity and matching capacity with aggregate demand. It costs Acme $.30 for every dollar of sales on any type of bridge design backlogged (delayed for completion at a later date) for one quarter. If it costs Acme $500 to hire

and train an engineer, $300 to lay off an engineer, and the beginning backlog in the first quarter is zero, which plan exhibits the least cost?

9. In Problem 7, The Brush and Roll Paint Company, the production department wants to consider another aggregate capacity plan with the new information—use a stable work force of 250 workers and overtime and inventory (beginning inventory is 5,000 gallons) as needed to meet demand. Overtime costs $5 per hour over and above straight-time pay and beginning inventory is 5,000 gallons. All other information in Problem 7 remains the same. **a.** What is the annual incremental cost of the proposed aggregate capacity plan? **b.** Which plan do you prefer?

10. The Hiway Trucking Company hauls commercial freight in Maricopa County, Arizona. Hiway estimates the aggregate quarterly demand for next year at 5,000, 7,500, 9,500, and 5,000 ton-miles. Trucking equipment owned by the company, rented trucks, and subcontracting can be used to supply capacity to meet Hiway's aggregate demand:

Source of Capacity	Ton-Miles per Quarter	Cost per Ton-Mile
Company trucks		
Straight-time	0–4,000	$.25
Overtime	4,001–6,000	.30
Work force changes	6,001–7,000	.35
Rented trucks		
(includes drivers		
and freight handlers	0–3,000	.40
Subcontracting	0–5,000	.42

a. Formulate this aggregate planning problem in a linear programming formulation and define the decision variables. In other words, write each decision variable and explain what one unit of the variable means. (Hint: There are 20 decision variables —5 sources of capacity for each quarter and one of these for each quarter—and 20 constraints—5 maximum sources of capacity for each quarter and one for each quarter.) **b.** Write the objective function. **c.** Write the aggregate demand constraints. **d.** Write the straight-time operation of company truck constraints. **e.** Write the overtime operation of company truck constraints. **f.** Write the operation of company trucks with work-force-changes constraints. **g.** Write the truck rental constraints. **h.** Write the subcontracting constraints.

Case

The Triple A Products Company

In Problem 2, The Triple A Products Company, the marketing department has informed the production department that a competitor has just introduced a new product that will effectively destroy the market for the A_1 product. Triple A is now trying to determine, in light of this new information, if levelized capacity or matching capacity with aggregate demand would be the best aggregate capacity plan. It costs Triple A $25 for every A_2 or A_3 product either backlogged or placed in inventory at the end of a quarter. Triple A begins the year with zero backlog and inventory. Each calendering machine operates only 75 hours per quarter, on the average, because of frequent repairs necessitated by corrosion in its mixing chamber. It costs $5,000 to either start up a calendering machine or shut one down whenever capacity is changed from quarter to quarter. It is Triple A's policy to fully utilize calendering machines whenever they are in service; in other words, partial use of a machine is not economical. It is also Triple A's policy, when demand exceeds production capacity, to satisfy the demand for the A_2 products within a quarter before the demand for the A_3 products is satisfied. When production capacity exceeds demand, the A_3 products are produced with the excess capacity.

Assignment

1. Compute the quarterly aggregate calendering machine hours capacity required to meet sales demand for the A_2 and A_3 products.

2. Compute the number of calendering machines required per quarter to meet sales demand for the A_2 and A_3 products.

3. Compute the amount of production above or below the sales demand for the levelized capacity plan, and compute its annual cost.

4. Compute the annual cost of starting up and shutting down calendering machines using the matching capacity with aggregate demand plan.

5. Which plan do you prefer? Justify your preference with as many factors as possible.

Selected Bibliography

Baker, K. R. *Introduction to Sequencing and Scheduling.* New York: Wiley, 1974.

Bowman, E. H. "Production Planning by the Transportation Method of Linear Programming." *Journal of Operations Research Society* 4 (February 1956): 100–103.

Buffa, E. S. "Aggregate Planning for Production." *Business Horizons* 10 (Fall 1967): 87–97.

Buffa, E. S., and W. H. Taubert. *Production-Inventory Systems: Planning and Control.* Rev. ed. Homewood, IL: Richard D. Irwin, 1972.

Conway, R. W., W. L. Maxwell, and L. W. Miller. *Theory of Scheduling.* Reading, MA: Addison-Wesley, 1967.

Day, James E., and Michael P. Hottenstein. "Review of Sequencing Research." *Naval Research Logistics Quarterly* 27 (March 1970): 11–39.

Eilon, Samuel. *Elements of Production Planning and Control.* New York: Macmillan, 1962.

Eisemann, K., and W. M. Young. "Study of a Textile Mill with the Aid of Linear Programming." *Management Technology* 1 (January 1960): 52–63.

Gelders, L., and P. R. Kleindorfer. "Coordinating Aggregate and Detailed Scheduling Decisions in the One-Machine Job Shop." *Operations Research* 22 (January–February 1975): 46–60.

Goodman, D. A. "A New Approach to Scheduling Aggregate Production and Work Force." *AIIE Transactions* 5 (June 1973): 135–141.

Holstein, W. K., and W. L. Berry. "The Labor Assignment Decision: An Application of Work Flow Structure." *Management Science* 16 (February 1970): 324–336.

Holt, Charles C., Franco Modigliani, John F. Muth, and Herbert A. Simon. *Planning Production, Inventories, and Work Force.* Englewood Cliffs, NJ: Prentice-Hall, 1960.

Schwarz, Leroy B., and Robert E. Johnson. "An Appraisal of the Empirical Performance of the Linear Decision Rule for Aggregate Planning." *Management Science* 24 (April 1978): 844–849.

Wight, Oliver W. *Production and Inventory Management in the Computer Age.* Boston: Cahners Books, 1974.

Chapter Outline

Introduction

Materials Management

Purchasing
Logistics
Warehousing
Expediting

Inventory Planning and Control

Purposes of Inventories
Behavior of Independent Demand Inventories
Inventory Costs
Fixed Order Quantity Systems
Optimal Order Quantities—Basic EOQ, EOQ with Gradual Deliveries, and EOQ with Quantity Discounts
Setting Order Points—Safety Stocks, Percentage of EDDLT, Square Root of EDDLT, and Effect of Safety Stock on EOQ
Fixed Order Period Systems
Some Realities of Inventory Planning

Summary

Review and Discussion Questions

Field Projects

Problems

Case: The Phoenix Wholesale Company

Selected Bibliography

9

Materials Management and Independent Demand Inventory Systems:
The Fundamentals

*The Arsenal needed not only the ships but also the neces-
sary gear and rigging. The task of outfitting the galleys was
facilitated by the warehousing of the equipment. All of it
was numbered and stacked in a designated space.*
Anonymous description of the Arsenal of Venice, 1450

Manufacturing is perhaps best understood by studying its material flows — the acquisition, storage, movement, and processing of raw materials, components, subassemblies, and supplies. Similarly, service systems such as retailing, warehousing, and transportation organizations are predominantly systems of material flows. In these systems all organizational functions tend to be either subordinate to or critically affected by planning and controlling material flows.

The importance of materials in POM can perhaps best be emphasized by understanding the proportion of product costs incurred in buying, storing, moving, and shipping materials. These costs typically range from 20 percent to 90 percent of total product cost depending upon the industry, but a good rule of thumb is about 70 percent of product cost. This represents a tremendous amount of money spent annually in this country in managing materials across all productive systems. Operations managers today are actively engaged in developing better ways of managing these functions so that product costs can be controlled and firms can survive in an increasingly competitive world.

Materials Management

A _material_ is any commodity used directly or indirectly in producing a product or service, such as raw materials, component parts, subassemblies, and supplies.[1] A _materials system_ is the network of material flows within a productive system, including materials at suppliers, in transit from suppliers, in receiving, in the raw materials warehouse, in in-process inventories, being processed in operating departments, being moved between operations, being inspected in quality control, in finished goods warehouses, and in transit to customers. In short, a materials system includes all materials present in the productive system between the suppliers and the customers.

Materials management is all the management functions related to the complete cycle of material flows, from the purchase and internal control of materials to the planning and control of work in process to the warehousing, shipping, and distribution of the finished products.[2] In many organizations materials management is the dominant activity that permeates and underlies all other activities.

Increasingly, organizations are tending to centralize their diverse materials management functions under one department that is headed by the _materials manager_. This executive position coordinates all the activities of the material system and bears total responsibility for the continuous supply of materials of low costs and specified quality when and where operating departments and customers require them. In some organizations the responsibility of the materials manager is immense, a reality underscored by their typically high salaries that rank with the highest industry positions.

The materials manager brings under one management umbrella the diverse materials activities that were until only recently typically dispersed throughout the organization. This dispersement was a continual source of frustration to operations managers because it seemed that no one was responsible for lost materials, damaged materials, and delayed shipments. Shipping blamed purchasing, purchasing blamed production, production blamed shipping, and so on. Where all the materials management functions are centralized in one department, there is no question where the buck stops — at the materials manager.

Materials management differs from organization to organization, but it usually includes these major activities — purchasing, logistics, warehousing, and expediting. These activities form the framework for studying the nature and scope of materials management.

Purchasing

Purchasing departments buy the raw materials, purchased parts and subassemblies, machinery, supplies, and all other goods and services either consumed or used in productive systems, from paper clips to steel bar stock to computers. Stop and think about the immensity of this activity. Over one half of the price manufacturers receive for their products may have been paid back to suppliers for materials. For example, a

---

[1] American Production and Inventory Control Society, _APICS Dictionary of Inventory Control Terms and Production Control Terms_, 3d ed. (Washington, DC: APICS., 1970), 25.

[2] Ibid.

large automobile manufacturer spends 49 percent of its revenues on purchases, a large food processor spends 67 percent, and a large farm implement manufacturer spends 59 percent. Across the totality of our country's industry and government, the amount of annual expenditures for purchased materials is indeed staggering. And yet purchasing department employees represent fewer than 1 percent of the total employees of organizations. Can you think of a more influential group of employees whose performance is so critical to organizational success?

Purchasing departments can be located at any level of the organization hierarchy. The *manager of purchasing* (or the *purchasing agent*) may report to the president, vice-president of operations, plant manager, or anyone in between. It is difficult to generalize about where purchasing will be assigned in the organization, except to say that its reporting level is generally directly related to the importance of its mission. In other words, if purchasing is critical to an organization's success, as with the large farm implement manufacturer who spends 59 percent of its sales revenues on purchased materials, then we would expect to see the purchasing department report to the vice-president of operations or even to the president. On the other hand, if purchasing has only a minor influence on organizational success, we would ordinarily expect the purchasing department to report relatively low in the organization, perhaps to the plant manager or manager of manufacturing.

Organizations tend to go through cycles of decentralization, centralization, decentralization, and so on. Purchasing has also been caught up in these cycles. It is believed that we are on the centralization upswing now. The tendency toward centralization of purchasing is probably encouraged today by the advances both in communication between plants and divisions of companies and in the information processing capabilities of computers. Among the advantages of centralization are:

1. Buying in larger quantities, which can mean better prices.

2. More clout with suppliers when materials are scarce, which means greater supply continuity.

3. Larger purchasing departments that can afford greater specialization of employees. For example, one buyer may specialize in buying only copper. This can lead to greater purchasing competence and lower material costs.

4. Combining small orders and thereby reducing duplication of orders, which can result in reduced clerical costs.

5. Reduction of transportation costs by combining orders and shipping larger quantities.

On the other hand, operations managers often complain that centralized purchasing departments that do not report to them are slow, bureaucratic and cumbersome, and unresponsive to the needs of operations.

Large companies typically have centralized purchasing departments, particularly when the amount of annual purchases is large relative to revenues and when expert purchasing technical knowledge is required. Additionally, even when other purchases are made at the plant level, buying of large capital assets, such as expensive production machinery, is usually centralized because of the long-term nature and amount of capital involved in these expenditures.

Regardless of its organizational location, purchasing follows rather standardized buying processes to acquire materials.

Purchasing Processes Figures 9.1 and 9.2 illustrate the processes of acquiring materials and capital goods in productive systems. These figures emphasize the interaction of the operations departments, purchasing, finance, and suppliers. Although some variation to these procedures exists between organizations, an amazing amount of similarity also is present.

Basic Purchasing Instruments The daily stock-in-trade of purchasing departments is material specifications, purchase requisitions, requests for quotations, and purchase orders. These instruments are fundamental to purchasing processes.

Figure 9.1
The Process of Acquiring Material Inputs

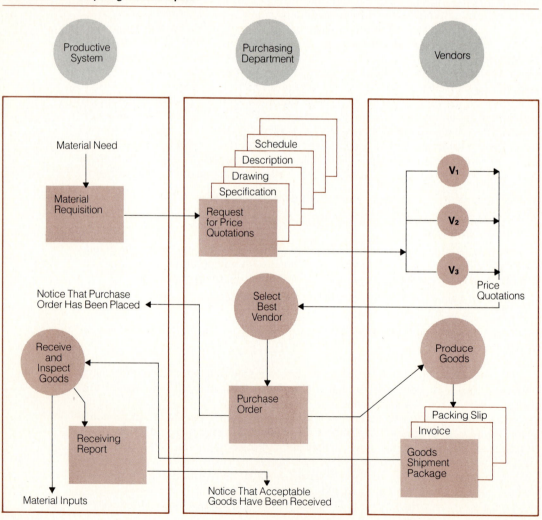

Figure 9.2
The Process of Acquiring Capital Goods Inputs

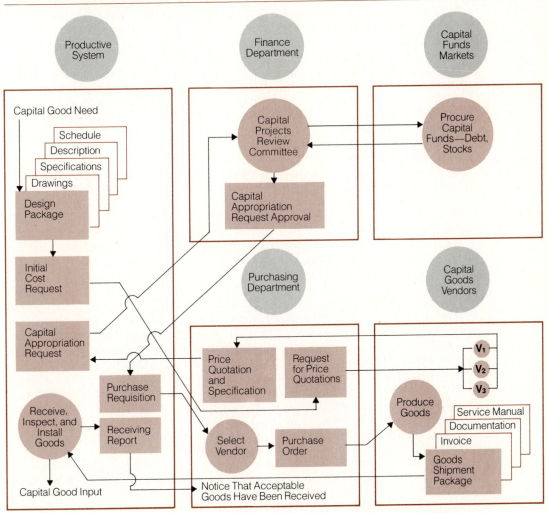

For every good to be purchased, purchasing departments must have a detailed description of that material. This detailed description is called a *material specification*. These instruments can include such descriptions as engineering drawings, chemical analyses, physical characteristics, and other details depending upon the nature of the materials.

Material specifications originate with the department requesting the material in its operations. Product engineers, process engineers, and other technical specialists of operations departments routinely supply purchasing departments with material specifications as products, parts of products, machinery, or other material that will ultimately be purchased are designed. As these original designs are modified, revised material specifications must be sent to the purchasing department so that the old specifications can be replaced with the new ones.

Value engineering or *value analysis* is an activity that typically occurs jointly between purchasing and the technical specialists of operations departments. This important activity is aimed at modifying the specifications of materials, parts, and products to reduce costs while retaining their original function. Value engineering is a continuing activity within purchasing today because this activity provides companies with a way of holding the line on materials costs in a time of spiraling inflation.

Material specifications are the fundamental means of communicating what materials operations wants purchasing to buy and what purchasing authorizes suppliers to supply. Suppliers use the specifications to guide them in the production of these materials, and finally these same specifications become the basis for determining whether the requested material was actually received. Material specifications are both the standards that purchasing buys to and the means of communication that guides the purchasing processes.

Purchase requisitions originate with the departments that will use the materials. They authorize purchasing to buy the goods or services. The requisitions usually include: identification of what is to be purchased, amount to be purchased, requested delivery date or schedule, account to which purchase cost is to be charged, where the purchased goods or services are to be delivered, and appropriate approval by manager charged with authority to approve purchase.

Requests for quotation are prepared by purchasing departments to be sent to suppliers that are believed to be capable of meeting the cost, quality, and schedule requirements of the requesting departments. This instrument invites prospective suppliers to bid or quote on the material. These forms usually include: material specification, quantity of purchase, delivery date or schedule desired, where materials are to be delivered, and date that supplier selection will be completed. Requests for quotation usually request the following from each prospective supplier: price per unit and total price, information on whether the supplier pays the freight costs, cash discounts and other terms of payment, delivery date or schedule, and any special conditions of the supplier.

Purchase orders are the most important single purchasing instrument. They are the basis of suppliers' authority to produce the goods or services, and they represent buyers' obligation to pay for the items. A legal commitment by the buyer is present when purchase orders are issued in response to quotations from a supplier. When a purchase order is issued in the absence of a request for a quotation, a legal commitment exists when a supplier acknowledges acceptance of the purchase order. These forms are usually designed to conform to the standards developed by the National Association of Purchasing Agents and the Division of Simplified Practice, National Bureau of Standards.

Purchase order forms usually include: purchase order number, quantity of goods or services, material specifications of goods or services, date and location for delivery of the items, shipping and billing instructions, price per unit and total price, cash discounts or other terms of payment, and any special terms of the purchase.

These instruments — specifications, requisitions, requests for quotation, and purchase orders — all form the framework for the procedures of actually buying the goods and services.

Purchasing Procedures Purchasing procedures differ depending upon the nature of the goods or service to be purchased. But these procedures tend to become more standardized as we classify the purchases into these homogeneous classes — high-volume continuously supplied materials, large unique purchases, small purchases, and regular purchases.

When materials are purchased in *high volume to be continuously supplied* throughout the year, purchasing departments typically issue requests for quotation to several prospective suppliers. When a supplier is selected, a *blanket purchase order* that covers the materials to be purchased for the entire year will be issued. The authorization for purchasing departments to purchase these materials stems from the inclusion of these materials in their purchasing budgets. Purchasing budgets may be prepared months ahead and are based on approved production schedules.

When operating departments need these materials, rather than issuing a purchase requisition to the purchasing department, a *release order* is sent directly to the supplier. The release order authorizes the supplier to ship a specific quantity of material in conformance to the original blanket purchase order.

This procedure allows organizations to *tie up* suppliers for long-term supply arrangements, resulting in the likelihood of both quantity discounts and continuity of supply. Additionally, release orders can be processed quickly straight to the supplier, thereby reducing the possibilities of needless delays in shipments. Suppliers usually like these release orders because the uncertainty of demand is reduced and better long-term production planning is possible.

Large computers, specialized machinery, and consulting services are examples of *large unique purchases*. Although purchasing departments coordinate the overall procedures, as Figure 9.2 shows, their main function is to provide the interface between the technical specialists of the requesting department and prospective suppliers. In these purchases price is often not the deciding factor in supplier selection. Instead, the ability of suppliers to deliver quality goods and services on a timely basis and to meet unique technological requirements is critical to the eventual choice of supplier. In these situations purchasing departments therefore bring the technical specialists who are requesting the purchase together with prospective suppliers and coordinate the activities of these parties. Once the final supplier is selected, purchasing departments proceed to negotiate a contract with the supplier and a purchase order is eventually issued.

Most purchasing departments do not wish to get involved with *small purchases* of such items as stationery supplies, blank checks, work gloves, and so on. These purchases are usually bought out of *petty cash accounts* by the originating departments directly from the supplier of their choice or from suppliers who hold *open purchase orders* that have been issued from the purchasing departments. Under this latter arrangement the requesting department issues a *release order* to the supplier listing the items to be purchased, quantity requested, and date needed. The price and other conditions of sale are specified on the original open purchase order. Purchases from petty cash or releases of items on open purchase orders are usually limited to very small purchases, say $50 or less per order. Otherwise, they must be processed according to the procedures of regular purchases.

In *regular purchases* buyers within purchasing departments are buying goods and services at the request of requesting departments. The procedure for these purchases is:

1. The requesting department issues a purchase requisition to the purchasing department.
2. The purchasing department issues requests for quotations to one or more suppliers.
3. The suppliers submit quotations and a supplier is selected.
4. A purchase order is issued by the purchasing department to the supplier.
5. The supplier supplies the item to the requesting department.

Although the procedures for these various classes of purchases generally cover getting the goods and services to the requesting departments, accounting can pay for the items only after it has been notified by the requesting departments how much of the item has been received of acceptable quality. The purchase order then becomes the basis of payment. One of the keys to the successful completion of these procedures is the competence of the buyers within purchasing departments.

Buyers and Their Duties *Buyers,* as the name implies, do the buying in purchasing departments. They are typically specialized according to commodities. For example, one buyer may buy all ferrous metals, another may buy all nonferrous metals, and yet another may buy all machinery and tools. This specialization allows buyers to become experts at purchasing their particular commodities. To be effective, buyers must know both the manufacturing processes of their own companies and those of their supplier companies. This is typically possible only through specialization according to commodities.

Buyers must know their markets—the going prices of commodities and their availability. Additionally, they must be cost and value conscious, strong negotiators who constantly push for the lowest prices possible with their suppliers. Knowledge of the laws that govern their areas of responsibility in purchasing is also a must. Contract law, misrepresentation and fraud, infringement of patent rights, damage claims against suppliers, and shipping regulations are only a few of the areas where laws and regulations must be understood by buyers.

Buyers must interview salespersons who call on them daily. The buyers' time is precious; so they must get the salespersons in and out as quickly as possible while maintaining a working relationship with the supplying organization. They must be both courteous and expeditious in processing salespersons. This is a daily challenge. But from these interviews comes information concerning new products and new services that may be of great importance to future purchases. The buyers remain open to salespersons' suggestions and continually pass along important information about new developments to operations departments. This feedback is an important function of buyers.

Officially, buyers process purchase requisitions and requests for quotation, make supplier selections, place purchase orders, and follow up on purchase orders. Additionally, they negotiate prices and conditions of sale on open purchase orders, blanket purchase orders, adjustments to purchase orders, and all other purchasing contracts. Generally, all operations departments go through buyers to contact suppliers unless otherwise authorized by buyers to contact suppliers directly.

Buyers are the backbones of purchasing departments: they are in a unique position of very high visibility. As one vice-president of operations recently stated:

"The good news is that buyers can *make* you. The bad news is that buyers can *break* you. Competence among buyers can be the difference between being very profitable or folding."

Contemporary Purchasing Issues A nagging problem within purchasing departments is the question of ethics among buyers. Salespersons deluge buyers with offers of free lunches, free liquor, free professional baseball tickets, free evenings on the town, free weekends at resorts, and occasionally even free summer homes in the Sierras. These attempts at offering gifts to buyers raise the question of how much is too much. At what point do gifts to buyers become unethical? Buyers hold great power, sometimes even economic life or death for salespersons and their organizations. Furthermore, buyers are not always compensated equitably with their responsibility. All the ingredients are present for temptation.

Some companies have laid down strict codes of conduct for buyers. No more than three bottles of liquor at Christmas, no gifts costing more than $25 per buyer per year from any one source, and no single gift exceeding $25 are examples of such rules of conduct. Policies covering gifts to company employees, whether they are buyers or not, certainly seem advisable. But perhaps more important is frequent communication within purchasing departments regarding what constitutes *ethical behavior*. The real worry here is that buyers may feel obligated to salespersons who have given them gifts and may not act in the best interests of their own organizations. This is a knotty problem that can start out small and grow to huge proportions. There are no easy answers, just diligence in keeping open the channels of communication and staying on top of problems to head off undesirable trends before the problems become irreversible. Generally, most companies strive to eliminate kickbacks, out-and-out bribes, and excessive gifts, which are carefully defined.

Here are some unethical, illegal, or questionable buying activities: taking advantage of obvious clerical or computational errors in quotations, fixing prices, collusion among bidders, playing favorites among suppliers in awarding orders, failing to respect personal obligations, and upgrading product samples with the intention of supplying lower-grade products.

Another issue that frequently surfaces within purchasing departments is reciprocity. *Reciprocity* means purposely buying products from a company because that company buys your products. In other words, "You scratch my back and I'll scratch yours." Most purchasing departments condemn the practice of reciprocity and most companies deny that they participate in it. You see, the difference between two firms honestly exchanging products and engaging in reciprocity is indeed a fine line. Reciprocity is the purchase of products or services from a firm while knowing that these purchases are a condition that must be met before that firm buys your products. The knowledge that reciprocity actually exists is often ignored or swept under the rug.

While the Federal Trade Commission (FTC) occasionally makes noise against reciprocity and other questionable buying practices, the FTC is not pushing the issue very hard. The practice of reciprocity exists and even thrives, but it is not talked about very much. These and other ethical and legal issues will continue to challenge purchasing departments in the future.

Purchasing is experiencing an increasing emphasis within organizations today:

Purchasing is an emerging frontier. Purchasing will be receiving greater organizational recognition due to increasing concerns regarding worldwide depletion of natural resources, spot shortages, increasing energy costs, changes in the relative costs of purchased items from country to country, ethical issues, and the increasing awareness of the need to maintain competitive position by better purchasing and materials management.[3]

These and other developments make the field of purchasing a challenging one for professional managers to consider for future jobs. You may too. Look at the want ads in your local urban newspapers; you may be surprised at the job opportunities in purchasing.

Once the materials are bought, materials managers must then decide the least expensive and most effective method of shipping goods to their organizations. Similarly, how to ship finished goods to customers is a critical question. These issues are central to the important materials management activity of logistics.

Logistics

Logistics is the organization function that manages the shipment of all incoming goods from suppliers and all outgoing goods to customers. Traffic departments in organizations routinely examine shipping schedules and select shipping methods, timetables, and ways of expediting these deliveries. The shipping costs to today's organizations represent such a huge proportion of revenues that manufacturing plants, warehouses, and other facilities are located with one overriding thought in mind: minimize incoming and outgoing shipping costs. In spite of these efforts, shipping costs alone can account for 50 percent or more of the sales price of some manufactured items.

The enormity of these expenditures has increasingly motivated organizations to staff traffic departments with professional managers and operations analysts who continually search for better techniques of shipping. Additionally, many companies have entered the transportation business (sometimes called *vertical backward and forward integration*), when economically feasible, in order to reduce their freight bills.

Example 9.1 demonstrates the savings that are possible through better logistics management. Think what large organizations could accomplish if this small manufacturer saved $175,000 annually in freight costs.

Logistics management is a specialized field requiring intensive technical training in the Department of Transportation (DOT) and the Interstate Commerce Commission (ICC) regulations and freight rates. This patchwork of *regs and rates* form the complex constraints that logistics experts must use to attack shipping costs. They must know the ins and outs of this complicated and changing field.

New developments are continually affecting logistics. Piggyback rail shipments, truck trailers on ships, and other unique shipping methods are examples of hybrids that have resulted in great freight savings. Lighter shipping containers, unitized loads, drop shipping, in-transit rates, consolidated shipments, deregulation of the trucking industry, and escalating fuel costs are examples of developments that are affecting logistics today, and new ones are coming every day. With the emergence of

---

[3] Robert M. Monczka, "The Purchasing Frontier," *Perspectives* 5(Fall 1977): 2–4.

Example 9.1

Flash Inc. Manufacturing Plant: Reducing Freight Costs

A small plant in northern California, Flash Inc., got a new plant manager. Upon examining the operating budgets for the plant, the new manager discovered that over $325,000 per year was being spent on incoming and outgoing freight bills. He immediately initiated a study of shipping methods and found that all shipping method decisions were being made by two clerks, a shipping clerk in the finished goods warehouse and an office clerk in the ordering department. Almost no materials or finished goods were shipped in whole carload or truckload quantities. Shipments were allocated to several trucklines to keep them happy. Additionally, no effort was made to develop unitized loading of goods and other means of reducing freight bills.

Two months later a new materials manager had turned the logistics situation around. Whole carloads and whole truckloads now accounted for 75 percent of incoming and outgoing shipments. Furthermore, the lowest cost form of shipment was utilized when feasible — for example, rail rather than truck and water rather than rail. Additionally, palletizing and other means of unitizing loads qualified the company for the lowest possible freight rates.

The result was indeed overwhelming to the new plant manager, who had hired the new materials manager: annual savings were $175,000 even after deducting the total expenses of the new materials manager's office.

computers in today's organizations, up-to-the-minute information is available on the status of each shipment. Additionally, the computer can be used to plan better networks of shipping methods in complicated distribution problems.

Linear programming was utilized in Chapter 5 to minimize the total costs of shipping products from several manufacturing plants to several warehouses or customers. These complex shipping problems can be and are analyzed routinely by standardized computer programs. The quantitative analysis of shipping problems will undoubtedly continue to grow because of the great outlay for freight costs and the resulting savings possible through intensive analysis.

Integral to questions of logistics are methods of warehousing materials and products once they are received from suppliers and before they are shipped to customers.

Warehousing

Warehousing is the management of materials from the point where they appear on the organization property until they depart the premises. It includes all aspects of receiving, moving, storing, dispersing, ordering, and accounting for all materials and finished goods from the beginning to the end of the productive process. The warehousing facilities may range from small stockrooms to large highly mechanized materials and finished goods storage facilities.

The importance of warehousing to operations managers cannot be overemphasized. Unfortunately, organizations may not always be conscious that their warehousing function is well managed; but when it is poorly managed, the awareness may be painful. Stockouts (running out of materials), damaged goods through improper handling, delayed in-plant deliveries, frequent emergency orders, delivery of the wrong materials, excessive inventory levels, and other undesirable conse-quences are the results of poor warehousing management. To avoid these and similar occurrences at the lowest cost is the goal of most warehousing managers.

Warehousing deals primarily with materials that directly support operations. The first problems that must be addressed are when to place an order for each material and how much to order. Numerous approaches exist for making these determina-tions, and the remainder of this chapter is principally devoted to these questions. Regardless of the techniques for these solutions, however, the orders are placed and shipments eventually appear in the receiving department, usually by either truck trailers or railroad cars.

Materials are routinely unloaded from delivery vehicles and held in temporary storage areas until quality control has tested them, confirmed their acceptability for use in operations, and released them. Materials handling equipment such as forklift trucks, conveyors, straddle trucks, and pump-forced pipelines are used to place the materials into *raw material inventory*. This inventory is stored on pallets (a small base frame on which bags and boxes of material are stacked), in high stacks, in storage tanks, or other means of holding raw materials. The raw material inventory is the reservoir of materials that operations use as required to begin the productive process.

In some firms, such as chemical processing plants, bulk materials are used as needed by operating departments without asking warehousing. In other facilities, however, a *stock requisition* is prepared in operations and forwarded to warehous-ing, requesting that materials be delivered to locations within the production system. In productive systems that use process layouts, where material moves intermittently through the facilities, *in-process inventories* are usually maintained. These aggregations of partially completed products that are in between processes are located at various designated locations throughout the productive system.

Warehousing may or may not be responsible for accounting for these in-process inventories, managing their movement, receiving and disbursing them, and control-ling what materials are put in and taken out. If the time that materials are in in-process inventory is short, operations usually retains control. If the time delay is long, however, or if other prevailing reasons exists, such as safety, governmental regulation, and so on, warehousing takes charge and maintains storerooms at various points within the productive system.

In systems that use product layouts, where material moves continuously through the facilities, in-process inventories are rare, and therefore operations maintains control of the in-process materials until they become finished products. At this point, after the materials have been transformed into finished goods inventory, they are again relinquished to warehousing in the finished goods warehouse.

Warehousing receives *shipping orders,* also called *factory orders,* from credit or marketing departments, which authorize the shipment of products to customers. Shipping departments within warehousing gather the various products included in the orders, prepare them for shipment, and load the orders onto outgoing freight vehicles.

This description of how the warehousing function manages materials all along the productive system is a general discussion of how these departments typically operate. In diverse productive systems, variation from this procedure occurs in practice because of great differences in materials, productive processes, products, markets, and organizational preferences of managers.

The record keeping within warehousing requires a *stock record* for each item that is carried in inventories. These individual items are called *stock-keeping units* (SKU). Stock records are running accounts that show the on-hand balance, receipts, disbursements, and any other changes that actually affect the usable on-hand balance for each SKU. Additionally, stock records may show such things as expected receipts, promises, or claims on SKUs even though they are still in inventory. This record keeping can be a clerical nightmare. Computers have allowed managers to improve the accuracy of these records, post changes to records more frequently as they occur, and have on-hand balance information instantaneously. Inventory record keeping was one of the first areas within large companies to be widely computerized in the 1960s, and this trend is continuing on down to even small operations today.

Warehousing managers require an interesting blend of knowledge and skills. Knowledge of computers and systems analysis, materials handling equipment, plant layout, safety, and packaging and a keen sense of humor are important attributes for these managers. The sense of humor is valuable for all managers because it allows them to keep problems and frustrations in a healthy perspective. Warehousing managers particularly need this attribute because they seldom get the recognition for a job well done. They tend to be victims of "we needed that part yesterday" from operations. Moreover, incoming material lead times are uncertain, and customer demand can vary all over the map. Then, when marketing or operations personnel say, "You always have too much of what we don't need and too little of what we do need," warehousing managers need a remarkable sense of humor.

New developments in warehousing are continuously modifying the management of these systems. Advances in computing systems are allowing on-line instantaneous record-keeping transactions. The automatic registering of products and prices at grocery stores is an example of these developments. Inventories are automatically adjusted as groceries are bought. Managers can remotely query the computing system and obtain instantaneous inventory balances. Motorola, Honeywell, Westinghouse, and other companies already have similar on-line systems for keeping stock records for all SKUs.

Ralston-Purina and Westinghouse have almost totally removed the human element from physically moving and storing materials at some of their newer locations. These automatic systems remove materials from raw material inventory, make up batches of complete material orders, and deliver them to the appropriate point within the production system, all without being touched by human hands. Other automatic systems similarly assemble shipping orders and move them to shipping areas. These and other developments promise to make warehousing even more effective in the future in meeting the quantity and scheduling needs of customers and operations departments.

In spite of the advances made in computing systems, the establishment of materials manager positions, and trends toward centralization of materials management functions for greater control, foul-ups still occur. Materials are not where they should be when they are needed, we discover that a stockout has occurred, or we anticipate that a stockout will occur. When these or similar situations arise, *and they do in all systems,* materials must be expedited.

Expediting

Expediting is the focusing of one or more persons' attention on a particular order or batch of materials with the goal of speeding up the order through all or part of the entire materials system. Expediting usually must occur because unforeseen events have caused an order for materials or products to be likely to be delinquent. Examples of some of these events are:

1. A customer increased the quantity of products ordered. The expanded order quantity now exceeds finished goods inventory, and additional products must be quickly produced.
2. A supplier fails to ship an order for materials when promised. Emergency shipping procedures must be employed in order to get the parts in-house in time to avoid a stockout or otherwise disrupt production processes.
3. Parts being processed in heat treat have encountered technical difficulties. The batch must be quickly transferred ahead of other materials if the annealing process is not to be delayed.

Expediting most often is necessary because of the uncertainties present in productive systems; customer demand, material delivery times, and in-house processing times are but a few of these uncertainties. Materials management must be flexible enough to accommodate this uncertainty by reacting quickly when the unexpected happens. Expediting is periodically performed by all materials management employees, and this activity helps make materials systems flexible.

Some managers and their organizations routinely operate by crisis management. *Every* activity is expedited. This approach to management is an excuse for poor planning, poor procedures, and poor management in general. When expediting becomes the dominant activity in materials management, something is wrong. Crisis management may have infringed on materials management. It can and does happen. Everyone and every productive system makes mistakes, and these can create the need for expediting when materials managers, buyers, warehousing managers, logistics personnel, and others in the materials system foul up. But expediting should be the exception to the rule, not the rule.

Expediting completes the materials cycle that proceeds from acquisition of materials to the delivery of the finished goods into customers' hands. The means to change procedures, override policy, make telephone calls and collect past favors, devise quick solutions as they occur, and other tactics of expediting are some of the important ways that managers make materials systems work effectively and get the right material to the right place at the right time.

Inventory Planning and Control

The variety of inventory situations in today's organizations is enormous. These situations vary not only in the number and nature of materials held, but also in the underlying purpose of the inventories and the degree of uncertainty of demand and supply of materials. Manufacturing presents perhaps the most comprehensive inventory-planning challenge. First, finished goods inventories are held as reservoirs of products expected to be demanded by customers. Forecasting customers' demand for products, ordering the right amount of products to replenish inventories on a timely basis, and building flexibility into inventory management in order to respond quickly to changing customers' demands are the principal finished goods inventory-planning problems. Inventory planning for retailing, warehousing, wholesaling, and other systems that store materials for customers' demand parallels manufacturing.

Manufacturing also must plan for in-process inventories that occur between production processing steps. These inventories, which generally occur because of different output rates of production operations, are indispensable to the continuous and efficient operation of productive systems.

The key in-process inventory-planning problem concerns how much material to carry before and after each step in production. Too few materials can lead to workers periodically running out of material to support their operations. Too many materials can lead to unsafe conditions around operations, confusion, damaged materials, increased levels of assets and reduced profitability and financial performance, and generally undesirable operating conditions. In-process inventories are generally unique to manufacturing, but they are also infrequently found in service systems with materials or technology emphases.

Manufacturing must forecast what products to hold in finished goods inventory and in what quantities they must be produced during future time periods so that products can be added to finished goods inventory to meet expected customer demand. These forecasts become the basis for production schedules for manufacturing plants, and the schedules create the need for raw materials inventories. Raw materials must be stocked to support the production schedules of on-going manufacturing operations. The inventory planning for raw materials inventories at the beginning of manufacturing systems is much like the inventory planning that must occur in service systems, such as hospitals, that stock supplies and materials to support their processes.

Because inventory planning in manufacturing encompasses most inventory problems encountered in other systems, this chapter will concentrate on manufacturing systems as the basis of developing inventory-planning concepts, issues, and analysis techniques. The novel characteristics of inventory systems from retailing, hospitals, transportation, and other service systems will be pointed out as the chapter progresses.

We shall examine in this chapter the inner workings of inventory systems, build an understanding of the various approaches to the fundamental issues in inventory planning, and develop several techniques for analyzing inventory problems. Central to understanding inventory planning are the purposes of holding inventories.

Purposes of Inventories

The purposes of inventories are an important consideration because inventories represent an investment, like any other asset in firms. Controllers and vice-presidents of finance monitor inventory levels in operations and argue for holding fewer materials in inventory. The reasons for wanting lower inventories are straightforward. First, it costs to insure, finance, store, and manage inventories. Second, larger

Table 9.1
Why Are Inventories Necessary?

Type of Inventory	Reasons
Finished goods	1. Variation in customer demand from period to period rules out planning flows of products in to exactly match flows of products out.
	2. It is more economical to hold inventory than constantly to place emergency orders to meet customers' demands.
	3. It is physically impossible to instantaneously produce or acquire products when demanded by customers.
	4. Backlogging of customers' orders may be unacceptable.
	5. Allows efficient scheduling of production. This refers both to economic production runs and to stable production levels that may not match seasonal or other erratic demand patterns.
	6. Allows the display of products to customers.
In-process	1. Production rates of processing steps are uneven.
	2. Allows the uncoupling of operations. Each operation is then somewhat independent of other operations. This allows flexibility in planning each operation.
	3. Allows large batches of materials to be moved at one time between operations, particularly with process layouts. This reduces materials handling costs.
Raw materials	1. It is physically impossible and economically infeasible to instantaneously supply raw materials and supplies when demanded by operations.
	2. Variation in demand for raw materials by operations from period to period and variation in delivery times of materials rule out planning flows of materials in that exactly match flows of materials out.
	3. Allows favorable unit prices through volume buying.
	4. Allows reducing of incoming unit freight costs through larger shipments.
	5. Allows more efficient materials handling through larger loads.

inventories tend to reduce return on investment. Inventory levels are therefore under constant scrutiny because they directly affect the profitability of operations.

At the other extreme, inventory levels that are too low can result in reduced production efficiency of operations, lost sales and dissatisfied customers, and increased raw material costs. So inventory levels that are too low also directly affect profitability. In a macro sense, therefore, too little or too much inventory is undesirable because profitability suffers.

How much material should be carried in inventory, then? Ah . . . that is the question. The answer is best developed by first looking at each stage of productive systems to examine why we hold inventories. Table 9.1 summarizes these reasons.

Finished Goods Inventories If we could precisely determine how much of each material would be demanded by customers in each time period, we could conceivably schedule quantities of products to flow in to exactly match the expected demand. Unfortunately, this is not the way customers ordinarily demand products. Demand is uncertain in most cases, thus making demand forecasting important in inventory planning. There is also usually some uncertainty about when products will be delivered to finished goods warehouses. The uncertainties of both supply and demand for finished goods therefore cause managers to hold a stock of finished goods to act as a buffer to be used when demand is greater than anticipated or when supply is less than expected in each time period. Buffer stocks are usually more economical than placing emergency special orders for meeting customer orders for items that are out of stock.

Customers may not always require instantaneous shipment of products when they are ordered. Tradition in some industries allows the routine *backlogging* of customer orders. The extreme situation is where firms wait until customers place orders before production is begun to produce the products. This is called *produce-to-order* in contrast to those firms who produce for inventory, which is called *produce-to-stock*. This is not to say that produce-to-order firms carry no finished goods inventory; they certainly do. But inventory levels are usually much lower because the function of buffer stocks tends to be replaced by backlogging of orders. Backlogs, when acceptable to customers or when backlogging is relatively inexpensive, even in produce-to-stock firms, encourage generally lower finished goods inventory levels.

Finished goods inventories often occur because of conscious decisions in POM to levelize production output even when demand patterns are seasonal. Figure 9.3

Figure 9.3
Production Leveling and Seasonal Demand

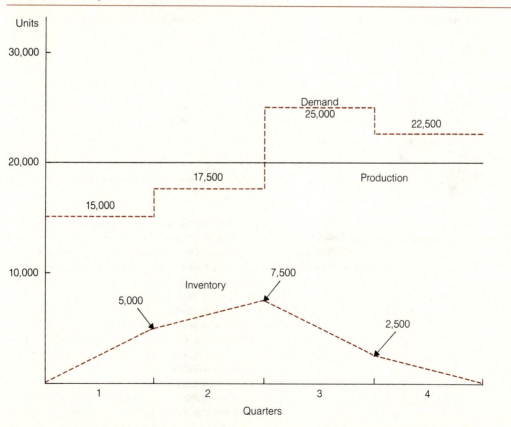

Figure 9.4
Cost per Unit vs. Length of Production Run

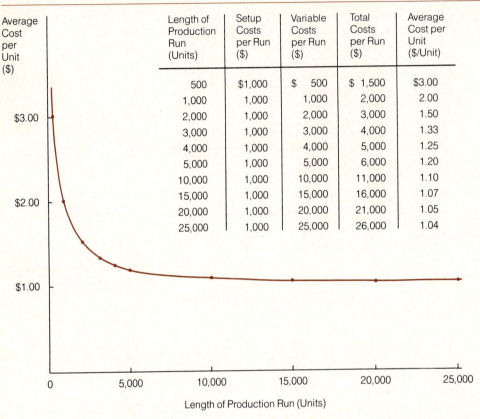

Length of Production Run (Units)	Setup Costs per Run ($)	Variable Costs per Run ($)	Total Costs per Run ($)	Average Cost per Unit ($/Unit)
500	$1,000	$ 500	$ 1,500	$3.00
1,000	1,000	1,000	2,000	2.00
2,000	1,000	2,000	3,000	1.50
3,000	1,000	3,000	4,000	1.33
4,000	1,000	4,000	5,000	1.25
5,000	1,000	5,000	6,000	1.20
10,000	1,000	10,000	11,000	1.10
15,000	1,000	15,000	16,000	1.07
20,000	1,000	20,000	21,000	1.05
25,000	1,000	25,000	26,000	1.04

shows how a manufacturer of a single product, such as ammonium nitrate fertilizer, may decide to schedule workers, raw materials, and facilities to produce at a uniform production rate of 20,000 tons per quarter. In periods when demand is less than production, finished goods inventory increases. When demand is greater than production, inventory declines. Levelized production output allows manufacturers to stabilize employment levels, thus avoiding hire-train-layoff worker cycles. Raw material deliveries can also be more programmed and thus more predictable. Overtime can be minimized because production peaks have been avoided. These and other economic factors make for efficient production and therefore lower labor, material, and variable overhead costs. These cost savings are somewhat offset by increased costs of holding the inventories that inevitably result when demand is not so level as production.

In production plants that produce many products—such as printing, household appliances, and garments—machines must be changed over to each product that is

Figure 9.5
Multiple Product Inventory Fluctuations Produced with the Same Machinery

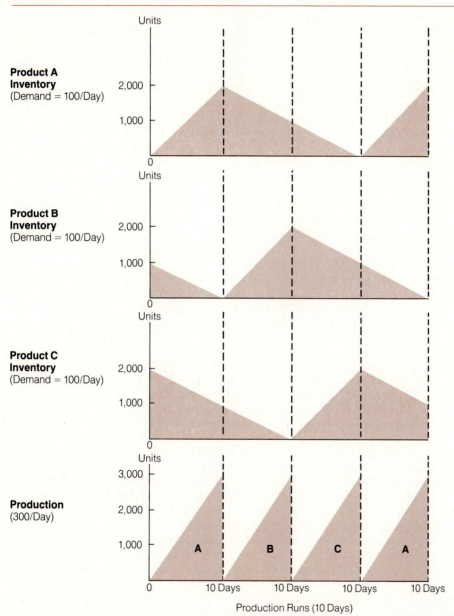

Product A
Inventory
(Demand = 100/Day)

Product B
Inventory
(Demand = 100/Day)

Product C
Inventory
(Demand = 100/Day)

Production
(300/Day)

Production Runs (10 Days)

to be produced, and the cost of these machine changeovers can be exorbitant if only a few units of each product are produced between machine changeovers. Figure 9.4 shows an example of an operation where each machine changeover, or setup, costs $1,000; variable costs (labor, material, and variable overhead) are $1 per unit; and production runs (number of units produced after each changeover) vary from 500 to 25,000 units. The average cost per unit, including setup and variable costs, is observed to decline as the length of production runs increases.

These conditions rationally lead managers to produce for extended periods (long production runs) on one product at rates of production greater than demand rates, thus allowing inventories to increase, then change the machines over to another product while finished goods inventory of the first product falls, and so on. Figure 9.5 is an example of a manufacturer that produces only three products, A, B, and C, each with demand rates of 100 units per day. The firm produces Product A for 10 days, changes over to Product B at night and produces Product B for 10 days, changes over to Product C and produces Product C for 10 days, and then repeats the cycle. Production is 300 units per day for each of the three products. Notice how the finished goods inventories of these products rise and fall as production switches from product to product.

Whether single products or multiple products are produced, levelized production outputs, economical production runs, and other scheduling efficiencies result in fluctuating finished goods inventory levels.

In retailing and even in some manufacturing firms, finished goods inventories are kept to display products to customers. There is an old saying in retailing: "You can't sell what you don't have." Products must be displayed, and thus finished goods inventories are a fundamental fact of retailing.

In-Process Inventories Rarely do successive operations produce at exactly the same output rate; when they do not, in-process inventories usually result. For example, Operation A is operated two shifts per day at a rate of 50 units per hour. Operation B operates one 8-hour shift per day and uses the output of Operation A at a rate of 100 units per hour. Operation C operates on two shifts per day and uses the output of Operation B at a rate of 50 units per hour. Look at Figure 9.6 to see how the in-process inventories between A and B and between B and C rise and fall.

Continuous productive systems, as described in Chapter 4 on process planning, use sequences of operations that are inseparably tied together; the output rates of the operations are the same, and thus no in-process inventories are present. This is the usual characteristic of assembly lines. One disadvantage of assembly lines is their inflexibility. For example, if one operation breaks down mechanically or one operation runs out of material, the whole line must sit idle while the one machine is repaired or material is supplied. Additionally, except during changeoves when lines are being purged, all successive machines must invariably produce the same product.

Many productive systems uncouple their operations. This uncoupling arrangement allows flexibility in scheduling different products through the facility — flexibility to continue operating even if one operation is idled because of mechanical breakdowns, material shortages, or other delays — and independence in planning the activities of individual operations. But this arrangement requires in-process

Figure 9.6
In-Process Inventories Resulting from Different Output Rates

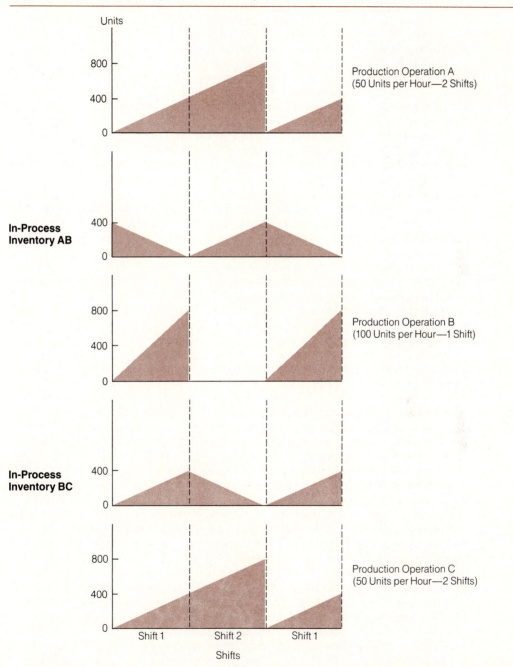

inventories between the operations so that the supply of partially completed materials to an operation is relatively independent of all other operations. The same principle of uncoupling applies where one manufacturing plant uses the output from another one. Inventories held between the two plants allow the two to plan their operations relatively independently of each other.

The large volumes of materials moved between operations that are uncoupled require that they be transported in batches to reduce the per-unit materials handling costs. This batch movement causes in-process inventories to develop both before and after successive operations.

One interesting phenomenon is observed concerning the relationship between the speed at which workers work and the amount of in-process inventory before and after their operations. Experienced foremen will tell you that workers have a preconceived notion about the optimal amount of in-process inventory before and after their operations. When these inventories are about at the optimal level, workers work at about their regular pace. But when the in-process inventory before their operation falls too low and/or when the in-process inventory after their operation gets too large, the natural tendency is for workers to slow their work pace. Conversely, when in-process inventories before their operation get too large and when in-process inventories after their operation get too low, workers tend to quicken their work pace.

Consider the results in operating efficiency when analysts develop programs to reduce in-process inventories with the goal of reducing the inefficiencies of excessive storage times, clumsy materials handling procedures, damaged materials, and excessive carrying costs. How confusing it would be to analysts to reduce in-process inventories expecting reduced operating costs, but find instead, because in-process inventories fall too low, workers slowing their work pace, with resultant increased operating costs. When we are analyzing the *things* of production — materials, machines, and so on — let us not overlook the impact upon the human behavior of our workers.

Raw Materials Inventories Planning the requirements for raw materials to support production schedules is an important activity within POM. *Material requirements planning* (MRP) are the buzz words applied to this rapidly developing POM specialty. (MRP will be discussed in detail in Chapter 11.) Raw materials cannot be instantaneously drawn out of a hat as if by magic. The process of sensing the need for raw materials, ordering them from suppliers, following their shipment, receiving and inspecting them, and moving them into production areas for use takes time and also involves some uncertainty. We may estimate that we can get Material A in 30 days, but it may take as few as 20 days or as many as 45 days. This uncertainty requires that we carry a buffer, or safety stock, in raw materials inventory just in case materials arrive later than expected. Early arrivals of orders cause raw materials inventories to climb.

Airfreight, helicopter deliveries such as those used in delivery of critical hospital supplies, and other emergency shipping methods can be used to get materials in a hurry. Although the exclusive use of these methods would conceivably reduce raw materials inventories, the expense would undoubtedly prove exorbitant. Thus raw materials inventories are normally used in conjunction with more conventional shipping methods such as rail, truck, and occasionally water. Emergency shipping methods are typically reserved for emergencies.

MRP, as we shall see in Chapter 11, seeks to reduce raw materials inventories by more closely matching the inflow of materials with the expected usage rates of production. Even with the most successful MRP applications today, however, perfect meshing of raw material inflows with outflows, which eliminates raw materials inventories, has proved impractical. Raw material inventories are used to accommodate both the uncertainties of production's use of materials and the uncertainties of delivery of materials.

Materials are almost universally bought *in quantity*. These volume purchases have become standard operating procedures because of economics. Lower purchase prices, lower freight rates, and lower materials handling costs motivate operations managers to buy materials in larger quantities. When these large batches of materials are received, a raw materials inventory is created because production does not use them instantaneously. Rather, they are used gradually, and the inventory levels decline until the next shipment is received.

We have shown that finished goods, in-process, and raw materials inventories are indispensable to the efficient and effective operation of productive systems. Let us now turn to a discussion of how these inventory systems operate in practice.

Behavior of Independent Demand Inventory Systems

We have described inventory planning as stocking the right amounts of materials, but this is the end result of effective planning rather than the beginning. **Two fundamental issues underlie all inventory planning:**

1. **How much to order of each material when orders are placed with either outside suppliers or production departments within organizations.**
2. **When to place the orders.**

The determination of *order quantities,* sometimes also called *lot sizes,* and when to place these orders, called *order points,* determine in large measure the amount of materials in inventory in any point in time. The study of the *inventory cycle*—materials are ordered, received, used, and the process is repeated—uses a terminology all its own; refer to Table 9.2 for an understanding of the meanings of these terms.

Inventories may contain materials that have either *dependent or independent demands.* **In independent demand inventories, the demand for an item carried in inventory is independent of the demand for any other item carried in inventory. Examples of independent demand inventories are finished goods inventories and parts that are shipped as end items to customers for spare parts or repair. The remainder of this chapter is aimed at the order quantity and order point decisions of independent demand inventories. Dependent demand inventories contain items whose demand depends upon the demands for other items also held in inventory. For example, the demand for a calculator case and shipping container, which are components, are both dependent upon the demand for the calculator, a finished good.** Typically, the demand for raw materials and components can be calculated if we know the demand for the finished goods that these materials go into. Order quantity and order point decisions for dependent demand inventories are therefore distinctly different from those of inde-

Table 9.2
Inventory Concepts and Terms

1. **Acquisition Cost (ac)** — The cost of purchasing or producing one unit of a material or product.

2. **Annual Acquisition Cost** — The total cost of either purchasing or producing a material for the entire year. Calculated by multiplying annual demand by the acquisition cost per unit.

3. **Annual Carrying Cost** — The total cost of providing inventories for the entire year. Calculated for a material by multiplying average inventory level by carrying cost per unit per year.

4. **Annual Demand (D)** — The number of units of a material estimated to be demanded per year.

5. **Annual Ordering Cost** — The total cost of acquiring inventory replenishments for the entire year. Calculated for a material by multiplying the number of orders per year by the ordering cost per order.

6. **Backlogging** — The process of holding customer orders to be filled later when they cannot be shipped immediately because of stockouts.

7. **Carrying Cost (C)** — The cost of financing, warehousing, damaging or losing, and any other cost directly related to holding materials in inventory. Calculated by multiplying the acquisition cost per unit by the estimated proportion of that cost attributed to carrying cost. Expressed in dollars per unit per year.

8. **Demand during Lead Time (DDLT)** — The number of units of a material demanded during the inventory replenishment process. The expected demand during lead time (EDDLT) is calculated by multiplying the average demand per day by the average lead time.

9. **Demand Rate (d)** — Also called the *usage rate*. The number of units demanded by customers or production departments per unit of time. Must be in the same units as the supply rate (p).

10. **Disbursements** — The act of physically removing materials from inventory. These transactions cause record-keeping adjustments that reduce inventory levels.

11. **Economic Order Quantity (EOQ)** — Also called *economic lot size* and *economic production quantity*. The quantity of materials ordered at each order point that

minimizes the total annual stocking costs for a material in a fixed order quantity inventory system.

12. **Finished Goods Inventory** — The reservoir of products held for customer demand.

13. **Fixed Order Period System** — The system of inventory planning that takes physical counts of materials in inventory at equal fixed time intervals. Orders are placed at these equally spaced reviews for varying quantities of each material depending upon inventory levels, maximum inventory targets, and expected demand during lead time.

14. **Fixed Order Quantity System** — The system of inventory planning that places orders for a material when the inventory level falls to a preestablished critical level. These orders are for fixed quantities of each material.

15. **In-Process Inventory** — Also called *work in process*. Work in various stages of completion between the processing steps of the productive system.

16. **Inventory Cycle** — The activities of sensing a need for ordering materials, placing an order, determining lead time for getting the material delivered, receiving the material, and using the material. This process is continuously repeated for a material and is thus cyclical.

17. **Inventory Level** — Amount of materials actually on hand in inventory that is ready for use.

18. **Inventory Planning** — All the management activities that result in stocking the right amount of each material. The principal concerns are order quantities, order points, and order periods.

19. **Lead Time (LT)** — The length of time required to replenish the inventory for a material from the time that a need for additional material is sensed until the new order for the material is in inventory and ready for use.

20. **Length of Production Run** — The number of units produced of a product at a processing step in the productive system between machine changeovers.

21. **Levelized Production** — Stabilizing production output levels from time period to time period. Even though this plan tends to increase finished goods inventory levels during periods of low demand, this excess inventory

Table 9.2 (continued)
Inventory Concepts and Terms

tends to be dissipated during periods of high demand. Employment levels, materials flows, and machine schedules are levelized, thus resulting in reduced operating expenses.

22. **Material Requirements Planning (MRP)** — The management technique of developing a raw materials delivery schedule that approximately matches raw materials inflows with production's demand for materials.

23. **Optimal Order Period (T)** — Also called the *economic time interval* and *optimal time interval*. The time, in fractions of a year, between reviews of the status of a material that exactly balances annual ordering costs with annual carrying costs in a fixed order period inventory system.

24. **Order Point (OP)** — A point in time when an order is placed for a material in a fixed order period inventory system. In fixed order quantity systems the order point refers to the preestablished inventory level that triggers a material order and is calculated by adding expected demand during lead time to safety stock.

25. **Order Quantity (Q)** — The quantity of a material ordered each time inventory is replenished. Q is constant in fixed order quantity systems and variable in fixed order period systems.

26. **Ordering Costs (S)** — The average cost of each inventory replenishment for a material, includes such costs as those of processing purchasing requisitions, purchase orders, machine changeovers, postage, telephone calls, and receiving.

27. **Produce-to-Order** — Productive systems are said to produce to order when production is not begun until customers' orders are in hand.

28. **Produce-to-Stock** — Productive systems are said to produce to stock when production proceeds and standardized products are placed in finished goods inventory before customers' orders are received.

29. **Quantity Discounts** — The reduction of purchase prices if raw materials are ordered in greater quantities. *Price breaks* are those quantities where price per unit changes.

30. **Raw Material Inventory** — The reservoir of raw materials held in warehouses until demanded by production or operations.

31. **Replenishment** — The process of adding material to inventory. It includes sensing the need for an order of materials, placing the order, production of the order, and shipment and receipt of the order.

32. **Safety Stock** — Also called *buffer stock*. Additional quantity of a material held in inventory to be used in time periods when demand is greater than expected or supply is less than expected.

33. **Setup Costs** — Also called *changeover costs*. The cost of changing a processing step in a productive system over from one product to another.

34. **Stockout** — When the usable inventory level for a material is reduced to zero.

35. **Stockout Cost** — The cost of stockouts, includes such costs as profits forgone by lost sales, cost of reclaiming disappointed customers, special expediting, special handling of backlogged orders, and additional production costs.

36. **Supply Rate (p)** — Also called *production rate*. The number of units per unit of time of a material supplied to inventory if delivered gradually. Must be in the same units as demand rate (d).

37. **Total Annual Material Costs (TMC)** — The total of annual acquisition costs and total annual stocking costs for a material.

38. **Total Annual Stocking Costs (TSC)** — The total costs of maintaining a material in inventory for one year. Includes annual carrying cost and annual ordering cost, but not annual acquisition cost.

39. **Two-Bin System** — A simple fixed order quantity system that uses two bins to physically hold a material in inventory. Material in the small bin is used only during lead time. Orders are triggered when the large bin is empty, and both are filled when inventory is replenished.

pendent demand inventories; these decisions will be treated in Chapter 11, Resource Requirements Planning Systems.

Two simple models demonstrate the behavior of independent demand inventories: fixed order quantity system and fixed order period system.

Fixed order quantity systems place orders for the same quantity of a material in each inventory cycle. Order quantity (Q) is a constant. However, *when* the order is placed is allowed to vary. Figure 9.7 demonstrates how these systems operate.

Inventories fall until a critical inventory level (OP) triggers an order. The order point (OP) that triggers orders is determined by estimating expected usage during lead time plus safety stock. When the inventory is replenished (R_1, an order is received), the fixed order quantity (Q_1) is placed in inventory. Note that $Q_1 = Q_2 = Q_3$, but that the elapsed times between orders are not necessarily equal.

The *two-bin system* of inventory control is a simple application of fixed order quantity systems. In the two-bin system each material has two bins that physically hold the material in the warehouse. As the material is used, material is withdrawn from a large bin until the large bin is empty. At the bottom of the large bin is a preprinted purchase requisition for another order of the material. This requisition is sent to purchasing and materials are used out of the small bin, which holds just enough material to last until the next inventory replenishment. The small bin contains the expected demand during lead time and safety stock. When the inven-

Figure 9.7
Fixed Order Quantity System

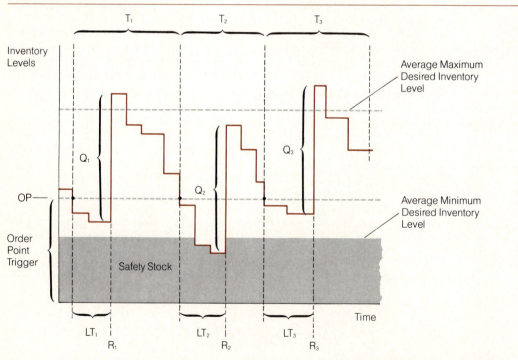

tory is replenished, a purchase requisition is placed in the bottom of the large bin, both bins are filled, and the cycle is repeated.

In fixed order quantity systems we usually assume perpetual inventory accounting. In *perpetual inventory accounting* additions and subtractions from inventory records are made at the time that materials are added to or removed from inventory. With this method, we can determine the amount of a material in inventory at any point in time by looking at its *inventory record,* a display of all of the inventory transactions that have affected that material. Such displays today are usually a part of the company's computer system and appear on a computer terminal display when called. Visualize how a fixed order quantity system would use the inventory record: the computer could be programmed to identify materials whose inventory levels have fallen to their critical levels, the fixed order quantities could be printed on computer printouts, or purchase orders could even be automatically prepared. Many firms have, in fact, computerized these inventory cycle decisions of how much to order and when to place orders. But the basis of determining order points and order quantities must first be programmed into the computer for each material. Various approaches to estimating these values exist in practice, and we shall examine several of these analyses later in this chapter.

Fixed order period systems review inventory levels at fixed time intervals and orders are placed for enough material to bring inventory levels back up to approxi-

Figure 9.8
Fixed Order Period System

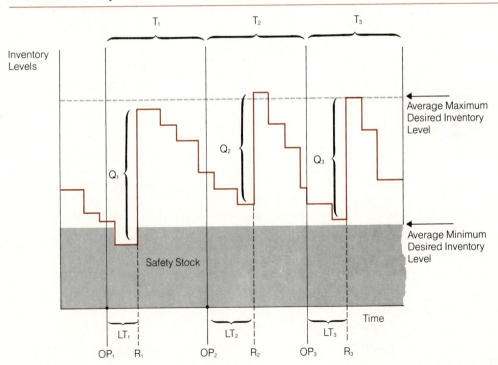

mately some predetermined level. Figure 9.8 demonstrates how these systems operate.

In Figure 9.8 orders are placed at equal time intervals so that $T_1 = T_2 = T_3$. The amount ordered in each cycle (Q_1, Q_2, and Q_3) is based on the inventory levels at the time of review, the average maximum desired inventory level including safety stock, and the expected demand during lead time. If at the time of review the inventory is relatively low, as at OP_1, larger order quantities (Q_1) are placed. If, on the other hand, inventories are high when reviewed, as at OP_2, smaller quantities (Q_2) are ordered ($Q_1 > Q_2$).

In this inventory system order quantities can be unequal, but order intervals are equal ($T_1 = T_2 = T_3$). In most real situations lead times and demand patterns are usually relatively uncertain. Note that once you have set the order interval, inventory level need not be monitored until the next review (OP_1, OP_2, or OP_3). Between these reviews, the uncertainties of both demand and lead time combine to make this system more subject to stockouts than the fixed order quantity system. This is because the fixed order quantity system bases its order points on estimates of demand only during the lead time period, whereas the fixed order period system bases its order points on estimates of demand during the entire period between reviews. The fixed order period system therefore usually requires more safety stock to accommodate this increased risk of stockouts.

The fixed order period system lends itself to inventories where it is more desirable to physically count inventory on a regular periodic basis, as in retail stores. In these situations, particularly with those goods that are in displays where perpetual inventory accounting may not be feasible, periodic counts of materials on hand may be the most practical system to use and the fixed order period system would be appropriate.

Both fixed order quantity and fixed order period systems have their strengths, and we observe both of these systems in practice. However, *hybrids* of these systems also exist. For example, some systems use inventory levels to trigger orders, as in fixed order quantity systems; but variable order quantities are based on inventory levels, materials promised in the near future, materials forecast to be needed, firm orders on hand for materials, and extraordinary events that are expected to affect lead times.

These and similar hybrids of the two simple inventory systems presented above tend to be the rules rather than the exceptions. This shouldn't surprise us. Nothing in POM is so simple and universal that we can lay out neat and simple formulas to describe its universal behavior in practice. What we can do is describe the way some systems operate to demonstrate concepts, issues, and techniques, while recognizing that between the extremes variety, rather than uniformity, dominates practice. The concepts, issues, and techniques that we have learned should guide us in adapting to the variety of practice.

Inventory Costs

Let us now address this question: How much should we order? The answer to this question is a function of the costs of ordering too much and the costs of ordering too little. The costs of ordering too much are those costs of carrying excessive quantities of materials in inventory for extended periods. These costs are *carrying costs,* and they include insurance, interest charges for financing the inventories, warehouse rental, utilities, taxes, lost and damaged materials, obsolesence, and any other out-of-pocket (cash actually expended) expense associated with holding materials in warehouses. Carrying costs are expressed as a percentage of cost of a material — usually between 15 and 35 percent — or as the actual dollar amount to carry a material in inventory for a year.

On the other hand, when too few materials are ordered, excessive annual *ordering costs* and *stockout costs* are encountered. Ordering costs are all of the out-of-pocket costs associated with an inventory cycle — typing the purchase order, any expediting required, postage, any other purchasing and warehousing labor for placing each order, setup costs if produced in the organization, record keeping, and receiving the order into the warehouse. Ordering costs are usually expressed as dollars per order and do not include the purchase cost of the materials.

Stockout costs are those costs directly attributed to running out of stock. A major part of these costs can be the lost profits of customer orders that cannot be filled. If the customers agree to backlogging of their orders — that is, holding the orders to be filled later — additional costs can result from extra paperwork, special handling of orders, and expediting. When raw materials arrive late and stockouts occur, production may have to shut down operations or take costly counteractions to avoid production delays. Additional sales costs can result when customers must be reclaimed after disappointments from unfilled orders. These and other costs associated with stockouts, difficult as they may be to quantify, are real costs of ordering too few materials at the order point. Not only do smaller orders result in lower inventory levels in general, but more inventory cycles per year are needed; and since stockouts usually occur during lead time, the likelihood of stockouts is increased.

Conceptually, managers order materials for raw material and finished goods inventories so that the cost of ordering too few materials is balanced against the cost of ordering too many materials on each order. Figure 9.9 demonstrates that annual carrying costs climb as the order quantities rise. This results from the direct relationship between order quantity and average inventory level: as order quantities increase, so do average inventory levels. On the other hand, as order quantities increase, the number of orders per year decline and thus the annual ordering costs fall. Similarly, as order quantities increase, the number of times that inventory is replenished per year declines and average inventory levels rise; therefore, the number of stockouts likely to occur declines.

As Figure 9.9 shows, when the annual carrying cost curve is added to the annual ordering and stockout cost curve, an annual total stocking cost curve results. This total cost curve demonstrates an important concept in inventory planning: **There exists for every material held in raw material and finished goods inventories an optimal order quantity where total annual stocking costs are at a minimum.** In this figure the optimum order quantity, traditionally called the *economic order quantity* (EOQ), appears to be approximately 524 units per order.

This concept is useful to operations managers, particularly if some version of the fixed order quantity system is used and some minimum inventory level triggers orders for fixed quantities of materials.

Figure 9.9
Balancing Carrying Costs against Ordering and Stockout Costs

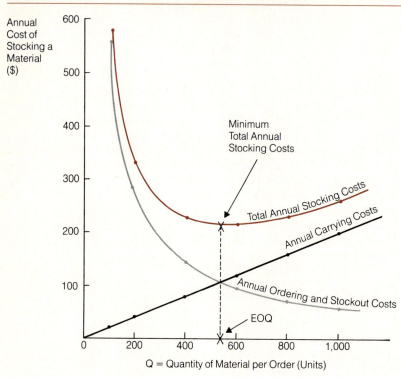

Q = Quantity of Material per Order (Units)

Fixed Order Quantity Systems

Order quantities and order points in fixed order quantity systems are ancient issues that have received acute attention since organizations have held inventories. Since the development of the economic lot size model (EOQ) by F. W. Harris in 1915, we have seen a growth in the variety and applications of such models.

Optimal Order Quantities When operations managers must decide the quantity of a material to order, either for raw materials or finished goods inventories in fixed order quantity systems, no single formula applies to all situations. Each situation requires analysis based on the characteristics of that particular inventory system. We shall develop here estimates of optimal order quantities for three inventory models: Model I—basic economic order quantity (EOQ), Model II—EOQ with gradual deliveries, and Model III—EOQ with quantity discounts.

Model I—Basic Economic Order Quantity (EOQ) Table 9.3 describes the assumptions, variable definitions, cost formulas, and EOQ formula for Model I. Study the assumptions of this model carefully, because this analysis may or may not be appropriate for analyzing some inventory problems in practice. The key question in

Table 9.3
Model I—Basic Economic Order Quantity (EOQ)

Assumptions

1. Annual demand, carrying cost, and ordering cost for a material can be estimated with precision.
2. Average inventory level for a material is order quantity divided by two. This implicitly assumes that no safety stock is utilized, orders are received all at once, materials are used at a uniform rate, and materials are entirely used up when the next order arrives.
3. There are no stockout costs.
4. Quantity discounts do not exist.

Variable Definitions

D = Annual demand for a material (units per year)*
Q = Quantity of material ordered at each order point (units per order)
C = Cost of carrying one unit in inventory for one year (dollars per unit per year)*
S = Average cost of completing an order for a material (dollars per order)
TSC = Total annual stocking costs for a material (dollars per year)

Cost Formulas

$$\text{Annual carrying cost} = \text{Average inventory level} \times \text{Carrying cost} = \left(\frac{Q}{2}\right)C$$

$$\text{Annual ordering cost} = \text{Orders per year} \times \text{Ordering cost} = \left(\frac{D}{Q}\right)S$$

$$\text{Total annual stocking cost (TSC)} = \text{Annual carrying cost} + \text{Annual ordering cost} = \left(\frac{Q}{2}\right)C + \left(\frac{D}{Q}\right)S$$

Economic Order Quantity Formula

The optimal order quantity occurs when the annual ordering costs for a material are exactly equal to the annual carrying costs (see Figure 9.9):

1. Set the annual carrying costs equal to annual ordering costs: $\left(\frac{Q}{2}\right)C = \left(\frac{D}{Q}\right)S$

2. Multiply both sides of equation by Q: $Q^2\left(\frac{C}{2}\right) = DS$

3. Divide both sides of equation by C/2: $Q^2 = \frac{2DS}{C}$

4. Take the square root of both sides of equation: $Q = \sqrt{\frac{2DS}{C}}$

5. The EOQ is therefore: $EOQ = \sqrt{\frac{2DS}{C}}$

---

* Note: In cases where a material has a seasonal demand, D could represent quarterly demand and C would represent per-unit carrying cost for one quarter. Thus, the order policies would vary from quarter to quarter as the seasonal demand varies.

applying this model is: Do the assumptions fit our inventory situation, or are the deviations from these assumptions only minor?

Three of these assumptions are critical: (1) Annual demand can be precisely estimated. (2) Average inventory level equals order quantity divided by two. (3) Quantity discounts do not exist. The number of units of a material expected to be demanded per year may be subject to great uncertainty, particularly if we have little experience on which to base our estimate. New products, products experiencing rapid growth or decline, and raw materials to support these highly variable products provide challenges to forecasters.

The demand for some materials and products is very stable and the estimates of their demand tend to be very accurate. The resulting order quantities for these materials also tend to be very precise. What about the demand for those materials that we are not too sure about? The order quantity estimates will be less precise, that's all. If we guess high (estimate D higher than actually experienced), the EOQ will be too high, annual carrying costs will be too high, and total annual stocking costs will be higher than optimal. If we guess too low (estimate D lower than actually experienced), the EOQ will be too low, the annual ordering costs will be too high, and the total annual stocking costs will be too high.

As demonstrated in Figure 9.10, an average inventory of Q/2 implies that there is no safety stock, orders are received all at once, materials are used at a uniform rate, and materials are entirely used up when the next order arrives. The presence of all these characteristics is rare in practice; but in spite of minor deviations, Q/2 may still be a reasonable estimate of average inventory levels for some materials. A quick check of the stock records of a material will either confirm or deny the validity of Q/2 as an estimate of average inventory levels. If another measure of average inventory

Figure 9.10
Average Inventory Level in Model I

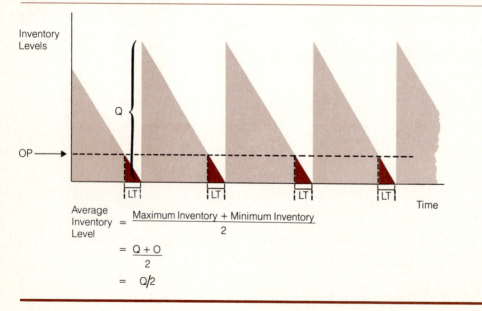

$$\text{Average Inventory Level} = \frac{\text{Maximum Inventory} + \text{Minimum Inventory}}{2}$$

$$= \frac{Q + 0}{2}$$

$$= Q/2$$

levels is found to be a more precise estimate, this new value could be substituted for Q/2 in the cost formulas, thus resulting in a slightly different EOQ formula.

Of all the variables that affect the order quantity decision, volume discounts is perhaps the most important factor that we consider in POM. Model III, covered later in this section, applies to those situations where suppliers quote lower prices for higher order quantities of materials. But since Model III is a modification of Model I, the basic EOQ formulation is a helpful starting point for analyzing a variety of inventory situations.

Example 9.2 applies the cost and EOQ formulas to one material purchased by a plumbing supply company. The simplicity of estimating an optimal order quantity, the present total annual stocking cost with present order quantity policy, and the new annual stocking cost by following the EOQ as a policy is impressive. The ease of calculation and understanding of the TSC and EOQ support the wide application of this analysis technique in POM.

Example 9.2

Use of Model I in a Plumbing Supply Company

The Don't Cuss — Call Us Plumbing Supply Company stocks thousands of plumbing items sold to regional plumbers, contractors, and retailers. Mr. Swartz, the firm's general manager, wonders how much money could be saved annually if EOQ were used instead of the firm's present rules of thumb. He instructs Mary Ann Church, an inventory analyst, to conduct an analysis of one material only (Material #3925, a brass valve) to see if significant savings might result from using the EOQ. Mary Ann develops the following estimates from accounting information: $D = 10,000$ valves per year, $Q = 400$ valves per order (present order quantity), $C = \$.40$ per valve per year, and $S = \$5.50$ per order.

Solution

1. Mary Ann calculates the present total annual stocking costs:

$$TSC_1 = (Q/2)C + (D/Q)S = \left(\frac{400}{2}\right).4 + \left(\frac{10,000}{400}\right)5.5 = 80 + 137.50 = \$217.50$$

2. The EOQ is calculated:

$$EOQ = \sqrt{\frac{2DS}{C}} = \sqrt{\frac{2(10,000)(5.5)}{.4}} = \sqrt{275,000} = 524.4 \text{ valves}$$

3. The total annual stocking costs if EOQ were employed are calculated:

$$TSC_2 = (Q/2)C + (D/Q)S = \left(\frac{524.4}{2}\right).4 + \left(\frac{10,000}{524.4}\right)5.5 = 104.88 + 104.88 = \$209.76$$

4. The estimated annual savings in stocking costs is calculated:

$$\text{Savings} = TSC_1 - TSC_2 = 217.50 - 209.76 = \$7.74$$

5. Mary Ann Church concluded that if the annual savings on this one material were applied to the thousands of items in inventory, the savings from EOQ would be significant.

Table 9.4
Model II — EOQ with Gradual Deliveries

Assumptions

1. Annual demand, carrying cost, and ordering cost for a material can be estimated with precision.
2. No safety stock is utilized, materials are supplied at a uniform rate (p) and used at a uniform rate (d), and materials are entirely used up when the next order begins to arrive.
3. There are no stockout costs.
4. Quantity discounts do not exist.
5. Supply rate (p) is greater than usage rate (d).

Variable Definitions

All of the definitions in Model I apply also to Model II.* Additionally:

d = Rate at which units are used out of inventory (units per time period)
p = Rate at which units are supplied to inventory (same units as d)

Cost Formulas

$$\text{Maximum inventory level} = \text{Inventory buildup rate} \times \text{Period of delivery} = (p - d)\frac{Q}{p}$$

$$\text{Minimum inventory level} = 0$$

$$\text{Average inventory level} = \frac{1}{2}(\text{maximum inventory level} + \text{minimum inventory level})$$

$$= \frac{1}{2}\left[(p - d)\frac{Q}{p} + 0\right] = \frac{Q}{2}\left(\frac{p - d}{p}\right)$$

$$\text{Annual carrying cost} = \text{Average inventory level} \times \text{Carrying cost} = \frac{Q}{2}\left(\frac{p - d}{p}\right)C$$

$$\text{Annual ordering cost} = \text{Orders per year} \times \text{Ordering cost} = \left(\frac{D}{Q}\right)S$$

$$\text{Total annual stocking cost (TSC)} = \text{Annual carrying cost} + \text{Annual ordering cost} = \frac{Q}{2}\left(\frac{p - d}{p}\right)C + \left(\frac{D}{Q}\right)S$$

Economic Order Quantity Formula

The optimal order quantity for a material occurs when the annual ordering costs are exactly equal to annual carrying costs (see Figure 9.9):

1. Set annual carrying costs equal to annual ordering costs:

$$\frac{Q}{2}\left(\frac{p - d}{p}\right)C = \left(\frac{D}{Q}\right)S$$

2. Multiply both sides of equation by Q:

$$Q^2\left[\frac{C}{2}\left(\frac{p - d}{p}\right)\right] = DS$$

3. Divide both sides of equation by $\frac{C}{2}\left(\frac{p - d}{p}\right)$:

$$Q^2 = \frac{2DS}{C}\left(\frac{p}{p - d}\right)$$

4. Take the square root of both sides of equation:

$$Q = \sqrt{\frac{2DS}{C}\left(\frac{p}{p - d}\right)}$$

5. The EOQ is therefore:

$$EOQ = \sqrt{\frac{2DS}{C}\left(\frac{p}{p - d}\right)}$$

* Note: See the note to Table 9.3.

Model II — EOQ with Gradual Deliveries Model II, EOQ with gradual deliveries, offers only one slight modification to Model I: orders are assumed to be delivered at a uniform rate rather than all at once. Table 9.4 presents the assumptions, variable definitions, cost formulas, and EOQ formula for Model II.

Figure 9.11 shows that orders are received at a uniform rate (p) during part of the inventory cycle and used at a uniform rate (d) throughout the cycle. Inventory levels build at a rate of $(p - d)$ during delivery and never reach the level Q as in Model I. Visualize a water tank with water flowing in at the top through a spigot at a rate of p and flowing out at the bottom through a spigot at a rate of d. The water level in the tank would rise at a rate of $(p - d)$, if p is greater than d, while the top spigot is open. The maximum water level would be determined by multiplying the buildup rate (p − d, in gallons per hour) by the time period the top spigot is open (Q/p, in hours). After the entire desired quantity of water (Q) is delivered, the top spigot is

Figure 9.11
Average Inventory Level in Model II

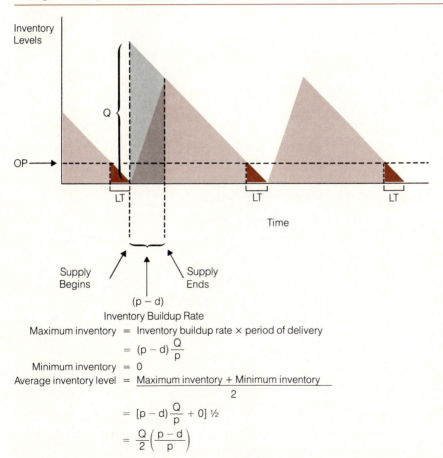

$$\text{Maximum inventory} = \text{Inventory buildup rate} \times \text{period of delivery}$$
$$= (p - d)\frac{Q}{p}$$
$$\text{Minimum inventory} = 0$$
$$\text{Average inventory level} = \frac{\text{Maximum inventory} + \text{Minimum inventory}}{2}$$
$$= [p - d]\frac{Q}{p} + 0]\ \tfrac{1}{2}$$
$$= \frac{Q}{2}\left(\frac{p - d}{p}\right)$$

closed and the tank is emptied at a rate of d. This analogy describes the dynamics of inventory levels when orders of materials are delivered gradually.

When materials are delivered gradually to either finished goods or raw materials inventories, two important developments result — larger order quantities and lower total annual stocking costs. Example 9.3 demonstrates these developments. Work through this example and compare the results to those of Example 9.2. Note that EOQ increases from 524.40 units to 642.26 units per order and TSC decreases from $209.76 to $171.26 per year as deliveries switch from orders received all at once in Example 9.2 to gradual deliveries of orders in Example 9.3.

Example 9.3

Use of Model II in a Plumbing Supply Company

Mr. Swartz of the Don't Cuss — Call Us Plumbing Supply Company wonders what effect on annual stocking costs will result if he allows his supplier to deliver the #3925 valve orders gradually rather than all at once. Mary Ann Church analyzes this request and develops these estimates: $D = 10,000$ valves per year, $C = \$.40$ per valve per year, $S = \$5.50$ per order, $d = 40$ valves per day (10,000 valves per year $\div$ 250 working days), and $p = 120$ valves per day.

Solution

1. Mary Ann calculates the EOQ:

$$EOQ = \sqrt{\frac{2DS}{C}\left(\frac{p}{p-d}\right)} = \sqrt{\frac{2(10,000)(5.5)}{.4}\left(\frac{120}{120-40}\right)} = 642.26 \text{ valves}$$

2. The new total annual stocking costs are calculated:

$$TSC_3 = Q/2\left(\frac{p-d}{p}\right)C + (D/Q)S = \frac{642.26}{2}\left(\frac{120-40}{120}\right).4 + \left(\frac{10,000}{642.26}\right)5.5$$

$$= 85.63 + 85.63 = \$171.26 \text{ per year}$$

3. The EOQ and total annual stocking costs from Example 9.2, when the #3925 valves were delivered all at once, were $EOQ = 524.4$ and $TSC_2 = \$209.76$.

4. The estimated savings to the plumbing supply company for allowing its supplier to deliver the #3925 valve gradually are calculated:

$$\text{Savings} = TSC_2 - TSC_3 = 209.76 - 171.26 = \$38.50 \text{ per year}$$

5. Mary Ann concluded the supplier should be allowed to deliver the #3925 valves gradually.

Model II is particularly useful in situations where products must be ordered from a production department within the organization. Production usually occurs at a specific rate greater than demand ($p > d$) and finished products are typically transferred gradually from production to finished goods inventory as they are produced. Therefore, this model is well suited for planning length of production runs for in-house production of products.

High-volume materials that are received in a specific shipping schedule arrangement often also fit the assumptions of Model II. The estimations of annual demand, demand rate, and supply rate are the principal variables affecting the precision of the computed optimal order quantity of this model.

Model III — EOQ with Quantity Discounts A critical concern in most decisions of order quantities is ordering enough material on each order to qualify for the best

---

Table 9.5
Model III — EOQ with Quantity Discounts

Assumptions

1. Annual demand, carrying cost, and ordering cost for a material can be estimated with precision.
2. Average inventory levels can be estimated at either:

   $Q/2$ — If the assumptions of Model I prevail: no safety stock, orders are received all at once, materials are used at a uniform rate, and materials are entirely used up when the next order arrives.

   $Q/2\left(\dfrac{p-d}{p}\right)$ — If the assumptions of Model II prevail: no safety stock, materials are supplied at a uniform rate (p) and used at a uniform rate (d), and materials are entirely used up when the next order arrives.

3. There are no stockout costs.
4. Quantity discounts do exist. As larger quantities are ordered, price breaks apply to all units ordered.

Variable Definitions

All the definitions in previous models apply to Model III.* Additionally:

TMC = Total annual material costs (dollars per year)

   ac = Acquisition cost of either purchasing or producing one unit of a material (dollars per unit)

Formulas

The EOQ and TSC formulas from either Model I or Model II are applied to Model III, depending upon which assumptions best fit the inventory situation.

$$\text{Annual acquisition costs} = \text{Annual demand} \times \text{Acquisition cost} = (D)ac$$

Total annual material costs (TMC) = Total annual stocking costs + Annual acquisition cost = TSC + (D)ac

Model I — Orders Delivered All at One Time	*Model II — Gradual Deliveries*
$EOQ = \sqrt{\dfrac{2DS}{C}}$	$EOQ = \sqrt{\dfrac{2DS}{C}\left(\dfrac{p}{p-d}\right)}$
$TMC = \left(\dfrac{Q}{2}\right)C + \left(\dfrac{D}{Q}\right)S + (D)ac$	$TMC = \dfrac{Q}{2}\left(\dfrac{p-d}{p}\right)C + \left(\dfrac{D}{Q}\right)S + (D)ac$

Procedures

1. Compute the EOQ using each of the sales prices. Note that C is usually a function of sales price. For example, C may be defined as 20 percent of sales price. Therefore, EOQ will change as C and ac change.
2. Determine which EOQ from Step 1 above is feasible. In other words, is the computed EOQ in the quantity range for its price?
3. The total annual material cost (TMC) is computed for the feasible EOQ and the lowest quantity of any volume ranges with lower sales prices.
4. The order quantity with the lowest total annual material cost (TMC) is the economic order quantity for the material.

---

* Note: See the note to Table 9.3.

Quantities	Prices	Feasible EOQ	Key Quantities to Investigate	Quantities	Prices	Feasible EOQ	Key Quantities to Investigate
0–399	$ 2.20			0–499	$ 6.95		
400–699	2.00	524.4	524.4	500–999	6.50		
700+	1.80		700	1,000–1,999	6.25	1,700	1,700
				2,000+	6.10		2,000
0–699	$43.50	590	590	0–599	$10.50		
700–1,499	36.95		700	600–749	7.50		
1,500+	35.50		1,500	750–999	7.25		
				1,000+	7.15	1,200	1,200

price possible, but not buying so much that carrying costs consume the savings in purchase costs. Model III attempts to achieve this objective: select the order quantity that minimizes the total annual costs of stocking and purchasing the material — total annual material costs (TMC). Table 9.5 lists the assumptions, formulas, and procedures of this model.

Model III utilizes either Model I or Model II TSC and EOQ formulas. If deliveries of orders occur all at once, Model I formulas are used. If deliveries are gradual, Model II formulas are used. Read the procedures of this model carefully. It is particularly important to recognize that the key quantities to consider are any feasible EOQ (the EOQ can actually be purchased for the price used to compute C in the EOQ formula) and any other minimum quantities of lower prices. Table 9.6 gives four different quantity discount/order quantity decision situations to demonstrate the procedures for identifying the quantities to be investigated by comparing the total annual material costs (TMC).

Example 9.4 applies Model III to our old friends at the plumbing supply company. In this example the manager must decide both the quantity and method of delivery — either gradual deliveries or orders received all at once — for one material. Follow through the steps of this example. It demonstrates both the procedures of Model III and the advantages accruing to gradual deliveries.

Example 9.4

EOQ with Quantity Discounts in a Plumbing Supply Company

The supplier of the #3925 valve has offered Mr. Swartz quantity discounts if he will purchase more than his present order quantities. The new volumes and prices are:

Range of Order Quantities	Acquisition Cost per Valve (ac)
0–399	$2.20
400–699	$2.00
700+	$1.80

Mr. Swartz asks Mary Ann Church to investigate the new prices under two sets of assumptions: Orders are received all at once or gradually.

Solution

Orders Received All at Once

1. Mary Ann has developed these estimates: $D = 10,000$ valves per year, $C = .2$ (ac) dollars per valve per year, and $S = \$5.50$ per order.

2. The EOQs are computed for each of the acquisition costs:

$$EOQ_{2.20} = \sqrt{\frac{2DS}{C}} = \sqrt{\frac{2(10,000)(5.5)}{.2(2.2)}} = 500$$

$$EOQ_{2.00} = \sqrt{\frac{2DS}{C}} = \sqrt{\frac{2(10,000)(5.5)}{.2(2.0)}} = 524.4$$

$$EOQ_{1.80} = \sqrt{\frac{2DS}{C}} = \sqrt{\frac{2(10,000)(5.5)}{.2(1.8)}} = 552.8$$

3. Mary Ann notes that only $EOQ_{2.00}$ is feasible because 524.4 valves per order can be purchased at \$2.00 per valve. The TMC at two quantities is therefore investigated: 524.4 and 700 units per order:

$$Q = 524.4: \quad TMC = \left(\frac{Q}{2}\right)C + \left(\frac{D}{Q}\right)S + (D)ac = \left(\frac{524.4}{2}\right).4 + \left(\frac{10,000}{524.4}\right)5.5 + (10,000)2$$

$$= 104.88 + 104.88 + 20,000 = \$20,209.76 \text{ per year}$$

$$Q = 700: \quad TMC = \left(\frac{Q}{2}\right)C + \left(\frac{D}{Q}\right)S + (D)ac$$

$$= \left(\frac{700}{2}\right)(.2 \times 1.8) + \left(\frac{10,000}{700}\right)5.5 + (10,000)1.8$$

$$= 126.00 + 78.57 + 18,000 = \$18,204.57 \text{ per year}$$

4. Mary Ann concludes that if orders are delivered all at once, then 700 valves should be ordered at each inventory replenishment.

Gradual Deliveries

1. Mary Ann has developed these estimates: $D = 10,000$ valves per year, $S = \$5.50$ per order, $C = .2$ (ac) dollars per valve per year, $p = 120$ valves per day, and $d = 40$ valves per day.

2. The EOQs are now computed:

$$EOQ_{2.20} = \sqrt{\frac{2DS}{C}\left(\frac{p}{p-d}\right)} = \sqrt{\frac{2(10,000)(5.5)}{.2(2.2)}\left(\frac{120}{120-40}\right)} = 612.4$$

$$EOQ_{2.00} = \sqrt{\frac{2DS}{C}\left(\frac{p}{p-d}\right)} = \sqrt{\frac{2(10,000)(5.5)}{.2(2.0)}\left(\frac{120}{120-40}\right)} = 642.3$$

$$EOQ_{1.80} = \sqrt{\frac{2DS}{C}\left(\frac{p}{p-d}\right)} = \sqrt{\frac{2(10,000)(5.5)}{.2(1.8)}\left(\frac{120}{120-40}\right)} = 677.0$$

3. Mary Ann notes that only $EOQ_{2.00}$ is feasible because 642.3 valves per order can be purchased at \$2.00 per valve. Two quantities are investigated, 642.3 and 700 units per order:

$$Q = 642.3: \quad TMC = \frac{Q}{2}\left(\frac{p-d}{p}\right)C + \left(\frac{D}{Q}\right)S + (D)ac$$

$$= \frac{642.3}{2}\left(\frac{120-40}{120}\right)(.2 \times 2.0) + \left(\frac{10,000}{642.3}\right)5.5 + (10,000)2.0$$

$$= 85.63 + 85.63 + 20,000 = \$20,171.26 \text{ per year}$$

$$Q = 700: \quad TMC = \frac{Q}{2}\left(\frac{p-d}{p}\right)C + \left(\frac{D}{Q}\right)S + (D)ac$$

$$= \frac{700}{2}\left(\frac{120-40}{120}\right)(.2 \times 1.8) + \left(\frac{10,000}{700}\right)5.5 + (10,000)1.8$$

$$= 84.00 + 78.57 + 18,000 = \$18,162.57 \text{ per year}$$

4. Mary Ann concludes that if gradual deliveries are used, 700 units per order should be purchased.

5. Given a choice, Mr. Swartz would prefer to have gradual deliveries of #3925 valves in quantities of 700 units per order because the TMC of gradual deliveries is less than that for orders delivered all at once.

Quantity discounts, when used with the EOQ formulas, begin to build more realism into these methods of analysis. Although some restrictive assumptions are still present in Model III, enough real inventory decisions approach the assumptions of this model to make it a valuable technique in POM. We have now estimated order quantities for materials in fixed order quantity inventory systems that operate under various assumptions. Let us now turn to the other fundamental issue in inventory planning — when to place the order.

Setting Order Points In fixed order quantity inventory systems, orders for materials are triggered by a perpetual inventory counting system when inventory levels fall to an established critical level. Five factors generally influence the setting of order points: (1) expected demand per day for the material during lead time, (2) variability or uncertainty of the demand per day, (3) expected lead time for the materials, (4) variability or uncertainty of the lead time, and (5) relative undesirability of stockouts. Order points are determined by first estimating the expected demand during lead time (EDDLT) — the product of average demand per day times the average lead time. The order point may equal the EDDLT at one extreme if the demand per day and lead time are relatively certain and if stockouts are not particularly undesirable. However, if stockouts are undesirable and demand and lead time are relatively uncertain, the order point is determined by adding a safety stock to the EDDLT:

Order point = EDDLT + Safety stock

In a general sense this equation always applies and safety stock in practice is observed to vary from zero to two or three times the EDDLT. Expected demand during lead time for a material can sometimes be estimated from historical records. The difficult part of setting order points is deciding on the proper amount of safety stock. Presented here are some rules of thumb used to set safety stock levels for raw material and finished goods inventories.

Percentage of EDDLT Perhaps the most common method involves setting safety stock levels at a percentage of EDDLT:

Order point = EDDLT + j(EDDLT), where j = a factor that varies from zero to 3.00

Materials are usually categorized according to classifications such as these:

Class	Description	j
1	Uncritical	.10
2	Uncertain – uncritical	.20
3	Critical	.30
4	Uncertain – critical	.50
5	Supercritical	1.00
6	Uncertain – supercritical	2.00

Classifications such as these would be custom-designed for a firm's inventory system and uniformly applied to most materials in finished goods and raw material inventories.

Square Root of EDDLT Another approach sets order points by uniformly applying this formula to all materials:

Order point = $EDDLT + \sqrt{EDDLT}$

This method selects safety stock levels that are large relative to EDDLT when EDDLT is small, but safety stocks are relatively small when EDDLT is large. This approach is usually applied when stockouts are not particularly undesirable or costly.

The percentage of EDDLT and square root of EDDLT methods for setting order points are demonstrated in Example 9.5. Although these methods are rough rules of thumb used in industry today, more precise methods do exist for setting order points; these methods are covered in the supplement to this chapter.

Example 9.5

Setting Order Points for Castings in Finished Goods Inventory for DAPPLE Manufacturing Company

DAPPLE Manufacturing Company produces bronze castings. One casting, #699, is held in inventory until customers order them from DAPPLE. Mr. George Dapple, DAPPLE's materials manager, is dabbling with various approaches to setting order points for materials. The #699 casting is selected as the principal material for investigation in the study. The following data were collected on #699: average demand per day is 6 castings; and average lead time is 10 days, the time needed to produce a lot of castings. Mr. Dapple's study requires the following: **a.** If safety stock is set at 20 percent of EDDLT, what is the order point? **b.** If safety stock is set at square root of EDDLT, what is the order point?

Solution

a. Order Point = EDDLT + .2 (EDDLT)

= Average demand per day $\times$ Average lead time + .2 (EDDLT)

= 6.0 (10) + .2 (6.0 $\times$ 10) = 60 + 12 = 72 castings

b. Order point = EDDLT + $\sqrt{\text{EDDLT}}$ = 60 + $\sqrt{60}$ = 60 + 7.75 = 67.75, or 68 castings

In Example 9.5 the two methods of computing order points develop safety stocks of 12 and 8 castings. Which one is correct? Both are mathematically correct, but the correctness of each of the order points can be tested only by experimentation—choose one and keep records on DDLT as time passes. This is the only true test of an order point: Does the safety stock give the level of protection against stockouts that is desired?

How does the use of safety stocks affect the order quantity (EOQ) in a fixed order quantity inventory system? Minimally if at all! However, total annual stocking costs would change because safety stocks cause these developments:

1. Increased annual carrying costs. This results from the fact that safety stocks are considered as dead stock: on the average they are never used. The additional inventory therefore results in higher annual carrying costs.

2. Lower annual stockout costs. The basic EOQ models do not include stockout costs, and for good reason: they are difficult to estimate. But conceptually we know that the costs of stockouts are real, and these would be reduced by safety stocks.

We have considered the determination of optimal order quantities and some rough estimates of order points in fixed order quantity inventory systems for both raw material and finished goods inventories. Let us now briefly consider techniques for computing optimal order periods in fixed order period inventory systems.

Fixed Order Period Systems

The selection of an optimal order period for materials in either raw material or finished goods inventories is the key determinant of the effectiveness of fixed order period inventory systems. If materials are reviewed too often, and therefore ordered too often, annual ordering costs and total annual stocking costs are excessive. On

---

Table 9.7
Model IV — Economic Order Period

Assumptions

1. Annual demand, carrying cost, and ordering cost for a material can be estimated with precision.
2. Average inventory is average order size divided by two. This implicitly assumes no safety stock, orders are received all at once, materials are used at a uniform rate, and materials are used up on the average when the next order is received.
3. There are no stockout costs.
4. Quantity discounts do not exist.

Variable Definitions

The variable definitions in Model I apply here.* Additionally:
T = Time between orders in fraction of a year

Cost Formulas

$$\text{Annual carrying costs} = \text{Average inventory} \times \text{Carrying cost} = \left(\frac{DT}{2}\right)C$$

$$\text{Annual ordering costs} = \text{Number of orders per year} \times \text{Cost per order} = \left(\frac{D}{DT}\right)S = \frac{S}{T}$$

$$\text{Total annual stocking costs (TSC)} = \text{Annual carrying costs} + \text{Annual ordering costs} = \left(\frac{DT}{2}\right)C + \frac{S}{T}$$

Optimal Order Period Formula

1. Set annual carrying costs equal to annual ordering costs:
$$\left(\frac{DT}{2}\right)C = \frac{S}{T}$$

2. Multiply both sides of equality by T:
$$T^2\left(\frac{DC}{2}\right) = S$$

3. Divide both sides of equality by $DC/2$:
$$T^2 = \frac{2S}{DC}$$

4. Take the square root of both sides of equality:
$$T = \sqrt{\frac{2S}{DC}}$$

---

* Note: See the note to Table 9.3.

the other hand, if the time between reviews of materials is too long, annual carrying costs and total annual stocking costs are too high and the probability of stockouts is increased. Therefore, we want to select an optimal time interval between reviewing materials so that annual carrying costs are exactly balanced against annual ordering costs. It is at this time interval that total annual stocking costs are minimal.

Table 9.7 states the assumptions and variable definitions and develops the cost formulas and optimal order period formula for Model IV — fixed order periods. When we have estimated the optimal order period, only one other important consideration is necessary in these systems — the order quantity. The determination of order quantity is straightforward:

Order quantity = Maximum inventory target − Inventory level + EDDLT

Order quantity is computed by subtracting the inventory level of the material under examination from the maximum inventory target (including safety stock) and adding the expected demand during lead time. This basic computation can also be adapted to include materials that are promised but not shipped, large customer orders expected in the near future, and so on. These amounts would be added onto the order quantity.

Example 9.6 applies the formulas for optimal order period and order quantity of this model to one material in a wholesaling company. Note that T, the optimal time interval for reviewing the status of a material and placing a material order, is expressed as a fraction of a year. This value must be adjusted to days, weeks, or months as desired. Note also that T is a computation that would be made only about once a year, whereas order quantity computations must be made for each order. In other words, T remains fixed for a long time and Q is allowed to vary from order to order.

Example 9.6

Optimal Order Period in Fixed Order Period Inventory System

The C, D & F Retailing Company routinely reviews the inventory levels of its products on display monthly and places orders for these products, if needed, from their suppliers. Mr. Bill Bailey, the regional manager, wonders if monthly reviews are optimal when considering both carrying costs and order costs.

One product is selected to be the focus of investigation — Goo-Goo, a jarred baby food cereal. The following information was developed for Goo-Goo: D = 29,385 jars per year, C = 30 pecent of acquisition cost, ac = $.29 per jar, and S = $10.90 per order. **a.** How often should Goo-Goo be ordered? **b.** At the first review after T has been computed in part *a*, if inventory level = 985 jars, maximum inventory target (including safety stock) = 3,220 jars, and expected demand during lead time = 805 jars, how many jars should be ordered?

Solution

a. $C = .3 \times .29$

$$T = \sqrt{\frac{2S}{DC}} = \sqrt{\frac{2(10.9)}{(29,385)(.3 \times .29)}} = .0923 \text{ years} = 33.7 \text{ days}$$

b. Order quantity = Maximum inventory target − Inventory level + EDDLT
$$= 3,220 - 985 + 805 = 3,040 \text{ jars}$$

The following generalizations can be deduced from the formula for T:

1. More expensive materials are reviewed more frequently.
2. Materials with higher usage rates are reviewed more frequently.
3. Materials with higher ordering costs are ordered less frequently.

These observations seem to be rational criteria for determining order intervals for materials.

We have now discussed order quantities, order points, and optimal order periods. Table 9.8 summarizes the models developed for these decisions. These are the fundamental issues in inventory planning, and our approach to these issues has been very traditional. Let us now discuss what we have done thus far in this chapter in view of the realities of today's productive systems.

Some Realities of Inventory Planning

The fundamentals of inventory planning are just that — fundamentals, basics, rules of thumb, and starting points for further study. We need to examine these fundamentals as practicing operations managers view them — in the light of the realistic conditions found in real world productive systems.

ABC Classification of Materials Not all materials are subjected to the analyses presented in this chapter, but others are analyzed much more intensely than covered here. What determines which materials receive intensive analysis and which ones receive little if any analysis? **Let's apply the 80–20 rule to inventories: in any aggregation of items, 20 percent of the items will account for 80 percent of a given characteristic.**

This rule, when used in inventory planning, states that only about 20 percent of the materials found in inventories account for about 80 percent of the total dollar value of the inventory. Now, strictly speaking, no one would argue these precise figures, but we do find in remarkable frequency that 15 to 25 percent of the materials in inventory do account for 75 to 85 percent of the value of inventory. Figure 9.12 shows that the ABC method of classifying materials actually is based upon the

Table 9.8
Summary of Inventory Planning Models

Variable Definitions

ac = Acquisition cost — cost of producing or purchasing one unit of a material (dollars per unit)

C = Carrying cost — cost of carrying one unit in inventory for one year (dollars per unit per year)

D = Annual demand for a material (units per year)

d = Rate at which materials are used out of inventory (units per time period)

DDLT = Demand during lead time (units)

EDDLT = Expected demand during lead time (units)

EOQ = Economic order quantity — the optimal quantity of material to order (units per order)

OP = Order point — the point at which materials should be ordered (units or point in time)

p = Rate at which materials are supplied to inventory (same units as d)

Q = Quantity of material ordered at each order point (units per order)

S = Average cost of completing an order for a material (dollars per order)

T = Order period — the time interval between orders for a material (fraction of a year)

TMC = Total annual material costs — the total annual costs of stocking and acquiring a material (dollars per year)

TSC = Total annual stocking costs — the total of annual carrying and annual ordering costs for a material (dollars per year)

Formulas

Fixed Order Quantity Inventory Systems

Model I — Basic EOQ (see Example 9.2)

$$EOQ = \sqrt{\frac{2DS}{C}} \qquad TSC = \left(\frac{Q}{2}\right)C + \left(\frac{D}{Q}\right)S$$

Model II — EOQ with Gradual Deliveries (see Example 9.3)

$$EOQ = \sqrt{\frac{2DS}{C}\left(\frac{p}{p-d}\right)}$$

$$TSC = \frac{Q}{2}\left(\frac{p-d}{p}\right)C + \left(\frac{D}{Q}\right)S$$

Order Points (see Example 9.5)

OP = EDDLT + j(EDDLT)   Percentage of EDDLT

OP = EDDLT + $\sqrt{EDDLT}$ Square root of EDDLT

Model III — EOQ with Quantity Discounts (see Example 9.4)

When assumptions of Model I apply:

$$EOQ = \sqrt{\frac{2DS}{C}} \qquad TMC = \left(\frac{Q}{2}\right)C + \left(\frac{D}{Q}\right)S + (D)ac$$

When assumptions of Model II apply:

$$EOQ = \sqrt{\frac{2DS}{C}\left(\frac{p}{p-d}\right)}$$

$$TMC = \frac{Q}{2}\left(\frac{p-d}{p}\right)C + \left(\frac{D}{Q}\right)S + (D)ac$$

In either case the procedures of Table 9.5 must be followed.

Fixed Order Period System

Model IV — Economic Order Period (see Example 9.6)

$$T = \sqrt{\frac{2S}{DC}} \qquad TSC = \left(\frac{DT}{2}\right)C + \frac{S}{T}$$

Q = Maximum inventory target − Inventory level + EDDLT

80 – 20 rule. These observations about the ABC classification explain the interpretation of this figure:

1. The A materials represent 20 percent of the materials in inventory and 75 percent of the inventory value.
2. The B materials represent 30 percent of the materials in inventory and 20 percent of the inventory value.
3. The A and B materials represent 50 percent of the materials in inventory and 95 percent of the inventory value.
4. The C materials represent 50 percent of the materials in inventory and 5 percent of the inventory value.

Figure 9.12
ABC Classification of Materials

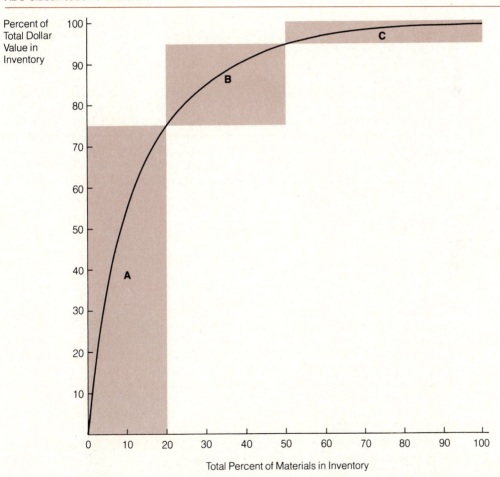

Percent of Total Dollar Value in Inventory

Total Percent of Materials in Inventory

This perhaps oversimplified classification suggests this question: What analysis is justified with each of these classes of materials? We would generalize by saying that the more inventory value a material represents, the more precision and more analysis can be justified. Class A materials would be analyzed extensively, Class B would be analyzed moderately, and Class C materials would be analyzed little if at all.

On the surface, linking levels of analysis to the value of inventories might seem reasonable, but be careful. Although it is true that we don't spend much time on analyzing order quantities and order points for paper clips, other relatively inexpensive materials can cause severe problems to productive systems if we experience stockouts. Similarly, some inexpensive items such as plastic moldings are subject to rapidly changing designs and these are usually ordered in small quantities with care taken to not be overstocked. Dollar value is an important consideration in classifying materials but other factors such as obsolescence, deterioration, and length of lead times must also be considered.

EOQ and Uncertainty Throughout this chapter, uncertainties have lurked just below the surface. Annual demand, usage patterns, usage rates, carrying costs, ordering costs, and stockout costs — these are all uncertain in most inventory planning situations.

Take annual demand, carrying costs, and ordering costs, for example. If we are in error when we estimate these values, what is the effect upon our order quantity decision? Look at Figure 9.9 again. Note that estimation errors in D, C, or S would move us to the right or left along the total annual stocking costs curve for a material. Moving in either direction increases our annual costs for stocking a material. In most circumstances this curve tends to be rather flat near the EOQ. For example, in Figure 9.9 if we order 400 or 600 units per order rather than 524 units, the EOQ, the total annual stocking costs would be:

Q	TSC
400	$217.50
524	$209.60
600	$211.67

The total impact of errors in estimating Q for one material does not appear to be critical. If, however, tens of thousands of items are carried in inventory, this could expand the impact of estimation errors to the critical point. Additionally, when quantity discounts are present, total annual costs can be much higher if we order the wrong quantity by just a slight amount.

Of perhaps greater concern to inventory decisions in POM is the cost of stockouts. Much of the cost of stockouts may be profits forgone in lost sales, lost customer goodwill, interruption of production schedules, and other costs that are impossible to precisely determine. The inability to precisely quantify the costs of stockouts does not deter us from conceptually including them in our inventory planning in POM. We know that stockouts are costly and thus we attempt to avoid them. Safety stocks are routinely carried on most materials, but even these buffer stocks cannot eliminate stockouts entirely. The uncertainty of usage rates and usage patterns causes us to run out of stock periodically.

Another pragmatic POM tactic is to devise means to replenish inventories quickly through emergency procedures. These emergency procedures usually allow us to avoid stockouts and carry lower levels of safety stocks. One good example of the use of emergency replenishment procedures is in hospitals. Many hospitals in the Western states have National Guard helicopters available on extremely short notice to supply critical materials as needed from other hospitals or hospital supply warehouses. These procedures are necessary because many hospital materials, such as whole blood, for example, have such short shelf lives that only a few of these materials are ordered at a time. When unexpected demand for these materials forces inventory levels too low, emergency procedures can usually deliver the materials within a couple of hours. Although inventory planners in manufacturing may not have helicopters flying in emergency supplies of materials, other less drastic emergency procedures do exist to allow these systems to successfully meet the uncertainties of demand and to avoid stockouts or at least minimize their impact.

Dynamics of Inventory Planning Order quantities in fixed order quantity inventory systems may not be as fixed as we have led you to believe in this chapter. Although we suggested that hybrid systems exist that do not operate with fixed order quantities, we should probably add that so-called fixed order quantities may be rare in practice. Almost all inventory systems continually review their ordering practices and modify order quantities, order points, and time intervals as required to give the kind of inventory performance desired in their particular situation. When we view inventory planning as a dynamic system that is continually modified as needed, less emphasis must be placed on any one computation. This view makes us realize that we do not have to live with a computed order quantity from now on.

Actually, although many firms say that they use EOQ as the basis for setting order quantities, they are observed in practice to set *initial* order quantities based on tradition, rough estimates, or other means. This is not surprising or particularly disturbing because these decisions are continually modified as time passes; order quantities are increased or decreased to fit their demand and supply patterns and thus the inventory systems empirically develop order quantities and order points that work. Neither excessive stockouts nor excessive inventories result.

Other Factors Affecting Inventory Planning The principal variables included in the models of this chapter for developing order points, order quantities, and time intervals were annual demand, carrying costs, ordering costs, production and demand rates, and quantity discounts. These factors are important but in practice other variables also operate in these decisions.

The quantity of a material that *can* be ordered may be determined by the capacity of an organization's warehouse. In the models of this chapter, warehouse capacity was implicitly assumed to be infinite or otherwise not a limiting factor. Another factor that may severely limit the size that an order for products *can* be is the capacity of the production department and the production schedules for other products. Once production schedules are set, they often cannot be changed quickly to work in an optimal order size for a material. We must often take the quantity of a material or product that we can get and not what we want because production capacity cannot be altered quickly, and the production department and its schedules are committed to producing quantities of other products.

Another factor than can give us more products or materials than we in POM would actually like to order is special buys on materials. When purchasing discovers a special buy, the savings from quantity discounts are often so spectacular that we just have to buy all we can get of that material. Many instances exist where we buy one or two years of supply of material on one order. Although this tends to play havoc with our warehousing and increases our annual carrying costs, ordering costs fall and the savings in purchase costs may be so great that we occasionally make these special buys.

These and other factors act on our order quantity and order point decisions in POM practice. These factors do not destroy the usefulness of the models presented in this chapter, but the results of these models are often modified as these other factors operate in the practical day-to-day operation of productive systems.

Automation and Inventory Planning   One of the first areas in business to receive the benefits of computerization was inventory planning. Computers' ability to store and retrieve huge quantities of information and to make lightning-quick and accurate calculations made them an almost sure success in inventory planning.

Today, inventory stock records are routinely maintained in the memory of computer systems. As changes in inventory levels occur, the computer files are modified to reflect the latest inventory transactions. Managers can query these files and instantaneously determine the status of each material's inventory level, what orders are outstanding, and other information critical to inventory management.

Order quantities, when orders should be placed, and automatic printing of purchase requisitions and purchase orders are routinely performed by computers in some organizations today. Now don't get the wrong idea — we can't totally turn over these inventory planning decisions to computers. Someone must still describe in detail the basis for order quantities (EOQ, etc.) and order points (EDDLT $+ .3 \times$ EDDLT, and so on). Computers just speed up the process and complete the calculations more quickly and accurately.

Complete computer software packages have been developed by the major computer producers and other software specialists that perform a wide range of inventory management functions. IBM's Inventory Management Program and Control Techniques (IMPACT), IBM's Communications Oriented Production Information and Control System (COPICS), and similar packages from Control Data Corporation, Xerox Computer Services, and other suppliers provide broad management information systems for operations managers. Not only do these and similar packages provide inventory planning information, this information is also integrated with other areas of the organization so that decisions about financial planning, production scheduling, and other critical areas are all considered when inventory decisions are made. This broader picture of how inventory planning and production scheduling, for example, are related and how a decision in inventory planning affects production scheduling and vice versa will be further developed in later chapters.

Summary

Materials management involves the management of material flows from the purchase and internal control, to the planning and control of work-in-process, to the warehousing, shipping, and distribution of finished products. Purchasing departments buy the materials for productive systems — any commodity used directly or indirectly in producing products or services. Logistics is the management of the shipment of all materials to the productive system and all finished goods to customers. Warehousing is the management of materials within productive facilities from the point where or when they are received until they are shipped as finished goods to customers. The materials system does not always act as planned: shipments from suppliers are delayed, customers' orders are greater than expected, materials are not processed in production as planned, and workers make mistakes. Expediting is the activity of solving these problems: some orders are moved ahead of others, different shipping methods are used, and other corrective actions are taken.

The inventory cycle is the central focus in traditional inventory planning. Materials are ordered, delivered, used, and the cycle is repeated. The key issues of inventory planning are how much to order of each material and when to place the order. Fixed order quantity inventory systems place orders for materials that involve fixed quantities from order to order. In these systems, material orders are triggered when inventory levels fall to an established critical level, the order point. In fixed order period inventory systems, material orders are placed at equal time intervals for enough materials to last approximately until the next material review. Traditional inventory theory attempts to balance the cost of carrying too much inventory (annual carrying costs) against the cost of carrying too little inventory (annual stockout and annual ordering costs).

Although the total annual stocking costs of materials is an important criterion for making inventory planning decisions, other factors can also be important. Among these are warehouse capacity, production schedules and capacity, and special buys on materials. Automation and computers play an increasing role in inventory planning.

Review and Discussion Questions

1. Define *materials, materials systems,* and *materials management.*

2. Define the position of a materials manager.

3. Describe these purchasing instruments or forms: **a.** material specification, **b.** purchase requisition, **c.** request for quotation, and **d.** purchase order.

4. Explain the procedures for purchasing these classes of purchases: **a.** high-volume continuously supplied materials, **b.** large unique purchases, **c.** small purchases, and **d.** regular purchases.

5. What is reciprocity?

6. Define *logistics.* Why have quantitative analyses been so often applied to logistics?

7. Define *warehousing.* What two fundamental questions must be answered in stocking materials in inventory?

8. Define *expediting.* Why is expediting necessary?

9. Name three purposes of carrying these inventories: **a.** finished goods, **b.** in-process, and **c.** raw material.

10. Define these terms: **a.** *backlogging,* **b.** *produce-to-order,* **c.** *produce-to-stock,*

d. *levelized production,* **e.** *order quantities,* **f.** *order points,* **g.** *inventory cycle,* **h.** *machine changeovers,* **i.** *length of production runs,* **j.** *uncoupling operations,* **k.** *lot sizes,* **l.** *order period,* **m.** *two-bin system.*

11. Compare and contrast fixed order quantity inventory systems with fixed order period inventory systems.

12. Define these terms: **a.** *carrying costs,* **b.** *ordering costs,* **c.** *stockout costs,* **d.** *annual carrying costs,* **e.** *annual ordering costs,* **f.** *total annual stocking costs.*

13. Name four assumptions of the basic EOQ — Model I.

14. Name five assumptions of the EOQ with gradual deliveries — Model II.

15. What units are these variables in? **a.** D, **b.** S, **c.** C, **d.** Q, **e.** EOQ, **f.** p, **g.** d.

16. Why is the maximum inventory level of a material greater when orders are received all at once than when orders are received gradually?

17. What are the purposes of safety stock? How will the use of safety stock affect the EOQ? How will the use of safety stock affect TSC?

18. What factors other than total annual stocking costs typically affect Q and T in practice?

Field Projects

1. Make an appointment with a materials manager or a manager directly affiliated with a materials system from one of these organizations: **a.** manufacturing — such as a maker of clothing, **b.** manufacturing — such as chemical processing, **c.** hospital, **d.** retailing, **e.** trucking, or **f.** warehousing. Interview this manager and define completely the three most important material problems that plague his or her organization.

2. From any organization interview one person from this list: **a.** purchasing agent, **b.** purchasing buyer, **c.** traffic or logistics manager, **d.** warehousing manager, or **e.** expediter. Determine as completely as possible the person's duties as viewed by the employee.

3. Interview a purchasing buyer from any organization. Determine the buyer's idea of what is and what is not ethical buying behavior relative to gifts. Do you agree or disagree with his/her point of view? Why or why not?

4. From any organization interview one person from this list: **a.** purchasing agent, **b.** traffic or logistics manager, **c.** warehouse manager, or **d.** expediter. What new developments are expected to have an important effect on the performance of this employee's duties witin the next five years? How will the person's duties be affected by these developments?

Problems

Model I — The Basic EOQ

1. Given: D = 5,000 units per year, C = $1 per unit per year, and S = $100 per order. Required: **a.** EOQ and **b.** TSC at EOQ.

2. Given: D = 300,000 units per year, C = 30 percent of acquisition cost per unit per year, S = $5.95 per order, and ac = $1.50 per unit. Required: **a.** EOQ and **b.** TSC at EOQ.

3. The Zartex Manufacturing Company produces ammonium nitrate fertilizer to sell to wholesalers. One raw material — calcium nitrite — is purchased from one supplier located near Zartex's plant; 5,750,000 tons of calcium nitrite are forecast to be required next year to support production. If calcium nitrite costs $22.50 per ton, carrying cost is 40 percent of acquisition cost, and ordering cost is $595 per order: **a.** In what quantities should Zartex buy calcium nitrite? **b.** What annual stocking cost will be incurred if calcium nitrite is ordered at EOQ? **c.** How many orders per year must Zartex place for calcium nitrite?

4. The Shady Lane Savings and Loan Company orders cash from its home office to meet daily counter transactions. If Shady Lane estimates that $5,000,000 will be needed next year, each order for cash costs $650, which includes clerical and armored car delivery costs, and idle cash costs 10 percent: **a.** What quantities of cash should Shady Lane include on each order? **b.** What total annual stocking costs would result from Shady Lane's following your recommendation in part *a*? **c.** How many days could Shady Lane operate with each order of cash if it stayed open 250 days a year and cash were ordered at the EOQ?

5. SWIMCO, a swimming pool retail supply firm in Phoenix, stocks pelletized chlorine that is sold to local pool owners. Chlorine is ordered from a regional wholesaler in Los Angeles at a uniform price of $95.60 per 100 pounds. Thirty tons of chlorine are estimated to be needed next year. SWIMCO orders chlorine in the 0–5,000 pounds per order range. Carrying costs are 30 percent of acquisition cost per pound per year, and ordering cost is $55 per order. If chlorine is ordered in quantities greater than 5,000 pounds, carrying cost falls to 20 percent of acquisition cost per pound per year because the supplier gives special late payment privileges which reduce the interest charges that must ordinarily be paid to finance the chlorine inventory at a local bank, but ordering cost increases to $75 per order because of extra handling costs. How many pounds of chlorine should SWIMCO order at each order point?

6. Several executives of the RAMCO Service Company, a maintenance contracting firm that services hydraulic pumping equipment, are reviewing some rather disturbing news at their monthly financial review meeting. The vice-president of finance states that the cost of financing the company's supplies inventories has increased 25 percent and the acquisition cost of its diaphragms has increased 5 percent. Increased labor rates and fringe benefits have caused ordering cost to rise 29 percent, and annual demand for diaphragms has declined 15 percent. Charlie McCullough, vice-president of Operations, sits quietly at the end of the conference table waiting for the inevitable question. Finally it comes from RAMCO's president: "Charlie, how much, percentagewise, will your order quantities change and how much will your total annual stocking cost change for diaphragms?" Can you answer for Charlie?

Model II — EOQ with Gradual Deliveries

7. Given: p = 500 units per day, d = 100 units per day, D = 10,000 units per year, S = $20 per order, and C = $.50 per unit per year. Required: **a.** EOQ and **b.** TSC at EOQ.

8. Given: p = 2d, C = ⅓(ac) dollars per unit per year, D = 100,000 units per year, ac = $5.95 per unit, and S = $100 per order. Required: **a.** EOQ and **b.** TSC at EOQ.

9. The Oklahoma Crude Oil Refinery buys crude oil from the Red Rock oil field located in eastern New Mexico, West Texas, and western Oklahoma. The refinery has been

guaranteed through long-term supply contracts that its needs for crude will be supplied from this field at $18.90 per barrel as long as 5,000 barrels per day are accepted by the refinery during shipping periods. The refinery uses crude oil at a rate of 1,500 barrels per day and plans to purchase 450,000 barrels from the Red Rock field next year. If the carrying cost is 20 percent of acquisition cost per unit per year and ordering cost is $2,500 per order: **a.** What is the EOQ for Red Rock crude? **b.** What is the TSC at EOQ? **c.** How many days of production are supported by each order of Red Rock crude?

10. The Continental Box Company produces fiberboard boxes for the Rocky Mountain states region. Continental buys reconstituted kraft paper stock that is made of scrap paper from FRAB Company, which is next door to its plant. FRAB produces its reclaimed paper for three such fiberboard box companies at a rate of 15,900 pounds per day and sells it to Continental for $.40 per pound. Continental uses 30,000 pounds of kraft paper per day, works 250 days per year, and 10 percent of its kraft is bought from FRAB. If carrying cost is 30 percent of acquisition cost per pound per year and ordering cost is $50 per order: **a.** What is the EOQ for FRAB's reclaimed kraft? **b.** What is the TSC at EOQ? **c.** How many orders per year will Continental place with FRAB?

11. The Central Iowa Electric Company buys coal from the Cedar Creek Coal Company to generate electricity. Cedar Creek supplies coal at the rate of 3,500 tons per day at a price of $10.50 per ton. Central Iowa Electric uses the coal at a rate of 800 tons per day and works 365 days per year. The annual carrying costs and annual ordering costs functions for the coal are:

Annual carrying costs = (C/5) multiplied by average inventory

$$\text{Annual ordering costs} = \frac{S}{1{,}000}\left(\frac{D}{Q}\right)$$

a. Derive a formula for TSC. **b.** Derive a formula for EOQ. **c.** What is the EOQ for coal if $C = \$2.50$ per ton per year and $S = \$5{,}000$ per order? **d.** What is the minimum TSC for coal?

Model III — EOQ with Quantity Discounts

12. Given: $D = 20{,}000$ units per year, $C = .3$ (ac) dollars per unit per year, $S = \$100$ per order, $ac_1 = \$2$ per unit for 0 to 2,999 units, and $ac_2 = \$1.90$ per unit for 3,000+ units. Required: **a.** What key quantities should be investigated? **b.** What is the EOQ? **c.** What is the minimum TMC?

13. Given: $D = 50{,}000$ units per year, $S = \$250$ per order, $C = .25$ (ac) dollars per unit per year, $p = 500$ units per day, $d = 200$ units per day, $ac_1 = \$5$ per unit for 0 to 5,999 units per order, $ac_2 = \$4.95$ per unit for 6,000 to 9,999 units per order, and $ac_3 = \$4.93$ per unit for 10,000+ units per order. Required: **a.** minimun TMC, **b.** EOQ, **c.** number of orders per year, and **d.** maximum inventory.

14. The T. F. Goodwealth Auto Supply Stores Company has a regional tire warehouse in Atlanta, Georgia. One popular tire—H78-15, 4-ply polyester, is estimated to have a demand of 25,000 tires next year. It costs the warehouse $100 to place and receive an order and carrying cost is 30 percent of acquisition cost. The supplier quotes these prices on this tire:

Q	ac
0–499	$21.60
500–999	20.95
1000+	20.90

a. What is the warehouse's EOQ? **b.** What is the minimum TMC?

15. Electronic Computing Services Inc. (ECS) is a computer center selling computing services to the banks in Miami, Florida. The center uses large quantities of computer printout paper #3225. ECS buys the paper from a regional warehouse of a large paper company. The warehouse has delivery trucks that make daily rounds to all the customers in its region. ECS receives 100 boxes of paper per day at a cost of $19.50 per box. ECS uses the paper at a rate of 50 boxes per day on a 5-day-per-week operation. It costs ECS $75 to place an order for the paper and carrying costs are 20 percent of acquisition cost. The supplier has recently put on extra delivery trucks and is offering one half of 1 percent discount if its customers will take 200 or more boxes per delivery day. You may assume that ECS can receive less than 100 or 200 boxes on the last delivery day of an order. **a.** What is ECS's present EOQ? **b.** What is ECS's present TMC? **c.** What would ECS's EOQ be if it accepted the supplier's discount offer? **d.** What would ECS's new TMC be under the discount arrangement? **e.** Should ECS accept the proposal?

Order Points

16. Given: j = 20 percent and EDDLT = 500. Required: **a.** safety stock using percentage of EDDLT method, **b.** order point using percentage of EDDLT method, **c.** safety stock using square root of EDDLT method, and **d.** order point using square root of EDDLT method.

17. Jay Houser is the director of maintenance at the United Silicon Chemicals Baton Rouge plant. Jay is meeting with his materials manager, Dick Blake, to plan inventories for their neoprene 6-inch spring seal, a commonly used repair item at the plant. Under consideration is the order point for this item and the appropriate level of safety stock. The plant operates under a policy of carrying 50 percent of EDDLT as safety stock across all items in the same class as this seal. Average demand per day is 5.4 seals, and average lead time is 30 days. **a.** How much safety stock should be carried for this seal? **b.** At what inventory level should an order for the seal be processed?

Model IV — Economic Order Period

18. Given: D = 30,000 units per year, S = $500 per order, and C = $5 per unit per year. Required: **a.** economic order period and **b.** TSC at economic order period.

19. The General Services Administration (GSA) is a government agency that buys and distributes supplies to other agencies. GSA maintains a regional supply warehouse in Chicago. One of its items is Form GSA #35,665 — a 15-part purchase order. GSA takes periodic inventory counts of its Chicago stock and places orders for materials needed. Inventory counts were taken today and inventory level was 300,000 forms. Maximum inventory target is 1,000,000, and expected demand during lead time is 200,000. Annual demand in the region is approximately 5,500,000 forms, ordering cost is $1,000 per order, acquisition cost is $.05 per form, and carrying cost is 35 percent of acquisition cost. **a.** When should the physical inventory count be taken next? **b.** How many forms should be ordered today?

The Phoenix Wholesale Company

The Phoenix Wholesale Company sells dry goods to regional retailers. Jethro Bleu, the president of the company, has just addressed the company's management team and has stressed the absolute necessity of reducing the cost of their warehousing operations. Mary Montgomery, the director of warehousing operations, is already investigating ways to respond to Mr. Jethro's pronouncement.

Mary's staff is considering proposing that a minicomputer be installed to assist them in converting the present fixed order period inventory system that depends upon periodic physical counts of inventory to a fixed order quantity system that assumes a perpetual inventory record system. The staff has developed these estimates for a single SKU that is believed to be representative of the many items in their warehouses:

Acquisition cost: $9.55 per unit

Ordering cost: $21.50 per order

Carrying cost: (40 percent of acquisition cost) $ per unit per year

Estimated annual sales: 57,500 units per year

Annual cost of physical counts of inventory for the item: $1,200 per year

Annual cost of minicomputer perpetual inventory system (portion of total cost of the system allocated to this SKU based on cost of goods sold): $250 per year

Assignment

1. Compute the estimated annual cost of the present inventory system for this SKU.

2. Compute the estimated annual cost for the proposed perpetual inventory system for this SKU.

3. What annual savings are likely to result from installing the new inventory system (savings for this single SKU alone)?

4. What difficulties prevent us from extrapolating the savings for this single SKU to the entire inventory in the warehouses? How can the information developed in No. 3 be used effectively in deciding whether to adopt the new inventory system?

5. What difficulties are likely to be encountered in implementing the new inventory system?

Selected Bibliography

American Production and Inventory Control Society. *APICS Bibliography of Articles, Books, Films, and Audio-Cassettes on Production and Inventory Control and Related Subjects*. Washington, DC: APICS, 1973.

American Production and Inventory Control Society. *APICS Dictionary of Inventory Control Terms and Production Control Terms*. 3d ed. Washington, DC: APICS, 1970.

Ballou, Ronald H. *Business Logistics Management*. Englewood Cliffs, NJ: Prentice-Hall, 1973.

Hadley, G., and T. M. Whitin. *Analysis of Inventory Systems*. Englewood Cliffs, NJ: Prentice-Hall, 1963.

Harris, F. W. *Operations and Costs*. Chicago: A. W. Shaw, 1915.

Heskett, James L., Nicholas A. Glaskowsky, and Robert M. Ivie. *Business Logistics*. New York: Ronald Press, 1973.

Hoyt, J. "Order Points Tailored to Suit Your Business." *Production and Inventory Management* 14(fourth quarter 1973): 42.

Mayer, R. R. "Selection of Rules-of-Thumb in Inventory Control." *Journal of Purchasing* 8(May 1972): 19–24.

Monczka, Robert M. "The Purchasing Frontier." *Perspectives* (Fall 1977): 2–4.

Peterson, R., and E. A. Silver. *Decision Systems for Inventory Management and Production Planning*. New York: Wiley, 1977.

Plossl, George W., and W. Evert Welch. *The Role of Top Management in the Control of Inventory*. Reston, VA: Reston Publishing, 1979.

Plossl, G. W., and O. W. Wight. *Production and Inventory Control*. Englewood Cliffs, NJ: Prentice-Hall, 1967.

Planning Safety Stock Levels

In Chapter 9 we discussed some rules of thumb that are used to set order points: percentage of EDDLT and square root of EDDLT. These approaches add a certain amount of safety stock to the expected demand during lead time to calculate the order point. These methods, although somewhat crude in their approach, at least recognize the uncertainty usually encountered in the reorder cycle and attempt to set safety stock levels to help protect the firm from running out of stock because of this uncertainty. Let us now explore more fully the nature of this uncertainty and ways of analyzing these reorder cycles so that we can develop more precise ways of setting safety stock levels and order points in fixed order quantity inventory systems. Study Figure 9S.1 to understand the relationship among the variables that we shall use in this section.

Accommodating Uncertainty in Inventory Planning

The methods presented here will seek to deal with the two principal sources of uncertainty in inventory planning — demand for products/materials and supply lead times. These two variables impinge on inventory managers at times that they are most vulnerable, when stock is relatively low and managers are waiting for a new order of materials to arrive. These uncertain situations arise almost universally during the reorder cycle. You may find it helpful to occasionally refer to Table 9S.1, which lists terms often used in analyses in inventory planning under uncertainty, as you progress through this section.

Figure 9S.1
Relationships between DDLT, EDDLT, SS, OP, and Probability of Stockouts for Each Reorder Cycle

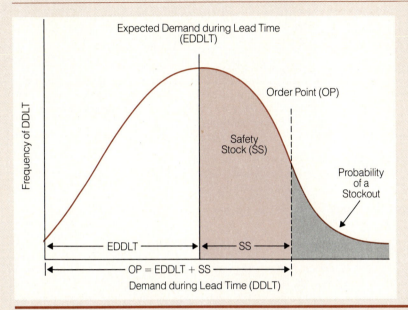

Figure 9S.2 shows that although the expected demand during lead time (EDDLT), the product of the average demand per day and average lead time, is the central focus of our inventory planning, the actual demand during lead time is subject to variation. Lead times less than average and demand per day less than average result in demands during lead time less than EDDLT and inventory still on hand when orders arrive. On the other hand, when lead time is greater than average and demand per day is greater than average, the demand during lead time is greater than EDDLT and stockouts occur unless adequate safety stock is maintained.

Safety stock is the central issue in this section. Given that demand during lead time is uncertain, how much safety stock should be carried in inventory to guard against stockouts? If we carry too much safety stock, the cost of continuously carrying these materials becomes excessive; however, when too little safety stock is carried, the cost of stockouts becomes excessive. This suggests that these two costs should be balanced to develop an optimal safety stock policy for each material. The principal obstacle to the concept of optimal safety stock levels is quantifying the costs of stockouts. Conceptually, we know that stockouts can cost. But how much? How much in profits is lost when we discourage a customer with stockouts? How much cost is incurred when production departments run out of a raw material and must shift schedules around to produce products that they have raw materials to support? These and other difficulties in estimating stockout costs have led analysts toward specifying minimum service levels under simplifying assumptions as workable solutions rather than optimal ones. Unless otherwise specified, the foregoing will apply to inventory systems where orders for inventories are triggered by minimum inventory levels — order points.

Table 9S.1
Terms Often Used in Analyses in Inventory Planning under Uncertainty

1. **Continuous DDLT Distributions**—Probability distributions of all possible demand during lead time (DDLT) values where DDLT is a continuous random variable. In other words, DDLT can take on any value continuously between the extreme DDLT values of the distribution. Examples of these distributions are normal, student's t, and exponential.

2. **DDLT Distribution Parameters**—the measures that describe the DDLT distributions. For example:

   EDDLT—Expected demand during lead time is the mean of the DDLT distribution.

   σ_{DDLT}—Standard deviation of demand during lead time is the measure of how the DDLT values are dispersed about their mean.

3. **Demand per Day (d) Distribution Parameters**—The measures that describe the d distributions. For example:

   $\bar{d}$—Mean demand per day.

   σ_d—Standard deviation of demand per day is the measure of how the d values are dispersed about their mean.

4. **Discrete DDLT Distributions**—Probability distributions of all possible demand during lead time (DDLT) values where DDLT is a discrete random variable. In other words, DDLT can take on only a few specific values between the extreme DDLT values of the distribution. Examples of these distributions are binomial, hypergeometric, Poisson, and a host of other empirically determined historical data distributions.

5. **Lead Time (LT) Distribution Parameters**—The measures that describe the LT distributions. For example:

   $\overline{LT}$—Mean lead time.

   σ_{LT}—Standard deviation of lead time is the measure of how the LT values are dispersed about their mean.

6. **Marginal Analysis**—A form of analysis of safety stock level and order point problems in inventory planning under uncertainty. This technique determines the cumulative probability that equates the expected long cost and expected short cost for DDLT. This probability is then used to identify the optimal DDLT in the cumulative DDLT probability distribution. The optimal safety stock level is deduced from the optimal DDLT or order point (SS = OP − EDDLT).

7. **Optimal Safety Stock Level**—The amount of safety stock, which is the order point (OP) minus the expected demand during lead time (EDDLT), that balances the expected long costs and expected short costs during lead time.

8. **Payoff Tables**—A form of analysis of safety stock level and order point problems in inventory planning under uncertainty. This technique computes the total of expected long and short costs per lead time for each order point strategy. The order point with the minimum total expected cost is the optimal order point. The optimal safety stock is then deduced (SS = OP − EDDLT).

9. **Service Level**—The portion of the time on the average that customers' or production departments' orders can be directly filled from inventory or production during lead time. For example, a 90 percent service level means that only 10 percent of the orders on the average cannot be filled.

Figure 9S.2
DDLT Uncertainty

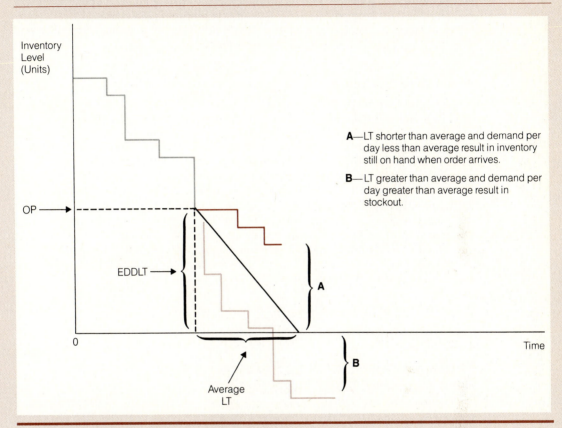

A—LT shorter than average and demand per day less than average result in inventory still on hand when order arrives.

B—LT greater than average and demand per day greater than average result in stockout.

Safety Stock Set at Service Levels

In many practical POM situations, actual safety stock levels are evolved over time. That is to say that managers determine the level of safety stocks that are not excessive while at the same time having enough of each material on hand during the reorder period to meet the demands of customers under most ordinary circumstances. These trial and error methods require experienced managers who are capable of exercising judgmental insight. Are other avenues available to set safety stock levels?

One approach requires managers in charge to specify the service levels they want their inventories to support during lead time. *Service levels* means the proportion of customers' orders that will be filled out of finished goods inventories or the proportion of production department orders that will be filled out of raw material inventories. Managers might specify, for example, "We want 90 percent of our customers' orders on the average to be immediately filled out of inventory." The corollary to this statement is that 10 percent of customers' orders will not be filled from inventory because stockouts will be experienced during lead times. These specifications of service levels are based on marketing policy in the case of finished goods inventory and on manufacturing policy in the case of raw materials inventory.

Let us describe some specific uncertain demand during lead time situations and develop techniques for setting safety stock levels.

DDLT Distributions

When enough information exists to develop historical data for the demand during lead time for a material, the setting of safety stock levels is straightforward. Example 9S.1 sets the safety stock level for a material whose demand during lead time (DDLT) has been classified into discrete classes. *Discrete DDLT distributions*, and the approach developed in Example 9S.1, are particularly helpful in situations where DDLT data have been grouped into discrete classes or when DDLT data are discrete and actually occur in finite steps as opposed to continuous measures. For example, when DDLT ranges from 3 to 15 units as shown in the first part of Figure 9S.3, a discrete distribution may more accurately describe the occurrence of DDLT since its values can only be integer values from 3 to 15 units. When the number of units in DDLT is very large, as shown in the second part of Figure 9S.3, or when units are divisible, as in the case of barrels of crude oil, *continuous DDLT distributions* accurately describe the occurrence of DDLT.

Example 9S.1

Setting Safety Stock at Service Levels for a Discrete DDLT Distribution

The Whipple Manufacturing Company produces office products that are sold through wholesaling distributors. One such product, a word processing small-business computer, is produced-to-stock and held in finished goods inventory until ordered by Whipple's distributors. Whipple's management wants to determine how much safety stock should be carried on this item and has uncovered the following information: average demand per day is 6.0 units, average production lead time is 10 days, and historical records show this frequency of actual demand during lead time:

Actual DDLT	Frequency
21–30	.05
31–40	.10
41–50	.15
51–60	.20
61–70	.20
71–80	.15
81–90	.10
91–100	.05

If Whipple's management wants to provide an 80 percent service level during lead time: **a**. What is the order point? **b**. What is the safety stock?

Solution

a. First, use the DDLT data above to develop a cumulative probability distribution of the service level:

Actual DDLT	Frequency	Service Levels (Probability of DDLT or Less)
11–20	0	0
21–30	.05	.05
31–40	.10	.15
41–50	.15	.30
51–60	.20	.50
61–70	.20	.70
71–80	.15	.85
81–90	.10	.95
91–100	.05	1.00

Next, graph this cumulative distribution:

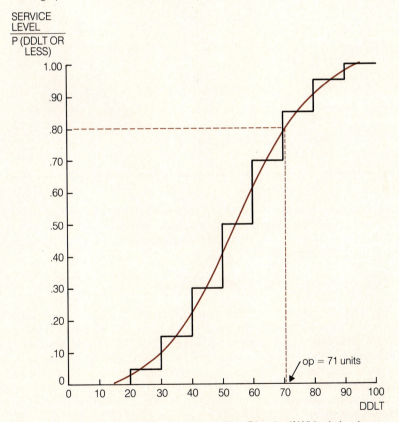

As we can see from this graph, the order point is 71 units. If Whipple begins a production lot of the computer when inventory falls to 71 units, stockouts will occur (DDLT > 71) about 20 percent of the time between the point in time when a production order for the units is begun and a production order is completed.

b. Determine the safety stock level:

$$OP = EDDLT + \text{Safety stock}$$

$$\frac{\text{Safety}}{\text{stock}} = OP - EDDLT = OP - [(\text{Average demand per day}) \times (\text{Average lead time})]$$

$$= 71 - (6.0 \times 10) = 71 - 60 = 11 \text{ units}$$

Figure 9S.3
DDLT distributions

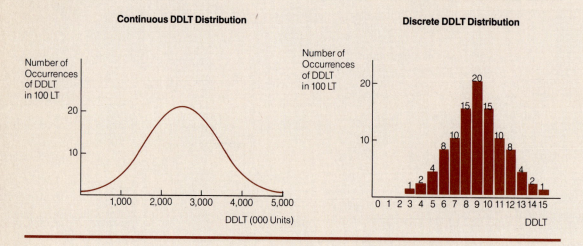

Example 9S.2 demonstrates how we would set safety stock levels when DDLT is depicted by a continuous distribution. This example assumes that the historical demand for a raw material is actually from a normal distribution of DDLT. Remember that we earlier defined order point as:

Order point = Expected demand during lead time + Safety stock

In this example we first use the historical data to compute the mean and standard deviation of the DDLT distribution (EDDLT and σ_{DDLT}). Next, we compute the value of DDLT that has a probability of 5 percent of being exceeded; this means that the probability of being less than or equal to this DDLT is 95 percent, the desired service level. This value of DDLT is our order point (OP). In other words, an order for resin #942 would be placed when inventory levels fall to 922.1 pounds. This order point would have 693.7 pounds used on the average during the reorder cycle. The safety stock level (SS) is therefore:

SS = OP − EDDLT = 922.1 − 693.7 = 228.4 pounds

Example 9S.2

Setting Safety Stock at Service Levels for DDLT That Is Normally Distributed

Billie Jean Bray, the materials manager for INJECTO Wholesale Plastics, is attempting to set the safety stock level for resin #942. This material is sold to INJECTO's customers, and its future use is believed to be accurately depicted by these historical DDLT data (in pounds): 632, 754, 429, 715, 949, 623, 555, 690, 740, and 850. Billie Jean believes that DDLT for resin #942 is really normally distributed and that these last ten DDLT occurrences are representative of the true DDLT normal distribution. **a.** What is the EDDLT for resin #942? **b.** What is the σ_{DDLT} for resin #942? **c.** If the production manager specifies that stock orders for resin #942 during lead time should be filled from inventory 95 percent of the time on the average, what safety stock should be maintained?

Solution

a. EDDLT is the mean of the ten historical DDLT occurrences:

$$EDDLT = \frac{\Sigma DDLT}{n} = \frac{(632 + 754 + 429 + 715 + 949 + 623 + 555 + 690 + 740 + 850)}{10}$$

$$= 693.7 \text{ pounds}$$

b. Standard deviation of DDLT is:

$$\sigma_x = \sqrt{\frac{\sum_{i=1}^{n} (X_i - \bar{X})^2}{n}} \qquad \text{(This is the formula for standard deviation.)}$$

$$\sigma_{DDLT} = \sqrt{\frac{\sum_{i=1}^{n} (DDLT_i - EDDLT)^2}{n}} \qquad \text{(This is the formula for standard deviation when applied to DDLT.)}$$

$$= \sqrt{\frac{1}{10} \begin{bmatrix} (632 - 693.7)^2 + (754 - 693.7)^2 + (429 - 693.7)^2 + (715 - 693.7)^2 + \\ (949 - 693.7)^2 + (623 - 693.7)^2 + (555 - 693.7)^2 + (690 - 693.7)^2 + \\ (740 - 693.7)^2 + (850 - 693.7)^2 \end{bmatrix}}$$

$$= 139.27 \text{ pounds}$$

Therefore, we have a normal distribution of DDLT with a mean of 693.7 pounds and a standard deviation of 139.27 pounds:

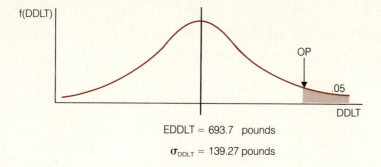

$$EDDLT = 693.7 \quad \text{pounds}$$
$$\sigma_{DDLT} = 139.27 \text{ pounds}$$

c. Compute safety stock (SS) to provide 95 percent service level; in other words, what is the DDLT level that has a probability of only 5 percent of being exceeded? This is the order point:

$$OP = EDDLT + Z(\sigma_{DDLT})$$

The Z value is read from Appendix A. Locate .95 (the area to the left of OP) in the body of the table and read off the Z value of 1.64. This is the number of standard deviations that OP is away from EDDLT:

$$OP = 693.7 + 1.64 \,(139.27) = 922.1 \text{ pounds}$$

The safety stock is then deduced:

$$SS = OP - EDDLT = 922.1 - 693.7 = 228.4 \text{ pounds}$$

This approach to setting safety stock levels is valid only if service levels are precisely set and if accurate DDLT historical data are available.

Constant Lead Time and Normally Distributed Demand per Day

There are times when it is difficult to obtain DDLT data. In these instances it is often satisfactory to obtain demand-per-day data and assume a constant lead time. Because historical demand-per-day data are usually abundantly available and lead time is ordinarily subject to less variation than the daily demand, this approach can be useful.

Example 9S.3 develops safety stock levels for a material while assuming constant lead time and a normally distributed demand per day. A normal DDLT distribution is developed by computing the expected demand during lead time (EDDLT) and standard deviation of demand during lead time (σ_{DDLT}):

$$EDDLT = LT(\bar{d}) \quad \text{and} \quad \sigma_{DDLT} = \sqrt{LT(\sigma_d)^2}$$

The resulting DDLT normal distribution is then analyzed to calculate the DDLT that provides the specified service level, and this DDLT is the order point (OP). The safety stock (SS) is then deduced: SS = OP − EDDLT.

Example 9S.3

Setting Safety Stock Levels at Service Levels for Constant Lead Time and Normally Distributed Demand per Day

Mr. Bob Fero is an operations analyst for Sell-Rite Discount Stores of Washington, D.C. He is currently studying the ordering and stocking policies at Sell-Rite's central warehouse for one of their best-moving items — the Zolo Blow Gun, a child's toy. An examination of historical supply and demand data for this stock-keeping unit (SKU) indicated an almost constant lead time (LT) of ten days because the supplier was located almost next door to the warehouse, and abundant production capacity allowed very consistent production and delivery times. Bob also discovered that the demand per day (d) was nearly normally distributed with a mean $(\bar{d})$ of 1,250 toys per day with a standard deviation (σ_d) of 375 toys per day. **a.** Compute the order point for the toy if the service level is specified at 90 percent during lead time. **b.** How much safety stock is provided in your answer in part *a*?

Solution

a. Compute the order point:

1. First, compute the EDDLT and σ_{DDLT}:

$$EDDLT = \text{Lead time} \times \text{Average demand per day} = LT(\bar{d}) = 10(1,250)$$
$$= 12,500 \text{ toys during lead time}$$

$$\sigma_{DDLT} = \sqrt{LT(\sigma_d)^2} = \sqrt{10(375)^2} = 1,185.85 \text{ toys during lead time}$$

2. EDDLT and σ_{DDLT} totally describe the DDLT distribution:

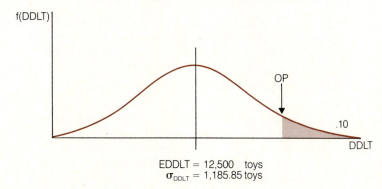

EDDLT = 12,500 toys
σ_{DDLT} = 1,185.85 toys

3. Next, we must determine Z, the number of standard deviations that OP is from EDDLT. Look up .900 in the body of the table in Appendix A and read off the corresponding Z value of 1.28.

4. Next, compute the order point:

$$OP = EDDLT + Z(\sigma_{DDLT}) = 12,500 + 1.28(1,185.85) = 12,500 + 1,517.89$$
$$= 14,017.89 \text{ toys}$$

Orders for the toy would be placed when the inventory level falls to 14,018 toys.

b. Compute safety stock (SS):

$$SS = OP - EDDLT = 14,018 - 12,500 = 1,518 \text{ toys}$$

All these approaches to explicitly dealing with uncertainty in inventory planning have relied on managers to specify service levels during lead time required to comply with either manufacturing policy or marketing policy. Let us now examine some techniques for determining optimal order points and safety stock levels.

Optimal Safety Stock Levels

Analysts may attempt to balance the costs of carrying too little or too much safety stock for a product or material. Conceptually, this leads to optimal safety stock levels.

Example 9S.4 uses *payoff tables,* which were discussed in Chapter 2, to minimize the total of expected long costs and short costs for each discrete order point alternative. This approach requires the following information:

1. Long cost — the cost of stocking one unit that is not demanded during lead time — is usually associated with carrying costs, the cost of special handling, and other expenses involved in carrying a unit from one period to another.

2. Short cost — the cost of not stocking a unit that is demanded during lead time — is ordinarily associated with stockouts — lost profits, special handling, expediting, and so on.

3. Either a historical discrete probability distribution of DDLT, a discrete probability distribution of DDLT based on near-continuous historical data (continuous data can usually be transformed into discrete classes, with each class then represented by its mean), or subjectively set discrete probability distributions of DDLT.

Example 9S.4

Developing Optimal Safety Stock Levels with Payoff Tables

A large hospital stocks supplies to support surgical operations. One such material, #711 surgical tape, is being studied. The following information has been developed: long costs = $20 per case not used during lead time, short costs = $60 per case short during lead time, and the following demand during lead time distribution. **a.** What order point for #711 surgical tape is optimal? **b.** What safety stock level is optimal?

DDLT (Cases of #711)	Occurrences	DDLT (Cases of #711)	Occurrences
3	1	6	2
4	4	7	1
5	3		

Solution

a. Compute optimal order point:

1. First, compute probabilities for each DDLT:

DDLT (Cases of #711)	Probability of DDLT	DDLT (Cases of #711)	Probability of DDLT
3	$1/11 = .091$	6	$2/11 = .182$
4	$4/11 = .364$	7	$1/11 = .091$
5	$3/11 = .273$		

2. Next, develop a long and short cost matrix:

DDLT (cases)

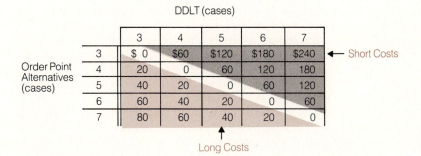

Order Point Alternatives (cases)	3	4	5	6	7
3	$ 0	$60	$120	$180	$240	← Short Costs
4	20	0	60	120	180
5	40	20	0	60	120
6	60	40	20	0	60
7	80	60	40	20	0

↑ Long Costs

Note: For example, if an order point of 5 cases were adopted and 3 cases were actually demanded during lead time, a long cost of $40 ($20 × 2 cases long) would result. If, however, an order point of 5 cases were adopted and 7 cases were actually demanded during lead time, a short cost of $120 ($60 × 2 cases short) would result.

3. Next, complete the payoff table analysis to find the order point:

		DDLT (cases)					Total Expected Long and Short Costs $EC = \Sigma [P(SN_i) \times C_{iJ}]$
S_i ＼ SN_i		3	4	5	6	7	
Order Point Alternatives (cases)	3	$ 0	$21.84	$32.76	$32.76	$21.84	$109.20
	4	1.82	0	16.38	21.84	16.38	56.42
	5	3.64	7.28	0	10.92	10.92	32.76
	6	5.46	14.56	5.46	0	5.46	30.94 ←
	7	7.28	21.84	10.92	3.64	0	43.68
$P(Sn_i)$		.091	.364	.273	.182	.091	

Note: The probability for each DDLT is multiplied times the long and short costs in the matrix in Step 2 above and recorded in this matrix. For example, the column for DDLT = 3 is computed by multiplying .091 times 0, 20, 40, 60, 80 from the 3 DDLT column in Step 2 to yield 0, 1.82, 3.64, 5.46, and 7.28. Each of the columns is similarly filled. The expected costs for each order point strategy are added horizontally across the matrix. For example: $109.20 = $0 + $21.84 + $32.76 + $32.76 + $21.84.

4. The order point alternative with the lowest expected long and short costs is 6 cases.

b. Compute the optimal safety stock level:

Safety stock = Order point − Average demand during lead time

$$SS = OP - EDDLT = 6 - \frac{1(3) + 4(4) + 3(5) + 2(6) + 1(7)}{11} = 6 - 4.82$$

$$= 1.18 \text{ cases}$$

Because the order point computed by the approach in Example 9S.4 is likely to be applied over and over from reorder cycle to reorder cycle, the minimization of total expected costs per reorder cycle is a useful criterion for selecting order points. The procedure in Example 9S.4 selects an order point of 6 cases of surgical tape as the optimal order point because it is 6 cases of surgical tape that exhibits the minimum total expected cost from among all the possible DDLTs that range from 3 to 7 cases. A safety stock of 1.18 cases is computed by subtracting EDDLT from the optimal order point.

Remember, in this example we are deciding what minimum inventory level (order point) to use as a guide indicating when to place an order for a material. We would like to place an order when the inventory level exactly equals what will be demanded while our order is being mailed, filled, received, and placed in inventory. Because we don't know with certainty how much will be demanded during this reorder period, we have to select an order point that equals some DDLT that tends to work out for us on average from one order period to the next. *Working out* means that the cost of ordering too soon when inventory is too high and having excessive inventory on hand when orders are received is balanced against the cost of ordering too late when inventory is too low and running out of material (stockout) before the order arrives. This decision obviously involves a trade-off between the advantages and disadvantages of high order points and low order points. The criterion of minimum total expected cost as the basis for choosing among order point alternatives achieves this trade-off.

In Example 9S.5 the same surgical tape safety stock problem is solved, but this time by *marginal analysis*. This approach computes the probability (P) that makes the expected long cost equal to the expected short cost for any DDLT. This P then is compared to the cumulative probability distribution—probability of at least DDLT being demanded. The lowest DDLT whose cumulative probability is greater than or equal to P is the optimal order point alternative. The safety stock is then computed as in Example 9S.4.

Example 9S.5

Developing Optimal Safety Stock Levels with Marginal Analysis

The study of #711 surgical tape from Example 9S.4 is now analyzed using marginal analysis.

MLC = $20 per case—long cost per case, the marginal cost of not using a case of #711 surgical tape during lead time

MSC = $60 per case—short cost per case, the marginal cost of being short a case of #711 surgical tape because of a stockout during lead time

P—probability of needing the nth case of #711 surgical tape during lead time; DDLT is equal to or greater than n cases.

$(1 - P)$—probability of not needing the nth case of #711 surgical tape during lead time; DDLT is less than n cases.

a. Derive a formula for P that exactly balances expected long costs and expected short costs.
b. Compute the order point for the #711 surgical tape. **c.** Compute the safety stock for the #711 surgical tape.

Solution

a. Derive the formula for P:

1. Set the expected short costs equal to the expected long costs and solve for P:

$$P(MSC) = (1 - P)(MLC)$$
$$P(MSC) = MLC - P(MLC)$$
$$P(MSC) + P(MLC) = MLC$$
$$P(MSC + MLC) = MLC$$

$$P = \frac{MLC}{MSC + MLC} = \frac{20}{60 + 20} = .250$$

2. When the probability of needing a unit is .250, the marginal cost of stocking that unit is exactly equal to the marginal cost of not stocking that unit.

b. Compute the order point for #711 surgical tape:

1. The optimal order point is determined by progressively increasing the order point, as long as the probability of needing the last unit added is equal to or greater than .250.

2. Develop the probability of at least each DDLT occurring:

DDLT (Cases of #711)	Probability of DDLT	Probability of at Least DDLT
3	.091	1.000
4	.364	.909
5	.273	.545
6	.182	.272
7	.091	.091

3. It seldom occurs that the probability of demanding at least any DDLT exactly equals the P computed in part *a*. Ordinarily, the appropriate DDLT to select, therefore, is the lowest DDLT whose probability of being demanded is equal to or greater than P. An order point of 6 cases would be selected in this example because $P(DDLT \geq 6) = .272$, which is the lowest DDLT whose probability of being demanded is $\geq$ P.

4. It can be shown that 6 is the optimal order point by comparing the expected cost of stocking 6 units with the expected cost of stocking 7 units:

OP = 6:   Total expected cost = Expected long cost + Expected short cost
$$= .091(60) + .364(40) + .273(20) + .182(0) + .091(60)$$
$$= 5.46 + 14.56 + 5.46 + 0 + 5.46$$
$$= \$30.94 \text{ during lead time}$$

OP = 7:   Total expected cost = Expected long cost + Expected short cost
$$= .091(80) + .364(60) + .273(40) + .182(20) + .091(0)$$
$$= 7.28 + 21.84 + 10.92 + 3.64 + 0$$
$$= \$43.68 \text{ during lead time}$$

c. Compute the safety stock level:

Safety stock = Order point − Average demand during lead time
SS = OP − EDDLT = 6 − 4.82 (4.82 was computed in Example 9S.4)
  = 1.18 cases

The data requirements for the marginal cost approach are exactly the same as with payoff tables—long cost per unit, short cost per unit, and discrete probability distribution of DDLT. Students seem to prefer the marginal cost approach over payoff tables because of speed and ease of computations. The two methods give comparable results but the payoff tables do offer an advantage: the total expected cost for each possible order point is clearly exhibited, thus allowing decision makers' insight into the sensitivity of total expected cost to changes in order points. For example, in the expected cost matrix in Example 9S.4, managers can see that the total expected cost per lead time increases from $30.94 to $43.68 if we increase the order point from 6 to 7 cases. Such information may allow managers more flexibility in their decisions because they must frequently suboptimize individual order point decisions in order to comply with warehouse capacities, marketing policies, customers' wishes, and other pressures not easily included in order point analyses.

In this supplement we have analyzed order point and safety stock level decisions while recognizing the uncertainty of demand per day and lead times for materials. Both management-specified service levels and optimal total expected cost per lead time have been used as criteria for these decisions. The key advantage to these analytic approaches has been their explicit addressing of uncertainty and the incorporation of this uncertainty into order point and safety stock decisions. Where data exist to support these kinds of analyses, more intelligent inventory planning decisions are almost sure to result.

Review and Discussion Questions

1. Explain what is meant by this statement: "The uncertainties of inventory planning almost always affect operations managers when they are most vulnerable—when inventory levels are at their lowest points."

2. Give a brief explanation for each of the following:
   - **a.** DDLT
   - **b.** EDDLT
   - **c.** σ_{DDLT}
   - **d.** discrete DDLT distributions
   - **e.** continuous DDLT distributions
   - **f.** $\overline{LT}$
   - **g.** σ_{LT}

3. Define *service levels*.

4. Assuming the DDLT distribution is normal, write the formula for computing: **a.** EDDLT and **b.** σ_{DDLT}.

5. What criteria are used to set optimal safety stock levels when payoff tables and marginal analysis are used?

6. Explain the relationship between these variables: order point, safety stock, and EDDLT.

Problems

1. Woopee Retailers traditionally has not carried safety stock. A party favor—the Woopee Cushion—is now being analyzed to set safety stock levels for this fast-moving item. Historical DDLT is:

DDLT (Cases)	Occurrences
3	8
4	6
5	4
6	2
	20

Construct a cumulative DDLT distribution. If service level is set at 80 percent during lead time: **a.** What is the order point? **b.** What is the safety stock level?

2. Jay Houser is the director of maintenance at the United Silicon Chemicals plant in Baton Rouge. Jay is meeting with his materials manager, Dick Blake, to plan inventories for their neoprene 6-inch spring seal, a commonly used repair item at the plant. Under consideration is the order point for this item and the appropriate level of safety stock. Average demand per day is 5.4 seals and average lead time is 30 days. Dick Blake suggests to Jay Houser that United Silicon is accumulating so much data in their computer that now may be the time to institute a more sophisticated approach to setting order points. He shows Mr. Houser the following information on past demands during lead time for this seal:

Actual DDLT	Occurrences	Actual DDLT	Occurrences
80–99	3	160–179	9
100–119	4	180–199	12
120–139	7	200–219	5
140–159	8		

Dick suggests that if a service level of 90 percent were specified, based upon historical DDLT, 90 percent of all demands for the seal could be met during lead time on the average. Mr. Houser instructs Dick to recommend the safety stock level and order point for the seal under the 90 percent service level policy. **a.** Compute the order point using the 90 percent service level. **b.** What safety stock is provided with your answer to part a above?

3. Given: EDDLT = 55.5 units, σ_{DDLT} = 12.5 units, DDLT is normally distributed, and service level is 95 percent. Required: **a.** OP, and **b.** SS.

4. The E–Z MONY Loan Company is a feeder operation servicing local Detroit industrial workers. It must periodically go to banks to trade loan paper for cash to use for short-term loans. E–Z wishes to know at what minimum level of cash inventory it should initiate order procedures for more cash from the banks. Mr. Slick, the president of E–Z, believes that the actual DDLT is really normally distributed and that the historical data for six previous periods are representative of what will be experienced in the future: 550, 520, 990, 780, 850, and 660 in thousands of dollars. If Mr. Slick specifies a service level of 85 percent: **a.** What is the order point? **b.** What is the safety stock level?

5. Given: LT = 6 days (constant), $\overline{d}$ = 100 units per day, σ_d = 20 units per day, d is normally distributed, and service level is 90 percent. Required: **a.** OP, and **b.** SS.

6. The maintenance department at the Blimp Tire Manufacturing Company stocks spare parts that are used to repair machines in production departments throughout the plant. One such part — #1520 bearing — has these demand-per-month historical data from ten previous periods: 21, 15, 22, 30, 18, 26, 23, 29, 25, and 19. If the lead time is so

predictable that it can be considered a constant 1.25 months, d is normally distributed, and if manufacturing's demand for the parts must be satisfied on the average of 90 percent of the time: **a.** What is the order point? **b.** What is the safety stock level?

7. Given: Long cost per unit = \$20, short cost per unit = \$30, and historical DDLT data in units are:

DDLT (Units)	P(DDLT)
6	.1
7	.3
8	.5
9	.1

Required: **a.** Use payoff tables to determine the order point. **b.** Use marginal analysis to determine the order point. **c.** Compute the safety stock.

8. The BIG University has a central work pool that supplies electrostatic copies for students at a price of \$.10 per unit. The actual cost of making the copies is \$.05. Ms. Stacey, the work pool manager, wants to determine what the optimal order point should be for the electrostatic paper if there are 20,000 sheets per case, the carrying cost from one reorder cycle to another is \$.03 per sheet, and past DDLT has been:

DDLT (Cases)	P(DDLT)	DDLT (Cases)	P(DDLT)
10	.10	12	.25
11	.20	13	.35
		14	.10

a. Compute the order point using payoff tables. **b.** Compute the order point using marginal analysis. **c.** Compute the safety stock.

Selected Bibliography

American Production and Inventory Control Society. *APICS Dictionary of Inventory Control Terms and Production Control Terms.* 3d ed. Washington, DC: APICS, 1970.

————. *APICS Bibliography, 1972–1973.* Washington, DC: APICS.

Hadley, G., and T. M. Whitin. *Analysis of Inventory Systems.* Englewood Cliffs, NJ: Prentice-Hall, 1963.

Pursche, S. "Putting Service Level into Proper Perspective." *Production and Inventory Management* 16(third quarter 1975): 69–75.

Chapter Outline

10

Scheduling Manufacturing and Service Operations:

Short-Range Scheduling Decisions

Gantt never patented the concept, nor profited from it, but his achievement did earn him the Distinguished Service Medal from the Government. A member of Gantt's consulting firm, Wallace Clark, popularized the idea of the Gantt Chart in a book that was translated into eight languages, formed the basis for the Russian central planners to control their five year plans, and provided the whole world with a graphic means of planning and controlling work.
Daniel A. Wren, 1972

Aggregate planning is the top management activity that results in a *capacity plan*—the scheme of providing workers, materials, machines, and other productive resources in each time period of the intermediate-range planning horizon. This capacity plan provides personnel departments with an overall plan for recruiting, training, layoffs, and overtime for workers. It also serves as a guide for purchasing departments to plan inflows of materials, thus indicating when to develop additional suppliers, cut back purchases from present suppliers, and so on. Capacity plans also indicate to production planning and control departments the planned productive capacity in each time period. Therefore, capacity plans generally set the aggregate output targets in each time period that constrain the detailed short-range schedules which are developed later.

The characteristics of scheduling systems that both plan and control the outputs from productive systems are determined in large measure by the productive systems themselves. For the unique nature of each productive system sets the general requirements of control systems employed to insure that outputs will be produced to meet customer requirements under conditions of high internal efficiency.

Manufacturing systems are classified into job shops (and other intermittent productive systems) and continuous productive systems for scheduling purposes.

Intermittent productive systems produce nonstandard products that are usually produced to customer orders and specifications in facilities that arrange workers, machines, supervision, and departments based on production processes. Customer orders are usually processed in small quantities requiring frequent machine change-overs and complicated scheduling and control systems.

On the other hand, continuous productive systems produce standard products in high volumes, usually on a produce-to-stock basis. Workers, specialized machines, supervisors, and departments are arranged according to products along assembly or processing lines. Machine changeovers are infrequent; in-process inventories are almost nonexistent.

Service systems are classified into custom and standard services for scheduling purposes. The scheduling techniques employed to schedule manufacturing systems may also be generally applied to service systems if we recognize the idiosyncrasies of service systems. The characteristics of job shop manufacturing systems are similar to those of custom service systems. Therefore, many scheduling approaches are interchangeable between these two types of systems. Standard service systems are similar to continuous productive systems except that custom service systems do not ordinarily produce to stock. Rather, like most other service systems, services are generated upon customer request. Additionally, service systems are usually dominated by workers as the chief productive resource; therefore, work force scheduling can be the principal scheduling concern in these systems.

The diversity of these productive systems precludes the development of a single scheduling approach or one set of techniques that comprehensively analyzes all scheduling decisions. On the contrary, the scheduling decisions of job shops, continuous productive systems, and service systems differ materially. Therefore, the analysis and control techniques used by managers to develop schedules must also differ.

Let us begin our study of scheduling by seeing how firms develop master production schedules — plans for producing end items or finished products.

Master Production Schedules (MPS)

Master production schedules (*MPS*) set the quantity of each end item to be completed in the productive system for each time period of the short-term planning horizon. End items are finished products, assemblies, or stocked parts that are shipped as end items to customers, stocked in inventory, shipped to branch warehouses, shipped to other intracompany locations, or used by marketing research and research and development (R & D) departments.

Master production scheduling is principally concerned with allocating productive capacity to satisfy a variety of end item demands. Inventory, customers, scrap, R & D, emergencies, and other factors all place claims upon productive capacity. These demands must be regularly estimated and productive capacity must be allocated among them with this goal in mind: fully utilize productive capacity and satisfy market needs.

Operations managers regularly, usually weekly, hold staff meetings to review market data and facility loading information and to approve master production schedules. The MPS is a plan for future production of end items over

Figure 10.1
The Master Scheduling Process

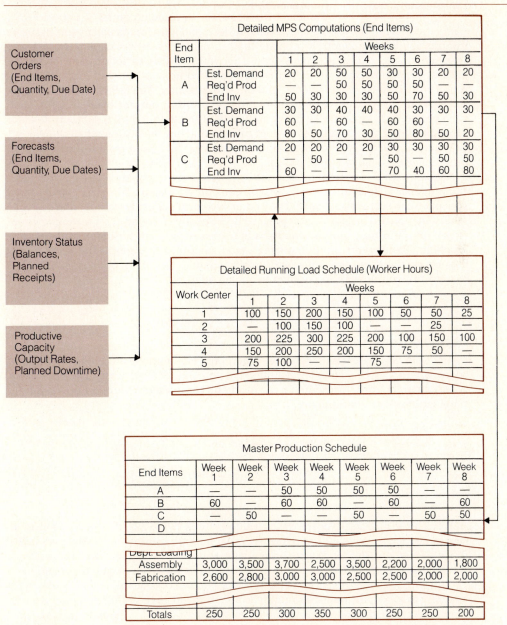

Customer
Orders
(End Items,
Quantity, Due Date)

Forecasts
(End Items,
Quantity, Due Dates)

Inventory Status
(Balances,
Planned
Receipts)

Productive
Capacity
(Output Rates,
Planned Downtime)

Detailed MPS Computations (End Items)

End Item		Weeks							
		1	2	3	4	5	6	7	8
A	Est. Demand	20	20	50	50	30	30	20	20
	Req'd Prod	—	—	50	50	50	50	—	—
	End Inv	50	30	30	30	50	70	50	30
B	Est. Demand	30	30	40	40	40	30	30	30
	Req'd Prod	60	—	60	—	60	60	—	—
	End Inv	80	50	70	30	50	80	50	20
C	Est. Demand	20	20	20	20	30	30	30	30
	Req'd Prod	—	50	—	—	50	—	50	50
	End Inv	60	—	—	—	70	40	60	80

Detailed Running Load Schedule (Worker Hours)

Work Center	Weeks							
	1	2	3	4	5	6	7	8
1	100	150	200	150	100	50	50	25
2	—	100	150	100	—	—	25	—
3	200	225	300	225	200	100	150	100
4	150	200	250	200	150	75	50	—
5	75	100	—	—	75	—	—	—

Master Production Schedule

End Items	Week 1	Week 2	Week 3	Week 4	Week 5	Week 6	Week 7	Week 8
A	—	—	50	50	50	50	—	—
B	60	—	60	60	—	60	—	60
C	—	50	—	—	50	—	50	50
D								
Dept. Loading								
Assembly	3,000	3,500	3,700	2,500	3,500	2,200	2,000	1,800
Fabrication	2,600	2,800	3,000	3,000	2,500	2,500	2,000	2,000
Totals	250	250	300	350	300	250	250	200

a given planning horizon. From these master schedules the detailed production schedules for all work centers in each department in each future time period of the planning horizon are determined.

Figure 10.1 describes the general process for developing an MPS. Detailed MPS computations require inputs of customer orders, end item forecasts, inventory status information, and productive capacity limitations (work center capacities, running load schedules, and so on). These inputs allow schedulers to determine preliminary MPS computations that are continuously checked against running load schedules for all work centers, departments, and the entire facility. The MPS computations are modified to insure that work centers are fully utilized but not overloaded in each time period. The final MPS is the compilation of the detailed MPS computations for all of the end items. The process would be repeated one week later when the Week 1 schedule is placed into production; one new week is added onto the end, and all other weeks are moved up one week.

When an MPS is prepared, schedulers do not have complete freedom to change the previous MPS. Earlier weeks will be considered frozen and cannot be changed except on the highest authority. The middle weeks are considered firm, and changes in this section are resisted. Later weeks can be easily changed. This arrangement of frozen and firm time period schedules is necessary to plan for material deliveries, machine changeovers, and employee work schedules to support the MPS. These supporting plans require some lead time to change; therefore, changes in the MPS may be difficult or even impossible to accomplish.

Detailed Computations in MPS

Figure 10.2 demonstrates how the detailed MPS calculations are made for two end items, A and B, over an 8-week planning horizon. Safety stock levels are 30 units for A and 40 units for B. EOQs are 50 for A and 60 for B. Follow through the computations for Product A carefully:

Week	Beginning Inventory − Total Demand = Balance			Required Production
1	70	20	50	——
2	50	20	30	——
3	30	50	(20)	50

In Week 1 the balance exceeds desired safety stock ($50 > 30$); therefore, no production is needed. In Week 2 the balance is also enough to provide the desired safety stock ($30 = 30$). But in Week 3 the balance is actually negative. Therefore, a production run of 50 units is planned. All other periods are computed similarly.

These procedures result in a schedule for each end item that when checked for capacity in all departments ultimately is summarized as the MPS. You may wonder about the level of confidence that we have in the customer demand figures. Customer demand is the force that drives all other MPS computations, and you *should* question the precision of these figures.

Figure 10.2
Detailed Computation in MPS

		\multicolumn{8}{c}{MPS Detailed Computations (End Items)}						
End Item		\multicolumn{8}{c}{Weeks}						
		1	2	3	4	5	6	7	8
A	Intracompany Orders				20	10	10		
	Branch Warehouse Orders			20					
	R & D Orders			10	10				
	Customer Demand (Forecast and Orders)	20	20	20	20	20	20	20	20
	Total Demand	20	20	50	50	30	30	20	20
	Beginning Inventory	70	50	30	30	30	50	70	50
	Required Production	—	—	50	50	50	50	—	—
	Ending Inventory	50	30	30	30	50	70	50	30
B	Intracompany Orders			10		10			
	Branch Warehouse Orders				20			20	
	R & D Orders					10	10		
	Customer Demand (Forecast and Orders)	30	30	30	20	20	20	10	30
	Total Demand	30	30	40	40	40	30	30	30
	Beginning Inventory	50	80	50	70	90	50	80	50
	Required Production	60	—	60	60	—	60	—	60
	Ending Inventory	80	50	70	90	50	80	50	80

Note: Safety Stock: EOQ:
         A = 30   A = 50
         B = 40   B = 60

Estimating Demand for End Items

If customer demand is wrong, we will not be producing the right end items in the correct quantities. However, the dynamics of the MPS usually cause us to have confidence in customer demand estimates for the earlier periods of the MPS; Figure 10.3 shows why. In Weeks 1 and 2 we have customer orders in hand to support the demand estimates. It is in the later periods of the MPS that we treat demand estimates as tentative because forecasts are the principal basis for estimating customer demand. **Accuracy of demand estimates is more important in the earlier periods of the MPS, however, because actions must have already been taken to provide resources to produce the end items scheduled for these earlier periods: materials have been ordered, workers have been scheduled to work shifts, and machine changeovers have been scheduled.** Money has already been spent or committed to producing the end items scheduled for these earlier periods.

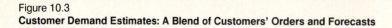

Figure 10.3
Customer Demand Estimates: A Blend of Customers' Orders and Forecasts

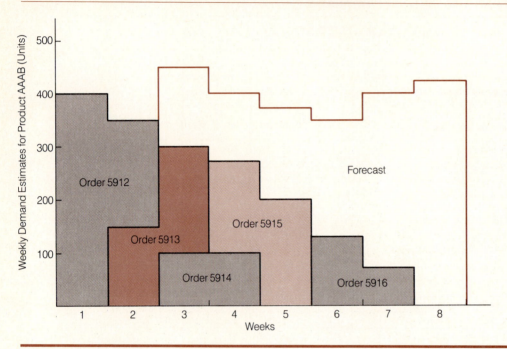

As time passes and the demand estimates of the later periods move forward in the schedule, a metamorphosis occurs — later periods' demand estimates based principally on forecasts become earlier periods' demand estimates based principally on in-hand orders. And this metamorphosis occurs because customer orders are flowing in as time passes, forecasts are being modified as time passes, demand estimates are being updated, and all of this is occurring before money must be committed to ordering materials, scheduling workers, and scheduling machine changeovers.

Master production scheduling is an important activity in POM. When it is poorly done, these symptoms can occur: (1) overloaded facilities, (2) underloaded facilities, (3) excessive inventory levels on some end items and frequent stockouts on others, (4) unbelievable schedules that production personnel do not follow, (5) unreliable delivery promises to customers, and (6) excessive expediting. When MPS is properly done, positive customer relations are developed, inventory levels are low (because we produce the right end items in correct quantities), and productive resources are fully utilized. Additionally, the MPS becomes the basis for detailed schedules for each production department and it anchors the material requirements planning system.

The description of the MPS above often mentioned the activities of schedulers. In some applications of the MPS today, some of these activities are performed by computers.

Computerized MPS

The MPS can be prepared by a computing system. In these cases scheduling department personnel input end item demand information, inventory status information (or this can be automatically deduced from inventory files), capacity constraints, demand forecasts, EOQs, and desired safety stock levels. The computer then performs the detailed MPS calculations, compares these figures to work center loads and capacity constraints, and finally generates an MPS. When many end items are produced in several production departments, the computer is not only economical, it is absolutely necessary to process all the data, particularly when a weekly MPS is generated. Use of computers has actually allowed some to use what is called a *net change MPS*. These schedules show only changes to the prevailing MPS on a real time basis.

The MPS is certainly the central focus in most computerized scheduling systems regardless of whether the programs are custom-designed for a productive system or whether they are a standard system from one of the computer hardware or software companies. *Communications Oriented Production Information and Control Systems* (*COPICS*) from IBM is an example of these computerized scheduling systems.[1] As Figure 10.4 shows, COPICS is more than just a computerized scheduling system in that it integrates forecasting, scheduling, inventory, and purchasing decisions into one large information system for planning and controlling all facets of the productive system.

The interdependence of inventories, scheduling, and purchasing is recognized in POM, but we have too often made these decisions independent of each other. Integrated information systems for POM should result in better-managed productive systems in the future.

Once we know from the MPS what end items must be produced from the entire facility, we must determine the detailed short-range work center production schedules required to support the MPS. The planning activities and techniques necessary to the development of these detailed schedules vary considerably from situation to situation, but they may be conveniently classified as job shop scheduling decisions, continuous productive system scheduling decisions, and work force scheduling decisions in services.

Job Shop and Custom Service Scheduling Decisions

The nature of job shops and some custom service systems creates the need for managers to make these key scheduling decisions:

1. If more than one customer order is waiting to be processed at a work center, in what sequence should the orders be processed?

2. Since customer orders can ordinarily be processed along a variety of paths through the productive facility, which orders should be assigned to which work centers to minimize both costs and throughput times?

---

[1] International Business Machines, *Communications Oriented Production Information and Control Systems* (*COPICS*), vol. 1: *Management Overview*, Publication G320-1974 (White Plains, NY: IBM, 1972).

472

Figure 10.4
COPICS

COPICS Manufacturing—Functional Flow

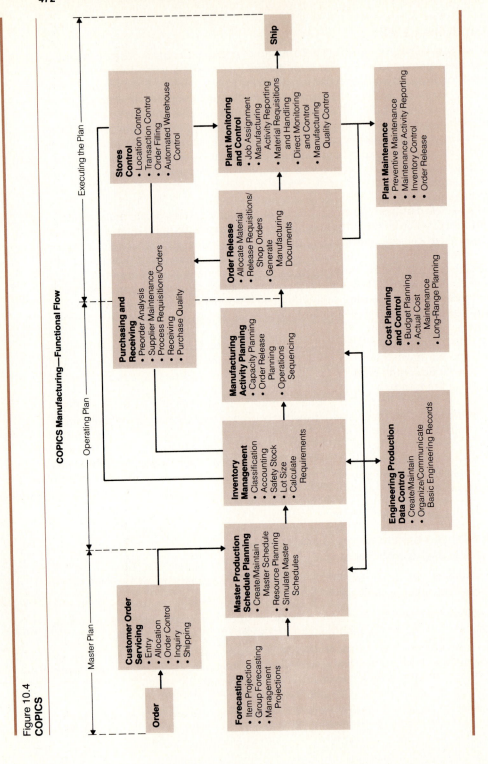

3. Given that numerous customer orders are being simultaneously processed in the productive facility and that times must be reserved for each customer order in downstream work centers, how can the work center schedules be coordinated?

Several approaches assist managers in making these scheduling decisions. We shall develop some of them here to analyze order sequencing problems, assignment problems, and coordinating work center schedules.

Order Sequencing Problems

Pretend that you are a production supervisor of a skilled machinist who operates a vertical boring mill in your department. He has just come to you to let you make a decision for him. He presently has four customer jobs to process at his operation. All of them seem important to him, but he cannot process all of them at once, so he wants to know in what order he should process the jobs. Unless the supervisor has a schedule that indicates the priorities assigned to the jobs at the vertical boring mill work center, confusion will more than likely exist. The order of processing the jobs at the work center is extremely important to determining how quickly all four jobs will be processed, and this directly affects the levels of in-process inventories, shop congestion, and customer service.

We will examine job sequencing decisions under four different situations: when changeover costs are independent of job sequence, when changeover costs are dependent upon job sequence, when several jobs must be processed through two work centers, and when many jobs must be processed through many work centers.

Changeover Costs Independent of Job Sequence Let us assume that the cost of processing the jobs at a work center is not dependent upon the sequence of processing the jobs. In other words, there is no economic reason that one job should follow another because of ease of machine changeovers.

Scheduling departments have developed many job sequencing rules that determine which job comes next at work centers. Some of the most frequently used rules are:

1. Process first the job that arrived first — first-come, first-served (FCFS).
2. Process first the job that has the shortest processing time among the waiting jobs at the present work center.
3. Process first the job that has the earliest due date through the entire facility.
4. Process first the job that has the shortest waiting line at its next work center.
5. Process first the job that has the least amount of downstream slack (time to due date minus total remaining processing time).
6. Process first the job that has the lowest critical ratio (time to due date divided by total remaining processing time).
7. Process first the job that is the most profitable.
8. Process first the job that belongs to the most valued customer.

Which of these sequencing rules performs best? These criteria are commonly used to evaluate the performance of sequencing rules:

1. *Average completion time*—the average amount of time each job spends in the facility.
2. *Average number of jobs in the system*—the average total number of jobs in the facility.
3. *Average job lateness*—the average amount of time that each job's actual processing time exceeds the allowed processing time that is set by its due date.

Let us demonstrate the use of sequencing rules and evaluation criteria in a simple one-work-center productive system. Example 10.1 describes a computer center that presently uses a first-come, first-served sequencing rule in processing customers' computer programs. The example compares shortest processing time (the job with the shortest processing time comes next) and the critical ratio (the job with the lowest critical ratio—time to promised delivery divided by downstream processing time remaining) sequencing rules with the present first-come, first-served policy.

Example 10.1

Evaluating Sequencing Rules in the Jiffy Computer Company

The Jiffy Computer Company processes computer programs for regional banks and savings and loans in Jacksonville, Florida. Numerous customer complaints have been received by Jiffy concerning excessive completion times for their jobs. Additionally, the computer center supervisors have complained that too many jobs seem to be in the center at any one time, thus confusing operations.

Jane Pinstripe, a systems analyst at the center, had taken some scheduling courses at the local university. She volunteered to study the problem. She suggested that a 24-hour period be studied at the center while using three sequencing rules—first-come, first-served (the present policy); shortest processing time; and critical ratio. These rules would be evaluated according to three criteria—average completion time, average number of jobs in the system, and average job lateness. Jane recommended that whichever rule seemed to perform best to these three criteria during the 24-hour study period should be adopted as the sequencing policy to be used over a longer operating period.

Jiffy's management authorized Jane to conduct the study. She selected a 24-hour period and prepared Tables 10.1 and 10.2.

Table 10.1 shows the estimated processing time remaining and the time to promised delivery for each of six computer jobs. The job sequence (order in which the jobs are to be processed), flow time (total time each job is in the system before completion), and lateness (time to promised delivery minus the flow time) are developed for each job under the three sequencing rules.

Table 10.2 compares the three sequencing rules according to three evaluation criteria—average completion time, average number of jobs in the system, and average job lateness. Average completion time is the average time that jobs are in the system and is computed by summing the

Table 10.1
Data and Computations of Three Sequencing Rules at Jiffy Computer Company

(1)	(2)	(3)	First-Come, First-Served			Shortest Processing Time			Critical Ratio			
			(4)	(5)	(6)	(7)	(8)	(9)	(10)	(11)	(12)	(13)
Computer Jobs	Estimated Processing Time (Hours)	Time to Promised Completion (Hours)	Job Sequence	Flow Time (Hours)	Lateness (Hours) [(3) − (5)]	Job Sequence	Flow Time (Hours)	Lateness (Hours) [(3) − (8)]	Critical Ratio [(3) ÷ (2)]	Job Sequence	Flow Time (Hours)	Lateness (Hours) [(3) − (12)]
A	2	4	1	2	—	1	2	—	2.00	2	6	2
B	5	18	2	7	—	5	18	—	3.60	5	20	2
C	3	8	3	10	2	2	5	5	2.67	3	9	1
D	4	4	4	14	10	3	9	5	1.00	1	4	—
E	6	20	5	20	—	6	24	4	3.33	4	15	—
F	4	24	6	24	—	4	13	—	6.00	6	24	—

Table 10.2
A Comparison of the Performance of Three Sequencing Rules at Jiffy Computer Company

Evaluation Criteria	First-Come, First-Served	Shortest Processing Time	Critical Ratio
Average completion time	$= \dfrac{2 + 7 + 10 + 14 + 20 + 24}{6}$ $= 12.83$ hours **Rank = 2**	$= \dfrac{2 + 5 + 9 + 13 + 18 + 24}{6}$ $= 11.83$ hours **Rank = 1**	$= \dfrac{4 + 6 + 9 + 15 + 20 + 24}{6}$ $= 13.00$ hours **Rank = 3**
Average number of jobs in system	$= \dfrac{2(6) + 5(5) + 3(4) + 4(3) + 6(2) + 4(1)}{24}$ $= 3.21$ jobs **Rank = 2**	$= \dfrac{2(6) + 3(5) + 4(4) + 4(3) + 5(2) + 6(1)}{24}$ $= 2.96$ jobs **Rank = 1**	$= \dfrac{4(6) + 2(5) + 3(4) + 6(3) + 5(2) + 4(1)}{24}$ $= 3.25$ jobs **Rank = 3**
Average job lateness	$= \dfrac{0 + 0 + 2 + 10 + 0 + 0}{6}$ $= 2.00$ hours **Rank = 3**	$= \dfrac{0 + 0 + 0 + 5 + 4 + 0}{6}$ $= 1.50$ hours **Rank = 2**	$= \dfrac{2 + 2 + 1 + 0 + 0 + 0}{6}$ $= .83$ hours **Rank = 1**

flow times for all of the jobs and dividing by the number of jobs. The average number of jobs in the system is computed by taking a weighted average. For example, in the first-come, first-served sequencing rule, 6 jobs are in the system for 2 hours, 5 jobs are in the system for 5 hours, and so on until only 1 job is in the system for 4 hours. Therefore, the average number of jobs in the system is computed thus:

$$\frac{[2(6) + 5(5) + 3(4) + 4(3) + 6(2) + 4(1)]}{24} = 3.21 \text{ hours}$$

The average job lateness is computed by summing the hours of lateness for each job and dividing by the number of jobs.

Jane reviewed the results of the study: shortest processing time received 1, 1, and 2 ranks; critical ratio received 3, 3, and 1 ranks; and first-come, first-served received 2, 2, and 3 ranks. She believed that shortest processing time should be recommended as the sequencing rule to be followed at Jiffy.

In the Jiffy Computer Company example, no single sequencing rule ranks first on all the evaluation criteria. This is also what we find in real world applications. *No single sequencing rule excels on all evaluation criteria.* We know from experience that:

1. First-come, first-served does not perform particularly well on most commonly used evaluation criteria. It does, however, in some cases give customers a sense of fair play, and equity can be an important consideration in service systems.

2. Shortest processing time does perform well on most evaluation criteria. It tends to perform best on average completion time and average number of jobs in the system. Although it does perform well in most circumstances on average job lateness, it may not do as well as critical ratio. The chief disadvantage of shortest processing time as a sequencing rule is that long duration jobs may be continuously pushed back in the schedule in favor of short duration jobs. Thus, long duration jobs may have excessive completion times from customers' viewpoints. Whenever this rule is used in practice, the long duration jobs must be periodically moved ahead and processed.

3. Critical ratio usually performs well on only the average job lateness criterion. However, critical ratio is intrinsically appealing: we want to first work on jobs that are most likely to be required before they can be finished. Additionally, critical ratio is a useful aid in identifying jobs that are likely not to meet due dates in the schedule. (Their critical ratios would be less than one.)

Scheduling departments usually perform test runs on their shops to measure the performance of different sequencing rules, as in our Jiffy Computer Company example. Once they have selected the rule that tends to perform best for them on the criteria most important to their organizations, the sequencing rule is uniformly applied for long periods. Although emergencies do occur that cause some jobs to have extraordinary priority, schedules at work centers set the sequence in which most jobs are processed. Supervisors and workers therefore ordinarily do not have to have lengthy discussions concerning the sequence of processing jobs when cost of changeovers is independent of job sequence.

Changeover Costs Dependent upon Job Sequence There are numerous situations in which the sequence of processing jobs at a work center is dictated by the economies of machine changeovers. For example, two jobs may use exactly the same major machine settings, jigs and fixtures (holding devices), and raw materials except for minor adjustments. Under ordinary circumstances, jobs that require similar machine setups and consequently require only minor adjustments to achieve a changeover from one job to another should follow each other at work centers.

Example 10.2 demonstrates a simple rule for determining job sequences in situations where the dominant factor in selecting a job sequence is minimizing the total cost of changeovers among the waiting jobs. The procedure selects the first and second job in the sequence by finding the lowest changeover cost among all the possible changeovers. From the second job on, the next job is always determined by selecting the lowest changeover costs from among the remaining jobs. This rule may not be optimal, but it usually performs well in practice.

Example 10.2

Changeover Costs and Job Sequence at Quick Printing Company

The Quick Printing Company does custom printing jobs for local firms, political candidates, and schools. Quick Printing is in the middle of an election year boom, and numerous political poster jobs are waiting to be processed at the offset press. Tom Skidoo does Quick Printing's job planning; he is currently developing a weekly printing schedule for the offset press. He has developed these changeover costs for the six waiting jobs. All jobs carry equal priority, so that the deciding factor in selecting a job sequence is the total changeover costs for the six jobs.

		Jobs That Precede					
		A	B	C	D	E	F
Jobs That Follow	A	—	$12	$15	$10	$35	$20
	B	$25	—	20	20	25	20
	C	27	15	—	12	20	15
	D	16	30	10	—	25	30
	E	35	20	25	30	—	30
	F	20	25	15	25	30	—

Tom uses this rule to develop a low-cost job sequence: *First, select the lowest changeover cost among all the changeovers. The next job will be selected that has the lowest changeover cost among the remaining jobs that follow the previously selected job.* Since there is a tie for the starting jobs (D–A and C–D), Tom develops two sequences:

1. A follows D ($10 is the minimum changeover cost, D is first and A is next).
   F follows A (read down A column; Job F has lowest changeover cost among the remaining jobs).
   C follows F (read down F column; Job C has lowest changeover cost among the remaining jobs).
   B follows C (read down C column; Job B has lowest changeover cost among the remaining jobs).
   E follows B (read down B column; Job E has lowest changeover cost among the remaining jobs).
   The job sequence is DAFCBE; its total changeover cost is 10 + 20 + 15 + 20 + 20 = $85.

2. Because there was a tie for the starting jobs above, the second job sequence is now developed:
   D follows C, A follows D, F follows A, B follows F, and E follows B.
   The job sequence is CDAFBE; its total changeover cost is 10 + 10 + 20 + 20 + 20 = $80.

Of the two sequences, CDAFBE is preferred because its total changeover cost is lower.

Now, Tom knows that this is not necessarily the lowest possible total changeover cost for the six jobs. In other words, the method does not guarantee an optimal solution. But the simpler rule is easy to understand and it gives satisfactory, if not optimal, results.

Other more mathematically sophisticated procedures will achieve optimal results. *Integer linear programming* can be used to minimize total changeover costs within a set of constraints that require all jobs to be assigned to the sequence once and only once. Linear programming procedures are usually practical only if computer services are available, because the number of variables and constraints becomes quite large when the number of waiting jobs increases beyond the trivial level.

Total enumeration can also yield an optimal solution, but this involves costing out all the possible job sequences. When only a few jobs are waiting, this procedure is simple; but when the number grows only slightly, total enumeration is impractical and is therefore rarely used. For example, here are the number of possible sequences when these numbers of jobs are waiting:

Jobs Waiting	Possible Job Sequences	Jobs Waiting	Possible Job Sequences
4	24	7	5,040
5	120	8	40,320
6	720	9	362,880
		10	3,628,800

The possible number of job sequences from among n jobs is $n!$:

$$n! = n(n-1)(n-2) \cdots (n-n+1)$$

When six jobs are waiting, as in the Quick Printing Company example, the number of possible job sequences is:

$$n! = 6(6-1)(6-2)(6-3)(6-4)(6-5)(6-6+1) = 6 \times 5 \times 4 \times 3 \times 2 \times 1 = 720$$

Computer search procedures short-cut the total enumeration procedures through following simple procedural rules as the computer searches for good job sequences. Although these methods may not be optimal from a purely mathematical standpoint, they do give good results in practice. They are useful in very large problems because of their quick, efficient, and near-optimal results.

One of the chief disadvantages of all these methods is that they are designed to select job sequences at work centers with only one goal in mind: minimize the total changeover cost. Although this is a worthwhile goal, what about the other evaluation criteria that we discussed previously — average completion time, average number of jobs in the system, and average job lateness? These criteria are fundamental in POM because in-process inventory levels, shop loading, throughput rates, shop congestion, and customer service are directly affected. How do we simultaneously consider these criteria while we seek to minimize total changeover costs?

One approach is to consider the job sequence determined by uniformly applying a sequencing rule such as shortest processing time and the job sequence determined by the total changeover cost procedures from Example 10.2 as alternatives. You must choose between the two alternatives based on which goal you hold most dear — minimizing total changeover cost or overall shop loading. Although some authors recommend this either-or approach, it seems from a practical standpoint that other job sequences could provide decision makers with alternatives that perform better across all the decision criteria of changeover costs and overall shop loading.

In practice, *schedulers* ordinarily first consider job sequences that result in low total changeover costs and then modify the sequence to a new compromise sequence as required to approximately conform to sequencing rules (critical ratio, shortest processing time, and so on) or special customer priority rules. Because sequencing decisions are increasingly an integral part of computerized scheduling systems in many organizations, the computation procedures must be programmed into the computer. These programs are written in practice to select job sequences that perform well across many criteria — total changeover costs, average completion time, average number of jobs in the system, average job lateness, special customer priorities, and so on.

Sequencing Several Jobs through Two Work Centers When several jobs must be sequenced through two work centers, the job sequence at each work center may be determined by the procedures presented above. Two job sequences would ordinarily result, one for the first work center and one for the second. The two job sequences would not be expected to be the same since the two sequencing decisions would ordinarily be treated as independent of one another. Occasionally, however, we want to select a job sequence that must hold for both work centers. This situation can be effectively analyzed by using *Johnson's rule*.[2]

---

[2] S. M. Johnson, "Optimal Two Stage and Three Stage Production Schedules with Setup Times Included," *Naval Research Logistics Quarterly* 1 (March 1954): 61–68.

Example 10.3 demonstrates the use of Johnson's rule in a two-work-center productive system—the Jiffy Computer Company. Customers' jobs must be processed through data encoding (Work Center 1) and data processing (Work Center 2) *in the same job sequence, the only requirement of Johnson's rule.* The job sequence that results has the minimum processing time through both work centers for all the jobs.

Example 10.3

Sequencing Computer Programs through Two Work Centers at Jiffy Computer Company with Johnson's Rule

There are two work centers at the Jiffy Computer Company, data encoding and data processing. Jiffy's management wishes to adopt a procedure that would routinely set a common sequence in which jobs would be processed through both work centers. Jane Pinstripe has been experimenting with Johnson's rule; she believes that Jiffy's situation can be effectively analyzed with this technique. Jiffy's management wants both work centers to change over to new jobs at the same time. In other words, if Work Center 1 completes its work on a job, it must wait until Work Center 2 has completed the job that it has been working on so that both work centers can begin new jobs simultaneously. The reason for this requirement is so that supervisors can give job instructions to both work centers at the same time about how to process the jobs.

Jane visits the computer center, noting that six jobs are waiting.

a. These data are developed for the six jobs:

Computer Job to Be Processed	Estimated Processing Times (Hours)		
	Work Center 1, Data Encoding	Work Center 2, Data Processing	Total for Both Centers
A	1.50	.50	2.00
B	4.00	1.00	5.00
C	.75	2.25	3.00
D	1.00	3.00	4.00
E	2.00	4.00	6.00
F	1.80	2.20	4.00

b. Johnson's rule is:

1. Select the shortest processing time.

2. If the shortest time is at the first work center, do the job first. If it is at the second work center, do the job last.

3. Eliminate the job assigned in Step 2 and proceed to repeat Steps 1 and 2 above until all of the jobs have been assigned a position in the sequence.

Jane then begins to follow the steps of the rule:

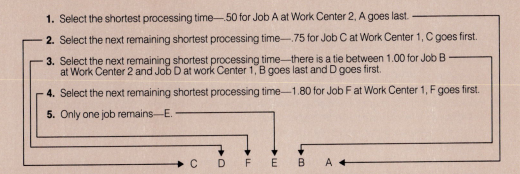

1. Select the shortest processing time—.50 for Job A at Work Center 2, A goes last.

2. Select the next remaining shortest processing time—.75 for Job C at Work Center 1, C goes first.

3. Select the next remaining shortest processing time—there is a tie between 1.00 for Job B at Work Center 2 and Job D at work Center 1, B goes last and D goes first.

4. Select the next remaining shortest processing time—1.80 for Job F at Work Center 1, F goes first.

5. Only one job remains—E.

C   D   F   E   B   A

c. This CDFEBA job sequence is further studied by developing the cumulative time to process all six jobs through both work centers. Jane knows that Jiffy's management wants the jobs to begin at the same time in both work centers:

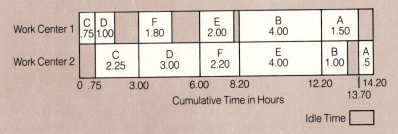

d. Jane can see that the CDFEBA job sequence allows both work centers to process all of the jobs in 14.20 hours. She plans to use this example to demonstrate to Jiffy's management the application of Johnson's rule.

Note in this example that if a tie for the shortest processing time occurs in different work centers, no difficulty is encountered in determining the job sequence. If a tie should occur within the same work center, however, two job sequences would need to be evaluated by comparing their cumulative processing times as in part c of the example. The job sequence with the lowest cumulative processing time would be the recommended job sequence. Note also in the example that if we wished to relax the requirement that all jobs must begin at the same time, *a constraint that is not required to use Johnson's rule*, the cumulative time for processing all jobs through both work centers would be reduced from 14.20 hours to 13.70 hours. Only the idle time (.50 hour) between Jobs B and A in Work Center 2 would be eliminated. Can you confirm the correctness of this 13.70 hours value by preparing a cumulative processing time figure as in Example 10.3? Johnson's rule can therefore be used with or without the requirement that all jobs must begin simultaneously in the two work centers.

Sequencing Many Jobs through Many Work Centers Job shops ordinarily must sequence many jobs through many work centers, a problem for which there are no easy analytical solutions. And yet operations managers and schedulers make these types of sequencing decisions daily; how do they go about making these complex decisions? Ordinarily, a sequencing rule such as shortest processing time, critical ratio, or earliest due date is uniformly applied periodically at each work center in the entire facility. This set of job sequences at each work center is then modified to take advantage of economies in changeovers. If some jobs are particularly late, change-over economies may have to be forgone in order to meet customer due date commitments.

Surprisingly, this nonoptimal approach is effective in practice: facilities are nearly fully loaded, high levels of customer service are maintained, low levels of in-process inventories result, and congestion in the shop is reduced to reasonable levels. Put simply, although this approach to setting job sequences is nonoptimal, it works in practice.

Research is continuing to explore mathematical methods to optimally solve these complex sequencing problems. Queuing theory, computer simulation, and computer search have all been used by operations research analysts to study sequencing problems. It is hoped that these and similar techniques will continue to mature as computer systems develop to provide managers with optimal or near-optimal sequencing decision support.

Assignment Problems

When many jobs are arriving in job shops that can be assigned to various work centers, determining which jobs should be assigned to which work centers is an important part of scheduling. These problems are commonly referred to as *assignment problems*.

Production planning and control departments develop routing plans or processing plans for jobs before they are placed in production in job shops. When one job is assigned to several work centers for processing, a certain amount of capacity in those work centers is then unavailable to be used by other jobs. Assignment of several jobs to work centers for optimal results, therefore, must be done for the whole group of jobs simultaneously.

In the Supplement to Chapter 5, the assignment method of linear programming was discussed and demonstrated in Example 5S.7. In that example, 5 jobs at the Mercury Electric Motor Company were assigned to 5 rewinding work centers. When n jobs must be assigned to only one downstream operation, as in the rewinding step at Mercury Electric, then the assignment method is an appropriate technique for analyzing such a problem. The assignment method is, however, seldom practical to use when job assignments must be made beyond the single-level case. Let us assume, for example, that each of the 5 jobs in the Mercury Electric example must be processed through 4 downstream work stations instead of the single rewinding operation. This assignment problem, involving 4 different sequential assignment decisions, is enormously complex to analyze mathematically because the jobs tend to emerge from each operation at random times. Computer simulation, covered in Chapter 13, is a technique that is appropriate for these analyses, but its application to multilevel job assignment problems is well beyond the scope of this text.

And yet, in spite of the difficulty of modeling these complex scheduling problems, schedulers routinely confront and solve similar problems in practice. These individuals have developed to a fine art the ability to prepare schedules for complex situations. Daily, schedulers efficiently load their shops with customers' jobs while juggling customer requests, machine breakdowns, delayed material shipments, upset supervisors, and so on. And somehow, their shops are near optimally loaded and customers are satisfied, and all of this in very complex scheduling situations.

When job assignments and job sequences have been determined as we have done thus far in this chapter, how do managers plan and coordinate the systematic flow of jobs through the facility? The coordination of work center schedules is the necessary planning and control activity that insures the orderly flow of jobs between work centers.

Coordinating Work Center Schedules

In intermittent productive systems, detailed schedules are prepared for each work center (an operation, processing step, small groups of operations, machine cluster, or other homogeneous groupings). These detailed schedules provide supervisors and workers with information regarding the sequences of jobs, when jobs should enter and leave each work center, standard worker-hours required, standard machine changeover times, and so on. An important missing ingredient in these detailed schedules, however, is the means to guide the set of jobs through the facility effectively.

How can supervisors develop a plan for changeover crews to follow, a plan that shows the work centers that require machine changeovers and the timing of each changeover? How can supervisors plan routine maintenance projects for each work center so that the activities occur during work center idle time? How can supervisors develop a plan for the movement of workers from work center to work center as needed to balance the load in the shop — in other words, move from slack work centers to overloaded work centers? These and other questions must be resolved by supervisors; detailed schedules for each work center cannot provide the answers.

Gantt charts, similar to those presented in Chapter 7 on project planning, can be used to display graphically the work loads in each work center in a department. Figure 10.5 is an example of a Gantt chart used to compare the weekly schedule for five work centers in a model shop (shops used to produce small quantities of experimental products for intracompany market research, engineering research, and process research). The jobs scheduled to be processed during the week are displayed with their beginning and ending times and allowed processing times represented by an open bar. As work progresses on a job, a solid bar shows how the work center is performing to the schedule. The time of the review is indicated by a vertical arrow.

Machine changes, routine maintenance projects, and other planned nonproductive work activities are indicated by an X. Blank spaces indicate idle time at the work center; work crews are not required during these periods and may be shifted to other work centers, or other jobs may be scheduled into these time slots later. Supervisors and production planners can see with a glance at the Gantt chart the progress of the work centers toward their schedules. For example, Figure 10.5

Figure 10.5
Gantt Chart for Coordinating Work Centers' Schedules

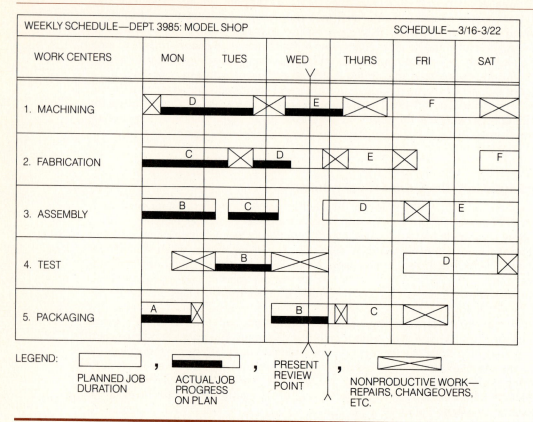

WEEKLY SCHEDULE—DEPT. 3985: MODEL SHOP   SCHEDULE—3/16-3/22

WORK CENTERS	MON	TUES	WED	THURS	FRI	SAT
1. MACHINING	☒ D		☒ E	☒	F	☒
2. FABRICATION	C	☒ D	☒ E	☒		F
3. ASSEMBLY	B	C		D	☒ E	
4. TEST	☒ B		☒		D	☒
5. PACKAGING	A ☒		B ☒	C	☒	

LEGEND: ▭ , ▬ , ⋏ PRESENT REVIEW POINT , ☒

PLANNED JOB DURATION   ACTUAL JOB PROGRESS ON PLAN   NONPRODUCTIVE WORK— REPAIRS, CHANGEOVERS, ETC.

shows that the time of the review is midafternoon on Wednesday. At this time the machining work center is ahead of schedule by about half a day on Job E, the packaging work center is ahead of schedule by about 2 hours on Job B, the test and assembly work centers are on schedule, and the fabrication work center is about 2 hours behind schedule on Job D. As a supervisor, how would information such as this guide your activities? These actions are suggested from Figure 10.5:

1. Check to see if Job F can be moved into the machining work center 4 hours early; also accelerate the changeover from Job E to Job F.

2. Investigate means of speeding up the performance of Job D in the fabrication work center. The use of packaging, testing, assembly, or machining workers may be feasible. If acceleration is infeasible, the schedules at fabrication and other downstream work centers must be slipped, that is, delayed.

3. Provide the workers at the packaging work center with 2 hours of other work.

Can you see now how Gantt charts provide operations managers with a practical way to coordinate the schedules of work centers? These graphical aids are found in most goods- and service-producing facilities, and although they are not often referred to as Gantt charts, they are extremely useful for coordinating a diversity of schedules of work teams, work centers, and major activities of projects.

Today detailed schedules are increasingly the outputs of computerized scheduling systems. Computer programs do output all the same information commonly found on Gantt schedules, and some of these programs actually output the Gantt charts. Other organizations routinely take the information off computer outputs and construct Gantt charts for departmental use. This reinforces the contention that the graphical nature of these charts makes the scheduling information easy to grasp and apply.

Computer packages for scheduling intermittent productive systems are growing in both number and frequency of application in today's productive systems.

Computerized Job Shop Scheduling Systems

Of course, you can buy or rent a computer and write your own computer programs that develop detailed schedules for each work center in your facility and for macro schedules that provide coordination of all the jobs to be processed. Or you can do as many other organizations have done, buy the ready-made software packages that are already tried and proven in a variety of scheduling situations. IBM, Xerox, and many other computer manufacturers and software companies have their own versions.

In some cases the scheduling packages are an integral part of a larger manufacturing information system—cost analyses, inventory information, and scheduling. All the areas of POM are tied together in a neat package. There is no denying that these computer packages are appealing, but don't jump to the conclusion that they can be adapted to a particular productive system quickly or easily just because the programs are already written and debugged. Many organizations have found, much to their disappointment, that it often takes months or even years to develop a system of information inputs that is necessary to feed the computerized system.

Other computer packages of less ambitious scope are principally designed to provide only scheduling information. Regardless of the scope of these packages, the scheduling portion of the programs ordinarily must:

1. Develop for each work center daily or weekly detailed schedules that indicate beginning and ending times for each job.
2. Develop departmental daily and weekly detailed schedules that are used to coordinate individual work centers.
3. Generate modified schedules as new customer or work center progress information surfaces.

Before these programs can be processed, the operations manager must set priority rules for determining the sequence of jobs at work centers, build the necessary set of rules for determining which jobs will be assigned to which work centers, and develop a system of follow-up and feedback within the facility for modifying schedules. These are not easy tasks. When computerized systems are installed, managers cannot play fast and loose with their scheduling decisions. One of the most common complaints from schedulers is that managers always seem to be changing the rules to save them from the latest customer's telephone call. Schedulers seem to be whipsawed between the changing orders from the top concerning which jobs are the hot ones in the current period. Computerized systems require that consistent rules must be developed and followed, rational approaches to routing and processing must be planned, and schedules must be followed if meaningful production planning information is to be delivered.

These requirements are often forced on some managers by the necessity of installing a computerized scheduling system. In short, we must clean up our scheduling acts in POM when computers are used to develop detailed schedules. Substantial improvements in customer service and internal operating efficiency are possible in these intermittent productive systems only if sequencing rules, routing plans, and other inputs are realistic and if schedules are followed.

We have now discussed and demonstrated several techniques for making decisions that either must precede detailed schedules or are helpful in developing and coordinating these schedules in intermittent productive systems. Let us now move from the job shop environment to the mass production environment of continuous productive systems and develop techniques of scheduling these systems.

Continuous Productive System and Standard Service Scheduling Decisions

The nature of assembly lines, continuous processing systems, and some standard service systems creates the need for managers to make these key decisions:

1. If products are produced in batches and multiple products are produced on the same assembly lines, how long should each product be produced before the line is changed over to another model? In other words, how many of each product model should be produced in each time period and when should changeovers be scheduled?

2. If products or services are produced to a specific delivery schedule, at any point in time how many cumulative units of output should have passed each upstream process step if future deliveries are to be on schedule?

We shall now develop some techniques to assist managers in resolving these scheduling-related problems — batch scheduling and scheduling and controlling production for delivery schedules.

Batch Scheduling

In Chapter 9 we discussed the concept of an economic order quantity (EOQ) when deliveries were gradual (p) and usage was at a constant rate (d). The EOQ then was based on striking a balance between annual carrying costs and annual ordering costs. The perspective developed was in the finished goods warehouse looking backward into the production departments. How many units of Product X should we order to replenish our finished goods inventory?

This same EOQ formula can be useful in estimating the length of production runs by developing a slightly different view. Picture yourself in the production departments looking toward the finished goods warehouse. How many units of Product X should we include in each production run to minimize annual carrying cost (still the same annual inventory carrying cost) and annual ordering cost (including ordering costs and changeover costs in production)? The length of production run problem is formulated in exactly the same way as the EOQ inventory replenishment problem from Chapter 9; the only difference is the perspective: $EOQ = \sqrt{(2DS/C)[p/(p-d)]}$. This EOQ formula is used in practice as a guide for determining the length of production runs for a single inventory item. As a comprehensive scheduling technique in batch scheduling, however, it is not entirely satisfactory because it fails to account for these facts:

1. Only so much productive capacity is available in each time period.
2. Inventory items share common productive capacity.
3. Length of production run decisions must be made simultaneously for all inventory items to be produced in each time period.
4. Length of production run decisions should be based on our most current information about demand rates and production rates and not upon annual ball park demand estimates as in EOQ.

These deficiencies of the EOQ to plan length of production runs have led to the development of the *runout method* for planning production schedules in production operations when batches of product models are produced on common assembly lines. This method attempts to use the total productive capacity available in each time period to produce just enough of each product model so that if we stopped producing, the finished goods inventory for each product would be depleted, or run out, at the same point in time.

Example 10.4 uses the runout method to develop a production schedule for five products of a pet food company. Notice in this example that the runout method does not attempt to set efficient lot sizes for individual products, a characteristic for which its approach is often criticized. In this example all 1,600 hours of extruder time per week are allocated among the five products so that if the weekly forecast demand materializes, the company would run out of each of the five products at exactly the same time.

Example 10.4

Runout Method of Production Scheduling at the Friendly Pet Food Company

The Friendly Pet Food Company is now planning its production for next week. All pet food products at Friendly must be processed through 20 mixer-extruders at its Hillsdale, Ohio, plant. Friendly has a total of 1,600 extruder hours per week of production capacity based upon its 6-month aggregate capacity plan. Friendly's scheduling department is reviewing the inventory levels, machine hours required per 1,000 pounds, and forecast usage for its five principal products. Develop a production schedule for the extruders by using the runout method.

Solution

1. First, convert inventory on hand and the forecasts into extruder hours:

(1) Product	(2) Inventory on Hand or in Production (000 Pounds)	(3) Extruder Time Required (Hours per 000 Pounds)	(4) Forecast Demand for Next Week (000 Pounds)	(5) Inventory on Hand (in Extruder Hours) [(2) × (3)]	(6) Forecast Demand for Next Week (in Extruder Hours) [(4) × (3)]
A	160.0	1.0	100.0	160.00	100.00
B	210.0	2.0	200.0	420.00	400.00
C	200.5	2.5	200.0	501.25	500.00
D	150.6	1.5	160.0	225.90	240.00
E	170.2	1.5	100.0	255.30	150.00
			Totals	1,562.45	1,390.00

2. Next, compute the aggregate runout time (in weeks). This value represents the amount of time that the last unit of an item would remain in inventory *beyond the week being planned*. This value is computed by dividing the inventory balance at the end of the week being planned (which is the numerator of the fraction that follows) by the demand per week:

$$\text{Aggregate runout time} = \frac{\left[\begin{array}{l}\textbf{(5)} \text{ Total} \\ \text{inventory on hand} \\ \text{(in extruder hours)}\end{array}\right] + \left[\begin{array}{l}\text{Total extruder} \\ \text{hours available} \\ \text{per week}\end{array}\right] - \left[\begin{array}{l}\textbf{(6)} \text{ Forecast demand} \\ \text{for next week} \\ \text{(in extruder hours)}\end{array}\right]}{\left[\begin{array}{l}\textbf{(6)} \text{ Forecast demand} \\ \text{for next week} \\ \text{(in extruder hours)}\end{array}\right]}$$

$$= \frac{1,562.45 + 1,600 - 1,390.00}{1,390.00} = 1.275 \text{ weeks}$$

3. Next, develop a weekly production schedule that uses the 1,600 hours of extruder time:

Product	(7) Desired Ending Inventory at End of Next Week (000 Pounds) [(4) × 1.275]	(8) Desired Ending Inventory and Forecast (000 Pounds) [(7) + (4)]	(9) Required Production (000 Pounds) [(8) − (2)]	(10) Extruder Hours Allocated to Products [(9) × (3)]
A	127.5	227.5	67.5	67.50
B	255.0	455.0	245.0	490.00
C	255.0	455.0	254.5	636.25
D	204.0	364.0	213.4	320.10
E	127.5	227.5	57.3	85.95
			Total	1,599.80

The runout method is a useful technique for planning production schedules because it allocates productive capacity to products in proportion to their demand and their inventory levels. However, if used as single-period short-run planning techniques, they may not allow rational material requirement plans if material lead times are long relative to the planning horizon of the production schedule. In the Friendly Pet Food Company example, planning weekly production schedules would not allow sufficient lead time under ordinary circumstances for acquiring the necessary raw materials to support the production schedules. This problem has led most organizations to use more than one-period schedules. For example, the Friendly Pet Food Company could have developed weekly production schedules for 5 or 6 weeks in advance. Raw materials could then have been ordered and received in time to support the production schedules.

Scheduling and Controlling Production for Delivery Schedules

When productive systems produce products or services to specific delivery schedules, some means to coordinate the performance of upstream processing steps is needed so that the integrity of the delivery schedule is insured. Productive systems often commit to a delivery schedule for their products. These *delivery schedules* can be a part of a purchase order or contract from a customer, a plan for shipping a product to a few customers, or the total demand for a product for many customers. If it is important that actual product deliveries match with the planned delivery schedule in any of these cases, a system must be devised to schedule and control all the processing steps of the productive system.

All too often an organization may be on schedule in terms of deliveries, but about to be delinquent on deliveries because the production pipeline will soon run dry of products. It is too late to take corrective action when this happens, because deliveries will necessarily cease until the pipeline can again be refilled with products. POM has successfully used *line of balance (LOB)* in a variety of goods- and service-producing productive systems to schedule and control upstream processing steps.

Example 10.5 shows how a snowmobile company uses a delivery schedule, manufacturing processing-step lead times, and cumulative production records at each processing step to develop a LOB analysis. Figure 10.6 shows the LOB charts for the company in the example.

Example 10.5

Line of Balance (LOB) in the Bigfoot Snowmobile Company

The Bigfoot Snowmobile Company produces snowmobiles in its Iceberg, Wisconsin, manufacturing plant. Bigfoot has just signed a contract for its total output to be sold to one of the giant retailing chains in the eastern United States. One of the stipulations of the contract was an ironclad delivery schedule:

Month	Units to be Delivered	Month	Units to be Delivered	Month	Units to be Delivered
January	1,000	May	1,000	September	2,000
February	1,000	June	2,000	October	2,000
March	1,000	July	2,000	November	2,000
April	1,000	August	2,000	December	2,000

The production processing steps, the relationships among the steps, and the lead times are shown on the flow chart below:

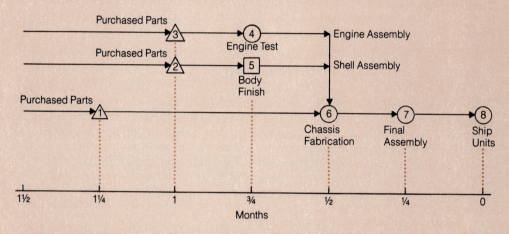

O = Company operation, □ = Subcontracted operation, △ = Purchased parts

After 8 months into the shipping schedule, these cumulative quantities of units have passed these processing steps in the production process:

Processing Step	Cumulative Production Quantity	Processing Step	Cumulative Production Quantity
⑧ Ship units	11,000	④ Engine test	12,000
⑦ Final assembly	11,000	③ Receive purchased parts	12,000
⑥ Chassis fabrication	11,500	② Receive purchased parts	14,000
⑤ Body finish	12,000	① Receive purchased parts	15,000

Develop a LOB chart and evaluate the status of production at each processing step.

Solution

1. First, construct a cumulative delivery schedule as shown in Figure 10.6.

2. Next, locate the review point on the cumulative delivery schedule in Figure 10.6. The review point is at 8 months. Proceed vertically upward until the cumulative delivery schedule curve is reached; proceed horizontally to the right until the last processing step ⑧ on the progress

Figure 10.6
Line of Balance Charts: Bigfoot Snowmobile Company

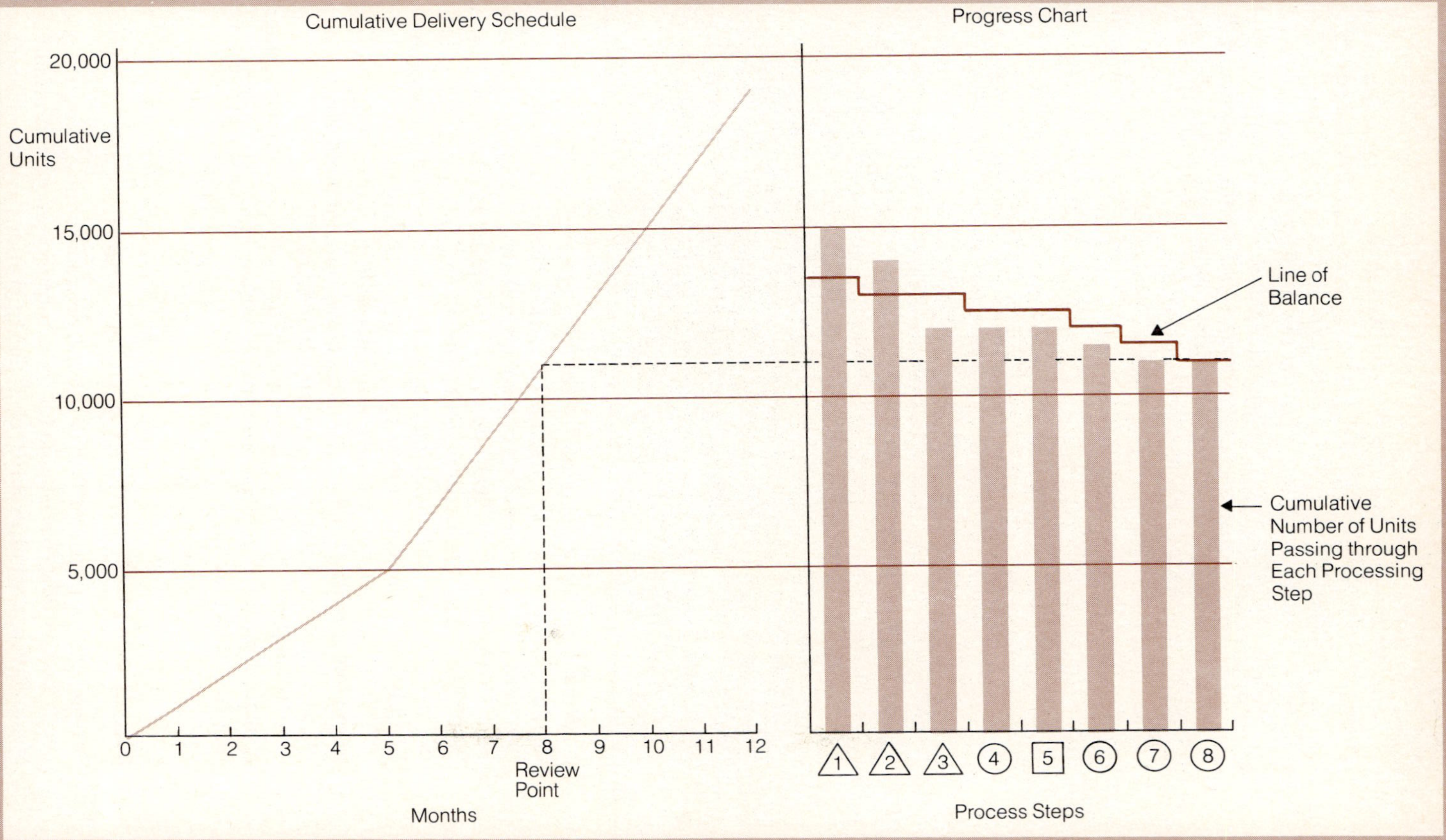

Cumulative Delivery Schedule

Progress Chart

Line of Balance

Cumulative Number of Units Passing through Each Processing Step

Cumulative Units

20,000

15,000

10,000

5,000

0   1   2   3   4   5   6   7   8   9   10   11   12

Months

Review Point

Process Steps

1   2   3   4   5   6   7   8

chart is reached. Draw a short horizontal line across the processing step ⑧ column at this level: this is the *line of balance* for processing step ⑧. To locate the line of balance for step ⑦, go *forward* (to the right) a quarter-month from the previous review point on the cumulative delivery schedule to 8¼ months and repeat the procedure. Why go forward in the schedule a quarter-month when step ⑦ is back upstream in the production process? Because the units that are at processing step ⑦ now should be shipped a quarter-month (the amount of lead time between steps ⑦ and ⑧) from now in the future, or at 8¼ months in the schedule. The line of balance is similarly drawn for all processing steps.

3. Next, draw a vertical bar for each processing step on the progress chart to indicate the cumulative number of units that have passed each step.

4. Next, evaluate the progress chart:
a. Bigfoot is on its delivery schedule: vertical bar for units shipped ⑧ exactly meets the line of balance. However, trouble looms ahead. **b.** Processing steps △2 and △1 are on schedule or ahead of schedule; that is, their bars either meet or exceed the line of balance. **c.** Processing steps ⑦, final assembly, and ⑥, chassis fabrication, are both 500 units behind schedule, probably because of engine assemblies and shell assemblies deficiencies. **d.** Processing step ⑤, subcontracted body finish, is 500 units behind schedule. The fault lies with the subcontractor and not purchased parts. **e.** Processing steps ④ and △3, engine assemblies, are 500 and 1,000 units behind schedule, respectively. Purchased parts is holding up engine test operation.

This evaluation suggests that management should immediately take corrective steps to accelerate purchase engines, engine test, and subcontracted body finish processing steps. Deliveries will be deficient by 500 units during the next review period (a quarter-month). Unless progress is made to accelerate △3 and ⑤, more serious delinquencies can be expected in the coming periods.

Once a delivery schedule is set, the cumulative delivery schedule does not change unless the delivery schedule is modified. Periodically (every quarter-month in Example 10.5), a new line of balance is drawn on the progress chart and vertical bars are extended to reflect additional units passing each processing step since the last review. Thus, a snapshot evaluation of each production step is taken at regular intervals. These periodic evaluations provide an operations manager with information about the performance of each step in its schedule.

This information is usually available well in advance of any deficiencies that might affect delivery schedules. Therefore, management corrective action is possible to insure the integrity of delivery schedules.

LOB achieves its greatest benefits when products or services are produced to specific delivery schedules, production involves many processing steps, and production lead times are long.

Work Force Scheduling in Services

Service systems generally have these characteristics: they do not hold finished goods inventories; the demand for their outputs is highly variable from hour to hour, day to day, and week to week; and their operations are labor intensive. Because the demand for services is so variable and because the services may be consumed as they are produced, great pressures rest on personnel scheduling because the principal means of performing the services is through personnel.

Scheduling Approaches in Services

How do operations managers in services cope with these variable demand patterns as they schedule personnel? Three approaches are usually used:

1. Let waiting lines that use a first-come, first-served priority buffer the difference between customer demand and the system capacity. This approach allows managers to schedule personnel such that the system's capacity is approximately uniform from period to period.

2. Use some means to level out the demand for services. Appointment schedules are commonly used in medical, legal, and other professional services for this purpose. Priority systems in medical clinics and hospitals allow certain types of patients, usually those cases that are emergencies or life threatening, to be scheduled first, and the remaining patients are admitted by appointments. This approach also allows operations managers to schedule personnel so that the system capacity is approximately uniform.

3. Develop personnel schedules to allow system capacities that approximately match the pattern of customer demand. This approach attempts to vary the system capacity by varying the number of personnel scheduled to work during each hour of the day. Because full-time personnel usually work 40 hours per week, some slack or personnel idle time is ordinarily introduced if full-time personnel are used exclusively.

From these scheduling approaches, we can see that operations managers may develop personnel schedules based on approximately uniform system capacities or highly variable system capacities. The uniform capacity approach must, however, be accompanied by other means of leveling out demand, such as appointment schedules, priority systems, and waiting lines.

Difficulties in Scheduling Personnel

Three general difficulties are encountered in scheduling personnel in services: demand variability, service time variability, and availability of personnel when they are needed. Consider, for example, how many attendants you would schedule to work during each hour of each day of the week in a health club. Figure 10.7 illustrates that the number of members at the club varies drastically throughout the day, the number of members at the club varies throughout the week, and the hourly pattern of the number of members at the club varies among the days of the week. If attendants are required to assist members in their exercises, provide guidance in their exercise programs, hand out supplies, and perform other duties, the number of attendants needed in each hour of the week is dependent upon the number of members at the club.

The amount of time required to complete the service for a customer can vary greatly from customer to customer. This is particularly true for custom services, and less true for standard services. When service times vary, even if the number of customers demanding service per hour was uniform, the capacity needs of the system would change hourly. This source of variability, when combined with variability in the number of customers arriving hourly, creates a situation of extreme demand variability in services.

Approaches that are based on a variable system capacity immediately encounter difficulty in finding the number and type of personnel needed to staff the service system. Full-time employees usually do not like strange-looking schedules. How would you like working from 6:00 a.m. to 10:00 a.m. and from 3:00 p.m. to 7:00 p.m. on Monday, Wednesday, Friday, Saturday, and Sunday? Such work schedules are ordinarily disliked by most employees, who usually want to work 5 consecutive days and 8 consecutive hours per day.

Because of the peaks and valleys in customer demand, operations managers are usually torn between two approaches to developing work schedules for employees in systems designed for variable capacity. The first approach is to use full-time employees exclusively. With this arrangement, more than enough employees will be scheduled in some periods, which will result in employee idle time in these periods. In other periods, not enough employees will be scheduled and overtime may be used or some means such as waiting lines will need to be used to level out demand. These periods when overstaffing and understaffing occur result from the inability of managers to develop work schedules that exactly match anticipated customer demand because of the desire of full-time employees for 5 consecutive days and 8 consecutive hours per day work schedules.

The other approach to developing work schedules for service systems with variable capacity is to use some full-time employees and some part-time employees to staff the system. If the part-time employees can be called in to work on short notice, so much the better. This approach avoids much of the planned overstaffing and understaffing in work schedules and provides operations managers a safety valve, other than the use of overtime and waiting lines, to service unexpectedly high levels of customer demand during some periods.

Appointment Schedules and Work Shift Scheduling

In some services even the use of appointment schedules and other efforts at levelizing demand are not entirely feasible, or in some cases not desirable. Although it is true that leveling demand does simplify scheduling personnel to staff these services, the nature of the service may dictate how much that customer demand can or should be controlled through appointment schedules and other means. In Example 10.6 the health club that we discussed earlier is used to illustrate how appointment schedules can be used to make customer demand conform to patterns that are more conducive to personnel scheduling, even if the resulting demand pattern is not entirely uniform. In this example we reshape the customer demand into a more manageable pattern through appointment schedules; then, we determine the number of attendants required in each day of the week, and schedule individual workers to work shifts.

Example 10.6

Personnel Scheduling at the Body Shop Health Club

Bob Builtright is studying the membership attendance records in Figure 10.7 with a view toward scheduling his attendants to work shifts at the Body Shop Health Club. The membership has recently voted to install a system of appointments at the club to avoid overcrowding during certain hours of the week and to avoid the extra cost of attendant overtime that has recently been used to excess at the club. Bob knows that the number of members at the club throughout the day tends to be low in the mornings and higher in the afternoon. In spite of this hour-to-hour pattern, Bob believes

Figure 10.7
Customer Demand Patterns for a Health Club

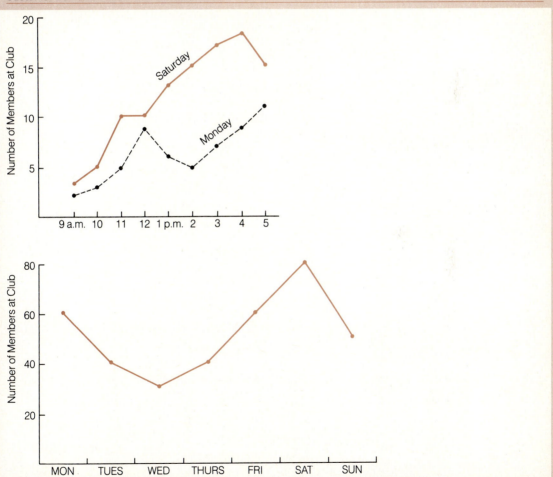

that the work load on the attendants is usually very uniform throughout the day because members who attend in the mornings tend to be on formal exercise programs and to require more assistance. Members who attend in the afternoons tend to participate in recreation activities and to require less assistance. Therefore, the hourly work load for attendants is approximately uniform.

Bob must now develop an appointment schedule and a work shift schedule for the attendants.

1. First, Bob converts the attendance information in Figure 10.7 to the number of attendants required daily. This conversion is shown in Figure 10.8 in two ways: without appointments and with appointments.

Figure 10.8
Requirements for Attendants at the Body Shop Health Club

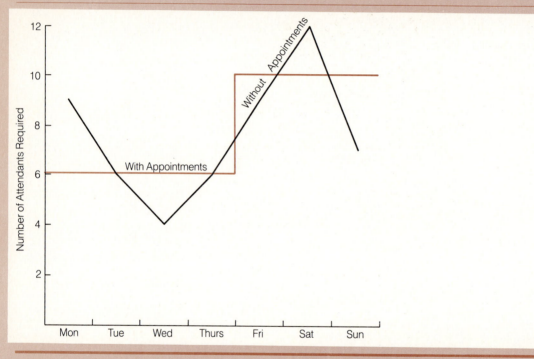

2. Next, Bob develops the number of attendants required daily with the appointment system:

Mon.	Tues.	Wed.	Thurs.	Fri.	Sat.	Sun.	Weekly Attendant Work Shifts
6	6	6	6	10	10	10	54

From this information Bob knows that he will need a theoretical minimum of 11 attendants. *Theoretical* minimum means that this number may not actually be attained in practice because of the 5-consecutive-days and 8-consecutive-hours-per-day constraint:

$$\frac{\text{Theoretical Minimum}}{\text{Number of Attendants}} = \frac{\text{Total number of attendant work shifts per week}}{\text{Number of work shifts per week per attendant}}$$

$$= \frac{54}{5} = 10.8 \text{ or } 11 \text{ attendants}$$

3. Next, Bob must develop a work shift schedule for the attendants. Table 10.3 shows the procedure used to develop the work shift schedule. This procedure uses the *work shift heuristic rule* to determine days off for each worker:

Work Shift Heuristic Rule: Choose two consecutive days with the least total number of work shifts required. In the case of ties, arbitrarily select a pair and continue.

Table 10.3
Work Shift Heuristic Procedure for Work Shift Scheduling of Attendants at the Body Shop Health Club

Attendant	Number of Attendant Work Shifts						
	Mon.	Tues.	Wed.	Thurs.	Fri.	Sat.	Sun.
1	(6	6*)	6	6	10	10	10
2	6	6	(5	5*)	9	9	9
3	(5	5*)	5	5	8	8	8
4	5	5	(4	4*)	7	7	7
5	(4	4*)	4	4	6	6	6
6	4	4	(3	3*)	5	5	5
7	(3	3*)	3	3	4	4	4
8	3	3	(2	2*)	3	3	3
9	(2	2*)	2	2	2	2	2
10	2	2	(1	1*)	1	1	1
11	1	1	1	1	0	0*	0**

* The pairs of days that are circled indicate the two consecutive days off for each attendant.

** This day will have one extra attendant. This is unavoidable slack because we have chosen to use all full-time employees and only 54 work shifts are required but 55 work shifts result from employing 11 attendants for five days per week.

The number of attendant work shifts required each day when Attendant 1's schedule is planned is taken from Figure 10.8 and is the same as used in Step 2 above. One work shift is subtracted from Attendant 1's work shifts to yield the total attendant work shifts required when Attendant 2's schedule is planned. This process is repeated for each attendant's schedule.

4. Next, from Table 10.3 Bob can now determine the shifts that each attendant will be scheduled to work during each week:

Attendant	Work Days	Days Off	Attendant	Work Days	Days Off
1	Wed.-Sun.	Mon.-Tues.	6	Fri.-Tues.	Wed.-Thurs.
2	Fri.-Tues.	Wed.-Thurs.	7	Wed.-Sun.	Mon.-Tues.
3	Wed.-Sun.	Mon.-Tues.	8	Fri.-Tues.	Wed.-Thurs.
4	Fri.-Tues.	Wed.-Thurs.	9	Wed.-Sun.	Mon.-Tues.
5	Wed.-Sun.	Mon.-Tues.	10	Fri.-Tues.	Wed.-Thurs.
			11	Sun.-Thurs.	Fri.-Sat.

Although the work shift heuristic procedure used does not guarantee optimal results, which means that the work shift schedule requires the least number of attendants possible, Bob knows that it does usually result in schedules with very little slack time. Additionally, Bob knows that other schedules may exist that are equally as good as the one developed by this heuristic procedure. He also knows that the work shift heuristic procedure may be used with or without appointment schedules.

Summary

The master production schedule—the MPS—sets the number of end items to be produced in each department in each time period. The MPS uses customer orders, forecasts, inventory status files, and productive capacity inputs to develop its detailed computation of required production in each time period. Once the MPS computations have been tested against production capacity and raw material availability, the modified MPS becomes the principal production management plan. The MPS is important in maintaining positive customer relations, reducing inventory levels, fully utilizing productive resources, and anchoring the material requirements planning system.

Managers in job shops and other intermittent productive systems must determine the sequence of processing jobs at work centers, assign jobs to work centers, and devise ways to simultaneously coordinate the schedules of many work centers. Sequencing rules, assignment algorithms, and Gantt charts have been developed in POM to assist managers in making these scheduling-related decisions.

Managers in continuous productive systems must determine length of production runs, devise systems of planning and controlling production of products for delivery schedules, and develop master production schedules. Economic order quantities

(EOQ), line of balance (LOB), and master production schedules (MPS) are used to assist managers in these scheduling situations.

Services do not hold finished goods inventories, the demand for services is highly variable, and their operations are labor intensive. These characteristics cause operations managers to place great emphasis on personnel scheduling. Choosing to schedule personnel such that the service system capacity is either uniform or approximately matches customer demand, personnel scheduling, appointment schedules, waiting lines, and work shift scheduling — all are important considerations in the management of these systems.

Review and Discussion Questions

1. Explain what purposes line of balance charts serve.
2. What are the inputs and outputs of an MPS?
3. Why must an MPS be frozen?
4. What three key scheduling decisions must managers make in job shops and other intermittent productive systems?
5. Name three common sequencing rules.
6. Name three criteria for evaluating sequencing rules.
7. How do managers select sequencing rules in practice?
8. What are the characteristics of sequencing decisions that are appropriate for applying Johnson's rule?
9. What is the key assumption of Johnson's rule?
10. Describe the circumstances in which it is appropriate to use the assignment method.
11. Describe three key decisions that operations managers must make in scheduling continuous production systems.
12. Evaluate EOQ as a technique for setting length of production runs. What are its advantages and disadvantages?
13. Explain how the runout method of scheduling improves upon the EOQ? What are its disadvantages?
14. Name three reasons why personnel scheduling in services is difficult.
15. Describe three ways that operations managers cope with the highly variable demand for services to schedule personnel.

Problems

1. The Jailbound Tax Service processes industrial customers' tax jobs on a first-come, first-served basis, but wonders if shortest processing time would be better. The jobs that are now waiting to be processed are listed in the order in which they arrived with their estimated processing times, time to promised completion, and the necessary computations:

| (1) | (2) | (3) | First-Come, First-Served | | | Shortest Processing Time | | |
| | | | (4) | (5) | (6) | (7) | (8) | (9) |
Cus-tomer Job	Estimated Processing Times (Days)	Time to Promised Completion (Days)	Job Se-quence	Flow Time (Days)	Lateness (Days) [(3) − (5)]	Job Se-quence	Flow Time (Days)	Lateness (Days) [(3) − (8)]
A	5	8	1	5	—	2	8	—
B	3	6	2	8	2	1	3	—
C	10	24	3	18	—	4	26	2
D	8	22	4	26	4	3	16	—

a. Rate the two sequencing rules on three evaluation criteria—average completion time, average number of jobs in the system, and average job lateness. **b.** Which sequencing rule would you recommend? Why?

2. The Hardtimes Heat Treating Service performs annealing, case hardening, water plunge, oil plunge, and other heat treating services on its customers' metal parts. Each job usually requires a different setup, and these changeovers have different costs. Today, Hardtimes must decide the job sequence for five jobs to minimize changeover costs. Below are the changeover costs between jobs:

Jobs That Precede

Jobs That Follow	A	B	C	D	E
A	—	$ 65	$80	$ 50	$62
B	$ 95	—	69	67	65
C	92	71	—	67	75
D	85	105	65	—	95
E	125	75	95	105	—

a. Use this rule to develop a job sequence: First, select the lowest changeover cost among all changeovers; this sets the first and second jobs. The next job will be selected that has the lowest changeover cost among the remaining jobs that follow the previously selected job. **b.** What is the total changeover cost for all five jobs?

3. The ATL Produce Company prepares and delivers produce to local grocery stores in Poteau, Oklahoma. Two separate work centers process each job at ATL: Work Center 1, which trims, ices, and packages, and Work Center 2, which loads, delivers, and returns. The times to process the jobs are listed below:

Job	Work Center 1 (Hours)	Work Center 2 (Hours)
Lettuce (L)	2.0	2.5
Celery (C)	2.1	2.4
Cabbage (Ca)	1.9	2.2
Chard (Ch)	1.8	1.6
Beans (B)	1.5	1.4

a. What is the key assumption of Johnson's rule? **b.** Apply Johnson's rule to the ATL Produce Company's job sequencing problem and set the sequence of processing the jobs. (Jobs must begin at the same time between the two work centers.) **c.** How much time is required to process the five jobs through both operations?

4. The Precise Manufacturing Company receives parts from suppliers to be used in their manufacturing departments. The quality control department must perform two operations when shipments are received: Operation 1 — draw a random sample, package, and deliver to testing, and Operation 2 — test the materials and issue a disposition report. The time estimates for processing six shipments through quality control are:

Shipment	Operation 1 (Hours)	Operation 2 (Hours)
A	.5	2.0
B	2.5	1.7
C	.2	2.4
D	1.7	.6
E	.5	.4
F	1.9	.9

a. Use Johnson's rule to set the sequence of processing the shipments through quality control. (Jobs need not begin at the same time between operations.) **b.** How much total time is required to process the six shipments through quality control?

5. The Gospel Bible Company prints bibles for churches, book companies, and other organizations on a 7-day-per-week basis. A production schedule is now being prepared for September. The printing jobs, estimated processing times, estimated changeover times, and the 12:00 noon, September 15 progress are shown below:

Work Center	Job Processing Times (in Days)					Changeover Times (in Days)	Sept. 15 Progress [Days Ahead or (Behind)]
	A	B	C	D	E		
Photo	—	—	9	13	10	2	—
Typeset	—	10	8	10	8	1	(2½)
Printing	5	5	5	5	5	3	½
Binding	6	4	5	5	4	1	½
Package	3	3	3	3	3	—	—

The printing company is just coming off a one-month vacation in August; therefore work centers will be phased in as needed. The jobs will be sequenced in this order: ABCDE. Draw a Gantt chart for the Gospel Bible Company that displays the September schedules for the work centers.

6. The Mad Toy Company produces five models of toys. The annual demand, setup and order costs, carrying costs, demand rates, and production rates for the toys are presented below:

Toy Model	Annual Demand (Toys)	Setup and Ordering Costs ($/Run)	Carrying Costs ($/Toy/Year)	Demand Rate (Toys/Day)	Production Rate (Toys/Day)
A	10,000	1,000	2.50	40	250
B	5,000	2,000	6.25	20	200
C	15,000	2,000	1.25	60	300
D	20,000	3,000	3.50	80	300
E	10,000	2,000	3.00	40	200

Compute the length of production run (the number of units in each production run) for each toy model while using the EOQ.

7. The Mad Toy Company produces five toy models—A, B, C, D, and E. It is now June 15, and Mad is planning its final assembly department schedule for the fall quarter—July, August, and September. The inventory on hand, final assembly hours required per toy, and forecast demand are shown below:

(1) Toy Model	(2) Inventory on Hand or in Production (Toys)	(3) Final Assembly Hours Required (Hours/Toy)	(4) Forecast Demand for Fall Quarter (Toys)
A	5,000	.040	3,000
B	2,000	.050	2,000
C	5,000	.033	5,000
D	5,000	.033	6,000
E	5,000	.050	4,000

The winter quarter demand forecast is the same as the fall quarter. If there are 900 final assembly hours available in each quarter, use the runout method to develop a final assembly production schedule for the fall quarter.

8. The Rawhide Boot Company has a contractual delivery schedule for hiking boots with one of the oil-producing nations on the Persian Gulf. Rawhide must meet the delivery schedule or the country will buy the boot company and produce the boots themselves. The delivery schedule calls for 5,000 pairs of boots to be delivered each week for 30 weeks. The production process for the boots has the lead times shown in

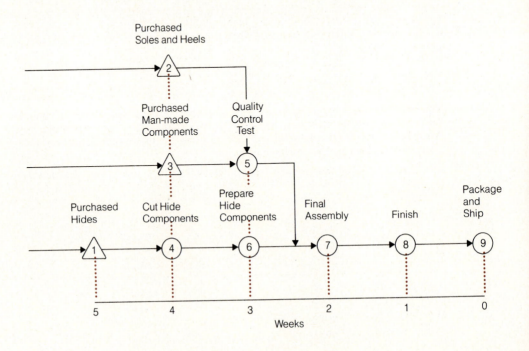

the accompanying illustration. Ten weeks into the delivery schedule, production records indicate that these cumulative quantities have passed the processing steps:

Processing Step	Cumulative Quantities (Pairs of Boots)	Processing Step	Cumulative Quantities (Pairs of Boots)	Processing Step	Cumulative Quantities (Pairs of Boots)
1	87,000	4	77,000	7	57,000
2	63,000	5	63,000	8	57,000
3	72,000	6	67,000	9	52,000

a. Prepare a cumulative delivery schedule chart, a progress chart, and a line of balance. **b.** Evaluate the prospects for future deliveries. Is the future bright for Rawhide, or are delivery problems looming on the horizon?

9. The Coverup Company produces various products used by typists to correct typing mistakes. Coverup develops master production schedules with 10-week planning horizons for its many products. One such product, Snowpac Correcting Fluid, has a beginning inventory of 1,400 cases, a weekly demand of 500 cases, a production lot size of 2,000 cases, and a minimum safety stock of 500 cases. Prepare the MPS detailed computations that result in the production schedule for Snowpac.

10. The Pharmy Company produces and markets three pharmaceutical products: Cremo (antacid), Dullo (aspirin), and Bendo (backache). The demands (in gross) for these products over the 8-week planning horizon are:

Product Demands	Weeks							
	1	2	3	4	5	6	7	8
Customers (Forecasts and Orders)								
Cremo	2,000	1,000	500	2,000	2,000	1,000	500	500
Dullo	4,000	2,000	2,000	6,000	8,000	5,000	4,000	4,000
Bendo	1,000	500	500	1,000	1,000	500	500	500
Branch Warehouses								
Cremo	1,000		1,000			2,000		
Dullo	1,000		2,000			3,000		
Bendo		1,000					500	
Market Research								
Cremo	500			500			500	
Dullo		500			500			500
Bendo			500			500		

The safety stock levels, minimum lot sizes, and beginning inventory levels for the products are:

Product	Minimum Lot Sizes (Gross)	Safety Stock (Gross)	Beginning Inventory (Gross)
Cremo	5,000	3,000	4,000
Dullo	8,000	5,000	4,000
Bendo	2,000	1,000	2,000

Prepare the next weekly MPS for Pharmy.

11. The Wet Look Barber Shop wants to convert totally from its *drop-in* system of customer arrivals to an appointment system. Gowen Bald, the shop's owner, has kept records of the numbers of daily customers and has estimated the number of appointments per day if only appointments were allowed:

	Mon.	Tues.	Wed.	Thurs.	Fri.	Sat.	Total
Customers (drop-in)	40	30	10	20	30	60	190
Customers (appointments)	32	32	32	32	32	32	192

Each customer requires an average of ½ hour of a barber's time. The barbers are all full-time employees and can work any 4 consecutive days per week from 8:00 a.m. to 5:00 p.m. Monday through Saturday. If only appointments are allowed: **a.** What is the theoretical minimum number of barbers required per week? **b.** Use the work shift heuristic procedure to plan weekly work shift schedules for the barbers. **c.** How many barbers do your schedules require? Are these schedules optimal?

12. The Big State Plaza Savings and Loan operates a thriving business in Gardendale, California, offering savings, checking, bill-paying, and other money services. The cashier clerks work the cash drawer counters from 9:00 a.m. to 6:00 p.m. Monday through Saturday. Ms. Begonia Spender is the manager of the cashier section and part of her responsibility involves developing work shift schedules for the cashier clerks. She has kept accurate records of customer demand and has estimated the number of cashier clerk work shifts required daily:

	Mon.	Tues.	Wed.	Thurs.	Fri.	Sat.	Total
Cashier clerk work shifts	8	6	4	5	8	10	41

All of the cashier clerks are full-time employees and according to company policy must be provided 4 consecutive days of work and 2 consecutive days off each week. **a.** What is the theoretical minimum number of cashier clerks required? **b.** Use the work shift heuristic procedure to develop weekly work shift schedules for the cashier clerks. **c.** How many cashier clerk work shifts of slack per week are present in your proposed schedules? How could this slack be avoided? Are your schedules optimal?

13. Mary Perkins is the store manager for Seattle's largest Buy-Right Food Store. She is now developing weekly work shift schedules for the counter clerks. She has summarized the daily need for clerk work shifts:

	Mon.	Tues.	Wed.	Thurs.	Fri.	Sat.	Sun.	Total
Day shift	6	5	5	6	8	10	6	46
Evening shift	5	4	4	5	6	7	4	35

The shifts are scheduled independently, the clerks' union contract calls for schedules based on 5 consecutive days and 8 consecutive hours per day, and only full-time clerks are employed. **a.** What is the theoretical minimum number of clerks required on both the day and evening shifts? **b.** Use the work shift heuristic procedure to develop work shift schedules for the clerks for both the day and evening shifts. **c.** How many clerk work shifts of slack per week are present in your day and evening shift schedules? How could this slack be avoided? Is your solution optimal?

Case

Quik Claim Services Company

The Quik Claim Services Company provides claims adjustment services to insurance agents and insurance companies in the Atlanta, Georgia region. The company's claims adjustors respond to insurance agents' requests for the resolution of damages to clients' properties in the region and collect fees from the insurance companies for this service. The service involves traveling to the client's property, observing the nature and extent of the damage, and affixing a reasonable amount that should be reimbursed by the insurance company. Quik Claim believes that the quick resolution of claims has been the cornerstone of its growth and success.

John Billingham is Quik Claim's operations manager in Atlanta. Recently numerous complaints have been received about the length of time required for a claims adjustor to complete the damage estimates. At a recent regional meeting, claims adjustors told John that they were working as hard and fast as humanly possible, but that on some days of the week the number of requests were so great that it could take a few days to get to some of these requests. All claims adjustors now work 5 days per week, 8 hours per day, Monday through Friday. John is considering a different scheduling arrangement for the adjustors that would result in their being available to answer requests 6 days per week, working 4 days per week and 10 hours per day, and having 2 consecutive days off per week not including Sunday (Sunday is never worked). Such an arrangement would allow the number of adjustors available to answer requests to better match the daily pattern of the volume of requests.

John has researched the latest forecasts of requests for claims adjustments from Quik Claim's marketing staff, and these daily averages seem to be reasonable estimates for the next several weeks:

	Mon.	Tues.	Wed.	Thurs.	Fri.	Sat.	Total
Number of requests	42	36	24	32	38	46	218

Each request is expected to require an average of about 4 hours of an adjustor's time. John wants to plan work shifts for the adjustors to approximately match the requests for service, but he wonders how this will affect the utilization of adjustors, group morale, and the time required to resolve clients' claims.

Assignment

1. What is the theoretical minimum number of adjustors required?

2. Use the work shift heuristic procedure to develop work shift schedules for the adjustors.

3. How much slack per week is present in your work shift schedules?

4. What ways could be used to reduce the amount of slack in your work shift schedules?

5. What factors should be considered in changes in work shift schedules such as the one that John Billingham is considering? Which of these factors is most important? Can you suggest how John should go about making the schedule changes that he is considering?

Selected Bibliography

Berry, William L., Thomas E. Vollman, and D. Clay Whybark. *Master Production Scheduling: Principles and Practice.* American Production and Inventory Control Society, 1979.

Buffa, E. S., and William H. Taubert. *Production-Inventory Systems: Planning and Control.* Rev. ed. Homewood, IL: Richard D. Irwin, 1972.

Clark, Wallace. *The Gantt Chart: A Working Tool of Management.* New York: Ronald Press, 1922.

Conway, R. W., W. L. Maxwell, and L. W. Miller. *Theory of Scheduling.* Reading, Mass.: Addison-Wesley, 1967.

Day, James, E., and Michael P. Hottenstein. "Review of Sequencing Research." *Naval Research Logistics Quarterly* 27 (March 1970): 11–39.

Fryer, John S. "Operating Policies in Multiechelon Dual-Constrained Job Shops." *Management Science* 19 (May 1973): 1001–1012.

Hershauer, James C., and Ronald J. Ebert. "Search and Simulation Selection of a Job-Shop Sequencing Rule." *Management Science* 21 (March 1975): 833–843.

Holloway, C. A., and R. T. Nelson. "Job Shop Scheduling with Due Dates and Variable Processing Times." *Management Science* 20 (May 1974): 1264–1275.

International Business Machines. *Communications Oriented Production Information and Control Systems (COPICS).* Vol. 1: *Management Overview.* Order Number G320–1974. White Plains, NY: IBM, 1972.

Johnson, S. M. "Optimal Two Stage and Three Stage Production Schedules with Setup Times Included." *Naval Research Logistics Quarterly* 1 (March 1954): 61–68.

Jones, C. H. "A Economic Evaluation of Job Shop Dispatching Rules." *Management Science* 20 (November 1973): 293–307.

O'Brien, James J. *Scheduling Handbook.* New York: McGraw-Hill, 1969.

Oral, M., and J. L. Malouin. "Evaluation of the Shortest Processing Time Scheduling Rule With Funcation Process." *AIIE Transactions* 5 (December 1973): 357–365.

Tibrewala, R. K., D. Philippe, and J. J. Browne. "Optimal Scheduling of Two Consecutive Idle Periods." *Management Science* 19, no. 1 (September 1972): 71–75.

Weeks, J. K., and John S. Fryer. "A Methodology for Assigning Minimum Cost Due Dates." *Management Science* 23 (April 1977): 872–881.

Wight, Oliver W. *Production and Inventory Management in the Computer Age.* Boston: Cahners Books, 1974.

Wren, Daniel A. *The Evaluation of Management Thought.* New York: Ronald Press, 1972.

Zimmerman, H. J., and M. G. Sovereign. *Quantitative Models for Production Management.* Englewood Cliffs, NJ: Prentice-Hall, 1974.

Chapter Outline

Introduction

Long-Range and Intermediate-Range Constraints
Resource Requirements Planning Systems
Terms Often Used in Resource Requirements Planning

Master Production Scheduling (MPS)

Objectives of the Master Production Schedule (MPS)
Relationships among MPS, CRP, and MRP
Short-Range End Item Demand
Independent and Dependent Demands
Estimating Demand for a Product
Lot-Sizing with Lumpy Demand
Length of Planning Horizons

Capacity Requirements Planning (CRP)

Objectives of CRP
Testing the Feasibility of the MPS
Answering Operating Questions through CRP
Load Schedules
Capacity Loading Hierarchy
CRP Computer Systems

Material Requirements Planning (MRP)

Objectives of MRP
Growing Use of MRP
Elements of MRP
Master Production Schedule
Bills of Material File
Inventory Status File
MRP Computer Program
Outputs of MRP
Case 11.1: The Green Thumb Water Sprinkler Company
MRP Issues
Net Change versus Regenerative MRP Systems
Safety Stock; Japanese *Just-in-Time* Methods
Lot-Sizing
Evaluation of MRP

Summary

Review and Discussion Questions

Problems

Case: The Yoko Company: Resource Requirements Planning in the Processing Industry

Selected Bibliography

11

Resource Requirements Planning Systems:

Master Scheduling, Capacity Requirements Planning, and Material Requirements Planning

A computer-based MRP system is the heart of modern logistics planning and operations management in a manufacturing enterprise, encompassing the key functions of inventory management, capacity requirements determination, and priority planning (scheduling and dispatching).
Joseph Orlicky, 1975

In Chapter 6 we discussed how long-range capacity plans were developed from long-range forecasts of customer demand, funds availability and business analysis, and capacity data and analysis. These long-range capacity plans resulted in production facilities plans, major subcontractor plans, and major machinery and process development plans. When such long-range capacity plans are set, they form capacity constraints for short-range and intermediate-range plans to be developed later.

In Chapter 8 we described how intermediate-range aggregate capacity plans were developed from intermediate-range forecasts of customer demand and long-range capacity constraints. These aggregate capacity plans resulted in employment plans, machinery and utility plans, subcontractor and material supply contracts, and facility modification plans. These aggregate capacity plans usually span time periods of from 6 to 18 months and form capacity constraints for short-range schedules to be developed later.

In Chapter 10 we illustrated how short-range master production schedules were developed and detailed work center scheduling decisions were made from estimated short-range customer demands, work center capacity constraints that were largely set when aggregate capacity plans were developed, inventory status information, and availability of materials information. These short-range schedules determine the number of each product, subassembly, and component to be produced in each work center in each week of the short-range plan.

The relationships among these long-range, intermediate-range, and short-range production plans were illustrated in Figure 8.1. What was not fully explained in either Figure 8.1 or in the discussion above is how firms plan for the resources required to support the short-range production schedules. In this chapter we shall present the concepts and techniques of resource requirements planning — the basis for planning for the materials, cash, personnel, and machine capacity needed to support the production schedules.

Figure 11.1 illustrates how the marketing, personnel, production, finance/accounting, purchasing, engineering, and the management information system (MIS) functions interact to determine a firm's resource requirements. It is important to recognize that resource requirements planning involves all of these functions. All of them work together to supply the information needed to develop the short-range resource requirements of the firm. When the master production schedule (MPS), capacity requirements planning (CRP), and material requirements planning (MRP) have been completed, each of these functions then receives output information about the resource requirements and production schedules.

This chapter is about resource requirements planning, both the overall process as depicted in Figure 11.1 and the details of master production scheduling, capacity requirements planning, and material requirements planning.

Figure 11.1
A Resource Requirements Planning System

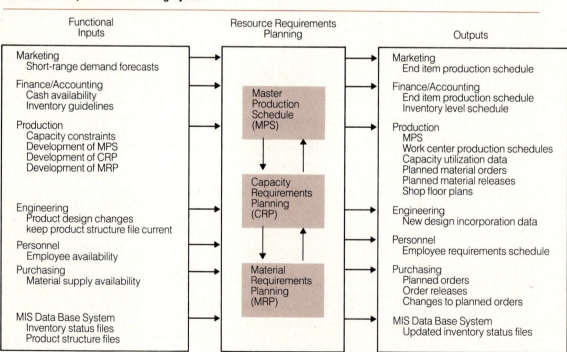

These topics have a language that has evolved with their growing use in industry today. The terms and their definitions that are a part of this language are found in Table 11.1. It may be helpful for you to refer to this table as these terms crop up in the sections that will follow in this chapter.

Table 11.1
Terms Often Used in Resource Requirements Planning

Allocated Inventory — Materials that are in inventory or on order but have been assigned to specific production orders in the future. These materials are therefore not available for use on other orders.

Available Inventory — Materials that are in inventory or on order that are not safety stock or allocated to other uses.

Bills of Material File — A file containing the bills of material for all end items; a major element of the MRP system. A bill of material is a listing of all raw materials, parts, subassemblies, and assemblies that go into an end item. The amount of each component that is required to produce one end item is included. The way that the components go together, or product structure, is also included.

Bucket — The principal unit of time measurement in MRP systems. The term refers to a particular period of time in the planning horizon. For example, time-bucket #6 means the sixth period, usually a week in duration, of the planning horizon.

Capacity Requirements Planning (CRP) — The process of reconciling the master production schedule to the labor and machine capacities of the production departments over the planning horizon.

Changes to Planned Orders — A primary output of MRP. These reports show how planned order schedules for a material should be changed. Orders may be delivered earlier, later, or canceled altogether, or quantities may be changed to adapt to a changed master production schedule.

Component — A term used to describe a subordinate relationship in a product structure. A component goes into a parent. For example, a part (component) goes into an assembly (parent).

Dependent Demand — Demand for a raw material, part, or other lower-level component that is dependent upon the demand for the end item into which the component goes.

End Item — A product, service part, or any other output that has a demand from customers, distributors, or other departments and that is independent of the demands for other components or end items.

Frozen MPS — The early periods of the MPS that can be assumed to not be subject to change. These frozen periods of the MPS allow operations managers to commit funds, order materials, and make other plans with the confidence that such plans will not need to be subsequently changed.

Gross Requirements — The quantity and timing of the total requirements for a particular material, not considering any availability of the material in inventory or scheduled receipts.

Independent Demand — Demand for a material that is independent of the demands for other materials. End items are usually assumed to have independent demands because they are not components of other parents; therefore, their demands are determined by customers outside of the organization and not by the demand for other, higher-level parents.

Inventory Status File — A major input to the MRP computer program. Material on hand or on order, planned orders, planned order releases, materials allocated, lot sizes, safety stock levels, lead times, costs, and suppliers are among the information included in this file about each material in the material system.

Load Schedules — A method used in capacity requirements planning to compare the amount of production capacity required by the MPS to the capacity available. These schedules are usually prepared in a hierarchy from the beginning to the end of the manufacturing system, department by department.

Lot Size Decisions — Given a net requirements schedule, decisions on how to group these requirements into production lots or purchase lots. The decisions usually include both the size and timing of the lots.

Lumpy Demand — The demand for a material that exhibits an irregular period-to-period pattern.

Master Production Schedule (MPS) — A schedule of the number and timing of all end items to be produced in a manufacturing plant over a specific planning horizon. An important input to the MRP computer program.

Material Requirements Planning (MRP) — A POM computer information system that determines how much of each material, any inventory item with a unique part number, should be purchased or produced in each future time period to support the MPS.

MRP Computer Program — A computer program that is the central processor of MRP information. It receives inputs from the MPS, inventory status file, and bills of material file. The

Table 11.1 (continued)
Terms Often Used in Resource Requirements Planning

program yields these primary outputs: planned order schedule, planned order releases, and changes to planned orders. Additionally, the program supplies transaction data to the inventory status file and secondary reports to operations managers.

Net Change MRP — MRP systems that generate outputs emphasizing only the changes to the last MRP outputs. Planned order schedules in these systems, for example, would indicate only the changes to the previous report and not a completely new schedule.

Net Requirements — The amount and timing of the need for a material that must be satisfied from production or purchasing. It is calculated by subtracting material available from gross requirements.

Offsetting for Lead Time — A term used in both MRP and CRP to describe the need to account for the time required to produce a production lot in-house or to receive a lot purchased from a supplier. A requirement in one time period will necessitate the release of the order in some earlier time period. The number of periods between the requirement and the release is the offset and is equal to the lead time.

On-Hand Inventory — The amount of a material actually in inventory. It may include safety stock and materials allocated to other uses, but it may not include materials on order.

Parent — A term used to describe a superior relationship in a product structure. For example, a part (component) goes into an assembly (parent).

Planned Order Receipts — The quantity of each material to be received in each time period of the planning horizon.

Planned Order Releases — The quantity of each material to be ordered in each time period of the planning horizon. This schedule is determined by offsetting the planned order receipts schedule to allow for lead times.

Planning Horizon — The number of periods included in the MPS, CRP, MRP, departmental schedules, and all other production planning.

Product Structure Levels — Strata of the hierarchy of the product structure. Level 0, for example, would be the final assembled end items, Level 1 would be all components that go into the final assembly, and Level 2 would be all of the components that go into Level 1 components.

Regenerative MRP — MRP systems that periodically generate one complete set of MRP outputs. In these systems, for example, a planned order schedule would be a complete report and not be comprised solely of changes to an earlier report.

Resource Requirements Planning — All of the planning that is directed at determining the amount and timing of productive resources, usually including personnel, materials, cash, and production capacity, needed in the short-range planning horizon. MPS, CRP, and MRP are important elements in this planning.

Safety Stock — A given quantity of each material held in inventory that is dedicated to but one use — emergency shortages arising out of uncertain demand or lead times. When demand for the material is greater than expected or when lead time is longer than expected during reorder periods, safety stock is intended to meet these extraordinary needs.

Scheduled Receipts — Materials that are on order from a supplier and scheduled to be received in a specific period of the planning horizon.

Service Parts — Materials that are demanded as end items when ordered by service centers to be used in repairing other end items. These materials usually also have dependent demands as they are assembled into other, higher-level components.

Master Production Scheduling

A master production schedule (MPS) is a schedule of end items to be completed in each week of a short-range planning horizon. End items are finished products, assemblies, or stocked parts that are to be shipped to customers, stocked in inventory for later shipment, shipped to branch warehouses or other company locations, or used by research departments within the company. A master production schedule for a manufacturing plant would include all of the end items, which could number into the hundreds, to be completed in each week over a time period that usually ranges from a few weeks to a few months.

In Chapter 10 we described the process of estimating short-range demand for an end item and developing a schedule of the number of end items to be completed in each week when the EOQ or lot size and safety stock were known. See Figures 10.1 and 10.2 for a review of these calculations. In that earlier discussion the relationship of the MPS to the running load schedules or production capacity was also discussed, but only in a general way. In this chapter the relationships among the MPS, capacity requirements planning (CRP), and material requirements planning (MRP) will be more fully explained.

The MPS is the core of all short-range manufacturing planning. In Joseph Orlicky's words: ''A MPS is to a MRP system what a program is to a computer.''[1] In other words, the MPS is the driving force behind production planning in manufacturing. Figure 11.2 illustrates the important role that the MPS plays in this process. In this figure we can see that a trial MPS is determined from estimated end item demand, availability of end items in inventory, lot-sizing and safety stock policies, and rough-cut capacity planning. These lot-sizing and safety stock decisions will be discussed later in this chapter. Next, two conditions can necessitate modification of the MPS before it becomes the actual MPS that will be put into action. First, we determine if the materials required to complete the end items in the MPS are available. If these materials are not available in the quantities required or when they are required, the MPS is modified accordingly. Second, we determine if there is enough production capacity in all of the work centers of the plant to complete the end items in each week of the MPS. This capacity is usually measured both in terms of worker availability and machine capacity. If the amount of capacity available in each week of the MPS is insufficient, then the MPS must be modified accordingly.

The means of checking a MPS for feasibility is material requirements planning (MRP) and capacity requirements planning (CRP). These two planning approaches will be covered in detail later in this chapter. The objective of a MPS should be not only to satisfy customer demand but also to promote the internal operating efficiency of the plant. These objectives can be achieved only if the MPS is both realistic and feasible: ''The MPS should be a statement of what *can* and *will* be produced, rather than what management wishes had been produced in the past and or would like to be able to produce in the immediate future.''[2] MRP and CRP provide the means of making the MPS both realistic and feasible, and therefore believable.

Short-Range End Item Demand

The demands for end items in the MPS are described as *independent demands.* This means that the demand for a material is independent of the demands for any other material. End items and parts stocked for sale to customers as service or repair parts are ordinarily considered to have independent demands. Other materials such as parts and assemblies that go into assembled end items have *dependent demands.* In other words, the demands for these materials are directly dependent upon the demands for the end items into which they are assembled. When a material has a dependent demand, the number of units of the material needed in a particular week can be calculated from the demand for the end items into which it goes. The concept

[1] Joseph Orlicky, *Material Requirements Planning* (New York: McGraw-Hill, 1975), 231.

[2] Ibid., 244.

Figure 11.2
Relationships among MPS, CRP, MRP, and Other Elements of the Production Planning System

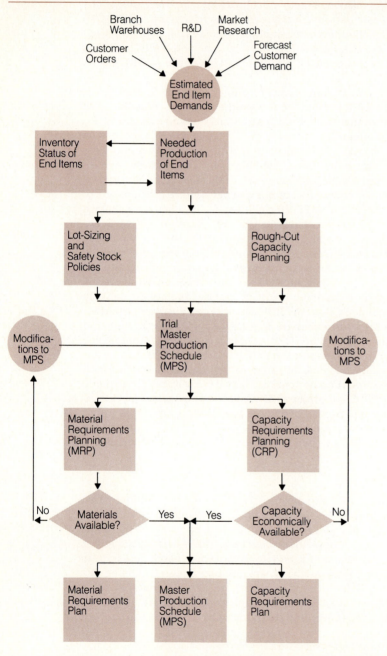

of dependent demand is at the heart of material requirements planning (MRP), which we shall expand upon later in this chapter.

Estimating the demand for an end item is the starting point for master production scheduling. Short-range forecasts of end item demand are combined with in-hand customer orders and intracompany orders to form the short-range estimated total demand for an end item. Table 11.2 illustrates how short-range estimated demand for a product is developed. In Week 1 of the 8-week schedule, estimated demand is the same as the in-hand orders. In the middle weeks of the schedule, estimated demand is a compromise between forecasts and in-hand orders. During the later part of the schedule, the forecasts are the basis for estimating demand.

Table 11.2
Estimating Demand for a Product

Week	Recent Short-Range Forecast of Demand	In-Hand Customer Orders	In-Hand Intracompany Orders	Estimated Demand
1	750	450	50	500
2	750	400	50	500
3	1,100	600	100	1,000
4	600	300	50	600
5	300	200	50	300
6	300	200	——	300
7	300	200	——	300
8	1,500	100	50	1,500

Note: In Week 1 the in-hand orders are used as the estimated demand. In Weeks 2 and 3 the estimated demand is a compromise between forecasts and in-hand orders. In Weeks 4 through 8, the forecasts prevail as estimated demand, because we have only a few in-hand customer orders for these later weeks.

As Table 11.3 shows, the estimated demands in each week of the schedule in Table 11.2 become the starting point for all MPS calculations. Next, any end items in inventory are used first to satisfy these demands early in the schedule. In Week 1,

Table 11.3
Master Production Schedule Computations for a Product with Lot-for-Lot (LFL)
Lot-Sizing

End Item		Weeks							
		1	2	3	4	5	6	7	8
	Estimated demand	500	500	1,000	600	300	300	300	1,500
	Beginning inventory	500*	300	300	300	300	300	300	300
#377	Net requirements	300	500	1,000	600	300	300	300	1,500
	Production lots	300	500	1,000	600	300	300	300	1,500
	Ending inventory	300	300	300	300	300	300	300	300

* Note: Safety stock is 300 units. This means that the ending inventory should never fall below 300 units.

500 units are in inventory. Of these, 300 are safety stock and should not ordinarily be used to satisfy this demand; therefore, only 200 units in inventory are used to reduce the demand of 500 units in Week 1 to 300 units of net requirements, which must be satisfied from production.

The presence of safety stock in the MPS suggests that the production of the product is a produce-to-stock manufacturing system where end items go into finished goods inventory until they are demanded by customers. The safety stock is a protection against stockouts when demand exceeds our estimates or when lead times are longer than expected. Safety stock would not ordinarily be used for end items in the MPS for produce-to-order manufacturing systems where end items are produced for customer orders that are already in-hand.

We can see in Table 11.3 that the net requirements are the same as estimated demands from Week 2 forward in the schedule because usable inventory was depleted in satisfying Week 1 demand and production is then the only remaining way of satisfying these demands.

One important part of master production scheduling is determining the timing and size of production lots from the net requirements. A *production lot* is a group of units continuously produced under the same operating conditions. In the case of end items, a production lot usually refers to a group of identical end items that are processed through the final assembly operation as a continuous batch. The decisions about how many end items should be processed in a batch and when these batches should be completed are often referred to as *lot-sizing decisions*. Table 11.3 assumes that a *lot-for-lot lot-sizing method* is used. This lot-sizing method adopts a schedule of production lots that exactly matches the net requirements schedule. Although this method is simple to apply, it may be too expensive to use when ordering or setup costs are high for an end item. Other lot-sizing methods are also used in industry today, and we shall study some of these methods more closely here.

Lot-Sizing with Lumpy Demand

In Chapter 9 we stated that only two basic decisions about a material were necessary to provide the amount of material necessary to satisfy a schedule of demands: how much to order of the material and when to place the order. How much to order was the object of order quantity or lot-size decisions and when to order concerned order point decisions — at what level of inventory should an order be placed? The order point decision involved determining the expected demand during lead time and the level of safety stock that gave the desired level of protection against stockouts during lead time. The approaches used to develop order point decisions in Chapter 9 also conceptually apply to master production scheduling decisions concerning the appropriate levels of safety stock for an end item. Lot-sizing decisions in the MPS are different from those in Chapter 9, however, because of one key factor — *lumpy demand*. Notice the period-to-period pattern of demand in the net requirements schedule in Table 11.3. The great variation in these weekly demands causes industry analysts to refer to these patterns as lumpy. One of the important assumptions of the economic order quantity (EOQ) models of Chapter 9 was that the demand for a material is uniform from week to week. When this assumption is violated as in the net requirements schedule of Table 11.3, the EOQ has been found to be a costly method of lot-sizing.

Other lot-sizing methods often exhibit lower costs. Among these methods are the *lot-for-lot method* and the *period order quantity (POQ) method*. Example 11.1 demonstrates the use of these methods when applied to the net requirements schedule of Table 11.3. Many other approaches have also been experimented with and may be used more extensively in the future. The nonoptimal methods of least total cost, least unit cost, and part-period balancing are discussed and described in Orlicky's book.[3] Heuristic methods by Gaither,[4] Groff,[5] and Silver and Meal,[6] though not optimal in their results, do provide good cost performance and are very efficient to use. The Wagner and Whitin method does yield optimal results, but it is based on dynamic programming and is difficult for analysts to understand, is very expensive to process on computers, and may not exhibit good cost performance when many changes to net requirements occur weekly.[7]

---

[3] Ibid., pp. 120–138.

[4] Norman Gaither, "A Near-Optimal Lot-Sizing Model For Material Requirements Planning Systems," *Production and Inventory Management* 22(fourth quarter 1981): 75–89.

[5] G. K. Groff, "A Lot-Sizing Rule for Time Phased Component Demand," *Production and Inventory Management* 20(first quarter 1979): 47–53.

[6] E. A. Silver and H. C. Meal, "A Heuristic for Selecting Lot Size Quantities for the Case of a Deterministic Time-Varying Demand Rate and Discrete Opportunities for Replenishment," *Production and Inventory Management* 14(second quarter 1973): 64–75.

[7] H. M. Wagner and T. M. Whitin, "Dynamic Version of the Economic Lot Size Model," *Management Science* 5, no. 1(October 1958): 89–96.

Example 11.1

Lot-Sizing Decisions for Materials with Lumpy Demands

The net requirements from Table 11.3 are:

	\multicolumn{8}{c}{Weeks}							
	1	2	3	4	5	6	7	8
Net requirements	300	500	1,000	600	300	300	300	1,500

The annual demand for this end item is estimated to be 30,000 units over a 50-week-per-year schedule, or an average of 600 units per week. It costs $500 to change over the machines in the final assembly department to this end item when a production lot is begun. It costs $.50 per unit when one unit of this product must be carried in inventory from one week to another; therefore, when one unit of this product is in ending inventory, it must be carried over as beginning inventory in the next week and incurs the $.50 per-unit carrying cost. Determine which of these lot-sizing methods results in the least carrying and changeover (or ordering) costs for the 8-week schedule: **a.** Lot-for-lot (LFL), **b.** economic order quantity (EOQ), and **c.** period order quantity (POQ).

Solution

a. Develop the total carrying and ordering costs over the 8-week schedule for the lot-for-lot method.

	Weeks								Costs		
	1	2	3	4	5	6	7	8	Carry	Order	Total
Net requirements	300	500	1,000	600	300	300	300	1,500			
Beginning inventory	0*	0	0	0	0	0	0	0			
Production lots	300	500	1,000	600	300	300	300	1,500	$0	$4,000**	$4,000
Ending inventory	0	0	0	0	0	0	0	0			

* For simplicity, the beginning inventory is assumed to be zero because the 200 units of usable inventory have been used to reduce the demand of 500 units in Week 1 to 300 units of net requirements, and the 300 units of safety stock and its associated carrying costs (8 × 300 × $.50 = $1,200) will apply to all lot-sizing methods. Therefore, safety stock will not be a factor in choosing *among* the methods.

** Ordering costs = Number of orders × $500 = 8 × 500 = $4,000.

b. Develop the total carrying and ordering costs over the 8-week schedule for the EOQ lot-sizing method.

First, compute the EOQ:

$$EOQ = \sqrt{2DS/C} = \sqrt{2(30,000)(500)/(.50)(50)} = 1,095.4 \text{ or } 1,095 \text{ units}$$

	Weeks								Costs		
	1	2	3	4	5	6	7	8	Carry	Order	Total
Net requirements	300	500	1,000	600	300	300	300	1,500			
Beginning inventory	0*	795	295	390	885	585	285	1,080			
Production lots	1,095	—	1,095	1,095	—	—	1,095	1,095	$2,495**	$2,500**	$4,995
Ending inventory	795	295	390	885	585	285	1,080	675			

* See the note concerning beginning inventory in the table in part *a* above.

** Carrying costs = Sum of ending inventories × $.50 = 4990 × .50 = $2,495
  Ordering costs = Number of orders × $500 = 5 × 500 = $2,500

c. Develop the total carrying and ordering costs over the 8-week schedule for the POQ method of lot-sizing.

First, compute the POQ:

$$POQ = \frac{\text{Number of weeks per year}}{\text{Number of orders per year}} = \frac{50}{D/EOQ} = \frac{50}{30,000 \div 1095.4}$$
$$= 1.83 \text{ or } 2 \text{ weeks per order}$$

					Weeks					Costs		
	1	2	3	4	5	6	7	8	Carry	Order	Total
Net requirements	300	500	1,000	600	300	300	300	1,500			
Beginning inventory	0*	500	0	600	0	300	0	1,500			
Production lots	800	—	1,600	—	600	—	1,800	—	$1,450**	$2,000**	$3,450
Ending inventory	500	0	600	0	300	0	1,500	0			

* See the note concerning beginning inventory in the table in part *a*.

** Carrying costs = Sum of ending inventories × \$.50 = 2900 × .50 = \$1,450
Ordering costs = Number of orders × \$500 = 4 × 500 = \$2,000

Among the lot-sizing methods considered, the POQ method exhibits the least carrying and ordering costs for the 8-week net requirements schedule.

Length of Planning Horizons

The planning horizons in master scheduling may vary from just a few weeks in some firms to more than a year in others. How does a firm decide how long its planning horizon should be? Although several factors impinge on this decision, one factor tends to be dominant: **the planning horizon should at least equal the longest cumulative end item lead time.**[8] *Cumulative end item lead time* means the amount of time to get the materials in from suppliers, produce all of the parts and assemblies, get the end item assembled and ready for shipment, and deliver it to customers. The end item with the greatest cumulative lead time therefore determines the least amount of time that a planning horizon should span. In practice, planning horizons are usually greater than this minimum to allow for adequate time to plan for the capacity needs to produce lower-level parts very early in the schedule.

Let us now consider how capacity requirement planning (CRP) is used to modify the MPS to insure that adequate production capacity is present to produce the end items in the MPS.

Capacity Requirements Planning (CRP)

Capacity requirements planning (CRP) is the short-range planning aimed at determining what production capacities will be required in each work center in each week to support the master production schedule (MPS). Equally important, however, CRP also allows operations managers to answer such week-to-week operating questions as:

1. How much overtime should be used in each work center in each week?
2. How many standby production machines should be activated in each week?

---

[8] Orlicky, op. cit., 158.

3. Should personnel be transferred between departments in some weeks?

4. Should work be shifted between work centers in some weeks?

5. Should work be subcontracted in some weeks?

6. Should the customer be notified that the order will be late?

The answers to such questions are natural outcomes of the CRP process.

In CRP the production capacity available in a given week is usually limited by two factors: the number of personnel possessing certain skills and the number of machine hours available in each work center. Although it is true that the number of labor hours in each week can be increased by working overtime and the amount of machine hours can be increased by activating standby machines or by subcontracting, there are practical limits beyond which short-range capacity cannot be economically expanded.

As Figure 11.2 indicated, CRP tests the feasibility of the trial MPS. In other words, through CRP we determine if all of the end items in the MPS *can* be produced, given the short-range personnel and machine capacity constraints in each week in all of the work centers. The principal means of testing the feasibility of the MPS is through work center load schedules. From these load schedules, we also determine the answers to the operating questions discussed above.

Load Schedules

A *load schedule* is a device for comparing the actual labor hours and machine hours required to produce the MPS against the available labor hours and machine hours in each week. Load schedules are usually prepared in a hierarchy from work centers at the beginning of the manufacturing system through successive stages to the end of the manufacturing system.

Figure 11.3 demonstrates that when end items are included in the MPS, this inclusion causes activities to be undertaken at successively earlier stages in the productive system. Beginning at the top of the figure in Week 5 in the Final Assembly work center, we find that 600 units must be processed through Final Assembly in Week 5. One week earlier, in Week 4, 600 units must be processed through Assemble Frame work center. The one-week lead time is required to perform the operations in the Assemble Frame work center and transport the units to Final Assembly.

In Week 3, 1800 #115 parts must be ordered from the supplier. Although ordering parts may not require any production capacity, the activity must begin in Week 3, thus demonstrating the need to offset the ordering activity by a lead time of one week from Assemble Frame. *Offsetting for lead times* between successive stages of the productive system is fundamental to resource requirements planning.

Notice in Figure 11.3 that we can determine the actual number of labor and machine hours that the MPS will require weekly in each work center for this product. When all end items from the MPS are included, the total labor and machine hours required weekly in each work center can be compared to the number available. Such comparisons allow operations managers to determine the feasibility of the MPS in each work center weekly and also answer operating questions about overtime, standby machines, subcontracting, and other overloading and underloading issues.

Figure 11.3
Loading Effects of MPS upon Work Center Capacities

Weeks	−2	−1	1	2	3	4	5	6	7	8
Final Assembly (Units)			800		1600		600		1800	
Labor Hours			400		800		300		900	
Machine Hours			240		480		180		540	

Weeks	−2	−1	1	2	3	4	5	6	7	8
Assemble Frame (Units)		800		1600		600		1800		
Labor Hours		320		640		240		720		
Machine Hours		280		560		210		630		

Weeks	−2	−1	1	2	3	4	5	6	7	8
Order Part #115 (Parts)	2400		4800		1800		5400			

Let us suppose that we have a trial MPS and we wish to test its feasibility through CRP. Load schedules such as the ones illustrated in Figure 11.4 may be used for this purpose. From such schedules we can determine the following:

1. The labor hours loading is out of balance in the Fabrication Department. It appears that some fabrication work needs to be shifted from Weeks 3, 4, and 8 into Weeks 5, 6, and 7. A review of the machine loading in the Fabrication Department in these weeks indicates that such a shift would not cause machine overloading.

2. The change suggested in Fabrication above would not adversely affect Final Assembly because all units in Fabrication move to Final Assembly one week later and overtime could be used to alleviate the labor hours overloading in Weeks 6, 7, and 8 in Final Assembly. The machine hour loading in all weeks in Final Assembly is not a limiting factor.

3. At the plant level, the later part of the schedule is overloaded on both machine hours and labor hours. Overtime could be used to relieve the labor hours overloading, and subcontracting or the use of less efficient standby machines could reduce the machine hour overloading. Another alternative is always present, however, and that is to modify the MPS to shift end items from the later part of the schedule to the earlier weeks.

If the MPS is modified, then the logic of the CRP would be applied again through a revised set of load schedules similar to Figure 11.4. In this process we develop a trial MPS and then modify it through CRP until not only is the MPS feasible, but also the

Figure 11.4
The Capacity Loading Hierarchy

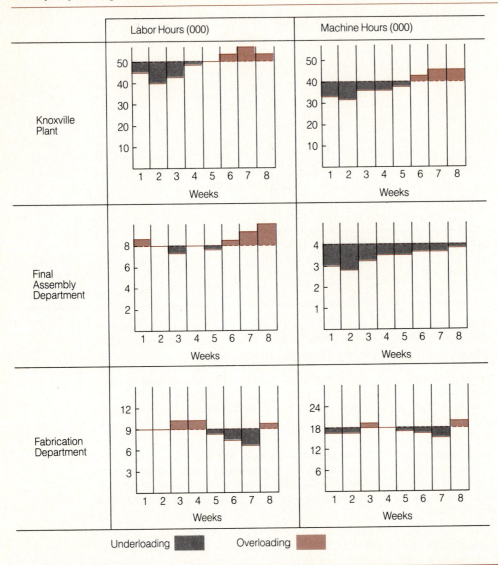

Underloading ▮   Overloading ▮

work centers are economically loaded, an achievement that promotes internal operating efficiency and low unit costs throughout the entire manufacturing system.

One trend in CRP is to use one of the many standard computer programs available from computer software suppliers. An example of such a system is the Capacity

Planning and Operation Sequencing System (CAPOSS – E) from IBM.[9] This and other approaches are likely to help overcome this knotty problem in CRP implementation in the future.

We have seen how the MPS attempts to achieve its dual objectives of satisfying customer demand on a timely basis while simultaneously promoting internal operating efficiency through CRP. The testing of the MPS, however, is not yet complete because we must also be assured that the MPS *can* be produced with the materials that are available. Material requirements planning (MRP) serves this purpose.

Material Requirements Planning (MRP)

Material requirements planning (MRP) is one of the hottest topics sweeping manufacturing organizations today. So many supporters of MRP abound and we have tended to attribute so many good results to MRP that it is little wonder that in some cases it has not quite lived up to its billing. Nothing could! However, MRP can offer many advantages over other inventory-planning approaches. As we discuss MRP in this section, you may find it helpful to refer to Table 11.1, Terms Often Used in Resource Requirements Planning.

MRP is a computer-based system that takes the MPS as given; explodes the MPS into the required amount of raw materials, parts, subassemblies, and assemblies needed in each week of the planning horizon; reduces these material requirements to account for materials that are in inventory or on order; and develops a schedule of orders for each material over the planning horizon.

Why have so many production organizations today adopted various forms of MRP systems? The objectives of MRP help explain why MRP has mushroomed in use.

Objectives of MRP

Operations managers adopt MRP in order to:

1. Improve customer service.
2. Reduce inventory investment.
3. Improve plant operating efficiency.

Improving customer service means more than just having products on hand when customer orders are received. To have satisfied customers also means meeting delivery promises and shortening delivery times. Not only does MRP provide the necessary management information to make intelligent delivery promises that have a high likelihood of being kept, but also the promises are locked into the MRP control system that guides production. Therefore, promised delivery dates become goals to be met by the organization, and in addition the probability of meeting promised delivery dates is improved. The improved control of raw material acquisition resulting from MRP tends to speed up customer orders because throughput rates tend to increase also.

---

[9] International Business Machines Corporation, *Capacity Planning and Operation Sequencing System — Extended,* Publication 5740 – M41 (OS/VS) and 5746 – M41 (DOS/VS), April 1977.

Because MRP systematically plans the timing of inflows of materials that closely match the needs of production, and because MRP systems quickly adapt to changing customer, production, and supplier needs, the need for large raw materials and in-process inventories is severely diminished.

Because MRP better controls the quantity and timing of deliveries of raw materials, parts, subassemblies, and assemblies to production operations, the right materials are delivered at the right time to production. Additionally, inflows can be slowed or accelerated in response to changes in production schedules. These controls of MRP result in reduced labor, material, and variable overhead costs because of:

1. Reduced numbers of stockouts and material delivery delays resulting in more output from production without corresponding increases in the number of employees and machines.

2. Reduction of the incidence of scrapped subassemblies, assemblies, and products resulting from the use of incorrect parts.

3. Increase in capacity of the production departments by increasing throughput rates as a result of decreased production idle time, increased efficiency of the physical movement of materials, and reduced confusion and planning delays.

Table 11.4 illustrates many of the improvements that have resulted from the installation of MRP systems in 326 firms. Inventory turns, delivery promises met, orders that need to be split because of material shortages, number of expediters required, and lead time from order to delivery have all improved. Furthermore, within these firms it is estimated that there is still room for other improvements in the future. With such glowing reports of MRP successes, it is little wonder that companies in growing numbers are installing or gearing up to install these systems. Let us now examine the general features of MRP systems.

Table 11.4
Material Requirements Planning: How Can It Help?

	Pre-MRP	With MRP (Current)	With MRP (Future)
1. Annual inventory turns*	3.5	4.7	5.6
2. Delivery promises met	64%	81%	93%
3. Orders that need to be split because of material shortages	32%	21%	13%
4. Number of expediters required	9.5	5.6	3.8
5. Lead time from order to delivery	64 days	57 days	42 days

* Annual inventory turns = Annual sales dollars divided by the dollar value of average inventory.

Source: "Material Requirements Planning: Who Can It Help?" John Anderson and Roger Schroeder, "The Trick of Material Requirements Planning," reprinted from the June 4 issue of *Business Week* by special permission, © 1979, p. 72, by McGraw-Hill, Inc., New York, NY 10020. All rights reserved.

The Elements of MRP

Figure 11.5 describes the operation of the MRP system. The *master production schedule* drives the entire MRP system. It is accepted as *given*. The *inventory status file* and *bills of material file* supply additional information about products included in the master production schedule. These inputs are fed into the MRP computer program, which generates the outputs. The inventory transactions resulting from the MRP actions are put back into the inventory status file so that current inventory

Figure 11.5
The MRP System

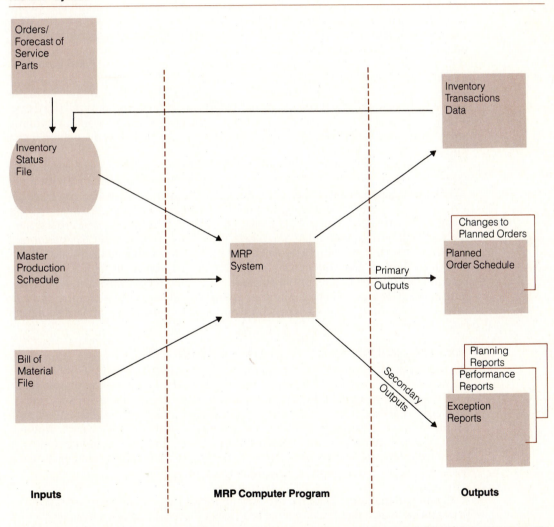

records are maintained. The *planned order schedule* and *changes to planned orders* are the primary outputs of MRP. Exception, performance, and planning reports are also frequently generated for management's use.

Master Production Schedule Master production schedules are devised to fill anticipated deficiencies in finished goods inventories or to directly meet customer demand. A MPS begins as a trial or preliminary schedule to be tested for feasibility through CRP and MRP. As these schedules are proved feasible, they become the MPS that is put into action. The early weeks of the MPS are understood to be *frozen*, the middle weeks are described as *firm*, and the later weeks are said to be *full* or *open*. The early weeks are frozen so that production departments can depend upon this portion of the plan to the extent that material can be ordered, personnel can be scheduled to work, and machine changeovers can be scheduled to support the MPS. If the early weeks of the MPS were allowed to be changed, material orders, personnel work schedules, and machine changeover schedules would also need to be changed. Such changes cause chaos in production departments and material control departments. After one period, usually a week, the MPS is revised by dropping off Week 1, since Week 1 would then be history, and adding a week onto the end of the schedule. This *rolling schedule* nature of the MPS must, however, observe the frozen character of the early weeks of the old MPS to allow for rational and systematic acquisition of material flows to support the schedule, *which is an absolute must in MRP*.

MRP cannot distinguish between feasible and infeasible master production schedules. That is to say, MRP assumes that the MPS can be produced within the production capacity constraints. MRP explodes the master schedule into material requirements. If these requirements cannot be met by the materials available from inventory, materials on order, or if insufficient time is available for new orders, then the MPS will need to be modified to a new MPS. This process of MRP is performed parallel to the CRP process. Refer to Figure 11.2 to clarify this point.

The MPS drives the MRP system and is the primary basis for the MRP system's planning for the acquisition of the required materials. As the MPS is modified, the MRP results are also modified. Material orders are speeded up or slowed down or canceled. When the MPS is frozen, the plan for the inflow of materials emanating from MRP is also frozen.

Bills of Material File A *bill of material* is a list of the materials and their quantities required to produce one unit of a product, or *end item*. Each product therefore has a bill of materials. In POM, bills of material are the basis for planning the amount of each raw material for each time period given a production schedule of end items.

A *bills of material file*, or *product structure file* as it is sometimes called, is a complete list of all finished products, the quantity of each material in each product, and the structure (assemblies, subassemblies, parts, and raw materials and their relationship) of products. Another term for a bill of material is *indented parts list*, a list in which the parent is in the margin and its components are indented to show structure.

The bills of material file is an up-to-date computerized file that must be revised as products are redesigned. Accuracy of the bills of material files is a major hurdle that must be overcome in most MRP applications. With the confidence that the file is current, once the MPS is prepared, end items in the MPS can be *exploded* into the assemblies, subassemblies, parts, and raw materials required. These units may either be purchased from outside suppliers or produced in downstream in-house production departments.

Inventory Status File The *inventory status file* is a computerized file with a complete record of each material held in inventory. These records include the inventory on hand, materials on order, and customer orders for the item. These records are kept up to date by inventory transactions such as receipts, disbursements, scrapped materials, planned orders, and order releases.

Another part of the file includes planning factors that are used by the MRP system. These factors include such information as lot sizes, lead times, safety stock levels, and scrap rates.

Some parts, subassemblies, and assemblies are carried as end items supplied to customers as replacement parts. These materials may not be a part of the master production schedule because they are purchased direct from suppliers and placed directly in inventory for customer demand; in other words, they are not *produced* so they are not included in the MPS. The orders or forecast orders for these materials, therefore, are fed directly into the inventory status file that directly becomes a part of the MRP system.

The inventory status file provides the MRP system not only a complete status record for each material in inventory but, additionally, the planning factors are used in the MRP computer program to project delivery dates of orders, quantities of each material to order, and when to place the orders.

MRP Computer Program The MRP computer program operates this way:

1. First, with the master production schedule it begins to determine the number of end items needed in each time period. Time periods are sometimes called *buckets* in MRP terminology.
2. Next, the number of service parts not included in the MPS but deduced from customer orders are included as end items.
3. Next, the MPS and service parts are exploded into gross requirements by time period into the future by consulting the bills of material file.
4. Next, the gross materials requirements are modified by the amount of materials on hand and on order for each period by consulting the inventory status file. The net requirements of each material for each bucket are computed as follows:

$$\text{Net requirements} = \frac{\text{Gross}}{\text{requirements}} - \left[\frac{\text{Inventory}}{\text{on hand}} - \frac{\text{Safety}}{\text{stock}} - \frac{\text{Inventory}}{\text{allocated to other uses}} \right]$$

If the net requirements are greather than zero, orders for the material must be placed.

5. Finally, the net requirements are offset to earlier time periods to allow for lead times at each step in the production process and supplier lead times.

This procedure results in inventory transactions data (orders released, changes in orders, and so on), which are used to update the inventory status file, the primary output reports (planned order schedules and changes to planned orders), and secondary output reports (exception, performance, and planning reports).

Outputs of MRP The outputs of MRP systems dynamically provide the schedule of raw materials for the future — amount of each material required in each time period to support the MPS. Two primary outputs result:

1. Planned order schedule — a plan of the quantity of each material to be ordered in each time period. These are used by purchasing to place orders with suppliers and by production to order parts, subassemblies, or assemblies from upstream production departments. These planned orders become a guide for future production at suppliers.

2. Changes in planned orders — modification of previous planned orders. Quantities of orders can be changed, orders can be canceled, or the orders can be slipped or advanced to different time periods.

The optional secondary MRP outputs provide this information:

1. Exception reports — reports that flag items requiring management attention in order to provide the right quantity of materials in each time period. Typical exceptions noted are reporting errors, out-of-bounds situations, late orders, and excessive scrap.

2. Performance reports — reports that indicate how well the system is operating. Examples of performance measures utilized are inventory turns, percentage of delivery promises kept, and stockout incidences.

3. Planning reports — reports used to plan future inventory planning activities. Examples of such planning information are inventory forecasts, purchase commitment reports, traces to demand sources, and long-range material requirements planning.

These are the major elements of MRP — the inputs, the MRP computer program, and the outputs. Let us now work through an example case to see how inventory planning can be affected by the use of MRP.

An MRP Case

Case 11.1 demonstrates how MRP can be applied to one product of a manufacturing firm to improve inventory planning, improve customer service, reduce inventory levels, and improve operating efficiency. Read the case and work your way through Figure 11.7, the MRP schedule, which is the heart of the case analysis. Make sure you understand how each piece of information is taken from the MPS (Table 11.5), the Bill of Material (Table 11.6), and Inventory Status Report (Table 11.7), to be used in the calculations of the MRP Schedule.

The Planned Order Schedule (Table 11.9) is the primary output of MRP. The *planned order schedule* is a schedule of planned future order releases over the entire planning horizon. This report indicates to purchasing and other materials management personnel what materials to order, what quantities of materials to order, and when to place the orders for every material in the productive system.

Case 11.1

The Green Thumb Water Sprinkler Company

Mr. Ever Verde, the president of Green Thumb Water Sprinkler Company, has just called a meeting of his key personnel to discuss new approaches to inventory planning at Green Thumb. Mr. Verde starts the meeting:

Mr. Verde: I've called this meeting to explore new avenues for inventory planning in our organization. The incidences of stockouts in our raw material inventory have led to lost business to the point that we just can't tolerate them any more. And the answer is not larger order quantities and higher safety stocks, because the interest charges for carrying our inventory are eating us alive. Somehow we've got to plan our acquisition of materials to mesh more closely with our cutomers' orders for finished products.

Bonnie Buck: I heartily agree, Mr. Verde. As production manager, may I say that when we in production place orders for materials from the warehouse, it seems they're out of stock as often as not. The warehouses are full—but of the wrong materials. Something has got to be done.

Bill Compton: Well, as materials manager, I'm obviously on the hot seat here. We've already concluded that our traditional system of fixed order quantities and order points is just not doing the job. Our individual customer orders are simply too large and spaced out to fit the assumptions of our present system. In anticipation of this problem, Joe Johnson, our inventory system analyst, has been attending a class in material requirements planning (MRP) over at the university at night. Joe has selected the #377 Lawn Sprinkler to demonstrate the MRP technique. Joe, will you show us the results of your analysis?

Joe Johnson: Thank you, Mr. Compton. I've prepared an MRP schedule for the #377 based upon our most recent master production schedule, #377 bill of material, and the inventory status of #377 and its components. The Planned Order Schedule summarizes the recommended timing and size of orders of #377 components.

After the group studies the results of the MRP analysis, Bonnie Buck has some clarifying questions:

Bonnie Buck: Joe, so I'll understand the mechanics of MRP, could you take just one component in the MRP Schedule (Figure 11.7) and explain your calculations?

Joe Johnson: Sure, Bonnie. Let's concentrate on Component C—the water motor. First, notice that our analysis of customer orders and forecasts of orders has resulted in Table 11.5, the Master Production Schedule for the #377 Lawn Sprinkler. One thousand units are needed in Week 4 and 2,000 units are needed in Week 8. Next, from the Bill of Material for the #377 (Table 11.6), we can see that one unit of Component C goes into each unit of Component M (water motor assembly) and one unit of Component M goes into each #377. This relationship can perhaps be seen more clearly in Figure 11.6—Product Structure: #377 Lawn Sprinkler. Next, looking at the MRP Schedule for the #377 in Figure 11.7, note that the number of #377 units available going into Week 4 is 200 units (the difference between the on-hand inventory balance and the safety stock). Because we need 1,000 #377 units in

Figure 11.7
MRP Schedule: #377 Lawn Sprinkler

Item Code	Level Code	Lot Size	Lead Time Weeks	On Hand	Safety Stock	Allocated		1	2	3	4	5	6	7	8
											Week Number				
377	0	LFL	1	500	300		Gross Requirements				1,000				2,000
							Scheduled Receipts								
							Available	200	200	200	200				
							Net Requirements				800				2,000
							Planned Order Receipts				800				2,000
							Planned Order Releases			800				2,000	
M	1	LFL	1	200			Gross Requirements			800			2,000		
							Scheduled Receipts								
							Available	200	200	200					
							Net Requirements			600			2,000		
							Planned Order Receipts			600			2,000		
							Planned Order Releases		600			2,000			
F	1	LFL	1	300			Gross Requirements			800			2,000		
							Scheduled Receipts								
							Available	300	300	300					
							Net Requirements			500			2,000		
							Planned Order Receipts			500			2,000		
							Planned Order Releases		500			2,000			
H	1	1,000+	2	1,500	200	1,000	Gross Requirements			800			2,000		
							Scheduled Receipts								
							Available	300	300	300	500	500	500	500	
							Net Requirements			500			1,500	1,500	
							Planned Order Receipts			1,000				1,500	
							Planned Order Releases	1,000				1,500			
A	2	50,000+	2	30,000	5,000	15,000	Gross Requirements		26,000				100,000		
							Scheduled Receipts	50,000							
							Available	60,000	60,000	34,000	34,000	34,000	34,000		
							Net Requirements						66,000		
							Planned Order Receipts						66,000		
							Planned Order Releases				66,000				
B	2	10,000+	1	5,000		2,500	Gross Requirements		3,300				12,000		
							Scheduled Receipts								
							Available	2,500	2,500	9,200	9,200	9,200	9,200	7,200	7,200
							Net Requirements		800				2,800		
							Planned Order Receipts		10,000				10,000		
							Planned Order Releases	10,000				10,000			
C	2	1,000+	2	1,000	500	800	Gross Requirements		600		1,000		2,000		
							Scheduled Receipts	1,000							
							Available	700	700	100	100	100	100		
							Net Requirements				900		1,900		
							Planned Order Receipts				1,000		1,900		
							Planned Order Releases		1,000		1,900				
D	2	10,000+	2	3,000		2,000	Gross Requirements		1,500				6,000		
							Scheduled Receipts	10,000							
							Available	11,000	11,000	9,500	9,500	9,500	9,500	3,500	3,500
							Net Requirements								
							Planned Order Receipts								
							Planned Order Releases								

Table 11.5
Master Production Schedule: #377 Lawn Sprinkler

	Week Number							
	1	2	3	4	5	6	7	8
Gross requirements				1,000				2,000

Table 11.6
Bill of Material: #377 Lawn Sprinkler

Parent Code	Component Code	Level Code	Description	Components Required per Parent
	377	0	#377 Lawn Sprinkler	
377	M	1	Water motor assembly	1
	F	1	Frame assembly	1
	H	1	#699 hose recept. assembly	1
M	A	2	½″ dia. ¹⁄₃₂″ alum. tube	10″
	B	2	½″ × ¹⁄₁₆″ metal screws	3
	C	2	Water motor	1
F	A	2	½″ dia. ¹⁄₃₂″ alum. tube	40″
	D	2	½″ × ½″ #115 plastic cap	3
	B	2	½″ × ¹⁄₁₆″ metal screws	3

Figure 11.6
Product Structure: #377 Lawn Sprinkler

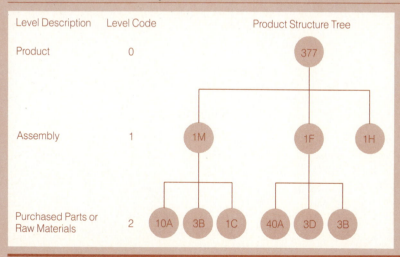

Table 11.7
Inventory Status Report: #377 Lawn Sprinkler

Item Code	On Hand	Safety Stock	Allocated	Lot Sizes*	Lead Times (Weeks)	Scheduled Receipts		Service Parts Orders	
						Qty.	Week	Qty.	Week
377	500	300		LFL	1				
M	200	0		LFL	1				
F	300	0		LFL	1				
H	1,500	200	1,000	1,000+	2				
A	30,000	5,000	15,000	50,000+	2	50,000	1		
B	5,000	0	2,500	10,000+	1				
C	1,000	500	800	1,000+	2	1,000	1	1,000	4
D	3,000	0	2,000	10,000+	2	10,000	1		

* Note: The plus (+) sign indicates that any quantity over the minimum may be ordered. For example, 1,000+ indicates that 1,000 or more may be ordered.

Week 4 and 200 units are available from inventory, we have a net requirement of 800 units in Week 4. Because it takes one week to process a batch of #377 units through final assembly operations, the 800 units must be started through final assembly in Week 3, one week earlier.

If 800 #377 units must begin final assembly in Week 3, 800 Component M units are needed in Week 3 and this need shows up as a gross requirement for Component M in Week 3. When this same logic is applied to Component M, 600 units of Component M must be started into production in Week 2 and this creates a gross requirement of 600 units of Component C in Week 2. The gross requirement for Component C in Week 6 similarly directly results from the #377 gross requirement in Week 8. The gross requirement of 1,000 units of Component C in Week 4 results from the need to ship service parts to customers. This information is found in Table 11.7—Inventory Status Report: #377 Lawn Sprinkler. This explains how the gross requirement for Component C was determined. A further explanation of all the gross requirements in the MRP schedule of Figure 11.7 is contained in Table 11.8—Gross Requirements Calculations for #377 Lawn Sprinkler.

The gross requirement of 600 units of Component C in Week 2 is met by the scheduled receipt of 1,000 units in Week 1, although only 700 of these units are available for use in Week 2 as we were 300 units short entering Week 1 owing to an overallocation of the on-hand inventory beyond the safety stock. The gross requirement of 600 units in Week 2 combined with the 700 units available in Week 2 results in 100 units available to meet the gross requirement of 1,000 units in Week 4. This leaves a net requirement of 900 units in Week 4 and 1,000 units, the minimum lot size, are planned to be received in Week 4. After offsetting for the 2 weeks of lead time to receive the shipment of Component C, we should release the order for 1,000 units in Week 2.

The gross requirement of 2,000 units in Week 6 is similarly computed. Now do you see how we work our way through Figure 11.7, the MRP Schedule?

Bonnie Buck: Yes. How do you know that the MPS and the Planned Order Schedule are feasible?

Table 11.8
Gross Requirements Calculations for #377 Lawn Sprinkler

Component Code	Parent Code	Components Required per Parent	Components Required for Parents' Production		Service Parts Required		Total Gross Requirements	
			Quantity	Week	Quantity	Week	Quantity	Week
M	377	1	800	3			800	3
M	377	1	2,000	7			2,000	7
F	377	1	800	3			800	3
F	377	1	2,000	7			2,000	7
H	377	1	800	3			800	3
H	377	1	2,000	7			2,000	7
A	M	10″	6,000	2				
A	F	40″	20,000	2			26,000	2
A	M	10″	20,000	6				
A	F	40″	80,000	6			100,000	6
B	M	3	1,800	2				
B	F	3	1,500	2			3,300	2
B	M	3	6,000	6				
B	F	3	6,000	6			12,000	6
C	M	1	600	2			600	2
C	—	—			1,000	4	1,000	4
C	M	1	2,000	6			2,000	6
D	F	3	1,500	2			1,500	2
D	F	3	6,000	6			6,000	6

In other words, how do you know that we have the production capacity to produce the MPS and how do you know that the materials will be available in time to allow us to produce the MPS?

Joe Johnson: That's a good question, Bonnie. We know that purchased materials will be available in sufficient quantities and in time to satisfy the Planned Order Schedule (Table 11.9) because we have double-checked with our suppliers. This method of checking whether materials can be supplied in time to make the production of the MPS feasible will be a continuing requirement in MRP. If we discovered that a material could not be supplied in time or in sufficient quantities to conform to the Planned Order Schedule, we would have only two alternatives: expedite the order and perhaps pay extra to have the order processed on an overtime basis at our suppliers, or change the MPS and go through the MRP process again. If the MPS is changed, the affected end item would have to be moved outward to later periods in the MPS.

The MPS has also been checked for production capacity feasibility. Load schedules like those in Figure 11.4 were developed for each production department at the plant. All of the products in the MPS were included, and it was clear that sufficient production capacity exists in each department to allow us to produce the

Table 11.9
Planned Order Schedule: #377 Lawn Sprinkler

Item Code	Week Number							
	1	2	3	4	5	6	7	8
377			800				2,000	
M		600				2,000		
F		500				2,000		
H	1,000				1,500			
A				66,000				
B	10,000				10,000			
C		1,000		1,900				
D								

MPS. This brings up an interesting point: How do we develop detailed weekly production schedules from the MRP Schedule that is Figure 11.7? Only items 377, M, and F, which are higher-level items, require in-house production. All other items are purchased from our suppliers.

The production departments where the 377, M, and F items will be produced include the planned order releases for these items in their load schedules. For example, 600 and 2,000 units of Component M must enter production in the Mechanical Fabrication and Assembly Department in Weeks 2 and 6, respectively. The amount of labor per unit and the amount of machine hours per unit are multiplied by these quantities, and the result is the amount of production capacity required in the department for Component M. When this same process is followed for all of our products, the loading can be compared to the labor and machine capacity of the department. The same loading analysis would also be applied to the Final Assembly Department and the Metal Fabrication and Assembly Department.

As you can see, capacity requirements planning (CRP), as this analysis is called, is a required part of the overall inventory-planning process. Additionally, the detailed production schedules of the production departments are picked off the MRP schedules. When all of the planned order releases are picked off all of the components of the MRP schedule that are to be produced in-house and classified according to their production departments, the result is departmental production schedules.

Do you see the connection between MRP and the departmental production schedules?

Bonnie Buck: Yes. Now would you summarize how MRP would be applied to all of our products in practice?

Joe Johnson: The procedure for our six major products would mechanically be the same as we demonstrated for #377. The big difference would be in computerizing the whole process. The figures that we've seen here today were all manually calculated. These could be the major tasks for us to get an MRP system operative: (1) Build an accurate computerized inventory status file for all our products. (2) Improve our forecasting methods so that we can combine anticipated customer orders with customer orders in hand to form a reliable basis for an accurate master production schedule. (3) Build an up-to-date computerized bills of material file for all our products. (4) Buy the services of ABM Computer Services to assist us in installing the MRP computer program and debugging the MRP system after it's installed. I would estimate that we could have an MRP system operating for all our products in about 6 months.

Mr. Verde: Joe, what are the major advantages of MRP over our present inventory-planning system, which is tied to economic order quantities and minimum inventory level order points?

Joe Johnson: (1) Better customer service, (2) lower inventory levels, and (3) higher operating efficiency in our production departments.

The group all agreed to give MRP a try by running the new system for one half of Green Thumb's products while the present inventory-planning system was used simultaneously on the other products. It was thought that this approach should give a practical comparison of the results of MRP and the present inventory-planning system.

Not all MRP systems are identical. Neither is MRP equally applicable to all productive systems. Several MRP issues are now being debated in POM. It is hoped that this debate will open new areas of application and clarify and refine MRP usage.

MRP Issues

The MRP issues treated here are not resolved. But any comprehensive treatment of MRP should inform you of important issues yet to be resolved by consensus in POM practice.

Net Change versus Regenerative MRP Systems Some organizations use what is called *net change MRP*. These systems update the master production schedule as major or even minor changes in the MPS occur. The MRP system is then activated to generate one set of MRP outputs. These outputs, however, are only the net changes to past MRP runs and not an entire set of MRP outputs. The planned order schedule report, for example, would indicate only changes to previous planned order schedules, not a completely new schedule. Although this concept is indeed tempting in theory, because it promises to serve as one big exception report that would greatly reduce the amount of information generated on each run, its incidence of application has been disappointing.

Many organizations continue to use what is called *regenerative MRP*. In these systems a complete MRP run is processed periodically, usually every one or two weeks. At these times a new MPS, an updated inventory status file, and an up-to-date bills of material file are fed into the MRP computer program, which generates a complete set of outputs. Although regenerative MRP systems are slightly more costly to prepare and process, they also apparently are easier to understand. Only time will tell which of these approaches will gain favor.

Safety Stock MRP users do not agree on whether safety stock should be used in MRP. Proponents for using safety stock in MRP argue that safety stock performs the same function in MRP systems as in other inventory-planning systems — avoiding excessive stockouts caused by uncertain lead times and daily demands. Those who oppose the use of safety stock in MRP argue that because MRP systems adapt to changing conditions that affect demand and lead times, safety stock will not actually be used under the vast majority of circumstances in MRP.

The use of safety stock can be justified only by the sources of uncertainty present during lead times. For higher-level items such as end items and components that are used as service parts, the uncertainty of demand compares with any other inventory item having independent demand. The uncertainty of lead times for these items seems more controllable if these items are produced in-house. On balance, the use of safety stock for end items in MRP systems can be justified on the same basis as in any other system — the presence of uncertain demand and uncertain lead times.

For lower-level items such as raw materials and parts, the uncertainty of demand is adequately controlled because the demand is a dependent demand. The MPS sets the weekly demand for these items. The only major uncertainties present during lead times are the uncertainty of lead time and the uncertainty of demand that occurs because of changes in the MPS. It appears that some safety stock can certainly be justified, even in raw materials, parts, and other lower-level items, although at significantly reduced levels. As one materials manager recently commented, "The only alternative to the use of safety stocks in MRP is an up-to-date resumé." This statement implies that safety stock saves his job when stockouts inevitably occur.

Some operations managers today, however, think that perhaps the biggest disadvantage of carrying safety stocks is not the extra cost of carrying these stocks, but the operations problems that the stocks help cover up. The Japanese use their *just-in-time* (Kanban) production methods to all but eliminate safety stocks; operations problems are then more obvious and more likely to be solved. Exhibit 11.1 describes these methods.

Exhibit 11.1
A Revolutionary Way to Streamline the Factory

The just-in-time (JIT) production system may be the most important productivity-enhancing management innovation since Frederick Winslow Taylor's time-and-motion studies at the turn of the century. It is a Japanese innovation, and key features were perfected by Toyota. But there is nothing uniquely Japanese about JIT production. It is usable anywhere.

JIT production means producing and buying in very small quantities just in time for use. It is a simple, hand-to-mouth mode of industrial operations that directly cuts inventories and also reduces the need for storage space, racks, conveyors, forklifts, computer terminals for inventory control and material support personnel. More important, the absence of extra inventories creates an imperative to run an error-free operation because there is no cushion of excess parts to keep production going when problems crop up. Causes of errors are rooted out, never to occur again.

In some ways, JIT production is nothing new. High-volume continuous producers — for example, steel, chemical and paper companies — employ it routinely. To do otherwise would bury them in inventory. Long-term predictability of materials needed makes it possible for continuous processors to arrange for materials to flow into and through their plants steadily without inventory buildups. The Anheuser-Busch brewery in St. Louis unloads a nearly continuous stream of trucks bringing in empty cans and uses them soon enough that, on the average, there is only a two-hour supply of unfilled cans on hand.

But cans of Budweiser don't come in many different models. In most of the rest of industry, plants produce an ever-changing variety of goods, and production scheduling is complicated and irregular. JIT streamlines and simplifies the stop-and-go production of most plant operations so that they resemble continuous processing. In so doing, it forces plan-

Exhibit 11.1 (continued)
A Revolutionary Way to Streamline the Factory

ners and analysts to get out of their offices and get out on the floor solving real problems.

The transformation begins with inventory removal. Fewer materials are bought, and parts and products are made in smaller quantities; so-called lot-size inventories thereby shrink. Buffer stocks or safety stocks—"just-in-case" inventory—are also deliberately cut.

The immediate result is work stoppages. Plenty of them. Production comes to a standstill because feeder processes break down or produce too many defectives—and now there is no buffer stock to keep things going. This is exactly what is supposed to happen. For now the analysts and engineers pour out of their offices and mingle with foremen and workers trying to get production going again. Now the causes—bad raw materials, machine breakdown, poor training, tolerances that exceed process capabilities—get attention so that the problem may never recur.

When one round of problems is solved, inventories are cut again so that more problems crop up and get solved. Each round of problem exposure and solution increases productivity—and quality, too. In Japan extensive quality control measures blend nicely with just-in-time production because many of the problems uncovered by inventory removal are quality problems.

Some people who have studied the just-in-time system conclude that it is suitable for high-volume producers but not for smaller-volume "job shops." But many companies that call themselves job shops have some semblance of a product line; those companies can become more productive by producing in smaller lots as continuously as possible. If they don't, chances are that a Japanese competitor will emerge and capture enough market share to become a high-volume repetitive producer jeopardizing the position of the stop-and-go producers; this is what is happening to Harley-Davidson, International Harvester and Hyster.

How can Western manufacturers become JIT producers? One way is "cold turkey": Remove inventories from the shop floor, dismantle distance-spanning conveyors, move machines close together and permanently reallocate floor space that once held inventory. Spasms of work stoppages for lack of parts will soon get everyone involved in solving underlying problems.

Most companies will want to take a more incremental approach. One way is to cut the cost of machine setup, a major reason why companies make parts in large batches. Setup times can be cut by simplifying dies, machine controls, fixtures and so forth. The term "quick die change" has been in the vocabulary of American production engineers for years. But American management only heard of it recently as stories have

trickled in from Japan about "single setup," which means a single-digit number of minutes, and "one-touch setup," which means zero setup (only load and unload) time.

The Kawasaki plant in Lincoln, Neb., uses another experimental approach. Occasionally it will deliberately draw down buffer stocks to near zero. The kinds of problems exposed will be recorded and assigned as improvement projects. Stocks will be allowed to build back up, and the improvement projects will proceed. As underlying problems are solved, stocks will then be permanently cut and storage floor space reallocated.

Geography is the big obstacle to just-in-time deliveries of purchased parts. When your supplier is across the country, the economies of full truck and rail car shipments often dictate infrequent large-lot buying. The Japanese companies that have opened subsidiary plants in North America—Sony, Honda, Nissan, Sanyo, Kawasaki, etc.—deal with this hurdle by resolutely seeking nearby suppliers.

Establishing those arrangements may take years of effort. In the meantime, consolidated loads from clusters of remote suppliers may permit a load to be delivered every day. Common carriers may be rejected in favor of contract shippers or company trucks, so that the day and maybe the hour of delivery may be strictly scheduled. And manufacturers must not tolerate the standard practice among U.S. suppliers of delivering plus or minus 10% of the agreed-upon purchase quantity. With no excess inventory, nor space to store it, the just-in-time company must insist on deliveries in exact quantities.

It is clear that geography is a deterrent, though not an intractable one. Aside from that, there are few obstacles. More money is not needed. The just-in-time approach features getting by with less of most of the costly resources that American manufacturers protectively surrounded themselves with in the days when capital was plentiful and interest rates were low.

Reorienting People's Thinking

The only significant obstacles to JIT are those that stand in the way of any major change in management system: reorienting people's thinking. Must of that task has been done. Just-in-time programs have been established at General Electric, the big-three auto makers, Goodyear, Rolm and various other American industrial companies.

Transforming our coughing, sputtering plants into streamlined just-in-time producers sounds like a 10- or 20-year project. It may not take that long because the innovating has been done for us. Taylor's innovation, scientific management, was readily exportable and implementable in Europe and Japan (and today the Japanese out-Taylor us all). The Japanese innovation, just-in-time, is equally transportable.

Lot-Sizing As Case 11.1 suggests, a variety of lot-sizing techniques can be used within MRP. Economic order quantity (EOQ), price breaks, or any other approach can be used in MRP. The discussion of lot-sizing techniques in the Master Production Scheduling section earlier in this chapter is also applicable to individual components in the MRP schedule. In other words, the net requirements line in the MRP schedule for each component is ordinarily analyzed to determine the timing and size of production lots or purchased lots by using one of the lot-sizing techniques mentioned earlier. The Planned Order Receipt line in the MRP schedule is the end result of these lot-sizing decisions.

One potential problem is said to exist when lot-sizing techniques are applied at every level in the product structure. Using lot-sizing in lower-level components (raw materials and parts) poses no serious problems, but when discrepancies between customer order sizes and economic lot sizes for higher-level components (end items and assemblies) exist, some MRP users believe that excessive inventory buildups in lower-level components can result.

For example, three components are related as follows:

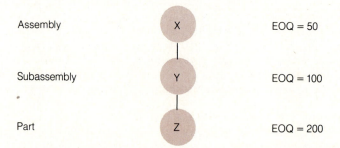

If a customer order of 25 units of X is received, no inventory is on hand for X, Y, and Z, and orders equal to EOQ are received from suppliers, then the inventory available for use immediately after shipping the customer order is:

Inventory of X = 25 units

Inventory of Y = 75 units

Inventory of Z = 175 units

Some MRP users argue, however, that excessive inventory levels are not reached. The larger economic lot size for Part Z in the example above is therefore based on a higher average inventory for these lower-level components. The per-unit cost of lower-level components leads to higher lot sizes and consequently higher inventory levels. These MRP users contend that higher inventory levels of lower-level components should not be surprising nor disturbing; the economic lot-sizing of all levels of components is therefore recommended.

The tendency among practicing materials managers is to use lot-for-lot (LFL) lot-sizing for end items and assemblies and minimum lot sizes for lower-level components such as raw materials and parts. The use of LFL in end items and assemblies avoids the inventory buildups in lower-level components described above. The use of minimum lot sizes for raw materials and parts suggests that for purchased components, some minimum amount of the material needs to be ordered to qualify for a price break or a transportation cost break. The minimum lot size for parts produced in-house suggests that at some minimum quantity the cost per unit of the item levels out (see Figure 9.4, Cost per Unit vs. Length of Production Run).

Evaluation of MRP

The advantages claimed for MRP over more conventional inventory-planning approaches such as fixed order quantities and order points have been demonstrated here and elsewhere in POM — improved customer service, reduced inventory levels, and improved operating efficiency of production departments. This sounds so good that we wonder why the whole world has not been "MRP'ed." There are good reasons that this isn't the case.

Table 11.10 lists the characteristics of productive systems that support the successful implementation of MRP. The presence of an effective computer system is an absolute must. This seems so obvious that it hardly needs elaboration. But would you believe that this may be the most serious impediment to MRP in most organizations? Two other characteristics that similarly seem almost automatic are accurate bills of material and inventory status files. The absence of these files and an ineffective computing system often pose the largest headaches for the implementation of MRP in practice. Correcting deficiencies such as these may take the bulk of the MRP team's time during MRP implementation programs.

Table 11.10
Desirable Characteristics of Productive Systems Suitable for MRP

1. An acceptable computer system.
2. Accurate computerized bills of material and inventory status files for all end items and materials.
3. A production system that manufactures discrete products made up of raw materials, parts, subassemblies, and assemblies that are processed through several production steps.
4. Production processes requiring long processing times.
5. Relatively short and reliable lead times for materials purchased from suppliers.
6. The master schedule frozen for a period of time sufficient to procure materials without excessive expediting and confusion.
7. Small lot sizes of materials as compared with variability.
8. Top management support and commitment.

MRP is conventionally applied only to manufacturing systems. These organizations process discrete products for which bills of material are possible, a requirement of MRP. This means that MRP is seldom applied to service systems, petroleum refineries, retailing systems, transportation firms, and other nonmanufacturing systems. Many of us in POM believe that MRP can be successfully applied to some of these nonmanufacturing systems.[10] These applications would do what MRP is designed to do — improve customer service, reduce inventory levels, and improve operating efficiency. When service systems require sets of raw materials to deliver

---

[10] This contention seems to be supported by the growing interest within the American Production and Inventory Control Society (APICS) in applying MRP to processing industries.

one unit of service (a pseudo bill of material), MRP potentially can be applied. Surgical operations in large hospitals, high-volume professional services, and other processes are likely to use MRP systems in the future.

MRP delivers the most benefits to systems that have long processing times because long in-house lead times make raw materials inventory planning more complex. Picture a hypothetical productive system that converts raw materials into finished goods instantaneously. Raw materials in this unlikely example would be ordered in to exactly match finished goods requirements. In most real productive systems, however, the in-house processing lead times can often exceed the lead times required to obtain the raw materials from suppliers. MRP's ability to offset planned order receipts to planned order releases to account for long and complicated lead times greatly simplifies inventory planning.

In order for MRP to be effective, supplier lead times must be short and reliable, and the MPS must be frozen for a time before actual production to the MPS is begun. This just means that what is to be produced, the MPS, must be known with certainty and the timing and quantity of raw material receipts must be dependable. When lot sizes of raw materials are large and variability in demand is small, the conventional (economic lot size and minimum inventory order point) inventory-planning systems tend to work quite well because their assumptions of uniform demand apply. MRP therefore offers more improvement in inventory planning when lot sizes are small and demand variability is large.

MRP has not been and will not be applied to all productive systems. In some POM applications, MRP is either unnecessary or economically unjustifiable. The frequency of MRP usage is, however, definitely on a dramatic upward trend. As we gain more experience with MRP, we realize that it is not a panacea. It doesn't solve all our inventory-planning problems, and in some cases it creates more problems than it solves. Basically, MRP is a POM computerized information system. When computer systems are ineffective, inventory status and bills of material files are inaccurate, master production schedules are undependable, and when the remainder of the organization is otherwise mismanaged, MRP—or any other technique—will not be of much help. It will generate greater volumes of inaccurate and unused information than previously thought possible.

MRP is best applied when productive systems are basically well managed and a more comprehensive inventory-planning system is needed, and it is seen as a way to *better* manage the material system.

Summary

Resource requirements planning is the planning for materials, cash, personnel, and machine capacity needed to support the short-range production schedules. In production departments within manufacturing firms, master production scheduling, capacity requirements planning, and material requirements planning form the nucleus of this planning.

Master production scheduling is the process of determining which end items will be produced in each week of the planning horizon and in what quantities. Among the principal issues to be resolved in MPS are estimates of short-range demand, transforming the net requirements to economical production lot sizes, and determining the length of the planning horizon. The MPS drives the MRP system.

Capacity requirements planning is the process of testing the MPS for feasibility while considering production capacity. Employee availability and machine capacity availability are the main elements of capacity considered. The trial MPS is tested by developing load schedules that compare the actual capacity requirements of the MPS against the employees and machine capacity available in each department. If the MPS is economically feasible, then CRP helps answer operating questions concerning the use of overtime, subcontracting, shifting work between departments, shifting work between weeks, and using standby machines. If the MPS is infeasible, then the MPS must be changed.

MRP is a computerized POM information system that develops a schedule of planned orders for each material — how much should be ordered of each material in each time period in the planning horizon. These plans are then periodically modified as supply conditions or production schedules change.

MRP is driven by the master production schedule (MPS), a multi-time period plan of end items to be produced. When combined with the inventory status file and bills of material file, the MPS is fed into the MRP computer program. This computer program explodes the end items included in the MPS into the raw materials, parts, subassemblies, and assemblies required for each time period. Then gross requirements are converted to net requirements after considering the materials available and offsetting them to different time periods to allow for supply lead times. The primary outputs of MRP are the planned order schedule, order releases, and changes in planned orders. Additionally, other outputs are transactions affecting the inventory status file and secondary outputs of exception, performance, and planning reports.

Several MRP issues defy consensus in POM. Among these hotly debated issues are the use of safety stock in MRP, lot sizes, and regenerative versus net change MRP. Although unresolved issues remain, we in POM agree that if the characteristics of productive systems are suitable for MRP, improved customer service, reduced inventory levels, and improved operating efficiency can result from its use.

Review and Discussion Questions

1. What is resource requirements planning?

2. What are the major elements of resource requirements planning in production departments of manufacturing firms?

3. What is a master production schedule? Describe the types of information included in a MPS.

4. Describe the general relationships among the master production schedule, capacity requirements planning, and material requirements planning.

5. What is lumpy demand? Name three methods of lot-sizing that are used when demand is lumpy.

6. Describe the general process of capacity requirements planning.

7. Define these terms: **a.** *bills of material file*, **b.** *inventory status file*, **c.** *master production schedule*, **d.** *MRP computer program*, **e.** *inventory transactions data*, **f.** *planned order schedule*, **g.** *changes in planned orders*, and **h.** *secondary outputs*.

8. What are the objectives of MRP?

9. The master production schedule identifies all the end items to be included in the MRP system. True or false? Why?

10. Explain how net requirements for a material in a bucket are computed.

11. Explain the differences between regenerative and net change MRP systems.

12. Define *capacity requirements planning*.

13. Name four characteristics of productive systems suitable for MRP.

14. What key characteristics of service systems must be considered as obstacles to MRP use?

Problems

Master Production Schedules (MPS)

1. The marketing department has just developed this forecast of customer demands:

	Weeks					
	1	2	3	4	5	6
Forecast demands (units)	50	110	130	100	70	80

The manufacturing plant has received these orders for units:

	Weeks					
	1	2	3	4	5	6
Customer orders (units)	30	90	70	60	50	20
In-house orders (units)	20	10	5	10	10	——
Total orders (units)	50	100	75	70	60	20

Although you have limited knowledge about the product and its sales patterns, develop an estimated demand schedule for MPS purposes.

2. If the beginning inventory for a product is 1,000 units, safety stock is 200 units, and estimated weekly demand is 500, 400, 300, 800, 1,000, and 500 units over a 6-week planning horizon, develop a net requirements schedule for the product.

3. If the weekly net requirements for a product are 0, 100, 300, 800, 1,000, and 500 units over a 6-week planning horizon, carrying cost per unit per week is $1 whenever a unit must be carried over into the next week, there are 52 work weeks per year, and ordering cost is $500 per order, develop a schedule of completed production lots and calculate the cost of your schedule by using these methods: **a.** Lot-for-lot (LFL), **b.** economic order quantity (EOQ), and **c.** period order quantity (POQ). You may disregard the effects of initial inventory and safety stock upon your calculations.

4. You are given this net requirements schedule:

	Weeks							
	1	2	3	4	5	6	7	8
Net requirements (units)	1,000	2,000	2,500	1,500	3,000	1,000	500	500

If it costs $5,000 to get the final assembly department ready to assemble batches of this product, it costs $26 to carry one unit in inventory for a year, and 52 weeks per year are worked by the final assembly department, develop a schedule of completed production lots for the product and calculate the cost of your schedule by using these methods: **a.** Lot-for-lot (LFL), **b.** economic order quantity (EOQ), and **c.** period order quantity (POQ). You may disregard the effects of initial inventory and safety stock upon your calculations.

Capacity Requirements Planning (CRP)

5. The Ever-Pure Water Company sits atop a spring in Blackwater, Arkansas. The company bottles the water for shipment to customers through a distributor network. Ever-Pure's management has developed this master production schedule for the next 6 months:

	Weeks					
	1	2	3	4	5	6
Water (gallons)	100,000	150,000	200,000	150,000	150,000	100,000

If Ever-Pure's labor and machine hours available and its production standards are:

	Labor	Machine
Monthly capacity available (hours)	17,333	25,000
Production standard (hours/gallon)	.10	.15

a. Determine the percent utilization (standard hours $\times$ 100 $\div$ hours of capacity) of the labor and machine capacity in each week. **b.** What suggestions would you make to Ever-Pure's management concerning their MPS?

6. The Silver Streak Iron Works produces three different models of wellhead valves for the petroleum industry. Each of the valves must be processed through three production departments: foundry, fabrication, and assembly. Approximately one week is required for a valve to be completely processed through each department. Silver Streak is now in the process of capacity requirements planning (CRP) and has just developed this MPS:

	Weeks							
Model	1	2	3	4	5	6	7	8
X-100	300	500	500	600	700	500	200	300
Y-101	500	300	400	200	300	500	300	400
Z-102	600	500	700	700	800	600	800	600

The weekly labor and machine capacities for the production departments are:

Models	Foundry		Fabrication		Assembly	
	Labor Standard (Hr./Unit)	Machine Standard (Hr./Unit)	Labor Standard (Hr./Unit)	Machine Standard (Hr./Unit)	Labor Standard (Hr./Unit)	Machine Standard (Hr./Unit)
X-100	2.0	3.0	1.5	2.0	1.5	1.0
Y-101	2.5	3.5	2.0	2.5	1.5	1.5
Z-102	3.0	3.5	1.5	2.5	2.0	1.5

a. Develop labor and machine load schedules for each department and the plant for the first 6 weeks of the MPS (remember to offset for lead times between departments). **b.** Interpret the meaning of your load schedule: Is the MPS feasible? Are the production departments efficiently loaded? Can you make suggestions for changing the MPS to improve loading?

Material Requirements Planning (MRP)

7. Product A is made of two B assemblies and two C assemblies. Each C assembly is made of one D subassembly, 3 E parts, and one F raw material. Each D subassembly is made of 2 E parts and 3 G raw materials. Each B assembly is made of one F raw material and 3 H parts. Construct a product structure tree for Product A.

8. Complete this MRP schedule for a component:

Lot Size	Lead Time (Weeks)	On Hand	SS	Allo- cated		Week Number				
						1	2	3	4	5
					Gross requirements			10,000		7,500
					Scheduled receipts	5,000				
5,000+	2	5,000	2,500	2,000	Available					
					Net requirements					
					Planned order receipts					
					Planned order releases					

9. A product has this product tree:

Level Description	Level Code	Product Structure Tree
Product	0	
Assembly	1	
Part	2	

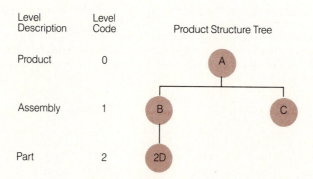

Complete this MRP schedule:

Item Code	Level Code	Lot Size	Lead Time (Weeks)	On Hand	Safety Stock	Allo-cated		Weeks					
								1	2	3	4	5	6
A	0	LFL	1	1,000	500		Gross Requirements				1,000	2,000	1,000
							Scheduled Receipts						
							Available						
							Net Requirements						
							Planned Order Receipts						
							Planned Order Releases						
B	1	LFL	1	200	100	100	Gross Requirements						
							Scheduled Receipts						
							Available						
							Net Requirements						
							Planned Order Receipts						
							Planned Order Releases						
C	1	LFL	1	500	100	100	Gross Requirements						
							Scheduled Receipts						
							Available						
							Net Requirements						
							Planned Order Receipts						
							Planned Order Releases						
D	2	1,000+	1	1,000	500	200	Gross Requirements						
							Scheduled Receipts						
							Available						
							Net Requirements						
							Planned Order Receipts						
							Planned Order Releases						

10. A product has this product tree:

Level
Code   Product Structure Tree

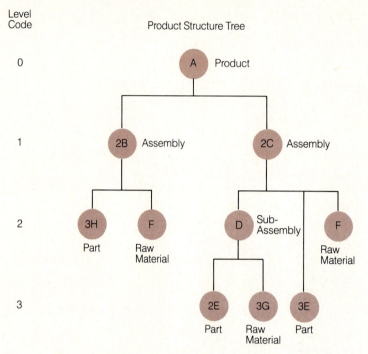

This inventory status report has just been issued for the product:

Product Status Report: Product A

Item Code	On Hand	Safety Stock	Allo-cated	Lot Size	Lead Time (Weeks)	Scheduled Receipts		Service Parts Orders	
						Quantity	Week	Quantity	Week
A	500	500	500	LFL	1	1,000	1		
B	1,000	200	500	LFL	1	1,000	2	1,000	3
C	1,000	500	200	LFL	1				
D	1,500	500	500	500+	1				
E	500	500		5,000+	1				
F	2,000	500	500	5,000+	3				
G	3,000	1,000	500	6,000+	2	6,000	1		
H	2,500	500	1,000	4,000+	2	4,000	2	5,000	6

Prepare an MRP schedule for all of the components in the product to cover a 6-week planning horizon if the MPS for Product A shows an estimated demand or gross requirements of 1,000 units in Week 5 and 1,500 units in Week 6.

11. In Case 11.1, the Green Thumb Water Sprinkler Company, the MPS is changed from 800 units in Week 4 and 2,000 units in Week 8 to 2,000 units in Weeks 4, 5, and 7. If all other data in the case remain unchanged: **a.** Prepare a MRP schedule. **b.** Is the MPS feasible from a material supply (purchased or produced components) perspective? **c.** What actions could be taken to allow Green Thumb to meet the material supply requirements of the MPS?

Case

The Yoko Company: Resource Requirements Planning in the Processing Industry

The Yoko Company is a pharmaceutical and food products manufacturer. Among its many products is an artificial egg product, called Yoko, which is produced in liquid bulk and sold to another company that markets it to persons who must have a low cholesterol diet. The company uses a 7-week planning horizon in its marketing and production plans and is now in the process of developing a master production schedule, material requirements planning, and capacity requirements planning. Its production planning department has just gathered this information to be used in these plans:

1. Estimated weekly demands or gross requirements for the Yoko product is 200, 1,000, 500, 1,000, 2,000, 2,000, and 1,000.

2. The bill of material for the Yoko product is:

Parent Code	Component Code	Level Code	Description	Amount of Component per Unit of Parent
	Yoko	0	Artificial egg product	
Yoko	A	1	Amino protein	20 pounds
Yoko	B	1	Polychlorine sulfate CN#2	30 pounds
Yoko	C	1	Carrier base #3389	50 pounds
A	D	2	Yellow color stock EE#78	.25 pounds
A	E	2	Salicton thickener	.50 pounds
A	F	2	Thetscon carrier	.28 pounds

Note: The standard unit of measure for the Yoko product is a 20-gallon half-barrel.

3. The product structure for the Yoko product is:

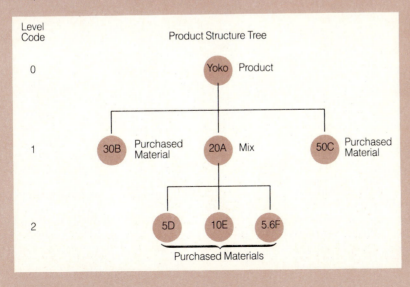

4. Capacity is limited in each week by 4,500 straight-time hours and 8,000 machine hours, although overtime may be used. The company policy on overtime allows up to 10 percent of the total weekly labor-hours capacity to be supplied by overtime. The production planning department has estimated the amount of labor and machine hours required by other products that must be manufactured to contractual schedules. The remaining hours may be used to manufacture the Yoko product.

Capacity Needed by Other Products	Weeks						
	1	2	3	4	5	6	7
Labor hours	3,635	4,050	3,800	3,400	3,100	3,700	4,500
Machine hours	6,645	7,050	6,900	6,000	6,100	6,700	7,900

Each 20-gallon half-barrel of the Yoko product requires .7 labor hour and .9 machine hour of capacity in the manufacturing plant. The production operation required to produce the Yoko product is a single mixing operation that is accomplished in two sequential steps: (1) Mix A is prepared by mixing D, E, and F materials, and (2) Mix A is combined with B and C materials. These mixing operations require only 1 week to complete. In other words, if 500 half-barrels of the Yoko product are required at the beginning of Week 3, all of the production of the product is begun in Week 2 and completed in Week 2.

5. The purchasing lead times for purchased materials are: B = 1 week, C = 1 week, D = 2 weeks, E = 2 weeks, and F = 2 weeks. D, E, and F can be shortened to 1 week with expediting and additional freight costs.

6. The inventory status report for the Yoko product is:

Item Code	On Hand	Safety Stock	Allo-cated	Lot Sizes	Scheduled Receipts	
					Quantity	Week
Yoko	500	250				
A	4,000#		1,500#	LFL		
B	3,000#		1,000#	LFL	30,000#	1
C	6,000#		2,000#	LFL	50,000#	1
D	5,000#	1,000#	2,000#	25,000#+	25,000#	1
E	4,000#	1,000#	1,000#	10,000#+	10,000#	1
F	3,500#	1,000#		5,000#+	5,000#	1

7. The Yoko Company operates 50 weeks per year and the annual demand for the Yoko product is 300,000 half-barrels. It costs $5,000 to flush the lines and set up to produce a production lot of the Yoko product, and it costs $10 whenever a half-barrel of the Yoko product must be carried in inventory into the next week.

Assignment

1. Prepare a set of master production schedule (MPS) calculations from estimated weekly demand (or gross requirements) to net requirements to production lots by using lot-for-lot (LFL), economic order quantity (EOQ), and period order quantity (POQ) as in Example 11.1. Select the lot-sizing method with the lowest total ordering and carrying costs. What are the total ordering and carrying costs of your production lot schedule?

2. Prepare an MRP schedule to test the MPS. The production lot schedule from the MPS in No. 1 above should be the same as the planned order receipts schedule for the Yoko product in the MRP schedule. Is the MPS feasible from the perspective of availability of materials? What expediting, if any, is required to allow The Yoko Company to meet the material requirements of the MPS?

3. Prepare load schedules of The Yoko Company plant for both labor and machine hours. Does your capacity requirements planning indicate that the MPS is feasible from the perspective of production capacity? What overtime, if any, is required? Is the overtime plan within company policy?

4. Summarize your resource requirements plan for The Yoko Company and outline any extraordinary measures required to render the MPS feasible.

Selected Bibliography

American Production and Inventory Control Society. *APICS Special Report: Materials Requirement Planning by Computer.* Washington, DC: APICS, 1971.

————. American Production and Inventory Control Society, *Capacity Planning and Control.* Washington, DC: APICS, 1979.

————. *APICS Bibliography, 1972–1973.* Washington, DC: APICS.

————. *APICS Dictionary, 1970.* Washington, DC: APICS.

Berry, W. L. "Lot Sizing Procedures for Requirements Planning Systems: A Framework for Analysis." *Production and Inventory Management* 13(second quarter 1972): 19–34.

Berry, W. L., and D. Clay Whybark. "Research Perspectives for Material Requirements Planning Systems." *Production and Inventory Management* 16(June 1975): 19–25.

Bevis, George E. "A Management Viewpoint on the Implementation of a MRP System." *Production and Inventory Management* 17(first quarter 1976): 105–116.

Bridgette, Ronald T. "MRP—Philosophy or Technique?" *Production and Inventory Management* 17(second quarter 1976): 118–120.

"Computer Takes on MRP, Savings Multiply." *Industrial Engineering* 11(March 1979): 26–27.

Gaither, Norman. "A Near-Optimal Lot-Sizing Model For Material Requirements Planning Systems." *Production and Inventory Management* 22(fourth quarter 1981): 75–89.

Groff, G. K. "A Lot-Sizing Rule for Time Phased Component Demand." *Production and Inventory Management* 20(first quarter 1979): 47–53.

International Business Machines Corporation. *Capacity Planning and Operation Sequencing System—Extended (CAPOSS–E).* Publications 5740–M41 (OS/VS) and 5746–M41 (DOS/VS), April 1977.

————. *Communications Oriented Production Information and Control Systems (COPICS).* Publications G320–1974 through G320–1981.

————. *The Production Information and Control System (PICS).* Publication GE 20–0280–2.

"The Material Requirements Planning Application." *IBM Systems/34 Manufacturing Accounting and Production Information Control Systems (MAPICS) Feature Education* SR30–0369–1, IBM(1979): 4-29 through 4-50.

Miller, Jeffrey G., and Linda G. Sprague. "Behind the Growth in Material Requirements Planning." *Harvard Business Review* 53(September–October 1975): 83–91.

Orlicky, Joseph. *Material Requirements Planning.* New York: McGraw-Hill, 1975.

Plossl, G. W., and Oliver W. Wight. *Material Requirements Planning by Computer.* Washington, DC: American Production and Inventory Control Society, 1971.

———. *Production and Inventory Control.* Englewood Cliffs, NJ: Prentice-Hall, 1967.

Ruch, William A. "Economic Lot Sizing in MRP: The Marriage of EOQ and MRP." *Proceedings 1976, APICS National Meeting, American Production and Inventory Control Society.* Atlanta, Georgia: 1976.

Silver, E. A., and H. C. Meal. "A Heuristic for Selecting Lot Size Quantities for the Case of a Deterministic Time-Varying Demand Rate and Discrete Opportunities for Replenishment." *Production and Inventory Management* 14(second quarter 1973): 64–75.

Wagner, H. M., and T. M. Whitin. "Dynamic Version of the Economic Lot Size Model." *Management Science* 5, no. 1(October 1958): 89–96.

Wight, Oliver W. *Production and Inventory Management in the Computer Age.* Boston: Cahners Books, 1974.

Part Four

Planning and Controlling Operations

Part Four of this text concerns the day-to-day decisions that operations managers make. With these managers rests the responsibility of getting production out the back door on time, within cost budgets, and within quality standards. Operations managers work hard to control their costs and product quality, not only because it is the professional or right thing to do, but also because their jobs are on the line. The fundamental management principle in real world organizations is: no alibis please, managers are accountable for every outcome in their areas of responsibility.

The objectives of operations managers (timely production, low costs, and acceptable product quality) would be relatively simple to attain if it were not for the inherent uncertainties. Will key personnel behave as expected? Will major pieces of equipment break down during next month's production peak? Will the natural gas supply be interrupted next month? Such questions require productive systems to be flexible and capable of adapting to these uncertainties so that products or services can be promptly and economically delivered to customers.

Perhaps more than any other factor, people — the workers in productive systems — directly affect costs, timely production, and quality. Because of their great impact, their jobs must be carefully planned and they must be skillfully managed. Similarly, facility layout — the physical arrangement of departments, personnel, and machines — also affects the performance of the productive system, and great attention is given to this important activity by operations managers. Maintaining the machines of production is another important aspect of controlling costs and quality. Knowing the concepts and techniques of preventive maintenance and related subjects helps to assure operations managers that machines will not interfere with their cost, timely production, and quality objectives.

Quality control varies in its importance within productive systems. Its function, however, is the same in each of these systems — to assure that the organization will produce products and services that meet its predetermined quality standards. The setting of these standards, inspecting outputs and comparing the actual product and service characteristics to these standards, and taking corrective actions as required are important parts of operations managers' daily jobs.

Although any one of these decisions about planning and controlling the day-to-day operations of the productive system may not be critical in and of itself to the long-range success and survival of the organization, the overall effect of all of these decisions is immense. If our industries are to survive foreign competition in the long run, they must improve the ways that they are planning and controlling their day-to-day operations. What this means to us is that the topics in Part Four of this text — Human Resource Management and Productivity, Facility Layout, Quality Control, and Maintenance Management and Reliability — when taken together may indeed prove crucial to the success and survival of our productive systems.

Chapter Outline

Introduction

Attitudes of Younger Workers toward Work

Importance of Worker Productivity in Fighting Foreign Competition

Human Behavior and Productivity

Definition of Worker Productivity

Major Factors Affecting Productivity

Maslow's Hierarchy of Needs and Its Meaning to POM

Does Satisfying Workers' Needs Result in Productivity?

Important Role of Labor Unions in Productivity

The Japanese and Lifetime Employment

What Rewards Can Supervisors Provide to Appeal to Workers' Higher-Level Needs?

Absenteeism, Turnover, and Productivity

Designing Workers' Jobs

Two Objectives in Designing Jobs

Some Practical Guidelines for Designing Workers' Jobs

Obstacles to Effective Job Designs

Work Methods Analyses

Approaching Analyses of Operations

Principles of Motion Economy

Techniques of Methods Analysis

Fitting the Methods Analysis Techniques to the Particular Operation

Work Measurement

Labor Standards

Techniques of Work Measurement

Workers' Health and Safety

Summary

Review and Discussion Questions

Problems

Case: Nilo Signal Company

Selected Bibliography

12

Human Resource Management and Productivity:

Behavior, Work Methods, and Work Measurement

There's nothing fundamentally wrong with our country except that the leaders of all our major organizations are operating on the wrong assumptions. We're in this mess because for the last two hundred years we've been using the church and Caesar's legions as our patterns for creating organizations. And until the last forty or fifty years it made sense. The average churchgoer, soldier, and factory worker was uneducated and dependent on orders from above. And authority carried considerable weight because disobedience brought the death penalty or its equivalent (excommunication for churchgoers and dismissal, blacklisting, and starvation for industrial workers).[1]
Robert Townsend, 1970

We've got two big problems concerning our industrial workers today. On the one hand, we need our workers to work harder and to be more productive so that we can get our production costs in line with the foreign competition. On the other hand, our workers today, particularly the younger ones, seem uncommitted to their jobs, change jobs often, are frequently absent from work, and appear to be disinterested in hard work, high productivity, and low production costs. The problem of the attitudes of our workers toward work and the problem of foreign competition are not new developments, but their simultaneous impingement upon operations management is causing us to look at the whole area of human resource management and productivity today with a fresh and genuine interest.

In this chapter we shall first develop an understanding of what productivity is and how human behavior is related to productivity and job design. Next, we shall develop the approach and techniques of how operations managers technically design workers' jobs so that the jobs themselves are efficient, in other words, so that the jobs require less physical effort from workers and at the same time allow many products and services to be produced. Finally, we shall examine the methods of measuring workers' productivity with a view to setting labor standards for cost control purposes and comparing alternative work methods. The overall purpose of

---

[1] Robert Townsend, *Up the Organization* (New York: Knopf, 1970), 137.

this chapter is to explore the setting in which operations managers today must achieve worker productivity and to develop some of the techniques that can be used to improve worker productivity.

Human Behavior and Productivity

Worker productivity means the amount of products or services produced by each hour of worker effort. In economics worker productivity is determined by dividing the real dollar value of all goods and services produced in a given year by the total labor hours used in producing those goods and services. The most common measure of productivity is the percentage of change from the previous year. If productivity goes up more than wage rates, production costs should be expected to fall, inflationary pressures should subside, and everyone should be better off. If productivity goes down, the reverse is true. In recent years the productivity of the United States has increased overall but at a slower rate of increase than its foreign competitors. The United Kingdom, Canada, France, Italy, West Germany, and Japan all have higher average rates of productivity increases than the United States over the last two decades. Unless this trend can be reversed, industries in the United States can continue to expect severe competitive pressure from foreign competitors through lower prices made possible by their lower production costs.

What causes workers to be more productive? Figure 12.1 shows the major factors that affect worker productivity. This illustration demonstrates an important truth: the causes of productivity are many and intricately related. We have not yet developed a set of formulas that precisely predict human behavior in general and productivity in particular. We have, however, begun to understand enough about worker behavior to remove some of the uncertainty about why workers are productive.

Two major factors affect worker productivity: employees' job performance and the machines, tools, and work methods that support and assist their work. Staff groups such as industrial, process, product, and systems engineering strive to develop better machines, tools, and work methods to enhance worker productivity. Most operations managers believe that productivity improvement through technological developments is at least equally important as motivation and behavioral factors in improving worker job performance.

Employee job performance is a complex topic because all people are different. Our abilities, personalities, interests, ambitions, energy levels, education, training, and experience vary widely. It is important for operations managers to consider these differences among us because blanket or universal approaches to improving job performance may not be effective for all workers. Personnel departments recognize these differences and attempt to select workers who have the desired abilities and to develop training programs to improve workers' skills.

Motivation is perhaps the most complex variable in the equation of productivity. Motivation is what prompts a person to act in a certain way. Maslow identified five levels of needs that prompt us to act: physiological, safety, social, esteem, and self-fulfillment.[2] The needs are arranged in a hierarchy from physiological at the

---

[2] A. H. Maslow, "A Theory of Human Motivation," *Psychological Review* (July 1943):370–396.

Figure 12.1
Major Factors Affecting Productivity

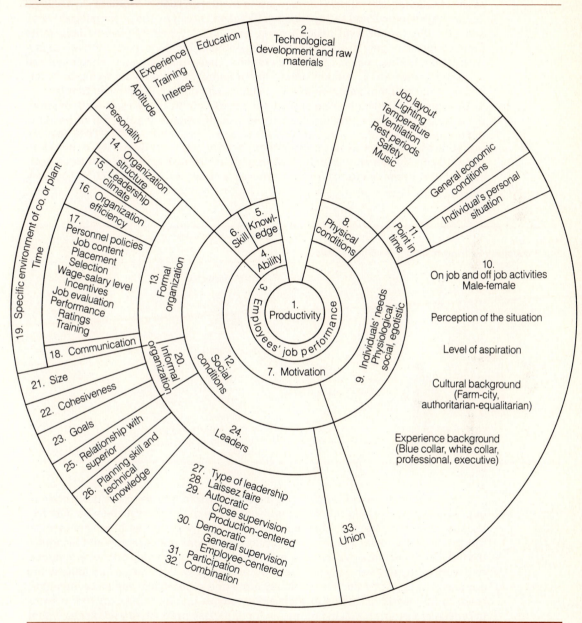

Source: Robert A. Sutermeister, *People and Productivity*, 2d ed. (New York: McGraw-Hill, 1969), ii.

lowest level to self-fulfillment at the highest level. Only unsatisfied needs are motivators, or cause people to act, and as each lower-level need becomes relatively satisfied, higher-level needs emerge as motivators. Today, workers' lower-level needs (physiological and safety) are mostly taken care of by the economic packages at work. The higher-level needs (social, esteem, and self-fulfillment) hold more promise for managers in their attempts to motivate most workers. Motivation is a tricky thing to diagnose in individual workers; therefore, managers should not run around from worker to worker acting like amateur psychologists trying to determine: "What will motivate you today?" Theory has not yet progressed that far.

How does an understanding of workers' needs help us to design a work environment that encourages productivity? If we can determine what class of needs is important to our workers, we can apply this framework: **If productivity is seen by workers as a means of satisfying their needs, high productivity is likely to result. Once workers have their needs satisfied through rewards that have been conditional upon productivity, the process is likely to be repeated.** Figure 12.2 illustrates this concept.

Figure 12.2
The Productivity Pathway to Satisfy Workers' Needs

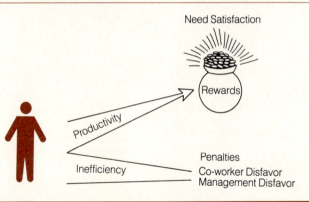

Labor unions and work groups can influence workers to be either productive or unproductive. If workers think that their work groups may treat them as outcasts because they have been productive, they may not cooperate with management in this productivity-reward-productivity cycle. Operations managers should recognize the influence that work groups have upon worker productivity and develop cooperative work groups by carefully selecting workers for these groups and by influencing group norms through effective communication and supervision. *Japanese managers seem to be way ahead of us in their ability to get unions to support productivity improvement programs.* A major reason for Japanese productivity advances is that both the unions and managers share the same key objective — stable employment for their workers. See Exhibit 12.1 for a description of how Toyota extends its concept of job security to "life security."

Exhibit 12.1
The Japanese Approach to Job Security and Lifetime Employment

Toyota City, Japan — Once known for its silkworm farms, Toyota City, Japan's automotive capital, is a model of how large Japanese industries wrap their workers in a cocoon of job and life security.

The paternal hand of Toyota Motor Co., Japan's largest automaker, reaches throughout this company town of 290,000, in facilities ranging from a free hospital to mountain resorts and cooking schools.

Cheap housing, a high school, a food cooperative and a large sports center are also available to the families of the 52,000 workers who work at eight Toyota plants in this city in central Japan.

Like most Japanese companies with ample funds, Toyota is committed to keeping its "family" content as part of the lifetime employment system where workers dedicate their working careers to one company in exchange for job security. Toyota officials say job turnover on the assembly line is only about 3 percent or 4 percent a year, with almost all engineers and upper level office workers staying on until retirement.

Since Kiichiro Toyoda founded the plant here in 1938, one of the biggest benefits in becoming a Toyota man or woman is good housing, the most elusive of material dreams on these crowded islands.

For new and single workers, there is dormitory space for 19,000 people at $6.38 a month. Fifty percent of food costs is paid by the company, so workers can eat three meals for around $4.25 a day.

Young marrieds often live in one of about 4,500 company apartments. Comfortable by Japan's pinched standards, the four-room units rent from $30 to $42.50 a month.

With cheap living, a company savings plan paying almost twice normal interest rates and average hourly wages of $9.75,

it is easy for workers to save, Toyota officials say. By their early 30s, workers are ready to buy a home, and many choose tracts developed by "Toyota Home," a company subsidiary which makes pre-fab units.

Prospective home owners can borrow $30,000 in low interest company loans, and another $12,766 if they buy a Toyota Home. A two-story house with a little land can be purchased for about $85,000.

Company spokesman Masamitsu Odaka also explained that residents of these "Toyota Heights" are always near a Toyota Cooperative, where food, clothing and other necessities are available at reasonable cost. The Cooperative, founded in 1945 with company backing, has 100,000 members, including noncompany residents of the area.

There is free medical and dental care at the 403-bed, 23-doctor Toyota Hospital, which costs the automaker about $15 million a year.

Hospital director Motoki Tanabe said about 10 Japanese companies have their own hospitals, "and ours is as good as any public hospital in the country." Pointing to a new, U.S.-made, million-dollar computer tomography machine for taking brain photos, Tanabe said, "you buy our cars, so we buy your medical equipment."

The outdoor showpiece is a 150-acre sports center including a 30,000-seat track and field stadium, completed six years ago at a cost of $14 million.

Workers and their families can unwind on 12 tennis courts, a 50-meter indoor swimming pool, two spacious baseball stadiums, an Olympic-quality gymnasium and athletic field and individual playing grounds for soccer, rugby, archery, sumo and softball.

Source: Jim Abrams, courtesy of the Associated Press.

The concept of *lifetime employment* has not yet caught on in the United States, but there are some signs that managers in this country are beginning to come around. One of the major U.S. automobile manufacturers announced in 1982 that some of its plants would adopt the lifetime employment concept — workers would not be fired because of economic conditions. Union-management-worker relations are sure to improve in this environment and joint productivity programs are more likely.

If higher-level needs (social, esteem, and self-fulfillment) hold promise for motivating workers today, what rewards are likely to satisfy these needs and cause workers to want to be more productive? (1) Opportunities for social interaction, companionship, and friendship from coworkers and supervisors on the job. (2) Recognition, respect, and status given by supervisors and coworkers on the job. (3) A sense of accomplishment, growth, and achievement from the work and an expectation of development and advancement. These rewards are usually available for use by all supervisors and thus can be offered as needed and deserved. Monetary rewards, on the other hand, can seldom be varied to adequately reward or penalize workers because wages are ordinarily set to apply universally to all workers and are beyond the day-to-day control of supervisors.

Why worry about satisfaction of workers' needs? What's in it for management and the organization? The obvious answer is an improvement in productivity, as we have discussed. Another equally important answer is that satisfied workers are less likely to be absent from work, less likely to leave their jobs for other ones, and more likely to produce high-quality goods and services. In today's working environment where absenteeism, turnover, and low quality of products and services are staggering problems, this reason alone seems sufficient to get operations managers interested in designing jobs in ways that provide for a broader range of workers' need satisfaction.

Designing Workers' Jobs

Behavioralists argue that the narrowly designed jobs of assembly lines are boring and monotonous and that workers are not satisfying their needs for socialization, ego, and self-fulfillment on these jobs. The high absenteeism and turnover among our highly educated and affluent young workers seem to validate these contentions. Proposals for remedying these narrow job designs range from minor modifications of assembly line job designs — job rotation, job enlargement, and supervision training — to major transformations of productive systems — job enrichment, automation, worker democracy, and regression to craftsmanship. These remedies have been experimentally applied with varying degrees of success and failure.

A burning issue remains: Can we simultaneously give workers the satisfaction they want from their work and still give the organization the productivity and efficiency it needs to survive economically? Is such a blend possible? How do we design jobs so that we integrate organizations' needs for high productivity and workers' needs for interesting work, self-direction, self-control, socialization, recognition, participation, and achievement? Are there practical guidelines that engineers and other technical specialists who design workers' jobs can follow to accomplish both of these necessary and worthwhile goals? Table 12.1 suggests several such guidelines for designing workers' job tasks, workers' immediate job setting, and the larger work environment.

Table 12.1 was developed upon the assumption that individual worker jobs have first been designed to be technically efficient and productive. These suggestions for modifying worker tasks have been practically applied in real world organizations to provide workers with opportunities for self-control, self-direction, and socialization. The remainder of this table offers other suggestions for modifying both the immediate job setting and the larger work environment in positive ways.

Table 12.1 and its suggested design guidelines illustrate the following points:

Table 12.1
**Some Practical Guidelines for Designing Workers' Jobs and
Work Environments That Accommodate Workers' Needs**

Elements of Workers' Jobs	Suggested Design Guidelines	Workers' Needs Affected
Workers' Job Tasks (the work itself—arrangement of machines, workplace layouts, work methods, and sequence of work tasks)	1. Avoid machine pacing of workers. Workers should determine, when possible, rates of output.	Self-control
	2. When practical, combine inspection tasks into jobs so that workers inspect their own output.	Self-control
	3. Work areas should be designed to allow open communication and visual contact with other workers in adjacent operations.	Socialization
	4. When economically feasible and generally desired by workers, combine machine changeovers, new job layouts, setups, and other elements of immediate job planning into workers' jobs.	Self-direction/control
Immediate Job Setting (the management policies and procedures that directly impinge upon workers' jobs)	1. Rotate workers where practical between jobs that are repetitive, monotonous, boring, and short cycled.	Variety and relief of boredom and monotony
	2. Assign new workers to undesirable jobs for fixed periods of time, then transfer them to more preferred jobs.	Equity
	3. Recruit mentally or physically handicapped, hard-core unemployed, or otherwise disadvantaged persons for jobs with high absenteeism and high turnover.	Interesting work *and* basic needs
	4. Provide workers with periodic rest periods away from repetitive jobs to relieve monotony.	Relief of boredom and socialization
	5. Set higher pay rates for undesirable jobs.	Physiological, security, equity, and achievement
Larger Work Environment (organizationwide policies, climate, management philosophy, structure, facilities, and programs)	1. Select and train supervisors who openly communicate on most issues that affect workers.	Recognition and socialization
	2. Develop supervisors who are comfortable with a participative environment, both with their superiors and with workers.	Participation, recognition, socialization, and achievement
	3. Create an organizational climate and management philosophy that recognizes workers as important elements of the organization. This tends to give workers an unspoken but understood sense of personal worth.	Recognition and achievement
	4. Develop formal and informal channels of communication between workers and all levels of management. These channels function best when used often, in all directions, and on a wide range of topics.	Participation, self-control, and recognition

1. Even slight modification of traditional job design principles that emphasize only technical efficiency can provide workers with a sense of self-control, self-direction, and opportunities for socializing with other workers on the job.

2. Workers' immediate job setting can be modified to relieve the monotony that can result from technically efficient work tasks. Additionally, approaches can be

developed to alleviate the high turnover and high absenteeism that can occur on highly repetitive jobs.

3. Larger work environments can be modified to provide workers with recognition, participation, and socialization.

Under most circumstances these modifications affect the technical efficiency of jobs either minimally or not at all. Thus workers can perform on jobs that are designed to be technically productive and under circumstances that support the satisfaction of many higher-level needs of workers.

What obstacles prevent us from following the guidelines found in Table 12.1? Although many exist, three dominant obstacles are notable:

1. Technical specialists who design most workers' jobs are often not trained to be sensitive to workers' needs. Their principal concern is for efficiency, not workers' need satisfaction.

2. Behavioralists emphasize worker job satisfaction to the exclusion of worker efficiency. After most behavioral experiments, organizations often revert to their former job design practices.

3. Labor unions are a strong force in affecting workers' attitudes toward work. Unions have been suspicious of managements' actions to make work more satisfying; thus workers and unions usually have not cooperated in enacting job design modification proposals.

How can we overcome these obstacles? Education is probably the answer to the first two obstacles. We must educate technical specialists in behavioral concepts. Educators can do this by enrolling them in behavioral management classes, speaking to classes, associating with them at their professional meetings, and visiting with them at their places of work.

Similarly, students who would become educated in behavioralist concepts should be trained in the concepts of worker productivity through job design. A ray of hope has emerged from the Center for Quality of Working Life at UCLA. Louis E. Davis and others at the center have developed an approach that seeks to improve worker satisfaction within the constraints of technical processes and worker productivity.[3] This is certainly a step in the right direction.

Union resistance will be overcome by persistently demonstrating trustworthiness in approaching job design. Additionally, union representatives can participate in studying job design modifications. Austria, Belgium, Denmark, West Germany, Norway, Sweden, Switzerland, and Yugoslavia have all developed intense management-union cooperative efforts to design worker jobs. In this country the United Automobile Workers (UAW) and General Motors, Ford, and Chrysler have established national-level joint union-management committees to study the improvement of workers' jobs. These committees "(1) review and evaluate management pro-

---

[3] For more on multicriteria job designs, see these two sources: Louis E. Davis and Albert B. Cherns, *The Quality of Working Life* (New York: Free Press, 1975), vols. 1 and 2; and Cecil H. Bell, Jr., Terence R. Mitchel, and Denis D. Umstot, "Goal Setting and Job Enrichment: An Integrated Approach to Job Design," *Academy of Management Review* 3(October 1978): 867–879.

grams directed at improving the work environment; (2) develop experiments and projects aimed at improved quality of working life; (3) report results to corporation and union; and (4) urge management and union to encourage their members and representatives to cooperate in experiments and projects."[4]

Although there do exist obstacles to designing workers' jobs that are both efficient and satisfying, experience shows that these obstacles can be overcome through education, cooperation, and persistence.

Work Methods Analyses

Figure 12.1 illustrated that the technological development of the job, which means the machines, tools, materials, and work methods used in the job, directly affect worker productivity. As one supervisor put it: "Workers can work their tails off, but if the machines, tools, and materials they use are poorly designed and if their own work methods waste energy and time, they might as well be loafing. The effect is the same."

Pretend that you were just hired at a large automobile assembly plant to work on the assembly line. You would more than likely be trained by an experienced worker for a few days and then be assigned a job such as attaching right front doors onto automobile assemblies. Your first few days would probably be hectic, tiring, and confusing; but the muscle soreness would soon go away and things would begin to settle down into a more predictable routine. You would probably soon be amazed at the amount of work that gets done each hour—materials moved, labor expended, inspections made, instructions given, and all manner of activities. This systematic whir of assembly line work is the result of years of work methods studies that have been continuously refined by industrial engineers, supervisors, and workers themselves.

The workers themselves are perhaps the most important source for improving the way they do their work. These people do their jobs daily, and they are the experts when it comes to determining whether new work methods will work as planned. Why not get them in on these studies in the beginning? Explain to them why their operations are being studied and what the objectives are. Ask them if they can suggest better ways to do their jobs; you'll be amazed at the results. Besides getting some valuable suggestions, workers who are allowed to participate in improving their own jobs will be more likely to make the new methods work.

Of course, some organizations have such poor management and worker relationships that this approach can lead to workers telling you: "I just work here, Mac. Tell me what to do and how to do it, and I'll turn out the work. It's your job to plan these operations." These situations are regrettable, but they are a fact of life. It is hard to overturn the patterns of several decades, but what harm is there in trying? Even though experience teaches us to approach these interactions carefully, most methods studies today can be carried out with a spirit of cooperation, even in union shops.

---

[4] Davis and Cherns, op. cit., vol. 1, 16.

Approaching Analyses of Operations

Industrial engineers, methods engineers, supervisors, and other personnel in productive systems usually attempt to improve work methods for three principal reasons—to increase the production capacity of an operation or group of operations, to reduce the cost of the operations, or to do both. Regardless of the reason for studying operations, the approach and techniques applied are essentially the same.

One key to successful methods analysis is the development of a questioning attitude about every facet of the job being studied. As the techniques of methods analysis that we shall cover later in the chapter are applied, every minute part of the work will be subjected to these questions: What? Who? Where? When? How? and Why? Table 12.2 presents questions about operations that should be asked as we analyze work methods. Adopting this questioning attitude leads analysts to accept nothing in an operation as sacred; everything about the job will be meticulously scrutinized.

Table 12.2
The Questioning Attitude of Methods Analysis

---

1. *What* is done? *What* is the purpose of the operation? *Why* should it be done? *What* would happen if it were not done? Is every part of the operation necessary?

2. *Who* does the work? *Why* does this person do it? *Who* could do it better? Can changes be made to permit a person with less skill and training to do the work?

3. *Where* is the work done? *Why* is it done there? Could it be done somewhere else more economically?

4. *When* is the work done? *Why* should it be done then? Would it be better to do it at some other time?

5. *How* is the work done? *Why* is it done this way?

Source: Adapted by permission from Ralph M. Barnes, *Motion and Time Study*, 4th ed. (New York: Wiley, 1958), 31.

When this questioning attitude is combined with tried and proven principles of motion economy, analysts can develop modifications in work methods that lead to increased output and reduced costs.

Principles of Motion Economy

Before we discuss the techniques of methods analysis, let us examine several principles of motion economy that have evolved. Although these fundamentals have their genesis in the work of Frank and Lillian Gilbreth, Frederick Taylor, and others of the scientific management period, they have since been profitably applied in almost every conceivable situation. Table 12.3 lists the principles of motion economy in the categories of use of the human body, arrangement of the workplace, and design of tools and equipment. Notice that the ideas in the principles not only provide for the efficient completion of work tasks (quick and timesaving) but also conserve the energy of workers, thus reducing fatigue. These concepts form a basis for a science of work (one of the elements in Taylor's principles of management) that can be applied through the techniques that follow.

Techniques of Methods Analysis

How do we go about analyzing work methods? Table 12.4 lists ten steps that are generally followed by methods analysts. Although the unusual characteristics of a

Table 12.3
Principles of Motion Economy

Use of the Human Body	Arrangement of the Workplace	Design of Tools and Equipment
The two hands should begin, as well as complete, their motions at the same time.	There should be a definite and fixed place for all tools and materials.	The hands should be relieved of all work that can be done more advantageously by a jig, a fixture, or a foot-operated device.
The two hands should not be idle at the same time except during rest periods.	Tools, materials, and controls should be located close in and directly in front of the operator.	Two or more tools should be combined whenever possible.
Motions of the arms should be made in opposite and symmetrical directions, and should be made simultaneously.	Gravity feed bins and containers should be used to deliver material close to the point of use.	Tools and materials should be prepositioned whenever possible.
Hand motions should be confined to the lowest classification with which it is possible to perform the work satisfactorily.	Drop deliveries should be used wherever possible.	Where each finger performs some specific movement, such as in typewriting, the load should be distributed in accordance with the inherent capacities of the fingers.
Momentum should be employed to assist the worker wherever possible, and it should be reduced to a minimum if it must be overcome by muscular effort.	Materials and tools should be located to permit the best sequence of motions.	Handles such as those used on cranks and large screwdrivers should be designed to permit as much of the surface of the hand to come in contact with the handle as possible. This is particularly true when considerable force is exerted in using the handle. For light assembly work the screwdriver handle should be so shaped that it is smaller at the bottom than at the top.
Smooth continuous motions of the hands are preferable to zigzag motions or straight-line motions involving sudden and sharp changes in direction.	Provisions should be made for adequate conditions for seeing. Good illumination is the first requirement for satisfactory visual perception.	
Ballistic movements are faster, easier, and more accurate than restricted (fixation) or controlled movements.	The height of the workplace and the chair should preferably be arranged so that alternate sitting and standing at work are easily possible.	Levers, crossbars, and hand wheels should be located in such positions that the operator can manipulate them with the least change in body position and with the greatest mechanical advantage.
Rhythm is essential to the smooth and automatic performance of an operation, and the work should be arranged to permit easy and natural rhythm wherever possible.	A chair of the type and height to permit good posture should be provided for every worker.	

Source: Reprinted by permission from Ralph M. Barnes, *Motion and Time Study,* 4th ed. (New York: Wiley, 1958), 214.

particular operation may dictate slight variations in these procedures, this general process is followed by many organizations today.

The following points may seem minor, but they are actually critical: (1) Workers and supervisors should participate early in the study. (2) Sell the proposed method to workers and supervisors. (3) Be willing to modify the proposed method at every step to guarantee acceptance and/or practicality. (4) Adequately train workers. (5)

Table 12.4
Procedures of Methods Analysis

---

1. Make an initial investigation of the operation under consideration.
2. Decide what level of analysis is appropriate.
3. Talk with workers, supervisors, and others who are familiar with the operation. Get their suggestions for better ways to do the work.
4. Study the present method. Use process charts, time study, and other appropriate techniques of analysis. (These techniques will be discussed later in this section.) Thoroughly describe and evaluate the present method.
5. Apply the questioning attitude, the principles of motion economy, and the suggestions of others. Devise a new proposed method by using process charts and other appropriate techniques of analysis.

6. Use time study if necessary. Compare new and proposed methods. Obtain supervisors' approval to proceed.
7. Modify the proposed method as required after reviewing the details with workers and supervisors.
8. Train one or more workers to perform the proposed method on a trial basis. Evaluate the proposed method. Modify the method as required.
9. Train workers and install the proposed method.
10. Check back periodically to insure that the expected savings are realized.

Follow up. Methods analysts who ignore these strategies are probably doomed to failure. The best proposed method may fall on its face unless workers and supervisors want it to work. Methods analysts are therefore advised to fully develop interpersonal relations skills.

Some useful work methods analysis techniques are flow diagrams and process charts, operation charts, simo charts, and multiactivity charts. These techniques will now be illustrated through examples that demonstrate the details of their use.

Flow Diagrams and Process Charts *Flow diagrams* and *process charts* are perhaps the most versatile techniques available for analyzing work methods. When used together, these two tools allow analysts to investigate a variety of situations: several operations being performed in sequence, flow of paper work, and a worker moving from place to place while doing work are examples of work that can be analyzed through the use of these techniques.

When we wish to eliminate or reduce delays, eliminate or combine tasks, reduce travel time or distance, or use other approaches that increase output or reduce costs, we first typically use flow diagrams and process charts. These analyses give us the big picture so that macro-modification of work methods can be made. This larger view often enables analysts to look beyond the minute details of the work to identify major inefficiencies involved in unnecessary tasks, excessive travel, unnecessary delays, and other elements of jobs that contribute to reduced output and increased costs.

Another versatile feature of flow diagrams and process charts is their ability to trace such diverse activities as the tasks of workers, processing of materials or products, flow of paper work, processing of patients in hospitals, flow and processing of customers in retail stores, and so on. This flexibility of application was demonstrated in Chapter 4 by our use of process charts to plan the processing of materials through production systems (Figure 4.14). Whether we focus on machine parts, restaurant customers, or clinic patients depends upon the operation under study and the principal object of our analysis. These tools' adaptability to many diverse operations and their ability to focus on numerous elements of these operations are probably their key strengths.

Case 12.1, American Insurance Company, illustrates how a large insurance company uses flow diagrams and process charts to improve work methods of clerks who prepare an authorization-to-investigate form for the claims department. Read this case carefully and note first that the present method is thoroughly documented by preparing a flow diagram (Figure 12.3) and a process chart (Figure 12.4). Next, a flow diagram (Figure 12.5) and a process chart (Figure 12.6) are prepared for the proposed method. Finally, Table 12.5 summarizes the comparison of the two methods. This general approach is typically used for improving work methods whenever we use these and other techniques of work methods analysis covered in this section.

Case 12.1

American Insurance Company

Bill Brown, manager of the property loss department at the home office of the American Insurance Company (AIC) in Los Angeles, has asked some of the key people to his office to discuss a departmental problem requiring analysis. These people were in attendance:

Betty Gray — section head, clerical services
Joe Millard — methods analyst, industrial engineering department
Gene Kuntz — manager, delayed billing department

Bill began the meeting.

Bill: I've asked you here to discuss what I consider to be a serious problem facing our department. The monthly cost of processing paper work to authorize investigations of property losses of our clients has grown to what both Betty and I believe to be unwarranted proportions. Something must be done. Our budget performance is intolerable.

Betty: Yes, our clerical staff which processes the authorization-to-investigate forms has grown to over 30. While we think we have the present procedure working pretty well, we believe that this work deserves another set of eyes to determine if improvements can be made.

Gene: I've come to this meeting at the request of Bill. We went through a similar methods study in our department last year. It worked out so well that our output increased 23 percent with the same number of clerical personnel. I think you'll be amazed at the results possible with Joe's help.

Joe: Thank you, Gene, but most of the credit must go to you and your people. About all I did was focus your department's attention on the methods problem. Once that was done, you really solved your own problem.

Bill: Well, Joe, how would you propose that we begin improving our work methods?

Joe: First, I would get your clerical personnel together to discuss with them the nature of the problem, get their suggestions, and outline what we propose to do.

Next, I would prepare a flow diagram and process chart of a single person completing one authorization-to-investigate form while following the present method.

Next, I would study the flow diagram and process chart to identify inefficiencies in the present method.

Then, I would discuss my ideas for improving the work methods of the operation with the clerical personnel. The proposed method would reflect any of their suggestions that seem reasonable.

Next, I would prepare a new flow diagram and process chart of the proposed method. The present and proposed methods could then be compared.

Finally, if you agree that the savings warrant converting to the new proposed method, I would train the personnel in adopting these modified work methods.

Bill: Betty, does this sound O.K. to you?

Betty: Yes, I think we can count on our clerical personnel to support us fully in this study.

Bill: Good. Let's get started right away.

Joe began his study. The present method was studied and documented in Figures 12.3 and 12.4, a flow diagram and process chart. The proposed method is described in Figures 12.5 and 12.6, also a flow diagram and process chart. A comparison of the two methods is found in Table 12.5.

Bill reviewed the results of the study with Joe and Betty. It was agreed that the savings that were expected from modifying the work methods justified immediate installation of the proposed method.

Figure 12.3
Flow Diagram: Present Method for Completing Authorization to Investigate Form

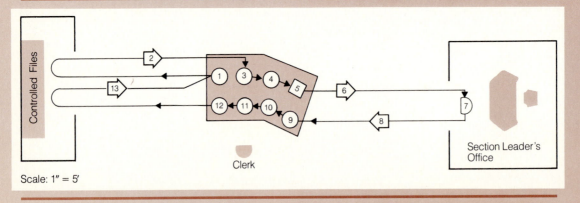

Figure 12.4
Process Chart: Present Method for Completing Authorization to Investigate Form

Operation Complete authorization			Sheet 1 of 1 Sheets	Summary	
Product to investigate form			Charted By Joe Millard	○ Operation	7
Depts. Property Loss				⇨ Transport	4
Drawing No. N.A. Part No. N.A.			Date 9/14	□ Inspect	1
Quantity One form in triplicate			Approved By Jim Street	D Delay	1
				△ Store	—
Present ✔ Proposed			Date 9/15	Vertical Distance	—
				Horizontal Distance	180 ft.
				Time (Hours)	16,000

No.	Dist. Moved (Feet)	Worker Time (Hours)	Symbols	Description
1		.200	○⇨□D△	Remove Claim Dept's request from in-basket and identify client.
2	55	3.250	○⇨□D△	Walk to filing area, locate file, and return to desk. Locate pertinent information in client file.
3		.500	○⇨□D△	Type information on authorization to investigate form (form no. 3355).
4		4.750	○⇨□D△	Inspect form.
5		.500	○⇨□D△	Walk to section leader's desk.
6	35	.200	○⇨□D△	Wait for signature.
7		.500	○⇨□D△	Walk back to desk.
8	35	.200	○⇨□D△	Tear form apart into separate sheets.
9		.200	○⇨□D△	Prepare regional investigator's copy for mailing, place in mail basket on desk.
10		1.750	○⇨□D△	Prepare Claims Dept's copy for routing, place in mail basket on desk.
11		1.500	○⇨□D△	Place one copy in client's file.
12		.200	○⇨□D△	Walk to filing area, refile, and return to desk.
13	55	2.250	○⇨□D△	
14			○⇨□D△	

Figure 12.5
Flow Diagram: Proposed Method for Completing Authorization to Investigate Form

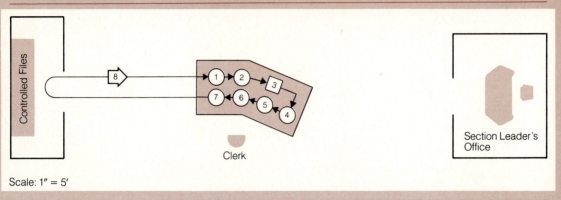

Scale: 1″ = 5′

Table 12.5
A Comparison of Present and Proposed Methods of Completing Authorization-to-Investigate Form — Property Loss Department

Comparison Factor	Present Method	Proposed Method	Estimated Savings
Feet traveled per form	180	55	125
Number of operations per form	7	6	1
Number of inspections per form	1	1	——
Number of delays per form	1	——	1
Minutes per form	16.000	12.250	3.750
Labor cost per form ($5.00 per hour)	$1.333	$1.021	$.312
Annual labor cost (300,000 forms per year)	$399,900	$306,300	$93,600

What are the principal improvements of the proposed method?

1. It eliminates retrieval of client's file by attaching claim department's claim form to request. All necessary client information is contained on this previously completed form.

2. It eliminates the necessity for clerk to obtain section leader's approval by utilizing existing interoffice mail service.

Figure 12.6
Process Chart: Proposed Method for Completing Authorization to Investigate Form

Operation	Complete authorization	Sheet 1 of 1 Sheets	Summary
Product	to investigate form	Charted By Joe Millard	
Depts.	Property Loss	Date 9/20	
Drawing No. N.A. Part No. N.A.		Approved By Jim Street	
Quantity One form in triplicate		Date 9/21	
Present Proposed ✔			

Summary:
○	Operation	6
⇨	Transport	1
☐	Inspect	1
D	Delay	—
△	Store	—
Vertical Distance		—
Horizontal Distance		55
Time (Hours)		12.250

No.	Dist. Moved (Feet)	Worker Time (Hours)	Symbols	Description
1		.200	○⇨☐D△	Remove Claim Dept's request with clients claim form attached from in-basket.
2		4.750	○⇨☐D△	Type information on authorization to investigate form.
3		.500	○⇨☐D△	Inspect form.
4		.100	○⇨☐D△	Attach routing slip to the completed form and place in mail basket on desk.
5		.200	○⇨☐D△	Remove approved form from in-basket and tear apart into separate sheets.
6		1.750	○⇨☐D△	Prepare regional investigator's copy for mailing, place in mail basket on desk.
7		1.500	○⇨☐D△	Prepare Claim Dept's copy for routing, place in mail basket on desk.
8	55	3.250	○⇨☐D△	Walk to filing area, locate client's file, place copy of form in file, and return.
9			○⇨☐D△	
10			○⇨☐D△	
11			○⇨☐D△	
12			○⇨☐D△	
13			○⇨☐D△	
14			○⇨☐D△	

Operation Charts The *operation chart,* sometimes called *operator chart* or *right and left-hand chart,* is a form of process chart that examines the coordinated movements of an individual worker's hands. This analysis tool is typically applied after the job has been studied through the use of flow diagrams and process charts to insure that the job efficiently fits into its overall production environment. Next, the individual worker's job is studied with operation charts (both present and proposed methods) to improve the efficiency of the worker's hand motions.

Figure 12.7 is an example of such an operation chart. In this chart the operator assembles U bolt cable clamps. This analysis clearly shows how the worker's two hands work together and separately to perform the operation, transportation, store, and delay elements of the assembly operation. The use of this technique allows analysts a microview of workers' work methods. Work methods can therefore be fine tuned by removing even small inefficiencies. Note that Figure 12.7 includes a workplace layout of the assembly operation. The sketches of workplace layouts thoroughly explain the methods used by the operator; additionally, they often suggest improvements for the way materials, machines, and tools are arranged in the workplace.

Simo Charts *Simo charts* are very similar in purpose to operation charts. Both charts are used to study the coordination of an individual worker's hands. When the cycle time — the total time to complete one unit of output — is very short, on the order of, say, .1 to .2 minutes (6–12 seconds), operation charts do not provide enough detail to adequately analyze a worker's hand movements. Simo charts are particularly valuable in analyzing these extremely short cycle-time operations.

Figure 12.8 illustrates a simo chart analysis of a bolt and washer assembly operation. Just as with an operation chart, the simo chart shows how the hands work separately and in concert to assemble three washers on a bolt. Additionally, the simo chart records a running clock time (in 2,000ths of a minute), elapsed time for each element (also in 2,000ths of a minute), and for each element the class of *therbligs* (*Gilbreth* spelled backwards with the *t* and *h* transposed, basic hand motions). Whereas the operation chart provides analysts with a microview of workers' work methods, the simo chart gives a mini-microview.

Multiactivity Charts There are several forms of *multiactivity charts,* but they all have one thing in common: they show how one or more workers work together and/or with machines. Figure 12.9, for example, is a *worker and machine chart.* This figure illustrates how a clerk in a grocery store works with a customer and with a coffee grinder machine to produce ground coffee for the customer. We can see clearly from this chart how the clerk coordinates each step of the work with the customer and the machine and the resulting degrees of utilization of the clerk, machine, and customer. These charts are helpful in minimizing worker and machine delay and in determining the optimal number of machines per operator.

Figure 12.10 shows how a multiactivity chart can be used to coordinate the work of several workers working as a team on an extrusion press operation. These charts are sometimes called *gang process charts,* and they show with clarity how all the participants work together and each of their utilizations. This technique affords methods analysts a unique way to coordinate the work of many workers, thereby often changing chaos into teamwork.

Flow diagrams, process charts, operation charts, workplace layouts, simo charts,

Figure 12.7
Operation Chart and Workplace Layout: Assembly of U Bolt Cable Clamp—Present Method

Operation Chart

No. _____
Page 1 of 1

Legend		Summary	Present		Proposed		Difference	
Row or Level		Per 1 Pieces	LH	RH	LH	RH	LH	RH
1st	2nd (A)	O Operations	3	10				
R7		ꝺ Transports	3	6				
R6		▽ Holds	12	0				
R5		D Delays	0	2				
R4		Total	18	18				
R3		Distance Ins.	32	46				

Right and Left Hand Chart

Operation __Assembly of U Bolt Cable Clamp__

☒ Present Method } Operator __A.G.B.__
☐ Proposed

Charted by __D.B.P.__ Date __6/20/__

R2	
R1	Nuts
C	Saddles
L1	U Bolts
L2	Fin. Work
L3	
L4	
L5	
L6	
L7	

Layout (workplace diagram showing L₂, L₁, C, R₁)

Parts Sketch
Bolt
Saddle
Nuts

Left Hand	O ꝺ ▽ D		O ꝺ ▽ D	Right Hand
To L₁	Oꝺ▽D	1	Oꝺ▽D	To C
Grasp Bolt	Oꝺ▽D	2	Oꝺ▽D	Grasp saddle
To above C while positioning	Oꝺ▽D	3	Oꝺ▽D	To above C while positioning
Hold bolt	Oꝺ▽D	4	Oꝺ▽D	Position with bolt
„ „	Oꝺ▽D	5	Oꝺ▽D	Place on bolt
„ „	Oꝺ▽D	6	Oꝺ▽D	To R₁
„ „	Oꝺ▽D	7	Oꝺ▽D	Grasp nut
„ „	Oꝺ▽D	8	Oꝺ▽D	To above C
„ „	Oꝺ▽D	9	Oꝺ▽D	Position with bolt
„ „	Oꝺ▽D	10	Oꝺ▽D	Screw on bolt
„ „	Oꝺ▽D	11	Oꝺ▽D	To R₁
„ „	Oꝺ▽D	12	Oꝺ▽D	Grasp nut
„ „	Oꝺ▽D	13	Oꝺ▽D	To above C
„ „	Oꝺ▽D	14	Oꝺ▽D	Position with bolt
„ „	Oꝺ▽D	15	Oꝺ▽D	Screw on bolt
To L₂	Oꝺ▽D	16	Oꝺ▽D	Wait for L.H.
Release Assembly	Oꝺ▽D	17	Oꝺ▽D	Wait for L.H.
	Oꝺ▽D	18	Oꝺ▽D	
	Oꝺ▽D	19	Oꝺ▽D	
	Oꝺ▽D	20	Oꝺ▽D	
	Oꝺ▽D	21	Oꝺ▽D	

Source: H. B. Maynard, *Industrial Engineering Handbook* (New York: McGraw-Hill, 1963), 2–41.
Reprinted by permission.

Figure 12.8
Simo Chart: Bolt and Washer Assembly — Present Method*

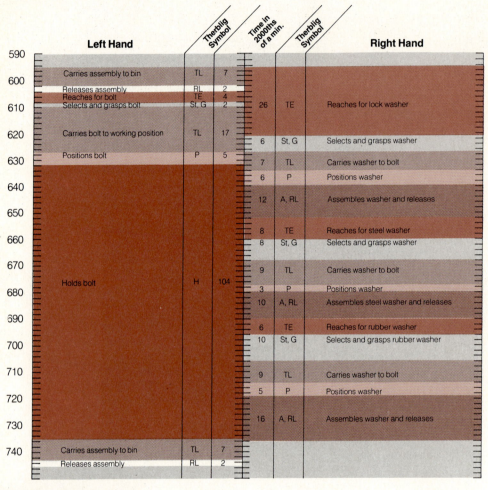

Left Hand	Therblig Symbol		Time in 2000ths of a min.	Therblig Symbol	Right Hand
Carries assembly to bin	TL	7			
Releases assembly	RL	2			
Reaches for bolt	TE	4			
Selects and grasps bolt	St, G	2	26	TE	Reaches for lock washer
Carries bolt to working position	TL	17	6	St, G	Selects and grasps washer
Positions bolt	P	5	7	TL	Carries washer to bolt
			6	P	Positions washer
			12	A, RL	Assembles washer and releases
			8	TE	Reaches for steel washer
			8	St, G	Selects and grasps washer
			9	TL	Carries washer to bolt
Holds bolt	H	104	3	P	Positions washer
			10	A, RL	Assembles steel washer and releases
			6	TE	Reaches for rubber washer
			10	St, G	Selects and grasps rubber washer
			9	TL	Carries washer to bolt
			5	P	Positions washer
			16	A, RL	Assembles washer and releases
Carries assembly to bin	TL	7			
Releases assembly	RL	2			

* Note: These are therblig definitions:
TL = Transport loaded   St = select
TE = transport empty   P = position
 G = grasp   H = hold
RL = release   A = assemble

Source: Reprinted by permission from Ralph Barnes, *Motion and Time Study,* 4th ed. (New York: Wiley, 1958), 158.

Figure 12.9
Multiactivity Chart (Worker and Machine): Purchasing Coffee at Grocery Store — Present Method

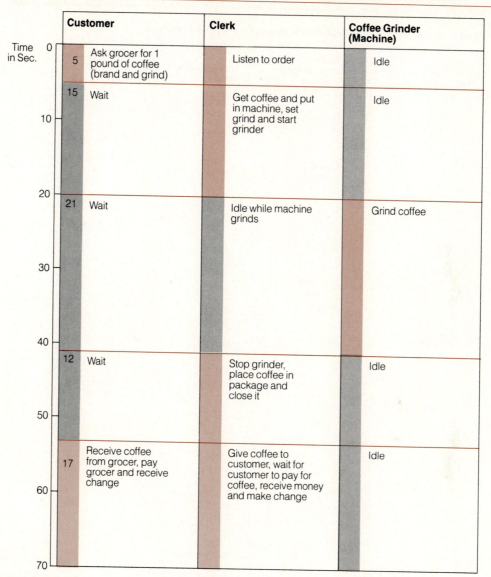

Time in Sec.	Customer	Clerk	Coffee Grinder (Machine)
0 / 5	Ask grocer for 1 pound of coffee (brand and grind)	Listen to order	Idle
15	Wait	Get coffee and put in machine, set grind and start grinder	Idle
21	Wait	Idle while machine grinds	Grind coffee
12	Wait	Stop grinder, place coffee in package and close it	Idle
17	Receive coffee from grocer, pay grocer and receive change	Give coffee to customer, wait for customer to pay for coffee, receive money and make change	Idle

SUMMARY

	Customer	Clerk	Coffee Grinder
Idle time	48 sec.	21 sec.	49 sec.
Working time	22	49	21
Total cycle time	70	70	70
Utilization in percent	Customer utilization	Clerk utilization	Machine utilization
	$\frac{22}{70} = 31\%$	$\frac{49}{70} = 70\%$	$\frac{21}{70} = 30\%$

Source: Reprinted by permission from Ralph Barnes, *Motion and Time Study,* 4th ed. (New York: Wiley, 1958), 80.

Figure 12.10
Multiactivity Chart (Gang Process): Hydraulic Extrusion Process — Proposed Method

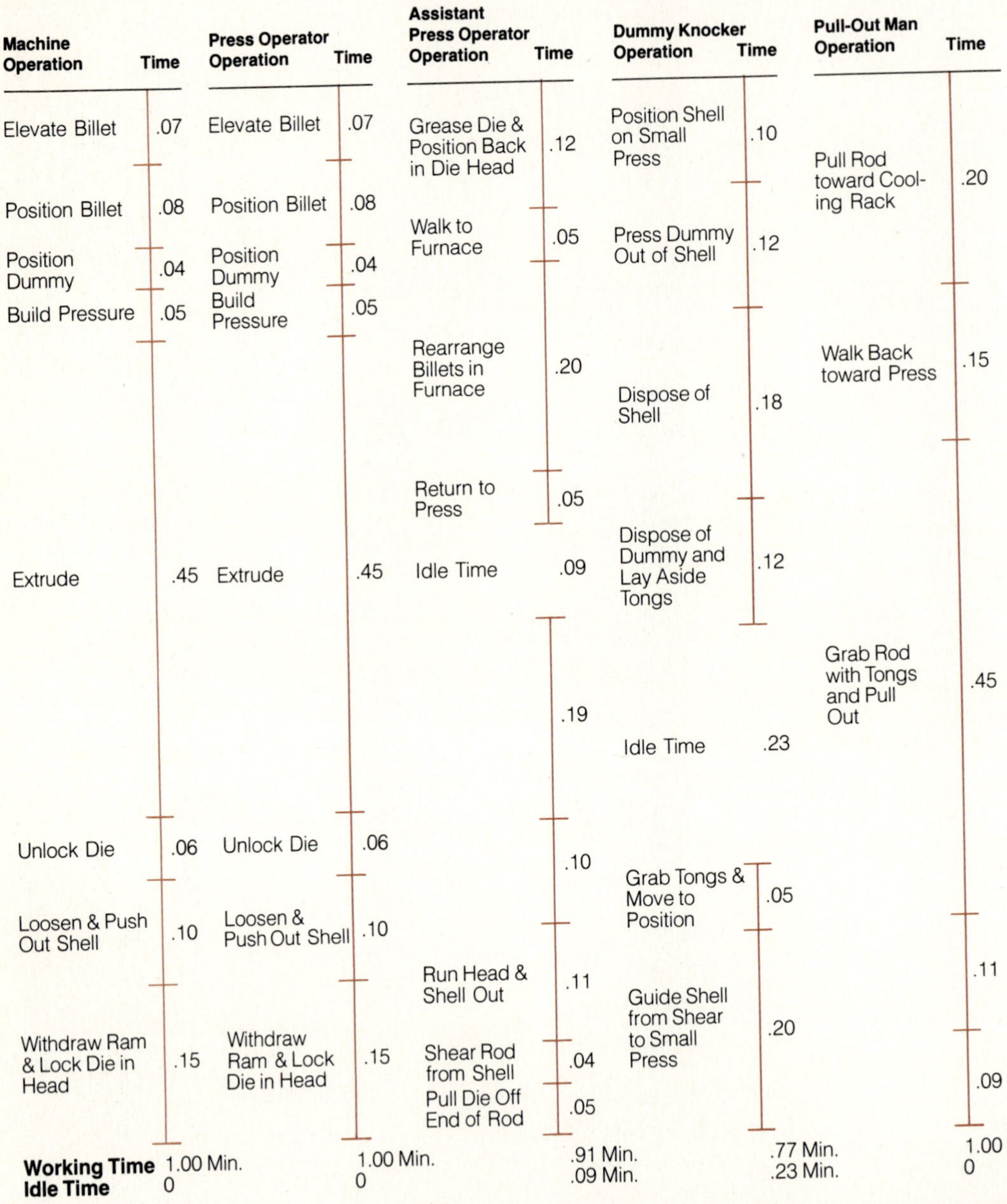

Machine Operation	Time	Press Operator Operation	Time	Assistant Press Operator Operation	Time	Dummy Knocker Operation	Time	Pull-Out Man Operation	Time
Elevate Billet	.07	Elevate Billet	.07	Grease Die & Position Back in Die Head	.12	Position Shell on Small Press	.10	Pull Rod toward Cooling Rack	.20
Position Billet	.08	Position Billet	.08	Walk to Furnace	.05	Press Dummy Out of Shell	.12		
Position Dummy	.04	Position Dummy	.04	Rearrange Billets in Furnace	.20			Walk Back toward Press	.15
Build Pressure	.05	Build Pressure	.05			Dispose of Shell	.18		
				Return to Press	.05				
Extrude	.45	Extrude	.45	Idle Time	.09	Dispose of Dummy and Lay Aside Tongs	.12		
					.19			Grab Rod with Tongs and Pull Out	.45
						Idle Time	.23		
Unlock Die	.06	Unlock Die	.06		.10				
Loosen & Push Out Shell	.10	Loosen & Push Out Shell	.10			Grab Tongs & Move to Position	.05		.11
				Run Head & Shell Out	.11	Guide Shell from Shear to Small Press	.20		
Withdraw Ram & Lock Die in Head	.15	Withdraw Ram & Lock Die in Head	.15	Shear Rod from Shell	.04				.09
				Pull Die Off End of Rod	.05				
Working Time	1.00 Min.		1.00 Min.		.91 Min.		.77 Min.		1.00
Idle Time	0		0		.09 Min.		.23 Min.		0

Source: Benjamin W. Niebel, *Motion and Time Study*, 5th ed. (Homewood, IL: Richard D. Irwin, 1972), 151. © 1972 by Richard D. Irwin, Inc. Reprinted by permission.

Table 12.6
Fitting the Methods Analysis Techniques to the Operation under Consideration

Characteristics of Operation Being Analyzed	Recommended Technique	Results Desired from Study
Several operations being performed in sequence	Flow diagram, process chart	Eliminate avoidable delays, reduce processing times by eliminating or combining tasks, reduce travel time and distance.
Flow of paper work	Flow diagram, process chart	Improve processing times, eliminate delays, reduce travel time and distance.
Worker moving from place to place while doing work	Flow diagram, process chart	Eliminate delays, reduce processing times, and reduce travel time and distance.
Worker performing work at fixed location (long cycle time)	Operation chart, workplace layout	Reduce fatigue, reduce processing times by simplifying method and reducing idle time.
Worker performing work at fixed location (short cycle time)	Simo chart, workplace layout	Reduce fatigue, reduce processing times by simplifying method and reducing idle time.
Worker operating one or more machines	Multiactivity chart, workplace layout	Balance worker and machine idle time, find optimal number of machines per worker.
Two or more workers working together as a team	Multiactivity chart, workplace layout	Reduce idle time, reduce processing times by eliminating or combining tasks and simplifying methods, reduce travel time and distance.

Source: Marvin E. Mundel, *Motion & Time Study,* © 1955, p. 46. Adapted by permission in *Handbook of Industrial Engineering and Management,* Ireson and Grant, Eds., © 1955, p. 288. Adapted by permission of Prentice-Hall, Inc., Englewood Cliffs, New Jersey.

and multiactivity charts are representative of a whole family of charts that are used to analyze work methods of workers. These techniques are effective in designing workers' jobs that are highly efficient — high output and low labor cost per unit of output result. These outcomes are necessary if productive systems are to remain competitive and, therefore, economically survive!

Once the general procedures of methods analysis are understood, we should consider the circumstances in which each of the methods analysis should be used. Table 12.6 describes several typical operations that are studied by methods analysis, appropriate analysis techniques, and the goals of these studies. Fitting the technique to the operation under consideration is fundamental to successful analyses.

Work Measurement

Although methods analysis is an important element in achieving high worker productivity, another technique is also helpful in this worthwhile goal — work measurement.

What units of measurement shall we use to measure human work? Foot-pounds, calories per minute, and other units historically have been used in the physical sciences to measure work. But we must use a unit of work in operations that is both easily measured and understood. The unit of measure that has evolved is *worker-minutes per unit of output.* In other words, how many minutes does it ordinarily take a well-trained worker to produce one component, subassembly, product, or service? *Work measurement* therefore refers to the process of estimating the amount of worker time required to generate one unit of output.[5] The ultimate goal of work measurement is usually to develop labor standards that will be used for planning and controlling operations and thereby achieving high worker productivity.

Labor Standards

A *labor standard* is the number of worker-minutes required to complete an element, operation, or product under ordinary operating conditions. Standards are hierarchical. In other words, each product has a labor standard, each major operation within each product has a labor standard, and each elemental task within each operation has a labor standard. Table 12.7 shows some of the hierarchical levels of labor standards for manufacturing a pair of office scissors.

Table 12.7
Hierarchy of Labor Standards for Office Scissors #325

Elemental Level		Operations Level		Product Level	
Element	Element Standard (Minutes)	Operations	Operation Standard (Minutes)	Product	Product Standard (Minutes)
a. Get	.100				
b. Operate	.150				
c. Turn	.050	1. Forge	.650		
d. Operate	.200				
e. Trim	.150				
		2. Grind	1.200	#325	3.750
		3. Polish	.550		
		4. Assemble	.700		
		5. Package	.650		

Ordinary Operating Conditions The term *ordinary operating conditions* refers to a hypothetical *average* situation — workers' ability, working speed, operation of machines, supply of materials, availability of information, and all other aspects of workers' jobs. Although workers may contend that conditions are never ordinary, conceptually the idea of an average condition is useful in developing standards.

Dynamic Nature of Standards Standards are dynamic. They must reflect the methods actually used in performing each element of work. When methods change, so must the labor standards change. If standards are not promptly modified as work methods change, their usefulness as planning and controlling aids is drastically diminished.

Planning and Controlling Aids Standards are absolutely necessary as planning tools. Estimating the number of workers required per week in each operation is computed by:

[5] One of the obstacles to widespread use of work measurement techniques in services is defining a unit of output. As shown in the examples of this section, however, some unit of measure of service can usually be found.

$$\text{Workers needed} = \frac{\left(\begin{matrix}\text{Number of products}\\ \text{to be produced weekly}\end{matrix}\right) \times \left(\begin{matrix}\text{Operation labor}\\ \text{standard per product}\end{matrix}\right)}{2{,}400 \text{ minutes per worker per week}}$$

Additionally, standards are routinely used to monitor labor performance. In this regard, the performance of individual workers, production departments, and manufacturing plants is routinely measured and compared to standard. This labor performance is usually computed as a percentage of standard:

$$\text{August departmental labor performance} = \frac{\left(\begin{matrix}\text{Number of products}\\ \text{produced}\end{matrix}\right) \times \left(\begin{matrix}\text{Labor standard}\\ \text{per product}\end{matrix}\right)}{\text{Actual minutes of labor used}}$$

A 90 percent performance would, for example, indicate a subpar performance and a 120 percent performance would indicate the efficient use of the department's personnel. Thus labor standards can provide operations managers with information about which individual workers, departments, and plants are performing above or below the labor standards.

Incentive Pay Systems Standards are also occasionally used as the basis for paying workers. Although *incentive pay systems* have diminished in popularity in recent years, their use is still common, particularly in mature firms and industries where tradition dictates incentive pay. Enormous variety exists in these systems and as union-management contract negotiations evolve, so also do these systems change. However, some generalities may be summarized from this patchwork of pay systems:

1. First, the percentage performance for each worker is computed for the pay period:

$$\text{Performance} = \frac{\text{Units produced} \times \text{Labor standard per unit}}{\text{Number of minutes worked}}$$

2. Next, the worker's performance is applied to the worker's hourly base pay:

$$\text{Actual hourly pay} = \text{Hourly base pay} \times \text{Performance}$$

3. Next, the worker's pay for the period is computed:

$$\text{Worker pay} = \text{Number of hours worked} \times \text{Actual hourly pay}$$

The process for paying workers described above is commonly called *gain sharing* or *bonus plans. Halsey plans, Rowan plans,* and *Gantt task and bonus plans* are of this type.[6] The important difference among these plans is in Step 2 above: How do you adjust the hourly base pay? Some plans guarantee the base rate, whereas others have a sliding-scale bonus formula to determine actual hourly rates. *Piece rate plans* determine workers' pay by computing a standard payment for each unit of output at each operation:

---

[6] For a good discussion of these and other commonly used bonus plans see Benjamin W. Niebel, *Motion and Time Study* (Homewood, IL: Richard D. Irwin, 1972), 605–617.

$$\text{Operation piece rate} = \frac{\text{Hourly base pay} \times \text{Operation labor standard per unit}}{60 \text{ minutes}}$$

This piece rate (dollars/unit) is then multiplied by the units produced by a worker to compute the pay for the period.

Incentive pay systems for workers are carefully watched over by workers, unions, and management. Elaborate and precise work measurement systems have evolved to compute the labor standards used in these systems. Precision is demanded here because we are dealing with workers' pocketbooks.

Certain plans such as the Scanlon, Kaiser, and Eastman Kodak plans allow workers to participate in the development of cost-cutting programs.[7] Workers and work groups are subsequently rewarded based upon the incentive rates worked out in these management-worker committees. The savings are shared between workers and the companies. These group systems are believed to promote cooperation between workers and management in increasing productivity.

Accounting Cost Standards Accountants routinely convert labor time standards to labor cost standards. This conversion is desirable because (1) the universal unit of measurement in accounting systems is dollars; (2) different operations may have different hourly pay rates, and conversion to operation labor cost standards makes operation standards additive; and (3) different shifts, departments, and plants may be aggregated for comparison to standard. These cost standards are particularly useful in cost estimates, labor cost variance reports, and pricing.

Cost estimates in POM occur routinely. How much will it cost to add an ear to our toy elephant? How much will it save if we eliminate Operation #104? These and other cost and savings questions must be answered, and labor cost standards help us to predict in advance of proposed actions what the cost outcomes will be. Labor variance reports are periodically prepared for each operating unit. For example, an August labor cost variance report may appear as follows:

	August Actual Labor Cost	August Standard Labor Cost	August Labor Cost Variance
Department 3251	$ 3,253	$ 3,100	$ (153)
Department 3252	4,922	5,522	600
Department 3253	10,153	8,965	(1,188)
Total section	$18,328	$17,587	$ (741)

These reports suggest potential labor performance problem areas. For example, the report above suggests that we should investigate why Departments 3251 and 3253 show unfavorable labor cost variances for August. Although rational explanations may exist for these variances, these reports flag potential problem areas for management investigation.

Labor cost standards are also used to set prices of new products. Although pricing decisions are a function of many variables, such as competition, the lower limits of prices are usually set in practice by our estimates of production costs. Labor cost standards can thus be used to estimate the total labor cost for a product. When

---

[7] For good descriptions of these and other sharing plans see A. J. Geare, "Productivity from Scanlon-type Plans," *Academy of Management Review* 1(July 1976): 99–108.

materials, overhead, shipping, and other costs are included, we have a good starting point for setting the lower limits of product and service prices.

Techniques of Work Measurement

If work measurement is primarily aimed at setting labor standards, how shall we go about setting these standards? Industry and government have traditionally used time study, work sampling, predetermined time methods, and subjective estimates.

Time Study *Time study* is the process of arriving at a labor standard for an operation based upon the actual timing of the elemental tasks of the operation. Time study analysts, who are usually industrial engineers, use stopwatches to physically observe the operation being performed by workers. The results of these observed timings are then converted into labor standards that are usually expressed in minutes per unit of output for the operation. Table 12.8 lists the steps generally employed by analysts in determining labor standards based upon time study.

Case 12.2 demonstrates the steps of computing a labor standard from a time study.

Table 12.8
Steps in Determining Labor Standards from Time Studies

1. Make sure that the operation being studied is being performed with efficient work methods that are to be used in the future.
2. Determine how many cycles to time. A *cycle* is one complete set of the elemental tasks included in the operation. Each company usually has its own policy, but, generally, the longer the cycle time, the fewer are the observations required; and the greater the number of units to be produced annually, the more numerous are the observations required.
3. Break the operation down into basic *elemental tasks* (get part, hold against grinder, adjust machine, etc.).
4. Observe the performance of the operation. Using a stopwatch, record the elapsed time for each element (in 100ths of a minute) for the minimum number of cycles.
5. Estimate the speed that the worker is working for each elemental task. If a worker is working normal speed, a *performance rating* of 100 percent is assigned; 120 percent indicates 20 percent faster than normal, and 80 percent indicates 20 percent slower than normal.
6. Compute the number of minutes per shift to be allowed for fatique, personal time, unavoidable delays, and other times when workers ordinarily cannot work through no fault of their own. This *allowance* is in minutes per shift.
7. Determine the *frequency of occurrence* of each elemental task (for example, 2/10, 5/10, 10/10).
8. Determine a *select time* for each elemental task that is representative of your observations (for example, mean, median, or mode).
9. Compute the *normal time for each elemental task:*

   Elemental normal time = Select time $\times$ Performance rating $\times$ Occurrence

10. Compute the *normal time for the entire operation*. This value is the sum of all of the elemental normal times in the operation.
11. Compute the *allowance factor* for the operation:

    Allowance factor = Total minutes per shift $\div$ (Total minutes per shift $-$ Allowance)

12. Compute the *labor standard* for the operation:

    Operation labor standard = Operation normal time $\times$ Allowance factor

---

Case 12.2
Setting Labor Standards with Time Study

Bob Richardson, Dean of Student Services at Metroville University, has received numerous complaints from students concerning confusion about how to register at the universty. Dean Richardson has asked a student advisory committee to suggest a solution. After thorough discussion, the committee designed a 12-page handout that explained to the students each registration step.

   This seemed like a good approach, but Dean Richardson wondered about the labor cost of the project. Although the individual sheets of the handouts were free to the university and could be collated in the university work pool by student workers at $5.00 per hour, labor budget funds were in critically short supply. Therefore, before an OK was given for the project, Dean Richardson had to estimate precisely the project's labor cost. Additionally, he had to know when the work should begin in order to complete the project before registration in the fall. An accurate labor standard was needed to estimate both the project labor cost and the number of work pool shifts required for the project.

   Dean Richardson asked Mary Delaney, a business student at the university, to study the situation and estimate a labor standard for the proposed handouts. Mary immediately set out to train a worker, Suzanne Ogden, in an appropriate method of collating the handouts. After Suzanne had mastered the procedure, a time study was conducted by observing the handouts being collated, recording the elapsed time for each element, estimating a performance rating for each element, and recording this information on an observation sheet (see Figure 12.11).

   Next, a select time was determined for each element (see Figure 12.12).

   The normal time for each element was then computed by multiplying the performance rating by the select time by the occurrence factor (see Figure 12.13).

Normal time = Performance rating $\times$ Select time $\times$ Occurrence factor

Mary worked out some estimates for allowances with Suzanne's supervisor. These allowances were converted to an allowance factor. Standard time was then computed for the handouts by multiplying normal time by the allowance factor (see Table 12.9).

Standard time or labor standard = Normal time $\times$ Allowance factor

The standard cost per handout and the number of handouts per shift were then computed. With the standard cost and production rate known, Dean Richardson can now accurately estimate the total labor cost for the project and when to begin production:

$$\begin{aligned}
\text{Total project labor cost} &= \text{Number of handouts} \times \text{Standard labor cost} \\
&= 30{,}000 \text{ handouts} \times \$.0363/\text{handout} \\
&= \$1{,}090
\end{aligned}$$

$$\begin{aligned}
\text{Shifts required to produce handouts} &= \text{Number of handouts} \div \text{Handouts per shift} \\
&= 30{,}000 \text{ handouts} \div 1{,}100.9 \text{ handouts per shift} \\
&= 27.3
\end{aligned}$$

Figure 12.11
Time Study Observation Sheet for Collating Handouts

Observation Sheet

Operation	Collate Materials for University Handouts				
Dept.	University Work Pool	Start	12:10	Date	8/15
Part		Stop	12:14	Shift	2
Size	12-page 8½" x 11" handout	Diff. (Elapsed Time)	4 min	Study	1
		Production	10 handouts	Sheet	1
		Est. Time	.400 min per handout		

Operator: Suzanne Ogden
M. F. ✓ Mary Delaney

Remarks: 12 stacks are arranged in two rows of 6 stacks each on a large table

Elements	Ele. No.	1	2	3	4	5	6	7	8	9	10	11	12	13	14	15	16	17	18	19	20	Rating Factor
Collate Row #1	1	10	9	9	8	8	9	7	10	8	9											100
Tap Handout on Edge	2	4	3	4	5	3	4	4	4	3	5											90
Collate Row #2	3	12	9	10	9	10	10	9	8	11	10											100
Tap Handout on Edge	4	4	2	3	5	3	4	4	3	5	4											90
Staple Handout	5	6	6	7	5	7	6	6	6	8	5											110
Aside	6	2	3	4	4	3	3	3	4	4	3											100
Miscellaneous Elements																						
Apply "Stickum" to Fingers	7					6																100
Straighten Stacks	8								21													100

Observer   Operator

Figure 12.12
Determining Elemental Select Times from the Time Study Observation Sheet

Element 1	
10	//
9	//// ✓
8	///
7	/

Element 2	
5	//
4	ⅣⅡ ✓
3	///

Element 3	
12	/
11	/
10	//// ✓
9	///
8	/

Element 4	
5	//
4	//// ✓
3	///
2	/

Elemental
Times
Observed

Occurrence
of Each
Elemental
Time

Element 5	
8	/
7	//
6	ⅣⅡ ✓
5	//

Element 6	
4	////
3	ⅣⅡ ✓
2	/

Elemental select times are usually determined by either of two methods: medians, as above, or arithmetic averages. The median method is generally preferred when the number of observed cycles is not small because either high or low extreme values do not unduly influence the select time. When the number of observed cycles is small (usually less than ten), arithmetic averages are generally preferred for determining elemental select times.

Table 12.9
Computing Labor Standard for Collating Handouts

Standard Cost Calculation

1. Total normal times (minutes) per handout (see Figure 12.13) = .385 minutes
2. Allowances (per shift)

Personal	24 minutes
Delay	10 minutes
Fatigue	12 minutes
Clean-up	10 minutes
Total	56 minutes

3. Allowance factor = Minutes per shift ÷ (Minutes per shift − Allowances)

$$= \frac{480}{480 - 56} = \frac{480}{424} = 1.132$$

4. Labor standard = Normal time × Allowance factor
$$= .385 \times 1.132 = .436 \text{ minutes}$$

5. Standard labor cost per handout = Labor cost per minute × Labor standard

$$= \frac{\$5.00}{60} \times .436 \text{ minutes} = \$.0363$$

6. Handouts per shift = Minutes per shift ÷ Labor standard
$$= 480 \div .436 = 1,100.9$$

Figure 12.13
Recap Sheet of Time Study for Collating Handouts

Recap Sheet

Dept. __University Work Pool__ Shift __2__ Date __8/15__ Sheet No. __1/1__
Operation __Collate Materials for University Registration Student Handouts__

Remarks __12 Stacks Are Arranged in Two Rows of 6 Stacks__		Operator __Ms. Ogden__
__Each on a Large Table__	Start __12:10__	Observer
Part & Size __12 Page 8½″ x 11″ Stapled Handout__	Stop __12:14__	Observer __Delaney__
Est. Time __.400 min__	Production __10__	
	Diff. __4 min__	

	Element	Select Time	Perfor Rating	Norm Time	Occ Factor	Adjusted Normal Time	
1	Collate Row #1	.09	100	.090	1/1	.090	
2	Tap Handout on Edge	.04	90	.036	1/1	.036	
3	Collate Row #2	.10	100	.100	1/1	.100	
4	Tap Handout on Edge	.04	90	.036	1/1	.036	
5	Staple Handout	.06	110	.066	1/1	.066	
6	Aside	.03	100	.030	1/1	.030	
7	Apply "STICKUM" to Fingers as Required	.06	100	.060	1/10	.006	
8	Straighten Stacks of Materials as Required	.21	100	.210	1/10	.021	

Total Normal Time / Handout   .385

Although time study offers great precision in determining labor standards, in most situations it does require a competent staff of analysts and is therefore expensive. Additionally, the labor standard cannot be determined before the operation is actually performed. These deficiencies have led to the development of other work measurement techniques that are less expensive and may be used in advance of the performance of the operation.

Work Sampling   *Work sampling* is a work measurement technique that randomly samples the work of one or more workers at periodic intervals to determine the proportion of the total operation that is accounted for in one particular activity. These studies are frequently used to estimate the percentage of workers' time spent in unavoidable delays (commonly called ratio-delay studies), repairing finished products from an operation, supplying material to an operation, and so on. The results of these studies are commonly utilized to set allowances used in setting labor standards, in estimating costs of certain activities, and in work methods investigations.

Work sampling is also infrequently used to directly estimate labor standards. This approach uses work-sampling studies to determine the proportion of the total operation accounted for in each of the operation's elements, converting the elemental proportions to average times in minutes (proportion $\times$ minutes per shift $\div$ units of output), assigning a performance rating to each element and using this rating to compute a normal time per unit, and completing the standard as we would in a time study. Work sampling offers few advantages over time study in directly determining labor standards. One exception might be in situations where large numbers of workers work together over a large geographical area. In these cases work sampling allows analysts to directly develop labor standards economically. However, when compared to time study, some sacrifice in precision usually is expected.

Example 12.1 demonstrates the mechanics of work sampling in the application of estimating crew sizes in an anticipated organizational change. In this example the manager wishes to know the proportion of 35 workers' time that is spent in performing credit checks. These types of applications of work sampling, as opposed to directly setting labor standards, are the most common. Work sampling, like time study, is also limited in application because the operation under study must be directly observed. Therefore, estimates cannot be determined in advance of the actual performance of the operation.

Example 12.1

Estimating Crew Sizes with Work Sampling

Joe Harper is section manager of the billing department for GASCO, a public utility company in Durham, North Carolina. Thirty-five billing clerks routinely audit customer bills, make manual adjustments, and perform credit checks on prospective new customers. GASCO has grown so rapidly in recent years that Mr. Harper wonders if it wouldn't be more efficient to separate the work of the department into two subdepartments, one that would do the billing, auditing, and adjustments and another that would perform the credit checks on new customers. He wonders how many of the present clerks should be assigned to the new credit check subdepartment.

Jean Holtz, a methods analyst from GASCO's industrial engineering department, was requested to assist Mr. Harper in this question. At issue is how much of the present billing clerks' work is credit checks. Jean recommends a work-sampling study of the 35 clerks to determine what percentage of the existing billing clerks' jobs involves credit checks. As a starting point, this percentage of the clerks could then be reassigned to the credit check subdepartment.

After conferring with the departmental personnel, Jean estimated that approximately 25 percent of the clerks' jobs involved credit checks. Referring to Table 12.10, "A Guide to Minimum Number of Work-Sampling Observations," a table commonly used by GASCO industrial engineers, she determined that a 95 percent confidence interval and ±3 percent absolute error would require about 833 total observations.

She immediately began to randomly observe the 35 clerks on 10-second intervals to determine if each observed clerk was or was not doing credit checks. The following data resulted from this work-sampling study.

Total Observations	Number of Observations Where Clerk Was Not Performing Credit Check	Number of Observations Where Clerk Was Performing Credit Check	
			$p = \dfrac{211}{900} = .234$ or 23.4 percent
900	689	211	

Jean met with Mr. Harper and explained the results of her work-sampling study. After 2½ hours of observation (6 per minute, 360 per hour) and 900 total random observations, 211 occurrences were credit checks. Therefore, she estimated that 23.4 percent of the present billing clerks' jobs involved credit checks. Thus, she recommended that 8 ($.234 \times 35 = 8.2$) of the existing billing clerks be reassigned to the new credit check subdepartment. She explained that one might assume that 9 should be reassigned. But she predicted that after some experience with the new job and with less switching back and forth from billing to credit and vice versa, some improved efficiency could be expected under the new arrangement. Thus, 8 clerks were recommended.

Table 12.10
A Guide to Minimum Number of Work-Sampling Observations

Activity Percentage [p or (1 − p)]	Absolute Error		
	±1%	±2%	±3%
1 or 99	396	99	44
5 or 95	1,900	475	211
10 or 90	3,600	900	400
15 or 85	5,100	1,275	567
20 or 80	6,400	1,600	711
25 or 75	7,500	1,875	833
30 or 70	8,400	2,100	933
35 or 65	9,100	2,275	1,011
40 or 60	9,600	2,400	1,067
45 or 55	9,900	2,475	1,099
50	10,000	2,500	1,111

Note: This table is based on a 95 percent confidence interval. Absolute error means the actual range of observations of p, the percentage of the total job devoted to a particular activity. For example, if p = 25 percent and the ±2 percent column were used, we could say that we were 95 percent confident that p ranged between 23 percent and 27 percent. Smaller absolute errors require larger numbers of work-sampling observations.

Predetermined Time Standards When labor standards must be determined in advance of actually performing an operation, *predetermined time standards* can be used. These methods utilize data that have been historically developed for basic body movements, elements of operations, and entire operations. When cost estimates or pricing information is required for new operations or new products for which organizations have labor standard experience, these methods are commonly used.

Many predetermined time standard systems are used today — Work Factor, Methods – Time Measurement (MTM), Basic Motion Timestudy (BMT), and a host of systems custom-designed for individual companies. To demonstrate the mechanics of these systems we shall demonstrate the development of MTM labor standards in Example 12.2. In this example a manager must estimate the labor cost for a newly imposed inspection for electrical diodes. MTM is an excellent choice when ultralight assembly work must be performed in an extremely small geographical area and when quick, accurate, and low-cost labor standards are required.

Example 12.2
Developing Labor Standards with MTM

Bill Rogers, production superintendent for ELECTEC, which manufactures diodes for the electronic industry, has just requested an estimate of additional labor costs if their XG1500 diode were to be inspected and cleaned. This request resulted from a few recent component failures in the field.

Table 12.11
MTM Labor Standard Calculation for XG1500 Diode Inspection and Cleaning Operation

Left Hand	MTM Code	TMU (1/100,000 Hour)	MTM Code	Right Hand
1. Reach to bin of electrical components.	R10C	12.9		
2. Grasp component to be tested.	G4B	9.1		
3. Move component to exposed inspection meter stop (10 inches).	M10A*	11.3		
4. Position component on test meter.	P2SS	19.7		
5. Observe electrical continuity light.	EF	7.3		
6. Transfer component to other hand.	G3	5.6	G3	Grasp component.
		9.2	M5C	7. Move component to abrasion wheel.
		19.7	P2SS	8. Position component on abrasion wheel.
		8.0	M5B	9. Move component to bin.
		2.0	RL1	10. Release component.

Total TMU = 104.8 units

= 104.8 ÷ 100,000 = .001048 hour

= .001048 × 60 = .0629 minute

* Look up this TMU in Table 12.12.

Ruth Bell, an industrial engineer, is briefed on how the new inspection operation would be performed. She tells Bill Rogers that she will have an estimate for him in an hour and disappears to her office.

Ruth Bell knows that although ELECTEC personnel had never performed the inspection and cleaning operation, a good labor estimate could be developed by using methods-time measurement (MTM). She got out her MTM manual, wrote down the right- and left-hand activities, estimated distances to be traveled, described the nature of the hand motions, and looked up the TMUs (time measurement units) for each activity. One TMU equals 1/100,000 of an hour. The results of this analysis are found in Table 12.11.

Because Ruth estimates that 80 minutes per shift will be unavoidably unproductive, she calculates the following:

Table 12.12
MTM — TMUs for Moving Objects with Hands and Arms (Move — M)

| Distance Moved Inches | Time TMU | | | | Wt. Allowance | | | Case and Description |
	A	B	C	Hand in Motion B	Wt. (lb.) Up to	Dynamic Factor	Static Con-stant TMU	
¾ or less	2.0	2.0	2.0	1.7				
1	2.5	2.9	3.4	2.3	2.5	1.00	0	
2	3.6	4.6	5.2	2.9				**A** Move object to
3	4.9	5.7	6.7	3.6	7.5	1.06	2.2	other hand or
4	6.1	6.9	8.0	4.3				against stop.
5	7.3	8.0	9.2	5.0	12.5	1.11	3.9	
6	8.1	8.9	10.3	5.7				
7	8.9	9.7	11.1	6.5	17.5	1.17	5.6	
8	9.7	10.6	11.8	7.2				
9	10.5	11.5	12.7	7.9	22.5	1.22	7.4	**B** Move object to
10	11.3	12.2	13.5	8.6				approximate or
12	12.9	13.4	15.2	10.0	27.5	1.28	9.1	indefinite loca-
14	14.4	14.6	16.9	11.4				tion.
16	16.0	15.8	18.7	12.8	32.5	1.33	10.8	
18	17.6	17.0	20.4	14.2				
20	19.2	18.2	22.1	15.6	37.5	1.39	12.5	
22	20.8	19.4	23.8	17.0				
24	22.4	20.6	25.5	18.4	42.5	1.44	14.3	**C** Move object to
26	24.0	21.8	27.3	19.8				exact location.
28	25.5	23.1	29.0	21.2	47.5	1.50	16.0	
30	27.1	24.3	30.7	22.7				
Additional	0.8	0.6	0.85		TMU per inch over 30 inches			

Source: Copyrighted by the MTM Association for Standards and Research. No reprint permission without written consent from the MTM Association, 16-01 Broadway, Fair Lawn, NJ 07410.

Allowance factor = Time per shift ÷ (Time per shift − Allowance)
= 480 minutes ÷ (480 minutes − 80 minutes) = 1.20

Labor standard = Normal time × Allowance factor
= .0629 minute × 1.20 = .0755 minute per XG1500 diode

Standard cost = Labor standard × Labor cost per minute
= .0755 minute × $.129 per minute = $.0097 per XG1500 diode

Ruth returned to the meeting and told Bill the results of her MTM analysis: the estimated labor standard for the proposed inspection and cleaning operation was .0755 minute per diode, and the estimated labor cost was $.0097 per diode. She took along the MTM table for the basic *Move* motions (Table 12.12) to demonstrate how the standard was estimated. She explained the third left-hand activity, M10A. To find this, look up the distance moved of 10 inches, go across to column A, and read the TMU—11.3, which is in 100,000ths of an hour. This is converted to hours and minutes by dividing by 100,000 and multiplying the result by 60.

Subjectively Set Labor Standards In some organizations labor standards are determined by rather gross estimates of the amount of work involved in each operation. In some cases *historical labor standards* are determined by using historical data from the actual performance of the operation. Although this procedure is low in cost, quick, and easy to understand, it has some rather fundamental flaws. First, this method implicitly assumes that past performance of the operation is *standard*. No formal methods studies are required such as time studies. Therefore, work methods and labor standards are not explicitly related. Second, no attempt at performance rating is present. These and other weaknesses in historical labor standards generally lead operations managers to use these types of labor standards only when the use of the standards is not crucial and precision is therefore not critical.

Like historical labor standards, other rough estimates have evolved. *Crew size standards,* for example, are determined by estimating the total number of workers required to produce the necessary output per shift. This total number of worker minutes per shift is then divided by the required output per shift. *Supervisor estimates* are occasionally used. These standards are based on supervisors' intimate knowledge of the operations for which they are responsible. These and other roughly estimated standards are commonly used in industry today. Their uses are, however, usually limited to those situations where more expensive techniques cannot be justified. Although the precision of these methods leaves much to be desired, their cost and speed make their use common when rough estimates are better than no standards at all.

Time study, work sampling, predetermined time standards, and subjectively set labor standards may all be appropriate work measurement techniques depending upon the nature of the job being considered. Table 12.13 describes some jobs for which each of these techniques is appropriate. Regardless of the work measurement techniques employed to develop labor standards, their ultimate goals are the same:

Table 12.13
Some Jobs for Which the Work Measurement Techniques Are Appropriate

Job	Appropriate Work Measurement Techniques
1. A job performed by a single worker in a fixed location. The job involves repetitive short cycles and is expected to continue relatively unchanged for long periods while producing large quantities of outputs. The resulting labor standards must be very accurate.	Time study
2. A job performed by a single worker in a fixed location. The job involves repetitive short cycles and will be changed periodically as customer orders for relatively small quantities of products change. The labor standards are used for accounting cost standards, pricing analyses, and production planning.	Predetermined time standards
3. A job performed by many workers over a compact area. The tasks may involve little repetition; but if repetitious, the cycles are usually very long. Workers must be observed by a single analyst. Although a moderate degree of accuracy in the labor standards is desired, time study would be too costly. Only large elements of work need to be observed; little detail is needed in setting the labor standards.	Work sampling
4. Any job or group of jobs in which labor standards are not required to be very accurate or in which the cost of time study, predetermined time standards, and work sampling is prohibitive.	Subjectively set labor standards

1. To set benchmarks or standards against which to measure the actual performance of operations. The objective is to improve worker productivity.

2. To establish estimates of labor content in operations as planning aids for operations managers.

Workers' Health and Safety

Hazards are inherent in most jobs. Workers can fall on slippery floors; fall from ladders; walk into protruding materials; get parts of their clothing or bodies caught in belts, gears, cutting tools, dies, and drill presses; be hit by flying pieces from grinding wheels and metal chips from lathes; and so on. Elevator shafts, stairs, balconies, heavy moving equipment, trucks, fires, explosions, high voltage electricity, molten metals, toxic chemicals, noxious fumes, dust and noise—all pose dangers to our workers. These and other hazards have always been around. They are not new. What perhaps is new is the growing body of governmental laws and regulations intended to provide workers with uniformly safe working conditions across all states, industries, and companies.

In modern times management has been concerned about the safety and health of workers. This concern was evident in the establishment of safety and loss prevention departments early in this century before laws rigidly forced employers to comply with government-imposed safety standards. The personnel management movement in the early 1900s and the human relations movement in the 1940s both contributed to this development. These movements emphasized the necessity to protect workers on the job and directly contributed to the growing number of formal safety programs in government and industry.

Two sets of laws have also critically affected workers' health and safety — the workmen's compensation laws and the Occupational Safety and Health Administration Act (OSHA). During the early 1900s the states gradually passed *workmen's compensation laws*. These laws provided for specific compensation amounts going to employees for various types of injuries incurred on the job. Employees no longer were required to bring suit through the courts and prove negligence by employers. Additionally, employers were protected by the maximum limitation on these settlements and court suits were all but eliminated.

Although workmen's compensation laws went a long way toward compensating employees after they were injured on the job, three facts detracted from their effectiveness in insuring safe working conditions:

1. Because the laws varied greatly among states and industries, this patchwork of regulation created great gaps in coverage and extreme variation in compensation for similar injuries.

2. Inflation and the enormous rise in the cost of health care have made compensation amounts of most of these laws inadequate.

3. The laws do not strike directly at the heart of the worker health and safety problem — creating a safe work environment for workers.

These and other deficiencies of the workmen's compensation laws and other contemporary developments led to the passage in 1971 of the *Occupational Safety and Health Administration Act (OSHA)*. OSHA established a federal agency whose primary functions were to set safety standards for all areas of the work environment for all industries and to enforce these standards through an inspection and reporting system. This law officially recognized, perhaps for the first time, the basic right of all workers to a safe working environment regardless of the state, industry, or firm in which they worked.

No company is beyond the reach of OSHA. Its inspectors routinely call on employers, conduct inspections, identify unsafe working conditions or violations of OSHA standards, require employer corrective actions, and can force compliance through the courts. OSHA is indeed a mighty force that management must deal with.

Cities, counties, and states also participate in regulating and/or inspecting the safety of working conditions of operations. In California, for example, a manufacturing plant can expect on a regular basis inspections concerning fire hazards from these sources: (1) in plant inspectors, (2) division and corporate inspectors, (3) city fire marshal, (4) county fire marshal, (5) state fire marshal, (6) OSHA, (7) insurance carriers, and (8) union inspectors. These and other sources of regulation of operations form a network of worker safety protection that for all practical purposes provides a guarantee of managements' continual diligence in designing jobs that are safe for workers. Experienced managers know, however, that even in this environment of overinspection, workers can still be injured and their health damaged. Managers therefore establish *safety and loss prevention departments*.

Sure, these departments interface with all of the sources of safety inspections, but also these specialists design safety devices and procedures aimed at protecting workers, raise worker awareness, and design advertising programs to minimize hazards resulting from human error. These and other activities are undertaken not just because it is the law, but because it is also the right and ethical thing to do. And besides — it is good business. When working conditions are safe, worker morale and worker productivity tend to be higher and the direct costs of accidents tend to be lower. Therefore, management has a large stake in maintaining a safe working environment for workers.

Summary

Today's productive systems are made up of jobs designed primarily for efficiency, maximizing the output from each hour of worker effort. This tradition from the scientific management era is being modified, however, to account for worker and customer needs. Workers want more interesting work and customers want low cost, timely deliveries, and high quality. The supreme challenge for POM today is to accommodate customer and worker needs while continuously trimming inefficiencies from operations and thereby surviving the onslaught of foreign and domestic competition.

Work methods analyses are studies of operations aimed at worker productivity and efficiency. These studies encompass the total working environment of workers — worker methods, materials, machines, layout of workplaces, lighting, and so on. The workers themselves are perhaps the most important source for improving work methods. They know the intricacies of each operation, and they are an invaluable source of suggestions if they will participate. Once the appropriate level of analysis has been determined, the procedures to follow, a questioning attitude, and the principles of motion economy guide methods analysts in their work.

Work measurement involves the estimation of the actual amount of human work required to produce one unit of output from an operation. The universal unit of work measurement is the amount of time in minutes ordinarily required for a well-trained worker to produce one unit of output. These worker-minutes per unit become labor standards. Labor standards are dynamic and must change as work methods change. They are used for incentive pay systems, accounting cost standards, and other planning and controlling applications. Time study, work sampling, predetermined time standards, and subjectively set labor standards are commonly used techniques of work measurement.

Useful guidelines have evolved for designing jobs that are both efficient and satisfying to workers. This growing body of knowledge is a provocative area in POM. While some work is being done on this important problem, much more remains to be done if we are to reduce worker turnover and absenteeism, increase quality of outputs, and improve morale.

Review and Discussion Questions

1. Describe the attitudes of the younger workers in industry toward their work. What explanation can you give for these attitudes?

2. Define *worker productivity*. Why should companies today be particularly concerned with worker productivity?

3. What two major factors affect worker productivity?

4. Under what conditions should we expect workers who have their needs satisfied to be productive?

5. Describe and explain Maslow's hierarchy of needs. What meaning does the hierarchy have for today's operations managers?

6. Make three suggestions for modifying workers' job tasks to improve workers' needs for self-control.

7. Make three suggestions for modifying workers' immediate job setting to make jobs more satisfying.

8. Make three suggestions for modifying workers' larger work environments to make jobs more satisfying.

9. Name three key obstacles to achieving the integration of workers' needs with productivity in job design.

10. Define and explain the questioning attitude of methods analysis.

11. Name five principles of motion economy concerning use of the human body.

12. Name five techniques of methods analysis.

13. Define *work measurement*. What is the universal unit of measure in work measurement?

14. Name five causes of allowances.

15. Name three uses of work sampling.

16. Define *job design*.

17. What two criteria must be used to evaluate job design remedy proposals?

18. Discuss the role of time study, work sampling, micromotion study, and other industrial engineering techniques in designing jobs for today's workers.

Problems

1. Bill Bonnet is Bratz Agricultural Chemicals' sales manager for the southern region. Twenty-two salespersons report to Bill and sell chemicals to jobbers throughout 12 southern states. During the past 5 years Bill has put together a team of salespersons that is second to none in its ability to cooperate. These salespersons appear to be happy with their jobs in all respects, including pay, supervision, attitudes toward the company, and morale. Bill feels that he has done everything in his power to make each salesperson in his group happy with his particular job.
   In recent months Bratz's sales in the southern region have declined 10 percent when compared to comparable periods in the past. Bill has racked his brain to come up with some reason, such as decline in the overall economy or competitor activity, to explain the sales decline. After much investigation, however, Bill has concluded that there has been a drop-off in productivity among the salespersons because of lack of motivation. **a.** Use motivation theory to explain how employees who are happy with their jobs could be unproductive. **b.** What was Bill doing wrong? **c.** What should Bill do to correct this situation? Give the specific steps that you would follow in improving the productivity of the southern region sales staff.

2. Mercury Electric manufacturers electric motors in Watertown, Connecticut. Mercury's industrial engineering department has been successful in designing assembly

line jobs that are highly specialized and technically efficient. The assembly line at Mercury is so refined, in fact, that its labor cost per unit is lower than that of any of its competitors in spite of its workers receiving the highest average annual pay in the industry. When Mercury's workers were recently interviewed by a national television commentator, their comments were:

—We like working at Mercury; we wouldn't work anywhere else.

—The pay is good and besides we like the way management treats us.

—Our foremen are great guys; you know we work hard but you can depend on them giving you a square deal and they stick up for you.

—If you screw up, they don't crucify you; sure, they point out what we did wrong and tell us to avoid the problem in the future, but they don't make a federal case out of it.

—When we do a good job, they're down here in a hurry to let us know that they appreciate the good work.

—If we've got a problem, we can walk right in to the boss's office and level with him. That gets results around here. And if he's got a rush order that needs to be produced and shipped quick, he'll come right down on the line and talk to us about it. We appreciate the way we can talk openly around here. It's a two-way street, you know?

—Sure, the work on the assembly line can get monotonous, but taking everything into consideration, this is the best job I've ever had.

—Quality is good, absenteeism is low, and turnover is low around here. Why not? It's a good place to work.

a. Are these workers satisfied with their jobs? Explain how these workers are satisfying their physiological, safety, social, esteem, and self-fulfillment needs. **b.** Why haven't the monotonous assembly line jobs at Mercury resulted in high absenteeism, high turnover, and low product quality? **c.** A new personnel manager at Mercury insists that he expects absenteeism and turnover to increase as new younger workers who have a lower tolerance for job boredom are gradually hired into the plant. What job design remedies should be tested at Mercury? Justify your proposals.

3. Mary Margret Tack manages a medium-sized garment factory in Cutandride, Texas. Worker turnover and absenteeism have plagued her operation during the 2 years she has been plant manager. The cost of hiring new workers and having standby workers to fill in for absent workers is excessive. With the help of some personnel and engineering persons from the home office in Oklahoma City, the following estimates of cost savings and cost increases from alternative job design remedies were made:

Job Design Remedy	Average per-Unit Cost Increase Due to Reduced Technical Efficiency	Average per-Unit Cost Savings Due to Reduced Turnover and Absenteeism
Job rotation	$.059	$.085
Job enrichment	.092	.129
Time away from jobs	.065	.055
Supervisor training	.057	.090

a. If only one of the proposals can be accepted, rank the remedies in order of desirability. **b.** Should Mary Margret reassign her industrial engineers to another plant because time studies will no longer be needed? **c.** Are the above remedies mutually exclusive, that is, in practice can only one of the remedies be applied at a time? What are some likely combinations?

4. Prepare a process chart for these operations: **a.** changing a flat tire on a bicycle, and **b.** patching a knee on a pair of work trousers.

5. Prepare an operation chart for making a double-dip ice cream cone. Can you make suggestions for improving your work method?

6. Prepare a flow diagram for batch processing a computer program at your school. How would you change this process to reduce travel distance and processing times?

7. Prepare a worker-machine chart for making three photocopies on a pay copy machine.

8. Using the principles of motion economy, design a method for these operations (document each method on an operation chart): **a.** buttering a piece of toast, **b.** replacing the ink element in a ball-point pen, and **c.** filling a stapler with staples.

9. Go to your school's library. Study the procedure for checking out books at the main desk. Prepare a process chart for the present method and for an improved proposed method. What are the estimated savings of the proposed method over the present method (in labor savings dollars and client time)?

10. A quality control technician performs a certain quality control (QC) test several times each day. A time study showed that the average time for the QC test is 12.55 minutes, the performance rating is 100, and allowances are 60 minutes per 8-hour shift: **a.** Compute the labor standard for the operation. **b.** If the technician performed only this test repeatedly, how many tests per 8-hour shift could be completed on the average? **c.** If the technician's labor rate is $9.75 per hour, what should the accounting department use as the standard labor cost per test?

11. A maintenance department of a large manufacturing plant routinely calibrates an electronic control unit for its production machines. A time study is performed on this operation, resulting in the data below (times are in 100ths of minutes):

Elemental Task	Cycles								Performance Rating
	1	2	3	4	5	6	7	8	
1. Get and position unit	10	12	15	10	9	14	12	10	105
2. Perform calibration	150	190	160	180	170	190	200	200	120
3. Perform standard tests	490	385	519	450	550	472	460	521	85
4. Update card and remove unit	50	60	70	60	60	50	80	60	100

Allowances per 8-Hour Shift:

Clothes change	12 minutes
Unavoidable delay	20 minutes
Lunch	30 minutes
Shower and change	20 minutes
Total	82 minutes

a. Compute the select time for each element in minutes by using the arithmetic average method. **b.** Compute the normal time for each element and for the total operation in minutes. **c.** Compute the allowance factor for the operation. **d.** Compute the labor standard for the operation.

12. A bead-taping operation for 14-inch passenger tires is repeated continuously by 25 operators at the Quality Tire Company in Chevron, Michigan. This operation was time studied, median method is used for developing select times except for Element 5, which uses arithmetic average, and times are in 100ths of minutes:

Elemental Task	Cycles										Performance Rating
	1	2	3	4	5	6	7	8	9	10	
1. Get bead, insert in clamp	10	8	10	12	11	9	8	10	11	10	90
2. Operate to roll bead	18	20	22	25	20	22	21	19	20	20	85
3. Get tape and insert	15	20	17	20	17	30	19	17	19	20	105
4. Operate to roll tape on bead	40	35	30	35	38	39	41	40	38	38	100
5. Straighten tape	—	20	—	—	22	—	—	20	—	—	110
6. Remove finished bead	10	8	6	8	9	8	8	7	8	8	100

Allowances per 8-Hour Shift:

Clothes change	10 minutes
Unavoidable delay	15 minutes
Rest periods	24 minutes
Area clean-up	10 minutes
Shower and change	20 minutes
Total	79 minutes

a. Compute the labor standard for this operation. **b.** If the labor rate is $8.90 an hour, what is the accounting standard labor cost for taping beads for each 14-inch tire if each tire has two beads? **c.** How many beads per operator should be expected for each 8-hour shift?

13. Receptionists at a medical clinic are estimated to spend approximately 5 percent of the time during each shift in answering telephone calls. A work-sampling study of the receptionists' jobs is proposed to determine more precisely how much time is actually spent on the telephone. If a 95 percent confidence interval and ±2 percent absolute error are acceptable, how many work-sampling observations are required?

14. A time study is being performed on an operation to set a labor standard. Problems have been encountered, however, in developing an allowance factor. The analyst knows that 60 minutes are normally devoted to coffee breaks and lunch, but an allowance for unavoidable delay must be estimated. A ratio-delay work-sampling study was conducted, with the following results:

Activity	Numbers of Observations
Unavoidable delay	52
Avoidable delay	39
Other	384

What allowance factor should be used in setting the labor standard if allowances include unavoidable delay, lunch, and coffee breaks? Assume 480 minutes per shift.

15. A work-sampling study was performed on an electronic assembly operation at

Oklahoma Instruments Inc. The study covered an 8-hour shift with a single worker. The results of the study were as follows:

Activity	Percent of Time
Assemble units	80
Allowances	20

If the worker received a performance rating of 120 on the assemble-units activity and 400 units were produced during the study, what is the labor standard for this operation?

16. A work-sampling study was conducted for a packaging operation in a mail order shipping room over a 40-hour week. During the study the operator completed 390 finished packages and was rated at 115 percent performance while packaging. The results of the study were:

Activity	Number of Observations
Packaging	375
Unavoidable delay	80
Rest periods	45

The second and third activities are to be included in allowances.

a. Determine the normal time per package. b. Determine the labor standard per package.

17. A company has a wage incentive gain-sharing or bonus plan for its hourly employees. Joe Blare, an employee in the tube-splicing department, has just completed a one-week pay period. The information on his time card is:

Total hours worked = 39.5
Total production = 550
Labor standard per unit = 5.386 minutes
Hourly base pay = $8.75 per hour

If the company uses the following formula to compute actual hourly pay, what is Joe Blare's pay for the period?

Actual hourly pay = Hourly base pay × Performance

18. Bill Bray, an employee of YELCO Manufacturing's machining department, operates a boring mill. YELCO has installed a straight piece-rate incentive pay system for its employees. A 2-week pay period has just ended and Bray is estimating his pay for the period from this information:

Total production = 1,200 units
Labor standard per unit = 4.500 minutes
Hourly base pay = $7.501 per hour

a. Compute Bray's piece rate for this product on the boring mill operation. b. Compute his pay for the period.

Case

Nilo Signal Company

Norbert Gailer is the new plant manager for the Nilo Signal Company of San Martin, California. The plant produces signal products for the highway, railway, and marine markets. Mr. Gailer is now confronted with a problem left over from his predecessor—low productivity within the bonnet operation. It is imperative to increase the output of this operation because it is the bottleneck operation for the entire assembly line of the plant. In fact, the bonnet operation's present production level is 20 percent below the capacity of all other operations on the assembly line. The excessive labor costs that result from underutilized personnel have caused the plant to operate in the red for several months and, furthermore, the plant's production level is inadequate to satisfy the demand of its customers.

Eight women per shift now staff the bonnet operation. In the distant past the operation was performed totally by hand and the workers' pay was based on the number of pieces produced by the group per shift. The workers now say that they never liked the incentive pay system. About a year ago some machines were installed in the bonnet operation as part of a plantwide program aimed at increasing plant capacity. It was estimated at the time that the production level of the bonnet operation would be increased by 30 percent. The number of women in the group was reduced according to plan, the machines were installed, and production levels did increase, but only by about 10 percent. About 3 months ago, when Mr. Gailer took over as plant manager, one of his first duties was to negotiate with the union representatives concerning the incentive pay system of the bonnet operation, the only such system in the plant. The system was done away with, and the bonnet operation workers were placed on hourly rates in line with similar work in other areas of the plant. The negotiations went well and all parties seemed satisfied with the outcome.

Mr. Gailer thought that the change in the pay system would trigger higher production levels in the bonnet operation, but the output remained below that of the other operations. Mr. Gailer met with the bonnet group and with individuals from the group to discuss the situation. Bernadine Murphy, the union steward for the plant and a member of the bonnet group, candidly indicated that the working relations between the former plant manager and the group had been strained. She seemed open and cooperative, not at all the trouble-maker described by the previous plant manager. Mr. Gailer spoke plainly to the group. "The plant is in trouble profitwise. We can't produce enough products to satisfy our customers and they are beginning to turn to our competitors. As I see it, the output of the bonnet operation is presently at the center of our difficulties. Time studies indicate that we should be able to get another 20 percent of production per shift out of the operation with just a fair day's work for a fair day's pay. Can't we work together to get the production level of your operation up? If I can assist you in any way, my door is open. Just walk across and tell me your needs and we'll get going." The group did not deny that production levels of the operation could be substantially improved. No immediate response came from the group, but during the next two weeks several personal contacts were made between individuals and Mr. Gailer:

1. Mary Malviola walked into Mr. Gailer's office during an afternoon break and said that the bonnet room was so hot that the women were all wrung out by the end of the shift. She thought that two or three fans would solve the problem. Mr. Gailer believed that the room was warm, perhaps a little warmer than some of the other operations' locations.

2. Mioke Kisama walked up to Mr. Gailer in the parking lot before work one morning and showed him her hands. Her fingernails were torn and broken and her hands had several nicks, scratches, and scrapes. She said that the new machines were chewing up the workers' hands

and that it was hard to make her own hands look pretty for her husband after they had been exposed to the machines all day long. She felt that some of the new-type gloves that she had seen at a local store would solve the problem and asked Mr. Gailer if he would supply the gloves to the group.

3. Mary Halalakala came into the main office during an afternoon break and asked Mr. Gailer if he would come over to the bonnet room. He accompanied her to a window on the west side of the room. She told him that the sun glared directly into the workers' eyes during the late afternoon and wondered if he would have a sunshade, blind, or awning installed.

4. Bernadine Murphy, the plant's union steward, entered Mr. Gailer's office during a morning break and asked him if he would support a plantwide Christmas party.

Assignment

1. Why is the production level depressed at the bonnet operation? Discuss the possible reasons for the development of the problem.

2. What should Mr. Gailer do about the requests from the bonnet group? Discuss the pros and cons of following your recommendations for responding to the requests. How are your recommendations directed toward the underlying problem?

3. What course of action should Mr. Gailer take to solve this problem and to avoid its recurrence?

Selected Bibliography

Alford, L. P., and H. Russell Beatty. *Principles of Industrial Management.* New York: Ronald Press, 1951.

Barnes, Ralph M. *Motion and Time Study.* 5th ed. New York: Wiley, 1968.

Bell, Cecil H., Jr., Terence R. Mitchel, and Denis D. Umstot. "Goal Setting and Job Enrichment: An Integrated Approach to Job Design." *Academy of Management Review* 3(October 1978): 867–879.

Davis, Louis E., and Albert B. Cherns. *The Quality of Working Life.* New York: Free Press, 1975, vols. 1 and 2.

Gears, A. J. "Productivity from Scanlon-type Plans." *Academy of Management Review* 1(July 1976): 99–108.

Maslow, A. H. "A Theory of Human Motivation." *Psychological Review* (July 1943): 370–396.

Maynard, H. B. *Industrial Engineering Handbook.* New York: McGraw-Hill, 1963.

Mundel, Marvin E. "Motion and Time Study." In *Handbook of Industrial Engineering and Management,* edited by William G. Ireson and Eugene L. Grant. Englewood Cliffs, NJ: Prentice-Hall, 1955.

———. *Motion and Time Study.* Englewood Cliffs, NJ: Prentice-Hall, 1960.

Niebel, Benjamin W. *Motion and Time Study.* Homewood, IL: Richard D. Irwin, 1976.

Sutermeister, Robert A. *People and Productivity,* 2d ed., p. ii. New York: McGraw-Hill, 1969.

Townsend, Robert. *Up the Organization.* New York: Knopf, 1970, 137.

Supplement to Chapter 12

Learning Curves

In 1925 the commander of the Wright-Patterson Air Force Base in Dayton, Ohio, observed that workers exhibited definite learning patterns in manufacturing operations.[1] Since these first studies, we now know that most aircraft manufacturing tasks experience an 80 percent learning rate. In other words, the average direct labor-hours required to assemble an aircraft is reduced by a factor of .8 as the production quantity is doubled. Figure 12S.1 shows how the learning of workers causes the average direct labor-hours per unit to fall as the number of units produced increases. If the first aircraft assembled requires 100 direct labor-hours, two aircraft would average $.8 \times 100 = 80$ labor-hours, four aircraft would average $.8 \times 80 = 64$ labor-hours, eight would average $.8 \times 64 = 51.2$ labor-hours, and so on.

The concept of the learning curve rests well with operations managers because they know through experience that in the beginning of production runs, workers are unfamiliar with their tasks and the amount of time required to produce the first few units is high. But as the workers learn their tasks, their output per day increases up to a point and then levels off to a rather constant output rate. Learning curves are therefore intuitively validated in POM experience. Additionally, learning curve concepts are based upon these conceptual underpinnings: (1) Where there is life, there can be learning. (2) The more complex the life, the greater the rate of learning. Worker-paced operations are more susceptible to learning or can give greater rates of progress than machine-paced operations. (3) The rate of learning can be sufficiently regular to be predictive. Operations can develop trends that are characteristic of themselves.[2] Workers are thus observed to improve eye and hand coordina-

---

[1] Miguel A. Reguero, *An Economic Study of the Military Airframe Industry* (Wright-Patterson Air Force Base, Ohio: Department of the Air Force, October 1957), 213.

[2] Winfred B. Hirschmann, ''Profit from the Learning Curve,'' *Harvard Business Review* 42 (February 1964): 118.

601

Figure 12S.1
Aircraft Assembly 80 Percent Learning Curve

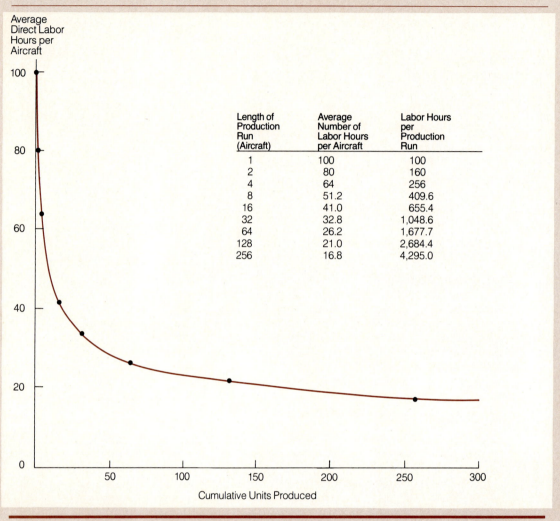

Length of Production Run (Aircraft)	Average Number of Labor Hours per Aircraft	Labor Hours per Production Run
1	100	100
2	80	160
4	64	256
8	51.2	409.6
16	41.0	655.4
32	32.8	1,048.6
64	26.2	1,677.7
128	21.0	2,684.4
256	16.8	4,295.0

tion, learn how to perform tasks, and develop technical skills as they gain more experience in performing certain operations. It is helpful in POM to be able to analyze these workers' learning situations and to be able to estimate: (1) the average number of labor-hours required per unit for N units in a production run, (2) the total number of labor-hours required to produce N units in a production run, and (3) the exact number of labor-hours required to produce the *n*th unit of a production run.

Three general approaches to learning curve analyses are found in practice; arithmetic analyses, logarithmic analyses, and handbook tables.

Arithmetic Analyses

The *arithmetic analysis* approach to learning curve problems is perhaps the most straightforward because its procedures are based directly upon this fundamental: *as the number of units produced doubles, the average labor-hours per unit declines by a constant factor.* This approach, introduced in the aircraft assembly operation of Figure 12S.1, is further demonstrated in Example 12S.1.

Example 12S.1

Arithmetic Learning Curve Analysis

Frances Blaylock, an industrial engineer for Z Lock Products Company, is preparing a labor cost estimate for producing 256 special bronze locking valves for a one-of-a-kind design that has never been produced before. She knows from experience, however, that products of this type can be expected to conform to an 85 percent learning curve in Z Lock's shop. One unit is produced in the model shop with 3.75 labor-hours required to complete the first unit. If labor rates are $12.75 per hour, what is Fran's labor cost estimate for the order?

Solution

1. First, prepare a table of length of production run, average labor-hours per unit, and labor-hours per production run:

(1) Number of Valves in Production Run (N)	(2) Average Labor-Hours per Valve	(3) Labor-Hours per Production Run (1) × (2)	(1) Number of Valves in Production Run (N)	(2) Average Labor-Hours per Valve	(3) Labor-Hours per Production Run (1) × (2)
1	3.750*	3.750	32	1.664	53.245
2	3.188	6.375	64	1.414	90.516
4	2.709	10.838	128	1.202	153.877
8	2.303	18.424	256	1.022	261.591
16	1.958	31.320			

* Note: $85 \times 3.750 = 3.188$; $85 \times 3.188 = 2.709$; and so on.

2. Next, compute the labor cost for the order:

Total labor cost = Labor-hours × Labor cost per hour = 261.591 × 12.75 = $3,335.29

Note in Example 12S.1 that the average labor-hours per unit and total labor-hours per production run estimates are easily developed for production runs equal to quantities that result from continuous doubling of previous quantities. (Production run = 2^i, where *i* is an integer that is increased from zero to ∞ in steps of one unit.) When the length of a production run does not exactly equal some doubled value, this approach is inadequate. Take, for instance, a production run of 100 units in Example 12S.1. What is the average number of labor-hours per unit? The graphical approach to learning curves allows us to answer this question about intermediate points on the curves.

Graphical Analyses

Figure 12S.2 shows *standardized* learning curves of from 75 to 95 percent for the average labor-hours per unit for production runs of varying lengths. Because the term *standardized* means that the first unit has been assumed to require one labor-hour in these curves, the actual labor-hours required for the first unit must be multiplied by the values of these curves. Example 12S.2 demonstrates the use of this figure and the graphical approach to learning curve problems.

Perhaps the greatest disadvantage of the graphical approach to learning curve problems is the imprecision introduced by the reading of values off the curves. Another disadvantage of both the arithmetic analysis and the graphical approaches is their inability to provide analysts with estimates of the labor-hours required to produce a specific unit of a production run. For instance, how many labor-hours are required to produce the 16th unit? Despite these deficiencies, these approaches are so straightforward that we find them used frequently in practice. However, the method that surpasses all others in both comprehensiveness and precision in analyzing learning curve problems is logarithmic analyses.

Figure 12S.2
Learning Curves: Average Labor Content per Unit

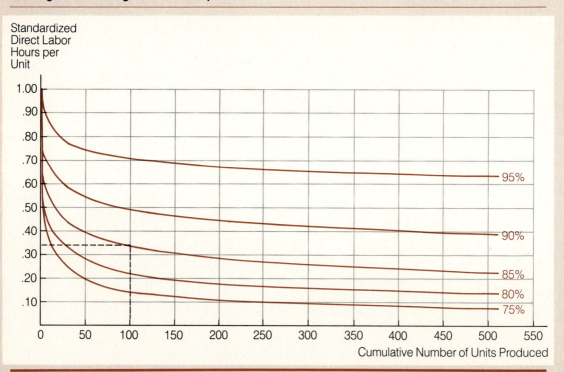

Example 12S.2

Graphical Approach to Learning Curves

Frances Blaylock (of Example 12S.1) wonders what the labor cost estimate for the order of Z Lock's bronze locking valves would be if the production run were reduced from 256 to 100 valves. The labor-hours required for the first unit is 3.75, an 85 percent learning curve is used, and the labor rate is $12.75 per hour. What is Fran's labor cost estimate for the order of 100 valves?

Solution

1. First, locate the 85 percent learning curve in Figure 12S.2 and read off the approximate average direct labor-hours per unit if the production order is 100 units. The value is about .340 labor-hour.

2. Next, convert the .340 labor-hour, which is standardized and assumes that the first unit required one labor-hour, to our situation. Because our first unit required 3.75 labor-hours, we must multiply the value from the curve by 3.75:

$$\begin{matrix} \text{Average} \\ \text{labor-hours} \\ \text{per unit} \end{matrix} = \begin{matrix} \text{Standardized} \\ \text{average} \\ \text{labor-hours} \\ \text{per unit} \end{matrix} \times \begin{matrix} \text{Actual labor-} \\ \text{hours required} \\ \text{for first unit} \end{matrix} = .340 \times 3.75 = 1.275 \text{ labor-hours}$$

3. Next, compute the total labor-hours for the order of 100 valves:

$$\begin{matrix} \text{Total labor-} \\ \text{hours for} \\ \text{the order} \end{matrix} = \begin{matrix} \text{Average} \\ \text{labor-hours} \\ \text{per unit} \end{matrix} \times \begin{matrix} \text{Number of} \\ \text{valves in} \\ \text{the order} \end{matrix} = 1.275 \times 100 = 127.5 \text{ labor-hours}$$

4. Next, compute the labor cost for the order:

$$\begin{matrix} \text{Total labor} \\ \text{cost for} \\ \text{the order} \end{matrix} = \begin{matrix} \text{Total labor-} \\ \text{hours for} \\ \text{the order} \end{matrix} \times \begin{matrix} \text{Labor} \\ \text{cost} \\ \text{per hour} \end{matrix} = 127.5 \times \$12.75 = \$1,625.63$$

Logarithmic Analyses

Logarithmic analyses allow us to answer most POM questions about learning curves. This method is based upon the formulas and variable definitions found in Table 12S.1. Note that the only real complexity introduced in these formulas is the necessity of using logarithms to solve for Y_N, the average number of labor hours per unit when N units are produced, thus the name *logarithmic analyses*. Your ability to

Table 12S.1
Logarithmic Learning Curve Formulas

Variable Definitions	Logarithmic Formulas
a = Labor-hours required to produce the first unit	$Y_N = aN^{-b}$ or $\dfrac{a}{N^b}$
b = Slope of the learning curve	$T_N = Y_N(N)$
N = Cumulative number of units produced	$y_n = T_N - T_{N-1}$
y_n = Labor-hours required to produce the nth unit	
Y_N = Average number of labor-hours per unit when N units are produced	
T_N = Total labor-hours required to produce N units	

work analyses of this type is dependent upon your memory of how to work with logarithms from your high school days or your having an electronic calculator that has logarithmic functions.

Example 12S.3 uses logarithmic formulas to estimate average labor-hours per unit (Y_N), total labor-hours for a production run (T_N), and labor-hours for one specific unit in a production run (y_n). These formulas use learning curve factor values of b and $(1 - b)$, which are developed in Table 12S.2. These factors result from solving the Y_N formula for b and sequentially substituting in values of learning curve rates.[3]

Table 12S.2
Learning Curve Factors

Learning Rate	b	$(1-b)$	Learning Rate	b	$(1-b)$
95%	.074	.926	75%	.415	.585
90	.152	.848	70	.515	.485
85	.234	.766	65	.621	.379
80	.322	.678	60	.737	.263

Note that these b and $(1 - b)$ values apply only if a = labor-hours for the first unit in the Y_N and y_n formulas.

[3] $Y_N = aN^{-b}$
$\log Y_N = \log a + (-b) \log N$

$b = \dfrac{\log a - \log Y_N}{\log N}$

Let a = 100 percent and Y_N = 80 percent and compute b for N = 2:

$b = \dfrac{\log (100) - \log (80)}{\log (2)} = \dfrac{2 - 1.9031}{.30103} = .322$, as found in Table 12S.2

Note that the .322 value for b applies as long as the labor-hours to produce the first unit (a) are substituted into the Y_N formula. If some other point of reference is selected (say the second unit labor-hours), then both b and a will change in the Y_N formula:

$b_2 = \dfrac{\log (80) - \log (64)}{\log (4)} = .1069$ and $Y_4 = 80(4)^{-.1609} = 64$

Example 12S.3

Logarithmic Learning Curve Analysis

Frances Blaylock, of the Z Lock Products Company, had developed labor cost estimates for 256 special bronze locking valves for a customer. Now the customer has some additional questions about the order: **1.** What is the total number of labor-hours required to produce 100 units? **2.** How many labor-hours would be required to produce the last unit (labor-hours for the 100th unit)? Remember that Z Lock had already estimated an 85 percent learning curve for this product in its shop, and the first unit required 3.75 labor-hours.

Solution

1. First, compute the average labor-hours per unit when $N = 100$ valves [read b from Table 12S.2: when an 85 percent learning curve is used, $b = .234$ and $(1 - b) = .766$]:

If we use a calculator to solve for exponential functions:

$$Y_{100} = \frac{a}{N^b} = \frac{3.75}{(100)^{.234}} = \frac{3.75000}{2.93765} = 1.27653 \text{ labor-hours}$$

If we use a calculator to solve for logarithms or if we use a table of logarithms:

$$Y_{100} = aN^{-b}$$

$$\log Y_{100} = \log a + (-b) \log N = \log 3.75 + (-.234) \log 100$$
$$= .57403 - (.234)(2) = .57403 - .46800 = .10603$$

$$Y_{100} = \text{antilog} \, (.10603) = 1.27653 \text{ labor-hours}$$

2. Next, compute the total labor-hours for the entire production run:

$$T_N = Y_N(N)$$

$$T_{100} = Y_{100}(100) = 1.27653(100) = 127.653 \text{ labor-hours}$$

3. Next, compute the labor-hours for the 100th unit:

$$y_{100} = T_{100} - T_{99}$$

If we use a calculator to solve for exponential functions:

$$Y_{99} = \frac{a}{N^b} = \frac{3.75}{(99)^{.234}} = \frac{3.75000}{2.93075} = 1.27954 \text{ labor-hours}$$

$$T_{99} = Y_{99}(99) = 1.27954(99) = 126.674 \text{ labor-hours}$$

$$y_{100} = T_{100} - T_{99} = 127.653 - 126.674 = .979 \text{ labor-hours}$$

If we use a calculator to solve for logarithms or if we use a table of logarithms:

$\log Y_{99} = \log (aN^{-b})$
$= \log a + (-b) \log N = \log 3.75 + (-.234) \log 99 = .57403 + (-.234)(1.99564)$
$= .57403 + (-.46698) = .10705$

$Y_{99} = $ antilog $(.10705) = 1.27953$ labor-hours

$T_{99} = Y_{99}(99) = 1.27953 (99) = 126.673$ labor-hours

$y_{100} = T_{100} - T_{99} = 127.653 - 126.673 = .980$ labor-hours

Note: The difference between .980 and .979 is rounding error in the logarithm calculations.

We have analyzed learning curve problems with arithmetic analysis, graphical approaches, and logarithmic analysis. Another method is frequently used in industry today — *handbook tables*. This method involves the analyst's using a handbook, which is available from many sources today, to determine the answers to the questions raised about learning curve problems in this section. Although beyond the scope of this book, these tables allow analysts to perform comprehensive learning curve analyses without the complex logarithmic calculations such as in Example 12S.3.

Uses and Limitations of Learning Curves

The use of learning curves in POM represents the understanding by managers that labor-hours per unit, labor cost per unit, and other costs related to these measures are not static, but rather they are dynamic. Labor-hours per unit can therefore be expected to decline as experience with a new product or operation increases. This concept is fundamental to many areas within POM.

Labor standards are expected to decline on many products and operations; thus cost standards, budgets, production scheduling, staffing plans, and prices are necessarily affected. Industrial engineers and other staff specialists routinely use learning curve theory to develop labor cost estimates for new products and services.

In job shops and custom service operations, learning curve theory is very important because:

1. Products and services tend to be one-time designs that require workers to start near the beginning to generate outputs.

2. Order quantities tend to be low; thus labor-hours per unit improves dramatically from the first to the last unit — unless, of course, only one of each unique design is produced.

3. Product and service designs tend to be complex; thus labor-hours per unit improves dramatically.

The application of learning curves to mass production and standard service operations is less significant because entirely new products or services are rare, and long production runs and simplified tasks combine to cause labor-hours per unit to improve only slightly.

Applying learning curves in practice can be difficult because:

1. It may be impossible either to develop precise labor-hour estimates for the first unit or to determine the appropriate learning rate. Large unique projects exhibit both of these difficulties.

2. Different workers have different learning rates. In a pure sense, learning theory applies only to individual workers, but little difficulty is encountered in applying learning curves to groups of workers by developing an *average* learning rate. But we can get into trouble when we apply learning curves to further aggregations such as direct labor cost per unit, indirect labor cost per unit, material cost per unit, and so on. Although these measures may be observed to improve as output increases, we must remember that workers learn and materials and machines do not. Application of learning curves to these aggregate measures must therefore be based on substantial historical evidence.

3. Few products are completely unique. Workers are usually well trained in the completion of tasks within their skill classifications. Past performance on related tasks therefore results in latent learning that is transferred to new products and services. The concept of a first unit can thus be a nebulous one in practice.

These and other difficulties cause us to use great care in applying learning curves. The simplistic analyses of learning curves are tempting to apply universally in POM, but experience teaches us that judgment must be exercised in using the results of these studies. Have we used good labor-hour estimates for the first unit? Is an 80 percent learning rate appropriate? Should we apply the learning rate to measures other than direct labor? Is this really a new operation? These and other questions must be answered and the results of learning curve analysis appropriately adjusted before operations managers can act on these studies in practice.

Review and Discussion Questions

1. As the number of aircraft doubles in production runs, what happens to the average labor-hours per unit?

2. Practically speaking, why does learning curve theory rest well with operations managers?

3. What three pieces of information do managers usually want to know about workers' learning situations?

4. Why are learning curves perhaps more beneficial in job shops, custom services, and other intermittent productive systems?

5. Give three reasons that problems can be encountered in using learning curves.

Problems

1. Given: Learning rate is 70 percent and first unit requires 2 labor-hours. Required: Use the arithmetic analysis approach to find: **a.** Average labor-hours per unit for a production run of 64 units. **b.** Total labor-hours for a production run of 64 units.

2. A repair facility at the White Plains Manufacturing Company is beginning to repair a group of 32 identical machines with identical malfunctions. It is estimated that the first unit will require 190 labor-hours, and an 80 percent learning rate is expected. **a.** Use arithmetic analysis to estimate the average labor-hours per unit for 32 machines. **b.** Use your answer from part *a* to estimate the total labor-hours for the whole job. **c.** Use the graphical approach to estimate the average labor-hours per unit for the order if the repair order is changed from 32 machines to only 25 machines. **d.** Use your answer to part *c* to estimate the total labor-hours for the whole order of 25 machines.

3. The Contrast Printing Company is now developing a price quotation on a special commemorative issue of *Life or Death Magazine.* The issue will have a special gold leaf and leather binding that involves all handwork for workers. It is estimated that the first unit will require 4 hours, and a 90 percent learning rate is expected. **a.** Use arithmetic analysis to estimate the average labor-hours per unit for 16 units. **b.** Use your answer in part *a* to estimate the total labor-hours for the 16 units. **c.** Use the graphical approach to estimate the average labor-hours per unit for an order of 200 units. Estimate the total labor-hours for the 200 units.

4. Specialty Metals Inc., a job shop that performs custom-machining services, has received an order for machining the impellers for 22 pump housings. Specialty estimates a total of 26 labor-hours for the machining operations on the first unit and a learning rate of 80 percent. Use the logarithmic analysis approach to: **a.** estimate the total number of labor-hours for the entire job, and **b.** estimate the labor-hours required for the 22d unit.

5. A valued customer has just called in a change in his order to Mercury Electric Motor Winding Service Company. The customer had first asked for a quote for 20 electric motors. Now, he wants only 12 or 13 motors repaired. To assist Mercury's management in responding to this customer, use logarithmic analyses to estimate: **a.** total labor-hours for the original 20 units if the first unit is estimated at 10 labor-hours and an 85 percent learning rate is expected, **b.** total labor-hours for 12 motors, and **c.** labor-hours for the 13th unit.

Selected Bibliography

Abernathy, W. J. "The Limits of the Learning Curve." *Harvard Business Review* 52(September–October 1974): 109–119.

Andress, Frank J. "The Learning Curve as a Production Tool." *Harvard Business Review* 32(January–February 1954): 87–95.

Hirschmann, Winfred B. "Profit from the Learning Curve." *Harvard Business Review* 42(February 1964): 118.

Holdham, J. H. "Learning Curves—Their Applications in Industry." *Production and Inventory Management* 11(fourth quarter 1970): 40–55.

Reguero, Miguel A. *An Economic Study of the Military Airframe Industry,* Wright-Patterson Air Force Base, Ohio: Department of the Air Force, 1957.

Chapter Outline

13

Facility Layout:
Planning the Arrangement of Facilities

The layout, or arrangement of equipment and work areas, is an inescapable problem in all industrial plants. We cannot avoid it. Even if we merely set the equipment inside the building, we have a layout of sorts. The question, therefore, is not "shall we have a layout?" Rather, we ask, "How good is the layout we have?"
Richard Muther, 1955

Facility layout **means planning for the location of all machines, employee work stations, customer service areas, material storage areas, and flow patterns of materials and people around, into, and within buildings.** When you arrange your furniture, you are deciding the layout of your living quarters. As you can attest, some of the layouts that you try are better than others; patterns of walking are convenient, more lounging space is provided, fewer steps are required between the dresser and the closet, and so on. But as you have also discovered, there is no single correct layout, but rather a few good layouts and a few bad ones. So it is with layouts in business and government. There are no absolutely correct layouts, but there are a few good ones. This chapter is intended to assist you in developing good layouts for a variety of facilities.

Facility layout decisions receive intensive attention in POM whether the facilities are goods producing or service producing. In both types of productive systems the physical arrangement of machines and equipment, storage areas, aisles, internal walls, human work areas, customer service areas, and other elements of productive facilities critically affect the operating efficiency, system capacity, system flexibility, and effectiveness of customer services. These factors in turn continuously affect the operating costs and degree of customer satisfaction. Although facility layouts can be occasionally changed, the frequency of these changes is limited by high changeover costs and the necessity of curtailing operations, thus reducing levels of customer service. Layout decisions are therefore also relatively long lasting.

Manufacturing Facility Layouts

When analysts study layout problems in manufacturing facilities, a multitude of factors are considered. Some of these are:

1. The required capacity per time period of the facility.
2. The size, number, and sequence of the machines that are necessary in the technology of the productive processes.
3. The required safety precautions, health care provisions, comfort needs, personal care needs, and other accommodations for employees.
4. Building and site constraints.
5. The expected growth trends of the organization.
6. The size, shape, weight, bulkiness, fragility, and other characteristics of the materials.

Although these and other factors are important, the overriding objective in most manufacturing layouts is to minimize the cost of processing, transporting, and storing materials throughout the productive processes.

Materials Handling

The materials used in manufacturing are many: raw materials, purchased components, materials-in-process, finished goods, packaging materials, maintenance and repair supplies, scrap and waste, and rejects or rework. These materials vary greatly in size, shape, chemical properties, and special features.

Most of this variety in material characteristics is determined by product design decisions. The layout of facilities is directly affected by the nature of these materials. Large and bulky materials; heavy materials; fluids; solids; flexible and inflexible materials; and materials requiring special handling to protect them from conditions such as heat, cold, humidity, light, dust, flame, and vibration — all affect the layout of facilities for handling, storing, and processing these materials.

A *materials handling system* is the entire network of transportation that receives materials, stores materials in inventories, moves them about between processing points within and between buildings, and finally deposits the finished products into vehicles that will deliver them to the ultimate customers. This system cuts across most departments of manufacturing and warehousing organizations.

Materials handling systems are expensive to purchase and operate. Obvious expenses are those of first costs, labor for operating the materials handling devices, and maintenance and repair costs. Other expenses that are not so obvious result from damaged or lost materials, delays in material deliveries, and accidents. These and other expenses are so large that the successful operation of these facilities demands acute management attention to the design and selection of materials handling systems.

Table 13.1
Materials Handling Principles

1. Materials should move through the facility in direct flow patterns, minimizing zigzagging or backtracking.
2. Related productive processes should be arranged to provide for direct material flows.
3. Mechanical materials handling devices should be designed and located and material storage locations should be selected so that human effort expended through bending, reaching, lifting, and walking is minimized.
4. Heavy or bulky materials should be moved the shortest distance through locating processes that use them near receiving and shipping areas.
5. The number of times each material is moved should be minimized.
6. Systems flexibility should allow for unexpected situations such as materials handling equipment breakdowns, changes in productive system technology, and future expansion of productive capacities.
7. Mobile equipment should carry full loads at all times; empty and partial loads should be avoided.

The design and layout of productive facilities must be integrated with the design of the materials handling system. For example, if overhead conveyors are to be used, the structure of the building must be strong enough to support the operation of these devices. Similarly, if heavy loads are to be transported on trucks, floors must have adequate support to withstand the constant stress of day-to-day pounding from these loads. Additionally, aisles must be wide enough to accommodate forklift trucks or other devices that will travel through the areas. Fixed position devices such as conveyors must also be provided floor space.

Certain principles have evolved to guide facility layout to ensure the efficient handling of materials. Table 13.1 summarizes some of these fundamentals. Al-

Table 13.2
Materials Handling Equipment

1. **Automatic transfer devices**—Machines that automatically grasp materials, hold them firmly while operations are being performed, and move them to other locations.
2. **Containers and manual devices**
   Hand carts—Unpowered wagons, dollies, and trucks pushed about by workers.
   Pallets—Base structures on which materials are stacked and moved about by materials handling vehicles.
   Tote boxes—Containers for holding loose parts or materials for storage and movements between operations.
   Wire bins—Containers for storing loose parts of materials in inventory.
3. **Conveyors**
   Belt—Motor-driven belt, usually made from rubberized fabric or metal fabric on a rigid frame.
   Chain—Motor-driven chain that drags materials along a metal slide base.
   Pneumatic—High volume of air flows through a tube, carrying materials along with the air flow.
   Roller—Boxes, large parts, or unitized loads roll atop a series of rollers mounted on a rigid frame The rollers can be either powered or unpowered.
   Tube—Chain with circular scraper blades drags materials along inside a tube.
4. **Cranes**—Hoists mounted on overhead rails or ground level wheels or rails; they lift, swing, and transport large and heavy materials.
5. **Elevators**—A type of crane that, while in a fixed position, lifts materials—usually between floors of buildings.
6. **Pipelines**—Closed tubes that transport liquids by means of pumps or gravity.
7. **Turntables**—Devices that hold, index, and rotate materials or parts from operation to operation.
8. **Trucks**—Electric, diesel, gasoline, or liquefied petroleum gas powered vehicles equipped with beds, forks, arms, or other holding devices.

though these are not hard and fast rules, they do provide effective guidelines for the efficient movement of materials in most facility layouts.

The process design and the principles of efficient materials handling provide the framework for selecting specific materials handling devices — the core of the materials handling system. Table 13.2 describes some of these devices.

Each of these devices has its own unique characteristics and advantages and disadvantages. Conveyors, for instance, are quite expensive to purchase, typically do not require operators, can be used to pace workers, follow fixed routes, and serve as temporary storage and holding devices. Trucks, on the other hand, are relatively inexpensive to purchase, follow no fixed routes, and provide the greatest materials handling flexibility.

The factors that ultimately affect the selection of specific devices for transporting materials in productive systems are product and process design, the estimated costs associated with purchasing and operating the devices, and the constraints imposed by the buildings and sites.

The three basic types of layouts for manufacturing facilities are process, product, and fixed position.

Process Layouts

Process layouts are designed to accommodate variety in product and process design. Figure 13.1 depicts two such products, X and Y, each with different product designs and different number, type, and sequence of processing steps. If a manufacturing facility produces a variety of nonstandard products in relatively small batches, as in a custom machine shop, chances are the facility will select a process layout.

Process layouts typically use general purpose machines that can be changed over rapidly to new operations for different product designs. These machines are usually arranged according to the type of processes being performed. For example, all punch presses would be in one department, all foundry machines in another department, and all lathes in another department. The materials handling equipment is

Figure 13.1
Process Layout for Producing Products X and Y

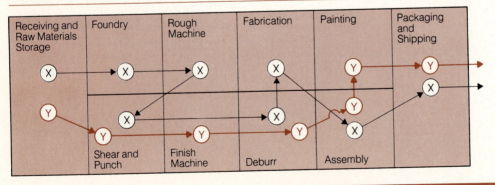

generally forklift trucks, cranes, and other mobile vehicles that allow for the variety of paths followed through the facility by the products produced.

The workers in process layouts must change and adapt quickly to the multitude of operations to be performed on each unique batch of products being produced. These workers must be highly skilled and require intensive job instructions and technical supervision.

Process layouts require ongoing planning, scheduling, and controlling functions to insure an optimum amount of work in each department and each work station. The products are in the productive system for relatively long periods of time, and large in-process inventories usually are present.

Product Layouts

Product layouts are designed to accommodate only a few product and process designs. Figure 13.2 depicts a facility that produces two products, X and Y. Although X and Y require different operations and different operation sequences, the layout is designed to allow a direct material flow through the facility for both products. Automobile manufacturing plants are good examples of facilities that use an assembly line or product approach to layout design.

Product layouts typically use specialized machines that are set up once to perform a specific operation for a long period of time on one product. To change over these machines to a new product design requires great expense and long down times. The machines are usually arranged into product departments. Within one product department several processes, such as forming, machining, and assembly, could be performed. Materials handling equipment is most often of the fixed position type, such as conveyors.

Workers in product layouts repeatedly perform a narrow range of activities on only a few product designs. The amount of skill, training, and supervision required is low. Although the planning and scheduling activities associated with these layouts are complex, they are not ongoing or continuously intense. Rather, planning and scheduling tend to be done intermittently as product changeovers, demand fluctuations, and special orders occur.

Figure 13.2
Product Layout for Producing Products X and Y

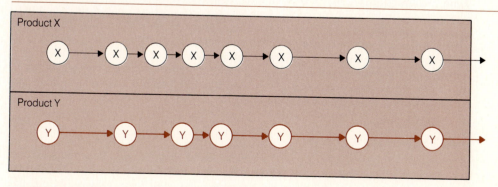

Figure 13.3
Fixed Position Layout

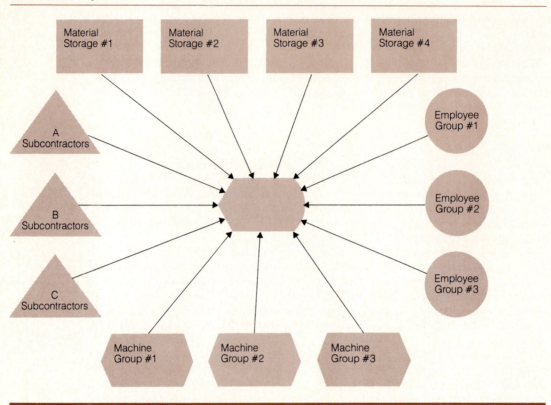

Fixed Position Layouts

Some manufacturing and construction firms use a layout for arranging work that locates the product in a fixed position and transports workers, materials, machines, and subcontractors to and from the product. Figure 13.3 demonstrates this type of layout. Missile assembly, large aircraft assembly, ship construction, and bridge construction are examples of *fixed position layouts*.

Although fixed position layouts are not common, they are used when a product is very bulky, large, heavy, or fragile. The fixed position nature of the layout minimizes the amount of product movement required.

Hybrid Layouts

Most manufacturing facilities use a combination of layout types. For example, one may basically adopt a process layout with one section of the facility using an assembly line, or vice versa. Figure 13.4 shows one such *hybrid layout* where the

Figure 13.4

Hybrid Layout for Producing Products X and Y

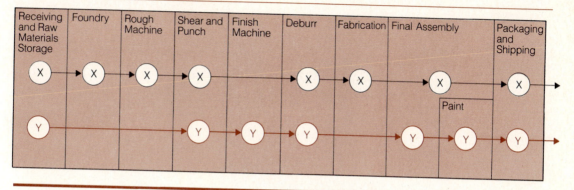

departments are arranged according to the types of processes, but the products flow through on a product layout.

In spite of these hybrids making the identification of layout types fuzzy, the importance of understanding the characteristics, advantages, and disadvantages of each type of layout should not be underestimated. As more complex productive system layouts are designed, the ability to classify these into either product, process, or fixed position layouts enhances our ability to develop comprehensive and effective layout designs.

Service Facility Layouts

The fundamental difference between service facility and manufacturing facility layouts is that service facilities principally exist to bring together customers and organizations' services. This chief difference results in service facility layouts that provide for easy entrance to these properties from freeways and busy thoroughfares. Similarly, large, well-organized, and amply lighted parking areas or garages are typically provided. Additionally, these facilities usually have wide, well-designed walkways to carry people to and from the parking areas.

Entryways and exits are typically well marked, easily located, and designed to accommodate large numbers of customers during peak visiting hours. Powered doors and escalators are often provided to ease the physical effort of opening doors and climbing stairs when armloads of merchandise must be transported.

A unique feature that often becomes the center for analyzing service facility layouts is lobbies or other such receiving or holding areas for customers, waiting lines, service counters, cash registers, and employee work stations. These direct customer receiving and service areas provide a basis for differentiating among types or classes of service facilities. Figure 13.5 shows that two extremes exist in layouts of service facilities: those that are almost totally designed around this customer receiving and servicing function and those that are designed around the technologies or processing of physical materials.

Figure 13.5
Types of Facilities Layout Emphases — Services

Customer/
constituent
receiving and
service
emphasis

Material or
technology
emphasis

Figure 13.6 shows a typical layout of a local branch savings and loan. The entire facility is primarily designed around customers — parking, easy entering and exiting, convenient waiting areas, waiting lines for standardized customer servicing, and individualized areas for customer savings account and loan customer servicing. The employee work areas for information processing and financial record keeping make up a secondary element of this type of service facility layout.

At the other extreme some service facilities are designed much like manufacturing and warehousing facilities; the central focus is on the technologies and physical materials processing. Figure 13.7 depicts a layout of a small hospital. Although some area of the layout is devoted to receiving patients, settling accounts, and releasing patients, the dominant consideration in this layout is the application of medical technologies such as surgery, radiology, laboratory tests, patient rest and recovery, patient feeding, and the effective application of doctors' and nurses' healing skills.

These two extremes in service facility layouts are near the endpoints in the continuum described in Figure 13.5. Other service facilities blend the characteristics of these two layouts. Layouts of exclusive restaurants, for example, typically emphasize customer receiving and individualized servicing perhaps more than the part of the facility that processes and prepares the food products. On the other hand, fast-food restaurant layouts tend to emphasize the processing and preparation of food instead of customer receiving and individual servicing. The mix of customer or technology and physical materials processing emphases varies according to the type of service offered and the operating strategies of each particular organization.

Another service facility that uses both customer receiving and servicing, and

Figure 13.6
A Savings and Loan Layout

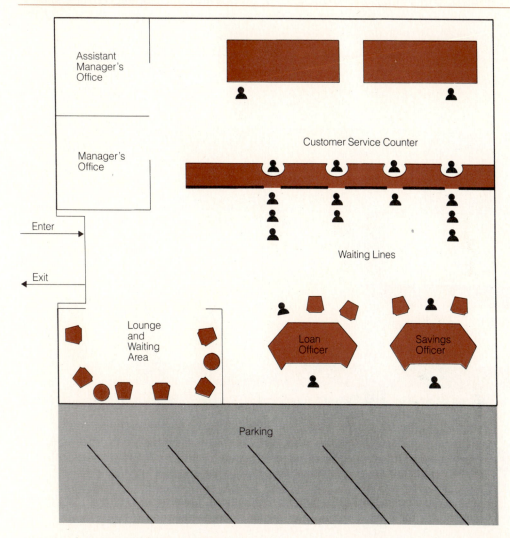

technologies and physical materials processing emphases is retail facilities. Figure 13.8 shows an example of the layout design for a retail grocery store. The entrance and exit, customer parking, the checkout channels, and the waiting areas near the front of the store have received the layout designers' intense attention. On the other hand, the design of the layout that displays the organization's products so that customers can easily locate them and want to buy them is a technology of retailing that also receives layout design emphasis. For example, the use of angular aisles to focus customers' attention on items located off main aisles, placement of high-profit items on the building's perimeter shelves, placement of sale items on the ends of aisles, and other store layout techniques are used to promote the sale of the organization's products.

Figure 13.7
A Hospital Layout

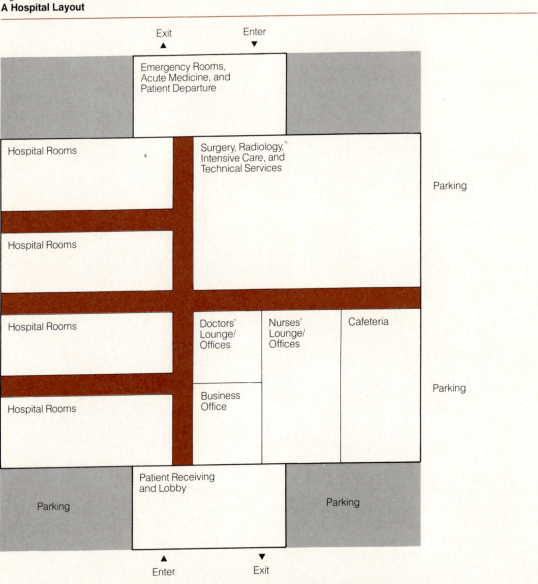

Figure 13.8
A Grocery Store Layout

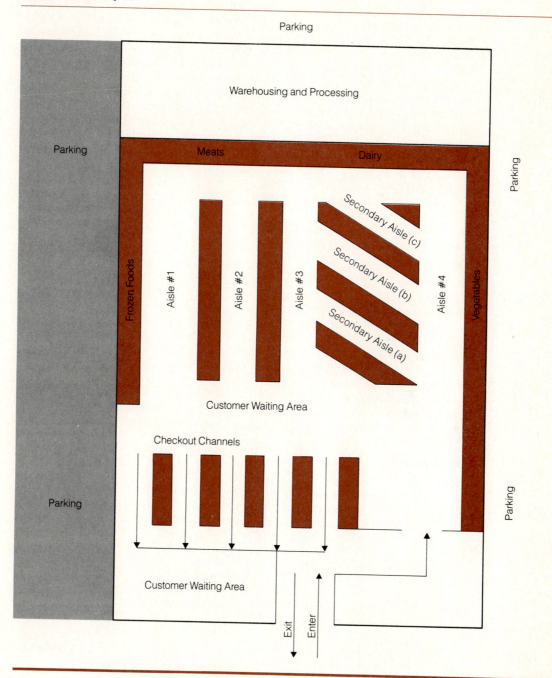

Those service facility layouts that are primarily oriented toward the technologies and physical materials processing can be viewed much like manufacturing layouts. Because service facilities almost always require great flexibility in accommodating a variety of processing paths through the facilities, the process layout depicted in Figure 13.1 dominates these layouts. Hospital layouts, for example, typically allow great variety in the processing steps for patients — surgery, radiology, blood chemistry testing, physical therapy, intensive care, and so on. The machinery and human work areas of hospitals are grouped and located according to their processing technologies in much the same way that a custom machine shop would lay out its machines and work stations. In both cases the layouts are designed to accommodate a variety of material (patient) flow patterns through the facilities while grouping employee skills and similar machinery logically according to the technical processes performed.

Let us now turn to some techniques that allow us to develop, analyze, and compare alternative layouts of facilities.

Techniques for Developing and Analyzing Facility Layouts

Perhaps the most common facility layout technique is that of using two-dimensional templates or machine cutouts on a building floor plan to determine the location of each element of the layout. Analysts slide these cutouts of machines, desks, and other equipment — which are drawn to the same scale as the building floor plan — to various positions. They achieve, through trial and error, a detailed layout in which materials and personnel can flow from place to place with little excess travel. The floor plan/template method is particularly useful in developing a layout for an existing department or building or when the configuration of the building is already established through other layout analyses.

Other layout techniques that more systematically develop layouts for productive facilities are also used. These techniques differ among three types of layouts — process and warehouse layouts, product layouts, and customer service layouts.

Process and Warehouse Layouts

The internal arrangement of buildings that use process layouts is usually first analyzed to systematically set the internal boundaries of operating departments and the external configuration of the building. Operations sequence analysis, block diagram analysis, load-distance analysis, and systematic layout planning (SLP) are techniques used to develop these layouts.

Operations Sequence Analysis An early approach to process layouts was the *operations sequence analysis*.[1] **This technique develops a good scheme for the arrangement of departments by graphically analyzing the layout problem.** Example 13.1 develops a general scheme for the arrangement of ten departments in a manufacturing facility.

---

[1] E. S. Buffa, "Sequence Analysis for Functional Layouts," *Journal of Industrial Engineering* 6(March–April 1955): 12–25.

Example 13.1

Operations Sequence Analysis

The Red Crystal Glass Products Company produces six distinct products that are transported between ten operating departments within its present production plant. Red Crystal is planning to build a new production facility at a new location next year and wishes to design a plant layout for the new facility. Will Dewey, Red Crystal's chief industrial engineer, is assigned this important layout assignment. Critical to the new layout is the total number of product movements per month among Red Crystal's operating departments:

Department Code	Department Description	Department Code					
		Grind 5	Paint 6	Drill 7	Rework 8	Glaze 9	Ship & Receive 10
1	Blow and mold	1,000		5,000		3,000	3,000
2	Heat treat	2,000	2,000				3,000
3	Neck		2,000			2,000	
4	Package	1,000		4,000			5,000
5	Grind		2,000				
6	Paint					2,000	
7	Drill				1,000		
8	Rework						1,000
9	Glaze						
10	Ship and receive						

Will must develop a schematic diagram of the general relationships among the operating departments by operations sequence analysis.

Solution

First, develop an initial solution schematic diagram with circles representing departments and lines representing product travel between departments. The number of product movements per month between departments is written on the lines:

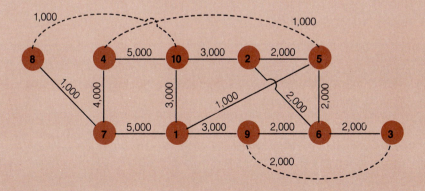

Next, restructure the initial schematic diagram to move departments closer to one another when the number of nonadjacent product movements between them is high, and move departments to a near rectangular shape. For example, Department 3 could be moved closer to Department 9 and Departments 8, 9, and 6 could be shifted to form a more rectangular shape:

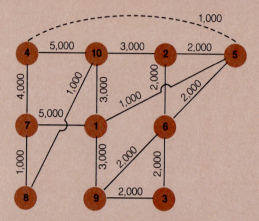

Further inspection of this schematic diagram reveals no changes in department locations that will substantially improve the layout.

Example 13.1 shows how we might develop a general set of relationships among operating departments when the external shape and dimensions of the building are not limiting factors.

Block Diagram Analysis   Example 13.2 takes the final schematic diagram from Example 13.1 and develops a **block diagram analysis, which sets the general shape and dimensions of the building and the location of the interior departmental boundaries.**

Example 13.2

Block Diagram Analysis

Will Dewey, chief industrial engineer at Red Crystal Glass Products Company, wishes to develop a departmental layout from the schematic diagram of Example 13.1. Whereas the schematic diagram of the last example shows the general relationships among the operating departments, Will must now determine the dimensions of the building and where the internal departmental boundaries will be. Critical to this building layout are the required areas for each department.

Department	Required Area (Square Feet)	Department	Required Area (Square Feet)
1. Blow and mold	200	6. Paint	200
2. Heat treat	200	7. Drill	400
3. Neck	400	8. Rework	200
4. Package	400	9. Glaze	200
5. Grind	900	10. Ship and receive	200

Will wishes to use a block diagram analysis to develop a departmental layout for Red Crystal's new building.

Solution

First, use the schematic diagram from Example 13.1 and place each department circle at the center of a square with the same relative area shown in the above table:

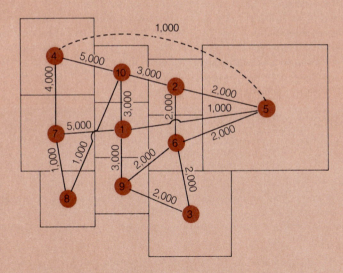

Notice that this layout retains the same general relationships among departments, but the external boundary of the facility is too irregular for functional building design.

Next, vary the shapes of the departments to fit the system into a rectangular building while retaining the required area of each department and the same relationships among departments:

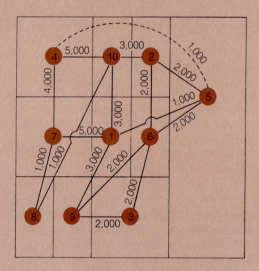

This block diagram is Will's proposed departmental layout for the new building.

Load-Distance Analysis Operations sequence analysis and block diagram analysis do not develop optimal — *the best* — layouts, only good layouts. It is not unusual for these analyses to develop two or more alternative block diagrams, each of which appears to be equally good. **Load-distance analysis is useful in comparing alternative layouts to identify the one with the least product or material travel per time period.** Example 13.3 compares two such layout alternatives.

Example 13.3

Analyzing Process Layouts with Load-Distance Analysis

Two layout alternatives are shown below. The facility's products, their movements between departments, and the distances between departments for each layout alternative are also displayed. Which layout alternative minimizes the monthly product travel through the facility?

Layout A

8	4	10	2	5
3	7	1	9	6

Layout B

7	1	9	6	3
4	10	2	5	8

Department Movement Combinations	Distances between Departments (Feet)		Department Movement Combinations	Distances between Departments (Feet)	
	Layout A	Layout B		Layout A	Layout B
1– 5	30	30	3– 9	30	20
1– 7	10	10	4– 5	30	30
1– 9	10	10	4– 7	10	10
1–10	10	10	4–10	10	10
2– 5	10	10	5– 6	10	10
2– 6	20	20	6– 9	10	10
2–10	10	10	7– 8	20	50
3– 6	40	10	8–10	20	30

Products	Department Processing Sequence	Number of Products Processed per Month	Products	Department Processing Sequence	Number of Products Processed per Month
a	1– 5–4–10	1,000	d	1– 7–8–10	1,000
b	2– 6–3– 9	2,000	e	2– 5–6– 9	2,000
c	2–10–1– 9	3,000	f	1– 7–4–10	4,000

Solution

1. First, compute the total travel for each product through each layout alternative:

Product	Department Processing Sequence	Compute Distance per Product (Feet)	
		Layout A	Layout B
a	1– 5–4–10	30 + 30 + 10 = 70	30 + 30 + 10 = 70
b	2– 6–3– 9	20 + 40 + 30 = 90	20 + 10 + 20 = 50
c	2–10–1– 9	10 + 10 + 10 = 30	10 + 10 + 10 = 30
d	1– 7–8–10	10 + 20 + 20 = 50	10 + 50 + 30 = 90
e	2– 5–6– 9	10 + 10 + 10 = 30	10 + 10 + 10 = 30
f	1– 7–4–10	10 + 10 + 10 = 30	10 + 10 + 10 = 30

2. Next, compute the total distance traveled per month for each product through each layout alternative:

Product	Products per Month	Distance per Product (Feet)		Distance per Month (Feet)	
		Layout A	Layout B	Layout A	Layout B
a	1,000	70	70	70,000	70,000
b	2,000	90	50	180,000	100,000
c	3,000	30	30	90,000	90,000
d	1,000	50	90	50,000	90,000
e	2,000	30	30	60,000	60,000
f	4,000	30	30	120,000	120,000
			Totals	570,000	530,000

3. Layout B results in the least total distance traveled per month through the facility by the products.

In Example 13.3, as well as in the previous layout examples of this section, the objective is to develop a layout that minimizes the product or material travel among production processes. This objective is usually dominant in goods-producing systems, but when material travel is not so important, as in service systems, other layout techniques can be used.

Systematic Layout Planning (SLP) In service systems, the amount of material that flows between departments may not be critical to developing a good facility layout. **In these service systems <u>systematic</u> <u>layout</u> <u>planning</u> (SLP) can be used.**[2]
SLP first develops a chart to rate the relative importance of each department being close to every other department. The ratings range from the extremes of absolutely necessary to undesirable. The ratings are based on a variety of reasons —type of customer, ease of supervision, common personnel, common equipment, and so on. Next, an initial schematic diagram, similar to the one in operations sequence analysis presented in Example 13.1, is developed. But this diagram connects the operating departments with color-coded lines to indicate closeness rating. This initial schematic diagram is modified through trial and error until departments with high closeness ratings are adjacent to one another and department and building space limitations are satisfied.

SLP is quite similar to operations sequence and block diagram analyses in both procedures and end results. The only significant difference among the three approaches is that SLP uses many reasons for assigning a closeness rating between departments whereas operations sequence and block diagram analyses use a single reason—product or material travel per time period.

The four layout analysis techniques presented—operations sequence, block diagram, load-distance analysis, and systematic layout planning—can be used whether the analyst is or is not restricted in the building configuration. These analyses begin with the production processes and develop a layout that sets the building configuration. Such a procedure is generally preferred because the operation of the facility is likely to be far more efficient than if we first begin with the building configuration and then work backward to see how we can fit the production processes into the building.

I recently worked with a municipal government to develop an improved layout and more efficient operations methods in a newly built jail complex in a large Western city. The jail was designed by a leading architect and was quite an imposing structure. But when the sheriff's department moved into the new facility, the staff found that they needed twice as many law enforcement officers to operate the new facility. I explained to the city administrators that they had fallen into the trap of first setting the configuration of the building and then trying to fit the operations into the building. They will be paying about $400,000 per year in excess labor costs for that error.

This is not to say, however, that layout analysts never begin with the building configuration. Often they do. Existing buildings and departments must frequently be converted to other uses. Sites can be so small or unusual in shape that buildings of only a certain shape are possible. Existing departments must be expanded. All these are only a few examples of *relayouts*. In cases like these, it is unavoidable that we begin with the building configuration and back into the layout design.

---

[2] Richard Muther and John D. Wheeler, "Simplified Systematic Layout Planning," *Factory* 120(August 1962): 68–77; (September 1962): 111–119; (October 1962): 101–113.

Computer Layout Analysis In recent years many computer programs have been written to develop and analyze process layouts. In the late 1960s three well-known computer analyses were developed — ALDEP, CORELAP, and CRAFT.[3]

ALDEP — automated layout design programs — and CORELAP — computerized relationship layout planning — are similar in that they use essentially the same procedures and logic as the systematic layout planning (SLP) that we discussed earlier. These programs maximize the total closeness rating for all the departments while complying with the required building characteristics. Very large and complex layout problems are feasible, and each analysis outputs a plotted floor-plan block layout.

CRAFT — computerized relative allocation of facilities — uses the same basic procedure and logic as operations sequence and block diagram analyses. CRAFT minimizes the total materials handling cost per time period for the layout. The material movements per time period are converted to cost per time period for movements of each material between departments. Analysts input an initial block layout, and CRAFT modifies the initial layout until no cost improvements are possible. New initial layouts yield different CRAFT layouts, so some experimentation is advised. The program also can handle complex, quite large layout problems while adhering to complex building characteristics. The outputs of the program are a plotted floor-plan block layout and the cost of the layouts.

These and other computer programs can save time and effort in large and complex layout problems, but their outputs are only the beginning of a finished layout. Their layouts must be smoothed by hand, checked for logic, and machines and other elements of the layout must usually be hand-fitted with templates and cutouts. Because heuristics are used and the number criteria used to compare layouts are few, analysts must double-check the outputs for logic flaws and for other quantitative and qualitative criteria.

Product Layouts

The analysis of assembly lines characterizes much of the analysis of product layouts. The product design and the market demand for the products ultimately determine the technological process steps and the required capacity of assembly lines. The number of personnel and the amount of work per person working on the assembly lines must then be determined. These kind of studies are known as line balancing.

Line Balancing *Line balancing* is the phase of assembly line study that determines which tasks each employee will perform and how the employees are grouped at work stations so that the total number of employees required on the assembly line is minimized. Table 13.3 summarizes some of the terms often used in line balancing. These terms will be used in the examples of this section.

The process that we follow to balance an assembly line is really conceptually quite simple. We determine what tasks are required to completely assemble one unit

---

[3] For further information about these analyses, see Jarrold M. Seehof and Wayne O. Evans, "Automated Layout Design Programs," *Journal of Industrial Engineering* 18(December, 1967): 690–695; Robert S. Lee and James M. Moore, "CORELAP—Computerized Relationship Layout Planning," *Journal of Industrial Engineering* 18(March 1967): 195–200; and Elwood S. Buffa and Thomas E. Vollmann, "Allocating Facilities with CRAFT," *Harvard Business Review* 42(March–April 1964): 136–150.

Table 13.3
Terminology of Assembly Line Analyses

1. Actual Number of Employees Required—The number of employees that must be employed by the firm to staff a work station. This total number includes the equivalent number of employees working and the equivalent number of employees idle at a work station.

2. Cycle Time—The time between units coming off the end of an assembly line.

3. Equivalent Number of Employees Idle—The amount of idle time at a work station that is expressed in number of employees. Four employee-hours among all of the employees assigned to a particular work station during an 8-hour shift would be the equivalent of one half of an employee who is idle.

4. Equivalent Number of Employees Working—The amount of work for employees to do at a work station expressed in number of employees. Twenty-nine employee-hours of work at a particular work station during an 8-hour shift would be the equivalent of 29/8 or 3.625 employees working.

5. Tasks—Very small elements of an employee's work. *Grasp pencil, position pencil on paper to write,* and *write the number 4* are examples of tasks. These tasks cannot usually be conveniently broken into smaller elements of work.

6. Task Times—The amount of time required for a well-trained employee to perform a task. Task times are usually expressed in 100ths of a minute.

7. Utilization of Employees—The percentage of the time that employees at a work station or along an entire assembly line are working. This is usually calculated by dividing the equivalent number of employees working by the actual number of employees required.

8. Work Station—Physical location where tasks are performed by one or more workers. Compatible tasks are combined into employee jobs at work stations. If more than one employee is assigned to a work station, all perform the same tasks.

of the product, and then we divide up the tasks among the workers so that all of the tasks get done and so that there is little unavoidable employee idle time. Table 13.4 explains this process in more detail.

The idea that tasks should be combined to form an employee's job at a work station only if the tasks are *compatible* is logical if you think about it. We would consider combining tasks if:

1. Two or more tasks use common materials. Such combinations can reduce the amount of material travel and number of material storage locations along the assembly line.

2. Two or more tasks do not create an unsafe condition. An example of an unsafe condition would be combining a task that uses materials that are classified as fuels with a task that uses materials classified as oxidants. These and other combinations can cause fires and other hazards.

3. Two or more tasks are adjacent to each other in the sequence of the assembly line. The first and last tasks of an assembly line, for example, would not ordinarily be performed by the same employee, unless, of course, we had a circular assembly line.

4. Two or more tasks are similar in their quality requirements. Two tasks would not ordinarily be combined, for example, if they require different precision levels in machine settings and labor skill. Additionally, greasy or dirty tasks would not be combined with those requiring a clean room environment.

5. Two or more tasks require the same machines.

6. Two or more tasks require the same levels of labor skill.

Table 13.4
The Line-Balancing Procedure

1. Determine what tasks must be performed to complete one unit of a finished product and the sequence in which the tasks must be performed.
2. Estimate task times (the amount of time it takes a worker to perform each task).
3. Determine which tasks can be combined. Some tasks should not be combined because of safety considerations, where they fall in the assembly sequence, etc.
4. Determine the cycle time (the amount of time that would elapse between products coming off the end of the assembly line if the desired hourly production were being produced).
5. Assign each task to a worker on the assembly line. This process results in determining the scope of each worker's

job or which tasks that he or she will perform. This combining of tasks into workers' jobs usually follows these steps:

a. Beginning at the beginning of the assembly sequence, combine tasks into workers' jobs so that the combined task times approach but do not exceed multiples of the cycle time.
b. When a combined task time is found that is very close to but does not exceed a multiple of the cycle time, these tasks will be performed by a worker and will determine the scope of the worker's job or the tasks that he or she will perform.
c. When tasks are combined into a worker's job, the number of multiples of the cycle time is the number of workers required at that work station, all performing the same job.

Tasks are logically separated into compatible groupings first, and then tasks within these groups are analyzed to determine which tasks should be combined to form employee jobs. Example 13.4 shows an analysis of an assembly line being planned to produce electronic calculators at Textech's Midland, Texas plant.

Example 13.4

Line Balancing within Product Layouts

Textech, a large electronics manufacturer, assembles Model AT 75 hand-held calculators at its Midland, Texas plant. The following assembly tasks must be performed on each calculator:

Task	Tasks That Must Immediately Precede	Time to Perform Task (Minutes)	Task	Tasks That Must Immediately Precede	Time to Perform Task (Minutes)
A. Place circuit frame on jig.		.18	J. Place and attach keyboard to inner frame.	I	.18
B. Place Circuit #1 into frame.	A	.12			
C. Place Circuit #2 into frame.	A	.32	K. Place and attach top body of calculator to inner frame.	J	.36
D. Place Circuit #3 into frame.	A	.45			
E. Attach circuits to frame.	B,C,D	.51	L. Place and attach power assembly to inner frame.	J	.42
F. Solder circuit connections to central circuit control.	E	.55	M. Place and attach bottom body of calculator to inner frame.	K,L	.48
G. Place circuit assembly in calculator inner frame.	F	.38	N. Test circuit integrity.	M	.30
H. Attach circuit assembly to calculator inner frame.	G	.42	O. Place calculator and printed matter in box.	N	.39
I. Place and attach display to inner frame.	H	.30		Total	5.36

The parts used in this assembly line are supplied by materials handling personnel to parts bins used in each task. The assemblies are moved along by belt conveyors between work stations. If 540 calculators must be produced by this assembly line per hour: **a.** Compute the cycle time per calculator in minutes. **b.** Compute the theoretical minimum number of employees required. **c.** How would you combine the tasks into workers' jobs to minimize operator idle time? Evaluate your proposal.

Solution

a. Compute the cycle time per calculator:

$$\text{Cycle time} = \frac{\text{Productive time/hour*}}{\text{Demand/hour}} = \frac{54 \text{ minutes/hour}}{540 \text{ calculators/hour}} = .100 \text{ minute/calculator}$$

b. Compute the theoretical minimum number of employees:

$$\begin{aligned} \text{Theoretical minimum} \\ \text{number of} \\ \text{employees} \end{aligned} = \frac{\text{Time for all tasks} \times \text{Demand per hour}}{\text{Productive time per hour}}$$

$$= \frac{5.36 \text{ employee-minutes/calculator} \times 540 \text{ calculators/hour}}{54 \text{ minutes/hour}}$$

$$= 53.60 \text{ employees}$$

c. Balance the line:

1. First, group the tasks according to compatibility of tasks: machines, labor skill, materials, precedence relationships, etc. (You may assume that this part of the analysis has already been performed. The task compatibility groupings have been determined as shown below.)

Group I:	Task A	Group IV:	Task I, J
Group II:	Tasks B, C, D	Group V:	Tasks K, L
Group III:	Tasks E, F, G, H	Group VI:	Tasks M, N
		Group VII:	Task O

These task groupings constrain the tasks that can feasibly be combined into work stations. For example, Tasks C and D could be combined into one work station whereas Tasks D and E could not.

2. Next, draw a network diagram of precedence relationships:

---

* An average of 6 minutes per hour in this example is not productive because of lunch, personal time, machine breakdown, and start-up and shut-down time.

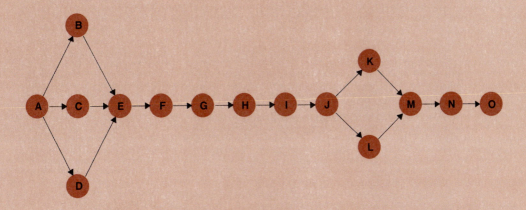

3. Next, combine tasks into workers' jobs within compatibility groups to minimize idle time. This is done by attempting to combine tasks that have combined processing times approaching but not exceeding multiples of the .100-minute cycle time (for example, .100, .200, .300). In the accompanying table we are searching for a combination of tasks so that the least number of employees can perform all of the tasks while strictly following the sequence of tasks (D must follow C, C must follow B, and so on). The *incremental utilization heuristic* is used in this example to group the tasks into workers' jobs. In this method tasks are

(1) Compatibility Group	(2) Work Station	(3) Tasks	(4) Employee- Minutes/Calculator	(5) Equivalent Number of Employees Working [(4) ÷ Cycle Time]	(6) Actual Number of Employees Required	(7) Utilization of Employees [(5) ÷ (6)]
I	1	A	.18	1.8	2	
II	2	B	.12	1.2	2	60.0%
	2	B,C	.12 + .32 = .44	4.4	5	88.0
	2	B,C,D	.12 + .32 + .45 = .89	8.9	9	98.9
III	3	E	.51	5.1	6	85.0
	3	E,F	.51 + .55 = 1.06	10.6	11	96.4
	3	E,F,G	.51 + .55 + .38 = 1.44	14.4	15	96.0
	4	G	.38	3.8	4	95.0
	4	G,H	.38 + .42 = .80	8.0	8	100.0
IV	5	I	.30	3.0	3	100.0
	6	J	.18	1.8	2	90.0
V	7	K	.36	3.6	4	90.0
	7	K,L	.36 + .42 = .78	7.8	8	97.5
VI	8	M	.48	4.8	5	96.0
	8	M,N	.48 + .30 = .78	7.8	8	97.5
VII	9	O	.39	3.9	4	

Total   55

combined in sequence until the utilization of the work station (equivalent number of employees working divided by the actual number of employees required) is observed to fall, and then a new combination is started. Look at Compatibility Group III and note that we first consider Task E alone (5.1 ÷ 6 or 85.0 percent); next we consider Tasks E and F as a combination (10.6 ÷ 11 or 96.4 percent), and then Tasks E, F, and G (14.4 ÷ 15 or 96.0 percent). Because the Task E and Task F combination has the highest utilization before the utilization is observed to fall, the other two alternatives are crossed out and Task E and Task F are performed by 11 workers at the third work station.

4. Draw a schematic of the work stations on an assembly line:

Compatibility Group	I	II	III		IV		V	VI	VII	
Tasks in Work Stations	A	B, C, D	E, F	G, H	I	J	K, L	M, N	O	
Work Stations	①→	②→	③→	④→	⑤→	⑥→	⑦→	⑧→	⑨→	
Actual Number of Employees Required	2	9	11	8	3	2	8	8	4	55 Total
Equivalent Number of Employees Working	1.8	8.9	10.6	8.0	3.0	1.8	7.8	7.8	3.9	53.6 Total
Equivalent Number of Employees Idle	.2	.1	.4	0	0	.2	.2	.2	.1	1.4 Total

5. Next, compute the efficiency of your proposal:

$$\text{Efficiency} = \frac{\text{Equivalent number of employees working}}{\text{Total actual number of employees required}} = \frac{53.6}{55} = .975 \text{ or } 97.5 \text{ percent}$$

Several methods exist for combining tasks within compatibility groups. Although linear programming, dynamic programming, and other optimal models have been used to determine these combinations, other nonoptimal methods are perhaps more commonly used.

Total Enumeration This method considers all of the possible combinations of tasks within a compatibility group. In Compatibility Group II in Example 13.4, for instance, four combinations are possible while strictly following the sequence of tasks (BCD, B-CD, BC-D, and B-C-D). The relationship between the number of possible combinations (X) and the number of tasks (n) is:

$$X = 2^{(n-1)}$$

Although this method can result in optimal solutions when n is very small, it becomes impractical as the number of tasks in a compatibility group increases because the number of possible combinations increases dramatically. For example, 25 tasks within a compatibility group results in 16,777,216 combinations. If we do not restrict the sequence of the tasks, then the number of combinations increases at an even faster rate ($X = n!$). This method is of little value in most realistic line-balancing problems.

Traditional Search Method The *traditional search method* involves trying certain combinations of tasks that "seem to make sense." For example, in Compatibility Group II in Example 13.4, Tasks B, C, and D are combined because no other combination results in fewer than nine employees required at the work station. We arrive at this combination by searching among the possible combinations for those that have combined task times approaching but not exceeding multiples of the cycle time. In this approach tasks that are prime candidates for combination are those that have task times just barely exceeding a multiple of the cycle time, as, for instance, .12, .32, and .45 in Example 13.4. By combining such tasks, we can develop combined task times that more closely approach multiples of the cycle time; for example, .12 + .32 + .45 = .89, which is very close to 9 times the .100 cycle time. The reason we want to combine tasks in this way is that as long as the combined task time is only slightly less than a multiple of the cycle time, the desired demand per hour can be achieved at a cost of only a little idle time. This principle is demonstrated in the examples of Table 13.5.

Table 13.5
Examples of Combined Task Times at a Work Station

(1) Combined Task Time within a Compatibility Group (Minutes)	(2) Equivalent Number of Employees Working to Produce 540 Calculators per Hour [(1) ÷ .100]	(3) Actual Number of Employees Required (Whole or Fractional Multiples of the Cycle Time)	(4) Equivalent Number of Employees Idle [(3) − (2)]
.300	3.00	3	0
.301	3.01	4	.99
.350	3.50	4	.50
.399	3.99	4	.01
.400	4.00	4	0
.410	4.10	5	.90

Note: Cycle time = .100 minute, 540 calculators per hour are demanded, and 6 minutes per hour are unproductive.

In these examples we can see that as the combined task time approaches a multiple of the cycle time, the equivalent number of employees idle decreases. When the combined task time exactly equals a multiple, then there is no built-in idleness. For example, when the combined task time is .300 minute, if three employees all perform the tasks at a work station, each employee will complete the combination of tasks in .300 minute, thus, one unit will be produced in an average of .100 minute. If the combined task time at the work station were .301 minute, three employees could not produce 540 units per hour and four employees would be needed to produce four units every .301 minute for an average of .075 minute per unit. This rate would result in a production rate of 720 units per hour (54 minutes per hour ÷ .075 minute per unit = 720 units per hour). Because upstream and downstream work stations are being designed to produce only 540 units per hour, the four employees would actually work only 40.5 minutes per hour and produce the required 540 units per hour (.075 minute per unit × 540 units per hour = 40.5 minutes per hour). This discussion reflects the thinking involved in traditional search methods.

Heuristic Methods In Example 13.4 we used a simple heuristic, the *incremental utilization heuristic,* to combine tasks within compatibility groups. Such heuristic methods are simple rules that when applied are not necessarily optimal (result in the fewest number of employees on the assembly line), but they are simple to use and they usually give very good results that are often optimal or nearly optimal. Several of these heuristics have been developed. Among these are the *largest number of following tasks* and *longest-operation time* rules. See the Buxey and Chase articles in the Selected Bibliography at the end of this chapter for a discussion of these and other heuristics.

There is some limit to the number of tasks that can be combined into workers' jobs. Assume, for example, that all of the tasks in Example 13.4 were combined into one super job. Superficially, it would appear that this combination requires only 54 employees ($5.36 \div .100 = 53.6$ or 54), which is one less than the solution of this example. This result is invalid because task times, under most circumstances, are based on some degree of labor specialization (jobs are broken down into small specialized tasks). Therefore, there exists, in addition to the compatibility limitations discussed earlier, some practical limit to the number of tasks that can be combined before the task times become invalid.

Example 13.4 is a line-balancing problem of only a few tasks. As the number of tasks increases, the ability of manual calculations to effectively analyze these problems diminishes. Computers are typically used to perform these line-balancing calculations on large problems.

Customer Service Layouts

The customer waiting lines at grocery stores that we have become accustomed to in recent years are not a necessary part of buying groceries. We wait in these lines either because managers have not hired enough checkout employees or because they do not have enough checkout counters.

More personnel can be hired to staff checkout counters and an abundance of checkout counters can be constructed, but these actions result in increased costs. Fewer checkout counters cost less, but customers must then wait in lines. If we have to wait in line too long, we may not come back to a particular store and this results in a cost to the store's management. Either too many or too few checkout counters can therefore become exorbitantly expensive. A balance must obviously be struck.

One compromise involves constructing an abundance of checkout counters but staffing them only as required when long waiting lines accumulate. When fewer checkout counters are needed, employees are used in other duties in the store or are on call at home. When other duties or being on call are both impractical, more precision is required in estimating the optimum number of staffed checkout counters if the costs of having too many and too few checkout counters are to be balanced.

Queuing theory, or waiting line theory, has evolved to assist managers in these kinds of questions: How many customer service channels should be staffed during each time period of the day? How much time will customers wait, on the average, if we staff a particular number of customer service channels during each time period of the day? How many customers will be in waiting lines on the average if we staff a particular number of customer service channels during each time period of the day?

And how much maximum room will we need for waiting lines if we staff a particular number of customer service channels?

These and other related questions can be important in customer oriented layouts and they can be analyzed by queuing theory, which is treated in the Supplement to Chapter 13. Standard formulas for manual computations, computer simulation, and standard computer programs can be applied to these problems.

Summary

Facility layout means planning the physical arrangement of all the elements of production in and around buildings. Many factors, such as material flows, customer processing, nature of materials, capacity, productive processes and technology, employee and service requirements, building and site constraints, and flexibility requirements affect the design of particular layouts. But among these factors, material flows dominate the design of layouts of facilities that process tangible goods; and customer processing dominates the design of layouts of service facilities.

Facilities that process tangible goods utilize product, process, or fixed position layouts. Materials handling, minimizing the number of employees, and minimizing employee idle time on assembly lines become the primary analysis bases for product layouts. Process layouts are typically analyzed to minimize the total product/service travel through alternative proposed layouts.

Customer oriented layouts are commonly analyzed to determine the optimum number of customer service channels during each time period of the day. Alternatively, if the number of customer service channels is set, the average number of waiting customers, the average waiting time per customer, and the maximum waiting space can be calculated. The basis of these analyses is called queuing theory or waiting line theory.

Review and Discussion Questions

1. Define *facility layout*.
2. Name five factors affecting manufacturing facility layouts.
3. Among the many factors that affect facility layout, what factor dominates the layout of facilities that process tangible goods?
4. Among the many factors that affect facility layout, what factor dominates the layout of service facilities?
5. Name four principles of materials handling.
6. Name five types of materials handling devices.
7. Name and describe three types of layouts for facilities that process tangible goods.
8. Compare and contrast the layout of a savings and loan with the layout of a hospital. How are they alike and how are they different?
9. Name five bases for combining tasks into work stations.

Problems

1. The business college at Upstate University is developing a layout of its classrooms. The eight classrooms are on a single floor of the proposed new building and the architect is planning to adapt the building configuration to the classroom layout. However, it is desirable to have a rectangular exterior building configuration. The layout should minimize the distance traveled between rooms by students. Here are the estimated student movements per day among the classrooms and the area requirements of the classrooms:

Number of Students Moving Daily between Classrooms

Classroom \ Classroom	1	2	3	4	5	6	7	8
1	—	400	0	400	400	0	400	0
2		—	200	0	0	400	0	100
3			—	0	0	100	100	300
4				—	400	0	400	200
5					—	0	400	200
6						—	0	200
7							—	0
8								

Classrooms	Required Area (Square Feet)
3 and 6	1,750
2 and 8	2,000
4, 5, and 7	2,500
1	5,000

An initial schematic diagram for the arrangement of the classrooms is shown below:

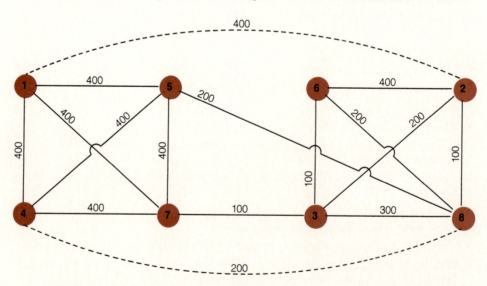

a. Use operations sequence analysis to develop a "best" schematic diagram for the classrooms. b. Use block diagram analysis to develop a layout for the classrooms.

2. The ABC Food Market has just purchased a building at a new location. This building has 80,000 square feet of floor space, measures 200 feet by 400 feet, and has ample parking. ABC's management has requested help from a local consultant to assist them in designing a facility layout for this store. The consultant is given this information:

Average Daily Customer Traffic between Departments

Department \ Department	A	B	C	D	E	F	G	H
A	—	2,000	1,000	0	500	1,500	200	300
B			500	1,000	500	500	0	500
C				500	1,500	200	0	300
D					0	500	500	500
E						0	500	0
F							500	1,000
G								500
H								

Department	Required Area (Square Feet)	Department	Required Area (Square Feet)	Department	Required Area (Square Feet)
A	5,000	D	8,000	G	16,000
B	5,000	E	4,000	H	12,000
C	10,000	F	20,000		

ABC's management has further indicated that the consultant could arrange the departments in any configuration within the building and that present entrances and exits could be modified to meet the needs of the layout. The firm wishes to minimize customer travel among departments. **a.** Develop an initial schematic diagram for the arrangement of departments within the food store facility. **b.** Use operations sequence analysis to develop a "best" schematic diagram for the departments. **c.** Use block diagram analysis to develop a final departmental layout. (Note: The areas for departments listed earlier include provisions for aisles.)

3. A warehouse processes six products monthly: a, b, c, d, e, and f. Two alternative layouts for the warehouse are being considered, A and B:

The products, their monthly production levels, their sequence of processing, and distances between processing departments are shown in the following table:

Product	Number of Products Processed/Month	Product Sequences	Sequence Distances (Feet)	
			Layout A	Layout B
a	1,000	R–1–S	70	50
b	3,000	R–2–S	70	50
c	2,000	R–3–S	50	30
d	3,000	R–4–S	50	30
e	2,000	R–5–S	30	70
f	2,000	R–6–S	30	70

Which layout alternative minimizes the monthly warehouse travel? (Use load-distance analysis.)

4. A manufacturing plant is adding a new wing to its building to manufacture a new product line with five models: a, b, c, d, and e. Two layout alternatives are shown below. The new wing's product models, their movements through six departments, and the distances between departments are also shown.
Which layout alternative minimizes the monthly product travel through the proposed new wing? (Use load-distance analysis.)

Layout A

1	2	3
4	5	6

Layout B

4	1	3
2	5	6

Product Model	Product Model Processing Sequence	Number of Products Processed per Month	Product Model Movements	Distances between Departments (Feet)	
				Layout A	Layout B
a	1–2–3	2,000	1–2	15	25
b	4–5–6	2,000	1–5	30	10
c	1–5–6	3,000	2–3	15	35
d	2–5–6	1,000	2–4	20	10
e	2–4–3	3,000	2–5	15	15
			3–4	35	25
			4–5	15	25
			5–6	10	10

5. In Problem 4 the industrial engineers have just come up with some additional information—the materials handling cost for each product. The cost of moving a single unit of each product between departments in the proposed wing differs because of the weight, bulkiness, and fragility of the products. These materials handling costs increase as the distance moved increases:

Product Model	Materials Handling Cost per Unit per Foot Moved	Product Model	Materials Handling Cost per Unit per Foot Moved
a	$.005	d	$.010
b	.003	e	.007
c	.001		

Which layout, Layout A or Layout B, minimizes the monthly materials handling cost for the proposed wing?

6. The Stratofit Manufacturing Company has just purchased an abandoned warehouse and plans to expand its manufacturing operations into this building. Two alternative layouts are being evaluated, Layout 1 and Layout 2, shown below. The company is a

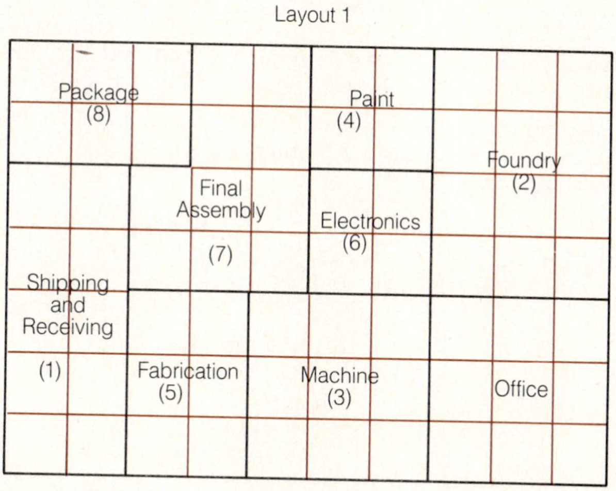

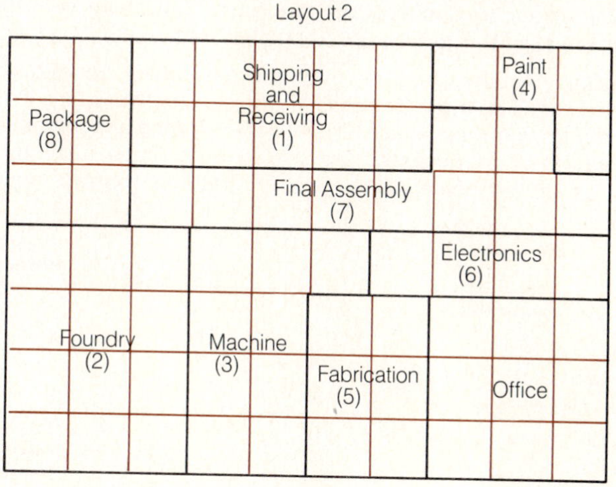

Layout 1

Layout 2

high-volume manufacturer of patented electromechanical devices used in several different industries. Because Stratofit's monthly volume is so high, the layout that is selected should minimize monthly product travel so that the cost and confusion of unnecessary materials handling is avoided. The two layouts shown are set on a 2,500-square-foot matrix background (in other words, the background squares are 50 × 50 feet), and products are assumed to travel in straight lines between centers of departments. Stratofit manufactures eight products at this location. The product model codes, the sequence of processing products through manufacturing departments, and the estimated monthly production of each model are shown below:

Product Model Code	Processing Sequence	Monthly Production (Units)	Product Model Code	Processing Sequence	Monthly Production (Units)
5555	1–2–3–4–7–1	5,000	8960	1–5–7–8–1	2,000
5285	1–3–5–7–8–1	5,000	9110	1–7–4–6–1	6,000
9560	1–5–6–8–1	10,000	2955	1–2–3–8–1	3,000
9999	1–2–3–5–4–7–1	4,000	6666	1–6–4–7–1	5,000

a. Use load-distance analysis to determine which layout should be adopted by Stratofit. **b.** Compare the two layouts; which one do you prefer? Why?

7. A firm is planning to set up an assembly line to assemble 300 units per hour, and 50 minutes per hour are productive. The time to perform each task and the tasks that must precede each task are:

Task	Tasks That Immediately Precede	Time to Perform Task (Minutes)	Task	Tasks That Immediately Precede	Time to Perform Task (Minutes)
A	—	.69	F	B	1.10
B	A	.55	G	C,D,E	.75
C	B	.21	H	G,F	.43
D	B	.59	I	H	.29
E	B	.70			

a. Draw a network diagram of precedence relationships. **b.** Compute the cycle time per unit in minutes. **c.** Compute the theoretical minimum number of assembly line employees required to produce 300 units per hour.

8. The Bulk Mail Specialty Company prepares, assembles, and mails advertising packages for customers on a contract basis. One such contract has just been signed and Bulk's production planner, Jesse Brown, is developing a layout for the assembly line. These tasks, their predecessor tasks, and task times have been identified and estimated as shown below. Jesse knows that the contract specifies that 10,000

Task	Tasks That Immediately Precede	Task Times (Minutes/Mailer)
A. Inspect materials for quality	—	.45
B. Prepare kits for assembly	A	.10
C. Get and fold industrial circular	B	.15
D. Assemble and glue envelopes	B	.22
E. Get and fold retail circular	B	.19
F. Put list of industrial outlets in circular	C	.31
G. Attach address to industrial envelope	D	.11
H. Attach address to retail envelope	D	.16
I. Put list of wholesale outlets in retail circulars	E	.20
J. Seal industrial circular into envelope	F,G	.41
K. Preassemble retail package into envelope	H,I	.10
L. Prepare plastic sleeve to fit over retail envelope	I	.05
M. Seal entire retail package into plastic sleeve	K,L	.19
N. Process addressed industrial and retail mailers through postage machine	J,M	.26
O. Combine mailers into bulk mail packages	N	.18

mailers must be processed in five working days, Bulk Mail Specialty works only one 8-hour shift per day, and employees are allowed two 15-minute coffee breaks per shift. **a.** Draw a network diagram of the precedence relationships. **b.** Compute the cycle time in minutes. **c.** Compute the theoretical number of assembly line employees required for the contract.

9. Pump Inc., a medical research laboratory, produces a standard heart substitute device on an assembly line basis. Six basic tasks are performed along an assembly line. The time to perform each task and the tasks that must immediately precede each task are:

Task	Tasks That Immediately Precede	Time to Perform Task (Minutes)	Task	Tasks That Immediately Precede	Time to Perform Task (Minutes)
A	———	5.40	E	D	17.10
B	A	3.20	F	E	12.80
C	———	1.50		Total	42.80
D	B,C	2.80			

If ten pumps per hour must be produced by the assembly line, 45 minutes per hour are productive, and all of the tasks are compatible except for precedence relationships and a maximum of two tasks can be combined into each work station: **a.** Draw a network diagram of the precedence relationships. **b.** Compute the cycle time per pump in minutes. **c.** Compute the theoretical minimum number of assembly line employees required. **d.** Combine the tasks into workers' jobs to minimize employee idle time by using the traditional search method and the incremental utilization heuristic. Evaluate your proposal.

10. Lectro Inc. assembles alternators for automobiles. Ten basic tasks must be performed along the assembly line. The time to perform each task and the tasks that must immediately precede each task are:

Task	Tasks That Immediately Precede	Time to Perform Task (Minutes)	Task	Tasks That Immediately Precede	Time to Perform Task (Minutes)
A	———	.10	G	D,F	.30
B	A	.15	H	G	.50
C	A	.20	I	H	.60
D	B,C	.30	J	I	.50
E	———	.40		Total	3.45
F	E	.40			

If 400 alternators per hour must be produced by the assembly line, 50 minutes per hour are productive, and all of the tasks are compatible except for precedence relationships and a maximum of three tasks can be combined into each work station: **a.** Draw a network diagram of the precedence relationships. **b.** Compute the cycle time per alternator in minutes. **c.** Compute the theoretical minimum number of assembly line employees required. **d.** Combine the tasks into workers' jobs to minimize employee idle time by using the traditional search method and the incremental utilization heuristic. Evaluate your proposal.

11. Serve Fast Inc., a fast-food restaurant in Los Angeles, will soon open its second store. Serve Fast's manager is now planning how to arrange the kitchen and food products

assembly area in the new store. Of utmost importance in this layout is the arrangement of tasks into employee work stations so that a minimum amount of employee idle time is experienced. Toward this goal the manager wants to develop a line-balancing analysis. The time to perform each task in constructing Serve Fast's principal product, the *Best Burger,* and the tasks that must immediately precede each task are:

Task	Tasks That Immediately Precede	Time to Perform Task (Minutes)	Task	Tasks That Immediately Precede	Time to Perform Task (Minutes)
A	—	.19	H	—	3.05
B	—	.15	I	—	.50
C	—	.20	J	H,I,G	.60
D	—	.10	K	J	.30
E	A,B	.23	L	K	.25
F	C,D	.20		Total	6.05
G	E,F	.28			

Two hundred burgers per hour must be prepared by the crew, 50 minutes per hour are productive, and these groups of compatible tasks have been established:

Compatibility Group	Tasks	Compatibility Group	Tasks
I	A,B,C,D	III	H,I,J
II	E,F,G	IV	K,L

a. Draw a network diagram of the precedence relationships. **b.** Compute the cycle time per burger in minutes. **c.** Compute the theoretical minimum number of assembly line employees required. **d.** How would you combine tasks into workers' jobs to minimize employee idle time? Use both the traditional search method and the incremental utilization heuristic. Evaluate your proposal.

12. The Suitcase Manufacturing and Export Company has just received an order for 1,500,000 leather briefcases from a large European distributor to be delivered over a period of 300 workdays. Because this product has never been produced before by the company, an assembly line must be planned to produce the order on a basis of one 8-hour shift per day. The company's employees are allowed to take two 15-minute coffee breaks per shift, they take 15 minutes per shift to clean up their immediate work area, and they lose an average of about 20 minutes per shift because of machinery breakdowns or material delivery delays. Suitcase's staff has identified these tasks and their predecessor tasks, and has estimated the time required for each task as shown in the table on the next page. Four production departments will do the work on the cases: Metals, Woods, Leather, and Final Assembly. The union contract does not allow workers to do work outside their own departments (for example, an individual employee could not do both leather and wood work), but they are allowed to do any work within their own production departments. **a.** Draw a network diagram of the precedence relationships. **b.** Compute the cycle time per case in minutes. **c.** Compute the theoretical minimum number of assembly line employees required. **d.** How would you combine tasks into workers' jobs to minimize employee idle time? (Use the incremental utilization heuristic.) Evaluate your proposal.

Task	Tasks That Immediately Precede	Task Times (Minutes/Case)
A. Process hide through cleaning bath	——	2.05
B. Cut wood components according to templates	——	.65
C. Process metal hinges through stamping operation	——	.45
D. Process metal closure components through stamping operation	——	.30
E. Process hide through tanning process	A	3.60
F. Trim wood components to dimension	B	.41
G. Tumble metal hinges to finish edges	C	.22
H. Tumble metal closure components to finish	D	.41
I. Cut hide into case blanks	E	2.15
J. Attach wood components into frame subassembly	F	1.02
K. Put metal hinges through plating process	G	.70
L. Put metal closure components through plating process	H	.80
M. Feather edges and sew corners of leather components	I	2.71
N. Rout out attaching grooves in wood frame subassembly	J	.79
O. Dye leather hide subassemblies	M	3.90
P. Bend metal handle and attach brackets	——	.61
Q. Assemble hinges, frame, closures, handle, and leather subassemblies	K,L,N,O,P	4.10
R. Assemble inner liner and shrink to case	Q	.71
S. Attach name plate	R	.30
T. Package for shipment	S	.21

Case
Acute Medical Clinic Layout

The Acute Medical Clinic needs to expand and has just purchased an existing one-story office building with 10,000 square feet of floor space. Acute is now developing plans for remodeling and equipping the building to fit its medical processes. A consultant has been hired to analyze the clinic's processes and recommend a layout for its building. The consultant has presented Acute with two alternative plans, Layout α and Layout β.

Acute's staff must now decide between the two layouts. As a first step, they have agreed on closeness ratings for locating departments close to one another. On a scale from 1 (not important) to 10 (very important), the closeness ratings are as shown in the accompanying table. These closeness ratings reflect many factors that make it desirable to locate departments adjacent to one another. Among these factors are the number of patients expected to flow between departments per month, the need to transport patients quickly between departments, the need to conserve doctors' time, the acuteness of the type of cases that flow between departments, the amount of materials that flow between departments, and the usual sequence of processing patients through the building.

The two layouts are set on a matrix background where one square represents 100 square feet. Acute's staff wants to minimize the total distance between departments as weighted by the

Layout β

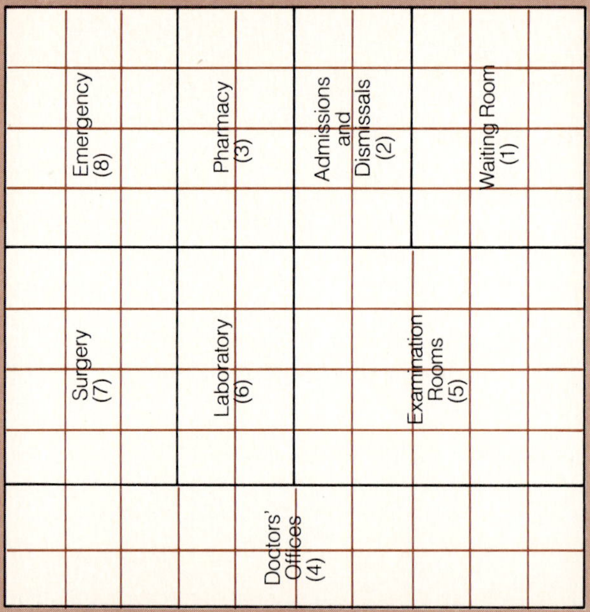

Doctors' Offices (4)							
Examination Rooms (5)				Surgery (7)			
	Laboratory (6)						
	Admissions and Dismissals (2)			Emergency (8)			
Pharmacy (3)			Waiting Room (1)				

Layout α

Emergency (8)							
Pharmacy (3)		Surgery (7)					
Admissions and Dismissals (2)	Laboratory (6)						
Waiting Room (1)	Examination Rooms (5)						
	Doctors' Offices (4)						

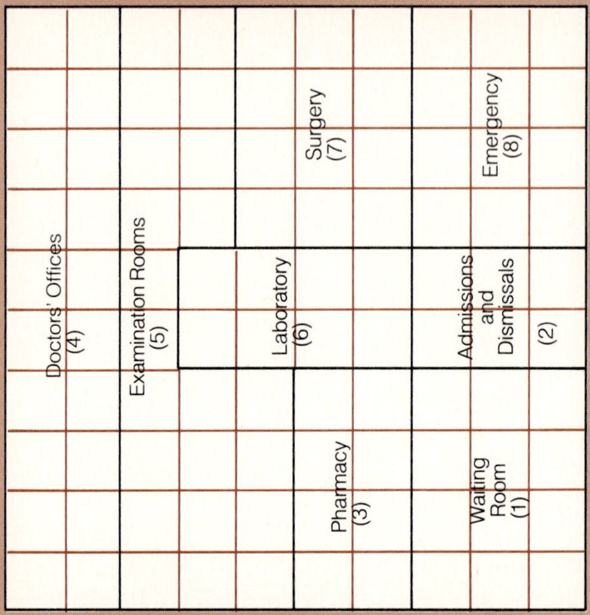

Department \ Department	Waiting Room (1)	Admissions and Dismissals (2)	Pharmacy (3)	Doctors' Offices (4)	Examination Rooms (5)	Laboratory (6)	Surgery (7)	Emergency Room (8)
1. Waiting Room	——	8	8	1	5	4	1	6
2. Admissions and Dismissals		——	8	3	5	4	1	7
3. Pharmacy			——	3	5	4	3	5
4. Doctors' Offices				——	9	2	6	3
5. Examination Rooms					——	5	6	7
6. Laboratory						——	9	8
7. Surgery							——	10

closeness ratings. In other words, the distance between two departments would be multiplied by the closeness rating for the pair to obtain a closeness-weighted distance. The distance between departments is assumed to be measured by straight lines that connect the approximate centers of the departments. The total closeness-weighted distance for the building would include the closeness-weighted distances for all possible combinations of pairs of departments:

$$\text{Number of combinations} = \sum_{i=1}^{n} (n - i), \text{ where n is the number of departments}$$

or 28 in this problem.

Assignment

1. Analyze the two layouts to determine which one minimizes the total closeness-weighted distance.

2. What changes in these layouts are suggested by your analysis?

3. Discuss how you would change the approach of this analysis in order to make it more realistic.

Selected Bibliography

Buffa, E. S., G. C. Armour, and T. E. Vollmann. "Allocating Facilities with CRAFT." *Harvard Business Review* 42(March–April 1964): 136–158.

Buffa, E. S., and William H. Taubert. *Production and Inventory Systems: Planning and Control.* Homewood, IL: Richard D. Irwin, 1972, 303–366.

Buxey, G. M., N. P. Slack, and R. Wild. "Production Flow System Design—A Review." *AIIE Transactions* 5, no. 1(March 1973): 37–48.

Chase, R. B. "Survey of Paced Assembly Lines." *Industrial Engineering* 6, no. 2(February 1974): 14–18.

Francis, R. L., and J. A. White. *Facility Layout and Location: An Analytical Approach.* Englewood Cliffs, NJ: Prentice-Hall, 1974.

Ignall, Edward J. "A Review of Assembly Line Balancing." *Journal of Industrial Engineering* 16(July–August 1965): 244–254.

Lee, Robert S., and James M. Moore. "CORELAP—Computerized Relationship Layout Planning." *Journal of Industrial Engineering* 18(March 1967): 195–200.

Maynard, H. B. *Industrial Engineering Handbook.* New York: McGraw-Hill, 1963.

Moore, James M. *Plant Layout and Design.* New York: Macmillan, 1962.

Muther, Richard. *Practical Plant Layout.* New York: McGraw-Hill, 1955.

Muther, Richard, and John D. Wheeler. "Simplified Systematic Layout Planning." *Factory* 120(August, September, and October 1962): 68–77, 111–119, 101–113.

Reed, R. *Plant Location, Layout, and Maintenance.* Homewood, IL: Richard D. Irwin, 1967.

Waiting Lines and Computer Simulation

Waiting Lines

Numerous situations occur in POM where waiting lines form while services are being performed. Here are just a few instances:

1. Computer programs are waiting to be processed at a computer center.
2. Workers are waiting to "clock in" at the company gate.
3. Customers are waiting to be served at a bank teller's window.
4. Parts are waiting to be processed at a manufacturing operation.
5. Machines are waiting to be repaired at a maintenance shop.
6. Customers are waiting to buy tickets at an airline ticket counter.
7. Trucks are waiting to unload their cargo at an unloading dock.

In these and other waiting line situations, managers don't necessarily plan for waiting lines to form; rather, waiting lines are an inevitable characteristic of these operations.

What causes waiting lines to form? When people, parts, machines, computer programs, or trucks are arriving at service centers irregularly and the capacity of service centers cannot be expanded or contracted to exactly meet the needs of these arrivals, waiting lines will always result. Even if managers *could* expand service center capacities to exactly meet the demands of these irregular arrivals, the pattern of this irregularity is often so unpredictable that managers can't respond fast enough to expand service center capacities; therefore, waiting lines form.

To further complicate the analysis of waiting lines, we don't usually know with certainty how long it will take to service each arrival. In banks, for example, some customers may take only about a minute to be served because they may only want to cash a small check or make a small deposit. Other customers may require 15 to 20 minutes to service, particularly if they have a whole moneybag full of commercial transactions to complete.

Waiting lines typically have these characteristics:

1. Arrival patterns are irregular or random. Although we may know the average number of arrivals per time period to expect, we don't know for certain how many will arrive in any specific time period.

2. Service times vary between arrivals. Although we may know the average time necessary to service an arrival, we don't know in advance how long it will take to service each arrival.

Generally speaking, practical managers plan service center capacities to meet the average condition plus a safety factor. For example, if a bank manager knows that about 50 customers per hour on the average must be serviced at teller windows, enough tellers, cash, supplies, open teller windows, and waiting areas would be provided to service about 70 average customers per hour. This safety factor approach is based upon the fact that, although 50 customers per hour arrive on the average, as few as 20 or as many as 90 customers can arrive in any one hour just through chance. Because arrival patterns are irregular or random, 20 minutes may go by without *any* customers and then 15 customers may flood through the doors.

Although the practical safety factor approach described above is observed in POM practice, more precise analysis techniques have evolved that provide managers with better information to plan waiting line service center capacities. The first recorded systematic study of waiting lines was performed by A. K. Erlang, a Danish mathematician working for the Copenhagen Telephone Company in 1917. Erlang's early work has been methodically expanded until today much is known about the behavior of waiting lines.

This body of knowledge about waiting lines is often referred to today as *queuing theory,* and waiting lines are called *queues.* Before we examine the concepts of queuing theory and its analysis techniques, study the terminology of queues in Table 13S.1.

Figure 13S.1 shows four queuing system structures: single channel, single phase; multichannel, single phase; single channel, multiphase; and multichannel, multiphase. A *single channel, single phase system* has only one waiting line, or channel, and the service is performed in only one step, or phase. Single booth theater ticket

Table 13S.1
Terminology of Queues

1. **Arrival**—One unit of the arrival rate distribution. Occurs when one person, machine, part, etc. arrives and demands service. Each of the units may continue to be called an arrival while in the service system.
2. **Arrival Rate** (λ)—The rate at which things or persons arrive, in arrivals per unit of time (e.g., persons per hour). Arrival rate is usually normal or Poisson distributed.
3. **Channels**—The number of waiting lines in a service system. A single channel system would have only one line and a multichannel system would have two or more waiting lines.
4. **Queue**—A waiting line.
5. **Queue Discipline**—The rules that determine the order in which arrivals are sequenced through service systems. Some common queue disciplines are first-come first-served; shortest processing time; critical ratio; and most valuable customers served first.
6. **Queue Length**—The number of arrivals waiting to be serviced.
7. **Service Phases**—The number of steps in servicing arrivals. A single phase service system would have only one service step, whereas a multiphase system would have two or more service steps.
8. **Service Rate** (μ)—The rate that arrivals are serviced, in arrivals per unit of time (e.g., per hour). Service rate is usually constant, normal, or Poisson distributed.
9. **Service Time** ($1/\mu$)—The time it takes to service an arrival, expressed in minutes (or hours, days, etc.) per arrival. The measure does not include waiting time.
10. **Time in System**—The total time that arrivals spend in system, including both waiting time and service time.
11. **Utilization** (P_n)—The degree to which any part of a service system is occupied by an arrival. Usually expressed as the probability that n arrivals are in the system.
12. **Waiting Time**—The amount of time an arrival spends in queue.

Figure 13S.1
Queuing System Structures

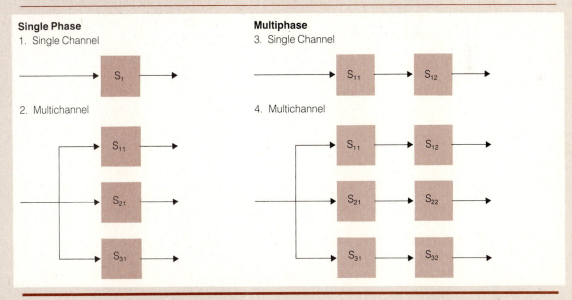

sales, machines waiting to be repaired at a repair center, and parts waiting to be processed at a manufacturing operation are examples of single channel, single phase queuing systems.

When more than one waiting line can form, as in checkout counters at supermarkets, multichannel queuing systems result. As the service performed becomes more complex, as in the case of two or more downstream manufacturing operations, more than one step is needed in performing services. These are referred to as *multiphase queuing systems.*

Real world waiting line situations in POM seldom fit the neat structures displayed in Figure 13S.1. Rather, real queuing systems tend to be combinations and hybrids of these structures. The fuzziness and complexity of real queuing systems have perhaps been the greatest obstacles to straightforward mathematical analysis of waiting lines in practice. As an introduction to queuing theory, we shall examine here some simple models that have been used to analyze waiting lines in POM. But first, what information do managers usually need to know about waiting lines?

1. Given that a service system has been designed to service a certain number of arrivals per hour on the average:
    a. What is the average number of units waiting?
    b. What is the average time each unit spends waiting?
    c. What is the average number of units waiting and being served — in other words, in the system?
    d. What is the average time each unit spends in the system?
    e. What percentage of time is the system empty?
    f. What is the probability that *n* units will be in the system?

2. Or, given that management sets policies that limit the average number of units waiting, average number of units in the system, average time each unit waits, average time each unit is in the system, and the percentage of time that the system is empty, what service center capacity is necessary to comply with these management policies?

This information can be deduced about a few waiting line situations in POM. We shall present here four models that have been used to study particular queuing systems. Tables 13S.2 and 13S.3 show the characteristics of these queuing systems, the formulas for analyzing them, and the definitions of variables that are introduced.

Table 13S.2
Definitions of Variables for Queuing Models

---

1. λ (lambda) = Arrival rate — average number of arrivals per unit of time

2. μ (mu) = Service rate — average number of arrivals that can be serviced per unit of time

3. n = Number of arrivals in the system

4. $\bar{n}_l$ = Average number of arrivals waiting

5. $\bar{n}_s$ = Average number of arrivals in the system

6. N = Number of channels in multichannel system

7. P_n = Probability that there are exactly n arrivals in the system

8. Q = Maximum number of arrivals that can be in the system (sum of arrivals being served and waiting)

9. $\bar{t}_l$ = Average time arrivals wait

10. $\bar{t}_s$ = Average time arrivals are in the system

Table 13S.3
Four Queuing Models and Their Formulas

Model Number	Characteristics of Service System			Examples	Formulas
	Number of Channels	Service Rate Distribution	Maximum Queue Length		
1	Single	Poisson	Unlimited	Single booth theater ticket sales, maintenance repair center	$\bar{n}_l = \dfrac{\lambda^2}{\mu(\mu - \lambda)} \qquad \bar{t}_l = \dfrac{\lambda}{\mu(\mu - \lambda)}$ $\bar{n}_s = \dfrac{\lambda}{\mu - \lambda} \qquad \bar{t}_s = \dfrac{1}{\mu - \lambda}$ $P_n = [1 - (\lambda/\mu)](\lambda/\mu)^n$
2	Single	Constant	Unlimited	Machine controlled manufacturing operation, automatic car wash	$\bar{n}_l = \dfrac{\lambda^2}{2\mu(\mu - \lambda)} \qquad \bar{t}_l = \dfrac{\lambda}{2\mu(\mu - \lambda)}$ $\bar{n}_s = \bar{n}_l + \dfrac{\lambda}{\mu} \qquad \bar{t}_s = \bar{t}_l + \dfrac{1}{\mu}$
3	Single	Poisson	Limited	Bank drive-in window, manufacturing operation with in-process inventories, parking lot of retail store, maintenance repair center	$\bar{n}_l = \left(\dfrac{\lambda}{\mu}\right)^2 \left[\dfrac{1 - Q(\lambda/\mu)^{Q-1} + (Q-1)(\lambda/\mu)^Q}{[1 - (\lambda/\mu)][1 - (\lambda/\mu)^Q]}\right]$ $\bar{n}_s = \left(\dfrac{\lambda}{\mu}\right)\left[\dfrac{1 - (Q+1)(\lambda/\mu)^Q + Q(\lambda/\mu)^{Q+1}}{[1 - (\lambda/\mu)][1 - (\lambda/\mu)^{Q+1}]}\right]$ $P_n = \left[\dfrac{1 - (\lambda/\mu)}{1 - (\lambda/\mu)^{Q+1}}\right](\lambda/\mu)^n$
4	Multiple	Poisson	Unlimited	Toll road pay booth, bank teller window, maintenance repair shop	$P_0 = \dfrac{1}{\displaystyle\sum_{n=0}^{N-1}\left[\dfrac{(\lambda/\mu)^n}{n!}\right] + \dfrac{(\lambda/\mu)^N}{N!\left(1 - \dfrac{\lambda}{\mu(N)}\right)}}$ $\bar{n}_l = P_0\left[\dfrac{\lambda\mu(\lambda/\mu)^N}{(N-1)!(N\mu - \lambda)^2}\right]$ $\bar{t}_l = \left(\dfrac{\lambda}{\mu}\right)^N\left[\dfrac{P_0}{\mu N(N!)\left(1 - \dfrac{\lambda}{\mu N}\right)^2}\right]$ $\bar{n}_s = \bar{n}_l + (\lambda/\mu)$ $\bar{t}_s = \bar{t}_l + (1/\mu)$

Note: All four models have single phase services and Poisson arrival rate distributions.

Model 1: Single Channel, Single Phase

Waiting lines that are single channel, single phase can usually be analyzed by *Model 1*. When the arrival rate (λ) and service rate (μ) are known, then the average number of arrivals in the line ($\bar{n}_l$), average number of arrivals in the system ($\bar{n}_s$), average time each arrival waits ($\bar{t}_l$), average time each arrival is in the system ($\bar{t}_s$), and the probability of exactly n arrivals being in the system (P_n) can all be computed. Example 13S.1 demonstrates how the formulas of this model are applied.

Example 13S.1

Analyzing Waiting Lines at XYZ Manufacturing Company

The XYZ Manufacturing Company produces artificial eardrum assemblies made of a specially developed material and processed through its own shop. The units are used in human eardrum transplant operations. The bottleneck operation (the operation with the lowest capacity) at XYZ is the ream, twist, and distort (RTD) operation. This information about the RTD operation is known:

$\lambda = 50$ units per hour arrive on the average

$\mu = 75$ units per hour can be serviced on the average

The arrival and service rates can be considered Poisson distributed, the system is single phase and single channel, and the maximum queue length is unlimited. **a.** Compute the average queue length. **b.** Compute the average number of units in the service system. **c.** Compute the average time units wait. **d.** Compute the average time units are in the system. **e.** Compute the probability that one or more units are in the system.

Solution

a. Compute the average queue length (use the formula for Model 1):

$$\bar{n}_l = \frac{\lambda^2}{\mu(\mu - \lambda)} = \frac{(50)^2}{75(75 - 50)} = \frac{2,500}{75(25)} = \frac{2,500}{1,875} = 1.33 \text{ units}$$

b. Compute the average number of units in the system:

$$\bar{n}_s = \frac{\lambda}{(\mu - \lambda)} = \frac{50}{75 - 50} = \frac{50}{25} = 2.00 \text{ units}$$

c. Compute the average time units wait:

$$\bar{t}_l = \frac{\lambda}{\mu(\mu - \lambda)} = \frac{50}{75(75 - 50)} = \frac{50}{75(25)} = \frac{50}{1,875} = .0267 \text{ hour or 1.6 minutes}$$

d. Compute the average time units are in the system:

$$\bar{t}_s = \frac{1}{(\mu - \lambda)} = \frac{1}{75 - 50} = \frac{1}{25} = .040 \text{ hour} = 2.4 \text{ minutes}$$

e. Compute the probability that one or more units are in the system.

First, compute the probability that the system is empty:

$$P_n = \left(1 - \frac{\lambda}{\mu}\right)\left(\frac{\lambda}{\mu}\right)^n, \text{ where } n = 0$$

$$P_0 = \left(1 - \frac{50}{75}\right)\left(\frac{50}{75}\right)^0 = \left(1 - \frac{50}{75}\right)(1) = 1 - \frac{50}{75} = 1 - .667 = .333$$

Next, because P_0 is the probability that the system is empty, $1 - P_0$ is the probability that one or more units are in the system:

$$1 - P_0 = 1 - .333 = .667$$

Model 2: Single Channel, Single Phase and Constant Service Times

When single channel, single phase waiting lines have *constant service times,* as in the case of an automobile car wash, an automatic coffee machine in an office building, or a machine-controlled manufacturing operation, *Model 2* is usually appropriate to study these systems. The $\bar{n}_1$, $\bar{n}_s$, and $\bar{t}_1$, and $\bar{t}_s$ measures are also computed from the formulas of this model. Note that these values are always less than in Model 1. Constant service times are therefore usually preferred over random service times. Example 13S.2 demonstrates the use of Model 2 formulas.

Example 13S.2

Changing the RTD Operation to a Constant Service Rate

The XYZ Manufacturing Company of Example 13S.1 is considering installing an automatic machine at the RTD operation that could process a constant 75 units per hour. An average of 50 units per hour arrive at the operation, arrivals are Poisson distributed, the system is single channel and single phase, and queue length is unlimited.

If the present average time each unit is in the system is 2.4 minutes and each minute that each unit is in the system on the average represents $10,000 per year, how much will the proposed machine save annually over the present RTD operation?

Solution

Compute the annual savings for the proposed machine.

First, compute $\bar{t}_s$ with the formula from Model 2:

$$\bar{t}_s = \bar{t}_1 + \frac{1}{\mu} = \frac{\lambda}{2\mu(\mu - \lambda)} + \frac{1}{\mu} = \frac{50}{2(75)(75 - 50)} + \frac{1}{75} = \frac{50}{2(75)(25)} + .0133$$

$$= \frac{50}{3,750} + .0133 = .0133 + .0133 = .0266 \text{ hour} = 1.6 \text{ minutes}$$

Next, compute the average number of minutes saved per unit:

$$\bar{t}_{s_1} - \bar{t}_{s_2} = 2.4 - 1.6 = .8 \text{ minute}$$

Finally, compute the annual savings:

Annual savings = (Minutes saved) ($ annual cost per minute) = (.8)(10,000) = $8,000/year

Model 3: Single Channel, Single Phase with Limited Waiting Line Length

When single channel, single phase waiting lines are limited in the maximum length that they can have, *Model 3* can usually be used. Waiting line lengths may be limited by such factors as waiting room area, size of parking lots, and size of conveyors holding parts waiting to be processed at manufacturing operations. The formulas of this model in Table 13S.3 are more complex to apply than those of previous queuing models.

Model 4: Multichannel, Single Phase

When more than one waiting line is used and services are single phase, *Model 4* can usually be used to provide managers with information about these systems. As in Model 3, however, the formulas of Model 4 are also more complex to use and apply. Computer programs such as those in Appendix C of this text have greatly simplified the application of this model because complex calculations are relegated to the computer. Analysts supply the computer with arrival rates, service rates, and number of waiting lines. The computer then performs the necessary calculations to supply analysts with P_n, $\bar{n}_1$, $\bar{n}_s$, $\bar{t}_1$, and $\bar{t}_s$.

An Evaluation of Queuing Theory in POM

The chief benefit from understanding the models presented in Table 13S.3 is the insight into the behavior of waiting lines that is gained through the use of these relatively simple models. The specific use of these formulas in POM practice is, however, severely limited because we seldom observe waiting lines that precisely fit the assumptions of the models.

These assumptions particularly limit the wide use of the queuing theory formulas:

1. Multiphase services may not be analyzed by the use of these formulas.
2. Arrival rates and service rates that are not from infinite Poisson distributions may not be analyzed by these formulas. When these rates are highly irregular, formulas cannot be developed.
3. First-come first-served queue discipline is assumed. Other disciplines such as shortest processing time, critical ratio, and most valued customers are known to be commonly used in practice.
4. Line switching is not allowed in multichannel systems.

These and other limitations on the use of the formulas of the models presented here continue to hamper their use in POM.

Another approach, though more involved and more time-consuming, has been developed that can be used to overcome the limitations noted above. *Computer simulation,* which is presented in this supplement, has become the universal tool for analyzing most real waiting line problems that occur in POM. This tool of modern computer technology allows analysts in POM to analyze any queuing system and provide managers with information about the behavior of even the most complex queuing systems.

Management and Waiting Line Alternatives

There are times when managers may indeed design service centers to accommodate the average arrival condition. When the number of arrivals is greater than average, waiting lines build up; and when the number of arrivals is less than average, waiting lines diminish until the service system is empty. This approach assumes an almost uniform service center capacity; personnel, machines, and waiting areas are all planned to provide a uniform capability to service arrivals. The formulas and the safety factor concept discussed earlier in this section reflect this general approach.

Managers are not, however, ordinarily restricted to using fixed capacity service centers in POM. In fact, we observe that managers routinely vary the capacity of service centers by having standby personnel and machines that can be assigned to specific service centers either to prevent excessive waiting lines from forming or to quickly work off excessively long lines. In grocery stores, for example, workers who ordinarily stock shelves can be called to standby checkout counters to activate additional channels or to speed up operating channels that have excessively long lines.

Part-time workers who are on call, standby equipment, and other contingency measures to avoid excessive line lengths and excessive waiting times are commonly used in organizations whose principal outputs are services. These service industries must avoid undesirable waiting line situations because their customers are the arrivals, and perhaps nothing irks customers more than to stand in line needlessly while waiting to be served.

The same management approaches to waiting lines may be used in both service industries and manufacturing. The factor of economics is present in both types of production systems: balance the cost of more service center capacity against the savings resulting from shorter waiting lines. But in service industries the cost of long customer waiting lines may be so high that it cannot be tolerated. Thus alternative, flexible service capacities and other schemes are evolving. Appointment schedules, express checkout counters, standby workers and facilities, "take-a-number" procedures, and other approaches have developed to ease the effects of waiting lines upon customer convenience.

Computer Simulation

Recent developments in industry lead us to believe that computer simulation may be emerging as one of the most frequently employed mathematical techniques by staff experts in production and operations functions today. One study showed that among manufacturing firms that used operations research techniques, 52 percent used computer simulation. These firms used simulation most often to analyze problems in waiting lines, inventory planning and control, production planning and control, capital investment decisions, and equipment maintenance and design.[1]

The flexibility of computer simulation to analyze a variety of different POM problems is perhaps its greatest virtue. These diverse problems, however, do share certain characteristics that make them targets for computer simulation analysis. Table 13S.4 lists six of these important characteristics. When these features are present and properly trained staff analysis specialists are available, computer simulation can be an effective tool to support decision making in POM.

Table 13S.4
Characteristics of POM Problems That Are Appropriate for Computer Simulation Analysis

1. Experimentation with the real system is either impossible or impractical.
2. The system being analyzed is so complex that mathematical formulas cannot be developed that provide information for management decisions.
3. The problem under consideration usually involves the passage of time. For example, policies are set and then executed as time passes. Although this characteristic is not absolutely mandatory, it is usually present.
4. The values of the variables of the problem are not known with certainty; rather, their values vary randomly through chance. We may know their average values and the degree of their variation, but their exact values at any point in time are not known in advance.
5. The severity of the problem justifies the expense of computer-based analysis.
6. The time available for analysis is long enough to permit computer-based analysis.

To demonstrate the use of computer simulation here, we shall identify the key steps in performing a computer simulation, work through a case study of a manual simulation analysis, and finally evaluate the usefulness of the techniques in POM.

The Procedures of Computer Simulation

Performing a computer simulation is not usually mathematically complex, but it can be very time consuming. Table 13S.5 lists the procedures for developing a computer simulation analysis. Although no single step in these procedures is particularly arduous, the entire list does describe a rather long process.

After the problem under consideration has been defined, the central activity of simulation is performed: building the mathematical model. Model building begins with determining which variables and parameters of the problem are important to its solution. Elements subject to variation when the real system operates are allowed to take on values that vary randomly in the model and are called *variables*. Elements that are constant in the operation of the real system (either because of management policies or for technological reasons) are assigned constant values and are called *parameters*. In most simulations the goal of the analysis is to produce a good set of parameter values (management policies) as the model simulates the operation of the real system.

Next, the *decision rules* of the model are specified. These rules answer questions such as: If this happens, then what? For example, if an arrival arrives at a multichan-

---

[1] Norman Gaither, "The Adoption of Operations Research Techniques by Manufacturing Organizations," *Decision Sciences* 6(October 1975): 797–813.

Table 13S.5
Procedures of Computer Simulation

1. Thoroughly define the problem under consideration — its nature, scope, and importance.
2. Build a mathematical model of the problem. This usually involves these principal activities:
   a. Identify the variables and parameters.
   b. Specify the decision rules.
   c. Gather data so that variables and parameters can be assigned realistic values.
   d. Specify the probability distributions for each variable and the value of the parameters.
   e. Specify the time incrementing procedures.
   f. Specify a procedure for summarizing the results of the simulation.
3. Write a computer program of the model and the summary procedures.
4. Process the program on the computer.
5. Evaluate the results of the computer simulation, modify parameter values, and rerun the program until a full range of parameter values has been evaluated.
6. Recommend a course of management action on the problem.

nel queuing system, which line does it go to — the shortest one, the quickest moving one, or the nearest one? These decision rules guide the operation of models and allow them to simulate how the real system operates.

Data gathering allows analysts to specify the frequency distributions of the variables and the constant values of the parameters. Next is a key part of the model, specifying the *time incrementing procedures*. A simulation analysis is a series (usually a long series) of snapshots (usually a thousand or more) of the model operating as time passes between the snapshots. The time incrementing procedure sets the time interval between these snapshots and the general rules for determining when a snapshot will be taken. At each snapshot each variable is randomly assigned a value, the decision rules are followed, and the results are recorded. The model is complete after a method of summarizing the results of all the snapshots is specified.

When the model has been written in a computer language such as BASIC or FORTRAN (or even some special computer simulation languages such as GPSS or SIMSCRIPT) and processed on a computer, the results are then evaluated. If other values of the parameters are to be analyzed (such as other crew sizes at service centers), a new set of parameter values is established, the simulation is run again, and its results are again evaluated. When a full range of parameter values has been evaluated, the *best* set — those values that are recommended management policies to solve the problem — are selected.

These procedures will perhaps be more easily understood if we use them in a computer simulation case study.

A Simulation Case Study

An outpatient clinic serves patients who arrive randomly. The number of patients arriving varies between six and ten per hour while the clinic is open. The clinic's daily schedule is from 8 a.m. to 5 p.m. Any patients who are waiting for doctors inside are served before the clinic closes. It takes between 6 and 30 minutes for a doctor to serve each patient, depending upon the nature of the patient's medical problem.

Two doctors presently serve on the staff of the clinic. But lately both patients and doctors have been complaining about the service. Patients complain about excessive waiting times before being served, and doctors complain about being overworked, not having any time between patients to rest or perform other duties such as charting, and not being able to leave work promptly at 5 p.m. The director of the clinic wonders how much patient waiting time and doctor idle time is being experienced now and how much things would improve if a third doctor were added to the staff.

A simulation will now be developed to analyze the director's staffing problem.

Problem Definition What does the director of the clinic need to know in order to solve the problem? He or she needs to know how much patient waiting time and doctor idle time result when two and three doctors are on the clinic's staff. Then the director can decide which staffing arrangement is best.

Build a Model A mathematical model of the clinic is developed by following the procedures of Table 13S.5, Step 2.

Identify the Variables and Parameters The key variables of the model are the number of patients arriving each hour, the number of minutes required for a doctor to serve each patient, the time patients must wait before being served, and the time doctors are idle. The key parameter is the number of doctors on the clinic's staff.

Specify the Decision Rules These rules will guide our simulation:

1. Patients are assumed to arrive rather uniformly through each hour. Patients do not wait and doctors are not idle because of irregular arrivals *within* each hour.

2. Doctors are assumed to serve patients on a first-come first-served basis. Any patients held over from previous periods are processed first before newly arriving patients are served.

3. Patient arrival patterns are assumed to be about the same for all hours of the day.

4. Patient waiting time or doctor idle time is computed hourly from this formula:
   $$T_n = t_i - (60N - W_{n-1})$$

where

T_n = Either patient waiting time or doctor idle time in Time Period n (if T_n is positive, it represents patient waiting time; if T_n is negative, it represents doctor idle time)

t_i = Service times for the ith patient arriving in Time Period n

W_{n-1} = Patient waiting time in last period or Time Period $(n-1)$

N = Number of doctors on the staff

Gather Data and Specify Variables and Parameters The simulation will compare two staffing arrangements: $N = 2$ and $N = 3$, the number of doctors on the staff. Records at the front desk of the clinic yield the historical information about patient arrivals and service times found in Figure 13S.2.

Specify Time Incrementing Procedures Each time increment will be one hour; enough time intervals will be simulated to cover one operating day from 8:00 a.m. to 5:00 p.m.

Specify Summarizing Procedures The patient waiting time and doctor idle time will be totaled across all time intervals of the simulation. Averages will then be computed for patient service time, patient waiting time, and doctor idle time.

Process the Simulation Because this simulation example will be processed manually, no computer program needs to be written as we would ordinarily do. What follows in this section would be the output of such a computer program. The essential elements in this simulation are determining how many patients arrive in each hour and how many minutes are required to service each patient.

Monte Carlo Arrivals *Monte Carlo* is a technique for generating random values from discrete distributions, such as the discrete distribution of patients arriving per hour in Figure 13S.2. Monte Carlo uses uniform random numbers (*uniform* means that each number has an equal chance of being drawn) to randomly select the number of patients arriving during any hour. First, in Table 13S.6, we set up ranges

Figure 13S.2
Historical Data for Arrivals per Hour and Service Times

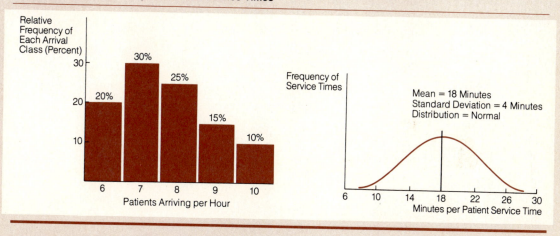

Table 13S.6
Establishing Random Number Ranges for Each Class in Discrete Arrival Distribution for Monte Carlo

Patients Arriving per Hour	Relative Frequency (Percent)	Random Number Range	Patients Arriving per Hour	Relative Frequency (Percent)	Random Number Range
6	20	0–19	9	15	75–89
7	30	20–49	10	10	90–99
8	25	50–74			

Table 13S.7
Table of Uniformly Distributed Random Numbers

6351	8348	2924	2414	8168	7280	0164	5466
1322	8739	0532	4546	2482	3980	1543	3442
6763	9603	6748	4061	3636	5266	8868	5817
5091	8188	3314	6192	7322	8207	3347	6218
7182	7128	8132	4638	4643	6119	4925	4476
2533	4910	6664	5793	4777	6530	6187	8349
4415	1347	8346	7957	2627	4151	1266	0237
0028	8040	7986	5559	1479	8844	9750	8901
5661	3854	2177	8376	0663	8592	5586	6187
6844	5383	0699	5749	8201	7467	0991	8737
3509	2418	2928	5803	8471	8598	5349	4714
0141	8418	9238	9667	4857	2140	9129	5517
0939	5977	7415	0690	7409	8244	2783	2502
9969	7295	4053	8663	5499	5024	0652	8698
6321	9644	0971	9037	5476	1527	9879	5530
4268	5837	6611	7137	3323	5702	4309	4533
8417	9699	2447	7390	2312	7368	3398	4075
3869	6536	4393	7533	5664	6182	6118	1073
1377	8599	9206	7842	4198	4608	9864	7713
7495	5559	5896	5344	8997	5889	4361	3166
9744	9971	2129	3036	9055	7011	0568	0312
6759	7744	5634	4107	3940	6674	4587	7455
3451	3612	0610	1156	1445	8261	6565	5042
1163	1599	9134	0409	0248	7807	4608	7382
2822	0493	7563	0939	7569	6966	3677	9366
3100	4307	7942	8883	1821	0982	9504	8185
3570	7757	4412	6664	0271	1656	7491	0047
2857	6721	4616	7207	1696	5314	6621	1898
1800	3717	6102	3159	4036	5780	8360	8142
3607	8366	7733	1108	7052	2340	0569	2354
9008	2860	6091	0800	9986	2712	6403	4006
6416	2438	6883	9360	4209	1018	8223	0181
7079	0844	1351	0508	0886	0747	6502	2293
5241	0807	7674	8782	3627	2728	3727	7805
3291	9499	7374	8751	6143	8100	3308	6951
1928	9013	6726	9241	4907	6275	3487	4448
5310	1826	3163	2545	6803	7911	6237	6225
1215	1270	6680	8651	1790	2881	1176	1130
6195	6999	6240	4452	0552	3239	4469	7658
5731	5461	1187	7973	7158	1193	2734	5666

of random numbers that correspond to the relative frequency of each class of the patient arrivals distribution.

Under this scheme the range of random numbers allocated to each class exactly equals the relative frequency of that class. Thus, 100 random numbers (0 to 99) are used to select one of the classes of patients arriving per hour from the distribution.

Table 13S.7 is a table of uniformly distributed random numbers. This means that any of the numbers from zero to nine all occur with equal frequency. They are not arranged in any order, and thus they are random. To use the table to select random numbers from zero to 99, as we want to do here, just pick a starting point anywhere in the table. For our purposes, begin at Row 8 and read from left to right: 00, 28, 80, 40, 79, 86, 55, 59, and 14 are nine random numbers (RN) that will be used to establish the number of patient arrivals during the nine daily operating hours of our simulation.

Table 13S.8 uses these random numbers to set the number of patient arrivals for each hour of the simulation. The first RN = 00 falls in the 0–19 range of the random numbers in Table 13S.6; this sets six arrivals for the first hour. RN = 28 falls in the 20–49 range for seven arrivals; RN = 80 falls in the 75–89 range of numbers for nine arrivals, and so on. This procedure is used to set the number of arrivals in all nine hours of the simulation. Remember that you can read uniformly distributed random numbers from Table 13S.7 in any sequence from any starting point in the table: up, down, right, or left—but be consistent.

Table 13S.8
Determining Number of Patient Arrivals for Each Hour of Simulation Using Monte Carlo

Hour	Uniform Random Number (RN)	Patient Arrivals	Hour	Uniform Random Number (RN)	Patient Arrivals	Hour	Uniform Random Number (RN)	Patient Arrivals
1	00	6	4	40	7	7	55	8
2	28	7	5	79	9	8	59	8
3	80	9	6	86	9	9	14	6

Note: Number of arrivals is determined by fitting RN into one of the random number ranges from Table 13S.6.

Normally Distributed Service Times Now we need to set the service times for our patients. But we cannot use Monte Carlo because our service times from Figure 13S.2 are normally distributed with a mean of 18 minutes and a standard deviation of 4 minutes. Table 13S.9 is a table of normally distributed random numbers that are Z scores—the number of standard deviations each service time is from the mean. This formula is used to compute the service time for each patient:

$$t_i = \mu + Z_i(\sigma) \quad \text{or} \quad t_i = 18 + Z_i(4)$$

Z is determined for each patient by selecting any starting point in Table 13S.9. For our purposes, let us begin at the upper left-hand corner and read from left to right: 1.21, −1.31, −1.12, 1.32, .86, and .31 are our Z scores for the six patients in the first

Table 13S.9
Normally Distributed Z Scores

1.21	−1.31	−1.12	1.32	.86	.31	−.77	1.90
.40	−.11	−1.63	−.75	.92	−.81	−1.12	1.28
1.40	−.49	.56	.10	−1.05	.48	1.00	−.35
−.04	1.21	1.80	−.21	−1.58	.15	−2.75	.45
.47	−.28	2.02	3.00	1.14	−.54	1.72	.60
.11	.77	1.14	.46	1.01	.04	−1.05	−.11
.22	1.94	−.11	1.02	−.79	−.24	.52	1.66
−1.80	.97	−.76	.31	1.27	.81	−.17	−.28
.09	−.60	−.63	.56	.09	1.08	−.60	2.10
1.66	−2.26	.10	1.66	−.85	−.34	.02	.73

Note: These numbers are not in any order and are normally distributed about a mean of zero.

hour of our simulation. Therefore, we can now compute the service times for these patients:

$t_1 = 18 + 1.21(4) = 22.84$ minutes

$t_2 = 18 − 1.31(4) = 12.76$ minutes

$t_3 = 18 − 1.12(4) = 13.52$ minutes

$t_4 = 18 + 1.32(4) = 23.28$ minutes

$t_5 = 18 + .86(4) = 21.44$ minutes

$t_6 = 18 + .31(4) = 19.24$ minutes

Total   113.08 minutes

By repeating this procedure, service times for all patients are computed and totaled for each hour of the simulation: 113.1, 135.1, 160.6, 112.8, 197.1, 180.3, 154.7, 159.2, and 98.8.

Performing the Simulation Now we are ready to perform the simulation. Table 13S.10 lists the number of patients arriving and total service time for each hour of the simulation. The patient waiting time and doctor idle time is computed for each hour for the two staffing arrangements. For example, in Hour 4:

Two doctors:

$T_n = t_i − (60N − W_{n−1})$ $T_4 = 112.8 − (120 − 55.7) = 112.8 − 64.3 = 48.5$

Because T_4 is positive, it represents patient waiting time.

Three doctors:

$T_n = t_i − (60N − W_{n−1})$ $T_4 = 112.8 − (180 − 0) = −67.2$

Because T_4 is negative, it represents doctor idle time.

    After all the patient waiting times and doctor idle times are similarly computed for all hours of the simulation, the totals and averages are computed. This summary information results:

Table 13S.10
Summary of Outpatient Clinic Simulation

Hour	Number of Patients Arriving	Total Service Time (Minutes)	Two-Doctor Staff		Three-Doctor Staff	
			Patient Waiting Time (Minutes)	Doctor Idle Time (Minutes)	Patient Waiting Time (Minutes)	Doctor Idle Time (Minutes)
1	6	113.1	0	6.9	0	66.9
2	7	135.1	15.1	0	0	44.9
3	9	160.6	55.7	0	0	19.4
4	7	112.8	48.5	0	0	67.2
5	9	197.1	125.6	0	17.1	0
6	9	180.3	185.9	0	17.4	0
7	8	154.7	220.6	0	0	7.9
8	8	159.2	259.8	0	0	20.8
9	6	98.8	238.6	0	0	81.2
Totals	69	1,311.7	1,149.8	6.9	34.5	308.3
Average per patient		19.0	16.7	.1	.5	4.5

	Two Doctors	Three Doctors
Average service time per patient	19.0 minutes	19.0 minutes
Average waiting time per patient	16.7 minutes	5.0 minutes
Average doctor idle time between patients	.1 minutes	4.5 minutes

The director agrees with the patients — too much patient waiting time results with a two-doctor clinic staff. The doctors also presently are probably overworked. The three-doctor staffing arrangement alleviates both problems.

This example of a manual simulation demonstrates the essential steps in developing a computer simulation without overpowering you with complex calculations. You should realize, however, that this example is simple compared to most computer simulations on at least three points: (1) Most simulated systems are far more complex than a two- or three-doctor outpatient clinic. (2) Decision rules are seldom as simple as those of this example. (3) The number of random variables and their patterns of randomness are usually more extensive. Poisson, exponential, and other distributions frequently must be represented in addition to the discrete and normal distributions of this example. But, in spite of the simplicity of our example, its procedures are similar in most respects to its real world counterparts.

An Evaluation of Computer Simulation

Computer simulation deserves our attention on at least three counts:

1. It is perhaps one of the most flexible analytical tools. In other words, it can be applied to a variety of POM problems.

2. It is frequently used in industry. Thus, the likelihood of encountering it in your future jobs is relatively high.

3. It is not highly mathematical and complex; rather, it uses a relatively simple experimental approach to analyzing problems.

These reasons support the contention that the use of computer simulation in POM will grow in years to come.

   Although computer simulation does not always necessarily yield *best,* or optimal, answers, good workable solutions can be developed by comparing alternative management policies. Although it is true that the technique requires well-trained staff specialists and an effective computer system, these elements are increasingly assumed in most organizations today.

Review and Discussion Questions

1. Give five examples of waiting lines in productive systems.

2. Why do waiting lines form?

3. List the assumptions of these queuing models: **a.** Model 1, **b.** Model 2, **c.** Model 3, and **d.** Model 4.

4. What techniques can be employed when queuing formulas are inappropriate?

5. What information about waiting lines do managers usually need to know?

6. How can managers vary service center capacities to avoid excessive waiting lines?

7. Name six characteristics of problems appropriate for computer simulation analysis.

8. Name six principal steps in computer simulation.

9. Name six activities in building a model for computer simulation.

10. Define *Monte Carlo.*

11. Define *uniformly distributed random numbers.*

12. Define *normally distributed random numbers.*

Problems

1. Given: Model 1, $\lambda = 5$ per hour, and $\mu = 10$ per hour. Required: **a.** $\bar{n}_1$, **b.** $\bar{n}_s$, **c.** $\bar{t}_1$, **d.** $\bar{t}_s$, and **e.** P_0.

2. Picture yourself as a teller at a single drive-in window at a local bank. If customers arrive one every 5 minutes on the average, and if you can serve customers in 3 minutes on the average: **a.** How long should customers expect to be at the bank facility on the average? **b.** How many cars would we expect to be in the drive-in facility on the average? (Assume one customer per car.) **c.** What is the probability that three or more cars will be in the drive-in facility?

3. The vice-president of Student Services at Moneycrunch University has ordered the operations manager to reduce the staff in the check-cashing booth at the student center. Although the average arrival rate of students to the single waiting line is

expected to remain at 40 students per hour, the average time required to cash a student's check is expected to increase from .5 minute to 1.4 minutes at the single cashing booth. Although the operations manager knows that the waiting line area is sufficient to accommodate the additional students, she wonders what changes this staffing change will cause in the average number of students in line, the average waiting time of students in line, and the proportion of the time that the staff will be at the window.

4. You are a supervisor of a maintenance repair shop, and you have just attended a staff meeting. A policy was set at the meeting that established 4 hours as the average time that each production machine to be repaired should be out of production. If it takes 8 hours on the average for a repair worker to repair a machine, one machine per hour on the average is failing, and Model 1 applies (assume that two workers can repair a machine in 4 hours, 4 workers can repair a machine in 2 hours, etc.): **a.** How many repair workers are needed in the repair shop? **b.** If each machine requires 20 square feet of floor space, how much area should be provided on the average for the repair facility? (Assume that repaired machines leave immediately.) **c.** In your answer to part *b*, what is the probability of overflowing the area?

5. Given: Model 2, $\lambda = 20$ per hour, and $\mu = $ a constant 30 per hour. Required: **a.** $\bar{n}_l$, **b.** $\bar{n}_s$, **c.** $\bar{t}_l$, and **d.** $\bar{t}_s$.

6. Billy White owns and operates White's Automatic Car Wash. The automatic washing mechanism takes exactly 12 minutes to wash each car. During weekdays the average arrival rate of cars is 3 per hour and on weekends the rate is 4.5 per hour. Each car takes approximately 20 feet of driveway length. **a.** How much driveway length will be required on the average for cars waiting to be washed? **b.** For what length of time will each customer be at the car wash on the average?

7. We would like to design an automatic night deposit box at the Flibynight Bank. The bank's board has set a policy of no more than two customers waiting to be served on the average. If ten customers per hour arrive on the average: **a.** In how many minutes should the automatic teller be designed to process customers? **b.** How many minutes will each customer be at the bank on the average? (Hint: The formula for the quadratic equation is: $X = (-b \pm \sqrt{b^2 - 4ac})/2a$.)

8. Given: Model 3, $\lambda = 10$ per hour, $\mu = 20$ per hour, and $Q = $ a maximum of 5 units in the system. Required: $\bar{n}_s$.

9. A popular student association, Business Students against Grade Inflation, is planning a car wash project to raise funds. A large shopping center has granted permission to use a portion of its parking lot with the understanding that no more than 100 feet of driveway length can be used. The students expect the 20-foot-long cars to arrive at the car wash one every 5 minutes on the average, and the car-washing team believes that it can wash a car in 4 minutes on the average. **a.** What proportion of the time will the students be able to rest? **b.** How many cars will be waiting in line at the car wash on the average?

10. Given: Model 4, $\lambda = 10$ units per hour, $\mu = 20$ units per hour, and $N = 4$ channels. Required: **a.** P_0 and **b.** $\bar{n}_l$.

11. Dixie Food Stores is opening a new store in Miami, Florida. Dixie has estimated that the new location will average 220 customers arriving per hour during peak shopping hours. During these peak periods all six checkout counters will be open and operating with a capability of serving an average of 40 customers per hour per counter. All checkout counters are assumed to be identical. **a.** What proportion of the time would we expect all of the checkout counters and waiting lines to be empty of customers?

b. How long would we expect customers to wait in line on the average? **c.** How many customers would we expect to be waiting in each line on the average?

12. Professor Goodguy keeps office hours between 2 and 4 p.m. one day per week. The number of students who take advantage of the assistance available during these periods is given in this relative frequency distribution:

Number of Students (n)	Relative Frequency F(n)	Number of Students (n)	Relative Frequency F(n)	Number of Students (n)	Relative Frequency F(n)
3	10	5	20	7	20
4	10	6	30	8	10

The amount of time required per student to provide assistance is approximated by a normal distribution with a mean of 15 minutes and a standard deviation of 5 minutes. Use these uniform random numbers to establish the number of students arriving in ten office hours periods: 6, 5, 1, 0, 2, 9, 5, 4, 7, 3. Use the normally distributed Z scores in Table 13S.9 to establish service times per student. (Begin in the upper left-hand corner of the table and read horizontally across the first line, return to the left margin, and repeat until completed.) Follow the procedures of the outpatient clinic case in this supplement to determine: **a.** The number of students arriving in each office hours period for ten periods. **b.** The total number of minutes required to assist students during each of the ten office hours periods.

13. The Red Snapper Fish Sales Company stocks fresh fish fillets daily for sale to its Boston customers. Its daily demand follows this pattern:

Cases of Fillets Demanded	Relative Frequency (Percent)	Cases of Fillets Demanded	Relative Frequency (Percent)
30	10	60	40
40	15	70	10
50	25		

Red Snapper can buy fillets only in multiples of 10-case quantities at a uniform cost of $25 per case. Red Snapper charges its customers $40 a case, and leftover fillets each day can be sold for cat food at $5 a case. Red Snapper's manager wishes to compare two rules for ordering fillets: (1) Order the quantity demanded today for tomorrow's sales. (Today's demand was 50 cases.) (2) Order a constant 60 cases per day. Use Monte Carlo to conduct a 20-day manual simulation to compare the average daily profit for the two decision rules. (These 20 uniformly distributed random numbers are read downward from the upper right-hand corner of Table 13S.7 — 66, 42, 17, 18, 76, 49, 37, 01, 87, 37, 14, 17, 02, 98, 30, 33, 75, 73, 13, and 66.)

Selected Bibliography

Bierman, H., Jr., C. P. Bonini, and W. H. Hausman. *Quantitative Analysis for Business Decisions*. 5th ed. Homewood, IL: Richard D. Irwin, 1977.

Carlson, J. G., and M. J. Misshauk. *Introduction to Gaming: Management Decision Simulations*. New York: Wiley, 1972.

Cosmetatos, G. P. "The Value of Queueing Theory — A Case Study." *Interfaces* 9, no. 3 (May 1979): 47–51.

Gaither, Norman. "The Adoption of Operations Research Techniques by Manufacturing Organizations." *Decision Sciences* 6(October 1975): 797–813.

Gross, Donald, and Carl M. Harris. *Fundamentals of Queuing Theory.* New York: Wiley, 1974.

House, William C. *Business Simulation for Decision Making.* New York: PBI Books, 1977.

McKeown, P. G. "An Application of Queueing Analysis to the New York State Child Abuse and Maltreatment Register Reporting System." *Interfaces* 9, no. 3 (May 1979): 20–25.

McMillan, C., and R. F. Gonzalez. *Systems Analysis: A Computer Approach to Decision Models.* 3d ed. Homewood, IL: Richard D. Irwin, 1973.

Meier, R. C., W. T. Newell, and H. L. Pazer. *Simulation in Business and Economics.* Englewood Cliffs, NJ: Prentice-Hall, 1969.

Nanda, R. "Simulating Passenger Arrivals at Airports." *Industrial Engineering* 4, no. 3 (March 1972): 12–19.

Naylor, T. H., J. L. Balintfy, D. S. Burdick, and K. Chu. *Computer Simulation Techniques.* New York: Wiley, 1966.

Petersen, Clifford. "Simulation of a Inventory System." *Industrial Engineering* 5, no. 6 (June 1973): 35–44.

Chapter Outline

Introduction

Effects of Product and Service Quality upon Organizations
**Some Products and Services and Their Principal Quality Control
  Concerns**
Quality Control throughout the Productive System

Quality Control Issues in Practice

Designing Quality Control Programs
High versus Low Quality
Organizing for Quality Control
How Many, How Often, and Where to Inspect

Japanese Quality Circles

Statistical Concepts in Quality Control

Sampling
Lots, Random Samples
Attributes, Variables
Single, Double, Sequential Sampling Plans
Central Limit Theorem and Quality Control
Sampling Distributions
Relationship to Control Charts and Acceptance Plans

Control Charts

Control Charts for Attributes
Keypunch Error Control Example, p Charts
Formulas and Variable Definitions for 3σ Control Limits
Control Charts for Variables
Box Weight Control Example, $\bar{x}$ and R Charts
Control Chart Factors for Variables

Acceptance Plans

Average Outgoing Quality (AOQ) Curves
Operating Characteristic (OC) Curves
Acceptance Plans for Attributes
Defective Ball Bearing Example
Formulas and Variable Definitions for Computing Acceptance Criteria for
  Acceptance Plans
Acceptance Plans for Variables
Concrete Core Sample Mean Example

Computers in Quality Control

Quality Control in Services

Summary

Review and Discussion Questions

Problems

Case: Gas Generator Corporation

Selected Bibliography

14

Quality Control:
Concepts and Control Methods

I'm afraid you've got a bad egg, Mr. Jones. Oh no, my lord, I assure you! Parts of it are excellent!
Punch, 1895

All organizations today are concerned with the quality of their outputs. This concern stems both from the desire to be known as high-quality producers and from the fact that the quality level of outputs can be an important element of their overall marketing strategy. Additionally, severe managerial problems can result when the quality of products and services is not carefully controlled.

When customers are dissatisfied with the perceived quality of products or services, they can react in a variety of ways: (1) They can just stop buying the product or service. (2) They can attempt to influence others not to buy the product or service through governmental or private consumer group agencies. (3) They can seek retribution through the courts by filing product liability suits to collect both economic losses and punitive damages. Production managers work hard to achieve the positive benefits of high-quality products and services — satisfied customers, reputation of being high-quality producers, and growing markets. They also work hard to avoid the negative consequences of poor-quality products and services — dissatisfied customers, reputation of being poor-quality producers, shrinking markets, product liability suits, product recall programs, and governmental sanctions. These positive and negative consequences that can result from product or service quality cause managers to pour time, money, and talent into establishing quality control departments.

Table 14.1
Some Products and Services and Their Principal Quality Control Concerns

Product/Service Organization	Quality Control Concerns
1. Commercial chemical fertilizer manufacturer	Does the product contain the correct amount of each chemical? Does the packaging avoid the absorption of excess moisture under ordinary conditions of use? Is particle sizing correct?
2. Hospital	Is the patient treated courteously by all hospital personnel? Does each patient receive the correct treatments at the correct times? Is each treatment administered with precision? Does the entire hospital environment support patient recovery?
3. University	Does each student take the prescribed courses? Is each student achieving acceptable performance in courses? Is each faculty member contributing to the growth and development of students? Does the university environment support high scholarship?
4. Automobile manufacturer	Does the auto perform as intended? Is its appearance pleasing? Is each part of the auto within the manufacturing tolerances? Is the design safe to operate? Does the auto have the intended endurance? Is the auto's gas mileage, pollution control, and safety equipment within government guidelines?
5. Bank	Is each customer treated courteously? Are each customer's transactions completed with precision? Do customers' statements accurately reflect their transactions? Does the bank comply with governmental regulations? Is the physical environment pleasing to customers?
6. Construction lumber mill	Is the lumber properly graded? Is the lumber within moisture content tolerances? Are knotholes, splits, surface blemishes, and other defects excessive? Is lumber properly packaged for shipment? Does the lumber comply with strength specifications?

POM is concerned with the quality of both products and services. The nature of each particular product or service determines the nature of this concern. Table 14.1 lists some common products and services and their principal quality control concerns. Managers usually want their products to meet certain physical, chemical, and performance specifications and tolerances, to be adequately packaged to protect their contents during shipment and handling, to be attractive in appearance, and to comply with governmental regulations and guidelines. Services must usually be delivered in courteous and accurate ways, within a total environment that is pleasing to customers, and within governmental regulations.

Quality control begins long before products and services are delivered to customers. As Figure 14.1 shows, quality control begins early in the productive system. Inputs must be of acceptable quality before they are allowed to be used. Materials must meet the appropriate specifications — strength, size, color, finish, appearance, chemical content, weight, and other characteristics. Personnel must also meet certain specifications — completion of training programs, possession of certain education certificates, passing of certain tests, and other evidences of skill, knowledge, and personality characteristics. Machines too must meet the appropriate performance specifications. The quality of these materials, employees, and machine inputs is fundamental to any successful quality control program.

As the inputs of the productive system proceed through the processing steps of the conversion subsystem, where they are sequentially converted into outputs, the quality of these partially completed units is monitored to determine whether the

Figure 14.1
Quality Control throughout the Productive System

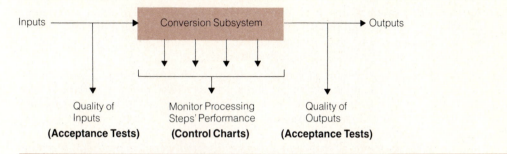

system is operating as intended. This monitoring is aimed at alerting managers that corrective action is required *before* poor-quality products and services are produced.

Finally, outputs are examined to determine their acceptability. This entire span of quality control activities from the beginning to the end of productive systems is an important part of POM. We shall study these activities by first discussing some realities of day-to-day quality control issues in productive systems. Then, we shall study how the Japanese have established *quality circles* for greater worker participation in quality control. Next, we shall explore the statistical underpinnings of quality control. Then, we shall develop the techniques of control charts and acceptance sampling. Finally, the use of computers in quality control and quality control in service organizations will be examined.

Quality Control Issues in Practice

Managers in charge of today's productive systems have already resolved most of the major quality control planning issues in their organizations. But in the past, such issues as how to design quality control programs; whether high- or low-quality targets were best; how to organize the quality control functions; and how often, how many, and where to inspect all had to be initially settled.

Designing Quality Control Programs

Quality control programs usually involve four major elements:

1. Quality control policies — top management issues directives about how the quality of its products and services are to mesh with the overall objectives of the organization. These general rules or guidelines provide direction and focus for all quality control activities.

2. Product or service design — the design of products and services sets the specifications for such things as raw material tolerances, product performance, and service requirements. The design also determines in large part how well the

product or service provides the intended function and its reliability.[1] This design ultimately becomes the basis for quality control standards that will govern the control of quality in production, distribution, and use.

3. Control in production — it is here that the well-known inspection and control techniques of quality control are found. Controlling incoming materials, production processes, and final product and service acceptability so that the quality standards are met is the main objective.

4. Distribution, installation, and use — packaging, shipping methods, and installation must be included in the program because poor product performance is perceived by consumers to be poor product quality, even if the product was damaged in shipment or improperly installed.

Each of these elements is crucial to a successful quality control program. Although we shall be emphasizing the third element here — control in production — let us not forget that top management policies, product or service design, and distribution and installation methods are also important aspects of product and service quality.

Although quality control programs provide the framework for achieving the desired quality levels of products and services, several nitty-gritty quality control questions must ultimately be resolved in POM before these plans can be effective.

High versus Low Quality

As consumers, we often complain about the poor quality of today's products and services. We yearn for earlier times when workers took pride in their work, producers cared about their customers, American products were better than their Japanese or European counterparts, and other familiar laments. But did it ever occur to you that products and services that are of low quality may not be that way because of shoddy workmanship, uncaring production management, or mismanagement?

Setting the quality level of products and services is a team decision that involves most functional areas of organizations — marketing, accounting and finance, production, and engineering. When products and services are initially designed, a fundamental determination must be made about the outputs. How much quality will customers pay for? What quality level and price best positions us in the market? What quality features allow us to best compete in the market?

Fundamentally, determining the appropriate level of quality is based on marketing considerations and estimated production costs. At one extreme, for example, nails are produced at very low quality levels, at very low production costs per unit, and in massive quantities. The resolution of the appropriate quality level of nails is therefore determined by the market: customers prefer low-cost and low-quality nails to higher-cost nails that are masterpieces. At the other extreme, Rolls-Royce automobiles are built to the highest quality specifications because their customers want high quality and are willing to pay handsomely for it.

Leaders of U.S. manufacturing firms are now talking about a concept called

---

[1] Reliability means the probability that a product will not fail in a given time period or number of trials under ordinary conditions of use. This definition will also be used in the machine design section of Chapter 15, "Maintenance Management and Reliability."

perfect quality. This concept involves producing products with no defects. Once the definition of a defect has been established, production of the product results in no defects. Years ago, government programs for producing military and aerospace products adopted a similar concept called *zero defects,* and it seems that the idea has spread to our industrial leaders of today. **Why should these leaders be thinking in terms of perfect quality instead of competitive quality? The answer lies in two important developments: (1) Many Japanese products today are approaching the point where consumers perceive that they are of perfect quality. (2) Industrial robots and other technological developments today make it feasible to produce products that are not only lower in cost but also higher in quality. Industrial technology and competitive market pressures may be the driving forces that move U.S. manufacturers toward making the idea of perfect quality a reality instead of just a concept that we are talking about.**
Determining the level of quality for a product or service is therefore a conscious marketing strategy choice that guides the entire quality control program. This strategy sets in large part the required organizational structure for quality control.

Organizing for Quality Control

Quality control departments are usually established in forms that parallel the structures of production or operations departments. This parallel relationship stems from the basic role of quality control departments, which is to monitor, measure, and report on the production or operation departments' quality performance. By designing quality control departments that parallel the structure of the production or operations departments, a balance of power is struck between these two functional areas. Quality control, on the one hand, continuously presses for production's conformance to quality specifications; production or operations, on the other hand, strives for low costs, high volume of outputs, and acceptable quality.

The size of quality control departments differs depending upon the scale of operations and the quality emphasis of the organization's products or services. Very large productive systems with a high quality emphasis would typically have very large quality control departments. When quality emphasis is high, the quality control organization structure has personnel who correspond to production personnel at almost all organizational levels. However, when quality emphasis is low, quality control departments tend to submerge within production or operations departments, and their size tends to shrink proportionally to the importance of their mission.

The watchdog nature of the relationship between quality control and production or operations personnel can cause numerous morale and cooperation problems. For instance, when quality control personnel interfere with the traditional authority of line supervisors by directing production workers to stop work, change work procedures, or improve their attentiveness, line supervisors resent these intrusions, to put it mildly. Workers can wonder from whom they should be taking orders — their supervisors or the quality control inspectors? Additionally, production workers who have their work checked by outside inspectors may tend to feel frustrated by their lack of ability to control their own work environments.

These frustrating and potentially explosive situations between quality control and production have led to clear-cut rules of conduct for quality control inspectors in most organizations. For example, inspectors must often contact production supervisors and relate quality deficiencies. These supervisors then direct production workers to take the necessary corrective actions. Such rules of conduct have evolved to form buffers between quality control and production personnel who may be thrust into seemingly adversary roles.

In some organizations, job enlargement experiments have combined the work of production workers and inspectors into enlarged jobs. The results of these experiments are mixed. In some cases, these enlarged jobs result in less efficiency and generally lower quality. In other cases, however, quality and efficiency improve. We want to watch and learn from these ongoing enlargement studies, but, for the present, quality control and production activities in most organizations are separated for one good reason — control.

Quality control departments are often divided into subdepartments that are differentiated by scientific disciplines. One company, for example, has mechanical, chemical, electronic, and hydraulic quality control subdepartments. Employees are grouped together in these units so that the necessary supervision, training, and flexibility in personnel assignments are facilitated. Quality control personnel are usually highly trained physical scientists from such disciplines as mechanical, electrical, civil, and chemical engineering; physics; biology; mathematics; and chemistry.

These scientists engage in two principal activities, inspection and testing. Inspections are performed at various points along the productive system to determine the acceptability of incoming raw materials, to monitor the quality performance of production processes, and finally to determine the acceptability of the final products. Inspection involves the careful measurement of raw materials, in-process parts, or finished goods against prescribed quality standards. Go-no-go gauges, surface finish gauges, scales, circuit continuity meters, and other measurement devices are used in these inspections.

Testing can be a highly specialized field within quality control. Chemical formulations are often verified in chemical tests, electronic instruments are tested for their resistance to vibration, concrete blocks are tested for their maximum compression pressure, and piston rings are tested for surface hardness. These and other quality control tests are usually performed in laboratories by scientists who are highly trained in their respective disciplines. Other routine tests may not require extensive scientific skills and may be performed by inspectors out in the production departments.

Regardless of the size and structure of quality control departments and the underlying scientific disciplines of their tests, determining how many, how often, and where to inspect is fundamental in quality control programs.

How Many, How Often, and Where to Inspect

How many of an organization's outputs to inspect is basically a question of economics. Figure 14.2 demonstrates that as more and more outputs are inspected, the costs of inspection increase while the costs of undetected defects decline. At some point some particular level of inspection results in an optimal trade-off where total quality control costs are minimized. Inspection costs include such costs as inspector training, managing of inspectors, inspection labor, conducting tests, maintenance of testing and inspection facilities, scrap, and rework. The costs of undetected defects

Figure 14.2
Trading off the Costs of Inspection against the Costs of Undetected Defects

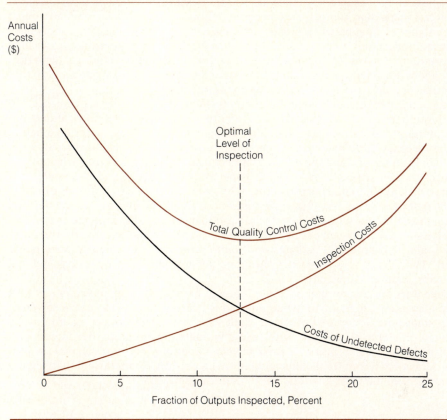

include such costs as customer complaints, loss of customer goodwill, product replacement costs, product liability suits, product recall programs, and returned products. Operations managers must balance these costs, conceptually at least, in deciding how many to inspect.

Practically speaking, in almost all products and services, we do not inspect all outputs. Not only would this be uneconomical, it would also be impossible in cases where destructive testing is employed. For example, when concrete blocks are crushed to determine their maximum compression strength, the product is destroyed. Ammunition, fire extinguishers, and intercontinental missile systems are similarly destroyed when tested. Obviously, these products must be tested by using sampling plans, which we shall discuss later in this chapter.

When to inspect during productive processes can usually be determined by following these general principles: (1) Inspect *after* operations that are likely to produce faulty items. (2) Inspect *before* costly operations. (3) Inspect *before* operations that cover up defects. (4) Inspect *before* assembly operations that cannot be undone. (5) On automatic machines, inspect first and last pieces of production runs but few in-between pieces. (6) Inspect finished products. The reasoning behind these principles is largely economic.

Inspection is done either at inspection stations within production departments or at central inspection centers. At inspection stations inspectors become an almost integral part of the productive process. In continuous systems where assembly lines are used, inspectors may look like any other worker in sequence along the line. Intermittent systems or job shops usually have inspection stations dispersed throughout the facility so that parts or products can be quickly inspected and so that materials handling to and from the stations is minimized.

Inspection requires judgment. Reading precision measurement instruments and interpreting the results of scientific tests require not only great skill and training, but the difference between a part passing or failing a test may be like splitting a hair in some rare cases. Judgment must be carefully exercised in these instances. One story is told over and over about the human frailty of inspectors. A supervisor who wanted to check out the inspection skills of his inspectors purposely placed 100 defects in a lot of parts without telling his inspectors. The inspectors found only 68 of the defects on the first pass. Determined that the inspectors should be able to find the defects, he again put the lot with 32 defects through inspection. This time the inspectors found many of the defects, but not all. After this process was repeated for the third, fourth, and fifth times, 98 defects were found. The other two defects were never found. They went to a customer. Another version of this same story had the inspectors finding 110 defects.

Inspectors are human beings and all human beings err. Human errors increase when inspectors are fatigued, when lighting is poor, when it is too hot or too cold, when inspectors do not feel secure in their jobs, and when inspectors are having personal problems at home or with fellow workers. These and other factors can affect workers' concentration or their physical ability to perform inspections and tests. Managers recognize that inspection can be partly judgmental and that inspectors must have the right environment to perform their jobs.

Japanese Quality Circles

Shortly after World War II Japanese products competed with U.S. and other countries' products on the basis of very low prices and shoddy quality. For too long we continued to assume that the Japanese would be content to follow this marketing and manufacturing strategy. In the 1970s and 1980s it became apparent not only that the Japanese were now in a position to be competitive with U.S. manufacturers on price and quality, but also that the Japanese now actually enjoyed a substantial quality advantage in mass-produced products. Exhibit 14.1 describes the extent of the Japanese quality advantage.

The turnaround in Japanese quality programs began in the 1950s but took a long time to develop to its successful status of today. Dr. Edward M. Deming, a professor at New York University, traveled to Japan after World War II at the request of the Japanese government to assist its industries in improving productivity and quality. Dr. Deming, a statistician and consultant, was so successful in his mission that in 1951 the Japanese government established the Deming Prize for innovation in quality control to be awarded annually to a company that distinguished itself in quality control programs.

Exhibit 14.1
Foreign-Made Goods' Quality Surpasses U.S.

NEW YORK (UPI) — At least half of all Americans are dissatisfied with American products and consider foreign products as good or better.

And to make domestic matters worse, the quality of American products has declined in the past five years while Japanese products have set new world standards for quality.

These are the conclusions of two surveys released recently, one by the American Society for Quality Control, based in Milwaukee, the other by Fortune magazine.

The Milwaukee society blamed industry's emphasis on profits, "uncaring workers" and the high costs of the present economy as the causes of the declining quality of American products.

The Fortune study put the blame on the same factors but added that Japanese cultural factors shape Japanese management attitudes.

"A Japanese executive expects to spend a lifetime with one company so its long-term success is his success," the article said. On the other hand "an American takes a more self-centered view of his career."

The Fortune article also quoted Stephen Moss, an executive of Arthur D. Little, Inc., the Cambridge, Mass., research firm, as saying the contrasting American and Japanese management attitudes play a big role in the decline in quality.

"The U.S. manager sets an acceptable level of quality and then sticks to it. The Japanese are constantly upgrading their goals," Moss was quoted as saying.

The Society for Quality Control said its latest survey showed that the only American industry given high marks for quality by the public today is drugs and pharmaceuticals. Makers of frozen foods and television receivers get fair marks.

The automobile manufacturers got the lowest mark, with only 17.6 percent of respondents saying American cars are good and 36.5 percent saying they are definitely inferior. Makers of toys and games and of household appliances got the next lowest marks.

On this score, Fortune noted that "a new American car is almost twice as likely to have a problem as a Japanese model. An American color TV needs repairs half again as often as a Japanese set and U.S.-made computer memory chips were judged in one test this year to be three times as likely to fail as Japanese chips."

Source: *The Houston Chronicle*, August 9, 1981, p. 3-29.

One outgrowth of Japan's continuous search for ways to improve the quality of its products was the concept of *quality circles,* or QC circles. "Basically, a QC circle is a small group of employees, the average number is nine, who volunteer to meet regularly to undertake work-related projects designed to advance the company, improve working conditions, and spur mutual self-development, by using quality control concepts."[2] QC circles are encouraged by Japanese companies and receive substantial training in quality control concepts and techniques. These groups often meet away from the job and combine their meetings with social or athletic activities. They tend to select their own projects for investigation and can generally count on the support of management in implementing their recommendations. The types of projects are varied and may extend beyond quality to such areas as productivity, tool design, safety, or environmental protection.

Membership in QC circles is voluntary and there are no direct cash incentives. Members give the principal reasons for belonging to the groups as personal satisfaction from achievement and recognition given at regional and national quality control meetings. The success of these circles is no less than phenomenal and their use is expanding to the United States, Britain, Brazil, Indonesia, and other countries. Korea is estimated to have more than 40,000 circles operating.

---

[2] "Japan: Quality Control & Innovation," reprinted from the July 20, 1981 issue of *Business Week* by special permission, © 1981, p. 32, by McGraw-Hill, Inc., New York, NY 10020. All rights reserved.

Figure 14.3
How QC Circles Work

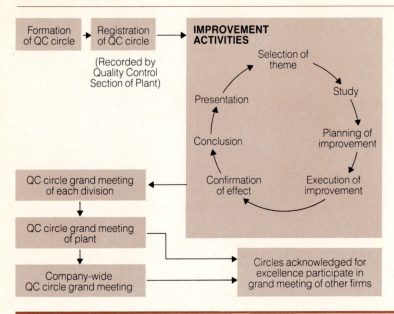

Figure 14.3 shows how these circles operate. Ask yourself this question: If there is no cash benefit from participating in these groups, why is there an almost 50 percent participation rate in Japan?

Part of the difficulty in answering this and similar questions lies in the cultural differences between this country and Japan. In Japan many employees work in an environment where they are guaranteed lifetime employment. They are provided many health, recreational, social, and economic opportunities by the company (see Exhibit 12.1 for one such company's program), and they generally view their relationship with the company with pride. In that environment the worker strives for cooperation and accommodation with the company's representatives. In this country all too often it appears that we see the worker-management relationship as an adversary relationship.

In spite of the cultural differences between Japan and the United States, QC circles are being organized in companies such as Motorola and Minnesota Mining and Manufacturing (3M). If these experiments are to succeed, a sincere trust and loyalty must exist between the worker and management. Such a relationship cannot be developed overnight, however; the groundwork for these programs had to have taken place years ago, and it is clear that the absence of positive labor-management relations will undoubtedly set back efforts at establishing QC circles in some companies. Nevertheless, companies in growing numbers are recognizing the importance of drawing their workers into the mainstream of their quality control programs. And this effort is sure to contribute to an overall elevation of quality control in the workers' consciousness, to result in unique and innovative solutions to quality problems, and to improve the likelihood of the workers cooperating in the implementation of programs to improve product quality.

Another reason for the superior quality of Japanese products is the extensive use of industrial robots on their assembly lines. This fact flies in the face of our traditional view that real product quality resulted from handcrafted products. Mercedes advertisements, for example, have emphasized that their products were handcrafted. Such promotions and our recollections of the distant past have led to our perception that anything produced by those cold, mechanical machines can never have the same quality as products that have been handcrafted. Such perceptions are just not true today. In fact, Japanese manufacturers and, more recently, U.S. manufacturers have found that product quality actually improves when industrial robots have been installed. At the Ford Motor Company, robots installed at its truck assembly plant in Norfolk, Virginia in 1980 have improved product quality and will permit a smaller work force. "Robotics is one of the most important technologies because the consistency of the robot ensures that the quality that is designed into the product will be built into it," said Robert S. Rennard, operations manager for Ford's body and assembly operations.[3] The use of robots as a competitive weapon in improving product quality may be the turning point for U.S. manufacturers in achieving parity with their Japanese counterparts.

Another important element of QC circles is training in the concepts and techniques of statistical quality control that was so strongly advocated to them by Edward M. Deming in the late 1940s. Here too, we shall need a brief review of certain statistical concepts that underlie quality control practices and thus are fundamental to the management of quality control programs.

Statistical Concepts in Quality Control

The ways that quality control departments achieve acceptable quality levels of products and services today have evolved over the past 100 years. The statistical underpinnings of today's quality control practices stem principally from the work of Shewhart, Dodge, and Romig at the Bell Telephone Laboratories during the 1920s. The techniques of random samples, statistical control charts, and statistical acceptance of products based on samples were developed by these men during this period. Their statistical sampling tables, although slowly accepted at first, are now widely used by quality control specialists in POM.

Sampling

Production departments routinely break the flow of products through their operations into discrete groups of units called *lots*. A lot of products will have been produced under the same conditions and will generally contain the appropriate number of units for economic control. For example, a lot of office scissors will include

---

[3] "Ford Says Robots Improve Quality of Truck Products," *The Houston Chronicle*, August 21, 1982, sec. 2, p. 3.

castings from a common lot, connecting rivets from a common lot, and paint from a common lot, and the scissors will be continuously produced under identical operating conditions. The maximum number of units in a lot of scissors may be limited to about 10,000 because of economics: as the number of units in a lot increases, the cost of physically keeping the lot together in production and storage becomes excessive. But as the number of units in a lot decreases, the sample represents too large a proportion of the lot and too large a percentage of the lot must be processed by inspectors and testing specialists; thus, very small lots are resisted. A compromise between very large and very small lots is struck in practice.

Lots of materials, assemblies, and finished products are sampled to determine if the lots meet desired quality control standards. *Random samples* are removed from these lots by inspectors and measured against certain standards. A random sample is one in which each unit in the lot has an equal chance of being included in the sample; thus, the sample is representative of the lot. Either attributes or variables can be measured and compared to standards.

Attributes are characteristics that are classified into one of two categories. In quality control, the two categories are usually *defective* and *nondefective*. For example, the lamp either lights up when connected to electrical current or it does not. *Variables* are characteristics that can be measured on a continuous scale. Inspectors who are inspecting for variables must measure the amount of a characteristic that is present and then determine if that amount is within the acceptable range before the unit can be passed. For example, the diameter of a motor shaft can be measured by a dial micrometer. If the diameter is within the minimum and maximum allowable diameters, the shaft passes the inspection.

An *acceptance plan* is the overall scheme for determining the acceptability of a lot based on sampling. The acceptance plan identifies both the size and type of samples and the criteria to be used to either pass or fail the lot. Samples may be either single, double, or sequential. *Single sampling plans* involve drawing one sample from a lot. If the number of defective units in the single sample does not exceed the maximum criteria of the plan, the lot passes.

Double sampling plans involve drawing one small sample initially. The lot is either accepted or rejected or another larger sample is drawn. If a second sample is required, the lot is either accepted or rejected, based on the total number of defects in both samples. The advantage of double sampling plans over single sampling plans lies in the possible reduction in inspection costs resulting from smaller initial sample sizes.

Sequential sampling plans carry the idea of smaller initial samples of double sampling plans one step further. Samples of increasing size are drawn sequentially as before and the lot is either accepted or rejected or another sample is drawn. This procedure is repeated until the lot is either accepted or rejected or the entire lot has been inspected by the sequential samples.

A concept that is important in applying sampling plans is the central limit theorem.

Central Limit Theorem and Quality Control

The *central limit theorem* may well be the most important single statistical concept in POM. Stated simply, this theorem is: *Sampling distributions can be assumed to be normally distributed even though the population distributions are not normal.* The only exception to this theorem is when sample sizes are extremely small. Computer studies show that in some cases even when sample sizes are as small as five, however, their *sampling distributions* are very close to normal distributions.[4]

Figure 14.4 compares a population distribution with its sampling distribution of sample means. We are obviously referring to variables in this figure since the population distribution includes all the possible measures of the variable x. The

Figure 14.4
A Comparison of Population and Sampling Distributions

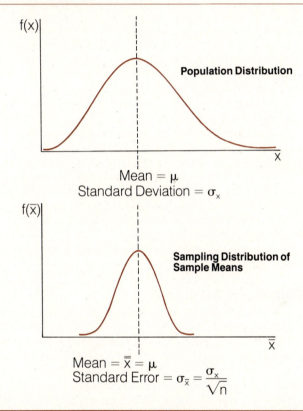

$f(x)$

Population Distribution

X

Mean $= \mu$
Standard Deviation $= \sigma_x$

$f(\bar{x})$

Sampling Distribution of Sample Means

$\bar{X}$

Mean $= \bar{\bar{x}} = \mu$
Standard Error $= \sigma_{\bar{x}} = \dfrac{\sigma_x}{\sqrt{n}}$

sampling distribution includes all the possible measures of sample means $\bar{x}$. We can make these generalizations about the sampling distribution:

1. The sampling distribution can be assumed to be normally distributed unless sample size (n) is extremely small.
2. The mean of the sampling distribution ($\bar{\bar{x}}$) is equal to the population mean (μ).
3. The standard error of the sampling distribution ($\sigma_{\bar{x}}$) is smaller than the population standard deviation (σ_x) by a factor of $1/\sqrt{n}$.

---

[4] Elwood S. Buffa, *Operations Management: Problems and Models,* 3d ed. (New York: Wiley, 1972), 616–617.

The power of the central limit theorem in quality control lies in its ability to allow quality control specialists to easily set limits for acceptance plans and control charts for both attributes and variables, which we shall discuss later in this chapter.

Two classes of quality control techniques are used almost daily in POM — control charts and acceptance plans. Let us now explore these two practical analysis and control decision-making tools.

Control Charts

Monitoring the processes that are producing an organization's products and services to be sure that outputs at any step in the productive system meet quality standards is an important part of all quality control programs. This ongoing activity of evaluating the quality characteristics of partially completed outputs produced from productive processes has one central purpose — to quickly discover when processes are going astray in their ability to produce products that comply with quality standards. Operations managers may then act to correct the malfunctions — replace worn tools, make machine adjustments, train and instruct workers, or deal with other problems that may be causing subquality outputs.

Control charts are useful aids to managers in monitoring the quality performance of the operations for which they are responsible. Managers can quickly glance at these charts and determine if the outputs of their operations are meeting quality standards and if unusual trends in quality should be investigated. Because of the flexibility of application of these tools, control charts are used in all types of business and governmental organizations today.

The way that control charts are constructed differs according to the quality characteristics that we wish to control.

Control Charts for Attributes

Defective or nondefective, yes or no, open or closed, pass or fail, and go or no-go are examples of attributes. Perhaps the most common attribute measurement in quality control is defective or nondefective. A control chart for controlling the percent of defectives in a sample, commonly called a *p* chart, is the principal chart for controlling attributes.

Constructing control charts involves three determinations: (1) center line, (2) upper control limit, and (3) lower control limit. After these three values are established, they become the benchmarks against which to compare future sample attribute values. Figure 14.5 is a *p* chart for controlling percent defectives in samples. This chart is used to plot the percent defectives in daily samples for the month of March. The upper control limit is slightly over 10 percent, the center line is 5 percent, and the lower control limit is 0 percent. As the daily sample percent defectives are plotted on this control chart, we can see that all the points are within the upper and lower control limits and no undesirable trends are present. Therefore, no management action to correct quality problems is necessary at this time.

Let us now try our hand at setting the center lines and control limits for control charts for controlling attributes. Example 14.1 requires a *p* chart for monitoring keypunch errors. Table 14.2 displays the formulas and variable definitions for the necessary calculations for control charts.

Figure 14.5
***p* Chart for Controlling Percent Defectives in Samples**

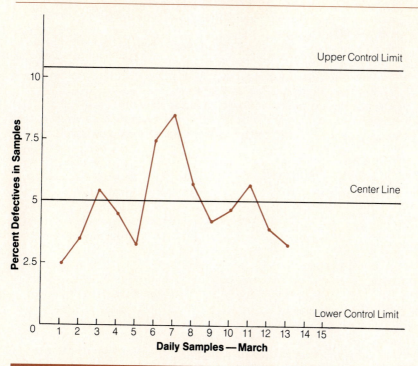

Table 14.2
**Formulas and Variable Definitions for Computing 3σ
Control Limits for Control Charts**

Type of Control Chart	Center Line	3σ Lower Control Limit	3σ Upper Control Limit
p	$\bar{p}$	$\bar{p} - 3\sqrt{\dfrac{\bar{p}(100 - \bar{p})}{n}}$	$\bar{p} + 3\sqrt{\dfrac{\bar{p}(100 - \bar{p})}{n}}$
$\bar{x}$	$\bar{\bar{x}}$	$\bar{\bar{x}} - A\bar{R}$	$\bar{\bar{x}} + A\bar{R}$
R	$\bar{R}$	$D_1\bar{R}$	$D_2\bar{R}$

p = Percent defectives in a sample
$\bar{p}$ = Average percent defectives across many samples
n = Sample size—number of observations in sample
$\bar{x}$ = A sample mean
$\bar{\bar{x}}$ = Mean of many sample means
R = A sample range
$\bar{R}$ = Mean of many sample ranges
A, D_1, D_2 = Factors from Table 14.3

Example 14.1

Constructing Control Charts for Attributes

Jane Morgan supervises 45 keypunch operators in their work at a large commercial computer center. Because of increasing problems with keypunch errors in recent months, Jane has decided to construct a control chart for each operator, draw daily samples of 20 cards (each card contains 5 keypunch transactions) for each operator, plot the sample error information on the control chart, and thereby monitor the quality performance of each operator. If the keypunch errors of any operator appear to be trending upward, Jane intends to provide training and counseling to help correct the problem. If, however, an operator consistently produces low levels of errors, special recognition and even bonuses may be provided. Jane knows that a well-trained keypunch operator should average 4 transactions that are in error in the 100 transactions contained in 20 computer cards of each sample. Jane wishes initially to construct a p chart with three standard deviation control limits for one operator to be used for a month. She has kept ten daily samples for one operator:

Sample Number	Number of Transactions in Error	Sample Number	Number of Transactions in Error	Sample Number	Number of Transactions in Error
1	4	5	1	8	12
2	3	6	9	9	4
3	3	7	5	10	3
4	6				

Solution

1. Compute three σ control limits for p:
   First, from Table 14.2 observe the control limits for p charts:

   Upper control limits $= \bar{p} + 3\sqrt{\dfrac{\bar{p}(100 - \bar{p})}{n}} = 4 + 3\sqrt{\dfrac{4(96)}{100}} = 4 + 3(1.9596)$

   $= 4 + 5.8788 = 9.88$ percent

   Lower control limits $= \bar{p} - 3\sqrt{\dfrac{\bar{p}(100 - \bar{p})}{n}} = 4 - 3\sqrt{\dfrac{4(96)}{100}} = 4 - 3(1.9596)$

   $= 4 - 5.8788 = -1.88$ percent or zero percent

2. Construct a p chart and plot the ten data points that Jane has collected.

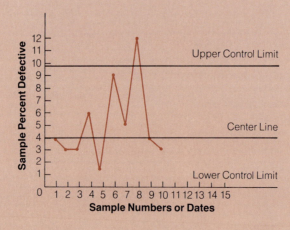

In this example the keypunch supervisor knows that experienced and well-trained operators should average 4 transactions in error in 100 keypunch transactions. This sets the center line at 4.0 percent for the p chart. Center lines are not always this easy to deduce. In cases when they are not, we usually draw samples from operators who are well trained and when processes are behaving normally. The mean percent defectives per sample is then used as the center line.

The control limits in Table 14.2 are 3σ control limits. This means that the control limits are three standard deviations from the center line. Because of the central limit theorem, we know that sampling distributions (control charts are sampling distributions) are normally distributed. In normal distributions three standard deviations either side of the mean includes 99.7 percent of the total observations. Therefore there is a 99.7 percent probability that sample data points will fall within the 3σ upper and lower control limits of control charts if the center line of the process being monitored has not changed. When data points are trending outside the control limits, we therefore tend to suspect that the underlying process is changing and management investigation is usually in order. Control limits for attributes could similarly be set at 95 percent, 90 percent, or any other confidence interval by substituting the appropriate Z scores from the normal distribution for the 3 in the formulas for p charts in Table 14.2. For example, 95 percent Z score = 1.96, 90 percent Z score = 1.64, and so on.

Don't make this classic mistake in constructing control charts: Someone gives you 30 sample data points, asks you to compute the center line and upper and lower control limits, asks you to plot the 30 sample data points on the control chart constructed from your control limit computations, and then asks you this question: Is the process in control? You just can't answer that question with the information you have. It is assumed that the 30 sample data points that were used to compute upper and lower control limits were drawn from a process that *was* under control. Even though an occasional data point can be outside the 3σ control limits just through chance, you should not have enough points outside the limits to indicate an out-of-control process when those same points were used to set the control limits.

The lower control limits in Example 14.1 are negative. Therefore, we set these limits at zero percent defectives. Lower control limits do not have to be negative or zero. On the contrary, they are often positive values. As it happens, however, we are seldom interested in lower control limits when controlling defectives. Exceeding lower control limits would indicate that the process being monitored had changed and that products of better quality than desired or expected were being produced. Managers do like to know when products of higher than expected quality are being produced. They may want to investigate the situation and determine the causes so that the condition can be continued, or higher quality in rare instances may indicate excessive costs if the condition continues.

Now let us move to constructing control charts for variables.

Control Charts for Variables

Variables are characteristics that take on values in varying degrees. Variables are measured in such units as pounds, gallons, feet, inches, and minutes. Samples are drawn from populations of products being produced from processes. These samples are usually described by sample means ($\overline{x}$) and sample ranges (R) for quality control purposes. Control charts are constructed for monitoring these variable values: $\bar{x}$ and R.

An $\bar{x}$ chart and an R chart are frequently used together to monitor the quality of products and services from a given process. The $\bar{x}$ chart monitors the average value of the variable being measured. The R chart monitors the variation among the items within samples. This dual monitoring therefore controls both average values and variation of values from their mean. Take, for example, the weights of boxes of cornflakes from a production line. An $\bar{x}$ chart may indicate that the sample average box weights are on target, but would you believe that without an R chart to monitor variation, box weights could range from zero to 10 pounds (assuming that a box would hold that much) within samples? This ridiculous example demonstrates that we usually cannot conclude that a process is in control just by monitoring sample means, but that variation within samples must also be monitored.

Example 14.2 demonstrates the construction of $\bar{x}$ and R charts in monitoring fill weights of boxes of cornflakes. Table 14.3 lists the control chart factors A, D_1, and D_2 for variables.

Table 14.3
Control Chart Factors for Variables

Sample Size n	Control Limit Factors for Sample Means	Control Limit Factors for Sample Ranges	
	A	D_1	D_2
2	1.880	0	3.267
3	1.023	0	2.575
4	.729	0	2.282
5	.577	0	2.116
10	.308	.223	1.777
15	.223	.348	1.652
20	.180	.414	1.586
25	.153	.459	1.541
Over 25	$.75(1/\sqrt{n})$*	$.45 + .001(n)$*	$1.55 - .0015(n)$*

* These values are approximations for student use in constructing control charts.

Source: *Economics Control of Manufactured Products* (New York: Litton Educational Publishing, Van Nostrand Reinhold Co., 1931). Copyright 1931, Bell Telephone Laboratories. Reprinted by permission.

Example 14.2 demonstrates an important truth in interpreting the information from control charts. Sometimes data trends are more important than the absolute values of the data. Trends can indicate the need for management corrective action *before* products and services of substandard quality are actually produced. Thus, managers carefully monitor the trends of control charts to discover potential quality problems in operations before they actually occur.

In contrast with this substandard quality prevention function of control charts, acceptance plans are devised to determine the acceptability of lots of products or materials *before* they are shipped to customers or used in production but *after* their quality is determined.

Example 14.2

Constructing Control Charts for Variables

The High Fiber Cereal Company has recently had numerous customer complaints about the fill weight of one of its products — 16-ounce packages of Peppy Corn Flakes. These complaints combined with increased government interest in High Fiber's operations have caused Bill Mallory, manager of High Fiber's quality control department, to direct Beverly Green to construct $\bar{x}$ and R control charts for the filling operation of 16-ounce Peppy Corn Flakes.

Beverly Green proceeds directly to the automatic filling operation. After first confirming that the process is operating properly, she begins to randomly select samples of 20 filled boxes hourly until 100 samples have been taken. The average of the 100 sample means is 16.1 ounces, and the average of the 100 sample ranges is 2.22 ounces.

Beverly now wishes to construct $\bar{x}$ and R charts and to begin plotting hourly sample means and ranges. These sample means and ranges were computed from samples subsequently taken from the filling operation:

Sample Number	Sample Means (Ounces)	Sample Ranges (Ounces)	Sample Number	Sample Means (Ounces)	Sample Ranges (Ounces)
1	16.2	2.0	7	16.0	2.9
2	15.9	2.1	8	16.1	1.8
3	16.3	1.8	9	16.3	1.5
4	16.4	3.0	10	16.3	1.0
5	15.8	3.5	11	16.4	1.0
6	15.9	3.1	12	16.5	.9

Beverly must determine whether the process is in control.

Solution

1. Compute the upper and lower control limits for the $\bar{x}$ and R charts:

   First, from Table 14.2 observe the control limits for an $\bar{x}$ chart ($\bar{\bar{x}}$ is the center line and equals 16.1 ounces; A is found in Table 14.3, A = .180 when n = 20):

   Upper control limit = $\bar{\bar{x}} + A\bar{R}$ = 16.1 + .180(2.22) = 16.1 + .400 = 16.500 ounces

   Lower control limit = $\bar{\bar{x}} - A\bar{R}$ = 16.1 − .180(2.22) = 16.1 − .400 = 15.700 ounces

   Next, from Table 14.2 observe the control limits for an R chart (D_2 is found in Table 14.3, D_2 = 1.586 when n = 20; D_1 is found in Table 14.3, D_1 = .414 when n = 20):

   Upper control limit = $D_2\bar{R}$ = 1.586(2.22) = 3.521 ounces

   Lower control limit = $D_1\bar{R}$ = .414(2.22) = .919 ounces

2. Plot the sample means and ranges on the $\bar{x}$ and R control charts:

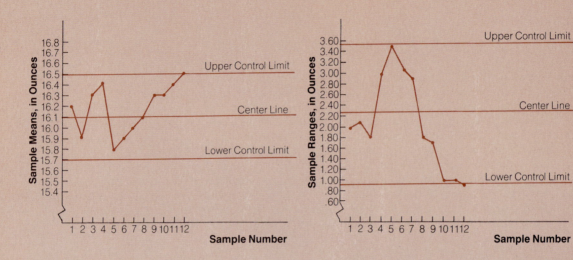

3. Is the process in control during the processing period of the 12 samples?

Although none of the sample means exceeded the control limits, the trend of the last 8 hours indicates a definite out-of-control situation. Unless this trend is reversed by management corrective action, excessive numbers of overfilled boxes will probably result. The R chart indicates that the sample ranges do not exceed the control limits. Curiously, however, the sample ranges of the last 8 hours have narrowed. This trend could be associated with the out-of-control situation of the sample means and should be investigated.

Acceptance Plans

Acceptance plans are used to decide whether lots of raw materials, subassemblies, or purchased parts received at the beginning, or lots of finished products at the end of productive systems meet the prescribed quality standards. Based on our accept-ance plan, we must either accept or reject each lot. If a lot of raw materials is accepted, we release the materials to the productive system or place them in inventory. If a lot of raw materials is rejected, the materials are returned to the supplier, the price of the materials is adjusted downward to allow for increased inspection and reworking costs, or some other mutually acceptable disposition of the rejected lot is made.

When a lot of finished products is accepted, it is either placed in finished goods inventory or shipped directly to customers. Depending upon the nature of the products, rejected lots may be thrown away or destroyed, ground up and reentered into the productive system at an earlier step, 100 percent inspected to save nonde-fective products, or some other *scrapping-out* procedure.

The key information in an acceptance plan is the criteria for accepting or rejecting a lot based on information deduced from a sample. In the case of attributes, what is the maximum percent defectives that we can find in a sample and still accept the lot? For variables, what is the largest and smallest sample mean and sample range that we can find and still accept the lot? The answers to these questions provide inspectors with the information they need to decide whether to accept or reject lots of materials.

Two approaches to setting acceptance criteria for samples are ordinarily used — (1) MIL STD, Dodge Romig, or other tables for attributes or (2) basic statistics to compute acceptance criteria for both attributes and variables. We know that many quality control departments exclusively use what they call *QC tables* for these decisions. However, because basic statistics underlies the construction of these tables, and because the basic statistical computations best teach us the principles of the application of acceptance plans, we shall develop these statistical approaches here.

Two important concepts are needed as background to acceptance plans when the characteristics being measured are attributes — average outgoing quality curves and operating characteristic curves.

Average Outgoing Quality (AOQ) Curves

Acceptance plans in quality control provide managers with the assurance that the average quality level or percent defectives actually going to customers will not exceed a certain limit. Figure 14.6 demonstrates this concept.

Figure 14.6
Average Outgoing Quality (AOQ) Curve

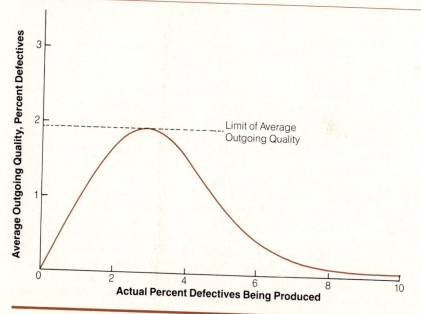

As the actual percent defectives in a production process increases—that is, moves along the horizontal from left to right in Figure 14.6—initially the effect is for lots to be passed even though the number of defectives has increased and the percent defectives going to customers increases. If this trend continues, however, the acceptance plan begins to reject lots. When lots are rejected, the lots are usually 100 percent inspected and the defective units are replaced with nondefective ones. The net effect of rejecting lots is therefore to improve the quality of the outgoing lots because the rejected lots that are ultimately shipped contain *all* nondefective units. As the actual percent defectives increases, the average outgoing quality improves because more and more lots are rejected. The extreme condition is when all lots are rejected and the percent defectives going to customers approaches zero.

Although each sampling plan exhibits a unique AOQ curve, this truth remains: **Acceptance plans protect an organization through limiting the percent of defective products that go to customers. This is an important consequence of acceptance plans and an important reason for implementing them.**

Operating Characteristic (OC) Curves

Four things can happen in applying acceptance plans, and two of them are bad. First the good news: we can accept good lots and reject bad lots. Now, for the bad news: we can accept bad lots and reject good lots. In the vast majority of cases, we do accept good lots and reject bad lots when we apply acceptance plans. But we know from experience that on rare occasions we also ship bad lots to customers even though our samples have met the acceptance criteria of our acceptance plans. Similarly, when we are reworking lots that have been rejected because the samples have not met the acceptance criteria, we occasionally find that these rejected lots were really good ones. These outcomes are unfortunate, but they are a fact of life in quality control programs.

When we stand before a lot of products, we just don't know with certainty the quality of all of the products. Even after drawing a random sample from the lot, we still don't know with certainty the quality of the products in the lot. All we do know is the quality of the products included in the sample. From this information about the small proportion of the products in a lot, we must infer the quality of *all* the products in the lot. This is a risky inference, but it is the nature of acceptance plans.

Operating characteristic (OC) curves describe an important feature of acceptance plans: *an OC curve shows how well an acceptance plan discriminates between good and bad lots.* Figure 14.7 shows such an OC curve. When the actual percent defectives in a lot is very low and the lot is good, say 2 percent, the probability of accepting the lot is 75 percent, and the probability of rejecting the good lot (*producer's risk*) is therefore 25 percent. If, however, the actual percent defectives in the lot is very high and the lot is bad, say 5 percent, the probability of accepting the bad lot (*consumer's risk*) is only 10 percent.

We want acceptance plans that pass good lots and fail bad lots. That is what we mean by an acceptance plan that discriminates between good and bad lots. We cannot, however, always have a sampling plan that achieves this objective to perfection. For example, a good lot of 10,000 items with only 5 defectives could conceivably produce a random sample of 100 units which contains all of the 5

Figure 14.7
An Operating Characteristic (OC) Curve

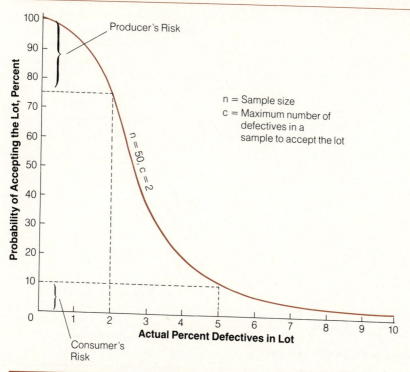

Note: A good lot in this acceptance plan is defined as a lot with 2 or less percent defectives, and a bad lot is defined as a lot with 5 or more percent defectives.

defectives. Thus, acceptance plans could reject the lot when the lot is actually good. Conversely, the lot could have 1,000 defectives and the random sample could have no defectives. In this case, a bad lot could be passed by the acceptance plan. Since these examples demonstrate how all acceptance plans can fail to discriminate between good and bad lots because of sampling error (random chance), how can managers modify acceptance plans to minimize these occurrences?

Perhaps the most obvious way is to increase the sample size. Figure 14.8 compares three different sampling plans: $n = 100$, $c = 4$; $n = 50$, $c = 2$; and $n = 25$, $c = 1$, where n is sample size and c is the maximum number of defectives in a sample from an acceptable lot. Note that even though each plan uses the same percent defectives as the maximum allowable for an acceptable lot (4/100, 2/50, 1/25 = .04 or 4 percent), the larger the sample size of the plan, the greater its discriminating power. Compare the $n = 25$ and $n = 100$ plans, for instance:

Figure 14.8
OC Curves for Different Sample Sizes — The Discriminating Power of Acceptance Plans (Ability to Reject Bad Lots and Accept Good Lots) Is Enhanced by Increasing Sample Size (n)

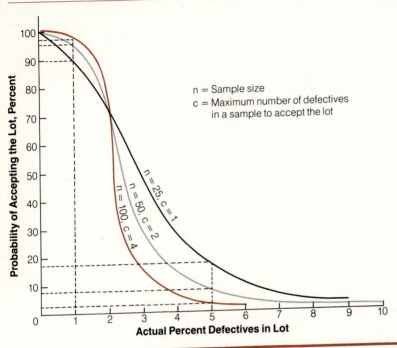

n = Sample size
c = Maximum number of defectives
    in a sample to accept the lot

Sampling Plan	Actual Percent Defectives in Lot	Probability of Accepting the Lot (Percent)	Sampling Plan	Actual Percent Defectives in Lot	Probability of Accepting the Lot (Percent)
n = 100	1	97.5	n = 25	1	90.0
	5	3.0		5	17.5

When n = 100, the probability of accepting very good lots (1 percent defectives) is 97.5 percent, and the probability of accepting bad lots (5 percent defectives) is only 3.0 percent. When n = 25, the corresponding probabilities are 90 percent and 17.5 percent. Acceptance plans with smaller sample sizes reject more good lots and accept more bad lots.

Why wouldn't we always have acceptance plans with large sample sizes? Because larger sample sizes cost more in inspection costs. Operations managers are therefore faced with this dilemma: we can avoid shipping bad lots and rejecting good lots but only at additional cost. What acceptance plan or sample size offers the best balance between inspection costs and costs of undetected defects as shown in Figure 14.2? The answer to this question is unique to each POM situation.

Are OC curves practical quality control tools in POM? If we mean by this question,

"Do quality control personnel actually use OC curves to make their day-to-day decisions?" then the answer is probably no. But OC curves and AOQ curves are useful in understanding the operation of acceptance plans, which we shall now discuss.

Acceptance Plans for Attributes

Example 14.3 demonstrates the steps in setting acceptance criteria for the percent defectives observed in samples of ball bearings. Table 14.4 exhibits the formulas and variable definitions in acceptance plans for attributes (percent defectives) and variables (sample means).

Table 14.4
Formulas and Variable Definitions for Computing Acceptance Criteria for Acceptance Plans

Characteristic Being Measured	Sample Measure	Acceptance Criteria
Attribute	Percent defectives (p)	$\bar{p} \pm Z\sqrt{\dfrac{\bar{p}(100 - \bar{p})}{n}}$
Variable	Sample mean $(\bar{x})$	$\bar{\bar{x}} \pm Z\sigma_{\bar{x}}$

α = Significance level or (1 − confidence interval); always is given assuming a two-tailed test, and includes total area in both tails.

p = Percent defectives in a sample

$\bar{p}$ = Average percent defectives across many samples

n = Sample size

$\bar{x}$ = A sample mean

$\bar{\bar{x}}$ = Mean of many sample means

Z = Z scores. These values depend upon the significance level (probability of sample measures exceeding acceptance criteria even though the lot is acceptable). $\alpha = .10$, $\alpha = .05$, $\alpha = .01$ are typically specified. The corresponding Z scores from the normal distribution are 1.64, 1.96, and 2.58.

$\sigma_{\bar{x}}$ = Standard error of the mean of the sampling distribution. $\sigma_{\bar{x}} = \dfrac{\sigma_x}{\sqrt{n}}$ or $\dfrac{\bar{S}_x}{\sqrt{n}}$, where σ_x is the population standard deviation deduced from past production records and $\bar{S}_x$ is the mean of many sample standard deviations $[S_x = \sqrt{\Sigma(x - \bar{x})^2/(n - 1)}$

Example 14.3

Setting Acceptance Criteria for Attributes

The Roll Perfect Bearing Company in Detroit produces ball and roller bearings of various sizes for automobile manufacturers. One such ball bearing, the ½" 5525 Chrome Polished Bearing—No. 3580, has been the subject of numerous customer complaints in recent months because of surface defects. Marsha Pool, the director of Roll Perfect's quality control department, has decided that an acceptance plan based on random samples should be established for this product. Marsha carefully researches past records when the surface polishing operation was known to be operating properly and finds that 2 percent of the No. 3580 ball bearings were defective. If a sample size of 200 bearings and a significance level of .05 is to be used: **a.** Set the acceptance criteria for the percent defectives in a sample. **b.** If a sample is drawn that has 7 defective ball bearings, should the lot be accepted?

Solution

a. Set the acceptance criteria for the percent defectives in a sample:

First, refer to Table 14.4 and observe that the acceptance criteria formula for the percent defectives is:

$$= \bar{p} \pm Z \sqrt{\frac{\bar{p}(100 - \bar{p})}{n}}$$

where $\bar{p}$ is the average percent defectives across many samples and equals 2 percent in this example. Because $\alpha = .05$, $\alpha/2 = .025$ is assigned to either tail of the normal sampling distribution and this fixes Z at ± 1.96.

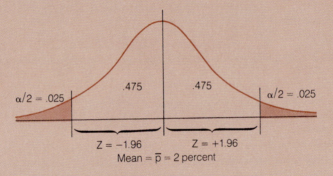

$\alpha/2 = .025$ .475   .475 $\alpha/2 = .025$

$Z = -1.96$ $Z = +1.96$
Mean $= \bar{p} = 2$ percent

Therefore, the acceptance criteria for p are:

$$= \bar{p} \pm Z \sqrt{\frac{\bar{p}(100 - \bar{p})}{n}} = 2 \pm 1.96 \sqrt{\frac{2(98)}{200}} = 2 \pm 1.96(.9899) = 2 \pm 1.9403$$

$$= .0597 \text{ and } 3.9403 \text{ or } .06 \text{ and } 3.94 \text{ percent}$$

b. A sample of 200 ball bearings has 7 defectives. Should the sample be accepted? Yes, because $7/200 = 3.5$ percent and falls within the acceptance criteria of .06 and 3.94 percent defectives.

Notice that the formula for acceptance criteria for percent defectives in Table 14.4 includes n, which is the sample size. If sample sizes vary from sample to sample, the acceptance criteria must also vary with n and therefore must either be computed for each sample or be reduced to tabular form for quick referral.

Acceptance plans for variables are not as commonly found in books of tables as those for attributes. Basic statistical computations therefore tend to be fundamental for establishing these acceptance plans.

Acceptance Plans for Variables

Example 14.4 shows how to set the acceptance criteria for the mean compression strength of core samples taken from a 10-mile section of a large interstate highway system.

Example 14.4

Setting Acceptance Criteria for Variables

The U.S. Department of Transportation (DOT) must accept sections of paving constructed by private contractors in the interstate highway system. These sections are usually 10 miles long, and they are accepted based on cores drilled from the concrete pavement at random intervals. DOT specifications require a compression strength in the roadway of 12,500 pounds per square inch.

Luis Gentry, head testing engineer for the third district, wishes to establish a statistical acceptance plan wherein sections of pavement would be accepted based on the mean compression strength of a sample of 50 cores removed from each section. Luis knows from experience that the standard deviation of compression strength for thousands of cores from hundreds of miles of pavement is 1,625 pounds per square inch. **a.** Set the acceptance criteria of DOT's acceptance plan if $\alpha = .01$. **b.** Fifty cores are pulled from a 10-mile section. The mean compression strength of the sample is 11,500 pounds per square inch. Should the section of pavement be accepted?

Solution

a. Set the acceptance criteria:

First, refer to Table 14.4 and observe that the acceptance criteria for sample means ($\bar{x}$) are:

$$= \bar{\bar{x}} \pm Z\sigma_{\bar{x}}$$

Because $\alpha = .01$, the Z score = 2.58.

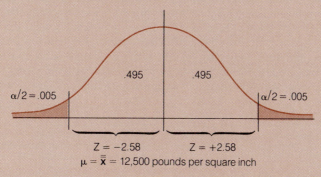

$$Z = -2.58 \qquad Z = +2.58$$
$$\mu = \bar{\bar{x}} = 12{,}500 \text{ pounds per square inch}$$

Because $\sigma_x = 1,625$ from the problem, $\sigma_{\bar{x}} = \sigma_x/\sqrt{n} = 1,625/\sqrt{50} = 229.81$ pounds per square inch. Therefore, the acceptance criteria are:

$$= \bar{\bar{x}} \pm Z(\sigma_{\bar{x}}) = 12,500 \pm 2.58(229.81) = 12,500 \pm 592.91$$
$$= 11,907.09 \text{ and } 13,092.91 \text{ pounds per square inch}$$

Luis Gentry is not concerned that a section of pavement might have a compression strength that is too high.

b. Should a section with a sample mean compression strength of 11,500 pounds per square inch be accepted?

No, because 11,500 falls outside the minimum sample mean acceptance criterion of 11,907.09 pounds per square inch.

Setting acceptance criteria in this example requires that the mean of sample means ($\bar{\bar{x}}$), significance level (α), and the population standard deviation (σ_x) must all be known. This, realistically speaking, is seldom the case. Rather, quality control specialists must usually establish the $\bar{\bar{x}}$ and σ_x values through field research. The $\bar{\bar{x}}$ could be established, for example, by reviewing the historical records of many sample means ($\bar{x}$) and averaging these $\bar{x}$s if the highway sections in these historical periods were good sections. Alternatively, the $\bar{\bar{x}}$ can be set as in this example by using a target, goal, or specification value. The σ_x must usually be deduced from historical information. A large group of cores from a number of acceptable sections could, for example, be tested and the standard deviation of these cores about their mean could be computed. This value could then be used as an estimate of σ_x.

The significance level (α) is usually specified as a management policy. Its value is usually based upon this reasoning: (1) If we would prefer to err on the side of accepting bad highway sections rather than rejecting good ones, we would select a small value of α, say about .01. (2) If, however, we would prefer to err on the side of rejecting good highway sections rather than accepting bad ones, we would select a large value of α, say about .10. (3) If we would wish to compromise between the two positions above, we would select an intermediate value of α, say about .05.

Although the computation of acceptance criteria in this section has been based on statistical concepts that you learned in your introductory statistics course, business organizations today usually determine acceptance criteria by consulting a book of sampling tables.[5] These tables require that managers specify such information as: (1) average percent defectives in lots generated when production processes are in control; (2) definition of bad lots (for example, lots with more than 5 percent defectives are bad) and the probability of accepting bad lots (consumer's risk); (3) definition of good lots (for example, lots with less than 2 percent defectives are good) and the probability of rejecting good lots (producer's risk); and (4) lot size. These specifications basically require managers to define a good lot and a bad lot,

[5] H. F. Dodge and H. G. Romig, *Sampling Inspection Tables* (New York: Wiley, 1959); and Munitions Board Standards Agency, U.S. Department of Defense, *Military Standard, Sampling Procedures and Tables for Inspection for Attributes* (Washington, DC: Government Printing Office, 1950).

determine the underlying percent defectives of the process, and the lot size. The tables then set the sample size and maximum number of allowable defectives.

Acceptance plans provide managers with a practical way of measuring quality levels of materials and products. When tests must be performed that destroy the materials and products, acceptance plans are the only feasible way of assessing quality levels and still having some materials and products survive for use and shipment. Additionally, acceptance plans are more economical than the alternative of 100 percent inspection. We as consumers should appreciate this advantage in lower prices. Acceptance plans also offer the last-ditch quality protection for consumers. The AOQ concept that was discussed earlier in this chapter demonstrated this principle: no matter what the quality level of the products coming out of productive systems, acceptance plans insure that there is an upper limit to the average percent defectives in outgoing lots. Acceptance plans are therefore a practical fact of life in most organizations today.

The record-keeping and computation activities in quality control departments that we have discussed thus far in this chapter have become increasingly laborious. Computers are taking over a growing share of these tasks.

Computers in Quality Control

In the late 1970s one tire manufacturer recalled millions of potentially faulty steel-belted radial tires. At about the same time an automobile manufacturer recalled hundreds of thousands of automobiles to correct potentially defective cruise control devices. Recall programs such as these require that manufacturers know information such as: (1) The lot numbers of raw materials, assemblies, and parts that are responsible for the potential defects, (2) an information storage system that can tie the lot numbers of the suspected raw materials, assemblies, and parts to the final product model numbers, and (3) an information system that tracks model numbers of final products to owner/consumers. In an industry such as the U.S. automobile industry, where each of the final products has between 5,000 and 10,000 parts and 8 to 10 million automobiles are produced each year, the information storage systems needed to support quality control records for potential recalls are indeed large. These systems must be computer-based information systems because manual transactions would not only be uneconomical but physically impossible.

Many industries such as the automobile industry are required under federal and state governmental regulations to retain such material lot records. Pharmaceutical firms, food manufacturers, and manufacturers of certain chemicals are also closely regulated in their record keeping. Even if an industry is not closely regulated by governmental agencies, however, such records are kept in order to limit its exposure in the event of product liability suits or the threat of such actions. Besides, it's just good business to be able to track your products from production through consumers' use, and this tracking is now more convenient and economical with the increasingly widespread use of computers.

Computers are also used to provide quicker information to managers about the quality of outputs coming from processes within productive systems. Control charts were described in this chapter as devices that indicate when product quality from a particular process is either substandard or developing worrisome trends that require management corrective action. The time lag between the time when materials, assemblies, parts, or products are inspected as they are leaving a particular process until they are measured, tested, the results posted on control charts, and finally, when managers review this information, can be too long for managers to take *timely* corrective action. Computers are now being used to reduce this time lag.

Computer terminals are located at inspection stations near production operations so that quality control inspectors can input measurements and test results to control chart computer programs. These programs automatically and quickly detect out-of-control sample results (beyond 3σ limits) and trends that require management attention. Because only those processes that require corrective action are highlighted by the computer system, managers' time is devoted less to data processing and more to corrective action, investigation, and planning. Thus, computers allow managers to manage rather than to process data and to manage on a more timely basis.

Similarly, computer programs are used to make decisions on whether lots should be accepted based on sample measurements. These programs are first used to set the criteria for acceptance. Then the sample measurements are inputted, and the acceptance decision is recommended by the programs. The time lags are reduced in these decisions, and thus products may be shipped to customers more quickly and materials may be moved more quickly into production.

The increasing role of computers in process control and acceptance decisions not only reduces time lags, but additionally makes possible certain cost reductions. The reduced calculations that were formerly required to manually prepare control charts and make acceptance plan decisions have freed up quality control personnel to perform other duties. In some cases the number of these personnel has actually been reduced. Inventory levels may be reduced because fewer lots are in quality control holding areas waiting for disposition. Reduced inventories can reduce holding costs, free up capital funds, and promote increased operating efficiency through reduced congestion.

The growth of computers in quality control departments has been spearheaded by a growing list of computer companies and computer software companies that provide standard quality control computer programs. These special programs are usually an integral part of larger management information systems and thus involve little out-of-pocket cost to users.

Computers and service industries are both becoming dominant forces in our economic system. Service systems must also be concerned with the quality of their outputs, but the nature of these systems defies the straightforward adoption of quality control programs from manufacturing.

Quality Control in Services

The outputs of service systems are usually intangible and the quality of these services is difficult to determine because quality standards are practically nonexistent. Take, for example, the problem airlines face when they try to determine the quality of the performance of flight attendants. Even if they could effectively measure the characteristics that relate to the quality of flight attendant services, they would not have any objective standards against which to compare those measurements. This subjectivity in determining the quality of services is the greatest obstacle to developing quality control programs in these organizations.

The perceived quality of services is often a function of the surroundings in which services are delivered to customers. Quiet, soft music, pleasant decor, comfortable furniture, convenient parking facilities, friendly atmosphere, cleanliness, and other features of the service facility itself can determine the perceived quality of the service more than the quality of the actual service. Better hospitals, banks, and restaurants, for example, all invest heavily in designing and maintaining facilities that develop particular feelings and impressions within their customers.

Services tend to be labor intensive and workers tend to come in direct contact with customers. In fact, in many services employees directly perform the service for customers. In these situations the performances of individual employees determine the quality of the services. And yet service organizations tend to be highly decentralized and geographically dispersed. Therefore, direct supervision of service personnel tends to be impractical. Many service organizations have determined that the most important element of their quality control programs is an intensive continuing education and training program for their employees. McDonald's Hamburger University and Holiday Inn's University are examples of service organizations that have established their own training centers.[6]

Even though services are more difficult to develop quality control programs for, can acceptance plans and control charts be used in service systems? Acceptance plans can be used, but usually only for accepting raw materials, supplies, and the like that are inputs to service systems. Because outputs are usually intangible, acceptance plans are not commonly used. Control charts are commonly used in service systems for the same purpose as in productive systems—to provide managers with information about when corrective action may be necessary at critical steps in the productive system. For example, automobile gas mileage, accounting errors, supplies cost per dollar of sales, tips per waitress per month, convictions or arrests for law enforcement officers, occupancy rates of motels, pulse rates in hospitals, and student and faculty evaluation factors are all displayed on control charts. The diversity of these measures emphasizes the flexibility of control chart applicability in controlling quality as well as costs and other dimensions of performance.

Summary

Statistical concepts form the foundation of today's quality control discipline. Material lots; random samples; attributes and variables; acceptance plans; single, double, and sequential sampling plans; and quality control tables are all based on the field of statistics. The central limit theorem allows quality control analysts to assume that sampling distributions are normally distributed. This is fundamental to control charts and acceptance plans.

Japanese firms have been very successful in encouraging their employees to

[6] W. Earl Sasser, R. Paul Olsen, and D. Daryl Wyckoff, *Management of Service Operations* (Boston: Allyn & Bacon, 1978), 17.

participate in improving the quality of their mass-manufactured products. They have used the concept of quality circles, volunteer groups of workers who develop projects for improving the quality of the products in their own areas. QC circles are now being used in this and other countries. It is hoped that some, if not all, of the benefits that Japan has enjoyed from these groups can be experienced here and elsewhere.

Control charts are used by managers to determine if the quality of products or services is in control during production processes or if worrisome trends are developing for which corrective action is needed. p charts are used to control percent defectives (an attribute) in a sample. $\bar{x}$ and R charts are used to control sample means and sample ranges (variables).

Average outgoing quality (AOQ) curves and operating characteristic (OC) curves both help explain the workings of acceptance plans. Although these plans are not foolproof — they can on rare occasions reject good lots and accept bad ones — they do offer operations managers a good compromise between economy and quality control protection. These plans set the acceptance criteria for samples so that inspectors can either accept or reject lots of materials or products. Attributes (p) or variables ($\bar{x}$ and R) can be measured from samples, and appropriate acceptance criteria can be developed for these plans.

Computers are being used increasingly in quality control departments. The information storage and retrieval capabilities of computers are used to retain the massive volume of records for material and product lots. Control chart information is also processed on computers, thus providing information to managers more quickly so that corrective action can be initiated while it is still possible to avoid production of poor quality products. Acceptance plan computations are also processed on computers. These uses of computers are providing quality control departments with lower costs and faster reaction time.

Quality control in services can be more difficult than in product systems because the outputs are often intangible and quality standards can be subjective. Additionally, the features of the service facilities may be more important in customer perception of quality than the quality of the actual service. Service firms are turning more and more to continuing education and training of their personnel as the key element of their quality control programs. Acceptance plans are commonly used in services to accept materials and supplies as inputs to these systems, but not for their outputs. Control charts are used to control a wide range of quality control measures in service systems.

Review and Discussion Questions

1. What are four elements of most quality control programs? Discuss the meaning of this statement: "You can't *inspect* quality into products."

2. Name two sources of morale or cooperation problems that can occur as quality control and production personnel interact.

3. What two sources of cost do managers attempt to balance when deciding how many — what proportion of total — products to inspect?

4. Define these terms: **a.** *lot*, **b.** *random sample*, **c.** *attribute*, **d.** *variable*, **e.** *acceptance plan*, **f.** *single sampling plan*, **g.** *double sampling plan*, and **h.** *sequential sampling plan*.

5. Define the *central limit theorem*. What are its principal uses in quality control?

6. Define a *quality circle*. Describe how it works.

7. What benefits do Japanese companies enjoy from QC circles?

8. Define these values. **a.** p, **b.** $\bar{x}$, **c.** R. Are they variables or attributes?

9. What is the purpose of control charts?

10. "Four things can happen in applying acceptance plans, and two of them are bad." Explain how these bad occurrences are possible.

11. Explain how you would decide what significance level to use in an acceptance plan.

12. What is the principal message that an average outgoing quality (AOQ) curve explains about an acceptance plan?

13. What is the most obvious way that acceptance plans can be modified to reduce the probability of accepting bad lots and rejecting good ones?

14. Name two factors that make quality control in service systems more difficult than in manufacturing.

15. What quality control strategy have service systems devised to deal with the fact that services tend to be labor intensive and geographically dispersed?

Problems

Control Charts

1. Given: $\bar{p} = 2.5$ percent and n = 25. Required: Compute 3σ control limits for p.

2. The southeastern distribution center for Jeans Inc. receives shipments of Western style denim trousers from manufacturers, places its own labels on the jeans, packages them, and ships them to its retail outlets throughout the southeastern United States. In recent months the center has received numerous complaints about the quality of the labeling operation. Labels are said to be too loose and some have even fallen off the garments. Janie Hochevar, director of production at the center, has decided to record the number of defective labels in random daily samples on control charts. If Janie estimates that 1.5 percent of loose labels is about normal, on the average, the sample size is 200 pairs of jeans, and a p chart is to be used: **a.** Compute the center line for the p chart. **b.** Compute the 3σ control limits for the chart. **c.** Plot these recent data collected from daily samples and decide if the labeling operation is in control: Number of defectives per sample = 2, 3, 5, 2, 7, 8, 3, 0, 5, 7, 9, 2.

3. Bill O'Fallon, vice-president for administrative services at Biltmore College, is concerned about the number of students who are dropping out of the college because of academic deficiencies each quarter. He believes that Biltmore should average about 285 academic drops per quarter out of a total stable student population of 9,500 students. Bill wishes to develop a control chart for the percent of academic drops in quarterly random samples of 500 students. The last ten quarters' records show these numbers of drops in random samples: 18, 18, 13, 10, 12, 9, 11, 8, 14, 8. **a.** Compute the 95 percent control limits. **b.** Plot the ten quarters of sample data on a control chart. **c.** Has there been a change in the percent of academic drops per quarter at Biltmore?

4. The average absenteeism rate for the clerical workers at the National Insurance Company (NIC) headquarters in Atlanta averages about 5 percent. Department heads voluntarily send data to the personnel department analytical records group to develop random samples of records for about 200 workers weekly out of a total clerical work force of 5,000 workers. These sample sizes and number of absences are received:

Sample Number	Sample Size	Number Absent	Sample Number	Sample Size	Number Absent
1	200	10	7	200	12
2	150	10	8	180	10
3	170	12	9	220	10
4	220	12	10	200	11
5	180	13	11	160	10
6	120	8	12	100	6

a. Construct a 3σ control chart for p and plot the sample data points. (Hint: The upper and lower control limits vary with sample size.) b. Has there been a change in the absenteeism rate at NIC?

5. Given: $\bar{\bar{x}} = 24$ inches, $\bar{R} = 5$ inches, and n $= 10$. Required: a. Compute 3σ control limits for $\bar{x}$. b. Plot these sample means on an $\bar{x}$ control chart: 24.1, 23.5, 24.7, 25.2, 25.8, 25.7, 26.1, 25.8, 26.7, 27.0. c. Is the process in control?

6. Given: $\bar{R} = 5.0$ inches and n $= 10$. Required: a. Compute 3σ control limits for R. b. Plot these sample ranges on a 3σ control chart for R: 2.9, 4.6, 6.9, 5.4, 1.6, 2.7, 6.9, 6.5, 8.1, 3.6. c. Is the process in control?

7. The Bi-State Trucking Company, a local deliverer of freight in Durham, North Carolina, has been experiencing customer complaints about late deliveries. Bi-State's management strives for an average delivery of local freight in 24 hours. Weekly samples of 20 customers are taken and exhibit an average range of 3.5 hours. Bi-State's management thinks this is about right. a. Compute 3σ control limits for $\bar{x}$. b. Plot these sample means on a 3σ control chart for $\bar{x}$: 23.4, 24.5, 23.9, 25.6, 26.5, 23.8, 23.7, 24.1, 25.1, 24.9. c. Is management's target of an average 24-hour delivery being met?

8. The No-Cal Bottling Company bottles soft drinks for sale to government commissaries. The bottles come in only one flavor (chocolate-lemon) and only one size (32 ounces). Joan Stickler, the quality control officer for the commissaries, wants to keep track of the fill weights of No-Cal and begins to draw daily samples of 100 bottles from the daily receipts. The first ten sample means and ranges are:

Sample	$\bar{x}$	R	Sample	$\bar{x}$	R
1	31.5	2.1	6	31.5	.7
2	31.2	2.5	7	31.7	1.2
3	32.1	3.0	8	31.2	2.0
4	30.9	1.6	9	32.8	1.7
5	32.7	1.7	10	31.9	0

If sample ranges ordinarily average 2.5 ounces: a. Compute 3σ control limits for sample means. b. Compute 3σ control limits for sample ranges. c. What would you conclude about the fill weights of No-Cal?

Acceptance Plans

9. Given: $\bar{p}$ = 10 percent, n = 200, α = .10, and c = number of defectives in a sample from a lot = 26. Required: Determine whether the sample percent defectives is large enough to reject the lot.

10. Betty Childress is regional quality manager for McDougal's Hamburgers. She wishes to establish an acceptance plan for hamburger cartons, with particular emphasis on the cartons' closing mechanisms. Several samples of normal carton shipments indicated that 5 percent of cartons from normal shipments had defective closing mechanisms. A sample of 500 cartons from a lot of 100,000 cartons had 6.5 percent defectives. If an α of .05 is used, should the lot be accepted?

11. The Rigid Beam Construction Company specializes in steel beam construction of high-rise buildings. Rivets are used by the thousands in this type of construction, and the tensile strength of the rivets is extremely important to the overall strength of these structures. Rigid draws random samples of rivets and subjects them to tensile force until they fail. If they fail after the force reaches 10,000 pounds, they pass. If they fail before the force reaches 10,000 pounds, they don't pass. Good lots of rivets average about 4 percent defectives. A lot of rivets from a new supplier has recently arrived. An inspector has just conducted a test of 100 rivets with 93 passing. If, given the choice, you would rather err on the side of rejecting good lots, should you accept the lot?

12. Given: μ = 28 ounces, σ_x = 4 ounces, n = 196, $\bar{x}$ = 27.40 ounces, and α = .10. Required: Determine whether to accept or reject the lot.

13. The Provo Steel Corporation buys coal from the Sun River Mining Company. Sun River ships low-volatility, low-sulfur coal from its mines at Howe, Oklahoma, via railroad cars. These cars are intended to hold precisely 60 tons because Provo Steel depends upon this weight as the primary basis for its blending operations prior to charging its coke ovens. Provo's records show that when Sun River is attentive, their cars of coal average 60 tons, a contractual requirement of Provo, with a standard deviation of 1 ton, and then the cars of coal can go directly into the coke ovens; but when Sun River is not attentive, Provo must unload the cars, weigh out exactly 60-ton charges of coal, and then charge the coke ovens. Provo wishes to take daily sample car weights and determine whether unloading and weighing the entire daily shipment is necessary. Ten cars are randomly selected from a day's shipment, and the mean car weight is 61.5 tons. If Provo would rather err on the side of accepting out-of-weight cars, should they accept the day's shipment from Sun River directly into the coke ovens?

14. Professor Knowitall keeps track of the grade point average (GPA) of his students from semester to semester. Overall he has found that his students average 2.5 out of 4.0 with a standard deviation of .25 among all his students, which is about the same as for the entire university. This semester, however, one of his classes of 75 students does not seem to be performing as well as they should on his standard exams. This class has a GPA of 2.43 and the professor wonders if this particular class might be academically below par. Use what you have learned in quality control analysis to help the professor resolve the issue.

Case

Gas Generator Corporation

Bill Blame has just received a big promotion to works manager and director of Gas Generator's largest plant, located in Carbondale, Illinois. The plant's products are gas generators that serve as power sources for the guidance systems for the most advanced U.S. missiles. After the euphoria of moving his family from California to the new location, meeting his new staff, and settling into his new office had passed, he got the bad news — one lot of the plant's products had just been rejected by its best customer. He noticed that the plant's staff members were not too concerned because, according to them, "It has happened before."

Mr. Blame called a meeting of all of the technical staff as soon as the test data from the customer had been received. He asked the following questions: (1) What was the nature of the test failure? (2) What caused the substandard products to be produced? (3) What should we have done differently in our production processes to have avoided the problem? (4) What is the impact of this failure on our operations? The staff summarized the nature of the failure this way. The products performed well under all conditions except the deep-freeze firing, and then the generators produced volumes of gas that were only slightly below standard. As for the other questions, the answers were the same: "We don't know!" Mr. Blame dispersed the group with instructions to develop the answers to his questions. He then called the home office to inform his boss, Mr. Don Billigan, that a potentially large problem loomed on the horizon and that he would keep him informed of the progress of the investigation.

The next morning the staff met again to discuss the problem. The news was much worse than Mr. Blame had thought. The entire finished goods inventory and in-process inventory back to the mixing stage of production were similarly substandard. Because it would take at least 3 months to introduce new materials at the mixing stage and process them through final assembly and delivery, the plant faced the prospect of 3 months of filling the pipeline without any revenue. The staff members were stumped, however, about the exact cause of the failure. Mr. Blame called Mr. Billigan and told him the bad news: "We won't have any finished products to ship for at least 90 days, we will have a net loss of about $500,000 before taxes during this period, we will be in default of our delivery contracts, and we don't know for sure what caused the problem or what needs to be done to correct it, but we are continuing the investigation."

Mr. Blame started with the mixing operation and worked forward through the production process to determine if their workers were following the *Manual of Standard Operating Procedures*. Two observers were assigned to every major operation in the process to verify that the procedures were being followed. It took only a week to determine that the workers were not following the procedures at the mixing operation. It took another week to verify that when the procedures were religiously followed, the in-process materials met the quality control performance specifications.

Assignment

1. What are the underlying causes of the quality control problem at the Gas Generator plant?

2. Discuss any difficiencies in the quality control program that are apparent from the case.

3. Why didn't the acceptance tests indicate the problem before the customer discovered it? Is such an occurrence possible? How would such a problem arise?

4. Discuss the appropriateness of the methods that Mr. Blame used to investigate the problem. How might he have acted to achieve better results?

5. Describe how a quality control program should operate so that such problems are avoided.

6. What changes should Mr. Blame make at the Gas Generator plant?

Selected Bibliography

Buffa, Elwood S. *Operations Management: Problems and Models*. New York: Wiley, 1972.

Dodge, H. F., and H. G. Romig. *Sampling Inspection Tables*. New York: Wiley, 1959.

Duncan, Acheson J. *Quality Control and Industrial Statistics*. 4th ed. Homewood, IL: Richard D. Irwin, 1974.

Economics Control of Manufactured Products. New York: Litton Educational Publishing, Van Nostrand Reinhold, 1931.

Grant, Eugene L., and Richard S. Leavenworth. *Statistical Quality Control*. 4th ed. New York: McGraw-Hill, 1972.

Hostage, G. M. "Quality Control in a Service Business." *Harvard Business Review* 53(July–August 1975): 98–106.

"Japan: Quality Control & Innovation." *Business Week*, July 20, 1981, 19–44.

Munitions Board Standards Agency, U.S. Department of Defense. *Military Standard, Sampling Procedures and Tables for Inspection for Attributes*. Washington, DC: Government Printing Office, 1950.

Sasser, W. Earl, R. Paul Olsen, and D. Daryl Wyckoff. *Management of Service Operations*. Boston: Allyn & Bacon, 1978.

Swartz, Gerald E., and Vivian C. Comstock. "One Firm's Experience With Quality Circles." *Quality Progress* 12, no. 9(September 1979): 14–16.

U.S. Department of Defense. *A Guide to Zero Defects: Quality and Reliability Assurance Handbook*—4415.12. Washington, DC: Government Printing Office, 1965.

Williamson, J. W. "Evaluating Quality of Patient Care." *Journal of the American Medical Association* 218(October 25, 1971): 564–569.

Chapter Outline

15

Maintenance Management and Reliability:

Concepts, Issues, and Function within POM

The purpose of maintenance management is to see that the plant and equipment are maintained in a way that enables a plant to produce its products with the lowest unit costs consistent with the safety and well-being of the working force. It is easy to see that maintenance management can actually be a profit-producing activity rather than merely a cost of doing business.
Charles V. Clark, Vice-President, H. B. Maynard and Company Inc.

The tires, shock absorbers, belts, wiper blades, wheel bearings, and spark plugs on your car must be either repaired or replaced as it ages and wears. So also must the machines and buildings of industry be repaired or replaced as they wear. Shafts break, bearings fail, electric motors burn out, gears strip, electrical and hydraulic controls malfunction, and hoses rupture in a seemingly endless and inevitable aging and wearing process. Both product and service industries have established maintenance departments to fight the potentially costly effects of these mechanical failures on productive systems.

Maintenance, in its broadest sense, is concerned with developing these essential elements:

1. A skilled staff of maintenance workers.
2. Stores of repair parts and supplies.
3. Specialized repair tools and machines.
4. An effective staff of design engineers and maintenance-planning specialists.

All these elements are coordinated and directed toward minimizing the long-term effects of wear, breakdowns, and malfunctions on the generation of products and services from productive systems. The success of maintenance departments is measured largely in terms of the combined total cost of downtime of production facilities when breakdowns occur and the cost of administering the entire maintenance program for an organization.

Maintenance departments are usually headed by a plant engineer who reports to a plant manager. Although these departments are considered to be staff, or support groups, their position in the organizational hierarchy ordinarily puts them on an equal footing with production departments. Generally speaking, maintenance departments are usually split into two major groups: buildings and grounds, and machine repair.

Buildings and grounds can include such workers as electricians, welders, pipefitters, steamfitters, painters, glaziers, carpenters, millwrights, and janitors. Machine repair may include such workers as mechanics, machinsts, welders, oilers, electricians, and electronic technicians. Of course, the degree of technology of the production processes, the amount of investment in plant and equipment, the age of the facilities, and other factors will directly affect the organizational location, reporting relationships, the required worker skills, and overall mission of maintenance departments.

The effectiveness of maintenance in productive systems has direct impact on these important POM performance elements:

1. Capacity—Machines idled by mechanical breakdowns cannot produce. Thus, the capacity of the system is reduced when machine breakdowns occur.
2. Variable costs—Workers idled by machine breakdowns cause direct labor and indirect labor costs per unit to climb.
3. Fixed costs—A large part of the maintenance department budget is fixed. Thus, the total facility fixed cost is increased when budgets are high.
4. Product and service quality—Poorly maintained equipment produces low-quality products. Also, equipment in disrepair experiences frequent breakdowns and cannot provide adequate service to customers.
5. Employee safety—Worn-out equipment is likely to fail at any moment, and these failures can be disastrous to worker safety.

Because of these critical outcomes from maintenance programs, maintenance departments engage in the activities of repair and preventive maintenance.

Repair and Preventive Maintenance

Workers, parts and supplies, along with specialized tools and machines, are all used and coordinated to repair production machines and buildings as breakdowns occur. Repairs can be performed on an emergency basis to prevent lost production time, unsafe working conditions, and scrap losses. In these critical situations maintenance workers work overtime, or they may be shifted from other, less critical projects. They are closely supervised and supported by supervisors and other staff specialists. The fundamental goal in this activity is to minimize the downtime of production or operating departments resulting from mechanical breakdowns. Quick response times and fast repair jobs are therefore required.

Other repairs may not be of an emergency nature. For example, standby machines may be quickly substituted for those that have failed; thus repairs may be performed in more controlled, systematic, and economic ways. Repair facilities that are managed much like production departments are used to routinely perform these nonemergency repairs. This activity is governed by the objective of minimizing the cost of repairs while providing acceptable repair services.

Whether repairs are made on an emergency basis or in a more controlled and systematic way, the principal problems related to repairs that managers in maintenance departments must resolve are:

1. Determining crew sizes for both emergency crews and repair facilities.
2. Scheduling maintenance workers and facilities to accommodate the number of required jobs in each time period.
3. Determining the number of standby machines and spare parts to hold for repairs.

Preventive maintenance involves those maintenance activities aimed at the prevention of breakdowns that can cause production downtime. These activities fall into three general classifications:

1. Servicing, adjusting, and lubricating production equipment according to routine schedules.
2. Regularly inspecting production machinery and buildings to identify needed repairs before breakdowns are likely to occur.
3. Performing repair overhauls and design enhancements that have been identified by periodic inspections. These repairs are usually done when interference with production is minimized — on weekends, midnight shifts, during vacation shutdowns, and so on.

The principal problems for managers in preventive maintenance activities are:

1. Scheduling and coordinating workers, materials, tools, and machines during major repair projects.
2. Determining how often to perform preventive maintenance to keep production equipment in peak operating condition and to minimize costs.
3. Determining policies about when to replace parts before failure, when experience shows definite breakdown patterns.

These problems will also be addressed later in this chapter.

Conceptually, operations managers must make a trade-off between the amount of effort to expend on repairs and the amount of effort to expend on preventive maintenance. As Figure 15.1 shows, some minimum amount of preventive maintenance is necessary to provide the minimal amount of lubrication and adjustments to avoid a complete and imminent collapse of the productive system. At this minimal level of preventive maintenance, the cost of breakdown (lost production time) and repair cost is so exorbitant that total maintenance cost is beyond practical limits. Such a policy is simply a remedial policy; in other words, fix the machines when they break. Most companies recognize that as movement is made from the origin to the

Figure 15.1
Total Maintenance Costs as a Function of Repair Cost and Preventive Maintenance Cost

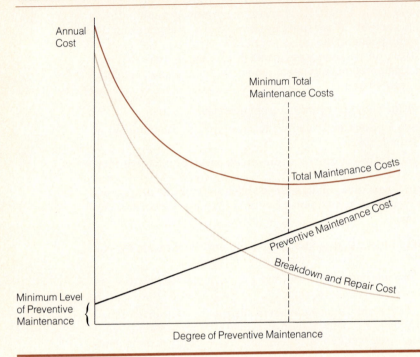

right in Figure 15.1, total maintenance costs decline. That is to say, preventive maintenance costs are a bargain in this region because such outlays actually reduce total costs.

Preventive maintenance programs are increasingly instituted as we move from left to right on the graph. Breakdown and repair cost declines, preventive maintenance cost increases, and total maintenance costs decrease. At some point additional spending for preventive maintenance is uneconomical because the additional money spent exceeds the amount of money saved in avoiding breakdowns. Thus, conceptually at least, an optimal level of preventive maintenance effort exists for any productive system that minimizes total maintenance costs.

One important element in maintenance management is the concept of machine reliability and system reliability. We shall now discuss these ideas particularly as they relate to the development of POM maintenance policies.

Reliability

Each part of a machine is designed for a given level of *component reliability,* which can be defined as the probability that a part will not fail in a given time period or number of trials under ordinary conditions of use. For example, if only 1 percent of automobile tires with an expected life of 30,000 miles fail within the 30,000 mile span, we would say that a tire has a reliability level of 99 percent.

When component parts are combined into a larger system such as a machine, the combined reliability of all the component parts forms the basis for *system reliability*. When critical component parts — those that can directly cause the large machine or system to fail — interact during the operation of the larger system, the system reliability is determined by computing the product of the reliabilities of all the interacting critical component parts. For example, four automobile tires, each with a reliability of 99 percent, would have a system reliability of 96.1 percent ($.99^4$ or $.99 \times .99 \times .99 \times .99 = .961$ or 96.1 percent).

The concept of system reliability is further demonstrated in Figure 15.2. If the critical components of a system have a reliability of 90 percent, the system reliability is almost zero if there are more than 50 critical component parts. Similarly, when component parts have a 99.5 percent reliability, system reliability falls to 60.6 percent when there are 100 critical component parts. The concept of system reliability is important in developing effective maintenance policies in POM because of this

Figure 15.2
System Reliability as a Function of Component Part Reliability and Number of Component Parts

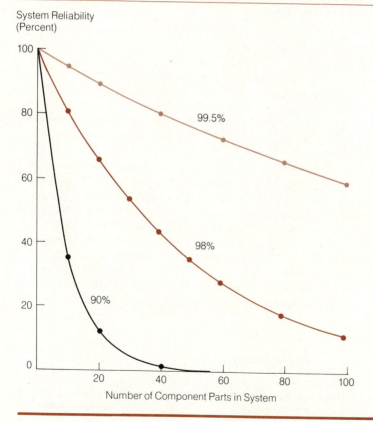

System Reliability (Percent)

Number of Component Parts in System

principle: *When machines are relatively simple (have only a few critical component parts) and when machines do not interact (as in job shops), overdesigning component parts to improve reliability may be a viable strategy in holding system reliability at acceptable levels; however, when machines are complex (have many critical component parts) and when many machines interact in complex machine systems (as in continuous productive systems), component part overdesign may not significantly improve system reliability.*

Even if overdesign of critical component parts warrants consideration, the cost of design, testing, and careful precision manufacture of the parts may be exorbitant. Thus, other alternatives besides extreme reliability of component parts must often be developed.

Table 15.1 describes some maintenance policies often used in POM to maintain system reliability at acceptable levels. Two general goals are pursued here — reduc-

Table 15.1
POM Maintenance Policies That Keep the Reliability of Productive Systems at Acceptable Levels

Goal of Policies	Maintenance Policies
1. Reduce frequency of failures	a. Preventive maintenance.
	b. Proper instruction of operators.
	c. Providing excess numbers of machines — underutilization.
	d. Early replacement of wearing parts.
	e. Overdesigning reliability into components of machines.
2. Reduce severity of failures	a. Increase crew sizes, stock of repair parts, and capacity of repair facilities to speed repairs.
	b. Utilize modular designs and easily replaceable parts to ease task of repairs.
	c. Provide standby machines to reduce downtime during repairs.

Source: Adapted from S. T. Hardy and L. J. Krajewski, "A Simulation of Interactive Maintenance Decisions," *Decision Sciences* 6 (January 1975): 92–105. Used by permission of the American Institute for Decision Sciences.

ing the frequency and reducing the severity of machine failure. Preventive maintenance, proper instruction of operators to avoid machine abuse, providing extra machines, and early parts replacement are alternative policies to overdesigning component parts in achieving reduced frequency of machine failure. Speedier repairs through greater repair capacity, simplified repairs through innovative machine designs, and standby machines are alternative policies often employed to reduce the severity of machine failures.

With this background in maintenance concepts, let us now examine several key maintenance problems that operations managers must frequently solve.

Key Maintenance Problems in POM

Although we know that many technical questions must be routinely answered as repair projects are undertaken — such as type of bearings to use, correct welding procedures for cast aluminum housings, and so on — our principal concern here is not engineering issues, but rather maintenance planning and control issues. There-fore, we shall examine those planning and control problems that are frequently encountered in POM as machine repairs and preventive maintenance programs are undertaken. These specific maintenance problems are described in this section:

1. Planning, scheduling, and controlling large-scale repair projects.
2. Determining the number of standby machines of each type and the number of spare parts to hold in stock.
3. Determining the optimal capacities for repair facilities.
4. Determining how often to perform preventive maintenance.
5. Determining optimal policies for early replacement of parts.

These maintenance problems have in recent years been targets of intensive quanti-tative analysis by operations analysis specialists. This underscores the importance of these problems in POM.

Planning and Controlling Large-Scale Repair Projects

Some repair projects in maintenance departments are long-lasting; involve many complex tasks; require many materials, workers, and subcontractors to be at the right place at the right time; require on-time completion; and are very costly. These characteristics apply to such massive repair projects as: (1) overhauling cracking units in an oil refinery, (2) remodeling an office building complex, (3) refurbishing a steel mill blast furnace, (4) overhauling a Banbury in an automobile tire plant, and (5) doing an oil refinery turnaround. These and other large-scale repair projects challenge managers to complete the work on time within the budgeted costs and with the desired improvements achieved. These projects involve two primary man-agement activities:

1. Planning — What tasks must be done, when each task should be begun and completed, how the tasks are related, what types of workers and how many workers are needed for each task, what materials are needed for each task, what subcontracting services are needed, arranging the overall scheme of the project so that it is completed within time and cost targets, and planning a system of control to insure conformance to the plan.
2. Control — Is the project progressing as planned in regard to time, cost, and quality? Are corrective actions needed? Should resources be shifted from one task to another to improve the likelihood of project success?

Planning and control of large-scale repair projects are effectively achieved by the project planning techniques discussed in Chapter 7. Foremost among these tech-niques are Gantt charts, milestone charts, PERT and CPM. *Gantt charts* and *mile-stone charts* are universally used to plan and control less complex projects and to summarize the aggregate activities of massive projects.

PERT and CPM are often used to plan and control very complex repair projects. These techniques provide maintenance managers with a systematic way of plan-ning the tasks of massive repair projects before the work is begun. Additionally, managers use the information systems of these techniques to keep informed about the current expected duration of the project, spotlighting the critical activities, determining the amount of slack for each activity, and evaluating the cost performance as the project progresses. Corrective action is therefore possible before the projects become prohibitively overbudget or late.

The critical nature of these projects thrusts them into the spotlight of management attention, because entire production facilities are often shut down until the repairs are completed. The urgency that surrounds these repairs is highlighted by their special organization arrangements. Project managers and project teams are often gathered together for the life of the project. These teams, which are made up of engineers, maintenance supervisors, workers, purchasing personnel, and other specialists, become the hub of management activities directed toward the project.

Large-scale maintenance projects and construction projects are principally responsible for the fact that PERT, CPM, and other project-planning and control techniques have emerged as the most frequently employed operations analysis techniques in POM.[1]

Determining the Number of Standby Machines and Spare Parts

When production machines break down, workers are idled and production output dries up until the machines that have failed can be repaired. In-process inventories can keep downstream production operations working while repairs are made in some intermittent systems. In service systems and continuous productive systems, however, in-process inventories frequently do not exist, and other alternatives must be adopted to lessen the severity of the effect of machine failures upon production operations.

Standby machines have been utilized in systems that use many machines of the same design. Some manufacturing plants, for example, have some production machines on a standby status on rollers with electrical cords, hydraulic hoses, and air lines with quick connect plug-ins. When a machine fails, one of these standby units is quickly rolled into position, connected to utilities, and adjusted to the product being processed so that production can soon be underway again.

Hard-to-get *spare parts* are often held in inventory in maintenance departments to be used to repair production machinery. When historical evidence shows that certain parts have high incidences of failure, these parts are almost always stocked in order to reduce the repair time of production machines.

A knotty problem for maintenance managers is how many standby machines and spare parts of each type to hold. If too few are held, idle workers and lost production costs are excessive. If too many are held, the costs of carrying and maintaining these items are excessive. Managers must therefore select a specific quantity of standby machines and spare parts of each type that strikes a balance between the excessive costs of holding too many or too few. The sticky part of these decisions is not knowing how many repairs will be required in each time period in the future.

[1] Norman Gaither, ''The Adoption of Operations Research Techniques by Manufacturing Organizations,'' *Decision Sciences* 6(October 1975): 797–813.

In cases where historical data exist on failure rates or when experienced managers can estimate the probabilities of failure rates, payoff tables or marginal analysis can assist in the decisions. Payoff tables were discussed in Chapter 2 and the Supplement to Chapter 9. Marginal analysis was also discussed in the Supplement to Chapter 9. Review the procedures of these techniques and their uses. Don't you agree that the determination of how many spare parts or standby machines to hold for each time period is really similar to deciding how much inventory to hold of an item when demand is uncertain?

Even when failure data do not exist, managers still conceptually apply the thinking employed in both payoff tables and marginal analysis: stock the number of standby machines and spare parts of each type that minimizes the expected total cost of lost production and idle workers *and* investment, carrying, and other holding costs. In other words, don't hold too many or too few; strike a balance between these costs.

Selecting Capacities for Repair Facilities

Many organizations have machine shops, electronic calibration facilities, welding shops, and other facilities that repair machines when they malfunction. These facilities receive repair jobs randomly as machine failures occur in production operations. The pattern of these failures causes repair facilities to be idle when only a few failures occur, and long waiting lines of broken machines form when many failures occur.

Managers must decide how many workers, how many specialized tools and repair machines, and other elements of capacity to provide for these facilities. Historical data such as these are important in their analyses: (1) cost of different capacity schemes, (2) failure patterns of machines, and (3) repair times of different capacity schemes. Waiting line analysis, or queuing theory, and computer simulation can be used to develop good capacity strategies for repair facilities. Queuing

Figure 15.3
Relative Cost Patterns Determine Repair Crew Sizes

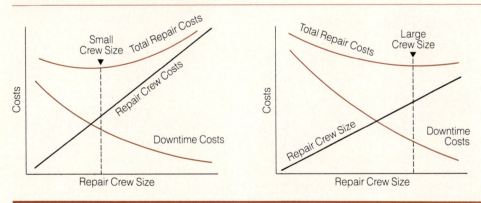

theory techniques and computer simulation were discussed in the Supplement to Chapter 13.

Again, the difficult part of these decisions is the uncertainty. How many failures will occur in each time period? Policies are therefore developed that, if followed across many time periods, should result in good average results. However, in any one time period either excessive idle time of repair facilities or excessive waiting lines of machines needing repairs can occur. The relative costs of repair crews and machine downtime determine in large part the size of repair crews. Figure 15.3 shows that when repair crew costs are high relative to machine downtime costs, we tend to prefer small repair crews. If, however, repair crew costs are low relative to machine downtime costs, we prefer large repair crews.

Determining the Frequency of Preventive Maintenance

As we discussed previously, preventive maintenance is regularly performed on production machines and buildings so that some costly breakdowns can be avoided. The decision of how often to perform preventive maintenance such as lubrication, servicing, adjustment, inspection, and repairs is an interesting one in POM.

If preventive maintenance is performed too infrequently, excessive breakdowns occur; and if it is performed too frequently, excessive monies are expended on preventive maintenance. To further complicate these decisions, managers are uncertain about how many machines will actually break down between preventive maintenance cycles.

Example 15.1 demonstrates how policies on *when* to perform preventive maintenance can be set when historical data and failure patterns are available. This approach develops for each policy a total cost that includes expected monthly cost of breakdowns and monthly cost of preventive maintenance.

Example 15.1

Setting Frequency of Preventive Maintenance

The Moldex Company has one production department with 20 injection molding machines. Bill Lee, the manager of maintenance at Moldex, is studying this group of machines with the goal of determining how often the department should shut down all the machines and perform preventive maintenance. The nature of the department and its processes causes preventive maintenance to be performed on all the machines at one time at a cost of $5,000 for the entire group of machines. When an individual machine breaks down, it costs about $500, on the average, to repair it. These historical failure data have been collected:

Months between Preventive Maintenance	Probability of a Breakdown for Each Machine	Cumulative Probability of Breakdown
1	.10	.10
2	.15	.25
3	.20	.45
4	.25	.70
5	.30	1.00

Bill Lee wonders whether preventive maintenance should be done every 1, 2, 3, 4, or 5 months. How often should preventive maintenance be performed?

Solution

1. First, compute the expected number of breakdowns for each of the preventive maintenance policies:

The formula for the expected number of breakdowns is:

$$B_n = N\sum_1^n p_n + B_{(n-1)}p_1 + B_{(n-2)}p_2 + B_{(n-3)}p_3 + B_{(n-4)}p_4$$

where:

B_n = Expected number of breakdowns for N machines when preventive maintenance is performed each n periods

p_n = Probability that a breakdown will occur between inspections when preventive maintenance is performed each n periods

Therefore:

$$B_1 = N(p_1) = 20(.10) = 2.00$$

$$B_2 = N(p_1 + p_2) + B_1(p_1) = 20(.10 + .15) + 2.00(.10) = 5.20$$

$$B_3 = N(p_1 + p_2 + p_3) + B_2(p_1) + B_1(p_2)$$
$$= 20(.10 + .15 + .20) + 5.20(.10) + 2.00(.15) = 9.82$$

$$B_4 = N(p_1 + p_2 + p_3 + p_4) + B_3(p_1) + B_2(p_2) + B_1(p_3)$$
$$= 20(.10 + .15 + .20 + .25) + 9.82(.10) + 5.20(.15) + 2.00(.20) = 16.16$$

$$B_5 = N(p_1 + p_2 + p_3 + p_4 + p_5) + B_4(p_1) + B_3(p_2) + B_2(p_3) + B_1(p_4)$$
$$= 20(.10 + .15 + .20 + .25 + .30) + 16.16(.10) + 9.82(.15) + 5.20(.20) + 2.00(.25)$$
$$= 24.63$$

2. Next, compute the expected breakdown cost, preventive maintenance cost, and total cost for each preventive maintenance policy:

(1) Preventive Maintenance Every n Months	(2) Expected Number of Breakdowns	(3) Average Number of Expected Breakdowns per Month [(2) ÷ (1)]	(4) Monthly Cost of Expected Breakdowns [(3) × $500]	(5) Monthly Cost of Preventive Maintenance [$5,000 ÷ (1)]	(6) Total Monthly Cost [(4) ÷ (5)]
1	2.00	2.00	$1,000	$5,000	$6,000
2	5.20	2.60	1,300	2,500	3,800
3	9.82	3.27	1,635	1,667	3,302
4	16.16	4.04	2,020	1,250	3,270
5	24.63	4.93	2,465	1,000	3,465

3. The optimal policy is therefore to perform preventive maintenance every 4 months.

Setting Early Parts-Replacement Policies

When repairs on production machines are being made, maintenance supervisors often must decide how much repair work should be done. In many cases parts that have not yet failed will be replaced because the cost of replacement now is less than if the part is allowed to fail while operating. Operations analysts study these situations to provide supervisors with policies to guide them in their decisions.

Take, for example, an electrostatic copier repairman who travels about from customer to customer performing preventive maintenance. When a copying machine shuts down, it would be desirable to know which of the following repair policies is optimal, that is, which one results in the lowest cost in the long run:

1. Repair or replace only parts that have failed.

2. Repair or replace all Class A and Class B parts that have failed and all Class B parts with 1,000 or more hours of service.

3. Repair or replace all Class A and Class B parts that have failed or that have 1,000 or more hours of service.

When analysts have data on failure patterns of parts, cost of repairs of failures, and cost of early replacement of parts before failure, these data can be analyzed to identify the lowest cost replacement policy. Computer simulation is frequently employed in such analyses today.

Secondary Maintenance Department Responsibilities

All maintenance departments are responsible for the repair of buildings and equipment and for performing certain preventive maintenance repairs, lubrication, and adjustments. Additionally, certain secondary responsibilities have traditionally been assigned to these departments.

Housekeeping, janitorial, window washing, groundkeeping, and painting services are usually performed by maintenance departments. These activities usually include all areas of the facility, from restrooms to offices to production departments to warehouses. In some plants, however, the area around each production worker's immediate workplace is cleaned by the worker. The appearance and cleanliness of all other areas are the responsibility of the maintenance department.

New construction, remodeling, maintaining safety equipment, loss prevention, security, and pollution control responsibilities have been assigned to some maintenance departments. But many of these duties are so different from ordinary repair and maintenance that one wonders how, for example, maintenance departments can be expected to be responsible for pollution control. In most cases the staff personnel of these specialties are grouped into subdepartments that are only indirectly related to other maintenance functions.

Trends in Maintenance

Production machinery today is far more complex than it was a decade or two ago. Computerized controls, new technology in metallurgy, more sophisticated electronic controls, new methods in lubrication technology, and other developments have resulted in many changes in the way we maintain complex machines.

Special training programs have sprung up to give maintenance workers the skills necessary to service and repair today's specialized equipment. An example of this training is found in the field of life support systems in hospitals. The engineers and technicians who design and perform maintenance programs for this sophisticated medical equipment must be involved in continuous training programs to stay abreast of new equipment developments. These training programs are conducted by individual hospitals, by cooperative health care groups, and by public and private educational institutions.

Subcontracting service companies have sprung up to supply specialized maintenance services. Computers, automobiles, office machines, and other products are increasingly serviced by outside subcontracting companies. Their specialized technical training and their fee structure, which is usually based on an as-needed basis, combine to offer competent service at reasonable cost.

Other technologies are developing that promise to reduce the cost of maintenance while improving the performance of production machines. An example of these developments is the network of computerized temperature-sensing probes connected to all key bearings in a machine system. When bearings begin to fail, they overheat, causing these sensing systems to indicate that a failure is imminent. The massive damage to machines that can happen when bearings fail — snapped shafts, stripped gears, and so on — can thus be avoided. This kind of automated technology promises to simplify managements' questions about when to perform preventive maintenance repairs.

As computers have been almost universally absorbed into management information systems in all types of organizations, maintenance departments have also been affected by this development. Five general areas in maintenance commonly use computer assistance today: (1) scheduling maintenance projects;[2] (2) mainte-

---

[2] One such maintenance scheduling program has been developed by General Electric Company. See *User's Guide to Preventive Maintenance Planning and Scheduling* (*FAME — Facilities Maintenance Engineering*) (New York: General Electric Company, 1973).

nance cost reports by production department, cost category, and other classifications; (3) inventory status reports for maintenance parts and supplies; (4) parts failure data; (5) operations analysis studies, which may include computer simulation, waiting lines (queuing theory), and other analytical programs. Information from these uses of computers can provide managers in maintenance with the necessary failure patterns, cost data, and other information fundamental to the key maintenance decisions discussed in this section.

Maintenance today in POM means more than simply maintaining the machines of production. As POM has broadened its perspectives from just minimizing short-range costs to other long-range performance measures such as customer service, return on investment, and providing for workers' needs, so also has maintenance broadened its perspectives. Today, maintenance means that the supply of products and services is what is maintained, and not merely machines.

Summary

It's a fact of life that buildings and equipment deteriorate; as they are used and grow older, age and wear eventually take their toll. Maintenance departments are established in both product and service industries to minimize the impact of this aging and wearing of machinery and buildings on production systems. Unless maintenance departments achieve this objective, capacity declines, variable and fixed costs climb, product/service quality declines, and employee safety declines.

Maintenance involves two principal activities — repairs and preventive maintenance. Maintenance operations are frequently analyzed by staff specialists to determine repair crew sizes, repair project schedules, number of standby machines and spare parts, how often to perform preventive maintenance, and policies about when to replace parts before failure.

The nature of maintenance operations has supported extensive analytical studies. Probability theory, PERT/CPM, payoff tables, marginal analysis, queuing theory, and computer simulation techniques are frequently employed in these studies. The results of these and other analysis techniques become valuable inputs to management decisions about maintenance operations.

As productive systems change, new trends are observed in maintenance — specialized training programs for maintenance workers, maintenance subcontracting, computerized sensing systems, and computerized maintenance information systems. These developments will provide managers with support to maintain the supply of products and services from productive systems, the ultimate goal of maintenance operations.

Review and Discussion Questions

1. What are four essential elements of maintenance?
2. What five POM performance elements are directly affected by maintenance?
3. Define *component reliability* and *system reliability*.
4. Name five key maintenance problems in most productive systems.
5. Name five secondary maintenance department duties.
6. Name four important trends in maintenance.

Problems

1. If your car has four spark plugs, each with a probability of failure of .01 over an expected life of 10,000 operating hours: **a.** What is the reliability level of each spark plug? **b.** What is the reliability of the spark plug system of your car?

2. The Numbacrunch Computing services company has ten regional computer centers in California. A preventive maintenance inspection and repair cycle costs a total of $7,000 on the average for all ten centers. If a breakdown occurs at any center, an average cost of $10,000 is incurred. The historical breakdown pattern for Numbacrunch is:

Weeks between Preventive Maintenance	Average Number of Breakdowns between Preventive Maintenance Cycles
1	.6
2	1.8
3	3.0
4	5.0
5	7.0

Recommend how often preventive maintenance should be performed.

3. It costs $400 for an engine overhaul and the probabilities of an engine failure with varying intervals between oil changes are:

Thousands of Miles between Oil Changes	Probability of Engine Failure
20	.05
40	.10
60	.20
80	.30
100	.35

If you have ten automobiles in your fleet and a custom oil change with filters, long-wearing oil, and careful adjustments costs $50 per auto at each oil change, which interval between oil changes would you select? (Hint: Looking at Example 15.1, base your analysis on cost per 1,000 miles for the fleet.)

Selected Bibliography

Abbott, W. R. "Repair versus Replacement of Failed Components." *Journal of Industrial Engineering* 19(January 1968): 21–23.

Conway, R. W., and Andrew Schultz, Jr. "The Manufacturing Process Function." *Journal of Industrial Engineering* 10(January–February 1959): 39–54.

Fabrycky, W. J., and P. E. Torgersen. *Operations Economy: Industrial Applications of Operations Research.* Englewood Cliffs, NJ: Prentice-Hall, 1966.

Gaither, Norman. "The Adoption of Operations Research Techniques by Manufacturing Organizations." *Decision Sciences* 6(October 1975): 797–813.

General Electric Company. *Users' Guide to Preventive Maintenance Planning and Scheduling (FAME — Facilities Maintenance Engineering)*. New York: General Electric Company, 1973.

Hardy, S. T., and L. S. Krajewski. "A Simulation of Interactive Maintenance Decisions." *Decision Sciences* 6(January 1975): 92–105.

Turban, Efraim. "The Complete Computerized Maintenance System." *Journal of Industrial Engineering* 1(March 1969): 20–27.

————. "The Use of Mathematical Models in Plant Maintenance Decision Making." *Management Science* 13(February 1967): 342–358.

Wilkinson, John J. "How to Manage Maintenance." *Harvard Business Review* 46(March–April 1968): 191–205.

Part Five

Conclusion

Chapter 16
Management of Productive Systems:
A Forward View

In Part Five, which includes only Chapter 16, "Management of Productive Systems: A Forward View," we explore some issues that will confront operations managers in the future and that will also affect you as you pursue your professional careers in business and government. The chapter presents no easy solutions to these contemporary problems, but it discusses what can be done and observes the likely outcomes. As this text nears its end, we hope that you have gained an appreciation of the essential elements of the field of operations management and have acquired a better understanding of the principal decisions that operations managers must make and the ways that they make them.

Chapter Outline

Introduction

Contemporary Developments and POM Practice Trends

Dominance of Service Systems
Governmental Regulation
Scarcity of Productive Resources
Spiraling Inflation and Financial Instability
Workers' Attitudes toward Work
Universal Use of Computers
Consumers' Demands on POM
Automation, Robotry, and Computerized Controls
International Scope of Productive Systems
Foreign Imports in U.S. Markets

Summary

16

Management of Productive Systems:

A Forward View

We are witnessing a reemergence of operations management into prominence among managers of organizations. Once again, the principal means of competing in world markets and achieving corporate objectives rests with operations managers. The challenge is there — now we must respond.
Norman Gaither

P OM today is a blend of practitioners, academics, researchers, and authors. Figure 16.1 shows how POM is divided into theory, practice, and research. Theory is the science that underlies practice; it explains how productive systems operate. Practice is the art of applying the theories of POM to the enormous variety of productive systems that we find about us today. Research is the study of productive systems with the goal of improving theory and practice.

POM is underpinned by management, finance and accounting, engineering, computer technology, decision theory, mathematics and statistics, and operations research. These disciplines are part and parcel of all practice, theory, and research in POM. The blending of these diverse disciplines into the management of complex operating systems makes POM one of today's most challenging professional activities.

POM has evolved from the relatively simple management tasks of Frederick Taylor's time to the extremely complex ones of today. As productive systems have become more complex and sophisticated, so also has the management of these systems. POM has responded and evolved to meet the developments and challenges of each era as it is continuing to evolve and adapt today. What new challenges are on the horizon that will shape what POM will be tomorrow?

729

Figure 16.1
POM: Its Divisions and Underpinnings

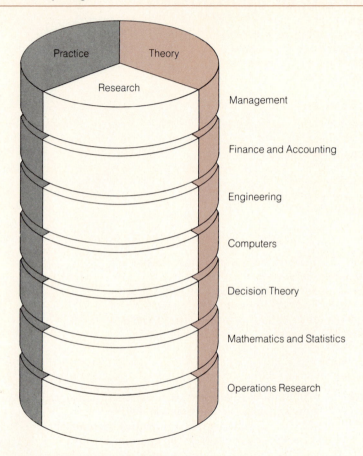

Contemporary Developments and POM Practice Trends

In Chapter 1, Table 1.6 listed some contemporary developments that are affecting present and future POM practice: (1) dominance of service systems, (2) governmental regulation, (3) scarcity of productive resources, (4) spiraling inflation and financial instability, (5) workers' attitudes toward work, (6) universal use of computers, (7) consumers' demands on POM, (8) automation, robotry, and computerized controls, (9) international scope of productive systems, and (10) foreign imports in U.S. markets. What can practicing managers do to meet the challenges of these developments? Although there are no simple formulas that apply in all cases, here are some principal concerns and/or ways that tomorrow's managers may be able to attack these problems.

Dominance of Service Systems

Of particular concern to managers of service systems is the dominance of personnel in determining the quantity and quality of these services. Although we have generally reduced the impact that human unpredictability has on goods-producing systems through standardization, training, automation, and other means, personnel remains the central focus in many service systems. Improving labor productivity in services is therefore perhaps one of POM's greatest challenges for the future.

Governmental Regulation

Organizations are expected to develop expanded staffs trained in the specialties required to understand and adapt to the growing presence of complex governmental regulations and highly trained on-site government representatives. Additional personnel, such as pollution control specialists, antitrust attorneys, tax accountants, lobbyists, and loss prevention specialists, will not come cheap. Substantial increases in these overhead expenses could make top-heavy organizations increasingly vulnerable to foreign competition.

Scarcity of Productive Resources

The shortage of productive resources is a growing concern in POM. What can organizations do to insure a dependable supply of inputs to their productive systems? For one thing, they can initiate programs of backward integration. This means that they can acquire other companies that supply their key inputs. Although these actions may be frowned upon by federal antitrust people, some latitude is usually possible.

Additionally, research and development programs to develop alternate inputs, buildup of inventories of these or substitute inputs, conservation, improved technologies and designs allowing raw material substitution, personnel training programs to improve skill flexibility, and other innovative approaches will be needed to adapt to these existing and anticipated input shortages.

A note of caution is warranted here. T. R. Malthus, the economist, proclaimed in 1799 a doomsday theory of scarcity of inputs to production: the finite supply of land, raw materials, and other inputs combined with an ever-increasing population would inevitably lead to starvation, depression, economic busts and booms, and eventual economic ruin. What Malthus overlooked, however, was man's ability to innovate through ever-improving technology. We must also recognize that man's creative ability is sufficient to overcome these anticipated scarcities. But such improvements are far from automatic. Today's managers must direct their best people and resources to these problems if tomorrow's managers are to be expected to be able to meet tomorrow's supply challenges.

Spiraling Inflation and Financial Instability

How can managers attack the inflation-induced cost-price squeeze? Did you know that the demand for certain staff personnel actually increases when firms are faced with these rising cost challenges? Industrial engineers, cost accountants, and others whose primary jobs are to reduce or control costs actually may be in more demand when business conditions get rough than when times are good. Staff groups undertake formal cost reduction programs to reduce scrap, increase labor efficiency, eliminate unnecessary overhead expenses, and initiate other cost-cutting projects. These activities should at least slow the pace of total cost increases in many organizations.

One old but still interesting dilemma continues to confront POM: Shall we substitute capital goods for labor or vice versa? During the 1940s, 1950s, and 1960s capital goods were substituted for labor in enormous proportions through formal mechanization and automation programs. In this period capital funds were readily available and cheap, but labor costs rose rapidly. Now capital funds are scarce and expensive. Although labor costs are also still rising, the opportunities for large-scale reduction of the use of labor through mechanization appear now not so economically attractive.

There may be continued pressure to reduce the quality of our goods and services in order to reduce total costs. Candy bars, for example, are now almost uniformly the size of postage stamps and seem to lack the good, wholesome, rich taste of those in bygone days. The substitution of lower-cost materials, such as plastic parts in automobiles, may be the expected trend of the future. Although we consumers may yearn for the good old days when quality was high, we are usually unwilling to pay for the high quality.

Workers' Attitudes toward Work

While we continue to strive for lower costs through worker efficiency and productivity, so also will we need to develop ways to reduce the cost impact of low worker morale. This is perhaps one of the greatest challenges to operations managers: How can we simultaneously attain high worker productivity and acceptable levels of worker morale? Much more work needs to be done on this problem. Be wary of those who prescribe simplistic fixes to existing job designs. There are no easy answers; if there were, we would already have solved this knotty problem. Management, unions, and government must ultimately make a commitment to the joint study of this critical problem if we are to see a light at the end of this long and difficult tunnel.

Universal Use of Computers

The many routine uses of computer-generated information in POM has made computers as much a part of most productive systems as the primary inputs of personnel, materials, machinery, and utilities. Fortunately, we have lived through the era when a forklift truck would deliver the day's load of computer output. Now we are beginning to carefully scrutinize what information managers need in order to manage and to provide only necessary information.

Novel uses of computers in POM will undoubtedly develop in the future. Computers' abilities to calculate, store, and retrieve information with lightning speed is indeed overwhelming, and these attributes will progressively be applied to a broader range of POM needs. On the other hand, the ability of computers (and computer personnel, for that matter) to differentiate between what information *can* be generated and what information *should* be provided is indeed underwhelming.

Operations managers must take charge of this critical activity and must not abdicate their responsibilities to others who may better understand the jargon of the experts. Operations managers must make computers work for them and not vice versa.

Consumers' Demands on POM

Flexibility is the key word to describe what is required of productive systems if they are to be responsive to their markets. Flexible product/service designs, production schedules, and shipping methods are a growing necessity today. How can POM make productive systems more flexible and responsive to the needs of markets?

Several POM strategies can increase system flexibility. Modular product designs standardize subassemblies and delay final assembly until customers' orders are in hand. These designs promise to yield low-cost operation through standardization of subassemblies *and* flexibility of final product design—the best of two worlds. Newer production scheduling and inventory-planning systems integrate raw material planning, production scheduling, and customer delivery. These information systems improve POM's ability to load production facilities economically *and* be very responsive to customers' needs.

Automation, Robotry, and Computerized Controls

Although these mechanical marvels may hold great promise for the future, they are not without their problems. First, can productive systems afford them? The low availability and high cost of capital funds may rule them out in favor of labor. Additionally, some of these devices require long production runs and may be too inflexible to survive the need for flexibility in adapting to varying customer demands. Newer designs, however, can be easily reprogrammed to adapt to the expected shorter production runs of the future. These and the as yet undeveloped smart machines of the future hold both great promise and great problems for operations managers. A major problem is: What will society do with employees displaced by machines? These and similar challenges await POM.

International Scope of Productive Systems

The refinement of transportation and communication systems has facilitated a proliferation of international operations. The growth of new and promising foreign markets has stimulated the exchange of outputs and inputs of their productive systems. This advancement offers both blessing and bane to POM. Inputs to productive systems that are lower in cost and available in greater supply may provide short-range operating advantages. However, the same export and import avenues that allow our domestic productive systems to gain competitive advantage also encourage foreign firms to do the same. Thus the importing of foreign outputs and the exporting of domestic inputs pose a threat to the survival of our country's productive systems. Our steel industry is a dramatic example of how the blessings of international competition may be overshadowed by the disadvantages. On the other hand, our computer industry is presently enjoying the advantages of enormous foreign markets.

Foreign Imports in U.S. Markets

U.S. manufacturers must fight fire with fire; that is, they must do a better job of managing their factories. The quality of their products must be improved and their costs must be reduced. Much can be learned from observing the Japanese and other foreign manufacturers. High production technology, better product designs, placing operations strategy on an equal footing with financial and marketing strategy, better production and industrial engineering, more effective production planning, and less factory and company overhead—all are needed today. Such efforts take time and money and lots of it, but these efforts are likely to be far more effective in the long run than cries for protection through import quotas or import fees.

Summary

POM today has evolved to its present form by adapting to past environmental developments. The practice, theory, and research of POM interact in today's organizations. Operations research, computers, mathematics and statistics, finance and accounting, engineering, management, decision theory, and other disciplines are used to manage productive systems. This evolution is continuing today as new developments shape this dynamic field.

The dominance of service systems, governmental regulations, scarcity of productive inputs, spiraling inflation and financial instability, workers' attitudes toward work, universal use of computers, consumers' demands on POM, automation, international scope of productive systems, and foreign imports are all interacting factors to which the practice of POM must adapt. These factors will make POM increasingly complex in the future; but management innovation, technology, and improved management information systems should allow us to modify our management of productive systems to meet these new and developing challenges.

Appendixes

Normal Probability Distribution

The table Areas under the Normal Curve gives the Z scores, or number of standard deviations from the mean, for each value of x and the area under the curve to the left of x.

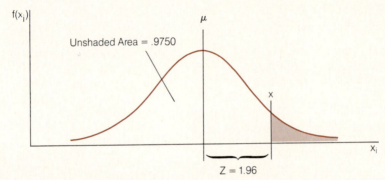

For example, in the figure above, if Z = 1.96, the .9750 figure found in the body of the table is the total unshaded area to the left of x.

The Z scores in the table are signless, that is, the Z scores can be either negative (−) or positive (+). We determine the sign of Z in each problem. In the figure above, Z was positive because x fell to the right of the mean (μ). In the figure below, x falls to the left of the mean (μ), and the area found in the body of the table lies to the right of x.

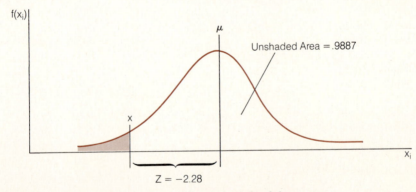

In this figure Z = −2.28 because x falls to the left of the mean.

In these examples Z scores of 1.96 and −2.28 were specified and the unshaded area to the left of x (positive Z scores) or to the right of x (negative Z scores) were read from the body of the table. The reverse process is often used: either the shaded area or unshaded area is specified and the Z score is read from the Z score column. For example, if the unshaded area = .90, the Z score is read from the table — Z = 1.28.

Areas under the Normal Curve

Z	.00	.01	.02	.03	.04	.05	.06	.07	.08	.09
.0	.50000	.50399	.50798	.51197	.51595	.51994	.52392	.52790	.53188	.53586
.1	.53983	.54380	.54776	.55172	.55567	.55962	.56356	.56749	.57142	.57535
.2	.57926	.58317	.58706	.59095	.59483	.59871	.60257	.60642	.61026	.61409
.3	.61791	.62172	.62552	.62930	.63307	.63683	.64058	.64431	.64803	.65173
.4	.65542	.65910	.66276	.66640	.67003	.67364	.67724	.68082	.68439	.68793
.5	.69146	.69497	.69847	.70194	.70540	.70884	.71226	.71566	.71904	.72240
.6	.72575	.72907	.73237	.73536	.73891	.74215	.74537	.74857	.75175	.75490
.7	.75804	.76115	.76424	.76730	.77035	.77337	.77637	.77935	.78230	.78524
.8	.78814	.79103	.79389	.79673	.79955	.80234	.80511	.80785	.81057	.81327
.9	.81594	.81859	.82121	.82381	.82639	.82894	.83147	.83398	.83646	.83891
1.0	.84134	.84375	.84614	.84849	.85083	.85314	.85543	.85769	.85993	.86214
1.1	.86433	.86650	.86864	.87076	.87286	.87493	.87698	.87900	.88100	.88298
1.2	.88493	.88686	.88877	.89065	.89251	.89435	.89617	.89796	.89973	.90147
1.3	.90320	.90490	.90658	.90824	.90988	.91149	.91309	.91466	.91621	.91774
1.4	.91924	.92073	.92220	.92364	.92507	.92647	.92785	.92922	.93056	.93189
1.5	.93319	.93448	.93574	.93699	.93822	.93943	.94062	.94179	.94295	.94408
1.6	.94520	.94630	.94738	.94845	.94950	.95053	.95154	.95254	.95352	.95449
1.7	.95543	.95637	.95728	.95818	.95907	.95994	.96080	.96164	.96246	.96327
1.8	.96407	.96485	.96562	.96638	.96712	.96784	.96856	.96926	.96995	.97062
1.9	.97128	.97193	.97257	.97320	.97381	.97441	.97500	.97558	.97615	.97670
2.0	.97725	.97784	.97831	.97882	.97932	.97982	.98030	.98077	.98124	.98169
2.1	.98214	.98257	.98300	.98341	.98382	.98422	.98461	.98500	.98537	.98574
2.2	.98610	.98645	.98679	.98713	.98745	.98778	.98809	.98840	.98870	.98899
2.3	.98928	.98956	.98983	.99010	.99036	.99061	.99086	.99111	.99134	.99158
2.4	.99180	.99202	.99224	.99245	.99266	.99286	.99305	.99324	.99343	.99361
2.5	.99379	.99396	.99413	.99430	.99446	.99461	.99477	.99492	.99506	.99520
2.6	.99534	.99547	.99560	.99573	.99585	.99598	.99609	.99621	.99632	.99643
2.7	.99653	.99664	.99674	.99683	.99693	.99702	.99711	.99720	.99728	.99736
2.8	.99744	.99752	.99760	.99767	.99774	.99781	.99788	.99795	.99801	.99807
2.9	.99813	.99819	.99825	.99831	.99836	.99841	.99846	.99851	.99856	.99861
3.0	.99865	.99869	.99874	.99878	.99882	.99886	.99899	.99893	.99896	.99900
3.1	.99903	.99906	.99910	.99913	.99916	.99918	.99921	.99924	.99926	.99929
3.2	.99931	.99934	.99936	.99938	.99940	.99942	.99944	.99946	.99948	.99950
3.3	.99952	.99953	.99955	.99957	.99958	.99960	.99961	.99962	.99964	.99965
3.4	.99966	.99968	.99969	.99970	.99971	.99972	.99973	.99974	.99975	.99976
3.5	.99977	.99978	.99978	.99979	.99980	.99981	.99981	.99982	.99983	.99983
3.6	.99984	.99985	.99985	.99986	.99986	.99987	.99987	.99988	.99988	.99989
3.7	.99989	.99990	.99990	.99990	.99991	.99991	.99992	.99992	.99992	.99992
3.8	.99993	.99993	.99993	.99994	.99994	.99994	.99994	.99995	.99995	.99995
3.9	.99995	.99995	.99996	.99996	.99996	.99996	.99996	.99996	.99997	.99997

Student's t Probability Distribution

This t distribution is a two-tailed probability distribution. Follow these rules to use the table to set confidence limits:

1. Select the desired confidence interval. Subtract this confidence interval from one. This will give the area in both tails outside the confidence interval. This area in the tails is shown in the figure below as the shaded area and is often referred to as the level of significance (α).

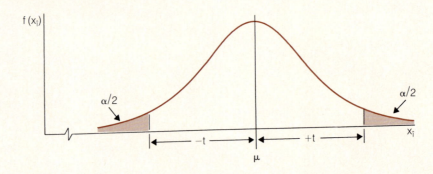

2. Find the column in the accompanying table with the appropriate level of significance heading.

3. Determine the degrees of freedom (d.f.). The d.f. usually equal $N - 1$ or $N - 2$, depending on the formula used, where N is the number of observations. Find the row in the table with the appropriate d.f.

4. The intersection of the level of significance column and the d.f. row is the t value. This t value means the number of standard deviations from the mean out to the shaded areas or the outer limits of the confidence interval.

5. The upper limit is computed by adding the product of the t value and the standard deviation to the mean. The lower limit is computed by subtracting this product from the mean.

Example

You have 25 observations with a mean of 32 and a standard deviation of 4.2. You wish to find the limits of a 90 percent confidence interval: $\alpha = .10$, $N = 25$, $\mu = 32$, and $\sigma_x = 4.2$. Upper limit = ? Lower limit = ?

Student's *t* Distribution

d.f.	.9	.8	.7	.6	.5	.4	.3	.2	.1	.05	.02	.01	.001
1	.158	.325	.510	.727	1.000	1.376	1.963	3.078	6.314	12.706	31.821	63.657	636.619
2	.142	.289	.445	.617	.816	1.061	1.386	1.886	2.910	4.303	6.965	9.925	31.598
3	.137	.277	.424	.584	.765	.978	1.250	1.638	2.353	3.182	4.541	5.841	12.941
4	.134	.271	.414	.569	.741	.941	1.190	1.533	2.132	2.776	3.747	4.604	8.610
5	.132	.267	.408	.559	.727	.920	1.156	1.476	2.015	2.571	3.365	4.032	6.859
6	.131	.265	.404	.553	.718	.906	1.134	1.440	1.943	2.447	3.143	3.707	5.959
7	.130	.263	.402	.549	.711	.896	1.119	1.415	1.895	2.365	2.998	3.499	5.405
8	.130	.262	.399	.546	.706	.889	1.108	1.397	1.860	2.306	2.896	3.355	5.041
9	.129	.261	.398	.543	.703	.883	1.100	1.383	1.833	2.262	2.821	3.250	4.781
10	.129	.260	.397	.542	.700	.879	1.093	1.372	1.812	2.228	2.764	3.169	4.587
11	.129	.260	.396	.540	.697	.876	1.088	1.363	1.796	2.201	2.718	3.106	4.437
12	.128	.259	.395	.539	.695	.873	1.083	1.356	1.782	2.179	2.681	3.055	4.318
13	.128	.259	.394	.538	.694	.870	1.079	1.350	1.771	2.160	2.650	3.012	4.221
14	.128	.258	.393	.537	.692	.868	1.076	1.345	1.761	2.145	2.624	2.977	4.140
15	.128	.258	.393	.536	.691	.866	1.074	1.341	1.753	2.131	2.602	2.947	4.073
16	.128	.258	.392	.535	.690	.865	1.071	1.337	1.746	2.120	2.583	2.921	4.015
17	.128	.257	.392	.534	.689	.863	1.069	1.333	1.740	2.110	2.567	2.898	3.965
18	.127	.257	.392	.534	.688	.862	1.067	1.330	1.734	2.101	2.552	2.878	3.922
19	.127	.257	.391	.533	.688	.861	1.066	1.328	1.729	2.093	2.539	2.861	3.883
20	.127	.257	.391	.533	.687	.860	1.064	1.325	1.725	2.086	2.528	2.845	3.850
21	.127	.257	.391	.532	.686	.859	1.063	1.323	1.721	2.080	2.518	2.831	3.819
22	.127	.256	.390	.532	.686	.858	1.061	1.321	1.717	2.074	2.508	2.819	3.792
23	.127	.256	.390	.532	.685	.858	1.060	1.319	1.714	2.069	2.500	2.807	3.767
24	.127	.256	.390	.531	.685	.857	1.059	1.318	1.711	2.064	2.492	2.797	3.745
25	.127	.256	.390	.531	.684	.856	1.058	1.316	1.708	2.060	2.485	2.787	3.725
26	.127	.256	.390	.531	.684	.856	1.058	1.315	1.706	2.056	2.479	2.779	3.707
27	.127	.256	.389	.531	.684	.855	1.057	1.314	1.703	2.052	2.473	2.771	3.690
28	.127	.256	.389	.530	.683	.855	1.056	1.313	1.701	2.048	2.467	2.763	3.674
29	.127	.256	.389	.530	.683	.854	1.055	1.311	1.699	2.045	2.462	2.756	3.659
30	.127	.256	.389	.530	.683	.854	1.055	1.310	1.697	2.042	2.457	2.750	3.646
40	.126	.255	.388	.529	.681	.851	1.050	1.303	1.684	2.021	2.423	2.704	3.551
60	.126	.254	.387	.527	.679	.848	1.046	1.296	1.671	2.000	2.390	2.660	3.460
120	.126	.254	.386	.526	.677	.845	1.041	1.289	1.658	1.980	2.358	2.617	3.373
∞	.126	.253	.385	.524	.674	.842	1.036	1.282	1.645	1.960	2.326	2.576	3.291

Level of Significance (α)

1. Level of significance = .10
2. d.f. = N − 2 = 25 − 2 = 23
3. t = 1.714
4. Upper limit = $\mu + t(\sigma_x)$ = 32 + 1.714(4.2) = 39.20
5. Lower limit = $\mu - t(\sigma_x)$ = 32 − 1.714(4.2) = 24.80

Two situations usually occur in using the t table:

a. You specify α and d.f. and you read t (the number of standard deviations to the right and left of the mean that spans the confidence interval or the unshaded area in the figure) from the body of the table.

b. You specify d.f. and t and read α from the top of the table.

C

Computer Programs

Introduction

Critical Path Method (CPM)
Program Evaluation and Review Technique (PERT)
Linear Programming
Input Instructions for Linear Programming Program LP
Program Listing for Linear Programming Program LP
Queuing

These programs are written in FORTRAN IV and are designed for batch processing. The reading device is 5 and the printing device is 6 in these programs. If your device codes are different, you will need to modify all read-and-write statements. The JCL statements appropriate for your location need to be added to all programs.

Critical Path Method (CPM)

```
C
C              CRITICAL PATH METHOD
C
C                 INPUT DATA FORMATS
C
C      CARD. 1        COLS 1-80      PROJECT NAME           (20A4)
C
C      CARD 2         COLS 1-4       NUMBER OF ACTIVITIES   (I4)
C                                        MAXIMUM OF 100
C
C                     COLS 5-10      CUSTOMER TIME REQUIRED   (F6.2)
C
C      CARD DECK 3      COLS 1-4      ACTIVTY DURATION        (F4.2)
C
C                       COLS 5-9      ACTIVITY IDENTIFIER    (I4)
C
C                       COLS 9-80     PRECEDENT ACTIVITIES   (18A4)
C                                        MAXIMUM OF 18
C
C
C         DEVICE 5 IS CARD READER
C         DEVICE 6 IS LINE PRINTER
C
C*****************************************************************
          INTEGER ACTS(100,19), STACK(100,20), NAME(20), PATH (10,101)
          INTEGER MAX,BLANK/4H    /
          REAL ES(100), EF(100), LF(100), LS(100), SL(100), LONG
          REAL TIME(100),T(100)
          IP=0
          READ (5,1) NAME
```

```
1      FORMAT(20A4)
       READ(5,2) MAX,CTIME
    2 FORMAT(I4,F6.2)
       DO 5 I=1,MAX
    5 READ (5,3) TIME(I),(ACTS(I,J),J=1,19)
    3 FORMAT(F4.2,19A4)
C*****************************************************************
C
C    COMPUTE ES AND EF FOR ALL ACTIVITIES  BY DETERMINING
C    LONGEST PATH.
C
C*****************************************************************
       DO 100 I=1,MAX
       DO 10 J=1,19
10     STACK(1,J)=ACTS(I,J)
       STACK(1,20)=2
       T(1)=TIME(I)
       TIME1=0
       M=1
20     N=STACK(M,20)
       IF (STACK(M,N).EQ.BLANK) GO TO 55
25     DO 50 K=1,MAX
       IF(STACK(M,N).NE.ACTS(K,1)) GO TO 50
       STACK(M,20)=N+1
       M=M+1
       DO 30 J=1,19
30     STACK(M,J)=ACTS(K,J)
       T(M)=TIME(K)
       STACK(M,20)=2
       GO TO 20
50     CONTINUE
       WRITE(6,4)(STACK(M,J),J=1,19)
    4 FORMAT('1',19A4,//,'PRECEDENT DOES NOT MATCH ANY ACTIVITY
      CIDENTIFIER',//,'CPM ABORT ERROR   ***',///)
       STOP
55     TIME2=0
       DO 60 J=1,M
   60 TIME2=TIME2+T(J)
       IF(TIME2.GT.TIME1) TIME1=TIME2
65     M=M-1
       IF  (M.EQ.0) GO TO 70
       N=STACK(M,20)
       IF(STACK(M,N).EQ.BLANK) GO TO 65
       GO TO 25
70     EF(I)=TIME1
       ES(I)=TIME1-TIME(I)
100    CONTINUE
       LONG=EF(1)
       DO 110 I=2,MAX
       IF(EF(I).GT.LONG)    LONG=EF(I)
110    CONTINUE
C*********************************************************
C
C    COMPUTE LS AND LF USING MAXIMUM EF AS MAX TIME
C
C*********************************************************
       DO 200 I=1,MAX
       TIME1=0
       DO 120 J=1,19
```

```
120     STACK(1,J)=ACTS(I,J)
        T(1)=TIME(I)
        M=1
123     K=1
  125 N=2
130     IF(ACTS(K,N).EQ.BLANK) GO TO 150
        IF(ACTS(K,N).EQ.STACK(M,1))  GO TO 135
        N=N+1
        IF(N.GT.19) GO TO 150
        GO TO 130
135     M=M+1
        DO 140 J=1,19
140     STACK(M,J)=ACTS(K,J)
        STACK(M,20)=K
        T(M)=TIME(K)
        GO TO 123
150     K=K+1
        IF(K.LE.MAX) GO TO 125
        TIME2=0
        DO 160 J=1,M
  160 TIME2=TIME2+T(J)
        IF(TIME2.GT.TIME1) TIME1=TIME2
        ALLOW=LONG-0.0001
        IF(TIME2.LT.ALLOW) GO TO 170
        IP=IP+1
        DO 165 J=1,M
165     PATH(IP,J)=STACK(J,1)
        PATH(IP,101)=M
170     K=STACK(M,20)+1
        M=M-1
        IF(M.LE.0) GO TO 195
        IF(K.GT.MAX) GO TO 170
        N=2
175     IF(ACTS(K,N).EQ.BLANK) GO TO 180
        IF(ACTS(K,N).EQ.STACK(M,1)) GO TO 135
        N=N+1
        IF (N.LE.19) GO TO 175
  180 N=2
        K=K+1
        IF(K.GT.MAX) GO TO 170
        GO TO  175
195     LS(I)=LONG-TIME1
        LF(I)=LS(I)+TIME(I)
200     CONTINUE
C***********************************
C
C     COMPUTE SLACK USING  LF - EF
C
C***********************************
        DO 300 I=1,MAX
300     SL(I)=LF(I)-EF(I)
C******************************
C
C     OUTPUT SECTION
C
C******************************
        WRITE(6,6) NAME,LONG,CTIME
6       FORMAT('1','PROJECT',2X,20A4,//,1X,'PROJECT CRITICAL PATH',
```

```
       C3X,F6.2,//,1X,'CUSTOMER REQUIRED TIME',F6.2,///)
       WRITE(6,7)
7      FORMAT(1X,'ACTIVITY',7X,'ACTIVITY',5X,'EARLIEST',5X,
       C'LATEST',4X,'EARLIEST',4X,'LATEST',7X,'SLACK')
       WRITE(6,8)
8      FORMAT(16X,'DURATION',6X,'START',7X,'START',6X,'FINISH',5X,
       C'FINISH')
       DO 310 I =1,MAX
       WRITE(6,9) ACTS(I,1),TIME(I),ES(I),LS(I),EF(I),LF(I),SL(I)
     9 FORMA,('0',2X,A4,9X,F6.2,7X,F6.2,6X,F6.2,5X,F6.2,5X,F6.2,6X,F6.2)
310    CONTINUE
       WRITE(6,11)
11     FORMAT('1',2X,'PROJECT CRITICAL PATHS')
       DO 320 J=1,IP
       K=PATH(J,101)
320    WRITE(6,12) (PATH(J,L),L=1,K)
12     FORMAT('0',(10(A4,4X)))
       WRITE(6,13)
13     FORMAT(///,'NORMAL EXIT OF CPM',///)
       STOP
       END
```

Program Evaluation and Review Technique (PERT)

```
C
C          PROJECT  EVALUATION AND REVIEW TECHNIQUE
C
C          INPUT DATA FORMATS
C
C          CARD 1    COL 1-80      PROJECT NAME                  (20A4)
C
C          CARD 2    COL 1-4       NUMBER OF ACTIVITIES          (I4)
C                                     MAXIMUM OF 100
C                    COL 5-8       CUSTOMER REQUIRED TIME        (F4.2)
C
C          CARD DECK 3   COL 1-4    OPTIMISTIC TIME              (F4.2)
C                        COL 5-8    MOST LIKELY TIME             (F4.2)
C                        COL 9-12   PESSIMISTIC TIME             (F4.2)
C                        COL 13-16  ACTIVITY IDENTIFIER          (A4)
C                        COL 17-80  PRECEDENT ACTIVITIES         (16A4)
C                                      MAXIMUM OF 16
C
C          DEVICE 5 IS CARD READER
C          DEVICE 6 IS LINE PRINTER
C
C*****************************************************************
       INTEGER ACTS(100,17),STACK(100,19),NAME(20),PATH(10,101)
       INTEGER MAX,BLANK/4H    /
       DIMENSION ET(100), VAR(100), VT(10,2)
       REAL ES(100),EF(100),LS(100),LF(100),SL(100), LONG
       REAL ATIME(100,3)
       READ (5,1) NAME
```

```
  1       FORMAT(20A4)
          READ (5,2) MAX,CTIME
      2 FORMAT(I4,F4.2)
          DO 5 I=1,MAX
          READ (5,3) (ATIME(I,L),L=1,3),(ACTS(I,J),J=1,17)
      3 FORMAT(3F4.2,17(A4))
          ET(I)=(ATIME(I,1)+(4.0*ATIME(I,2))+ATIME(I,3))/6.0
      5 VAR(I)=((ATIME(I,3)-ATIME(I,1))/6.0)**2.0
C****************************************************************
C
C     COMPUTE ES AND EF FOR ALL ACTIVITIES  BY DETERMINING
C     LONGEST PATH.
C
C****************************************************************
          IP=0
          DO 100 I=1,MAX
          DO 10 J=1,17
 10       STACK(1,J)=ACTS(I,J)
          STACK(1,18)=2
          STACK(1,19)=I
          TIME1=0
          M=1
 20     N=STACK(M,18)
          IF (STACK(M,N).EQ.BLANK) GO TO 55
 25       DO 50 K=1,MAX
          IF(STACK(M,N).NE.ACTS(K,1)) GO TO 50
          STACK(M,18)=N+1
          M=M+1
          DO 30 J=1,17
 30       STACK(M,J)=ACTS(K,J)
          STACK(M,18)=2
          STACK(M,19)=K
          GO TO 20
 50       CONTINUE
          WRITE(6,4)(STACK(M,J),J=1,17)
      4 FORMAT('1',17(A4,1X),//,'PRECEDENT DOES NOT MATCH ANY ACTIVITY
          CIDENTIFIER',//,'PERT ABORT ERROR     ***',///)
          STOP
 55       TIME2=0
          DO 60 J=1,M
 60       TIME2=TIME2+ET(STACK(J,19))
          IF(TIME2.GT.TIME1) TIME1=TIME2
 65       M=M-1
          IF(M.EQ.0) GO TO 70
          N=STACK(M,18)
          IF(STACK(M,N).EQ.BLANK) GO TO 65
          GO TO 25
 70       EF(I)=TIME1
          ES(I)=TIME1-ET(I)
100       CONTINUE
          LONG=EF(1)
          DO 110 I=2,MAX
          IF(EF(I).GT.LONG)     LONG=EF(I)
110       CONTINUE
C****************************************************************
C
C     COMPUTE LS AND LF USING MAXIMUM EF AS MAX TIME
C
C****************************************************************
```

```
          DO 200 I=1,MAX
          TIME1=0
          DO 120 J=1,17
120       STACK(1,J)=ACTS(I,J)
          STACK(1,18)=I
          STACK(1,19)=I
          M=1
123       K=1
  125 N=2
130       IF(ACTS(K,N).EQ.BLANK) GO TO 150
          IF(ACTS(K,N).EQ.STACK(M,1))  GO TO 135
          N=N+1
          IF(N.GT.17) GO TO 150
          GO TO 130
135       M=M+1
          DO 140 J=1,17
140       STACK(M,J)=ACTS(K,J)
          STACK(M,18)=K
          GO TO 123
150       K=K+1
          IF(K.LE.MAX) GO TO 125
          TIME2=0
          VAR2=0
          DO 160 J=1,M
          VAR2=VAR2+VAR(STACK(J,18))
160       TIME2=TIME2+ET(STACK(J,18))
          IF(TIME2.GT.TIME1) TIME1=TIME2
          ALLOW=LONG-0.0001
          IF(TIME2.LT.ALLOW) GO TO 170
          IP=IP+1
          DO 165 J=1,M
165       PATH(IP,J)=STACK(J,1)
          PATH(IP,101)=M
          VT(IP 1)=VAR2
          VT(IP,2)=VAR2**.5
170       K=STACK(M,18)+1
          M=M-1
          IF(M.LE.0) GO TO 195
          IF(K.GT.MAX) GO TO 170
          N=2
175       IF(ACTS(K,N).EQ.BLANK) GO TO 180
          IF(ACTS(K,N).EQ.STACK(M,1)) GO TO 135
          N=N+1
          IF (N.LE.17) GO TO 175
  180 N=2
          K=K+1
          IF(K.GT.MAX) GO TO 170
          GO TO  175
195       LS(I)=LONG-TIME1
          LF(I)=LS(I)+ET(I)
200       CONTINUE
C*******************************
C
C      COMPUTE SLACK USING  LF-EF
C
C*******************************
          DO 300 I=1,MAX
300       SL(I)=LF(I)-EF(I)
```

```
C**********************************************************
C
C     OUTPUT SECTION
C
C     FOR EACH ACTIVITY THE OPTIMISTIC TIME, MOST LIKELY TIME,
C     PESIMISTIC TIME, MEAN TIME, AND VARIANCE WILL BE OUTPUT.
C     ALSO THE ES, LS, EF, LF, AND SLACK WILL BE OUTPUT.
C
C     FOR EACH CRITICAL PATH IN THE NETWORK THE ACTIVITIES
C     ON THE PATH, VARIANCE AND STANDARD DEVIATION OF THE PATH,
C     AND THE NUMBER OF STANDARD DEVIATIONS AWAY FROM THE
C     REQUIRED TIME THE PATH IS, WILL BE PRINTED.
C
C**********************************************************
      WRITE(6,6) NAME,LONG,CTIME
6     FORMAT('1','PROJECT: ',20A4,//,1X,'PROJECT CRITICAL TIME: ',
     CF6.2,//,1X,'CUSTOMER REQUIRED TIME: ',F6.2)
      WRITE(6,7)
7     FORMAT('0',//,2X,'ACTIVITY',4X,'OPTIMISTIC',4X,'MOST-LIKELY',
     C4X,'PESSIMISTIC',5X,'MEAN',4X,'VARIANCE',4X,'EARLIEST',5X,
     C'LATEST',3X,'EARLIEST',4X,'LATEST',7X,'SLACK',/,17X,'TIME',
     C11X,'TIME',11X,'TIME',8X,'TIME',18X,'START',6X,'START',5X,
     C'FINISH',5X,'FINISH',/)
      DO 310 I=1,MAX
      WRITE(6,8) ACTS(I,1),(ATIME(I,L),L=1,3),ET(I),VAR(I),ES(I),LS(I),
     C EF(I),LF(I),SL(I)
    8 FORMAT('0',4X,A4,7X,F6.2,9X,F6.2,9X,F6.2,6X,F6.2,4X,F6.2,6X,
     C F6.2,6X,F6.2,5X,F6.2,4X,F6.2,6X,F6.2,2X)
310   CONTINUE
      WRITE(6,9)
9     FORMAT('1','PROJECT CRITICAL PATHS'///)
      DO 320 I=1,IP
      M=PATH(I,101)
      WRITE(6,11) (PATH(I,J),J=1,M)
11    FORMAT('0',10(A4,4X))
      WRITE(6,12) LONG,VT(I,1),VT(I,2)
12    FORMAT('0','DURATION: ',F6.2,/,1X,'VARIANCE: ',F6.2,/,1X,
     C'STANDARD DEVIATION: ',F6.2)
      IF(CTIME.EQ.0) GO TO 320
      SD=(CTIME-LONG)/VT(I,2)
      WRITE(6,13) SD
13    FORMAT('0','# OF STANDARD DEVIATIONS OFF REQUIRED TIME: ',F6.2//)
320   CONTINUE
      WRITE(6,14)
14    FORMAT(/////,'NORMAL EXIT OF PERT'/////)
      STOP
      END
```

Linear Programming

Input Instructions for Linear Programming Program LP

A set of linear programming data input instructions is given below. These instructions assume that the program has been placed in storage and the user calls the stored program (LMN, LP: L 11000001). This procedure seems to work well for student use. Users will, of course, need to modify the JCL statements (!JOB, !LIMIT, !RUN, !DATA, and !EOD) to those appropriate for their locations. The program does not require that a load module or other forms of stored programs be used.

CONTROL CARDS (starting in card column 1):

!JOB¢11030000,BA(student's last name),7
!LIMIT¢(TIME,1),(CORE,5)
!RUN¢(LMN,LP:L,11000001)
!DATA

NOTE: "¢" stands for a blank card column.

DATA CARDS:
1. Title: up to 80 columns of problem's name, etc.
2. cc 1–2, number of constraints, exclusive of object function, up to 20 constraints.

   cc 3–4, number of variables exclusive of slack and artificial variables, up to 40 variables.

   cc 5–6, + 1 for maximum
           − 1 for minimum

3. For each constraint and in the order in which the constraints are read in (see No. 4 below):
   '¢1' less or equal constraint
   '¢¢' strict equality
   '−1' greater or equal constraint

   All on one card in subsequent fields of 2 starting in cc 1, the '' do not need to be input.

4. For each constraint:
   cc 1–8 right side constraint
   cc 9–16 coefficient of x_1
   cc 17–24 coefficient of x_2
   cc 25–32 and on through cc 73–80 for the coefficients of x_3 through x_9

   If more than nine variables, then second card contains the coefficients of x_{10} to x_{19}, third card contains the coefficients of x_{20} to x_{29}, etc.

   If one constraint requires more than one card, all other constraints must have the same number of cards, even if the coefficients on some cards are all zero. Zero coefficients may be left blank.

5. Objective function:
   cc 1–8 blank
   cc 9–16 cost coefficient associated with x_1
   cc 17–24 cost coefficient associated with x_2, etc., as in No. 4 above.

   Any number of problems may be stacked behind each other.

   !EOD

Program Listing for Linear Programming Program LP

```
C        CARD 1        TITLE ALL 80 CARD COLUMNS
C        CARD 2
C                 CC 1-2      NUMBER OF EQUATIONS
C                 CC 3-4   NUMBER OF STRUCTURAL VARABLES.
C                 CC 5-6 SPACE FOR MAXIMUM, '-1' FOR MIN.
C                 CC 7-8 SPACE FOR ONLY FIRST AND LAST ITERATION TO PRINT
C                        ANY NEUMERIC PUNCH FOR ALL ITERATIONS PRINTED
C
C        CARD 3        EQUATION TYPES.
C                 ' ' SPACE FOR EQUAL TO
C                 '+1' FOR LESS THAN OR EQUAL TO
C                 '-1' FOR GREATER THAN OR EQUAL TO.
C
C        CARD DECK 4        RHS AND STRUCTURAL VARABLES  10 PER CARD  10F8.0
C                           CC 1-8 IS THE RIGHT HAND CONSTRAINT. CC 9-80
C                           PLUS NEXT CARD(IF NECESSARY) FROM CC 1-80  ARE
C                           STRUCTURAL VARABLES
C
C        CARD DECK 5        OBJECTIVE FUNCTION.
C                 CC 1-8 SPACE
C                 CC 9-80  COSTS OR PROFITS FOR STRUCTURAL VARABLES,
C                          COST ARE ENTERED WITH '-' PROFITS ,PLUS.
C                          IF YOU GO TO CARD 2 START IN CC 1-80.
C
C        MAXIMUM NUMBER OF EQUATIONS 20 , MAXIMUM NUMBER OF VARABLES 40
C
C
C        DEVICE 108 IS LINE PRINTER
C        DEVICE 105 IS CARD READER
C
         INTEGER EQNUM,VARNUM
         INTEGER ROWNUM(21,2),COLNUM(2,63)
         INTEGER RHS,Z,S,IAR,X,C
         DIMENSION ASUB(22,63),NAME(20),NUMBER(63)
         COMMON T
         DATA RHS,Z,S,IAR,X,C/'RH','-Z','S','A','X','C'/
         DATA NUMBER/' 1',' 2',' 3',' 4',' 5',' 6',' 7',' 8',' 9','10',
        1'11','12','13','14','15','16','17','18','19','20','21','22','23',
        2'24','25','26','27','28','29','30','31','32','33','34','35','36',
        3'37','38','39','40','41','42','43','44','45','46','47','48','49',
        4'50','51','52','53','54','55','56','57','58','59','60','61','62',
        5'63'/
           T=.001
 1000    CONTINUE
         READ(5,1,END=170) NAME
    1    FORMAT(20A4)
   10    READ(5,2,END=185) EQNUM,VARNUM,MAX,NPRINT
    2    FORMAT(4I2)
         IZ = EQNUM + 1
         IW = EQNUM + 2
            DO 15 I = 1,22
               DO 15 J = 1,63
   15    ASUB(I,J) = 0.0
         READ(5,3,END=175)(ROWNUM(I,1),I = 1,EQNUM)
```

```
     3    FORMAT(20I2)
          VARNUM = VARNUM + 1
               DO 20 I = 1,IZ
    20    READ(5,4,END=180)(ASUB(I,J),J = 1,VARNUM)
     4    FORMAT(10F8.0)
          COLNUM(1,1) = RHS
          COLNUM(2,1) = S
               DO 25 J = 2,VARNUM
          COLNUM(1,J) = X
    25    COLNUM(2,J) = NUMBER(J-1)
          ROWNUM(IZ,1) = C
          ROWNUM(IZ,2) = Z
          K = EQNUM + VARNUM
               DO 55 I = 1,EQNUM
          J = I + VARNUM
          ASUB(I,J) = 1.0
          IF(ROWNUM(I,1)) 40,35,30
    30    COLNUM(1,J) = S
          ROWNUM(I,1) = S
          COLNUM(2,J) = NUMBER(I)
          ROWNUM(I,2) = NUMBER(I)
          GO TO 55
    35    COLNUM(1,J) = IAR
          COLNUM(2,J) = NUMBER(I)
          ROWNUM(I,1) = IAR
          ROWNUM(I,2) = NUMBER(I)
          GO TO 45
    40    K = K + 1
          COLNUM(1,J) = IAR
          COLNUM(2,J) = NUMBER(I)
          COLNUM(1,K) = S
          COLNUM(2,K) = NUMBER(I)
          ROWNUM(I,1) = IAR
          ROWNUM(I,2) = NUMBER(I)
          ASUB(I,K) = -1.0
    45    ASUB(IW,J)  = 1.0
          DO 50 J=1,K
    50    ASUB(IW,J) = ASUB(IW,J) - ASUB(I,J)
    55    CONTINUE
          DO 60 J =  1 , K
    60    ASUB(IZ,J) = -ASUB(IZ,J)
          ITNUM = 1
          CALL PRINT(ASUB,ROWNUM,COLNUM,NAME,IZ,K,ITNUM)
    65    IPV  = 0
          JPV  = 0
          CALL ACHX(ASUB,ROWNUM,COLNUM,EQNUM,JPV,IPV,K)
               IF(JPV.NE.0)  GO TO 140
          DEL  = -1000000.
          IOBJ=IZ
          DO 70   J1=1,K
               IF(COLNUM(1,J1).EQ.IAR) GO TO 70
          IF(ASUB(IW,J1)+T.GE.0) GO TO 70
          IOBJ=IW
          GO TO 75
    70    CONTINUE
    75    DO 125 J = 2, K
               IF(IOBJ.EQ.IW) GO TO 85
    80    IF(MAX.LT.0) GO TO 90
    85    IF(ASUB(IOBJ,J)) 95,125,125
    90    IF(ASUB(IOBJ,J).LE.0) GO TO 125
    95    IF((COLNUM(1,J)-IAR).EQ.0) GO TO 125
```

```
100    IR = O.
       BI = 1000000.
       DO 115 I = 1,EQNUM
       IF(ASUB(I,J).LE.O) GO TO 115
105    BX   = ASUB(I,1)/ ASUB(I,J)
       IF((BX-BI).GE.O)   GO TO 115
110    IR = I
       BI = BX
115    CONTINUE
       BXX=ABS(BI*ASUB(IOBJ,J))
       IF((BXX-DEL).LE.O)    GO TO 125
120    DEL    = BXX
       JPV  = J
       IPV  = IR
125    CONTINUE
       IF(JPV.NE.O)  GO TO 140
130    IF(NPRINT.NE.O) GO TO 1000
135    CALL PRINT(ASUB,ROWNUM,COLNUM,NAME,IZ,K,ITNUM)
       GO TO 1000
140    CONTINUE
       ITNUM = ITNUM + 1
       ROWNUM(IPV,1)   = COLNUM(1,JPV)
       ROWNUM(IPV,2)   = COLNUM(2,JPV)
       PIV    = ASUB(IPV,JPV)
       DO 145 J = 1,K
145    ASUB(IPV,J)   = ASUB(IPV,J)/PIV
       DO 160 I = 1, IOBJ
       IF((I-IPV).EQ.O)GO  TO 160
150    IF(ASUB(I,JPV).EQ.O)  GO TO 160
155    PIV    = ASUB(I,JPV)
       DO 161 J = 1,K
       ASUB(I,J) = ASUB(I,J) - PIV*ASUB(IPV,J)
  161 CONTINUE
160    CONTINUE
       IF(NPRINT.EQ.O) GO TO 65
165    CALL PRINT(ASUB,ROWNUM,COLNUM,NAME,IZ,K,ITNUM)
       GO TO 65
  170 WRITE (6,5)
  5    FORMAT ('O',//,1X,'** NORMAL EXIT OF LP **')
       CALL EXIT
  175 WRITE (6,6)
  6    FORMAT ('O',//,1X,'** # OF EQUATIONS SPECIFIED ON CARD2 NOT FOUND'
      1,/,1HO,'** LP RUN ABORTED **')
       CALL EXIT
  180 WRITE (6,7)
  7    FORMAT ('O',//,1X,'** # OF STRUCTURAL VARIABLES SPECIFIED ON CARD'
      1'2 NOT FOUND **',/,1HO ,'**   LP RUN ABORTED **')
       CALL EXIT
  185 WRITE (6,8)
  8    FORMAT ('O',//,1X,'** CARD2 MISSING OR DECK OUT OF ORDER **',/,
      11HO ,'**   LP RUN ABORTED **')
       CALL EXIT
       STOP
       END
       SUBROUTINE PRINT(ASUB,ROWNUM,COLNUM,NAME,IZ,K,ITNUM)
       INTEGER ROWNUM(21,2),COLNUM(2,63)
       DIMENSION ASUB(22,63),NAME(20)
       COMMON T
       WRITE(6,1)
1      FORMAT(1H1)
       WRITE(6,2)
```

```
2          FORMAT (1X,'* * LINEAR PROGRAM  * *',//)
           WRITE(6,3) NAME,ITNUM
3          FORMAT(20A4,//,11X,'ITERATION NO.',I3,///)
           WRITE(6,4) ((COLNUM(I,J),I = 1,2),J = 1,K)
4          FORMAT(13X,2A2,7X,12(2A2,4X),/,(24X,12(2A2,4X)))
              DO 15 I = 1,IZ
           WRITE(6,6)
6          FORMAT(1H0)
    15     WRITE(6,7) (ROWNUM(I,J),J = 1,2),(ASUB(I,J),J = 1,K)
7          FORMAT(2X,2A2,1X,F11.2,2X,12F8.2,/,(20X,12F8.2))
           RETURN
           END
           SUBROUTINE ACHX(ASUB,ROWNUM,COLNUM,EQNUM,JPV,IPV,K)
           DIMENSION ASUB(22,63)
           INTEGER EQNUM
           INTEGER ROWNUM(21,2),COLNUM(2,63)
           INTEGER IAR
           DATA IAR/'A'/
           DO 10  I=1,EQNUM
              IF(ROWNUM(I,1).NE.IAR) GO TO 10
              IF(ASUB(I,1).NE.0.) GO TO 10
           DO 5  J=2,K
              IF(COLNUM(1,J).EQ.IAR) GO TO 5
              IF(ASUB(I,J).EQ.0.) GO TO 5
           JPV=J
           IPV=I
              IF(ASUB(I,J).GT.0.) GO TO 15
    5      CONTINUE
   10      CONTINUE
   15      CONTINUE
           RETURN
           END
```

Queuing

```
C
C          MULTIPLE-CHANNEL  SINGLE-PHASE QUEUING
C
C
C          INPUT DATA FORMAT
C
C          CARD 1     COLS 1-2    NUMBER OF CHANNELS         I2
C                     COLS 3-8    AVERAGE ARRIVALS PER UNIT TIME (LAMBDA)
C                                 F6.3
C                     COLS 9-14   AVERAGE NUMBER OF SERVICES EACH
C                                 CHANNEL CAN PERFORM PER UNIT TIME (MU)
C                                 F6.3
C                     COLS 15-16  NUMBER OF UNITS IN LINE WHICH YOU
C                                 WANT PROBABILITIES         I2
C
C
C          DEVICE 5 IS CARD READER
C          DEVICE 6 IS LINE PRINTER
C
C********************************************************************
```

```
        REAL LAMBDA,MU,LQ,L
        READ (5,1) N,LAMBDA,MU,MAX
      1 FORMAT(I2,2F6.3,I2)
        WRITE(6,2) N,LAMBDA,MU
      2 FORMAT('1','NUMBER OF CHANNELS:',18X,I2,/,1X,'AVERAGE ARRIVALS',
       1' PER UNIT TIME:',5X,F7.3,/,1X,'NUMBER OF SERVICES EACH',/,
       2' CHANNEL CAN PERFORM PER UNIT TIME:',2X,F7.3)
        D=LAMBDA/MU
        B=0
        NFAC=1
        DO 10 I=1,N
     10 NFAC=NFAC*I
        IF(N.EQ.1) GO TO 15
        DO 30 I1=2,N
        I=I1-1
        IFAC=1
        DO 20 J=1,I
     20 IFAC=IFAC*J
     30 B=B+(D**I)/IFAC
        E=(D**N)/(NFAC*(1-D/N))
        PO=1/(B+E)
        GO TO 35
     15 PO=1.0-D
     35 LQ=PO*((D**(N+1))/((NFAC/N)*((N-D)**2)))
        L=LQ+D
        WQ=LQ/LAMBDA
        W=L/LAMBDA
        WRITE(6,3) PO,LQ,L,WQ,W
      3 FORMAT('0','PROBABILITY OF IDLE SYSTEM',19X,F9.6,
       1/,1X,'AVERAGE NUMBER OF UNITS IN WAITING LINE',5X,F10.6,
       2/,1X,'AVERAGE NUMBER OF UNITS IN SYSTEM',11X,F10.6,
       3/,1X,'AVERAGE UNIT WAITING TIME IN LINE',11X,F10.6,
       4/,1X,'AVERAGE UNIT TIME IN SYSTEM',17X,F10.6)
        DO 80 K=1,MAX
        KFAC=1
        DO 50 J=1,K
     50 KFAC=KFAC*J
        IF(K.GT.N) GO TO 60
        PIN=((D**K)/KFAC)*PO
        GO TO 70
     60 PIN=((D**K)/(NFAC*(N**(K-N))))*PO
     70 WRITE(6,4) K,PIN
      4 FORMAT('0PROBABILITY OF ',I2,3X,F8.6)
     80 CONTINUE
        WRITE(6,5)
      5 FORMAT(/////'NORMAL EXIT OF QUEUING')
        STOP
        END
```

D

Answers to Odd-Numbered Problems

Chapter 2

(1) a. 119,048 ton-miles; b. $2,065,483. **(3)** a. $P_a = \$33,000$, $P_b = \$59,000$; b. $Q_a = 25,352$ hours, $Q_b = 22,892$ hours; c. $TR_a = \$760,560$, $TR_b = \$766,882$. **(5)** b. Blanket contract has lowest expected cost; c. $250,000, $300,000, or $350,000. **(7)** b. Bid low on the research contract and bid the production contract; c. $1,050,000, $200,000, $700,000, or ($150,000). **(9)** 40 thousand pounds. **(11)** 150 classrooms. **(13)** 30 standby machines. **(15)** a. Expand jail services (C/B = .737), expand patrol services (C/B = .716); b. expand jail services.

Chapter 3

(1) $a = 83$, $b = 15$, $Y_6 = \$173,000$, $Y_7 = \$188,000$. **(3)** $a = 48.286$, $b = 4.429$, $Y_8 = 83.7$ personnel. **(5)** a. $a = -39.735$, $b = 11.1796$, $Y_7 = \$13.37$ million; b. $r^2 = .994$. **(7)** b. AP = 8 has the least total absolute forecast error over the 10 months of data; c. $F_{25} = 95.1$ maintenance calls. **(9)** b. $\alpha = .5$ results in the least total absolute forecast error over the 16 months of data; c. $F_{17} = \$.851$. **(11)** a. $Y = 106.25$; b. the number of parts per order, the number of past orders, and the number of pounds per part explain 79.5 percent of the variation in the number of production engineering hours per order. **(13)** a. $Y_8 = 83.718$ personnel; b. UL = 88.302 personnel and LL = 79.134 personnel; c. our forecast for next year is 84 research personnel, there is only a 10 percent probability that more than 89 or less than 79 personnel could be required just due to chance if past trends continue. **(15)** a. $Q_1 = 15.75$ million pounds, $Q_2 = 14.51$ million pounds, $Q_3 = 21.59$ million pounds, and $Q_4 = 27.19$ million pounds; b. UL = 29.32 million pounds; c. lease the warehouse. **(17)** a. $a = 91.33$, $b = 21.58$, $Y_{11} = 328.71$ units, $Y_{12} = 350.29$ units, $Y_{13} = 371.87$ units, $Y_{14} = 393.45$ units, and $Y_{15} = 415.03$ units; b. $s_{yx} = 17.12$ units, $UL_{15} = 446.87$ units; c. Cycle 1 peaks at 115 percent of trend, Cycle 2 peaks at 90 percent of trend, Cycle 3 peaks at 108 percent of trend, and Cycle 4 will peak at about 94 percent of trend; d. UL = 1,931 units, LL = 1,788 units.

Chapter 4

(7) In-house cost = $75,000, outside cost = $87,500; heat treat in-house. **(9)** a. install robotry process; b. robotry overtakes Springy in Year 2, robotry overtakes conventional in Year 3; c. $12,700,000. **(4S.1)** $3,375, $4,950, $4,725, $4,725, and $4,725. **(4S.3)** $118, $173, $165, $165, and $165. **(4S.5)** $60,000, $110,000, $155,000, $195,000, $230,000, $260,000, $290,000, $320,000, $350,000, $375,000, $400,000, $425,000, $450,000, $475,000, $500,000. **(4S.7)** a. $620.90; b. $4,329;

c. \$3,991. **(4S.9)** \$3,619.66. **(4S.11)** Payback period is 2.4 years, make the bolts. **(4S.13)** NPV = (\$63,689), do not build the store. **(4S.15)** Payback period exceeds 5 years, additional first cost of the Z computer cannot be justified, buy the Y computer. **(4S.17)** $PI_A = 1.25$, $PI_B = 1.18$, buy design A.

Chapter 5

(1) a. No, the mix of the three woods is beyond the mill's control; b. No. **(3)** max $Z = 700X_1 + 500X_2$, $X_1 \le 100$ (soybean acreage), $1,000X_1 + 2,000X_2 \le 200,000$ (pounds of fertilizer), $X_1 = $ acres to be planted in soybeans this season, $X_2 = $ acres to be planted in milo this season. **(5)** max $Z = 20,000X_1 + 30,000X_2$, $X_1 + X_2 \le 20$ (total personnel), $X_1 \le 15$ (1st qtr. personnel), $X_2 \le 10$ (2d qtr. personnel), $X_1 = $ number of research personnel to be assigned to project during 1st quarter, $X_2 = $ number of research personnel to be assigned to project during 2d quarter. **(7)** min $Z = 5/100X_1 + 3/100X_2$; $100X_1 + 100X_2 \ge 4,000$; $200X_1 + 400X_2 \ge 10,000$; $200X_1 + 100X_2 \ge 5,000$; $X_1 = $ pounds of oats to be fed to each head of cattle per day; $X_2 = $ pounds of corn to be fed to each head of cattle per day. **(9)** max $Z = 10X_1 + 6X_2$, $\frac{1}{4}X_1 + \frac{1}{8}X_2 \le 480$, $\frac{1}{6}X_1 + \frac{1}{4}X_2 \le 480$, $\frac{2}{7}X_1 \le 480$, $X_1 = $ number of hardback books to be produced per shift, $X_2 = $ number of paperback books to be produced per shift. **(11)** $X_1 = 100$, $X_2 = 50$, $Z = \$95,000$. **(13)** $X_1 = 10$, $X_2 = 10$, $Z = \$500,000$. **(15)** $X_1 = 1,440$, $X_2 = 960$; $Z = \$20,160$. **(5S.1)** The 3rd tableau is optimal, $X_2 = 375$, $X_1 = 500$, $Z = 125,000$. **(5S.3)** The 4th tableau is optimal, $X_1 = 50$, $S_1 = 100$, $S_2 = 200$, $Z = 1,000$. **(5S.5)** a. $X_1 = $ sales calls per day per salesperson to petroleum industry customers, $X_2 = $ sales calls per day per salesperson to chemical industry customers; b. max $Z = 500X_1 + 200X_2$, $8X_1 + \frac{8}{3}X_2 \le 8$, $40X_1 + 30X_2 \le 60$; c. max $Z = 500X_1 + 200X_2 + 0S_1 + 0S_2$, $8X_1 + \frac{8}{3}X_2 + S_1 + 0S_2 = 8$, $40X_1 + 30X_2 + 0S_1 + S_2 = 60$; d. the 3rd tableau is optimal, $X_1 = .6$, $X_2 = 1.2$, $S_1 = 0$, $S_2 = 0$, $Z = \$540$ average daily profits. **(5S.7)** a. $X_1 = $ urban renewal spending next year, $X_2 = $ health services spending next year, $X_3 = $ fire department spending next year; b. max $Z = .4X_1 + .3X_2 + .35X_3$, $X_1 \le 7$, $X_2 \ge 3$, $X_3 \le 8$, $X_1 + X_2 + X_3 \le 10$; c. max $Z = .4X_1 + .3X_2 + .35X_3 + 0S_1 - MA_2 + 0S_3 + 0S_4 + 0S_2$, $X_1 + 0X_2 + 0X_3 + S_1 + 0A_2 + 0S_3 + 0S_4 + 0S_2 = 7$, $0X_1 + X_2 + 0X_3 + 0S_1 + A_2 + 0S_3 + 0S_4 - S_2 = 3$, $0X_1 + 0X_2 + X_3 + 0S_1 + 0A_2 + S_3 + 0S_4 + 0S_2 = 8$, $X_1 + X_2 + X_3 + 0S_1 + 0A_2 + 0S_3 + S_4 + 0S_2 = 10$; d. the 4th tableau is optimal, $X_1 = \$7,000,000$, $X_2 = \$3,000,000$, $X_3 = 0$, $Z = \$3,700,000$, $S_1 = 0$, $S_2 = 0$, $S_3 = \$8,000,000$, $S_4 = 0$. **(5S.9)** a. and b. See Problem 9 above; c. max $Z = 10X_1 + 6X_2 + 0S_1 + 0S_2 + 0S_3$, $\frac{1}{4}X_1 + \frac{1}{8}X_2 + S_1 + 0S_2 + 0S_3 = 480$, $\frac{1}{6}X_1 + \frac{1}{4}X_2 + 0S_1 + S_2 + 0S_3 = 480$, $\frac{2}{7}X_1 + 0X_2 + 0S_1 + 0S_2 + S_3 = 480$; d. the 4th tableau is optimal, $X_2 = 960$, $X_1 = 1,440$, $S_3 = 68\frac{4}{7}$, $S_1 = 0$, $S_2 = 0$, $Z = \$20,160$. **(5S.11)** a. Plant 100 acres of soybeans, 50 acres of milo, profits will be \$95,000 next season, and all acreage and fertilizer will be used; b. X_1 and X_2 are in the solution, one acre change in soybean RHS will change Z by \$450, one pound change in fertilizer RHS will change Z by \$.25. **(5S.13)** a. 10 personnel should be assigned during the 1st quarter, 10 personnel should be assigned during the 2nd quarter, profits will be \$500,000, 5 personnel less than the maximum of 15 will be assigned in the 1st quarter, no slack in either 2nd quarter or total personnel; b. X_1 and X_2 are in the solution, one person change in project personnel allowance RHS will change Z by \$20,000, one person change in 1st quarter personnel allowance RHS will not affect Z, and one person change in 2nd quarter personnel allowance RHS will change Z by $10,000. **(5S.15)** a. Feed each head of cattle 10 pounds of oats and 30 pounds of corn per day, daily feeding cost will be $1.40 per head, and 4,000 excess mineral units per head per day will result; b. X_1 and X_2 are in the solution, one calorie change in RHS will change Z by $\frac{1}{100}$¢, one vitamin unit change in RHS will change Z by $\frac{1}{50}$¢. **(5S.17)** a. Produce 1,440 hardbacks and 960 paperbacks per shift for a contribution of $20,160 per shift, there will be 68$\frac{2}{3}$ minutes of unused framing capacity per shift; b. X_1 and X_2 are in the solution, one minute change in printing capacity RHS will change Z by $6, one minute change in cover capacity RHS will change Z by $36. **(5S.19)** a. Transportation table No. 3 is optimal, (A-1) = 100, (B-1) = 100, (B-3) = 400, (C-1) = 100, (C-2) = 800; b. cost = $940. **(5S.21)** Transportation table No. 6 is optimal, (A-4) = 9,000, (B-3) = 14,000, (B-4) = 3,000, (C-1) = 3,000, (C-2) = 10,000, (C-3) = 1,000; b. cost = $23,500. **(5S.23)** a. See the solution in Problem 5S.21 above; b. the starting solution is optimal. **(5S.25)** a. Al to 4, Ben to 1, Cal to 2, Dan to 3; b. cost = $1,600.

Chapter 6

(1) a. 12,500 textbooks; b. $150,000; c. $15,000; d. $9.50. **(3)** b. Build the large plant, EV = $3,950,000; c. $5,000,000, $2,500,000, or $1,000,000. **(5)** NPV = ($63,689), do not build the store. **(7)** Annual after-tax savings in buying is $12,800, payback period = 7.81 years, lease the building. **(9)** San Antonio: 0–250,000 units, Dallas: 250,000–500,000 units, Houston: 500,000+ units. **(11)** a. Los Angeles: min $Z = 170X_1 + 100X_2 + 190X_3 + 150X_4 + 200X_5 + 160X_6 + 130X_7 + 180X_8$, $X_1 + X_2 + X_3 + X_4 = 50,000$, $X_5 + X_6 + X_7 + X_8 = 50,000$, $X_1 + X_5 = 25,000$, $X_2 + X_6 = 25,000$, $X_3 + X_7 = 25,000$, $X_4 + X_8 = 25,000$, San Jose: min $Z = 170X_1 + 100X_2 + 190X_3 + 120X_4 + 200X_5 + 160X_6 + 130X_7 + 170X_8$, constraints are same as for Los Angeles; c. $Z_{LA} = $14,500,000$, $Z_{SJ} = $13,750,000$; d. select San Jose because the annual cost of shipping trailers from the two plants to the four warehouses is less than the Los Angeles alternative; e. 25,000 from Stockton to San Jose, Portland to Seattle, Stockton to San Francisco, and Portland to San Diego. **(13)** The ultimate selection should be based upon weighing the strengths and weaknesses of each location, each with its good and bad points, and upon which factors you believe are important.

Chapter 7

(3) Activity f (Field Test) is complete and is 2 weeks ahead of schedule at the end of February, Activity g (Production Design) is 2 weeks behind schedule. **(5)** The project now has four more personnel than planned and the project is projected to be overstaffed by five personnel through July. **(11)** c. Path b-f-h-i and 48 days. **(13)** *Time:* Activities a and b are completed within the original schedule, Activities c and d have slipped 1 and 2 weeks, respectively, Activity e has been compressed 2 weeks, Activity f is projected to be completed within its original estimate of 5 weeks, Activities c and d are critical and have no slack and the project's completion has therefore been extended 3 weeks from 12/15 to 1/7; *cost:* project is estimated to overrun target by $6,000, Activities a and b have $2,000 and ($1,500) variances, respectively, and are closed, Activities c and d are in progress and are expected to overrun target by $3,500 and $5,000, respectively, Activities e and f have not begun but are projected to overrun targets by $1,000 each. **(15)** a. 25, 29.5, 17.17, and 18 days; b. 2.78, 1.36, .69, and 0; c. path's expected duration is 89.67 days, path's variance is 4.83. **(17)** Path 2 offers the greatest risk of overrunning contract deadline of 48 weeks, but only by a small amount (1 percent).

Chapter 8

(1) Q_1: 374.4, 842.4, 1,716.0, and 2,932.8; Q_2: 468.0, 780.0, 1,872.0, and 3,120.0; Q_3: 374.4, 936.0, 1,560.0, and 2,870.4; Q_4: 312.0, 780.0, 1,560.0, and 2,652.0. **(3)** a. Q_1: 310,145 hours, Q_2: 453,987 hours, Q_3: 363,461 hours, Q_4: 534,830 hours; b. Q_1: 220,490 hours, Q_2: 324,595 hours, Q_3: 258,658 hours, Q_4: 380,997.5 hours. **(5)** a. 799.24 employees per quarter; b. Q_1: 596.43, Q_2: 873.05, Q_3: 698.96, Q_4: 1,028.52. **(7)** levelized: $33,400, matching: $40,950; the levelized capacity plan has the least annual incremental cost. **(9)** a. $164,619; b. the levelized capacity plan is more economical and exhibits other stable work force advantages.

Chapter 9

(1) a. 1,000 units; b. $1,000. **(3)** a. 27,573.135 tons; b. $248,158.22; c. 208.5 orders. **(5)** 6,860.84 pounds, TSC = $1,311.80. **(7)** 1,000 units; b. $400. **(9)** a. 29,160.59 barrels; b. $77,158.92; c. 19.44 days. **(11)** a. $\text{TSC} = Q[C/10(p - d)/p)] + \text{SD}/(1,000Q)$; b. $\text{EOQ} = \sqrt{\text{SD}/(100C)[p/(p - d)]}$; c. 2,751.431 tons; d. $1,061.26. **(13)** a. $251,447.5; b. 10,000 units; c. 5 orders; d. 6,000 units. **(15)** a. 1,000 boxes; b. $255,450; c. 818.54 boxes; d. $254,614.78; e. yes. **(17)** a. EDDLT = 162 seals, SS = 81 seals, b. OP = 243 seals. **(19)** a. 52.6 days; b. 900,000 forms. **(9S.1)** a. 5 cases; b. 1 case. **(9S.3)** a. 76 units; b. 20.5 units. **(9S.5)** a. 662.71 units; b. 62.71 units. **(9S.7)** a. and b. 8 units; c. .4 units.

Chapter 10

(1) a. Shortest processing time ranks first on all three criteria; b. shortest processing time, but must deal with long jobs. **(3)** a. The two operations must use the same job sequence; b. Ca-L-C-Ch-B; c. 12 hours. **(7)** A: 72.76 hours, B: 127.30 hours, C: 210.05 hours, D: 285.05 hours, E: 204.60 hours. **(9)** Production: 2,000 units in Weeks 2, 6, and 10. **(11)** a. Three barbers; b. Barber 1: Wed.-Sat., Barber 2: Fri.-Tues., Barber 3: Mon.-Thurs.; c. three barbers, yes. **(13)** a. Day shift: 9.2 or 10 clerks, evening shift: 7 clerks; c. day shift: 4 shifts slack per week, evening shift: 5 shifts slack per week.

Chapter 11

(1) 50, 100, 100, 100, 70, and 80 units. **(3)** a. $2,500; b. 671 units in Weeks 2, 4, and 6, and 858 units in Week 5, $3,155; c. 400 units in Week 2, 1,800 units in Week 4, and 500 units in Week 6, $2,800. **(5)** a. Labor: 58, 87, 115, 87, 87, and 58 percent, machines: 60, 90, 120, 90, 90, and 60 percent; b. labor is feasible with overtime in third month, machine loading is infeasible, third month's production should be spread to earlier and later months. **(9)** Planned order releases — A: 500 in Week 3, 2,000 in Week 4, and 1,000 in Week 5, B: 500 in Week 2, 2,000 in Week 3, and 1,000 in Week 4, C: 200 in Week 2, 2,000 in Week 3, and 1,000 in Week 4, D: 1,000 in Week 1, 3,700 in Week 2, and 2,000 in Week 3. **(11)** a. Planned order releases — #377: 1,800 in Week 3, 2,000 in Weeks 4 and 6, M: 1,600 in Week 2 and 2,000 in Weeks 3 and 5, F: 1,500 in Week 2 and 2,000 in Weeks 3 and 5, H: 1,500 in Week 1 and 2,000 in Weeks 2 and 4, A: 116,000 in Week 1 (must be expedited to compress lead time from 2 weeks to 1 week) and 100,000 in Week 3, B: 10,000 in Weeks 1 and 2 and 10,800 in Week 4, C: 2,900 in Week 1 (must be expedited to compress lead time from 2 weeks to 1 week), 1,000 in Week 2, and 2,000 in Week 3, D: 10,000 in Week 3; b. no, not unless expediting can compress lead times of A and C components; c. expedite A and C components.

Chapter 12

(3) a. Job enrichment, job rotation, supervisor training, and time away from jobs; b. no; c. no. **(11)** a. Element 1: .115 min., Element 2: 1.800 min., Element 3: 4.809 min., and Element 4: .613 min.; b. .121 min., 2.160 min., 4.088 min., .613 min, and 6.982 min.; c. 1.206; d. 8.420 min. **(13)** 475 observations. **(15)** 1.440 min./unit. **(17)** $432.05. **(12S.1)** a. .235 hour; b. 15.059 hours. **(12S.3)** a. 2.62 hours; b. 41.99 hours; c. 1.760 hours and 352 hours. **(12S.5)** a. 99.21766 hours; b. 67.08923 hours; c. 4.242 hours.

Chapter 13

(3) Distance of A: 650,000 feet per month, distance of B: 630,000 feet per month, Layout B is preferred. **(5)** Materials handling cost of A: $1,975 per month, materials handling cost of B: $1,855 per month, Layout B is preferred. **(7)** b. .167 min./unit; c. 31.86 employees. **(9)** b. 4.5 min./pump; c. 9.51 employees; d. both methods require ten employees or 95.1 percent utilization. **(11)** b. .250 min./burger; c. 24.20 employees; d. both methods require 26 employees or 93.1 percent utilization. **(13S.1)** a. .5; b. 1; c. 6 min.; d. 12 min.; e. .50. **(13S.3)** Present: $\lambda = 40$/hour, $\mu = 120$/hour, .167 students, .25 min., .333; proposed: $\lambda = 40$/hour, $\mu = 42.86$/hour, 13.05 students, 19.6 min., .933. **(13S.5)** a. $\frac{2}{3}$; b. $\frac{4}{3}$; c. 2 min.; d. 4 min. **(13S.7)** a. $\mu = 12.07$ customers/hour, $1/\mu = .0829$ hour or 4.97 min./customer; b. 16.97 min. **(13S.9)** a. 27.1 percent; b. 1.25. **(13S.11)** a. .001693; b. 2.34 min.; c. 8.59 customers. **(13S.13)** a. Cost is $10,500 for 20 days; b. cost is $10,300 for 20 days; order the quantity demanded today for tomorrow's sales.

Chapter 14

(1) 0 and 11.87 percent. **(3)** a. 1.50 and 4.50 percent; c. the trend is downward. **(5)** a. 22.46 and 25.54 inches; c. no, the sample means are changing rapidly and the process is out of control on the upward side. **(7)** a. 23.37 and 24.63 hours; c. no, too many sample means are above the upper limit, and therefore delivery times exceed 24 hours. **(9)** 13.0 percent, do not reject lot. **(11)** $\alpha = .10$, .79 and 7.21 percent, do not reject lot. **(13)** $\alpha = .01$, 59.18 and 60.82 tons, reject the lot.

Chapter 15

(1) a. 99 percent; b. 96.1 percent. **(3)** Perform preventive maintenance every 40,000 miles.

Index